W9-BTN-197

MANAGING FINANCIAL RISK

A Guide to Derivative Products, Financial Engineering, and Value Maximization

Managing Financial Risk

A Guide to Derivative Products, Financial Engineering, and Value Maximization

---

Charles W. Smithson
CIBC Wood Gundy
School of Financial Products

Clifford W. Smith, Jr.
William E. Simon Graduate
School of Business,
University of Rochester

with

D. Sykes Wilford
Bankers Trust

Chicago • London • Singapore

Senior sponsoring editor: Amy Hollands Gaber
Project editor: Lynne Basler
Copy editor: Michael O'Neal
Production manager: Laurie Kersch
Interior designer: Michael Warrell
Cover designer: Tim Kaage
Art manager: Kim Meriwether
Compositor: BookMasters, Inc.
Typeface: 11/13 Times Roman
Printer: Buxton Skinner Printing Co.

Library of Congress Cataloging-in-Publication Data

Smithson, C. W. (Charles W.)
Managing financial risk : a guide to derivative products, financial engineering, and value maximization/Charles W. Smithson, Clifford W. Smith, Jr., D. Sykes Wilford.
p. cm.
Rev. ed. of: Managing financial risk / Clifford W. Smith Jr., Charles W. Smithson, D. Sykes Wilford. ©1990.
Includes bibliographical references and index.
ISBN 0-7863-0440-5, ISBN 0-7863-0433-2, ISBN 0-7863-0849-4 (Special CIBC edition)
1. Business enterprises—Finance. 2. Risk Management. I. Smith, Clifford W. II. Wilford, D. Sykes. III. Smith, Clifford W. Managing financial risk. IV. Title.
HG4026.S63 1995
658.15—dc20 94–21824

Printed in the United States of America
6 7 8 9 0 BX 1 0 9 8 7 6

About the Authors

Charles W. Smithson is a Managing Director and head of the CIBC Wood Gundy School of Financial Products. His career has spanned the gamut, with positions in the private sector, in academe and in government. Prior to joining CIBC, Mr. Smithson was a Senior Vice President of the Chase Manhattan Bank, where he was responsible for risk management research. He was also a Managing Director of the Continental Bank, where he directed research for the global trading and distribution sector. Mr. Smithson taught for nine years at Texas A&M University and later directed the Ph.D. program in finance at the University of North Texas. In government, he served with both the Federal Trade Commission and the Consumer Products Safety Commission. Charles Smithson is the author of numerous articles in academic journals on subjects ranging from regulation to labor market discrimination to financial engineering. He is the author of three other books, *The Doomsday Myth, Managerial Economics,* and *The Economics of Mineral Extraction,* and is one of the editors of *The Handbook of Financial Engineering.* He has been cited in newspapers from *The Des Moines Register* to *The Wall Street Journal.* Charles Smithson served as a member of the working group for the Global Derivatives Project sponsored by the Group of Thirty.

Clifford W. Smith, Jr., Clarey Professor of Finance at the William E. Simon Graduate School of Business Administration at The University of Rochester, has published over 40 papers and 5 books in the fields of option pricing, corporate financial policy, and financial intermediation. Students gave Mr. Smith their Superior Teaching award nine times, and he was chosen from among the University of

Rochester faculty as one of 10 university mentors in recognition of his scholarship and teaching. He is an editor of the *Journal of Financial Economics,* associate editor of the *Journal of Financial and Quantitative Analysis,* the *Journal of Accounting and Economics,* the *Journal of Real Estate Finance and Economics,* and *Financial Management,* a member of the editorial review board of the *Journal of the American Real Estate and Urban Economics Association,* and is a member of the advisory board of the Continental Bank *Journal of Applied Corporate Finance.*

D. Sykes Wilford is the Chief Investment Officer of the Bankers Trust Global Private Bank. Further, as a member of the Asset Allocation Committee of Bankers' Global Investment Management Co., he is responsible for general asset allocation, the development of quantitative and judgmental asset allocation approaches to both institutional and private portfolios.

Previously he held the position of Managing Director of Chase Manhattan Bank N.A. as global component executive for the Portfolio Strategies Group in the Risk Management Sector of the Bank. In this function he was responsible for developing and managing the Bank's Global Enhancement Management business and chairing its Investment Committee.

Prior to that, he directed Chase's Global Commodity Risk Management and European Index Linked Derivative Products businesses and was Director of the Chase Europe Development Institute as Head of Chase's global Treasury product development and education efforts. He was an Economist with the Federal Reserve Bank of New York as well as Chief International Fixed Income Strategist for Drexel Burnham Lambert in London.

Wilford, whose main research interests are monetary economics and international finance, has written in both the academic and popular press. His articles have appeared in research journals such as the *American Economic Review* and the *Journal of Finance* as well as market oriented publications. He has both authored and edited several books, ranging from economic policy in developing countries to *Managing Financial Risk.*

His interest is not limited to research; he is an active consultant for corporations, central banks and governments, explaining and lecturing about financial innovations and methodologies for analyzing international markets. He has lectured at several universities, including New York University, The University of New Orleans, and The City University of London. Wilford holds a B.A., M.A., and Ph.D in Economics.

To all our colleagues who helped develop the concept for this book, and to Cindy, who helped transform the concept into a book.

PREFACE

Much of this book deals with the use of *derivatives* either to change a firm's *risk profile* or to construct *new financial products.* This process—often referred to as *financial engineering*—sounds like something that you need a degree from MIT or CalTech to do. But, if we look at these innovative financial products as combinations of some basic financial building blocks, much of the mystery, and apparent complexity, is removed. Indeed, the principle message of this book is:

This stuff is not as hard as some people make it sound.

The financial markets have some complicated features, but good common sense goes a lot further than mathematical flash and dash.

This book has its roots in a program that Sykes Wilford pioneered and the three of us taught to client executives of the Chase Manhattan Bank. For the learning experience that all of us went through, I want to thank all of those colleagues—some still at Chase and some who, like us, subsequently left Chase. I do want to single out a few people at Chase for particular mention. Mark Grier, then the executive vice president in charge of the financial risk management business at Chase (now the CFO of the Prudential Insurance Co.), was extremely supportive of this project. A number of Chase people contributed their time to review portions of the manuscript: Michael Davis; Ottho Heldring; Jim Mevay; Lucia A. Rosato; and Kate Smith. But most of all, I want to single out the people I worked within the risk management research group: Kwok Chung (William) Chan; Nancy Durso; Kathy Falconio; Greg Hayt; and Chris Turner, who devoted hours to looking up missing references, responding to the copyeditor, and reviewing page proofs.

But, it wasn't only Chase people who helped put this book together. Don Chew, the editor of *The Journal of Applied Corporate Finance,* helped with the construction of some chapters and the review of others. David Mengle and Derik Hargraves of J.P. Morgan were particularly helpful in constructing some of the data sets and figures. The manuscript benefited from the comments and suggestions provided by a large number of readers who are actively involved in the risk management business. These readers included: Susan Berra; Mark Brickell, J.P. Morgan; Halsey Bullen, FASB; Lee Choo, Enron Gas Services; Christopher Culp, then with the Federal Reserve Bank of Chicago; Robert O. Gurman, Swiss Bank Corporation; Robert Mackay, VPI; Jeffrey D. Sherman, Toronto-Dominion Bank; and Peter L. Smith, Securities & Exchange Commission.

The change that most distinguishes this book from the edition published in 1989 is the addition of applications written by market practitioners. I very much appreciate the hard work of these people: John P. Behof, Federal Reserve Bank of Chicago; Steve Bloom, Susquehanna Investment Group; Halsey Bullen, Financial Accounting Standards Board; Martin Cooper, Chase Manhattan Bank; Tracy Corrigan, The Financial Times; Daniel P. Cunningham, Cravath, Swaine & Moore; Satyait Das, TNT Group; Kosrow Dehnad, Chase Manhattan Bank; David Fiedler, Eastman Kodak; Mahlon Frankhauser, Lord Day & Lord, Barrett Smith; Peter D. Hancock, J.P. Morgan; Frank Hankus, McDonald's; Greg Hayt, Chase Manhattan Bank; James P. Healy, Credit Suisse Financial Products; R.K. Hinkley, British Petroleum; Walter Hosp, Ciba-Geigy; Matthew Hunt, Chase Manhattan Bank; Ira G. Kawaller, Chicago Mercantile Exchange; Kenneth Lehn, University of Pittsburgh; Ellen Levinson, Lord Day & Lord, Barrett Smith; Victor I. Makarov, Chase Manhattan Bank; John Martin, TNT Group; Constance Mitchell, *The Wall Street Journal;* Allen R. Myerson, The *New York Times;* Nancy Newcomb, Citibank; Tony Pearl, McDonald's; J. Matthew Singleton, Arthur Andersen; Fred Stambaugh, Chase Manhattan Bank; Jacques Tierny; and Ronald D. Watson, Bear Stearns.

I also want to thank Lee Macdonald Wakeman, president of The Mutual Group Financial Products. Lee is the coauthor of a number of the articles that are the precursors to chapters of this book, but; more generally, Lee has had a profound impact on the way that I look at the risk management business.

My biggest debt is, however, to my wife, Cindy. There wasn't a part of the process of creating this book with which she was not involved.

Charles W. Smithson

CONTENTS

7 Using Forwards to Manage Financial Price Risks 164

8 Futures 183

9 Using Futures to Manage Financial Prices Risks 210

10 Swaps 234

11 Using Swaps to Manage Financial Price Risks 267

CHAPTER

1 The Evolution of Risk Management Products*

Unpredictable movements in exchange rates, interest rates, and commodity prices can not only affect a firm's reported quarterly earnings but may even determine whether a firm survives. Over the past two decades, firms have been increasingly challenged by such financial price risks. It's no longer enough to be the firm with the most advanced production technology, the cheapest labor supply, or the best marketing team; price volatility can put even well-run firms out of business.

Changes in exchange rates can create strong new competitors. Similarly, fluctuations in commodity prices can drive input prices to the point that substitute products—products made from different inputs—become more affordable to end consumers. Changes in interest rates can put pressure on the firm's costs: firms whose sales are hurt by higher interest rates may find themselves in financial distress as sales plummet and borrowing costs skyrocket.

Not surprisingly, the financial markets have responded to increasing price volatility. A range of financial instruments and strategies that can be used to manage the resulting exposures to financial price risk have evolved over the past 20 years.

At one level, financial instruments now exist that permit the direct transfer of financial price risk to a third party more willing to accept that risk. For example, with the development of foreign exchange futures contracts, a U.S. exporter can transfer its foreign exchange risk to a firm with the opposite exposure or to a firm in the business of managing foreign exchange risk, leaving the exporter free to focus on its core business.

*This chapter is based on Rawls and Smithson (1989).

At another level, the financial markets have evolved to the point that financial instruments can be combined with a debt issue to unbundle financial price risk from the other risks inherent in the process of raising capital. For example, by coupling their bond issues with swaps, issuing firms are able to separate interest rate risk from traditional credit risk.[1]

The World Becomes a Riskier Place

There is general agreement that the financial environment is riskier today than it was in the past. Figure 1–1 provides some dramatic evidence of the change in the form of what must be regarded as long price series, the retail price index for England from 1666 to the mid-1980s. From the 17th century until the late 20th century, the price level in England was essentially stable. Prices did go up during wartime; the data series reflects conflicts like the one the British had with "that French person" in the early 19th century, but prices fell to prewar levels once the conflict ended.

In marked contrast, the price history for the second half of the 20th century indicates that the financial environment has changed. For the first time, prices have gone up—and stayed up. This phenomenon is evident not only for the United Kingdom; a similar pattern of price-level behavior exists for the United States, albeit, as

FIGURE 1–1 Retail Price Index for England from the 17th to the 20th Century (1850 = 100)

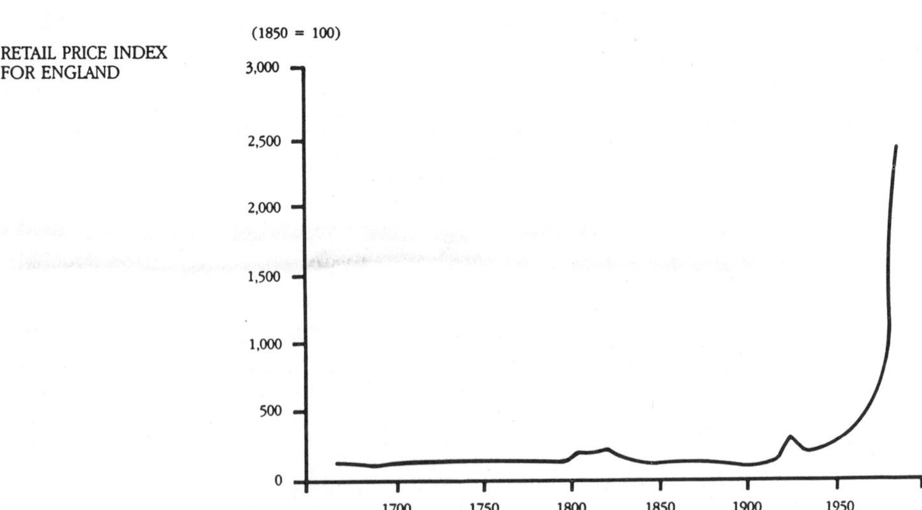

our British colleagues point out, with fewer data points. (See Figure 1–2.) In fact, during this period of general uncertainty, the developed economies generally have begun to experience unexpected price changes—primarily increases.

In short, financial markets have been confronted by increased price uncertainty. Growing uncertainty about inflation has been quickly followed by uncertainty about foreign exchange rates, interest rates, and commodity prices.

FIGURE 1–2 U.S. Price Index, 1800–1985 (1967 = 100)

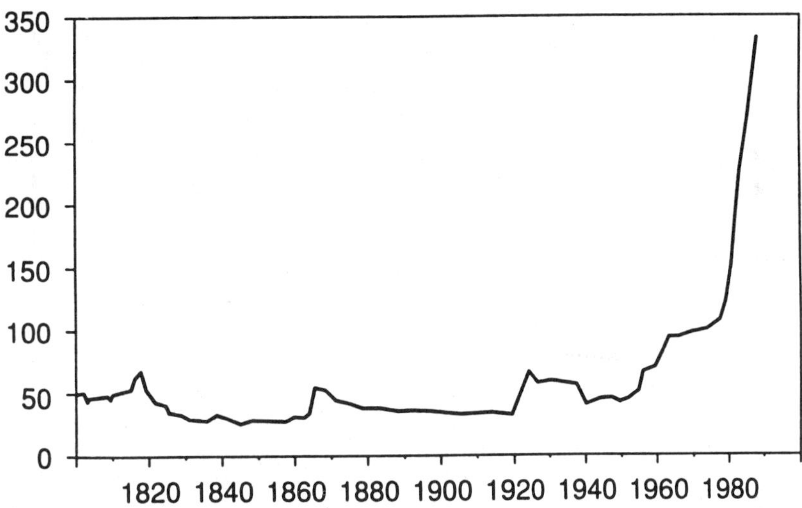

Volatility of Foreign Exchange Rates

Figure 1–3 shows monthly percentage changes in the U.S. dollar–deutsche mark exchange rate since 1960. This figure clearly indicates that the foreign exchange market has become riskier. What is equally evident is the reason for the increased volatility of foreign exchange rates in the early 1970s: the breakdown of the Bretton Woods system of fixed exchange rates.[2]

Under the fixed-exchange-rate system of Bretton Woods, importers knew what they would pay for goods in their domestic currency, and exporters knew how much they would receive in their local currency. If the importer could sell at a profit to the consumer, and the exporter's costs were below the export price, then gains from trade were had by all.

With the breakdown of Bretton Woods, the rules have changed. Both sides to the transaction now face exchange rate risk. Each firm wants to transact in its own

FIGURE 1–3 Percent Change in Deutsche Mark–U.S. Dollar Exchange Rate

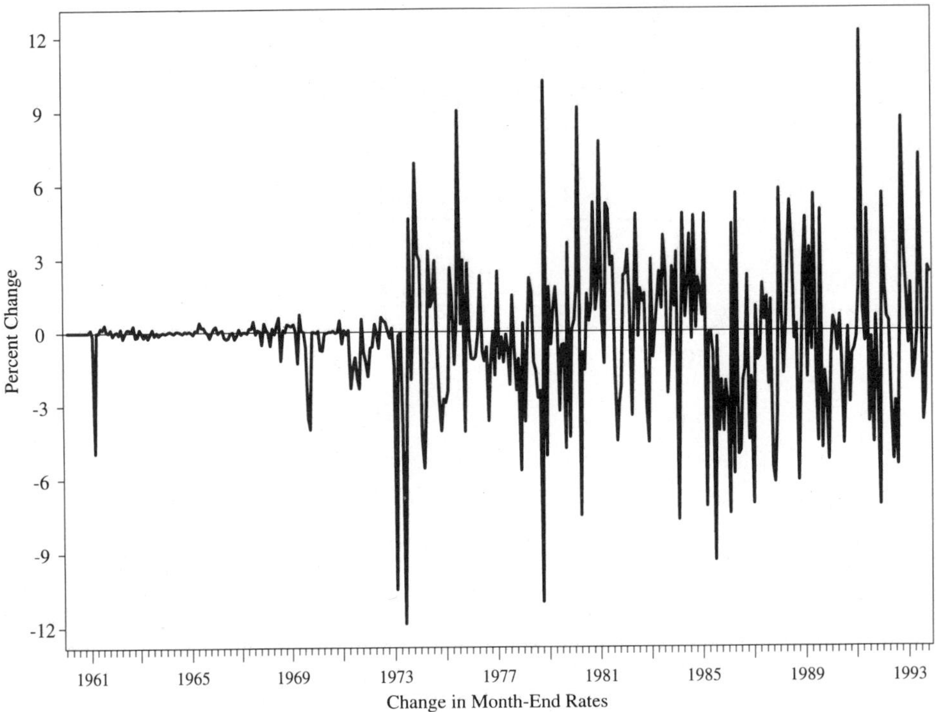

currency to prevent being "whipsawed" by the market. Importers' profit margins can, and often have, evaporated if their currency weakens sharply and the imported goods are priced in the exporter's currency.

Volatility of Interest Rates

Surprisingly, the increased volatility evident in the foreign exchange market did not spill over into the U.S. domestic money market at first. Indeed, compared with the early 1970s, interest rates actually became more stable immediately after the collapse of the Bretton Woods accord. As shown in Figure 1–4, interest rate volatility[3] declined during the period 1977–79, even though interest rates were rising in response to the inflation rate.

However, as illustrated in Figure 1–4, uncertainty hit U.S. interest rates with a vengeance in the early 1980s. On October 6, 1979, newly appointed Federal Reserve Board Chairman Paul Volcker abandoned the Fed practice of targeting

FIGURE 1–4 Percent Difference Five-Year U.S. Treasuries

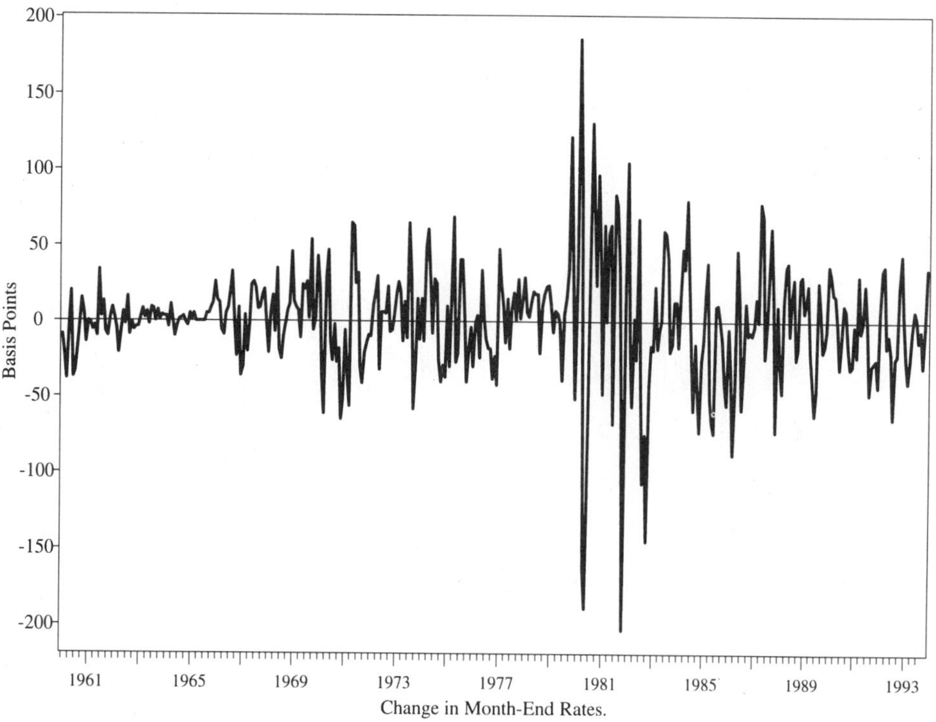

interest rates and began to target money supply growth instead. As a consequence, interest rates became extremely volatile.

Volatility of Commodity Prices

Volatility also increased in the commodity markets. Figure 1–5 indicates that the price of petroleum products became more volatile in the 1970s (as did the prices of most basic commodities).

The Impact of Increased Financial Price Risk on Firms

Over the past eight years, we have talked to hundreds of managers about the way that they view their firms' exposures to financial price risk. We have heard about several very different kinds of risk.

FIGURE 1–5 Percent Difference in U.S. Crude Oil Price

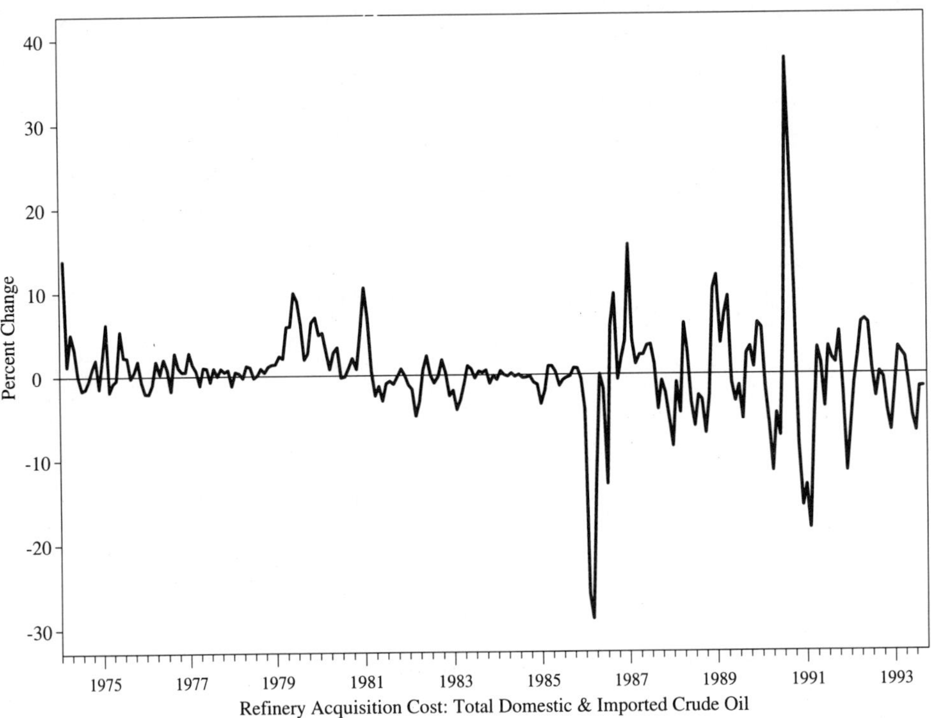

Virtually every firm considers accounting-based exposures—those exposures that would be reflected directly in the firm's financial statements. Within these accounting-based exposures, *transaction exposures* receive the most attention. A transaction exposure exists when a change in one of the financial prices will change the amount of a receipt or expense. Obviously, the amount of a transaction—a receipt or an expense—would be determined by price per unit and the number of units sold or purchased:

$$\text{Receipt or expense} = P \times Q \tag{1–1}$$

Transaction exposures focus on only the direct effect of a price change—the impact of price changes on quantity is ignored.

Traditionally, the accounting profession has focused only on those transaction exposures where the transaction is a "firm commitment." However, a number of firms have transactions that, while not committed, are predictable with a high degree of certainty—for example, a firm that has been doing business through its subsidiary in Germany for the past 20 years knows with a great deal of certainty how many deutsche marks it will receive in each of the four quarters of next year. The Financial Accounting Standards Board recognizes this as well and is considering the degree to which it would be willing to permit hedge accounting for "forecasted transactions."

Moving beyond the strict accounting-based exposures, some firms have begun to consider their firm's *economic exposures*—also referred to as *competitive exposures*. In the context of Equation 1–1, changes in foreign exchange rates or interest rates or commodity prices will change the firm's receipts or expenditures not only because of the direct price change but also because the price change will change the amount that the firm sells or buys. This view of financial price risk recognizes changes in foreign exchange rates, interest rates, or commodity prices on the firm's sales and market share and then on the firm's net profits (net cash flows).

Whether the exposure is accounting-based or economic, changes in foreign exchange rates, interest rates, or commodity prices can change the real cash flows of the firm. The increased volatility in financial prices evident in the 1970s has led more firms to recognize their exposures to financial price risk. A case in point is Eastman Kodak.

Risk Management in Practice

The Management of Exchange Risk

David Fiedler

Eastman Kodak Company has a deep and far-reaching global presence in the markets that we serve. Almost half of our sales from our three major groups—imaging, health, and chemicals—are outside the United States.

Kodak recognized that the rules of the game relative to foreign exchange changed with the breakdown of the Bretton Woods Agreement in the early 1970s. For a number of years, we dealt with foreign exchange risk by focusing on the company's balance sheet transaction exposures (receivables, payables, etc.). However, throughout the 1980s, it became clear that a number of broad economic influences were dramatically altering the nature of the exchange risk problem:

The Management of Exchange Risk continued

- The foreign exchange market (and most financial markets) became significantly more volatile and therefore riskier.
- World financial markets became increasingly less regulated, allowing for a free flow of capital around the world. (This influence has been reflected in the exchange markets by a shift from the early 1980s, when the majority of transaction volume was trade-related, to the late 1980s, when the majority of volume is capital-flow-related.)
- U.S. GNP as a percentage of world output has declined steadily since the end of World War II (from about 50 percent in the late 1940s to less than 25 percent by 1990). For U.S. companies this implies an increasing probability that the competition is a foreign company.

All of these influences contributed to Kodak concluding that exchange risk needed to be looked at differently going forward. Specifically, Kodak realized that foreign exchange represents a strategic variable for the company, which has the potential to affect the value of the firm over time.

In 1988, Kodak began implementation of a new corporate policy that defined the exchange risk problem as one of economic exposure. We define *economic exposure as the extent to which exchange rate movements affect the discounted dollar cash flows of the consolidated corporation*. This definition represents a significant departure from the U.S. accounting model of exchange risk. Whereas it includes the accounting notion of transaction exposure—foreign-currency-denominated receivables, payables, and so on—because these are cash flow exposures, it excludes the translation of the balance sheet, which is not cash flow exposure but rather, in essence, a mark-to-market or valuation of the dollar value of our foreign investments.

But, more importantly, the economic notion of exchange exposure is not confined to currently recorded cash flows. In fact, the essence of the economic model is focused on future, yet unrecorded, cash flows. Whereas currently recorded cash flows are indeed economic exposure, it is the combined impact of the future, unrecorded cash flows that has the ability to affect the viability of the firm over time.

To put into operation our definition of economic exposure, we have defined two components of economic risk, which we simply refer to as tactical exposure and strategic exposure. Our approach to the management of the two components is quite different.

Tactical Exposure

Tactical exposure includes the worldwide balance sheet transaction exposure of the company for all currencies that have viable, external forward markets.

The Management of Exchange Risk continued

(Currencies that do not have viable forward markets are handled separately). In addition, certain unrecorded but comparatively shorter-dated exposures are included in this component. All exposures are netted on an after-tax basis (since they emanate from various tax jurisdictions) using a commercially available PC-based software package.

Tactical exposure is managed centrally at our headquarters in Rochester, New York, by the Foreign Exchange Planning Department. The department has direct accountability for the financial result on tactical exposure as measured against a 100 percent hedge standard (the dollar outcome that would result if the exposure were simply hedged forward). It should be noted, however, that this is a standard, not an objective. The objective is to attempt to add some value to the corporation as compared to the standard, within some predefined risk parameters.

A full range of strategies is used in the management of tactical exposure (including leaving exposures unhedged, forwards, proxy hedges, options strategies, etc.). In the case of options, there is no option premium budget; however, the financial outcome versus the standard includes any premium cost incurred.

It should be noted that taking a totally centralized approach to the management of tactical exposure has required distinguishing between statutory, externally reported results for subsidiaries around the world and the measurement of the performance of operating managers. This distinction is necessary because the statutory result of exchange rate movement on the underlying exposure and the statutory result of any hedge of the worldwide net exposure will generally be on the books of different legal entities. Whereas it would be possible to overcome this mismatch through the use of intercompany hedging contracts, we believed that generating internal paperwork that did not affect the economic result would be a value-eroding activity and that it was more productive to deal with the performance measurement issues directly.

Strategic Exposure

The other component of economic risk, strategic exposure, is composed exclusively of future, unrecorded cash flows. Unlike tactical exposure, which we manage centrally, we have defined the ownership of strategic exposure as belonging to our operating units. (Kodak is organized along a line of business structure; for example, Consumer Imaging, which has a worldwide responsibility for that product line.)

In that context, the Foreign Exchange Planning Department serves as a consultant to the operating units. The consulting role includes extensive education

The Management of Exchange Risk concluded

of operating units regarding the nature and intricacies of strategic exposure, performing analytic studies of the exposure on behalf of the operating units, proposing hedging strategies where appropriate, implementing the strategies when the hedge is a financial hedge, and managing the hedges after implementation. Importantly, however, the decision to hedge and the cost and benefits of any hedges remain with the operating units. If they were to decide not to hedge, we would not implement a hedge at the corporate level.

The rationale for this approach is that strategic exchange risk is an integral part of a business and inseparable from other strategic business issues. For example, decisions to change where raw materials are sourced, where to manufacture, markets to serve, and so on, all will change the nature of the risk embedded in the business. In addition, there are times when the optimal solution to an exposure may be a nonfinancial hedge that is under the direct control of the operating unit.

Where financial hedges are appropriate, we will always use option-oriented strategies, principally for two reasons. First, our approach to strategic risk management is not forecast based. We do not profess to know where exchange rates will go over multiyear time horizons, nor do we believe that such information is discoverable. For example, events such as the reunification of Germany, the dissolution of the Soviet Union, and the Gulf War all significantly impacted capital markets. These events attest to the important but unpredictable impact that political events can have on the work economy. As a consequence, our approach is exposure-management- rather than forecast-based. Secondly, a forward-based hedge is too unforgiving in dealing with strategic risk. A hedged dollar result that is acceptable today may not be tomorrow as a result of unforeseen competitive actions.

Summary

Our approach to the management of tactical risk is well entrenched in the way that we do business. On the strategic side, whereas we have made very satisfying progress, the consulting approach that we feel is necessary and the complexity of fully weaving the management of strategic risk into the fabric of how we do business dictate that our progress will be evolutionary in nature. However, unless capital markets undergo future, unforeseen changes resulting in a return to Bretton Woods–like stability, we believe that a clear focus on strategic exposure will become increasingly common among global corporations.

David Fiedler is the director for Investor Relations at the Eastman Kodak Company. He previously directed foreign exchange planning at Kodak. He holds a B.A. in economics from the University of Minnesota. In 1984, he spent a year working in the foreign exchange trading room of a major New York City money center bank (as an Eastman Kodak Company employee) before assuming his foreign exchange planning role.

Unfortunately, other firms have been forced to recognize their exposures the hard way: Exposures to financial prices have caused them financial difficulties or, in some cases, put them out of business.

Exchange Rate Risk

In the context of foreign exchange rate risk, transaction exposures have received the lion's share of attention. A transaction exposure will often lead to trouble when there is a mismatch in revenues and expenses. A classic example—the one cited by almost every risk management marketer we have ever met—is Laker Airlines:

Illustration 1–1

Laker Airlines an FX Risk*

In the late 1970s, Laker Airlines had a problem, but it was a problem we all might like to have—there were more British vacationers lining up for Laker's flights than he had seats to fill. (At the time, the U.S. dollar was weak, so a U.S. vacation was a bargain.) Freddie Laker solved the problem by buying five more DC-10s, financing them in U.S. dollars.

Laker Airline's revenues were primarily in pounds—from those British vacationers—but the payments for the new DC-10s were in dollars. The result for Laker Airlines was a mismatch on revenues and expenses.

In 1981, the U.S. dollar strengthened and the FX transaction exposure became evident as Laker's expenses increased. With the stronger dollar, Laker had to pay more pounds to make the payments on the debt. While not the only factor, this FX transaction exposure contributed in sending Laker into bankruptcy.†

*This illustration was taken from a story in *Business Week* (1982) and from Millman (1988).

†And we haven't told you all the story. Laker Airlines also had an economic exposure. With the stronger dollar, U.S. vacations were no longer the "bargain" they had been in the late 1970s, so at the same time Laker's expenses were increasing, revenues were declining.

Foreign exchange transaction exposures would be reflected in the firm's income statement. (We will look at some of the ways in which exposures are reflected in accounting data in Chapter 5.) A parallel exposure—one that also focuses only on the direct effects of a price change—that would be reflected in the firm's balance sheet is referred to as a *translation exposure*. A translation exposure reflects the change in the value of the firm as foreign assets are converted to home currency. Most of the firms we have talked with make a point of noting that they do not manage translation exposures.[4]

The evidence indicates very clearly that changes in foreign exchange rates can have a significant negative impact on a firm's ability to compete. Another classic illustration—indeed, the companion piece to the Laker Airlines story in the risk management marketer's litany of horror stories is the Caterpillar story:

Illustration 1–2

Caterpillar'S FX Whammy*

Throughout the early 1980s, Caterpillar cited the strong dollar as the primary cause of its difficulties. As the 1982 annual report put it,

> The strong dollar is a prime factor in Caterpillar's reduced sales and earnings. . . .

As the dollar strengthened relative to the yen, the price of Caterpillar equipment rose relative to Komatsu equipment, giving Komatsu a competitive advantage on Caterpillar.

*This illustration was adapted from Hutchins (1986).

And versions of the Caterpillar story continue to be repeated. In late 1993, for instance, competitive exposures related to the yen/dollar exchange rate were again in the news, only the competitive exposure was the other way around.

Interest Rate Risk

Transaction exposures are normally associated with foreign exchange rate risk. However, changes in interest rates can also have the same kind of impact on accounting statement income. While changes in interest rates could impact either receipts or expenses, most firms focus on interest expense. Perhaps the most widely cited example of interest rate transaction exposures—the interest rate counterpart to the Laker Airlines and Caterpillar stories—is the experience of the U.S. savings and loan association industry (S&Ls).

And changes in interest rates can also result in economic exposures. In contrast to interest rate transaction exposures, where we focus on the firm's expenses, interest rate economic exposures are somewhat more likely to be observed on receipts—changes in interest rates can change the quantities that the firm sells.[5]

Commodity-Price Risk

Our experience has been that firms are more likely to distinguish between *transaction* and *economic* exposures for foreign exchange rates and interest rates than for commodity prices.[6] Despite this hazy characterization, firms can be confronted with exposures to commodity prices. Such exposures moved from being possible

Illustration 1–3

A Summer of Discontent for Japanese Manufacturers

In the sense of the curse of "living in interesting times," Japanese manufacturers must have regarded 1993 as an "interesting time."

The value of the dollar (in yen) for the first three quarters of 1993 is provided below:

Japanese Yen per US Dollar (New York Close)

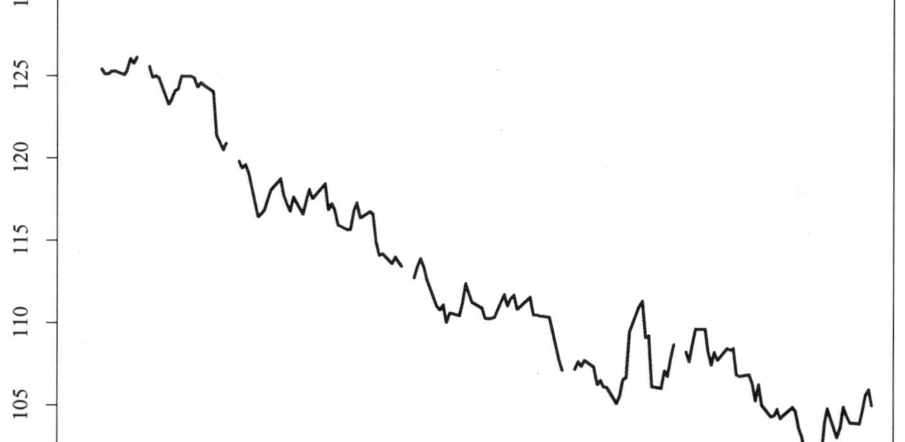

By April, the dollar had fallen to the 113–114 yen per dollar range. And, as was reported by the *New York Times*, the weakening dollar was beginning to hurt Japanese

A Summer of Discontent for Japanese Manufacturers continued

The New York Times

Rising Yen Rings Alarms in Tokyo

By JAMES STERNGOLD

Special to The New York Times

TOKYO, April 6 — For most of the last two months, the Japanese yen has been edging up in value to its strongest level of the postwar era, sending waves of anxiety through the Government and the business world.

The dollar fell to 113.40 yen at one point here on Friday, closing at 114. Some experts say it could plummet soon to 100 yen, less than half its value a decade ago.

Slight Gain in New York

On Monday, the dollar slipped to 113.70 in New York, its third consecutive postwar low. Today, the dollar recovered a bit, rising to 113.85 yen in New York. [Page D18.]

The dollar's steep drop has set off alarms here, with some experts arguing that the rising yen threatens the Japanese economy's fragile recovery and could undermine markets from Tokyo to Wall Street. But after a month of fretting, others are concluding that the stronger yen could ultimately prove an economic boon, giving Japanese consumers price breaks from cheaper imports they have long been denied.

Japan's soaring trade surplus and a sharp decline in the country's overseas investments are believed to be among the reasons for the yen's strength. The dollar has lost around 8 percent of its value against the yen this year, and that decline is already having a big impact on corporate policies.

A weak dollar is having a big impact on Japanese business.

The Toyota Motor Corporation is said to be preparing to slice some $700 million from its production costs in the next few months; the Sharp Corporation has said it will move all its personal computer production out of Japan to lower costs, and the Daiei Corporation, a leading retailer, has said that for the first time it will substitute less expensive imported suits from China for some Japanese-made suits.

The yen's rise comes as a harsh blow to Japanese exporters in particular, because Japanese goods are becoming more expensive for Americans and other foreigners. But it helps American companies, which is why the Clinton Administration has largely supported the movement.

Less demand for Japanese goods is expected to force manufacturers to take stern measures to reduce their costs and to improve their efficiency, difficult steps at a time when profits have been battered by an economic slowdown. The Industrial Bank of Japan has estimated that the stronger yen could reduce economic growth as much as half a percentage point this year.

The uncertainty over exchange-rate movements also disrupts Japanese investment plans overseas. Some experts worry that the unease could encourage a flight of Japanese capital from America back to Japan. The value of American securities has already dropped sharply in terms of the yen, in many instances below what the investors paid for them.

'One Big Risk'

"The one big risk is a chain reaction of fear if Japanese investors decide they have to get out of dollar assets," Richard Koo, a senior economist at the Nomura Research Institute, said. "At these exchange rates, all the dollar-denominated paper they own is under water, and there is already some inclination to sell now before the exchange rate gets worse. That could become scary."

Japanese Government officials had clearly supported the yen's apprecia-

firms that export to the U.S. The *Times* noted that Japanese manufacturers would have to "take stern measures to reduce their costs and to improve their efficiency." Singled out was Toyota Motor Corporation.

By June, the foreign exchange market had gotten still worse for Japanese manufacturers as the dollar had fallen to about 110 yen to the dollar. The *Asian Wall Street Journal* reported that Japanese manufacturers had large foreign exchange bets on the table. They were not hedging their foreign exchange exposure, expecting—betting—that the dollar would recover.

THE ASIAN WALL STREET JOURNAL.

WEDNESDAY, JUNE 9, 1993, PAGE 9

MONEY AND INVESTING

Most Japanese Firms Hold Off Hedging Their Currency Needs

A Summer of Discontent for Japanese Manufacturers concluded

As the summer neared its end, the bet was going against the Japanese manufacturers. Instead of recovering, the dollar had fallen as low as 100 yen per dollar.

The New York Times was reporting that Japanese manufacturers were shifting production from Japan.

THE NEW YORK TIMES

SUNDAY, AUGUST 29, 1993

Japanese Moving Production Abroad

And *The Wall Street Journal* reported that Standard & Poor's was considering a downgrade for Toyota, Nissan, and Honda. As the *Journal* noted, "Japan's economic slump and the yen's strengthening against the dollar in the past few months have hurt the companies' profits, leading to dismal earning results."* In July, Japanese exports of automobiles were 14 percent below the level a year before.

Nissan, Toyota And Honda Face S&P Downgrade

---

*Honda had posted a 55 percent drop in pretax profit for the quarter ending June 30, Toyota posted a 25 percent decline in pretax profits for the year ending June 30, and Nissan reported a pretax loss for the year ending March 31.

Illustration 1–4

From Money Machines to Money Pits : U.S. S&Ls

In the 1970s, S&Ls looked like money machines. The U.S. yield curve was upward sloping—and had been for as long as most of the S&L bankers could remember. In such an environment, S&Ls could earn a steady profit by making long-term fixed-rate mortgage loans and financing these assets by taking in short-term passbook deposits. Looking at the income statement, the S&Ls' receipts would be insensitive to interest rate changes, but changes in the short-term interest rate would have a direct effect on expenses—increases in rates would lead to increases in expenses. The S&Ls had a significant interest rate transaction exposure. But, in the 1970s, the market was going their way and the big interest rate bet was paying off for the S&Ls.

In the 1980s the market turned against the S&Ls. The yield curve inverted—short-term interest rates rose dramatically—and S&Ls changed from money machines to money pits. The short-term rates the S&Ls had to pay on their passbook deposits exceeded the fixed rate they were receiving on their loans to homeowners.

Illustration 1–5

Inherent Exposures to Interest Rates: Residential Construction

The firms that construct residential real estate and the firms that supply materials and fixtures to these construction firms are inherently exposed to interest rate risk—regardless of the manner in which the firms are financed. One of the primary determinants of the demand for housing is the level of interest rates. When interest rates are high, the demand for housing declines (and may decline dramatically). Consequently, the net incomes reported by the construction firms and their suppliers will move inversely with interest rates.

The *New York Times* provided a concrete example of this situation when it reported on the problems that the USG Corporation—the big Chicago-based maker of gypsum wallboard—faced in 1991.* In 1991, U.S. interest rates were high and the real estate market was depressed. Consequently, the demand for USG's main product, Sheetrock, had tumbled.

And it wasn't enough that USG's revenues were low. In 1988, USG had beat back a hostile takeover by taking on increased debt. Therefore, high interest rates meant not only that revenues were decreased, but also that the interest expense on the floating rate portion of USG's debt increased. As the *Times* put it, USG was choking on its borrowings.

---

*"USG's Struggle to Buy Time," by Eric N. Berg, *The New York Times* (Market Place column), March 20, 1991.

in theory to being a reality with the spike in oil prices during the Iraq–Kuwait conflict in 1990. These transaction exposures to oil prices appeared in the firms' income statements via increased receipts for producer firms or increased expenses for the firms that use oil.

Illustration 1–6

A Gulf War Casualty: Continental Airlines*

On August 2, 1990, Iraq invaded Kuwait. By October, the price of jet fuel had more than doubled from its preinvasion level, and Continental Airlines was certainly feeling the pinch. Continental's fuel costs in October were $81 million higher than they had been in June. This extra fuel expense hit Continental particularly hard because it was also servicing an extremely high debt load. (Continental's debt/capital ratio was almost twice the industry average.) On October 24 Continental announced a management shakeup and plans to sell some of its jets and routes to stem the red ink but said that it had "no intention of filing for bankruptcy protection."[†]

While fuel costs moderated a little in November, they were still 80 percent higher than the preinvasion levels.

On December 3, 1990, Continental Airlines visited the U.S. Bankruptcy Court—for a second time [‡]—filing for Chapter 11 protection from its creditors.[§] The following headline appeared in *The Wall Street Journal* on December 4:

Debt-Burdened Continental Air, Citing Rising Fuel Costs, Files Under Chapter 11

Binge of Borrowing in '80s to Finance Acquisitions Brings 2nd Visit to Court

*This illustration is based on a story that appeared in *The New York Times*: "Continental Bankruptcy Study Seen," October 24, 1990, and two stories in *The Wall Street Journal*: "Troubled Continental Plans Asset Sales," October 24, 1990, and "Debt-Burdened Continental Air, Citing Rising Fuel Costs, Files Under Chapter 11," December 4, 1990.

†*The New York Times*, Wednesday, October 24, 1990.

‡Continental Airlines had sought protection from its creditors in September 1983.

§Continental Airlines emerged from Chapter 11 protection in April 1993.

The Forecasters Flunk

So far, we have told you two facts: First, in the 1970s and 1980s, financial prices became more volatile. Second, this increased financial price volatility has had a detrimental impact on a number of firms.

It is not surprising that senior management at a number of firms decided to solve the problem by getting better forecasts for the various financial prices. While we weren't privy to the meetings, we believe that the decision at many U.S. multinationals must have gone something like:

> If the deutsche mark–U.S. dollar exchange rate is more volatile, and if increases (or decreases) in this rate could have a significant impact on the viability of my firm, then I need to get more accurate forecasts about the DM–USD exchange rate.

However, as the following set of clippings from the mid-1980s demonstrated, this was easier said than done.

The Forecasters Flunk

Poor predictions give once prestigious pundits a dismal reputation

"I'm thinking of quitting and becoming a hockey goalie"

TIME, August 27, 1984

THE WALL STREET JOURNAL, TUESDAY, OCTOBER 16, 1984

Maybe Economists Should Be a Little Less Positive

BY DOUGLAS L. BENDT AND CAROLYNE LOCHHEAD

THE ECONOMIST'S NEW CLOTHES

Economic forecasters have fallen into disrepute because they keep trying to do the impossible.

■ Economists and economics have taken a lot of heat recently. What sensible businessmen have long suspected is now obvious: the economist has no clothes.

In trying to predict the future values for foreign exchange rates, interest rates, and commodity prices, the forecasters flunked. The mid-1980s was a particularly active period of "economist bashing," but pointing out the errors in economists' forecasts is a pastime that continues. For example, a recent story *The Wall Street Journal*[7] noted that economists have been particularly bad at predicting major turning points in interest rates:

> Robert Beckwitt, a portfolio manager at Fidelity Investments, noted that between 1982 and 1992, the consensus forecast on which way long-term interest rates were heading over the next six months was right five times and wrong 17 times.

Even when an economist gets the forecast right, one year's hero often turns into the next year's goat.

> Edward S. Hyman . . . was tops in mid-1991 on the basis of his forecasts of interest rates in the second half of that year. . . . But Mr. Hyman ranked dead last among 42 forecasters in the mid-1992 survey for his second-half interest-rate forecasts.

Nonetheless, we do not find this lack of success in forecasting exchange rates, interest rates, and commodity prices to be at all surprising. The markets for these financial prices are all markets that would be characterized as *efficient markets*. An efficient market is a market characterized by:

- A homogeneous product.
- Liquid primary and secondary markets (i.e., a large number of market participants and the ability of the participants to enter and exit the market freely).
- The ability to contract for current delivery or for delivery at some date in the future.
- Low transactions (e.g., contracting) costs.

In an efficient market, the price of the commodity or asset reflects all currently available public information. In such an environment, price *changes* will be random. And if price changes are random, there is no way to accurately forecast prices. To see how this works, let's look at a market that has the characteristics of an efficient market.

Illustration 1–7

Making Millions Trading Wheat Futures

A recent addition to the American scene (and one we have seen nowhere else in the world) is The Weather Channel—a 24-hour cable channel devoted entirely to weather reports. Basic economics tells us that the market price of wheat must be determined by the demand for and supply of wheat. And since the supply of wheat is in large part determined by weather conditions, shouldn't we be able to use those weather forecasts from The Weather Channel to make money?

More specifically, let's devise a trading strategy: If The Weather Channel forecasts bad weather (e.g., hail in Kansas), we will contract to buy wheat in the future at the price prevailing today. Then, when the bad weather conditions reduce the supply of wheat, the price of wheat will consequently rise. And (here comes the good part), when our contract matures, we will accept delivery of the wheat at the low price we contracted for today and immediately sell it at a higher price.

Making Millions Trading Wheat Futures concluded

How much money would you expect to make on this strategy? (If you said anything greater than zero, write us, because we have some land deals to offer you.) The problem with this simple trading strategy is that it is based on available public information, while today's wheat price already reflects all of the available public information. As soon as any new information relevant to wheat is available, it will be reflected in wheat prices. What then will change the price of wheat? It follows from everything we have said so far that wheat prices will change when the available information changes.

The upshot is that if we want to be able to predict wheat prices, we need to be able to predict the new information *before it is available*. And if new information is really "new," it must be random. So predicting wheat prices would require us to predict a random variable.

There are people who have made a million in the futures market. But with the strategy we proposed above—one with trades based on available public information—the one who is making the millions is the broker executing the trades. In trying to predict the market, the forecasters flunked.

As Illustration 1–7 indicates, you are unlikely to be successful trying to outpredict an efficient market. In an efficient market, the best forecast of the price in the future is the price today.

> In an efficient market, the price of the commodity or asset reflects all currently available, public information. In such a market, price changes are random, so the best forecast of the future price is the current market price.

The very things that economists are usually called on to predict are the prices of assets or commodities traded in markets that are very efficient—the money markets (interest rates), foreign exchange markets (foreign exchange rates), and commodity markets (the prices of gold, copper, wheat, and so on). Therefore, it is not very surprising that economists have not done very well at forecasting these prices.

Note, however, that our illustration does not mean that it is impossible to make money in an efficient market. (Indeed, in our example our broker did make money.)[8] However, our example implies that one way to make money is to be the first one to get the information—to get the weather forecast. Such a line of reasoning might lead you to suspect that maybe it is the weather forecasters who are making the killings in the commodity markets—an idea that also occurred to the editors of *The Wall Street Journal*:[9]

Since forecasting did not solve the problem of financial price risk, the firms that were confronted with financial price risk turned to methods of transferring the risk, the topic we explore next.

Some Meteorologists Reap Windfall from Crop Futures Markets

From the Tuesday, July 13, 1993 "Money & Investing" column, *The Wall Street Journal.* Reprinted by permission of *The Wall Street Journal* © 1993 Dow Jones & Company, Inc.

The Markets' Response: Tools to Manage Financial Price Risk

Exchange Rate Risk Management Products

Foreign exchange forward contracts have been available for decades. But not surprisingly, it was only in the early 1970s that this financial instrument came into its own. In Chapters 2 and 6 we will demonstrate that a forward contract involves the extension of credit. Consequently, by the 1970s the forward foreign exchange market had become primarily an interbank market, and for this reason, many firms confronted with foreign exchange risk were unable to take advantage of the forward market.

As illustrated in Figure 1–6, the financial market responded to the need for greater access to the forward market by creating a range of risk management instruments. The first to appear was futures contracts on foreign exchange. In May 1972, the International Monetary Market of the Chicago Mercantile Exchange (CME) began trading futures contracts on the British pound, Canadian dollar, deutsche mark, Japanese yen, and Swiss franc.[10]

Currency swaps were next to appear. In Chapter 10, we will note that precursors to swaps, such as back-to-back and parallel loans, had been used since the onset of volatility in foreign exchange rates. However, the World Bank–IBM swap of August 1981 is generally regarded as the public introduction of currency swaps.

Option contracts on foreign exchange followed closely on the heels of swaps. In December 1982, the Philadelphia Stock Exchange introduced an option contract on the British pound, which was followed by options on the Canadian dollar, deutsche mark, Japanese yen, and Swiss franc in January and February 1983.[11]

The Chicago Mercantile Exchange followed with the introduction of options on foreign exchange futures in these currencies:

Deutsche mark, January 1984;

British pound and Swiss franc, February 1985;

Japanese yen, March 1986; and

Canadian dollar, June 1986.[12]

FIGURE 1–6 Evolution of Exchange Rate Risk Management Tools

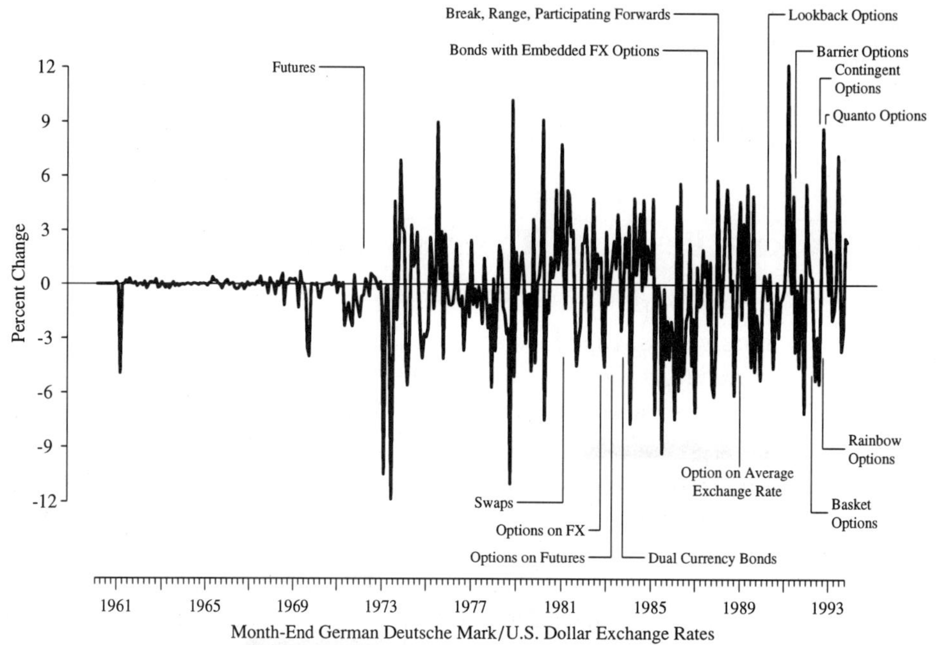

Commercial banks responded by offering their clients over-the-counter foreign exchange options. As we will describe in Chapter 15, the banks also created forward foreign exchange contracts with optionlike characteristics. Break forwards, range forwards, and participating forwards had all entered the market lexicon by 1987.

Once the market had developed the basic building blocks—forwards, futures, swaps, and options—the next step was to introduce combinations of the building blocks and more complex forms of the basic instruments.

In Chapter 15 we will examine the evolution of more complex forms of the instruments. In Figure 1–6, we have illustrated the appearance of path-dependent options—options on average exchange rates, lookback options, barrier options, and contingent options—and multifactor options—rainbow options, quanto options, and basket options—in the 1990s.

In addition to the financial instruments themselves, rising foreign-exchange-rate volatility spawned a number of the "hybrid securities." We will discuss these in Chapter 16. Hybrid securities can be viewed as a combination of a standard debt instrument and one or more of the financial instruments. In Figure 1–6 we note the introduction of dual currency bonds[13] in 1984 and bonds with embedded foreign exchange options in 1987.

Interest Rate Risk Management Products

As uncertainty about interest rates increased in the 1970s, financial institutions became less willing to make long-term rate commitments. Instead, lenders turned to floating-rate loans, which first appeared after the period of rising rates and volatility in 1973–74 and had become widely used by the 1980s.

Floating-rate loans helped banks and S&Ls manage their exposure to interest rate movements, but only by passing the interest rate risk to the borrower.[14] Better tools for managing interest rate risk were required, and as indicated in Figure 1–7, they were not long in coming.

In contrast to the foreign exchange market, there had been no long-established forward market for interest rates. Consequently, financial futures were the first financial instrument designed to help firms manage their interest rate risk. The progression of futures contracts on U.S. dollar interest rates introduced on the

FIGURE 1–7 Evolution of Interest Rate Risk Management Tools

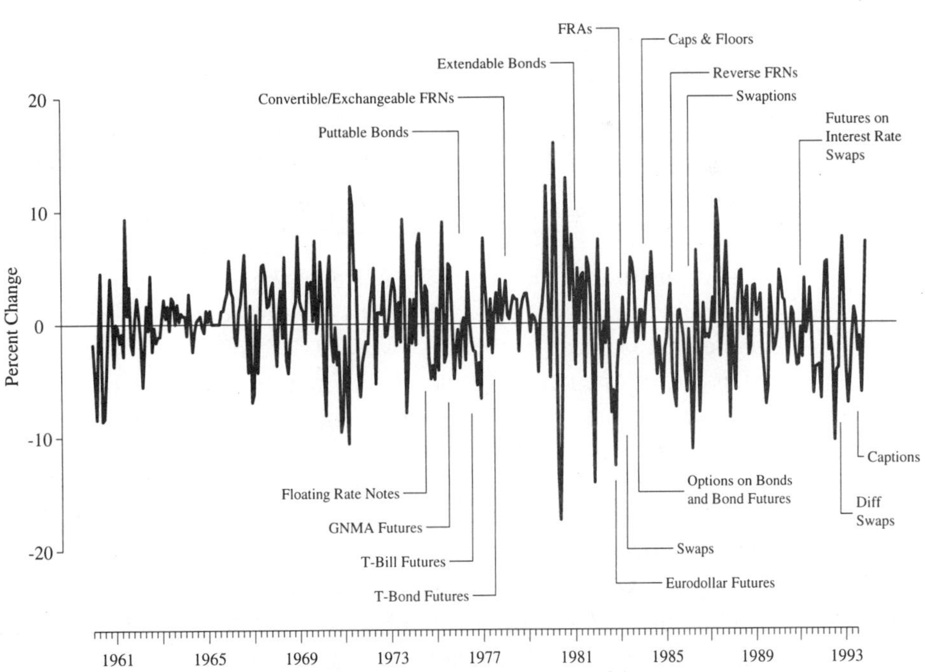

Chicago Board of Trade (CBOT) and the Chicago Mercantile Exchange is presented below:

First Day Trading	*Underlying Asset*	*Exchange*
October 1975	GNMA	CBOT
January 1976	U.S. T-Bills	CME
August 1977	U.S. T-Bonds	CBOT
December 1981	Eurodollar	CME
May 1982	T-notes	CBOT

Although the futures exchanges had established a large lead in the field of interest rate risk management products, banks responded to the demand for these products in the 1980s. Interest rate swaps came first, in 1982. Then in early 1983 banks provided the missing forward market for interest rates with the introduction of forward-rate agreements (FRAs).

As was the pattern in the foreign exchange markets, the introduction of options followed quickly. Option contracts on the U.S. Treasury bonds and notes appeared on the Chicago Board Options Exchange (CBOE). Options on futures on the underlying asset were introduced on both the CBOT and the CME:

First Day Trading	*Underlying Asset*	*Exchange*
October 1982	T-Bond Futures	CBOT
October 1982	T-Bond	CBOE
March 1985	Eurodollar Futures	CME
May 1985	T-Note Futures	CBOT
July 1985	T-Note	CBOE
April 1986	T-Bill Futures	CME

And again as in the case of foreign exchange, banks responded to the exchanges by introducing interest rate options in over-the-counter form: caps, floors, and collars began to appear in 1983. As we will describe in Chapter 15, caps, floors, and collars are combinations of individual interest rate options. In other words, a two-year cap on three-month LIBOR is made up of seven options on three-month LIBOR, one with a maturity of three months, one with a maturity of six months, and so on until the final option, which has a maturity of 21 months.

As was the case with foreign exchange risk management products, we also saw the introduction of *hybrid securities*, debt with embedded interest rate risk management derivatives. In Figure 1–7, we note a few of the hybrids we will examine in Chapter 16: puttable bonds in 1976, convertible/exchangeable floating-rate notes in 1985, extendable bonds in 1982, and inverse floating-rate notes in 1986.

Most recently, we have seen the introduction of combinations and more complex forms of the basic interest rate risk management products: swaptions (an option on a swap), captions (an option on an interest rate cap), futures on interest rate swaps, and diff swaps (swaps on the differential between two interest rates). These instruments will be described in Chapter 15.

Commodity-Price Risk Management Products

As they did with foreign exchange and interest rates, financial markets responded to the increased commodity-price risk with new instruments. The evolution of financial instruments to manage petroleum price risk is traced in Figure 1–8.

Given the preponderance of long-term contracting in the oil industry, forward contracts per se had never been a significant feature of the petroleum market. But as oil prices became more volatile, futures contracts were not long in appearing. Heating oil futures appeared on the New York Mercantile Exchange (NYMEX) in November 1978, and futures on West Texas Intermediate (WTI) crude oil appeared there in March 1983.

FIGURE 1–8 Evolution of Petroleum Price Risk Management Tools

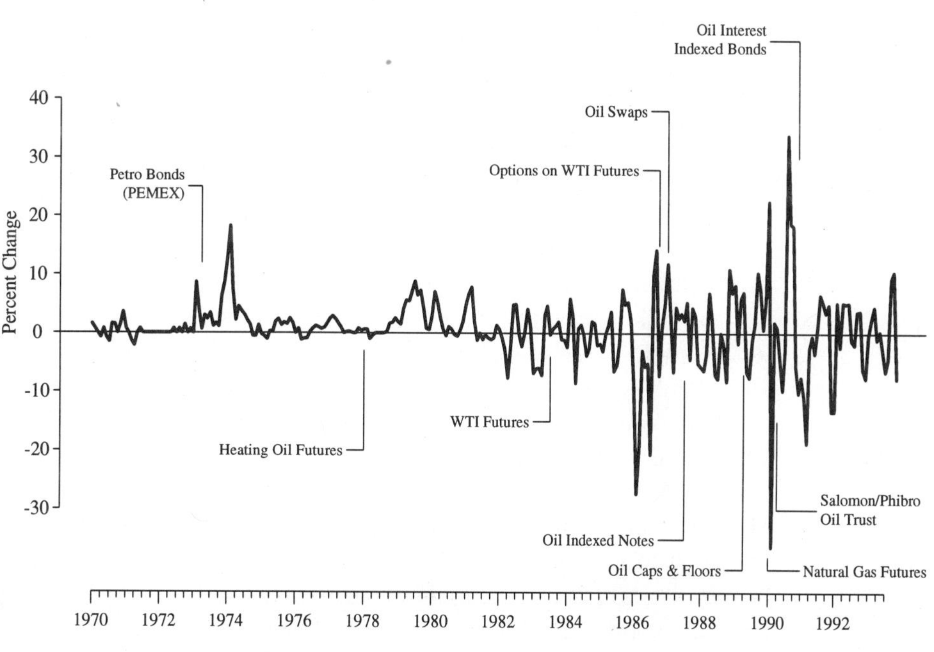

Percentage Change in the Producer Price Index of Light Oil

And as with all the other risk management markets we have observed, options followed quickly. Options on WTI crude oil futures were introduced in November 1986, and options on heating oil futures followed in June 1987.

Commercial banks began providing commodity price risk management products in 1986, when The Chase Manhattan Bank arranged the first oil swap. However, in 1987, the Commodity Futures Trading Commission (CFTC) challenged the legality of bank activity in this market in the United States.[15] Not surprisingly, the CFTC action had a "chilling effect on new product development"[16] and led to the business moving overseas. It was not until 1993 that the CFTC passed rules that provided comfort to this market and product development began again in earnest.

Hybrid securities involving commodities have also evolved. The earliest petroleum hybrid was the so-called "Petrobonds" issued by Pemex in 1973. As we will describe in Chapter 16, these Petrobonds can be viewed as straight debt plus a long-dated forward contract on oil. With its June 1986 issue of oil-indexed notes, Standard Oil made the first inroad into bonds with embedded oil warrants. And bonds with interest payments indexed to the price of petroleum products appeared in 1991.[17]

Recently, new futures contracts and new products have appeared. We have seen the addition of a futures contract on natural gas, now listed on the NYMEX. And we witnessed the development of several investment products based on petroleum prices—the Salomon/Phibro Oil Trust and the Goldman Sachs Commodity Index.

How Much Is Really New?

So far in this chapter, we have traced the evolution in the 1970s and 1980s of financial structures that have come to be called innovations in the capital markets. Forward-rate agreements; futures contracts on foreign exchange rates, interest rates, metals, and petroleum; currency, interest rate, and commodity swaps; options on foreign exchange rates, interest rates, and petroleum; and hybrid securities—all these represent innovations in the sense that they provide firms with the ability to deal with an increasingly risky financial environment.

But it is misleading to think of these financial instruments as recent discoveries. If anything, these risk management instruments have been *rediscovered* in the 1970s and 1980s.

For example, while futures contracts have been traded since 1865 on the Chicago Board of Trade, futures contracts are actually much older.[18] Historians suggest that futures contracts first appeared in Japan in the 1600s. The feudal lords of Japan used a market they called *cho-ai-mai*—rice trade on book—to manage the volatility in rice prices caused by weather, warfare, and other sources.[19] Formal futures markets also appeared in Europe—in the Netherlands—during the 1600s. Among the most notable of these early futures contracts were the tulip futures that developed during the height of the Dutch "tulipmania" in 1636.[20]

7 PER CENT COTTON LOAN
OF THE
Confederate States of America,
FOR 3 MILLIONS STERLING OR 75 MILLIONS FRANCS.
Series A
No. 1347
£1,000
F25,000
40,000 lbs. COTTON.

J. HENRY SCHRÖDER & Co.

ÉMILE ERLANGER & Cie.

THE CONFEDERATE STATES OF AMERICA are indebted to the Holder of this Bond in the Sum of ONE THOUSAND POUNDS Sterling, with Interest at the rate of Seven per Cent. per Annum, payable on the First Day of March and the First Day of September in each Year, in Paris, London, Amsterdam, or Frankfort °/M against delivery of the corresponding Coupon, until redemption of the Principal.

THIS BOND forms part of an issue of Seventy-five Millions of Francs, equal to Three Million Pounds Sterling, with Coupons attached till first September, 1883, inclusive, and redeemable at par in the course of twenty years by means of half-yearly drawings, the first of which takes place first March, 1864, the last first September, 1883.

At each drawing, one-fortieth part of the amount unredeemed by Cotton as indicated below is to be drawn; and all Bonds then drawn will be repaid at the option of the holder, in Paris, London, Amsterdam, or Frankfort °/M.

The Holder of the Bond, however, will have the option of converting the same at its nominal amount into Cotton, at the rate of sixpence sterling per pound—say 40,000 lbs. of Cotton in exchange for a Bond of £1000—at any time not later than six months after the ratification of a Treaty of Peace between the present belligerents. Notice of the intention of converting Bouds into Cotton to be given to the representatives of the Government in Paris or London, and sixty days after such notice the Cotton will be delivered, if peace, at the ports of Charleston, Savannah, Mobile, or New Orleans; if war, at a point in the interior within 10 miles of a railroad or stream navigable to the ocean. The delivery will be made free of all charges and duties, except the existing export duty of one-eighth of a cent per pound. The quality of the Cotton to be the standard of New Orleans middling. If any Cotton is of superior or inferior quality, the difference in value shall be settled by two Brokers, one to be appointed by the Government, the other by the Bondholder: whenever these two Brokers cannot agree on the value, an Umpire is to be chosen, whose decision shall be final.

The said issue and the above conditions are authorised by an Act of Congress, approved 29th January, 1863, a certified copy of which is deposited with Messrs. FRESHFIELDS & NEWMAN, in London, the Solicitors to the Contractors, and the faith of the Confederate States is pledged accordingly.

In Witness whereof, the Agent for the Loan of the Confederate States in Paris, duly authorised, has set his hand, and affixed the Seal of the Treasury Department, in Paris, the first day of June, in the year of Our Lord One Thousand Eight Hundred and Sixty-three.

LES ÉTATS CONFÉDÉRÉS D'AMÉRIQUE doivent au Porteur de cette Obligation la somme de MILLE LIVRES STERLING ou VINGT-CINQ MILLE FRANCS, portant intérêt à raison de Sept pour Cent l'an, payable le premier Mars et le premier Septembre de chaque année à Paris, Londres, Amsterdam et Francfort s/M, contre le Coupon respectif jusqu'à remboursement du Capital.

CETTE OBLIGATION fait partie d'une émission de Soixante-et-Quinze Millions de Francs, égale à Trois Millions de Livres Sterling, avec Coupons jusqu'au premier Septembre 1883 inclus, et remboursable au pair dans l'espace de vingt années moyennant des tirages semestriels, dont le premier aura lieu le premier Mars 1864, et le dernier le premier Septembre 1883.

Chaque tirage comprendra la quarantième partie du capital non-remboursé selon le mode indiqué ci-après, et chaque Obligation sortie sera remboursée au choix du Porteur à Paris, Londres, Amsterdam et Francfort s/M.

Le Porteur de l'Obligation aura le droit de réclamer le remboursement du montant nominal en Coton, au prix de sixpence sterling par livre de Coton, soit 40,000 livres par Obligation de £1000 (Frs. 25,000), et ceci, en tout temps, jusqu'aux six mois qui suivront la ratification d'un Traité de Paix entre les belligérants. La déclaration de convertir l'Obligation en Coton devra être faite aux réprésentants du Gouvernement à Paris ou à Londres, et soixante jours après le Coton sera délivré, en cas de paix, dans les ports de Charleston, Savannah, Mobile ou de la Nouvelle-Orléans, et, en cas de guerre, dans l'intérieur du pays, à une distance de dix milles au plus d'un chemin de fer ou d'une rivière navigable jusqu'à la mer. La livraison sera faite libre de tous frais et impôts, à l'exception du droit d'exportation actuellement en vigueur de ⅛ cent américain par livre. La qualité du Coton devra être le type de "New Orleans middling." Si tout ou partie du Coton est de qualité supérieure ou inférieure, la différence en valeur sera réglée par deux Courtiers, l'un désigné par le Gouvernement et l'autre par le Porteur de l'Obligation. Dans le cas où ces deux Courtiers ne pourraient s'accorder, un Arbitre sera choisi et sa décision sera définitive.

Ladite émission et les conditions ci-dessus indiquées sont autorisées par un Acte du Congrès approuvé le 29 Janvier 1863, dont une copie légalisée est déposée chez Messrs. FRESHFIELDS & NEWMAN, à Londres, Solicitors des Contractants: en conséquence les États Confédérés sont engagés.

En Foi de quoi, l'Agent pour l'Emprunt des États Confédérés à Paris, dûment autorisé, a signé et apposé le Sceau du Trésor à Paris, le premier Juin l'an mil huit cent soixante-et-trois.

CONTRACTORS.

AGENT FOR THE LOAN.

AGENTS TO THE CONTRACTORS IN LONDON.

(Countersigned.)

COMMISSIONER.

ON 1st SEPTEMBER, 1883, a further Sum of **£35** will be paid by Messrs. J. HENRY SCHRÖDER & Co., London; or **Frs. 875** by Messrs. EMILE ERLANGER & Co., Paris; or the equivalents at the Exchange of the day by Mr. RAPHAEL ERLANGER, Frankfort o/M, and Messrs. B. H. SCHRÖDER & Co., Amsterdam; together with the principal Sum of **£1000**, or **Frs. 25,000**, on surrender of this BOND and WARRANT.

This is a facsimile of a bond issued in 1863 by the Confederate States of America.

The forward contract is even older. Historians suggest that forward contracts were first used by Flemish traders who gathered for trade fairs on land held by the counts of Champagne. At these medieval trade fairs, a document called a letter *de faire*—a forward contract specifying delivery at a later date—made its appearance in the 12th century.[21]

Of the financial instruments, options were the last to appear and therefore seem to be the most innovative. But options, too, are not new. As early as the 17th century, options on a number of commodities were being traded in Amsterdam.[22]

Even the hybrid securities are not new. In other periods of uncertainty, similar securities have appeared. Since we are Southerners, we would conclude by reminding you of the "cotton bonds" issued by the Confederate States of America.

In 1863, the Confederacy issued a 20-year bond denominated not in Confederate dollars but in French francs and pounds sterling. The most interesting feature of this bond, however, was its convertibility (at the option of the bondholder) into cotton.[23] In the parlance of today's investment banker, the Confederate States of America issued a dual-currency, cotton-indexed bond.

Concluding Remarks

The financial environment of the 1970s stimulated demand for new financial instruments, and the changes that resulted are important in understanding today's financial markets. The financial environment is the key determinant of the kinds of instruments that will be successful in the marketplace. In short, financial innovation is a demand-driven phenomenon.

If the financial environment is stable, the market will use simple instruments. In the late 1800s, for example, the financial instrument of choice was the consol, a bond with a fixed interest rate but no maturity; it lasted forever. Investors were quite happy to hold infinite-lived British government bonds because British sovereign credit was good and expected inflation was nil. Confidence in price-level stability led to a stable interest rate environment and therefore to long-lived bonds.

But in financial environments fraught with uncertainty, we can expect a proliferation of new risk management instruments and hybrid securities. Uncertainty, though disruptive and rife with problems, has stimulated much valuable financial innovation. Through this process of innovation, financial intermediaries can expand their activities by offering customers products to manage risk, or even the ability to turn such risk into an advantage. Moreover, through innovation, financial institutions can better evaluate and manage their own portfolios. Because price uncertainty cannot be eliminated, the clear trend now is to manage risk actively rather than to try to predict price movements.

Notes

1. This decoupling of interest rate risk and credit risk is stressed in Arak, Estrella, Goodman, and Silver (1988).
2. A description of the Bretton Woods system and its effect on prices is contained in Putman and Wilford (1986).
3. For exposition, Figure 1–4 provides the monthly first difference in the rate rather than percentage change or some other measure more closely related to volatility.
4. As we will note when we discuss the evolution of swaps in Chapter 10, U.S. firms were a lot more interested in translation exposures in the 1970s—before Accounting Statement FAS 7 was replaced by FAS 52. Under FAS 7, changes in the value of the asset induced by changes in foreign exchange rates would be reflected in the firm's income. Hence translation exposures would result in volatile income.
5. In the context of traditional economics, an economic exposure to interest rates would result if the firm produces a good that is interest elastic.
6. Whether the cause of this difference or not, it may be useful to note that while almost all of the firms we have talked to manage their exposures to interest rates and foreign exchange rates in the treasury, exposures to commodity prices are likely to be managed in other parts of the firm—for example, a purchasing department.
7. Herman (1993).
8. The function of a dealer (a broker) is to bring together buyers and sellers. For doing so, the dealer is rewarded with the bid/ask spread. As we will discuss throughout this book, in the risk management markets, dealers receive a bid/ask spread for facilitating the transaction. The dealer's task is then to manage the risks so that, at the maturity of the transaction, the dealer has retained as much of this spread as possible.
9. Getler (1993).
10. CME futures contracts on other currencies followed: French franc, September 1974; European Currency Unit, January 1986; and Australian dollar, January 1987.
11. Option contracts on the French franc began trading in 1984, followed by the ECU in 1986 and Australian dollar in 1987.
12. Options on futures are not traded on the CME for French francs, the ECU, or Australian dollars.
13. In Chapter 16 we will demonstrate that a dual currency bond can be viewed as a combination of a standard bond and a long-dated foreign exchange forward contract.
14. While floating-rate loans dealt with the immediate problem of interest rate risk, they did not turn out to be the panacea some expected. By passing the market risk to the borrower, floating-rate loans increased the default risk of the borrower.
15. Commodity Futures Trading Commission (1987).
16. Response of the SEC to the CFTC, August 19, 1988, p. 6.
17. The behavior of the price of metals differs from that of foreign exchange, interest rates, and oil prices in that the price volatility of metals increased in the 1950s as well as in the 1970s. Given what we have seen so far, then, it should come as no surprise that a forward contract on zinc was introduced on the London Metal Exchange (LME) in 1953. (Forward contracts on copper had been traded on the LME since 1883.) With the increase in volatility in the 1970s, forward contracts began trading on the LME on aluminum in 1978 and nickel 1979.

    Futures contracts appeared later on the Commodity Exchange (Comex)—on copper in July 1983 and on aluminum in December 1983. An option on copper futures began trading on the Comex in April 1986.

    Hybrids that modify the timing of the options embedded in the bond have also begun to appear. Magma Copper Company's November 1988 Copper Interest-Indexed Senior Subordinated Notes, for example, were a 10-year issue paying a quarterly interest payment that varied with the prevailing price of copper.
18. The Board of Trade opened in 1842, but in its early years forward rather than futures contracts were traded, according to Chicago Board of Trade (1988).
19. Teweles and Jones (1987).
20. Garter (1986).
21. Teweles and Jones (1987).
22. International Chamber of Commerce (1986).
23. At a set rate of sixpence sterling per pound of cotton.

CHAPTER

2

An Overview of the Risk Management Process

A Building Block Approach to Forwards, Futures, Swaps, Options, and Hybrid Securities*

An Overview of the Risk Management Products

The increased economic uncertainty first evident in the 1970s has altered the way financial markets function. As foreign exchange rates, interest rates, and commodity prices have become more volatile, corporations have discovered that their value is subject to various financial price risks in addition to the risk inherent in their core business.

To illustrate the effect of changes in a given financial price on the value of a firm, we use the concept of a **risk profile**. Figure 2–1 presents a case in which an unexpected increase in financial price P (that is, the T-bill rate, the price of oil, or the dollar price of a yen) decreases the value of the firm (V). In Figure 2–1, the difference between the actual price and the expected price is shown as ΔP, while ΔV measures the resulting change in the value of the firm. Had ΔP remained small, as it did before the 1970s, the indexed changes in firm value would have been correspondingly small. But for many companies, the increased volatility of exchange rates, interest rates, and commodity prices (large ΔPs) in the 1970s and 1980s has been a major cause of sharp fluctuations in share prices (large ΔVs). With this greater potential for large swings in value, companies have begun exploring new methods for dealing with financial risks.

Confronted with the increased volatility of financial prices, companies found that the first and most obvious approach was to try to forecast future prices more accurately. If changes in exchange rates, interest rates, and commodity prices could be predicted with confidence, companies could avoid unexpected swings in value.

*This chapter is adapted from Smithson (1987).

In the context of Figure 2–1, if the actual price could be completely anticipated, ΔP would equal zero and the value of the firm thus would be unchanged. However, economists were generally unsuccessful in predicting changes in interest rates, foreign exchange rates, and commodity prices.

This shouldn't be surprising; attempts to outpredict markets as efficient as the financial markets are unlikely to succeed. Because forecasting cannot be relied on to eliminate risk, the remaining alternative is to *manage* the risks. Financial risk management can be accomplished by using on-balance-sheet transactions. For example, a company can manage a foreign exchange exposure resulting from foreign competition by borrowing in the competitors' currency or by moving production abroad. But such on-balance-sheet methods can be costly and, as firms like Caterpillar have discovered, inflexible.[1]

Alternatively, financial risks can be managed with the use of off-balance-sheet instruments: forwards, futures, swaps, and options. When you first begin to examine these financial instruments, you are confronted by what seems an insurmountable barrier to entry: participants in the various market and the trade publications seem to possess specialized expertise applicable in only one market to the exclusion of all the others. Adding to the complexities of the individual markets themselves is a welter of jargon—ticks, collars, strike prices, straddles, and so forth. Indeed, it appears to the novice like a Wall Street version of the Tower of Babel, with each group of market specialists speaking a different language.

FIGURE 2–1 A Risk Profile Relating the Expected Change in Firm Value (ΔV) to Unexpected Changes in a Financial Price(ΔP)

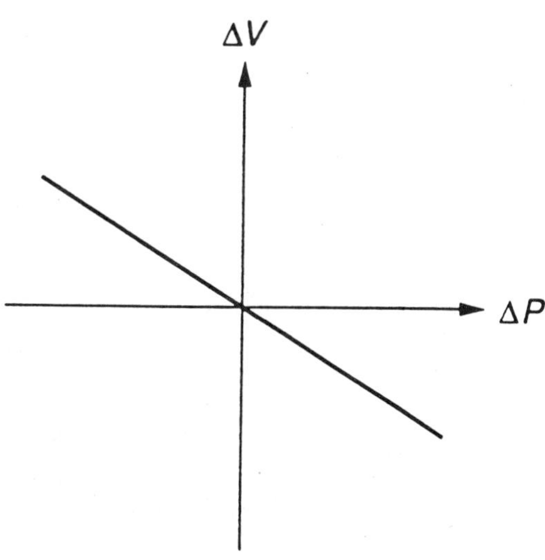

In marked contrast to this specialist approach, this text presents a generalist approach. We treat forwards, futures, swaps, and options not as four unique instruments but rather as four closely related instruments to deal with a single problem—managing financial risk. Indeed, we are going to show how the off-balance-sheet instruments are like those plastic building blocks children snap together: you can build the instruments from one another (or combine the basic instruments into larger creations).

Forward Contracts

Of the four instruments we consider in this text, the forward contract is the most straightforward and, perhaps for this reason, the oldest. A forward contract obligates its owner to buy a given asset on a specified date at a price (known as the *exercise or forward price*) specified at the origination of the contract. If, at maturity, the actual price is higher than the exercise price, the contract owner makes a profit; if the price is lower, the owner suffers a loss.

In Figure 2–2, the payoff from buying a forward contract is superimposed on the original risk profile. If the actual price at contract maturity is higher than the expected price, the firm's inherent risk will lead to a decline in the value of the firm, but this decline will be offset by the profit on the forward contract. Hence, for the risk profile illustrated, this forward contract provides a perfect hedge. (If the risk

FIGURE 2–2 Payoff Profile for Forward Contracts

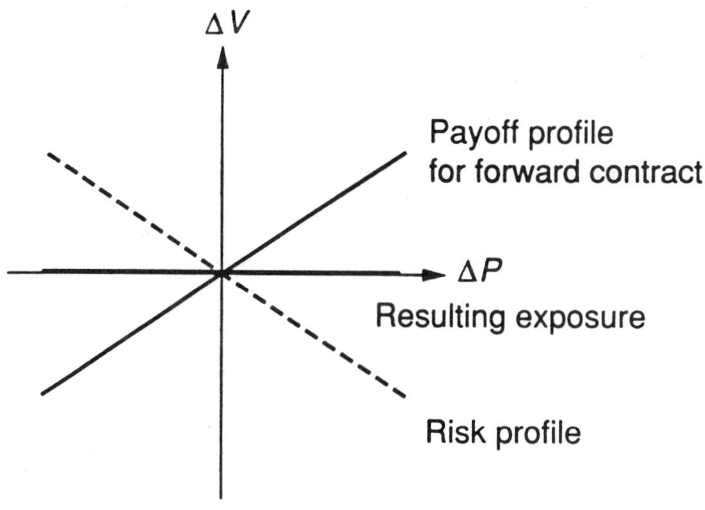

profile were sloped positively instead of negatively, this risk would be managed by selling instead of buying a forward contract.)

In addition to its payoff profile, two features of a forward contract should be noted. First, the default (or credit) risk of the contract is two-sided. The contract owner either receives or makes a payment, depending on the price movement of the underlying asset. Second, the value of the forward contract is conveyed only at the contract's maturity; no payment is made either at origination or during the term of the contract.

Futures Contracts

Although futures contracts on commodities have been traded on organized exchanges since the 1860s, financial futures are relatively new, dating from the introduction of foreign currency futures in 1972. The basic form of the futures contract is identical to that of the forward contract: a futures contract obligates its owner to purchase a specified asset at a specified exercise price on the contract maturity date. Thus, the payoff profile for the purchaser of a forward contract as presented in Figure 2–2 could illustrate equally well the payoff to the holder of a futures contract.

Like the forward contract, the futures contract also has two-sided risk. But in marked contrast to forwards, futures markets use two devices that virtually eliminate credit risk. First, instead of conveying the value of a contract through a single payment at maturity, changes in the value of a futures contract are conveyed at the end of the day in which they are realized. Look again at Figure 2–2. Suppose that on the day after origination the financial price rises and, consequently, the contract has a positive value. In the case of a forward contract, this value change would not be received until contract maturity. With a futures contract, this change in value is received at the end of the day. In the language of the futures markets, the futures contract is *cash settled,* or *marked-to-market,* daily.

Because the performance period of a futures contract is reduced by marking-to-market, the risk of default declines accordingly. Indeed, since the value of the futures contract is paid or received at the end of each day, it is not hard to see why Fischer Black likened a futures contract to "a series of forward contracts. Each day, yesterday's contract is settled, and today's contract is written."[2] That is, a futures contract is like a sequence of forwards in which the "forward" contract written on day 0 is settled on day 1 and is replaced, in effect, with a new "forward" contract reflecting the new day-1 expectations. This new contract is then itself settled on day 2 and replaced, and so on until the day the contract ends.

The second feature of futures contracts that reduces default risk is the requirement that all market participants—sellers and buyers alike[3]—post a performance bond called *margin*. If your futures contract increases in value during the trading day, this gain is added to your margin account at the day's end. Conversely, if your contract loses value, this loss is deducted. And if your margin account balance falls below some agreed-upon minimum, you are required to post an additional bond—your margin account must be replenished or your position will be closed out.[4] Because this process generally closes any position before the margin account is depleted, performance risk is materially reduced.[5]

Note that the exchange itself limits the default risk exposure of its customers. Yet while daily settlement and the requirement of a bond reduce default risk, the existence of an exchange (or clearinghouse) primarily transforms risk. More specifically, the exchange deals with the two-sided risk inherent in forwards and futures by serving as the counterparty to all transactions. If you wish to buy or sell a futures contract, you buy from or sell to the exchange. Hence, you need only evaluate the credit risk of the exchange, not the credit risk of some specific counterparty.

From the point of view of the market, the exchange does not reduce default risk; the expected default rate is not affected by the existence of the exchange. However, the existence of the exchange can alter the default risk faced by an individual market participant. If you buy a futures contract from a specific individual, the default risk you face is determined by the default rate of that specific counterparty. If instead you buy the same futures contract through an exchange, your default risk depends on the default rate not just of your counterparty but on the rate of the entire market. Moreover, to the extent that the exchange is capitalized by equity from its members, the default risk you face is reduced further because you have a claim not against some specific counterparty but rather against the exchange. Therefore, when you trade through the exchange, you are in a sense purchasing an insurance policy from the exchange.

The primary economic function of the exchange is to reduce the costs of transacting in futures contracts. The anonymous trades made possible through the exchange, together with the homogeneous nature of the futures contracts—standardized assets, exercise dates (four per year), and contract sizes—enable the futures markets to become relatively liquid. However, as was made clear by recent experience of the London Metal Exchange, the exchange structure, marking-to-market, and margin accounts do not eliminate default risk. In November 1985, the "tin cartel" defaulted on contracts for tin delivery on the London Metal Exchange, thereby making the exchange liable for the loss.[6]

In sum, a futures contract is much like a portfolio of forward contracts. At the close of business each day, in effect, the existing forwardlike contract is settled and a new one is written.[7] This daily settlement feature combined with the margin requirement allows futures contracts to reduce substantially the credit risk inherent in forwards.

Swap Contracts[8]

Because they were publicly introduced only in 1981, swaps are commonly portrayed as one of the latest financing innovations. But as we hope to be able to convince you, a swap contract is in essence nothing more complicated than a portfolio of forward contracts. We will also demonstrate that the credit risk attending swaps is somewhat less than that of a forward contract with the same maturity but greater than that of a comparable futures contract.

As implied by its name, a swap contract obligates two parties to exchange, or swap, some specified cash flows at specified intervals. The most common form is the *interest rate swap*, in which the cash flows are determined by two different interest rates.

Panel (a) of Figure 2–3 illustrates an interest rate swap from the perspective of a party who is paying out a series of cash flows determined by a fixed interest ($\bar{R}_T$) and receiving a series of cash flows determined by a floating interest rate ($\tilde{R}$).[9]

Panel (b) of Figure 2–3 demonstrates that this swap contract can be decomposed into a portfolio of forward contracts. At each settlement date, the party to this swap

FIGURE 2–3 **(*a*) An Interest Rate Swap** **(*b*) An Interest Rate Swap as a Portfolio of Forward Contracts**

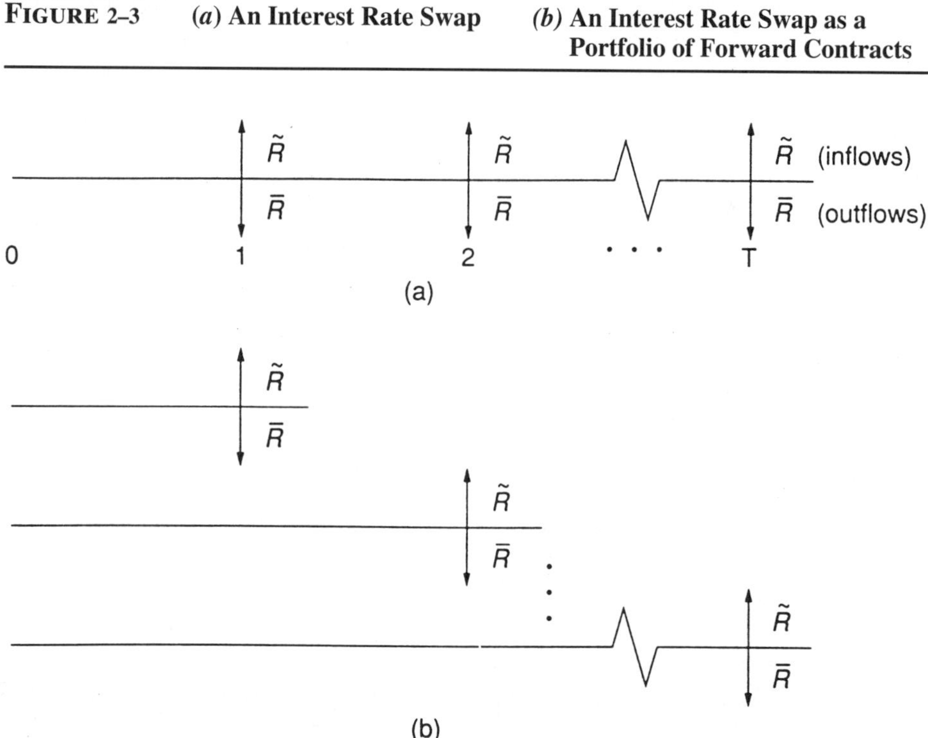

has an implicit forward contract on interest rates: The party illustrated is obligated to sell a fixed-rate cash flow for an amount specified at the origination of the contract. Also in this sense, a swap contract is like a portfolio of forward contracts.

In terms of our earlier discussion, this means that the solid line in Figure 2–2 also represents the payoff from a swap contract. Specifically, the solid line in Figure 2–2 illustrates a swap contract in which the party receives cash flows determined by P (say, the U.S. Treasury bond rate) and makes payments determined by another price—say, London InterBank Offer Rate (LIBOR). Thus, in terms of their ability to manage risk, forwards, futures, and swaps all function in the same way.

But similar payoff profiles notwithstanding, the instruments differ with respect to their default risk. As we know, the performance period of a forward is equal to its maturity; because no performance bond is required, a forward contract is a pure credit instrument. Futures reduce the performance period (to one day) as well as requiring a bond, thus virtually eliminating credit risk. Swap contracts typically use only one of these mechanisms to reduce credit risk; they reduce the performance period.[10] This point becomes evident in Figure 2–3. Although the maturity of the contract is T periods, the performance period is generally not T periods long but is instead a single period. Thus, given a swap and a forward contract of roughly the same maturity, the swap is likely to impose far less credit risk on the counterparties to the contract than the forward. This credit risk difference between swaps and forwards is analogous to that between an amortized loan and a zero-coupon bond.

At each settlement date throughout a swap contract, the changes in value are transferred between the counterparties. To illustrate this in terms of Figure 2–3, suppose that interest rates rise on the day after origination. The value of the swap contract illustrated has risen. This value change will be conveyed to the contract owner not at maturity (as would be the case with a forward contract) nor at the end of that day (as would be the case with a futures contract). Instead, at the first settlement date, part of the value change is conveyed in the form of the "difference check" paid by one party to the other. To repeat, then, the performance period is reduced from that of a forward, albeit not to so short a period as that of a futures contract.[11] (Keep in mind that we are comparing instruments with the same maturities.)

At this point let us stop to summarize the two major points made thus far. First, a swap contract, like a futures contract, is like a portfolio of forward contracts. Therefore, the basic payoff profiles for each of these three instruments are similar. Second, the primary differences among forwards, futures, and swaps are the settlement features of the contracts and amount of default risk these instruments impose on counterparties to the contracts. Forwards and futures represent the extremes, with a swap being the intermediate case.

It is important to note that swaps do impose some credit risk. For this reason it is not surprising that commercial banks have become increasingly active in a market that was initiated, for the most part, by investment banks. The sharp difference of opinion that has arisen between commercial and investment banks over the "most advisable" evolutionary path for the swap market to follow is also understandable. Because investment banks are not in the business of extending credit, they would much prefer swaps to become more like futures—that is, exchange-traded instruments with bonded contract performance. Commercial banks, by contrast, have a comparative advantage in credit extension and thus stand to benefit if swaps remain credit instruments. Accordingly, they would prefer the credit risk to be managed by imposing capital requirements on the financial institutions arranging the swaps.

Option Contracts

As we have seen, the owner of a forward, futures, or swap contract has an *obligation* to perform. In contrast, an option gives its owner a *right*, not an obligation. An option giving its owner the right to buy an asset—a call option—is provided in Figure 2–4. (Here, once again, the financial price *P* could be an interest rate, a foreign exchange rate, the price of a commodity, or the price of some other financial asset.) The owner of the contract illustrated has the right to purchase the asset at a specified future date at a price agreed upon today. Consequently if *P* rises, the value of the option also goes up. But the value of the option remains unchanged (at zero) if *P* declines because the option contract owner is not obligated to purchase the asset if *P* moves to an unfavorable price.[12]

FIGURE 2–4 The Payoff Profile of a Call Option

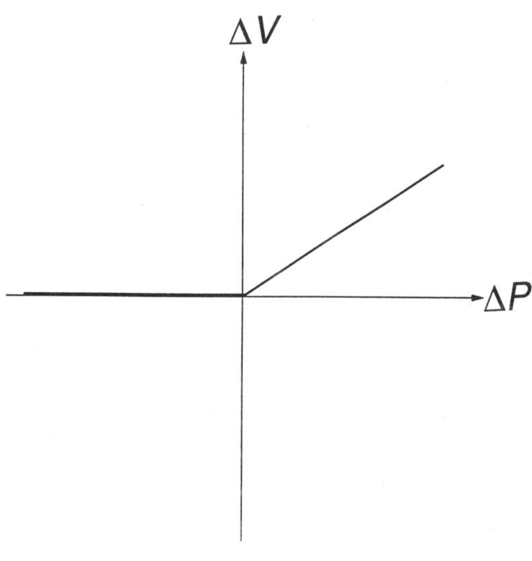

The payoff profile for the owner of the call option is repeated in panel (a) of Figure 2–5. In this case, the contract owner has bought the right to buy the asset at a specified price—the exercise (strike) price. (In Figures 2–4 and 2–5, the exercise price is implicitly equal to the expected price.)

The payoff profile for the party who sold the call option (also known as the call writer) is shown in panel (b). Note that in contrast to the buyer of the option, the seller of the call option has the *obligation* to perform. For example, if the owner of the option elects to exercise his or her option to buy the asset, the seller of the option is obligated to sell the asset.

Aside from the option to buy an asset, there is also the option to sell an asset at a specified price, known as a *put* option. The payoff to the buyer of a put is illustrated in panel (c) of Figure 2–5, and the payoff for the seller of the put is shown in panel (d).

In many instances, jargon does more to confuse than to make clear, and this is particularly true in the buy/sell, call/put jargon of options. Suppose you were

FIGURE 2–5 Payoff Profiles of Puts and Calls

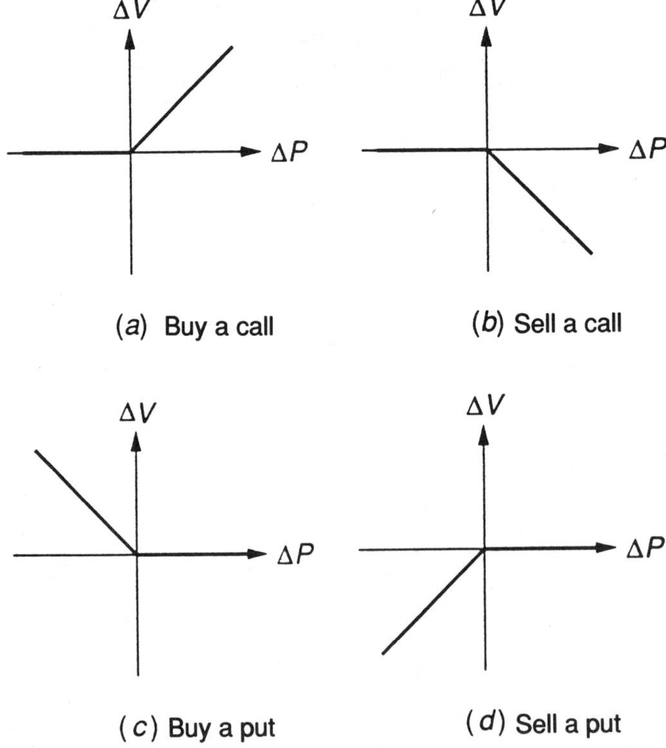

exposed to rising interest rates—that is, an increase in interest rates reduced your wealth. As illustrated by the left side of Figure 2–6, you could eliminate the downside exposure by buying a call on the interest rate (that is, you could buy an interest rate cap). Expressed in terms of bond prices, however, the proper strategy for hedging the same exposure would be to buy a put on bonds. As Figures 2–6 illustrates, a call on interest rates is equivalent to a put on bonds. The same thing occurs, moreover, in the foreign exchange market; a put on DM/$ is equivalent to a call on $/DM. (There have been times when two persons arguing about whether something was a put or a call were, in fact, both right.)

To this point, we have considered only the payoffs for the option contracts. Figures 2–4 through 2–6 assume in effect that option premiums are neither paid by the buyer nor received by the seller. By making this assumption, we have sidestepped the thorniest issue, the valuation of option contracts. We now turn to option valuation.

The breakthrough in option pricing theory came with the work of Fischer Black and Myron Scholes in 1973. Conveniently for our purposes, Black and Scholes took what might be described as a building-block approach to the valuation of options. Look again at the call option illustrated in Figure 2–4. For increases in the financial price, the payoff profile for the option is that of a forward contract. For decreases in the price, the value of the option is constant, like that of a riskless security such as a Treasury bill.

The work of Black and Scholes demonstrates that a call option could be replicated by a continuously adjusting (dynamic) portfolio of two securities: (1) forward contracts on the underlying asset and (2) riskless securities. As the financial price

FIGURE 2–6 Hedging Exposures with Options

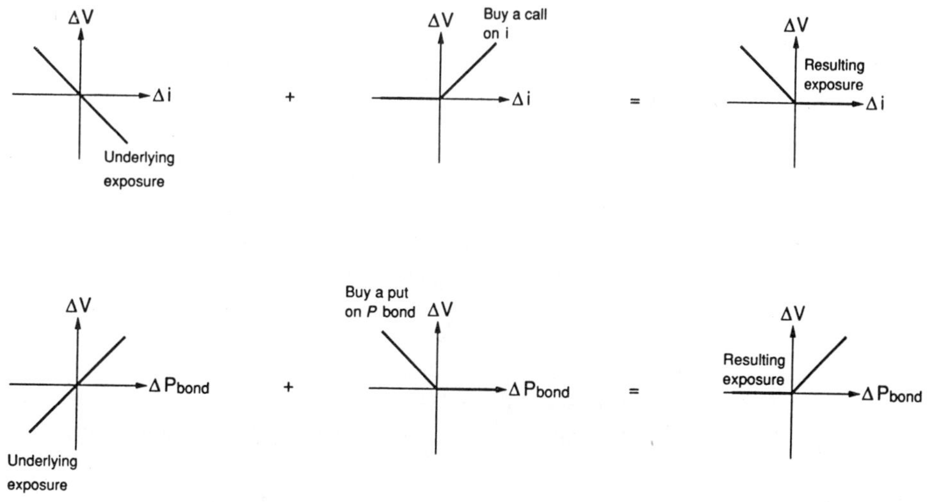

ΔV
Δi
Underlying exposure
+
ΔV
Buy a call on i
Δi
=
ΔV
Resulting exposure
Δi

ΔV
Δ P_{bond}
Underlying exposure
+
Buy a put on *P* bond
ΔV
Δ P_{bond}
=
ΔV
Resulting exposure
Δ P_{bond}

rises, the call-option-equivalent portfolio contains an increasing proportion of forward contracts on the asset. Conversely, the replicating portfolio contains a decreasing proportion of the asset as the price of the asset falls. Because this replicating portfolio is effectively a synthetic call option, arbitrage activity should ensure that its value closely approximates the market price of exchange-traded call options. In this sense, the value of a call option—and thus the premium that would be charged its buyer—is determined by the value of its option-equivalent portfolio.

Panel (a) of Figure 2–7 illustrates the payoff profile for a call option that includes the premium. This figure (and all of the option figures thus far) illustrates an *at-the-money option,* an option for which the exercise price is the prevailing expected price. As panels (a) and (b) of Figure 2–7 illustrate, an at-the-money option is paid for by sacrificing a significant amount of the firm's potential gains. However, the price of a call option falls as the exercise price increases relative to

FIGURE 2–7 *(a), (b)* **"At-the-Money" Option** *(c), (d)* **"Out-of-the-Money" Option**

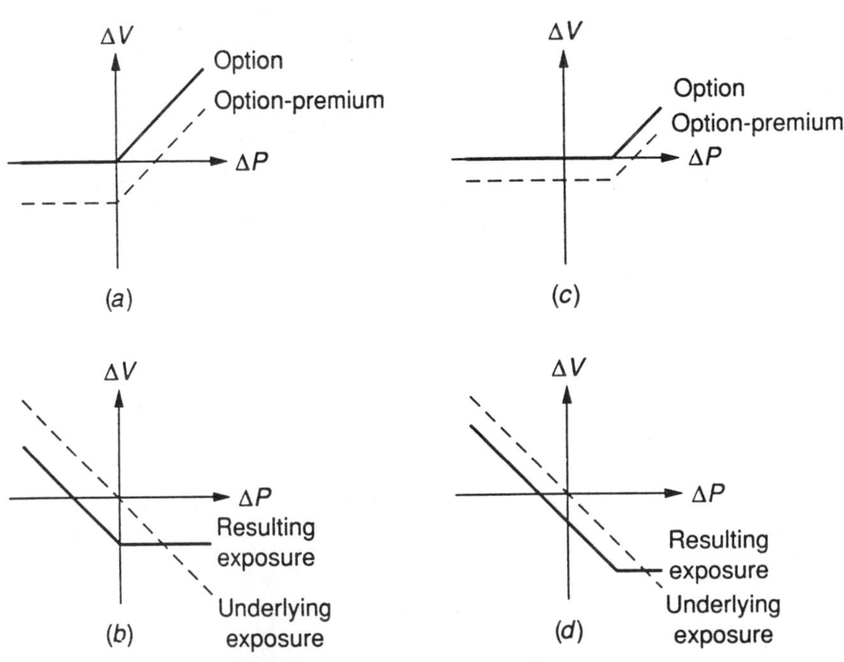

(a) The payoff profit for buying an at-the-money call option. The dashed line reflects the premium.
(b) The resulting exposure from buying the at-the-money option.
(c) The payoff profit for buying an out-of-the-money call option.
(d) The resulting exposure from buying the out-of-the-money option.

the prevailing price of the asset. This means that an option buyer who is willing to accept larger potential losses in return for paying a lower option premium should consider using an out-of-the-money option.

An out-of-the-money call option, illustrated in panel (c) of Figure 2–7, provides less downside protection than other instruments, but the option premium is significantly less. The lesson here is that option buyers can alter their payoff profiles simply by changing the exercise price.

For the purposes of this discussion, however, the most important feature of options is that they are not as different from other financial instruments as they might first seem. Options do have a payoff profile that differs significantly from that of forward contracts (or futures or swaps). But option payoff profiles can be duplicated by a dynamically adjusted combination of forwards and risk-free securities. Thus, we find that options have more in common with the other instruments than is immediately apparent. Futures and swaps, as we saw earlier, are in essence nothing more than particular portfolios of forward contracts; options, as we have just seen, are very much akin to portfolios of forward contracts and risk-free securities.

This point is reinforced if we consider ways that options can be combined. Consider a portfolio constructed by buying a call and selling a put with the same exercise price and maturity. As the top row of Figure 2–8 illustrates, the resulting

FIGURE 2–8 Put-Call Parity

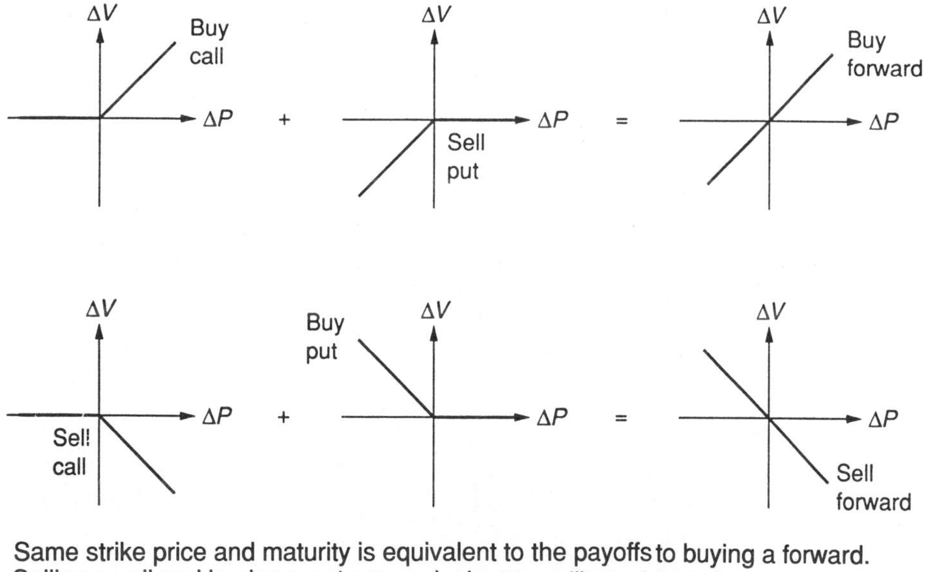

Same strike price and maturity is equivalent to the payoffs to buying a forward. Selling a call and buying a put are equivalent to selling a forward.

portfolio (long a call, short a put) has a payoff profile equivalent to that of buying a forward contract on the asset. Similarly, the bottom row of Figure 2–8 illustrates that a portfolio constructed by selling a call and buying a put (short a call, long a put) is equivalent to selling a forward contract. The relation illustrated in Figure 2–8 is known more formally as put-call parity. The special import of this relation, at least in this context, is the building-block construction it makes possible: two options can be "snapped together" to yield the payoff profile for a forward contract.

At the beginning of this section, then, it seemed that options would be very different from forwards, futures, and swaps; in many ways they are. But we discovered two building-block relations between options and the other three instruments:

1. Options can be replicated by "snapping together" a forward, futures, or swap contract with a position in risk-free securities.
2. Calls and puts can be "snapped together" to become forwards.

The Box of Financial Building Blocks

Forwards, futures, swaps, and options—to the novice, they all look so different. And if you read the trade publications or talk to the participants in the four markets, the apparent differences among the instruments are likely to seem even more pronounced. It looks as if the only way to deal with the financial instruments is to pick one and then become a specialist in that market, to the exclusion of the others.

However, it turns out that forwards, futures, swaps, and options are more like building blocks—to be linked together into complex creations—and less like standalone, individual constructions. To understand the off-balance-sheet instruments, you don't need a lot of market-specific knowledge; you just need to know how the instruments can be linked to one another. As we have seen: (1) futures are built by snapping together a package of forwards; (2) swaps are similarly built by snapping together a package of forwards; (3) options can be built by snapping together a forward with a riskless security; and (4) options can be snapped together to yield forward contracts, or forwards can be snapped apart to yield a package of options.

Figure 2–9 characterizes each of the four instruments we have been discussing according to the shapes of their payoff profiles. It also reminds us of the put-call parity relation between options and forwards, futures, or swaps. In so doing, Figure 2–9 in effect provides the instruction manual for our box of financial building blocks. A quick look shows that though there can be many pieces in the box, there are only six basic shapes with which to concern yourself. The straight pieces come in three colors; we know we can obtain a forward payoff profile either with forwards (the red ones), futures (the yellow ones), or swaps (the blue ones). The kinked pieces are all the same color (white) because options can be combined to replicate a forward, a future, or a swap.

FIGURE 2–9 The Financial Building Blocks

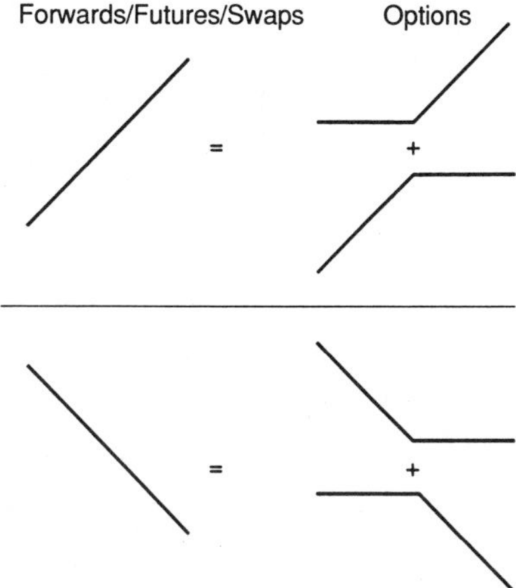

In forthcoming chapters, we examine the individual risk management instruments in detail. Chapters 6 and 7 deal with forwards. Chapters 8 and 9 describe futures. Swaps are discussed in Chapters 10 and 11, and Chapters 12–14 cover options. We do want you to have some detailed information about how each of the instruments, as well as the market within which it is traded, work. But in the chapters to come, we don't want you to lose sight of the building-block nature of these financial instruments. Indeed, we follow these chapters about the individual building blocks with two chapters (Chapters 15 and 16) that could best be described as a blueprint for constructing complicated financial instruments (the so-called hybrid securities) building block by building block.

Notes

1. See "Caterpillar's Triple Whammy," *Fortune,* October 27, 1986.
2. See Black (1976).
3. Keep in mind that if you buy a futures contract, you are taking a long position in the underlying asset—i.e., the value of the futures position appreciates with increases in the value of the asset. Conversely, selling a futures contract is equivalent to taking a short position.
4. When the contract is originated on the U.S. exchanges, an "initial margin" is required. Subsequently, the margin account balance must remain above the "maintenance margin." If the margin account balance falls below the maintenance level, the balance must be restored to the initial level.
5. Note that this discussion has ignored daily limits. If there are daily limits on the movement of futures

prices, large changes in expectations about the underlying asset can effectively close the market. (The market opens, immediately moves the limit, and then is effectively closed until the next day.) Hence, there could exist an instance in which the broker desires to close out a customer's position but is not able to do so immediately because the market is experiencing limit moves. In such a case, the statement that performance risk is "eliminated" is too strong.

6. A description of this situation is contained in "Tin Crisis in London Roils Metal Exchange," *The Wall Street Journal,* November 13, 1985.
7. A futures contract is *similar* to a portfolio of forward contracts; however, a futures contract and a portfolio of forward contracts become identical only if interest rates are *deterministic*—that is, known with certainty in advance. See Jarrow and Oldfield (1981) and Cox, Ingersoll, and Ross (1981).
8. This section is based on Smith, Smithson, and Wakeman, (1986).
9. Specifically, the interest rate swap cash flows are determined as follows: the two parties agree to some notional principal, P. (The principal is notional in the sense that it is only used to determine the magnitude of cash flows; it is not paid or received by either party.) At each settlement date, 1, 2, . . . , T, the party illustrated makes a payment $\bar{R}_T = \bar{r}_T P$, where $\bar{r}_T$ is the T-period fixed rate that existed at origination. At each settlement, the party illustrated receives $\tilde{R} = \tilde{r}P$, where $\tilde{r}$ is the floating rate for that period—that is, at settlement date 2, the interest rate used is the one-period rate in effect at period 1.
10. There are instances in a which bond has been posted in the form of collateral. As should be evident, in this case the swap becomes more like a futures contract.
11. We will show in Chapter 10 that unlike futures for which all of any change in contract value is paid or received at the daily settlements, swap contracts convey only part of the total value change at the periodic settlements.
12. For continuity, we continue to use the ΔV, ΔP convention in figures. To compare these figures with those found in most texts, treat ΔV as deviations from zero ($\Delta V = V - 0$) and remember that ΔP measures deviations from expected price ($\Delta P = P - \bar{P}$).

CHAPTER

3

The State of the Risk Management Market

The markets for risk management products grew dramatically throughout the 1980s, and the growth continues in the first years of the 1990s. A 1993 study of derivatives activities conducted jointly by the Board of Governors of the Federal Reserve System, the Federal Deposit Insurance Corporation, and the Comptroller of the Currency reported that, over the five-year period between the end of 1986 and the end of 1991, open positions in exchange-traded futures and options grew over 500 percent. During the same period, use of over-the-counter (OTC) products grew even more rapidly, multiplying almost eightfold.

The markets for risk management products have flourished, moreover, in spite of a variety of obstacles ranging from the unfamiliarity and apparent complexity of the instruments themselves to tax accounting and legal uncertainties to regulatory concerns about the risk of default by individual counterparties and its potential effect on the international payments system.

In this chapter, we describe the patterns of price volatility that continue to spur demand for derivative products and the consequent recent growth of both exchange-traded and over-the-counter products. We then examine the end-users, looking not only at what they use, but also at why they use them. We also look at the dealers. We will then look at the recent regulatory challenges faced by the derivatives markets, tracing the evolution and highlighting the issues. We conclude this chapter with brief descriptions of current accounting policies and tax regulations.

The Financial Environment Remains Volatile . . .

In Chapter 1, we argued that the *financial price volatility* of the 1970s and early 1980s was the primary impetus for the evolution and subsequent growth of the risk management products:

> The collapse of the Bretton Woods fixed exchange rates in 1973 caused an abrupt rise in foreign exchange rate volatility which, in turn, spawned financial futures—foreign exchange rate futures on the Chicago Mercantile Exchange—and, later, currency swaps and options.
>
> When the U.S. Federal Reserve decided, in 1979, to target money supply rather than interest rates, the volatility in U.S. interest rates rose dramatically, leading to the rise of exchange-traded interest rate futures and options, and to OTC derivatives like forward rate agreements, interest rate swaps, and OTC options (caps and floors).
>
> The oil price shocks arising from the Arab oil embargo in the early 1970s, the Iran–Iraq war in the late 1970s, and the U.S. deregulation of oil prices in the early 1980s have given rise to exchange-traded futures and options, as well as the development of OTC derivatives—swaps and options—on a variety of commodities.

What has happened during the late 1980s and early 1990s? And, more importantly, what can we expect in the future? Can we anticipate a return to pre-1970s stability?

In the following sections we examine evidence that makes us believe that the financial environment will, at least in the near term, be characterized by moderately higher underlying levels of volatility—punctuated by episodic "spikes" in price volatility.

Interest Rates

As illustrated in Figure 3–1, the *level* of U.S. interest rates—using six-month U.S. dollar LIBOR and the 10-year U.S. Treasury interest rate as proxies—reached lows in the early 1990s. However, the story for *volatility* was not as reassuring. When the Fed began lowering interest rates in December 1991, the volatility of interest rates—both historical and implied—increased significantly. Over the period 1987–1991, implied volatility averaged around 15 percent (not high by the standards of the turbulent early 1980s, but certainly higher than the average 8 percent that prevailed in the 1970s). Beginning in late 1991, however, the markets began to signal their expectation of a return to greater volatility; the volatility for six-month U.S. dollar LIBOR *implied* in the traded prices of two-year U.S./LIBOR interest rate caps increased sharply, rising from less than 15 percent in mid-1990 to over 20 percent near the end of 1993.

Foreign Exchange Rates

The story for foreign exchange rates is even more dramatic than that for interest rates. At the end of the 1980s, the picture of the future being painted by politicians and some forecasters was of a world of more stable foreign exchange rates. Supposedly, the influence of the G-7 and the "inexorable" movement toward a unified European Monetary System was leading us back toward stability.

FIGURE 3–1 U.S. Dollar Interest Rates

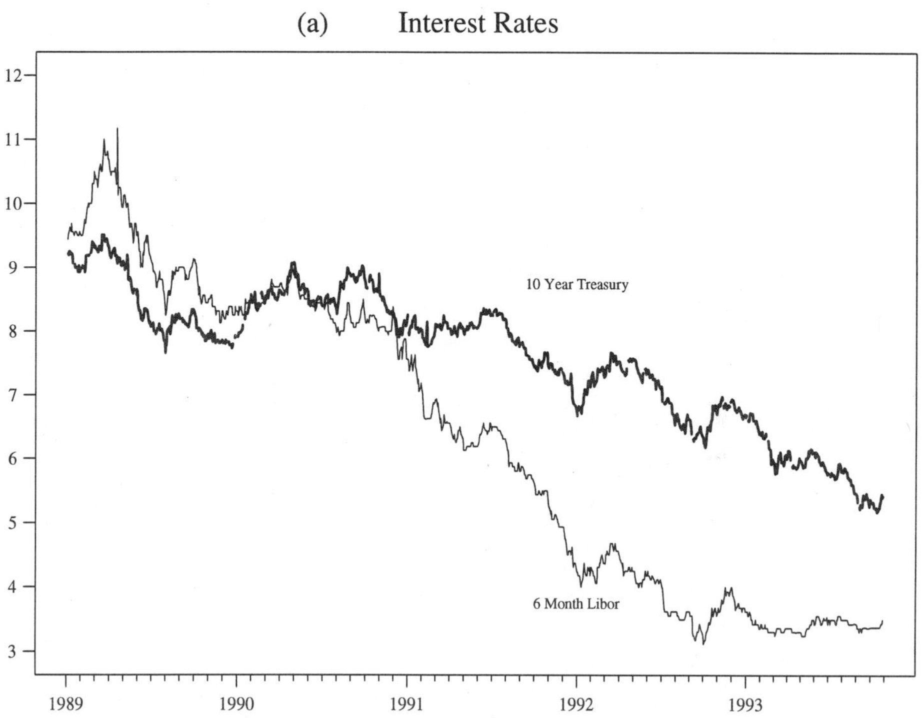

But, as is so often the case, the truth turned out far different from the rosy predictions. Panel (a) of Figure 3–2 illustrates recent history for three exchange rates. There were only modest changes in the level of rates for some currencies—the U.S. dollar strengthened only modestly against the deutsche mark over the early 1990s. But, the change for other rates was more dramatic—the dollar strengthened significantly against sterling and by the end of 1993, the level of the U.S. dollar had reached postwar lows against the yen.

When we look at volatility, the view of the tranquil environment is dispelled further. In panel (b) of Figure 3–2, we have illustrated actual and implied volatility for the deutsche mark–U.S. dollar exchange rate. Volatility has been low—except when something happens. Our figure illustrates such a period of extreme volatility when sterling withdrew from the EMS as the result of the currency upheavals in September 1992.[1] A smaller spike occurred at the end of July 1993, when there was yet another surge in general currency volatility when pressure from currency traders on the French franc effectively forced a sus-

Illustration 3–1

Volatility*

So far, when we have talked about "volatility," we have tried to convey to you some mental picture of movement. But, we need to begin to define the concept.

In the context of financial risk management, volatility provides a measure of the degree of uncertainty about the future path of a financial price—an interest rate, a foreign exchange rate, or a commodity price—or the yield on a financial asset.

As will be demonstrated in Chapter 12, volatility is a crucial factor in the pricing of options. Market practitioners talk about two distinct types of volatility—historical volatility and implied volatility. Historical volatility is measured using past economic data, while implied volatility is "backed out" of market prices for options.

Historical volatility is approximated by the square root of variance. Let's look at a simple example.

Suppose we have three observations on the underlying variable:

Observation	*Value of Variable*
1	4
2	8
3	6

The first step to working out the volatility is to find the average—the mean—of the observed values. For our simple example, the average is equal to the sum of the observed values (4 + 8 + 6 = 18), divided by the number of observations (3):

$$\text{Mean} = (4 + 8 + 6)/3 = 6$$

Next, we calculate the deviation from the mean for each observation and then square the deviations (so the resultant volatility cannot be negative).

Observation	*Value of Variable*	*Deviation from Mean*	*Squared Deviation*
1	4	$4 - 6 = -2$	4
2	8	$8 - 6 = +2$	4
3	6	$6 - 6 = 0$	0

The variance is calculated by adding the squared deviations together and dividing this sum by the number of observation points minus one:†

$$\text{Variance} = (4 + 4 + 0)/(3 - 1) = 8/2 = 4$$

The standard deviation—historical volatility—is the square root of the variance

$$\text{Standard deviation} = \sqrt{\text{Variance}} = \sqrt{4} = 2$$

The problem in calculating historical volatility is preventing one large price movement from making the overall result unhelpful. There are many models that allow volatility to be sensitized to "outliers," which can distort volatility results.

In Chapter 12, we will see that five factors are needed to value an option—the spot price, the strike (exercise) price of the option, the maturity of the option, the risk-free interest rate corresponding to the maturity of the option, and the volatility in the underlying price. Of these, the first four are *parameters*—they are observable in the market or are defined by the option contract. Volatility is the "free variable."

If I give an options trader the spot price, the strike (exercise) price of the option, the maturity of the option, the risk-free interest

Volatility continued

rate, *and the volatility*, the trader can give me the value of the option—the option premium. Conversely, if I give a trader the spot price, the strike (exercise) price of the option, the maturity of the option, the risk-free interest rate, *and the premium someone just offered for the option*, the trader can give me the volatility *implied* by that premium. Indeed, in the course of a business day, traders will constantly be looking at option premiums being quoted in the market and will then run those premiums through their own opt[illegible] models to determine the implied volatility being offered by other professionals.

---

*This discussion is adapted from the "Learning Curve" column by Paul O'Keefe, which appeared in the November 2, 1992 issue of *Derivatives Week*, an Institutional Investor, Inc. Publication©.

†This subtraction avoids mathematical bias in the result.

pension—some would say the demise of—the EMS when the trading bands were widened.

Commodity Prices

Once the U.S. inflation of the late 1970s and early 1980s was damped out, commodity prices stabilized somewhat. Panel (a) of Figure 3–3 illustrates that oil prices have been reasonably stable over the past five years—except for the huge jump in response to Iraq's invasion of Kuwait in late 1990. Over the same period, the prices of natural gas and copper were a little less stable. And, as 1993 neared its end, we were seeing increased volatility in the price of gold.

When we look at the volatility of the price of oil, illustrated in panel (b) of Figure 3–3, we see the now-familiar picture—moderately higher volatility punctuated by "spikes." (Looking at this picture, it is easy to pick out the invasion of Kuwait by Iraq and Operation Desert Storm.)

. . . And the Use of Derivatives Continues to Grow[2]

At the outset of this chapter we noted that the past five years have seen remarkable growth in both exchange-traded and over-the-counter derivatives. Put more concretely, New York Federal Reserve economist Eli Remolona noted that over the five-year period 1987–1991, "the stock of financial derivatives outstanding worldwide . . . multiplied fivefold to approach $10 trillion at the end of 1991."

FIGURE 3–2 Foreign Exchange Rates

(a) Foreign Exchange Rates

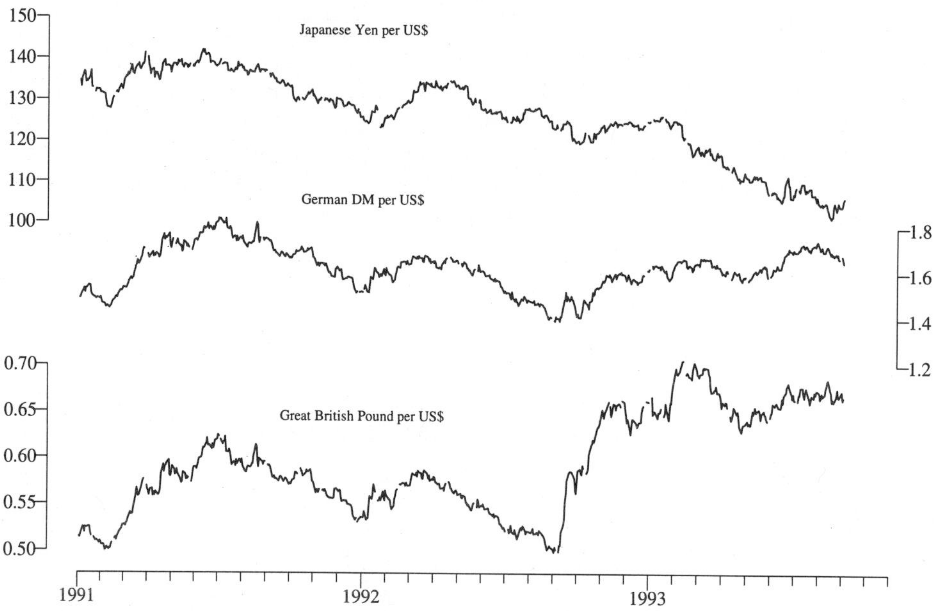

(b) Volatility of US Dollar, German Deutsche Mark Exchange Rate

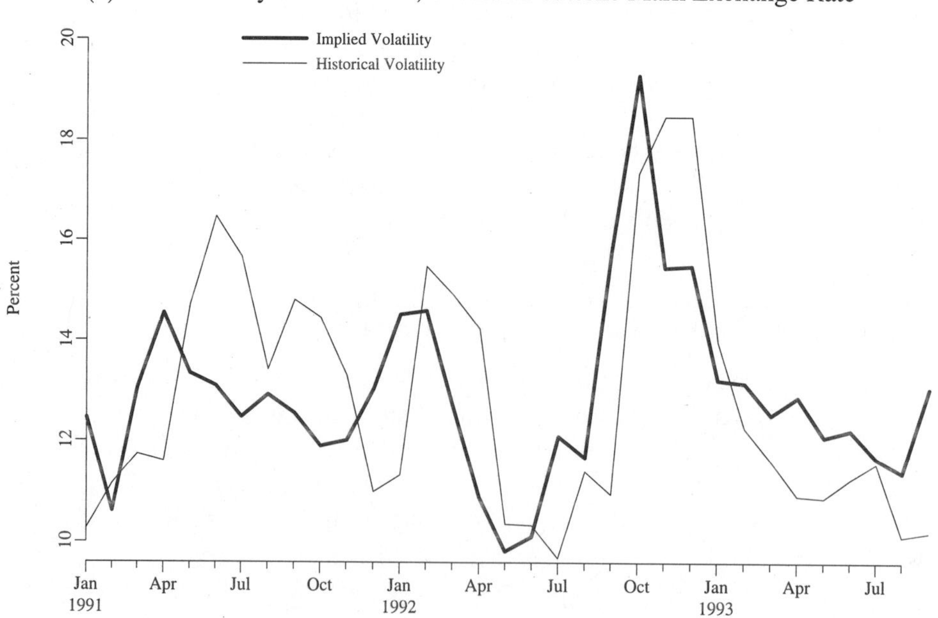

FIGURE 3–3 Commodity Prices

(a)

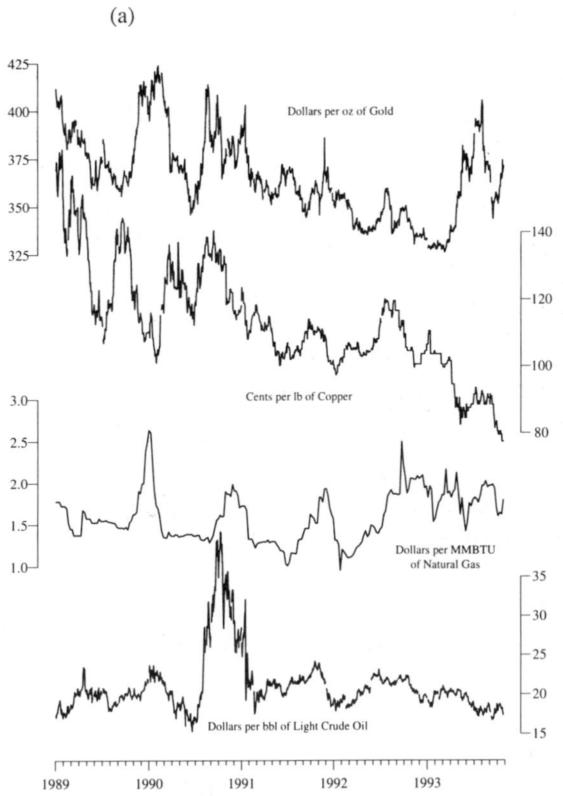

(b)

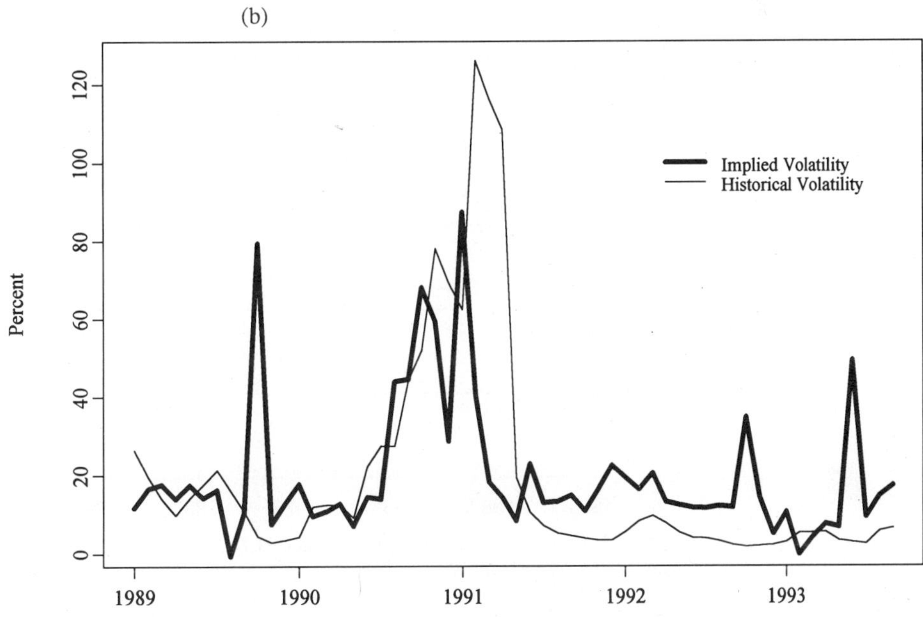

Remolona points out, however, that it is misleading to compare the open interest of the exchange markets with the notional principal of OTC products. When an OTC swaps user "unwinds" an earlier swap by means of another, offsetting, swap, the original transaction remains on the books and the new swap is counted as an addition to notional principal. By contrast, the unwinding of positions in exchange markets reduces open interest. Hence, to assess the relative rates of growth in the exchange-trade versus the OTC markets, it may make more sense to compare trading volumes in the exchange-traded markets with notional principal in the OTC markets.

Interest Rate Derivatives

Recent growth in both exchange-traded and OTC derivatives in the past five years has been dominated by the growth of interest rate products.

As shown in Figure 3–4, trading in exchange products—notably interest rate futures contracts—grew at about 20 percent per year from 1986 to 1992. Remolona observes that most of this growth was concentrated in the Eurodollars futures contract on the Chicago Mercantile Exchange[3] and the relatively new futures on French and German government bonds.[4]

Among OTC interest rate products, interest rate swaps grew at an average rate of over 40 percent annually. As presented in Table 3–1, the annual surveys con-

FIGURE 3–4 Exchange-Traded Interest Rate Derivatives (Annual Trading Volume of Futures and Options Contracts)

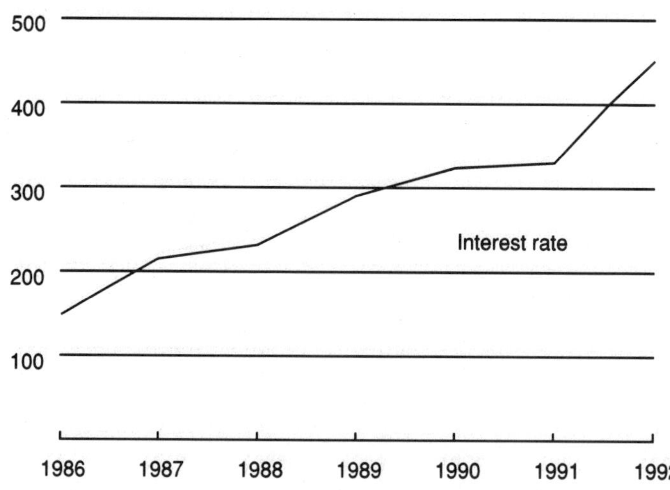

SOURCE: Eli M. Remolona, "The Recent Growth of Financial Derivative Markets," *Quarterly Review,* Federal Reserve Bank of New York, Winder 1992–93 (Chart 2).

ducted by ISDA indicate that the amount of interest rate swaps written (notional principal) increased from $388 billion in 1987 to $3.851 trillion in 1992.

OTC interest rate options—caps, floors, and collars—have been growing even more rapidly than swaps, averaging over 80 percent a year during the same period.[5] As shown in Table 3–2, at the end of 1992, the total notional principal of caps, floors, and collars was $507 billion.

TABLE 3–1 Interest Rate Swaps Outstanding

	1987	*1988*	*1989*	*1990*	*1991*	*1992*
Number of contracts	34,127	49,560	75,223	102,349	127,690	151,545
Notional principal in billions of U.S. dollars	$ 682	$ 1,010	$ 1,539	$ 2,311	$ 3,065	$ 3,850

SOURCE: International Swaps and Derivatives Association, Inc.

TABLE 3–2 Caps, Floors, and Collars Outstanding
(Notional Principal in Billions of U.S. Dollars)

Year-End	*1989*	*1990*	*1991*	*1992*
Caps				
U.S.$	177	251	225	232
Non-U.S.$	77	68	92	105
Subtotal	253	319	317	337
Floors				
U.S.$	54	76	73	62
Non-U.S.$	32	34	56	76
Subtotal	86	110	129	138
Collars				
U.S.$	35	33	13	14*
Non-U.S.$	4	5	10	18*
Subtotal	39	38	22	32*
Total	378	467	468	507

*1992 figures also include participations, options on caps/floors, and specialized combinations

SOURCE: International Swaps and Derivatives Association, Inc.

Foreign Exchange Derivatives

The growth in foreign exchange derivatives, although steady, was much less spectacular than that for interest rate products. However, the data for foreign exchange derivatives does exhibit a striking difference between exchange-traded and OTC products.

Exchange trading of currency futures and options grew by only about 8 percent a year over the period 1986–1992. Figure 3–5 portrays this slow growth graphically.

At the same time, however, OTC currency swaps grew at roughly the same rate as did interest rate swaps. As shown in Table 3–3, the notional principal of currency swaps grew from $183 billion in 1987 to $860 billion by the end of 1992.

Remolona suggests that the disparity between the growth rates of currency swaps and futures is that currency futures, initiated by the CME in 1973, are now

FIGURE 3–5 Exchange-Traded Interest Rate and Foreign Exchange Derivatives
(Annual Trading Volume of Futures and Options Contracts)

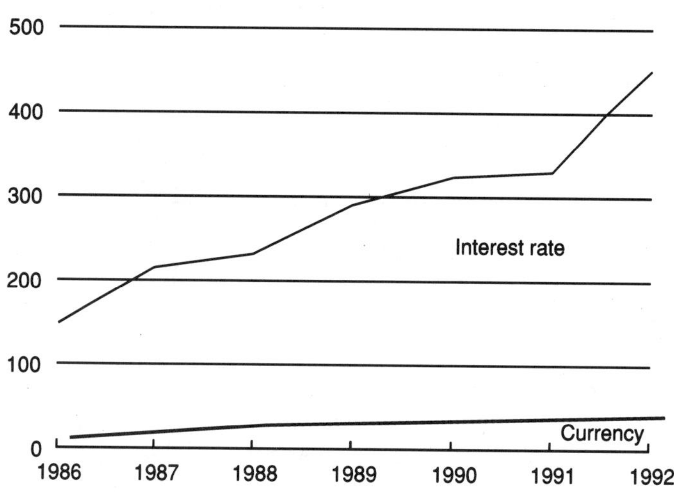

SOURCE: Eli M. Remolona, "The Recent Growth of Financial Derivative Markets," *Quarterly Review,* Federal Reserve Bank of New York, Winder 1992–93 (Chart 2).

TABLE 3–3 Currency Swaps Outstanding

	1987	*1988*	*1989*	*1990*	*1991*	*1992*
Number of contracts	6,612	10,271	15,285	22,717	31,035	32,841
Notional principal in billions of U.S. dollars	$ 183	$ 317	$ 435	$ 578	$ 807	$ 860

SOURCE: International Swaps and Derivatives Association, Inc.

a considerably older and thus more "mature" market than the market for currency swaps—a market that did not really get underway in earnest until the early 1980s.

Commodity Derivatives

The first survey of the level of activity in commodity swaps and options was published by ISDA for year-end 1992 activity. As shown in Table 3–4, at the end of 1992, the notional principal of commodity swaps was estimated to be $18 billion, while the notional principal for commodity options was $12 billion. Energy—oil and natural gas—dominate the swaps; but activity in metals exceeds that for energy options.

TABLE 3–4 Commodity Swaps and Options—1992 (Notional Principal in Billions of U.S. Dollars)

	Between Dealers	*With end users*	*Total*
Commodity swaps			
Energy	$5	$10	$15
Metals	—	3	3
Subtotal	5	13	18
Commodity options			
Energy	$2	$ 3	$ 5
Metals	2	5	7
Subtotal	4	8	12
Total	**$9**	**$21**	**$30**

SOURCE: International Swaps and Derivatives Association, Inc.

Equity Derivatives

Somewhat newer derivatives are those on various stock market indexes. These derivatives allow money managers to hedge the value of their equity portfolios, while also providing market makers, speculators, and arbitragers with a low-cost means of trading baskets of stocks.

So far, we have seen pictures of continuous growth. However, as is illustrated in Figure 3–6, this is not the case for exchange-traded equity index derivatives. Stock index derivatives, especially futures, were widely used in the "portfolio insurance" strategies in place prior to the 1987 stock market crash. "Portfolio insurance" was supposed to protect investors against just such a collapse; but the "dynamic hedging" strategies that would call for the sale or purchase of large numbers of futures contracts in response to falls or rises in stock prices failed to func-

FIGURE 3–6 Exchange-Traded Equity Derivatives

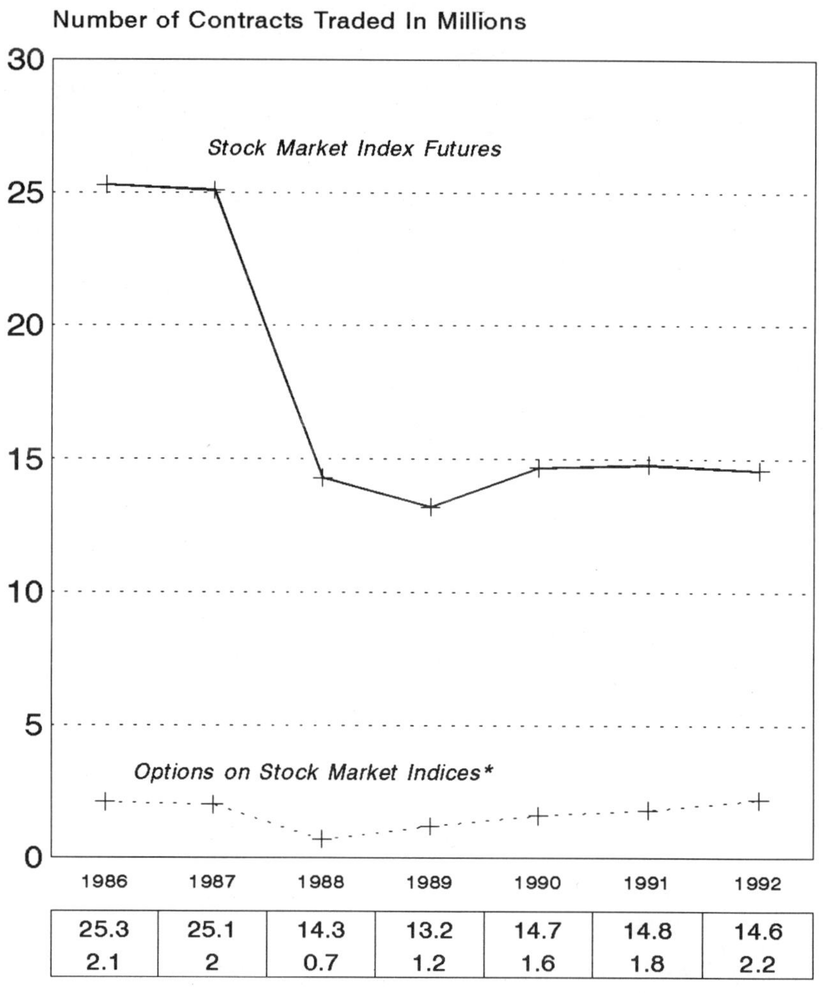

1986	1987	1988	1989	1990	1991	1992
25.3	25.1	14.3	13.2	14.7	14.8	14.6
2.1	2	0.7	1.2	1.6	1.8	2.2

SOURCE: Data provided by the Futures Industry Association.

tion as expected. The sudden loss in liquidity in the derivatives markets made the large trades required by the programs impossible to execute. With the demise of "portfolio insurance," the use of stock index futures declined sharply. But, after that temporary setback, the growth of these instruments has resumed. Remolona reports that between 1988 and 1992, trading volumes in equity index contracts increased 14 percent a year. Much of the new growth in index contracts, however, can be attributed to new contracts, especially Nikkei index futures and options at the Osaka Securities Exchange.[6]

Following the development of exchange-traded equity derivatives came, predictably, OTC equity index swaps and options. Such equity derivatives were designed by investment houses either for their own trading or hedging purposes (known as the "off-the-peg" segment of the business) or tailored for their investor clients (referred to as the "bespoke" segment). Although the OTC equity products are only a small fraction of the exchange-traded market, their growth in the past few years has been explosive. The most recent estimate by the ISDA puts the current outstanding notional principal of equity swaps at $10 billion and OTC equity options at $66 billion. (See Table 3–5.)

TABLE 3–5 Equity Swaps and Options—1992 (Notional Principal in Billions of U.S. Dollars)

	Between Dealers	*With End Users*	*Total*
Equity swaps—Indexes by country			
Japan	$ 3	$ 3	$ 6
U.S.	1	1	2
Other	—	1	1
Baskets & individual stocks	—	1	1
Subtotal	4	6	10
Equity options—Indexes by country			
Japan	$11	$ 9	$20
U.S.	3	8	11
U.K.	6	5	11
Germany	4	2	6
France	3	2	5
Other	2	2	4
Baskets	—	2	2
Individual stocks	1	6	7
Subtotal	30	36	66
Total	**$34**	**$42**	**$76**

SOURCE: International Swaps and Derivatives Association, Inc.

Putting Derivatives in Context

So far, our discussion has focused on "how large" the derivatives markets have become. And it is important to note that the growth has been nothing short of astounding:

Over the period 1987 to 1991, the open interest of exchange-traded derivatives grew 36 percent a year to reach \$3.5 trillion.[7]

The OTC derivatives market—as measured by notional principal outstanding for interest rate and currency swaps, interest rate options, and commodity and equity swaps and options—has grown from \$866 million in 1987 to almost \$5 trillion in 1992.

While the OTC market appears larger when notional principal outstanding is compared to open interest, activity in the exchange-traded markets still dwarfs that in the OTC markets. Within the markets for the OTC derivatives, interest rate swaps dominate. Of the \$5 trillion outstanding notional principal in 1992, 68 percent was for interest rate swaps. The new OTC derivatives—commodity and equity swaps and options make up only a tiny fraction of total activity. In 1992, outstanding notional principal for commodity and equity swaps and options was \$106 billion—2 percent of the total outstanding notional principal for OTC derivatives.

Moreover, in assessing the growth of risk management products, it is important to keep in mind that the derivative markets are still quite small relative to the underlying asset markets. In Figure 3–7 we have reproduced a figure developed by Derik Hargraves at J.P.Morgan that illustrates this graphically. As of the end of 1991, the total notional principal outstanding for interest rate and currency swaps (\$4.5 trillion) and the open interest of exchange options and futures (\$3.3 trillion) amounted to less than one third of the world's outstanding debt and equity (almost \$25 trillion).

End Users

Insights into the composition of participants in the OTC derivatives markets is provided in Figure 3–8. While the end users of the derivatives include financial institutions and governments, we will in this section focus our attention on the corporate users of risk management.

What Derivatives Are End Users Using and Why?

Over the past few years, end users have been surveyed on a number of occasions. In this section, we will attempt to draw together several of these surveys to give you some perspective on what end users are saying.

In 1989, William Millar surveyed 173 subscribers—principally large multinational corporations—of Business International publications.[8] When asked to rank risk management among various other financial objectives, the Business International subscribers placed risk management second only behind maintaining or improving the firm's credit standing.

FIGURE 3–7 Selected Global Financial Markets (Outstandings in Trillions of Dollars Data for End of 1991)

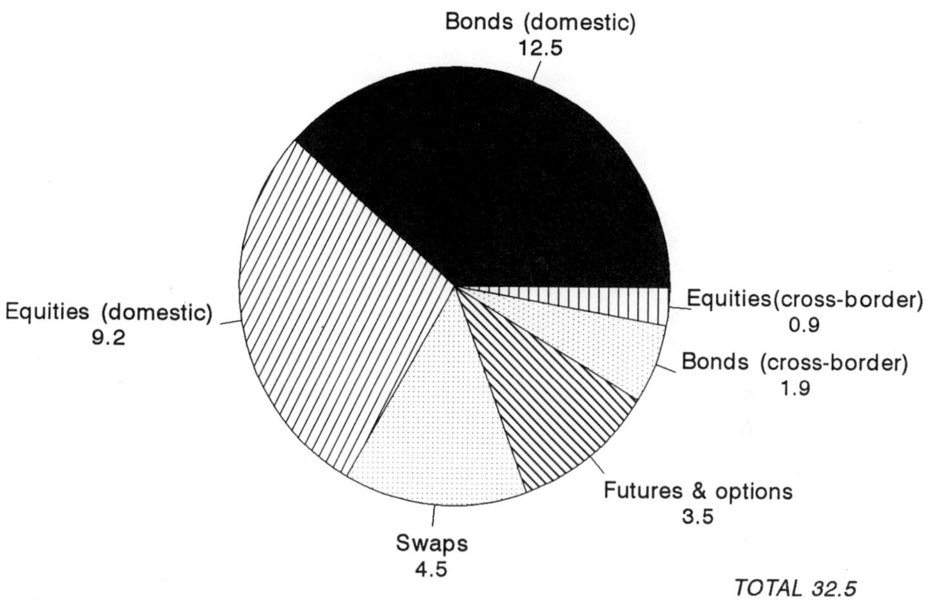

SOURCE: Adapted from *World Financial Markets,* J.P. Morgan.

Also in 1989, Henry Davis surveyed 255 members—mainly medium-sized companies—of the Financial Executives Institute.[9] The FEI respondents ranked "minimizing borrowing costs" as their primary financial objective, but put risk management in a virtual tie for second place with maintaining credit standing.

Surveys of readers have recently been published in two of the trade magazines. *Institutional Investor* published a survey of chief financial officers in 1992.[10] In 1993, *Treasury Magazine* published the results of a survey of 95 firms, 74 percent of which were users of derivatives.[11]

In 1992, Greenwich Associates released a survey of 325 American companies.[12] In the Greenwich survey, 45 percent of the firms surveyed reported having used risk management products in the past year.[13]

In Tables 3–6 through 3–8, we have tried to collect results from all five of the surveys. In doing this we have taken some liberties with the individual surveys, collecting results under general headings. Where there was a substantial difference between our heading and the question actually asked in the survey, we have shown the text of the actual survey question or heading in a footnote.

FIGURE 3–8 OTC Currency Derivatives

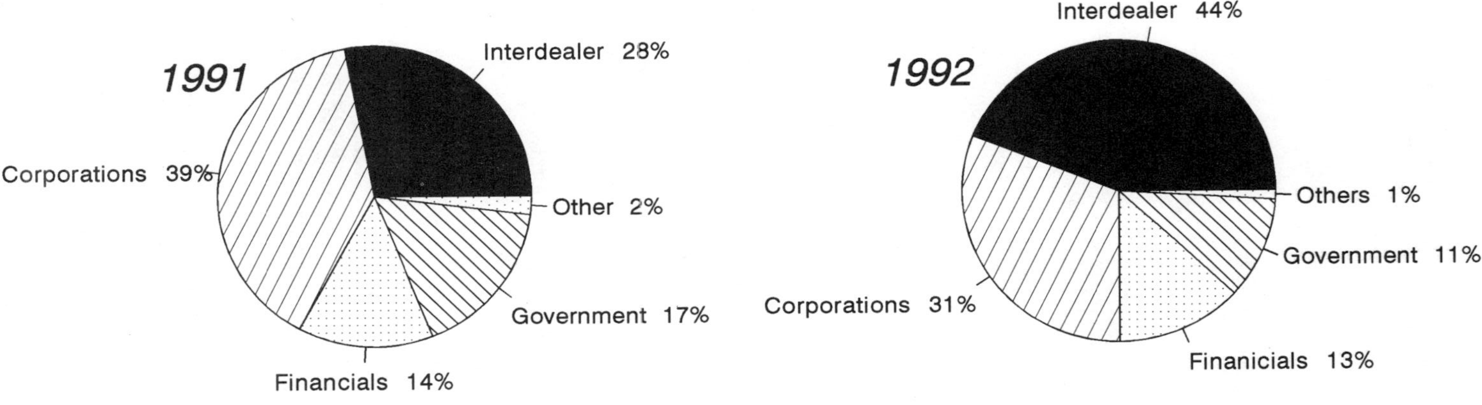

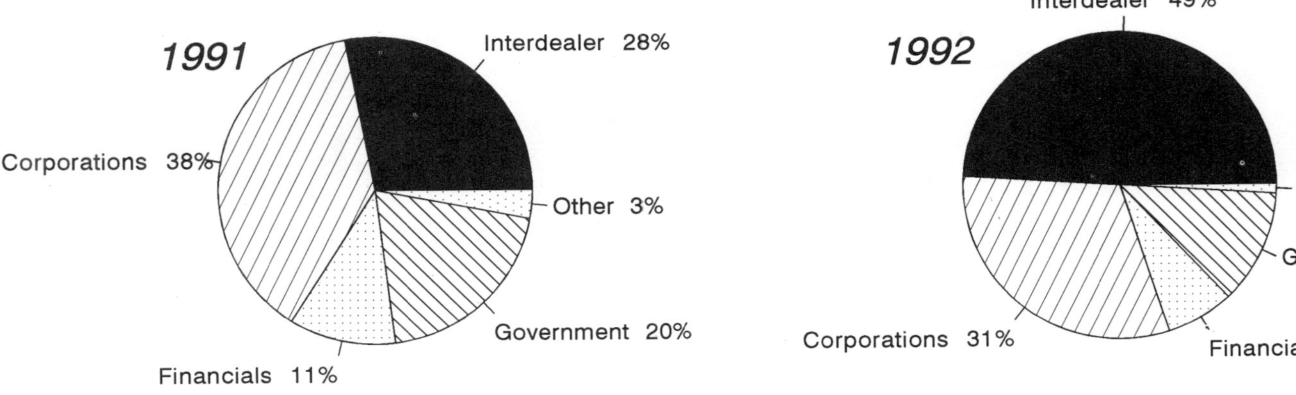

SOURCE: International Swaps and Derivatives Association.

Why do corporations use financial derivatives? As summarized in Table 3–6, the results of these surveys indicate that corporations are using derivatives for four major reasons:

1. Transaction hedges: Firms are hedging foreign exchange transaction exposures or hedging a particular debt issue. In the BI survey, almost 60 percent of the respondents aimed to eliminate *all* currency and interest rate risk. Only 1 percent of these firms said they made no effort to manage financial risk. For FEI companies, by comparison, hedging was considerably less in evidence; and when practiced, it was generally "selective" rather than "complete." In the Greenwich study, it was interesting that whereas financial institutions tend to hedge interest rate risk, industrials are more likely to be managing currency risk. Moreover, in the Greenwich report, almost half the firms that manage currency risk attempt to hedge expected cash flows as well as transactional exposures, while a third hedge translation and balance sheet exposures.

2. Strategic hedges: Also known as "economic" hedging, these firms are using derivatives to protect cash flows or value of the corporation from movements in financial prices.

3. Corporations continue to use the derivatives to reduce funding costs. The most widely cited category under this heading was the creation of "synthetic debt." In Chapters 11 and 14, we will show how derivatives can be used to create synthetic debt instruments which have lower coupons than "standard" debt. A distant second was accessing foreign markets to reduce funding costs. And, a still more distant third was the use of tax or regulatory arbitrage to lower funding costs. In Chapter 11, we will argue that tax and regulatory arbitrage was a major force in the

TABLE 3–6 Why Do Corporations Use Financial Derivatives?

	FEI 1989	*BI 1989*	*Greenwich 1992*	*II 1992*	*Treasury 1993*
Transaction hedges					
FX transactions	34%	59%	21%*	37%†	77%
Debt issues	31	58	25	53	56
To reduce funding costs					
by creating synthetic debt		29%	—	44%	54%
by accessing foreign markets		—	—	15	10
via tax or regulatory arbitrage		4	4%	—	—
Strategic hedging			20%	40%‡	43%§
To trade for profit		7%	8%	—	—

*Manage currency exposure of cash flow.

†To hedge overseas investments.

‡To achieve strategic asset-liability management.

§To hedge income/profits.

initial development of the OTC derivatives, especially swaps. However, the survey results bear out our belief that the importance of these arbitrages has declined dramatically as the OTC derivatives markets have matured.

4. Trading derivatives for profit: Respondents to the surveys cite this reason for using the derivatives last. This is supported by questions asked about the organization of the treasury function within the firm. As illustrated below, very few of the respondents had profit-center treasuries:

Survey	*Percent of Firms Where Treasury Unit Is a Profit Center*
Business International	16%
Financial Executives Institute	7
Treasury survey	20

What derivatives do corporations use? In Table 3–7, we have grouped these responses according to type of derivative: foreign exchange derivatives, interest rate derivatives, commodity price derivatives, and equity derivatives.

For managing currency exposures, forwards were far and away the most widely used instrument. Except for the FEI survey, currency swaps and OTC currency

TABLE 3–7 What Derivatives Do Corporations Use?

	FEI 1989	*BI 1989*	*Greenwich 1992*	*II 1992*	*Treasury 1993*
Foreign Exchange Derivatives					
Forward contracts	45%	99%	91%	64%	70%
Ex-traded futures or options	14	20	—	11	9
Currency swaps	9	64	51	—	6*
OTC options	9	48	45	40	53
Interest Rate Derivatives					
Forward rate agreements (FRAs)	—	35%	11%	—	—
Ex-traded futures or options	8%	25	12	29%	17%
Interest rate swaps	24	68	35	79	83
OTC options (caps, floors, etc.)	24	43	19	14	16
Commodity Price Derivatives					
Ex-traded futures or options			7%	—	—
Commodity swaps			6	15%	10%
Equity Derivatives					
Ex-traded futures or options				10%	3%
Equity swaps				5	6

*Others, such as currency swaps.

options were in a virtual tie for second place, with exchange-traded futures and options third.

In 1993, Business International again surveyed their subscribers, this time in association with Emcor. As is illustrated below, the new data bear out the earlier results.

Foreign Exchange Derivatives Usage

	BI: 1989	*BI/Emcor: 1993*
Forward contracts	99%	75%
Ex-traded futures or options	20	22
Currency swaps	64	52
OTC options	48	45

For managing interest rate exposures, interest rate swaps are the preferred instrument. OTC options (caps, floors, collars, and the like) are virtually tied with exchange-traded futures and options. The studies do not provide enough data for us to say very much about the use of FRAs.

With respect to interest rate risk management, the Greenwich study also reported that the demand for interest rate options is growing, particularly among smaller companies. Furthermore, U.S. corporations that practice risk management with derivatives use, on average, about three different products and four different banks. Large users use more than twice as many products, and almost four times as many banks, as small users. Large users tend to use foreign, typically European banks, as well as money-center American banks, whereas small users rely almost exclusively on U.S. banks.

What keeps corporations from making more use of the financial derivative? Several of the surveys also asked companies about difficulties or concerns about using the derivatives. In Table 3–8 we have collected the results from three of the surveys.

Concerns about credit risk are clearly evident. This concern is further reflected in the survey results obtained when *Institutional Investor* and *Treasury* asked about the minimum credit rating the corporation requires for their counterparties:

Lowest-Rated Counterparty with Which You Would Deal

	AAA	*AA*	*A*	*BBB*
Institutional Investor	6%	43%	43%	7%
Treasury	10	31	48	11

To be a dealer, the financial institution must be rated A or better. Indeed, in the Greenwich survey, roughly 10 percent of the firms said they were considering switching from OTC to exchange-traded products either to reduce counterparty risk (24%), to lower transactions costs (15%), or to get increased liquidity (29%).

TABLE 3–8 What Keeps Corporations from Making More Use of the Financial Derivatives?

	Greenwich 1992	*II 1992*	*Treasury 1993*
Credit risk		58%	66%
Accounting treatment of derivatives			64
Transaction costs		25	46
Liquidity risk	7*	32	
Insufficient knowledge about derivatives	18	34†	
My own knowledge			19
My staff's knowledge			16
My board of directors' knowledge			46

The Greenwich survey looked at "Reasons for not using swaps." The *Institutional Investor* survey asked "What concerns you about using derivatives?" *Treasury* magazine asked about major corporate concerns about using derivative instruments from two perspectives (1) internal worries and (2) external worries.

*Difficulty of unwinding.
†Complexity in pricing.

The style of the FEI survey was a little different; the researchers asked respondents to rank the difficulties encountered implementing a risk management program. These results are similar to those in Table 3–8.

FEI Survey—Ranking of "Difficulties"	
#1	No suitable instrument
#2	Lack of knowledge
#3	Transaction costs
#4	Resistance by senior management or board of directors
#5	Accounting or legal difficulties

The results of these surveys, together with our own conversations with a large number of corporate managers, indicate that one of the primary reasons that corporations do not manage financial price risk is "lack of knowledge" about derivatives. However, as the results of the FEI and *Treasury* surveys indicate, the real obstacle may not be so much management's inability to comprehend derivatives as the prospect of its having to explain risk management products and practices to corporate boards and shareholders.

Another interesting recent study was conducted by Walter Dolde of the University of Southern Connecticut.[14] Dolde conducted a survey of the risk management practices of the Fortune 500 in the summer of 1992. Of the 244 companies that responded to his survey, he found that 85 percent of these companies had used swaps, forwards, futures, or options on at least one occasion. Moreover, as suggested by the Greenwich survey, there also appeared to be a pronounced positive correlation between the size of the companies and the use of derivatives: the larger the company, the greater the use of derivative products. Dolde notes that this finding confirms the experience of risk management practitioners that the corporate use of derivatives requires an appreciable upfront investment in personnel, training, and computer hardware and software; for this reason, companies are likely to perceive scale economies in the use of derivatives. But, as we will also argue in the next chapter, there are also reasons why the demand for risk management products should actually be greater for small firms than for large—primarily, because the risk of default from price risk tends to be greater and equity ownership tends to be more concentrated (and hence less diversified) in smaller companies.

Dolde's survey provides an interesting piece of evidence in support of this argument. Smaller companies reported hedging greater percentages of their FX and interest rate exposures than the larger companies. Put another way, larger companies appear more inclined to "self-insure" their FX or interest rate risks.

To the extent this finding confirms a stronger economic rationale for hedging by smaller companies, it suggests that it may be only a matter of time before small and medium-sized companies begin to move themselves further down the formidable "learning curve" and increase their use of derivative products. As we suggest later, this may be the growth market of the future.

End Users Are under Increasing Pressure to Hedge

As the financial environment became—and has remained—volatile, there is increasing pressure on the firm to hedge, because there is more risk. This was most evident in the early 1990s in the case of foreign exchange rate risk. In Chapter 1, we discussed the impact of the dramatic move in the level of the U.S. dollar–Japanese yen exchange rate. However, the increased volatility evident in the European currency markets caused a number of firms to take notice.

Even though the level of risk had increased, there was a time when the management of a firm could effectively shrug off financial price risk. Not so long ago it was okay for management to lay off the blame for poor results on the movement of the dollar or unforeseen interest rate changes or commodity price shocks. After all, financial price movements were something that the management of the firm couldn't do anything about.

But with the advent of the financial derivatives, shareholders and bondholders realize that management *can* do something to protect the firm. And, there are some indications that shareholders and bondholders may hold management accountable.

Risk Management in Practice

Currency Upheaval Wins Converts

Tracy Corrigan

Many companies have now been using derivative products of various sorts for more than a decade. They have advanced further down this route than investment managers, but there is still considerable scope for growth.

Most large companies—such as British Petroleum, which runs its large treasury operation as a separate bank—are already sophisticated users of derivatives. But smaller companies are also venturing into the market.

In a recent survey in *Institutional Investor,* more than a third of U.S. companies questioned said they use derivatives to hedge overseas investments. More than 82 percent had been using derivatives for more than 2 years, including 12 percent for more than 10 years.

The turmoil in Europe's foreign currency markets during the autumn of 1992 created more converts. Treasurers can no longer feel comfortable with large exposures to foreign currencies.

Companies are "suddenly much more aware of the risks. The dealings and profits which a company has at any moment can be wiped out in hours, let alone days," according to Mr. Les Halpin, a director of Record Treasury Management.

A survey by the management consultants Touche Ross showed that 85 percent of companies had selective hedging cover last year. Interest has grown even more sharply in recent months. "We advise 25 of the FT-SE 100 companies, and quite a large number have increased their hedging activity since Black Wednesday," said Mr. Derek Ross, a Touche Ross partner.

This is excerpted from a story by the same title that appeared in the December 8, 1992 issue of *Financial Times*.

Risk Management in Practice

Do Corporations Have a Duty to Hedge? *Brane v. Roth* and *In re Compaq*

Daniel P. Cunningham

A 1992 decision by an Indiana court and a class action suit filed in 1991 by the U.S. District Court for the Southern District of Texas have led some to question whether there may exist in some circumstances a duty for corporations to hedge their exposures to changing commodity prices and currency values. Following is an analysis of these two cases and a discussion of how the law should develop on this issue.

Brane v. Roth

In *Brane v. Roth,* 590 N. E. 2d 587 (Ind. Ct. App. 1992), a case decided by the Indiana Court of Appeals in 1992, the plaintiffs held shares in a grain elevator cooperative that received 90 percent of its operating income from the sale of grain. A decline in grain prices resulted in large losses to the cooperative—losses that could have been mitigated through the use of hedging contracts. The Indiana Court of Appeals held that the failure to hedge constituted a breach of the fiduciary duty of care owed by the directors to the cooperative's shareholders.

Absent self-dealing, a corporate director can satisfy his or her fiduciary duty to shareholders by exercising good faith and honest judgment. The business judgment rule provides a presumption that informed decisions made in good faith shall not be judicially reviewed, even if the results of such decisions indicate that the choices were unwise or inexpedient.

The *Brane* court reasoned that the directors of the grain cooperative did not enjoy the protection of the business judgment rule because they failed adequately to inform themselves about the hedging opportunities that could have prevented their losses. In Delaware, there is some argument that directors must be *fully informed* in order to enjoy the protection of the business judgment rule. *See Smith v. Van Gorkom,* 488 A.2d 858 (Del. 1985). New York law also requires that corporate decisions be informed, but the standard is arguably lower, since New York courts will respect business decisions which reflect the "exercise of honest judgment." *See Auerbach v. Bennett*, 419 N.Y.S. 2d 920, 926 (N.Y. 1979). Since the directors in the *Brane* case were found to have breached their fiduciary duty to the shareholders, the directors were liable for the losses incurred due to the failure to hedge.

If read broadly, *Brane* would inject the specter of judicial second-guessing into the day-to-day operational decisions of corporations, because courts would be forced to examine the substance of decisions to hedge or not to hedge. In *Brane*, the grain cooperative derived 90 percent of its income from grain sales, so the court simply assumed that hedging was a necessary activity to reduce the risk of a decline in grain prices. In essence, the court posited the failure properly to hedge as evidence that the managers were ill-informed about hedging, thus giving rise to liability.

The duty of care, however, is violated only by uninformed decisions, and not merely by decisions that have negative results. By blurring the distinction between the procedural steps taken to reach a decision and the substance of the decision itself, *Brane* invites shareholders and judges to substitute their judgment, with the benefit of hindsight, for the judgment of the board of directors. Given these problems, *Brane* may stand alone as an anomalous departure from the mandate of the business judgment rule.

Though *Brane* has prompted some concerns in the financial community, the case has not been cited, favorably or otherwise, by any other court since it was decided over one year ago.

In re Compaq

A class action suit, *In re Compaq Securities Litigation,* No. H-91-9191 (S.D. Tex. May 16, 1991), recently brought by shareholders of Compaq Computer Corporation against that corporation's chief executive officer and chairman of the board of directors, raises many of the same problems as the *Brane* case. The causes of action in *Compaq,* however, are based on alleged violations of Federal securities laws. The plaintiffs had purchased shares in Compaq based on its president's statements regarding the future prospects for the company. Soon thereafter, the stock dropped 20 percent in value in response to a disappointing earnings report. The plaintiffs charged that the public statements made by the president had been materially misleading (within the meaning of Section 10 (b) of the Securities Exchange Act of 1934 and Rule 10-b5 promulgated thereunder). The claim was based in part upon the corporation's failure to disclose its lack of adequate foreign currency hedging mechanisms to protect against a drop in the value of foreign currencies against the U.S. dollar. The absence of currency hedges allegedly was material because Compaq derived 54 percent of its revenues from foreign markets.

The plaintiffs in *Compaq* must show that the failure to disclose the absence of hedging contracts was "material." Information is material is there is a sub-

Do Corporations Have a Duty to Hedge? Brane v. Roth and In re Compaq continued

stantial likelihood that a reasonable shareholder would consider it important in deciding how to invest. The absence of hedging could only be material if the court decides that there was a reason that Compaq should have been hedging. Therefore, though pleaded as a 10b-5 claim, the *Compaq* case, much like *Brane,* requires the court to look at the underlying substance of the decision not to hedge and determine the reasonableness of that decision.

Analysis

As noted earlier, *Brane* might be limited to its facts and therefore have little significance as precedent. Likewise, the *Compaq* litigation has not yet been set for trial in the District Court for the Southern District of Texas, and there is the question of whether the plaintiffs' novel claims will be successful at trial.

Nevertheless, if the plaintiffs in *Compaq* are successful and courts begin to cite *Brane* as meaningful precedent, the two cases could be interpreted to introduce a "duty to hedge" against business risks through the use of financial derivatives. Such a duty, however, would represent a significant judicial intrusion into the day-to-day corporate decision-making process. A more narrow reading of the *Brane* ruling and the concerns raised by *Compaq* would not create a two-tiered procedural requirement to be followed by directors in making hedge-related decisions. The following approach most likely would satisfy the requirements of these two cases if they were considered controlling precedent.

First, at a minimum, directors would need to understand their corporate risks and set up proper mechanisms to address those risks. This requirement would not force all corporate directors to become educated in the nuances of financial derivatives; rather, the directors would need to ensure that the responsibility rested with a knowledgeable party who could adequately assess corporate risks and develop proper responses. Directors would be insulated from liability by relying on the decisions and actions of knowledgeable employees, and would not be confronted with the problem faced by the *Brane* directors, who delegated the hedging issue to an uninformed subordinate. By becoming adequately informed and creating a structure to address risk management issues, directors should enjoy the protection of the business judgment rule, even under an expansive application of *Brane*.

Second, after implementing a system to make informed hedging decisions, directors should disclose those hedging decisions that might be considered material. This disclosure could help to avoid Rule 10b-5 claims from disgruntled shareholders. The required disclosure will differ depending upon the

Do Corporations Have a Duty to Hedge? Brane v. Roth and In re Compaq continued

facts, and more disclosure may be necessary if the corporation makes optimistic predictions.

By making a good faith effort to become informed about corporate risk management, properly delegating the risk assessment and management tasks to qualified employees, and then disclosing hedging decisions that might be considered material to the reasonable investor, corporate directors should be able to avoid the type of liability that arose in *Brane v. Roth* and that is alleged in *In re Compaq*.

Daniel P. Cunningham is a partner of the law firm of Cravath, Swaine & Moore. He was the firm's resident London partner from 1986 to 1990. Upon his return to New York in July 1990, he became the firm's managing partner. His corporate finance practice includes derivative instruments, mergers and acquisitions, and receivables finance.

Mr. Cunningham has participated since 1984 in the preparation by the ISDA Documentation Committee of standard master agreements for derivative transactions. As ISDA's general counsel, Mr. Cunningham served as legal coordinator for the preparation of memoranda under U.K., U.S., Canadian, French, German, Italian, Japanese, Dutch, Swedish, and Belgian law examining the status of 1987 ISDA master agreements with counterparties that have become insolvent under the laws of those nations. Those legal memoranda will be updated this year to cover the 1992 ISDA master agreements.

Mr. Cunningham received a B.A. degree from Princeton University in 1971. In 1975 he graduated from Harvard Law School, where he was an editor of the *Harvard Law Review*.

We find the preceding discussion important because we believe that firms should tell the market about their risk management policies—what the firm is doing and why. As we will describe in the next section, we believe that the market will reward firms for managing risk.

However, there were—we hope it is "were" and not still "are"—firms who hesitated to tell the market what they were doing because they believed that the market would penalize them if they let it be known that they were using derivatives. They believed that if they told the market they were using derivatives, the market would assume that they were speculating rather than hedging.

And there were cases where corporate treasuries "went rogue." Perhaps the most widely cited instance was Allied-Lyons.

But, the Allied-Lyons case is not unique. On the western side of the Atlantic, a similar event happened to a firm with a similar name—Allied Signal.

And, more recently, currency options became a point of contention between the Dell Computer Corporation and a security analyst.[15]

We continue to believe that firms need to tell the market what they are doing with respect to financial price risk. And, one of the important things that must be communicated to the market is that controls are in place.

Illustration 3–2

Allied-Lyons*

During fiscal 1991, Allied-Lyons Plc, a British drinks and food group, incurred losses of £147 million trading in foreign exchange derivatives.

In mid-1989, Allied-Lyons's treasury unit expanded its foreign exchange hedging activities, including the writing of foreign currency options. During 1990, the scale of options trading grew substantially beyond the company's foreign currency cash flows.

These developments occurred without the knowledge or authorization of Allied-Lyons's board.

*From "Credit Implications for Firms that Use Derivatives," Moody's Special Comment, November 1991. For more on this, see "Allied-Lyons' Deadly Game," *Euromoney,* April 1991.

Illustration 3–3

Allied-Signal*

Allied-Signal thought its hedging activity involving all types of derivatives was airtight. Its policy, after all, was clear: nobody outside of the company's Morristown, New Jersey, headquarters could hedge anything—period. But it found that from 1991 through [February 1992] the controller of Allied-Signal's Norplex Oak Europa subsidiary, based in Wipperfurth, Germany, racked up roller coaster gains and losses by secretly trading currencies in the company's name.

The scam began in 1991 when the controller forged a colleague's signature in order to open the first of a number of new accounts in the company's name. The accounts were set up as subaccounts of Norplex's main bank account—a common practice in Germany. What was unusual is that activity in these subaccounts was not netted against Norplex's other accounts at the bank. Instead, statements were mailed separately and were intercepted by the controller.

The controller began drawing on the line, thus enabling himself to establish [secret] trading positions in the currency markets.

*This discussion is an excerpt from "Allied-Signal's Case of the Crooked Controller and His Secret Accounts," by Gregory J. Millman, which appeared in the June 1993 issue of *Corporate Finance*.

End Users Recognize That the Market Rewards Risk Management

In Chapter 19 we will provide a careful description of the available evidence about the degree to which the market recognizes the extent of a firm's exposure to financial price risk and rewards a firm for hedging these risks. At this point we only want to note that end users recognize that financial price risk matters to their shareholders and bondholders.

The reason end users recognize that financial price risk matters to their shareholders and bondholders is that more and more people are recognizing the importance of risk management to the value of the firm.

Firms themselves recognize that risk management goes beyond hedging a receivable or swapping a loan from floating to fixed: "The concept is not just to buy financial hedges, but to protect the dollar value of the business."[16]

The business press recognizes the link between financial price risk and the value of the shares. "[A] quick run-up in the dollar can dent a company's foreign sales and quarterly profits and even cause a sudden drop in the stock price."[17]

And, the rating agencies recognize the relation between financial price risk management and the creditworthiness of the firm. "[D]erivatives are potentially powerful tools to help firms manage financial and business risks. In so far as firms are able to utilize them prudently and effectively for these purposes, derivatives can contribute to users' financial stability—a positive factor for their credit quality."[18]

The Dealers

Dealing in derivatives has tended to concentrate among principals possessing not only the requisite technology and know-how but also ample capital and credit experience. To give you some idea who the dealers are, we have in Table 3–9 provided a ranking of the largest 20 dealers of foreign exchange forwards, interest rate and currency swaps, and interest rate options as of 1991.

The six largest foreign exchange forward dealers were all U.S. money-center banks: Citicorp, Chemical, Chase, Bankers Trust, BankAmerica, and J.P. Morgan. These were followed by a number of Canadian, European, and Australian banks. Only one investment bank—Goldman Sachs—made the top 20 for FX forwards.

For interest rate and currency swaps, the six U.S. money-center banks again appear in the top 20; but this time the list is headed by a European bank—Paribas. As with forwards, other European banks as well as a number of Canadian and Australian banks made the list. For swaps, two investment banks made the top 20—Merrill Lynch, Morgan Stanley. One insurance company—AIG—also made the list.

In terms of interest rate options, the six U.S. money-center banks again appear. As with swaps, the list is headed by a French bank; but this time it is Societe Generale. The list again includes other European banks; but for interest rate options nei-

TABLE 3–9 Top 20 Derivatives Dealers

Foreign Exchange Forwards			Interest Rate and Currency Swaps			Interest Rate Options		
Rank	*Firm*	*Amount*	*Rank*	*Firm*	*Amount*	*Rank*	*Firm*	*Amount*
1	Citicorp	584,771	1	Campagnie Financiers de Paribus	353,992	1	Societe Generale	196,666
2	Chemical Banking	512,434	2	JP Morgan	329,131	2	Chemical Banking	169,347
3	Chase Manhattan	378,722	3	Bankers Trust	296,137	3	JP Morgan	125,708
4	Bankers Trust	220,915	4	Citicorp	257,021	4	Bankers Trust	123,775
5	BankAmerica	220,653	5	Chemical Banking	244,544	5	Citicorp	109,401
6	JP Morgan	215,009	6	Chase Manhattan	230,395	6	Chase Manhattan	74,998
7	Westpac	198,620	7	Credit Lyonnais	205,010	7	Chapagnie Financiers de Paribus	69,618
8	Royal Bank of Canada	164,882	8	Merrill Lynch	163,039	8	Continental Bank	53,268
9	Champagnie Financiers de Paribus	157,337	9	Indosuez	153,593	9	Credit Agricole	43,338
10	Credit Lyonnais	152,796	10	Security Pacific	144,302	10	Credit Lyonnais	40,409
11	Security Pacific	150,661	11	Westpac	121,169	11	BankAmerica	36,067
12	First Chicago	123,510	12	Royal Bank of Canada	100,719	12	First Chicago	33,442
13	Bank of Montreal	115,394	13	Morgan Stanley	95,000	13	Merrill Lynch	32,321
14	National Australia Bank	114,897	14	BankAmerica	94,182	14	Indosuez	27,110
15	Goldman Sachs	113,018	15	Canadian Imperial Bank	93,713	15	Security Pacific	21,561
16	Canadian Imperial Bank	106,817	16	Bank of Nova Scotia	74,175	16	Banque Nationale de Paris	20,633
17	Indosuez	106,630	17	First Chicago	71,846	17	Union Euro-peenne de CIC	20,157
18	Toronto Dominion	104,090	18	American International Group	62,836	18	Bank of Boston	15,880
19	Den Danske Bank	103,446	19	Union Euro-peenne de CIC	57,538	19	First Interstate	14,282
20	Kredietbank	103,154	20	Continental Bank	56,456	20	Republic New York	10,386

SOURCE: This data is based on a ranking in *The World's Largest Derivatives Dealers* (Swaps Monitor Publications, Inc., New York) for year end 1991. The ranking is only of those firms which publish audited data on their interest rate options outstandings.

ther Canadian nor Australian banks make the top 20. Of the investment banks, only Merrill Lynch makes the top 20 list.

Summarizing Table 3–9, the largest dealers tend to be commercial banks; but the list of the largest dealers also contains investment banks, securities firms, and some insurance companies.[19] Moreover, these rankings are by no means static. No single firm dominates activity, and the relative positions of the leaders appear to be continually shifting.

The Function of a Dealer[20]

A derivatives dealer is a classic intermediary. The dealer provides over-the-counter risk management products to end users. As financial intermediaries, banks have traditionally offered foreign exchange and interest rate management products to their customers. By tailoring derivative products to their customers' needs, the dealers are able to provide more flexibility than that offered by exchange-traded derivatives, especially for hedging longer-term exposures.

Since the dealer is an intermediary, the credit standing of the dealer is very important. Several dealers have created special-purpose derivatives product companies that benefit from the support of a strong parent or shareholder. Other dealers, including Goldman Sachs, Merrill Lynch, Salomon Brothers, Morgan Stanley, Banque Paribas, and Westpac, have established separately capitalized, triple-A rated derivative vehicles.[21]

By providing OTC derivatives to end users, the dealers expose themselves to a number of risks:[22]

Credit risk: the risk that the end user (the dealer's counterparty) defaults.

Market (or price) risk: the risk that unhedged inventories of OTC products decline in value substantially.

Legal risk: the possibility that contracts are not enforced by the courts.

Administrative or operating risk: the possibility that internal controls over trading activity may prove inadequate.

The dealers have not always accepted all of these risks. In the days of the first currency and interest rate swaps, investment banks, commercial banks, merchant banks, and independent broker/dealers acted mainly as intermediaries for their corporate clients by finding counterparties with offsetting requirements in terms of notional amount, currencies, type of interest to be paid, and maturity. Acting as agent or broker for a fee, the institutions arranging the swaps took no principal position in the transactions and, hence, were exposed to neither credit nor market risk.

But most financial institutions discovered that they could expand their business by offering themselves as counterparties (or principals). Transactions designed to meet a given customer's requirements were immediately matched by entering into an offsetting transaction such as a "matched swap." Because each pair of transactions was dealt with separately and discretely, the dealer's book of business was relatively simple to monitor and manage. This new role, however, required a commitment of capital, since dealers now faced credit risk and some limited market risk.

The next step in the evolution of dealer activities was the "warehousing" of derivatives transactions. In this phase of development, dealers would temporarily hedge a swap—typically with a cash security or futures position—until a matched transaction could be found to replace the temporary hedge. This advance in risk management practice increased the ability of dealers to accommodate customer needs.

Today, major dealers have moved from the "warehouse" approach to a "portfolio" approach in which the dealer simply takes the customer's transaction into its portfolio (or "book") of derivatives and manages the residual risk of its overall position.

Risk Management in Practice

The Evolution of Market Risk Management

Nancy S. Newcomb

In the old days, over-the-counter derivative transactions—mainly interest rate and currency swaps—were quite straightforward. They were almost always immediately offset with opposing transactions. Each set of transactions was separate, credits tended to be of top quality, and management review, accounting, and controls were fairly routine.

The initial evolutionary step in the growth of derivatives was the introduction of "warehousing": instead of immediately offsetting each transaction, dealers would temporarily hedge the swap with a cash, security, or futures position until an offsetting transaction could be found. These hedging transactions—and subsequent unhedging transactions—complicated the recording and accounting processes, but were still very straightforward. What was needed was a good inventory process to record the additions and subtractions from inventory. However, now there was the additional problem of accumulating offsetting yet still discrete transactions over different time periods. Computer systems were developed and enhanced to keep track of the variations in the timing and the different types of transactions.

The next big evolutionary step in the developing derivatives business was the transition from a warehouse environment to a portfolio approach. Under the portfolio approach, each new transaction gets decomposed into its component cash flows and aggregated with all the other transactions already in the portfo-

The Evolution of Market Risk Management continued

lio. Management focus changes from managing the warehouse to managing the portfolio. This calls for even more powerful computer systems for managing portfolios on an aggregate basis.

The portfolio approach dramatically improved dealers' abilities to accommodate a broad spectrum of customer transactions. It also improved the trading manager's ability to monitor the various components of market risk, regardless of what kind of transaction those components were derived from. Computer models were developed to disaggregate risk components to enable the evaluation of the underlying, inherent risks, which is now so critical for evaluating market risk and aggregate counterparty credit risk.

Ms. Newcomb is principal financial officer of Citicorp, responsible for liquidity, funding, capital and worldwide treasury oversight. She is also chairman of the Market Risk Policy Committee, which is responsible for establishing policy, standards, and limits for price and liquidity risks throughout the corporation. She has held her current position since January 1988.

From 1986 to 1988, Ms. Newcomb was senior executive vice president of AMBAC, a municipal bond insurance company that was then a Citicorp subsidiary. From 1982 to 1986 she was a senior credit officer for Citibank's U.S. investment bank. Prior to that she had a range of assignments in Citicorp, including corporate restructurings, corporate lending, strategic planning, and economics. She joined Citicorp in 1968.

Ms. Newcomb received a B.A. from Connecticut College, an M.A. in economics from Boston University, and completed the PMD at Harvard Business School.

As we will illustrate in Chapter 18, each transaction is broken down by the warehouse manager into its component cash flows to yield a measure of its net, or *residual,* exposures arising from all its positions. The residual exposures can then be hedged by entering into other OTC transactions, taking positions in the cash market, or using exchange-traded instruments. By thus improving their ability to monitor and manage the various components of their own market risk, this shift by dealers to a portfolio approach has significantly increased their ability to provide their customers with a broad and continually expanding range of transactions. In a business that has become increasingly competitive, moreover, dealers also realize higher returns for the financial engineering that goes into developing the highly customized and structured transactions. (For an account of the most recent "structured" transactions, see Chapters 15 and 16.)

In the process of providing products for end users, dealers also provide liquidity by quoting bid and offer prices. To supply the immediacy demanded by end users, dealers either use their own inventory or establish new positions and manage the resulting risk. They are compensated by the bid-ask spread. In addition, some dealers take market risk positions with the expectation of profiting from anticipated movements in prices or rates. Some dealers also provide an arbitrage function, identifying and exploiting anomalies between derivatives and underlying cash market instruments, thereby enhancing market liquidity and pricing efficiency.

Risk and Opportunities[23]

Derivatives have proved to be profitable products for the dealers. The derivatives businesses generate profits in and of themselves. For example, Union Bank of Switzerland (UBS) notes that the derivatives business "is at the very upper end in terms of the return on equity that one has in a bank."[24] Moreover, the derivatives are also useful in the dealer's own core activities: underwriting, trading, asset management, and asset/liability management.

However, dealers face a number of risks in derivative products. In addition to the credit risk, market risk, legal risk, and operation risk noted earlier, Moody's added some additional concerns:

Derivatives dealing uses the firm's debt capacity, thus affecting its ability to place its debt and leading to potentially greater funding risks.

Regulation is still in an early stage. New or altered regulations could adversely affect previously existing derivatives positions.

The liquidity of many derivatives is not particularly good, thus decreasing participants' overall liquidity.

The increasing number of derivatives dealers and the maturation of some products are squeezing margins.

Competition among Dealers

As Moody's noted, competition among the dealers is becoming more intense. *American Banker* put it a little more colorfully when they observed:[25]

> Newcomers Pile into Booming Swaps Field

The newcomers listed by *American Banker* include NationsBank, First Union, and Wachovia.[26] In addition to these U.S. commercial banks, the new entrants to the derivatives business include commercial banks from Europe, Canada, Australia, and Japan, as well as investment banks and insurance companies.

One of the most evident dimensions of this increasing competition will be on product development. Dealers will attempt to be the first to market the newest of the new products. (A topic we will return to in Chapter 15.) As a way of accomplishing this, a number of commercial banks are joining forces with trading companies:

Swiss Bank Corporation formed an alliance with options firm O'Connor Associates;[27]

Chase Manhattan Bank formed a joint venture with Susquehanna Partners;

NationsBank recently acquired Chicago Research and Trading, a 750-person options trading firm; and

Republic New York acquired the staff of Mercadian Group, a derivatives firm affiliated with New England Mutual Life.

Regulation, Legislation, and Litigation

No examination of the state of the derivatives market could ignore the recent response to derivatives by another set of interested constituents—regulators, legislators, and lawyers.

The Regulators Express Concern

The opening barrage in the regulatory assault occurred in a speech delivered by the president of the New York Federal Reserve Bank, Gerald Corrigan, in January 1992.[28] Speaking to the New York Bankers Association, Corrigan first voiced his concern about derivatives:

> High-tech banking and finance has its place, but it's not all that it's cracked up to be.

And sent his first warning to his audience:

> You had all better take a very, very hard look at off-balance sheet activities

Later on, if there was anyone in the audience who was still unclear about Corrigan's position, he made it crystal clear:

> I hope this sounds like a warning, because it is.

Corrigan even went on to make sure that his audience knew that the warning was addressed not to the people who were directly involved in derivatives activities but to the senior management of the banks:

> Off-balance-sheet activities . . . must be understood by top management, as well as by . . . rocket scientists

In October 1992, the Bank for International Settlements issued what has come to be called the "Promisel Report."[29] This report reinforced Corrigan's concerns, urging banks to improve their controls over derivatives and regulators to increase their surveillance of banks.

And the barrage continued. In December, it was Treasury Secretary Nicholas Brady. When he delivered a speech at the Kennedy School of Government at Harvard, the headline that appeared on the wire was:[30]

> Treasury Secretary Warns about Risks from Swaps

Secretary Brady's comments were echoed by New York Stock Exchange chairman William Donaldson, who called the swaps market a weak link in the financial industry.[31]

All of these barrages led to action. In 1992 and 1993, the OTC derivatives markets were subjected to intense scrutiny. The OTC derivatives were the focus of a joint study by the Board of Governors of the Federal Reserve System, the Federal Deposit Insurance Corporation and the Office of Comptroller of the Currency, a study by the Commodities Futures Trading Commission, a study by the Securities and Exchange Commission, and a study by the General Accounting Office.

One source of the bank regulators' concern was the size of the notional principal of OTC products. Looking at the notional principal outstanding amounts reported by the largest dealers—look again at Table 3–9—it is not hard to understand why regulators and legislators feared that a few defaults could cause the insolvency of some large financial institutions, leading not only to taxpayer losses but perhaps even imperiling the entire financial system.

With respect to notional principal, we in the derivatives industry had shot ourselves in the foot. Notional principal is not a very good measure of activity; it greatly overstates the amount of credit risk involved in intermediating swaps. A better measure is the market value (replacement cost)—for example, in the case of an interest rate swap, the replacement cost of a swap is the net present value of all remaining payments owed by one counterparty to the other based on current interest rates. But in the early 1980s, when the swaps market was just getting started, the industry participants relied on notional principal—rather than the much smaller market value—as a way of advertising that the market was "for real."

In retrospect, this turned out to be a mistake. Among the people who have chastised the industry for this mistake is Richard Breeden, then chairman of the Securities and Exchange Commission:[32]

> The widespread use of "notional amounts" is the worst thing market participants have done, because the specter of *trillions* of dollars in "notional amount" has scared many people, including a few members of legislative bodies.

But Chairman Breeden did recognize that the actual risk for the OTC derivatives is much smaller than the notional amounts would suggest:

> The amounts actually at risk in these markets do not appear to be unusually large compared to the size of exposures that banks, broker-dealers and insurance companies maintain for their traditional business. Actual risk is represented by the replacement cost or the mark-to-market value of the contract, which is typically only 2 percent to 3 percent of the notional amount.

Table 3–10 examines this relation between replacement cost and notional amount for the 50 largest U.S. bank holding companies. Over the period 1990–92,

TABLE 3–10 Derivatives Exposure by Lead Banks of 50 Largest U.S. Bank Holding Companies: Gross Replacement Costs (Year-End 1990–1992)

	Interest Rate Contracts		Currency Contracts		Combined Exposure
Year	*$ Billion*	*Percent of Notional Principal*	*$ Billion*	*Percent of Notional Principal*	*$ Billion*
1990	26.2	1.15	76.3	2.82	102.5
1991	47.8	1.61	99.4	3.70	147.2
1992	49.7	1.61	94.3	2.98	144.0

SOURCE: Consolidated Reports of Condition and Income. The gross replacement cost is the mark-to-market value for OTC derivatives contracts with positive replacement cost, including swaps, forwards, purchased options, when-issued securities and forward deposits accepted. Exchange-traded contracts and foreign exchange contracts with less than 14 days' maturity are excluded.

the gross replacement cost of the interest rate derivatives held by the 50 largest U.S. banks ranged between 1.2 percent and 1.6 percent of the notional amount of the contracts. For currency derivatives, the ratio of gross replacement cost to the notional amount was larger, but still ranged only between 2.8 percent and 3.7 percent.

Looked at another way, the $144 billion in gross replacement cost at the end of 1992—roughly $94 billion in currency contracts and $50 billion in interest rate contracts—represents less than 11 percent of the market value of the assets of these banks and 120 percent of their total capital.[33]

Another source of concern to the regulators was the concentration of derivatives activities. They pointed to the fact that at the end of 1991, the top 8 U.S. banks accounted for 86 percent of the OTC interest rate derivatives and 88 percent of OTC currency derivatives outstanding among 50 of the largest American banks.

The response of the industry was that such statistics ignore the increasingly international character of the OTC markets. While accounting for almost 90 percent of the U.S. markets, the eight largest U.S. banks accounted for only 56 percent of worldwide interest rate and currency derivatives. Moreover, the market share of non-U.S. dealers appears to be growing steadily.

Courts and Legislatures Challenge Enforceability

Ultra Vires is a Latin phrase—rough translation "beyond power"—that lawyers use to describe the situation when one's counterparty is legally incapable of entering into the contract.

The concern is that the contract or entire class of contracts would be declared illegal or unenforceable. This is precisely what happened in 1991.

Illustration 3–4

Hammersmith and Fulham*

In January 1991, the United Kingdom House of Lords held that the London borough of Hammersmith and Fulham lacked the necessary capacity to enter into interest rate swap contracts in had entered into during the 1980s and therefore was not liable to make payments on those contracts on which it would otherwise have suffered large losses.

The Local Government Act of 1972, from which local authorities derive their powers, does not include any express power for local authorities to enter into derivatives transactions, and the House of Lords found no implied powers—whether for hedging or for other purposes.

*This discussion is adapted from that contained in the Report of the Group of Thirty Global Derivatives Project.

OTC Derivatives as Illegal Futures Contracts? In the United States, another source of legal risk for derivative products is the requirement by the Commodity Exchange Act (CEA) that "futures contracts" be traded on organized exchanges. In the context of the CEA, the terms "commodity" and "futures" have been broadly interpreted. The upshot is that futures and options on a broad range of underlying assets—including interest rates and foreign exchange rates as well as soybeans and pork bellies—have come within the regulatory purview of the Commodities Futures and Trading Commission (CFTC).

The language of the CEA led to concerns that OTC derivatives could be ruled to be illegal off-exchange futures. If swaps or other OTC derivatives were construed by the courts to be futures, then those counterparties who owed money could potentially walk away from the contracts without meeting their obligations.

And, as we mentioned in Chapter 1, these fears were realized in 1987. In an Advance Note of Proposed Rulemaking, the CFTC questioned the legality of commodity swaps. The immediate impact was that the commodity swaps business immediately went offshore.

Moreover, a series of lawsuits further increased the uncertainty about the legal status of OTC derivatives.

Since the Brent crude oil market was not designated by the CFTC as a contract market, the 1990 finding of the court in *Transnor* meant that the Brent forwards could have been construed as illegal futures contracts—and, hence, unenforceable.

As in *Transnor*, the ruling of the court in *A-Mark* was that OTC contracts could be viewed as futures contracts subject to the CEA.

Illustration 3–5

Transnor*

In December 1985, Transnor (Bermuda) Ltd. purchased two cargoes of North Sea crude oil for delivery in Scotland in March 1986, at an average price of $24.50 per barrel. However, at contract maturity, Transnor refused to take delivery of these cargoes because their market value had declined after Transnor entered into the contracts.

Transnor claimed that Conoco Inc., Conoco (U.K.) Ltd., and Exxon Corporation conspired to cause a decline in crude oil prices by jointly selling cargoes of Brent blend crude oil at below-market prices. Transnor claimed that Conoco and Exxon violated the Sherman Act and the Commodity Exchange Act.

Conoco and Exxon moved for summary judgement on several grounds, including that the defendants' conduct was neither governed by nor in violation of the CEA. Conoco and Exxon contended that the Brent transactions were "cash forward contracts" specifically exempted from the scope of the CEA.

U.S. District Judge William Conner noted that the CFTC has jurisdiction over "contracts of sale of a commodity for future delivery," but that the CEA provides that "the term future delivery shall not include any sale of a cash commodity for deferred shipment or delivery." So, the court viewed the Brent contract to be a hybrid of a futures contract and a forward contract.

After examining the distinctions between the two and the relevant case law, Judge Conner concluded that Transnor's 15-day Brent transactions were indeed futures contracts within the meaning of the CEA.

*This discussion is adapted from the decision written by Judge William Conner, United States District Court, Southern District of New York, April 18, 1990 (86 Civ. 1493).

Illustration 3–6

A-Mark*

In 1979, A-Mark Precious Metals, Inc., a wholesale metals dealer, began doing business with Keith Bybee, a retail metals dealer. A-Mark offered Bybee a "deferred delivery/margin" contract, which called for an immediate down payment and for payment of the remaining balance within two years. The balance due A-Mark was secured by a lien on

A Mark continued

all undelivered metals bought under the deferred delivery plan.

In April 1982, Bybee began making purchases of silver from A-Mark for his own account using the "deferred delivery/margin" contract. He also began informing his customers that they need not take delivery of metals for which they had paid in full; instead, A-Mark would store their metals free of charge for up to two years. The customers, however, were unaware that the metals "stored" with A-Mark were subject to the lien securing Bybee purchases for his personal account.

As silver declined in value, A-Mark issued margin calls to Bybee, who initially satisfied them from his personal assets. Later, he borrowed from friends and customers to meet further margin calls. By May 1986, Bybee was unable to satisfy new margin calls and resold all metals that he had purchased on margin, including the metals that Bybee's customers had paid for in full but were being "stored" at A-Mark.

After deducting Bybee's indebtedness, A-Mark remitted to Bybee some $300,000, which he then invested in the futures market and lost.

Soon thereafter, Bybee filed for bankruptcy.

The bankruptcy trustee charged that A-Mark's "deferred delivery/margin" contract was in fact an illegal off-exchange futures contract. Consequently, the trustee sought to recover from A-Mark all money Bybee and his customers had lost in connection with the A-Mark/Bybee deferred delivery purchases.

The bankruptcy court concluded that A-Mark's contract *was not* a futures contract because it was not offered to the general public by A-Mark.

The trustee then appealed to a U.S. district court, which also concluded that A-Mark's deferred delivery contract *was not* a futures contract.

The trustee then appealed to the court of appeals. In September 1991, a three-judge panel of the court of appeals concluded that the deferred delivery contract marketed by A-Mark to Bybee *was* a futures contract under the CEA.[†]

---

*This description is excerpted and edited from the discussion which appeared in Chapter V of "OTC Derivative Markets and Their Regulation," the Report of the Commodity Futures Trading Commission to Congress, October 1993, pp. 141–43.

[†]Nonetheless, the court held that the CEA's prohibition against off-exchange futures trading did not apply because the A-Mark/Bybee contracts came within the cash forward contract exclusion of the CEA

In *Dr. Tauber* the courts made what appeared to be a clear ruling. Some might argue that this should be the end of the story; but like many things involving the law, questions remain.

Illustration 3–7

Dr. Tauber*

Over the course of two and one-half years Dr. Laszlo N. Tauber, a surgeon from Virginia, entered into almost three thousand foreign exchange transactions with Salomon Forex, Inc. Dr. Tauber's trading with Salomon Forex was just one aspect of his extensive dealings in foreign exchange—during the relevant period, Dr. Tauber traded with more than a dozen other companies, exchanging billions of dollars worth of currency.

In March 1991, the value of Dr. Tauber's transactions, particularly in Swiss francs, declined sharply, and Salomon Forex demanded that Tauber cover his open positions.

When Dr. Tauber failed to do so, Salomon Forex ceased trading with him. Just over $25 million became due and payable under 68 contracts that matured in July and August, 1991, leaving Dr. Tauber owing $30 million to Salomon Forex. After applying $4 million in collateral that it was holding to this balance, Salomon Forex billed Tauber for almost $26 million.

When Tauber refused to pay, Salomon Forex brought suit. Tauber responded that the transactions he negotiated with Salomon Forex were illegal under the Commodities Exchange Act and that therefore he should not be held responsible for them.

The central issue in this case is whether Congress intended transactions such as those between Salomon Forex and Dr. Tauber to be regulated by the CEA.

The CEA provides that no person shall enter into, or offer to enter into, a transaction involving the sale of a "commodity for future delivery," unless it is conducted on or through a board of trade designated and regulated by the CFTC. However, in the opinion of the U.S. Circuit Court which heard this case, Congress never purported to regulate "spot" or "cash forward" transactions (in which the commodity is presently sold but its delivery is, by agreement, delayed or deferred).

Moreover, when Congress expanded the scope of the CEA in 1974, the Department of the Treasury proposed explicit recognition of an exception to CEA coverage—that off-exchange trading of foreign exchange futures was not to be regulated under the CEA. To establish the recommended exclusion, the Treasury Department proposed an amendment, which was ultimately codified.

> Nothing in this chapter shall be deemed to govern . . . transactions in foreign currency, security warrants, security rights, resales of installment loan contracts, repurchase options, government securities, or mortgages and mortgage purchase commitments, unless such transactions involve the sale thereof for future delivery conducted on a board of trade.

It is on this "Treasury Amendment" that Salomon Forex based its contention that the transactions between it and Tauber are exempted from the CEA.

---

*This discussion is excerpted from the decision written by Paul Niemeyer, judge of the United States Court of Appeals for the Fourth Circuit, October 18, 1993.

The district court that heard this case concluded that Tauber's transactions were exempted from CEA regulation by the Treasury Amendment, which exempts from regulation all off-exchange "transactions in foreign currency."

Dr. Tauber continued*

When the case was appealed, the U.S. Court of Appeals noted that the CEA excludes from its regulation "transactions in foreign currency" unless they involve sales "for future delivery conducted on a board of trade." So the question was whether "transactions in foreign currency" included the type traded in by Salomon Forex and Tauber. The court of appeals concluded that the Treasury Amendment applies to all foreign exchange transactions; so, the court was satisfied that off-exchange transactions in foreign currency are exempted from regulation by the CEA.

Legal Status of OTC Derivatives Clarified

The prospect that an OTC derivative transaction could be viewed as an "illegal off-exchange futures" is one that—to say the least—was very unsettling for OTC derivatives participants. However, since 1987, a great deal of progress has been made.

In 1989, the CFTC reversed its position on the status of swaps. In July 1989, the commission, led by the recently appointed chairman Wendy Lee Gramm, published a policy statement that noted that, while swaps possess some elements of futures contracts, they were not appropriately regulated as futures contracts under the CEA. The commission also recognized a nonexclusive "safe harbor" for swaps. In the same month, the CFTC adopted rules which exempted hybrid instruments from commission regulation.

In 1992, Congress passed the Futures Trading Practices Act reauthorizing the CFTC and giving it explicit authority to exempt swaps from regulation under the Commodity Exchange Act.

In January 1993, the CFTC used this new exemptive authority to clarify that swaps have a separate legal identity, distinct from futures and hence exempt from the CEA's exchange trading requirement. This exemption went a long way toward clearing up the uncertainty introduced by the legal challenges. Moreover, in its October 1993 report to Congress, the CFTC recognized these issues and noted that it will continue to monitor how the *A-Mark* decision is used and interpreted.[34]

OTC Derivatives Released from the Infectious Diseases Ward

With the reauthorization of the CFTC and the resultant reduction in uncertainty about the legal status of OTC derivatives contracts, the regulatory tide began to turn. The news for participants in the OTC derivatives markets was much better in 1993 than it had been in 1992.

Risk Management in Practice

Thumbnail Sketch of CFTC Reauthorization Bill

Mahlon M. Frankhauser
Ellen S. Levinson

After almost a four-year period of gestation, or rather indigestion, the fourth reauthorization of the Commodity Futures Trading Commission (CFTC) finally occurred on October 28, 1992. The fact that "authorization" expired on September 30, 1989, has been irrelevant since Congress continued to appropriate the CFTC's budget—notwithstanding House and Senate rules that prohibit appropriations for programs that are not "authorized."

At the outset of the reauthorization process, there were some optimists who prophesied a one-line reauthorization similar to those that occur with the authorization for the Securities and Exchange Commission. However, with the revelations of the Chicago sting operation early on in the process, and the later turf battle over first stock index futures and then off-exchange derivative products—hybrids and swaps—a major legislative battle was joined that was not concluded until the very last days of the 102nd Congress.

A contentious issue that blocked progress on this legislation was the regulation of swaps. Swaps dealers asked Congress for an automatic statutory exclusion from the act, and the Chicago exchanges argued that if swaps were excluded, then a futures exchange should also be able to trade swaps free from CFTC regulation. Title V of the bill reflects a compromise on these various derivative product intermarket issues.

In general, the CFTC was granted new authority to exempt by rule, regulation, or order any agreement, contract, or transaction that is otherwise subject to the act from any provision of the act, if the CFTC determines the exemption would be in the public interest. The bill explicitly states that a board of trade is eligible to seek or to be granted an exemption under this new provision.

To provide an exemption for a transaction, agreement, or contract from the requirement that a futures contract be traded on a designated board of trade, the CFTC must determine that (a) such an exemption would be consistent with the public interest and the purposes of the Act, (b) the transactions will be between "appropriate persons" and (c) the transactions will not have a material adverse effect on the ability of the CFTC or a contract market to carry out their regulatory duties. "Appropriate persons" include business entities with a net worth exceeding $1 million or total assets exceeding $5 million, a bank or trust company, an investment company, a commodity pool, a regulated broker-

Thumbnail Sketch of CFTC Reauthorization Bill continued

dealer, a regulated FCM or commodities floor broker or trader, and "such other persons that the [CFTC] determines to be appropriate in light of their financial or other qualifications."

The legislation specifically authorizes the CFTC to *promptly exempt* from the act (1) hybrid instruments that are predominantly securities or depository instruments, and (2) swaps agreements that "are not part of a fungible class of agreements that are standardized as to their material economic terms."

The report accompanying the bill states that the purpose of the new exemptive powers is to give the CFTC "a means of providing certainty and stability to existing and emerging markets so that financial innovation and market development can proceed in an effective and competitive manner." It encourages the CFTC by rule, regulation, or order, to exempt swaps, forwards, bank deposits, and hybrid instruments, but for other instruments or markets, the CFTC should use its general exemptive authority "sparingly."

Mahlon M. Frankhauser is managing partner of the Washington, D.C. office of the New York law firm of Lord Day & Lord, Barrett Smith, where he specializes in securities and commodities regulation, related litigation, and legislation. Mr. Frankhauser began his career with the Securities and Exchange Commission. He subsequently served as a vice president of the New York Stock Exchange, executive vice president and General Counsel of CBWL-Hayden Stone, Inc. (more recently known as Shearson Lehman Brothers, Inc.), and a partner in the law firm Kirkland & Ellis, before joining Lord Day. A graduate of the University of Pennsylvania Law School, Mr. Frankhauser has taught on the faculties of St. John's University Law School, Catholic University Law School, and Georgetown Law Center.

Ellen S. Levinson is government relations advisor at Lord Day & Lord, Barrett Smith, where she provides advice regarding legislative and administrative procedures, as well as assisting Lord Day clients with matters before Congress and federal agencies. Ms. Levinson's practice covers a wide range of areas, including commodity futures, agriculture, and trade.

Fed/OCC/FDIC Report to Congress. Early in 1993 the joint study by the Board of Governors of the Federal Reserve System, the FDIC, and the OCC[35] gave banks' derivatives operations a "cautious thumbs up."[36] This study, which was conducted in response to an inquiry by Senate Banking Committee Chairman Donald Riegle, concluded:

> Whether a bank's management of the risks associated with its derivatives activities is prudent depends critically on the strength of its related policies, procedures, risk controls and management information systems. To date, these management procedures have been generally successful.

Although a number of money-center banks have reportedly experienced losses, no bank has failed as a result of derivatives trading. Moreover, a number of banks and other dealers have recently raised additional capital to strengthen their credit ratings in order to support further dealings in derivatives. No major dealer has withdrawn from dealing or scaled-back operations.

Group of Thirty Report. One of the forces from within the derivatives industry that responded to and thereby helped assuage the fears of the regulatory community was a Study Group on Global Derivatives sponsored by the Group of Thirty—a group of leading bankers, regulators, and academics from major industrial nations. The Steering Committee for the Derivatives Project was chaired by Dennis Weatherstone, chairman of J.P. Morgan. The working group, co-chaired by David Brunner of Paribas Capital Markets and Patrick de Saint-Aignan of Morgan Stanley, was made up of individuals from academia, dealer firms, end-user firms, law firms, accounting firms, and the FASB.

The G-30 Derivative Project examined and reported on the different types of risk confronting the industry—market risk; credit risk; legal enforceability; systems, operations and controls; and accounting—as well as commenting on the systemic risk from derivatives.[37] However, the central feature of the G-30 report was a set of 20 "good-practice" recommendations for dealers and end users. These recommendations, presented in Figure 3–9, offer a benchmark against which participants can measure their own practices.

CFTC Report to Congress. The conference committee of Congress which dealt with the 1992 reauthorization of the CFTC directed the CFTC to conduct a study of the OTC derivatives market. This report was presented to Congress in October 1993. As with the Fed/OCC/FDIC study, this study gave the market a cautious clean bill of health. The commission concluded that "no fundamental changes in regulatory structure appear to be needed. . . . "

. . . But, Regulatory and Legislative Attention Continues

In 1993, the news for the OTC derivatives markets did get much better. However, the regulatory and legislative focus on derivatives certainly did not end.

Indeed, on the very day that the CFTC's report was being delivered to Congress (October 27, 1993), the Office of the Comptroller of the Currency (OCC) instituted additional controls on national banks engaged in financial derivatives activities with the issue of Banking Circular 277. While encouraging banks to use derivatives to meet business objectives, this circular set out a set of guidelines that the bank should follow: *Senior Management and Board Oversight.* BC-277 holds senior management and the bank's board of directors more accountable than did previous guidelines. According to BC-277, the board should approve the bank's entry into derivatives activities and ensure that sufficient capital is maintained. The bank should establish a comprehensive set of written risk management policies that should be reviewed annually by senior management. Senior management and the board should ensure that a risk management system is developed with an independent risk management function; and the board should develop an audit program to check for weaknesses.

Market Risk Management. The bank should have adequate systems to evaluate risks. BC-277 would permit (with approval from the OCC) national banks to trade physical commodities to manage the risks arising from the intermediation of commodity risk management derivatives.

Credit Risk Management. The bank should have systems and mathematical models in place to quantify presettlement risk, including current and potential exposures. BC-277 also contained a "suitability" guideline which would make the bank responsible for making sure that a particular transaction is appropriate for a particular customer.

On December 20, 1993, the Board of Governors of the Federal Reserve System issued SR Letter 93-69, which contained guidance to its examiners that was very similar to that contained in BC-277 from the OCC. SR Letter 93–69 focused on three crucial factors: *Oversight by the Board of Directors and Management, The Risk Management Process,* and *Internal Controls and Audits.*

The legislators have also continued to focus on derivatives. Congressman Henry B. Gonzalez (D-TX), Chairman of the Committee on Banking, Finance, and Urban Affairs of the U.S. House of Representatives, has been vocal in his concern about derivatives:

> I have long believed that growing bank involvement in derivative products is . . . like a tinderbox waiting to explode. . . .
>
> We must work to avoid a crisis related to derivative products before, once again . . . the taxpayer is left holding the bag.[38]

On November 22, 1993, Congressman James A. Leach (R-IA), the ranking Republican on the House Banking Committee, released a list of 30 recommendations for regulatory and legislative guidance, which were based on a six-month, 900-page study of financial derivatives. Congressman Leach recommended that an interagency commission be established to coordinate regulations related to capital, accounting, disclosure, and suitability for dealers and end users of OTC derivatives, that cross-industry and cross-border standards be harmonized, and that active derivatives dealers be required to demonstrate both adequate capitalization and sophisticated technical capacity. In January 1994, Congressman Leach went a step further by introducing legislation to set up a Federal Derivatives Commission to establish principles and standards for the supervision of financial institutions engaged in derivatives activities.

Figure 3–9 Group of Thirty Derivatives Project Good Practice Recommendations

Recommendation 1: The Role of Senior Management
Dealers and end users should use derivatives in a manner consistent with the overall risk management and capital policies approved by their boards of directors. These policies should be reviewed as business and market circumstances change. Policies governing derivatives use should be clearly defined, including the purposes for which these transactions are to be undertaken. Senior management should approve procedures and controls to implement these policies, and management at all levels should enforce them.

Recommendation 2: Marking to Market
Dealers should mark their derivatives positions to market, on at least a daily basis, for risk management purposes.

Recommendation 3: Market Valuation Methods
Derivatives portfolios of dealers should be values based on mid-market levels less specific adjustments, or on appropriate bid or offer levels. Mid-market valuation adjustments should allow for expected future costs such as unearned credit spread, close-out costs, investing and funding costs, and administrative costs.

Recommendation 4: Identifying Revenue Sources
Dealers should measure the components of revenue regularly and in sufficient detail to understand the sources of risk.

Recommendation 5: Measuring Market Risk
Dealers should use a consistent measure to calculate daily the market risk of their derivatives positions and compare it to market risk limits.

- Market risk is best measured as "value at risk" using probability analysis based upon a common confidence interval (e.g., two standard deviations) and time horizon (e.g., a one-day exposure).
- Components of market risk that should be considered across the term structure include: absolute price or rate change (delta); convexity (gamma); volatility (vega); time decay (theta); basis or correlation; and discount rate (rho).

Recommendation 6: Stress Simulations
Dealers should regularly perform simulations to determine how their portfolios would perform under stress conditions.

Recommendation 7: Investing and Funding Forecasts
Dealers should periodically forecast the cash investing and funding requirements arising from their derivatives portfolios.

Recommendation 8: Independent Market Risk Management
Dealers should have a market risk management function, with clear independence and authority, to ensure that the following responsibilities are carried out:

- The development of risk limit policies and the monitoring of transactions and positions for adherence to these policies (See Recommendation 5.)
- The design of stress scenarios to measure the impact of market conditions, however improbable, that might cause market gaps, volatility swings, or disruptions of major relationships, or might reduce liquidity in the face of unfavorable market linkages, concentrated market making, or credit exhaustion. (See Recommendation 6.)
- The design of revenue reports quantifying the contribution of various risk components, and of market risk measures such as value at risk. (See Recommendations 4 and 5.)
- The monitoring of variance between the actual volatility of portfolio value and that predicted by the measure of market risk.
- The review and approval of pricing models and valuation systems used by front and back-office personnel, and the development of reconciliation procedures if different systems are used.

Recommendation 9: Practices by End Users
As appropriate to the nature, size, and complexity of their derivatives activities, end users should adopt the same valuation and market risk management practices that are recommended for dealers. Specifically, they should consider: regularly marking to market their derivatives transactions for risk management purposes; periodically forecasting the cash investing and funding requirements arising from their derivatives transactions; and establishing a clearly independent and authoritative function to design and assure adherence to prudent risk limits.

Recommendation 10: Measuring Credit Exposure
Dealers and end users should measure credit exposure on derivatives in two ways:

- Current exposure, which is the replacement cost of derivatives transactions, that is, their market value.
- Potential exposure, which is an estimate of the future replacement cost of derivatives transactions. It should be calculated using probability analysis based upon broad confidence intervals (e.g., two standard deviations) over the remaining terms of the transactions.

Recommendation 11: Aggregating Credit Exposures
Credit exposures on derivatives, and all other credit exposures to a counterparty, should be aggregated taking into consideration enforceable netting arrangements. Credit exposures should be calculated regularly and compared to credit limits.

Recommendation 12: Independent Credit Risk Management
Dealers and end users should have a credit risk management function with clear independence and authority, and with analytical capabilities in derivatives, responsible for:

- Approving credit exposure measurement standards.
- Setting credit limits and monitoring their use.
- Reviewing credits and concentrations of credit risk.
- Reviewing and monitoring risk reduction arrangements.

Recommendation 13: Master Agreements
Dealers and end users are encouraged to use one master agreement as widely as possible with each counterparty to document existing and future derivatives transactions, including foreign exchange forwards and options. Master agreements should provide for payments netting and close-out netting, using a full two-way payments approach.

Recommendation 14: Credit Enhancement
Dealers and end users should assess both the benefits and costs of credit enhancement and related risk-reduction arrangements. Where it is proposed that credit downgrades would trigger early termination or collateral requirements, participants should carefully consider their own capacity and that of their counterparties to meet the potentially substantial funding needs that might result.

Recommendation 15: Promoting Enforcebility
Dealers and end users should work together on a continuing basis to identify and recommend solutions for issues of legal enforceability, both within and across jurisdictions, as activities evolve and new types of transactions are developed.

Recommendation 16: Professional Expertise
Dealers and end users must ensure that their derivatives activities are undertaken by professionals in sufficient number and with the appropriate experience, skill levels, and degrees of specialization. These professionals include specialists who transact and manage the risks involved, their supervisors, and those responsible for processing, reporting, controlling, and auditing the activities.

Recommendation 17: Systems
Dealers and end users must ensure that adequate systems for data capture, processing, settlement, and management reporting are in place so that derivatives transactions are conducted in an orderly and efficient manner in compliance with management policies. Dealers should have risk management systems that measure the risks incurred in their derivatives activities including market and credit risks. End users should have risk management systems that measure the risks incurred in their derivatives activities based upon their nature, size, and complexity.

Recommendation 18: Authority
Management of dealers and end users should designate who is authorized to commit their institutions to derivatives transactions.

Recommendation 19: Accounting Practices
International harmonization of accounting standardization for derivatives is desirable. Pending the adoption of harmonized standards, the following accounting practices are recommended:

- Dealers should account for derivatives transactions by marking them to market, taking changes in value to income each period.
- End users should account for derivatives used to manage risks so as to achieve a consistency of income recognition treatment between those instruments and the risks being managed. Thus, if the risk being managed is accounted for at cost (or, in the case of an anticipatory hedge, not yet recognized, changed in the value of a qualifying risk management instrument should be deferred until a gain or loss is recognized on the risk being managed. Or, if the risk being managed is marked to market with changes in value being taken to income, a qualifying risk management instrument should be treated in a comparable fashion.
- End users should account for derivatives not qualifying for risk management treatment on a mark-to-market basis.
- Amounts due to and from counterparties should only be offset when there is a legal right to set off or when enforceable netting arrangements are in place.

Where local regulations prevent adoption of these practices, disclosure along these
lines is nevertheless recommended.

Recommendation 20: Disclosures
Financial statements of dealers and end users should contain sufficient information about their use of derivatives to provide an understanding of the purposes for which transactions are undertaken, the extent of the transactions, the degree of risk involved, and how the transactions have been accounted for. Pending the adoption of harmonized accounting standards, the following disclosures are recommended:

- Information about management's attitude to financial risks, how instruments are used, and how risks are monitored and controlled.
- Accounting policies.
- Analysis of the credit risk inherent to those positions.
- Analysis of positions at the balance sheet date.
- For dealers only, additional information about the extent of their activities in financial instruments.

SOURCE: *Derivatives: Practices and Principles,* Global Derivatives Study Group, Group of Thirty, Washington, D.C., July 1993

And the White House was not to be left out. As 1993 rolled into 1994, Treasury Secretary Lloyd Bentsen resurrected the Working Group on Financial Markets, a high-profile interagency committee originally formed to study the 1987 stock market crash. Secretary Bentsen instructed this group to work toward coordinating government policy in regulating the OTC derivatives markets.[39]

Accounting[40]

Financial derivatives transactions have raised many new questions that accountants have found difficult to resolve. Moreover, new kinds of instruments and transactions, increased volatility in financial markets, and changes in the financial services industry raised questions about the adequacy of present accounting standards.

In the United States the accounting issues raised by the new financial instruments are being dealt with by the Financial Accounting Standards Board (FASB), its Emerging Issues Task Force (EITF), and the American Institute of Certified Public Accountants (AICPA). (As some indication of the scale of these problems, almost half of the more than 260 issues considered by the EITF since its formation in 1984 have been concerned with financial instruments, financial institutions, or off-balance-sheet financing.)

The FASB's constituents made clear their dissatisfaction with inconsistent accounting treatment for similar transactions and their support for improved accounting for financial instruments by all reporting entities. Those points have been recognized internationally as well, as evidenced by the efforts of Australian, Canadian, British, Japanese, and international accounting standard setters, among others, that have each undertaken projects on accounting for financial instruments.

The FASB's Financial Instruments Project

The FASB added the project on financial instruments and off-balance-sheet financing to its agenda in 1986. The project was initially divided into three separate though related parts: disclosure, recognition and measurement, and distinguishing between liabilities and equity.

The first part was designed as an interim step to improve disclosures about financial instruments while the Board considers the more difficult (and time-consuming) issues of recognition and measurement. Work on disclosures has so far resulted in FASB Statement No. 105, *Disclosure of Information about Financial Instruments with Off-Balance-Sheet Risk and Financial Instruments with Concentrations of Credit Risk* in March 1990, and FASB Statement No. 107, *Disclosure about Fair Value of Financial Instruments*, in December 1991.

In September 1991, the FASB issued a Research Report—*Hedge Accounting: An Exploratory Study of the Underlying Issues*—which examines the issues raised by hedging relationships. In November 1991, the FASB issued a Discussion Memorandum—Recognition and Measurement of Financial Instruments—as a basis for further consideration of the financial accounting and reporting issues of recognition and measurement raised by financial instruments. In response to urgent requests for action in these troublesome areas, the recognition and measurement phase of the financial instruments project resulted in the issuance of FASB Statements No. 114, *Accounting by Creditors for Impairment of a Loan*, and No. 115, *Accounting for Certain Investments in Debt and Equity Securities*, in May 1993—as well as FASB Interpretation No. 39, *Offsetting of Amounts Related to Certain Contracts*, in March 1992.

FASB began deliberations on accounting for hedging and other risk-adjusting activities in January 1992. This project addresses the accounting for hedging, other risk-adjusting activities (e.g., asset-liability management and synthetic instrument creation), and derivative financial instruments. If the tentative Board decisions are eventually adopted into a final statement, that statement would likely replace the present incomplete and inconsistent hedge accounting standards contained in FASB Statements No. 52, *Foreign Currency Translation* and No. 80, *Accounting for Futures Contracts* and the positions embodied in various consensus reached by the FASB Emerging Issues Task Force.

The aim of developing broad, conceptually consistent accounting standards for financial instruments requires reconsidering many generally accepted accounting principles and changing some of them. Figure 3–10 highlights some of the authoritative accounting literature subject to reconsideration.

Accounting for Hedging Activities

Hedge accounting is a special accounting treatment that alters the normal accounting for the components of a hedge so that counterbalancing changes in the fair values of the hedged item(s) and the hedging instrument(s) are included in earnings in the same period. Concern has arisen that the explosion of hedging instruments and hedging strategies has outpaced accounting guidance.

Hedge accounting arose initially as a practical "fix" for anomalous situations in which two items related by a hedging strategy were accounted for differently. While some of these situations have been resolved by improvement in normal recognition or measurement standards and practices, anomalies continue to exist.

Hedge accounting creates problems in itself, leading some to question whether it is worthwhile. The prevailing opinion is that some form of hedge accounting must continue to be available but must be limited to qualifying transactions. However, which transactions should qualify, which other criteria must be met, and exactly how hedge accounting should work are controversial issues.

Demand for hedge accounting arises because of differences in the way hedged items and hedging instruments are normally recognized or measured. Special

FIGURE 3–10 Some of the Authoritative Literature That May Be Affected by the Recognition and Measurement Part of the Financial Instruments Project

Document	*Title*	*Area That May Be Modified*
APB Opinion No. 10	Omnibus Opinion-1966	The effect of the right of set off-relationship is being re-examined.
APB Opinion No. 21	Interest on Receivables and Payables	Accounting and scope restrictions are being reconsidered in initial and subsequent measurement issues.
FASB Statement No. 5	Accounting for Contingencies	Impairment of receivables for collectibility is being reconsidered in subsequent measurement issues.
FASB Statement No. 12	Accounting for Certain Marketable Securities	Entire statement is being reconsidered in subsequent measurement issues.
FASB Statement No. 15	Accounting by Debtors by Creditors for Troubled Debt Restructurings	Entire statement is being reconsidered in subsequent measurement and derecognition issues.
FASB Statement No. 52	Foreign Currency Transaction	Subsequent measurement of forward exchange contracts and hedge accounting provisions are being reconsidered.
FASB Statement No. 60	Accounting and Reporting by Insurance Enterprises	Subsequent measurement of investment assets and perhaps certain insurance liabilities is being reconsidered.
FASB Statement No. 65	Accounting for Certain mortgage loans, mortgage-backed securities	Subsequent measurement and derecognition of and the sale of loans with servicing retained are being reconsidered.
FASB Statement No. 76	Extinguishment of Debt	Entire statement is being reconsidered in derecognition issues.
FASB Statement No. 77	Reporting of Transferors for Transfers of Receivables with Recourse	Entire statement is being reconsidered in derecognition issues.
FASB Statement No. 80	Accounting for Futures Contracts	Hedge accounting provisions are being reconsidered.
FASB Statement No. 91	Accounting for Non-refundable Fees and Costs Associated with Originating or Acquiring Loans and Initial Direct Costs of Leases	Entire statement is being reconsidered in derecognition issues.

accounting for hedges arose as a means of compensating for anomalies—situations in which counterbalancing changes in values of hedge components would otherwise be reported in earnings in different periods—that arise from applying existing recognition and measurement standards.

Recognition anomalies arise because some assets and liabilities are recognized in the statement of financial position, while others, such as some derivative financial instruments and firm commitments, are not. Measurement anomalies arise because existing accounting standards use different measurement attributes for different assets and liabilities. Some assets and liabilities are measured based on historical prices, others are measured based on current prices, and still others are based on a combination of historical and current prices—the lower-of-cost-or-market (LOCOM) values. Under the existing mixed attribute accounting system,[41] the effects of changes in prices or interest rates on many assets and liabilities are not recognized in income until they are realized. Yet, for many instruments measured fully or partially at current prices, for example, trading instruments, "speculative" instruments, or instruments held for sale, the unrealized gains and losses that arise from changes in prices are recognized in income as market price change.

Numerous hedging recognition anomalies arise because many derivative financial instruments, which are commonly used as hedging instruments, remain unrecognized. With the exception of futures contracts, for which FASB Statement No. 80, *Accounting for Futures Contracts,* requires recognition of gains and losses as realized by daily settlement of the variation margin, and forward contracts for foreign currency, covered by FASB Statement No. 52, *Foreign Currency Translation,* no accounting standards for derivative financial instruments have as yet been codified in FASB Statements. In current practice, many types of derivative instruments remain unrecognized, while others are recognized and measured, some at market value, others based on historical prices.

Problems with Hedge Accounting: Evolution of an Impasse

Hedge accounting has previously been addressed in FASB Statement No. 8, *Accounting for the Translation of Foreign Currency Transactions,* Statement 52 (which superseded Statement 8) and Statement 80. Those statements present hedge accounting guidance—and permit deferral hedge accounting—for hedges of foreign exchange risk (Statement 52) and for hedges with exchange-traded futures contracts other than for foreign exchange (Statement 80). However, those statements do not explicitly cover many of the instruments used today, such as commodity forwards and interest rate swaps.

Further, Statements 52 and 80 have important conceptual inconsistencies.

One of these deals with *hedge accounting for anticipated future transactions.* Statement 52 limits hedge accounting for foreign currency transactions to those anticipated transactions that are firmly committed. Statement 80 extends hedge accounting with futures contracts to anticipated transactions that are not firmly committed provided certain underlying hedge criteria are met.[42]

In 1986 the American Institute of Certified Public Accountants published Issues Paper 86-2, *Accounting for Options,* which focused on hedge accounting in a variety of circumstances. The paper proposed criteria and hedge accounting techniques, some of which were consistent with those in Statement 52, others of which were consistent with those in Statement 80, and still others that were consistent with neither statement. One of the advisory conclusions would permit hedge accounting for hedges of anticipated transactions that were not firmly committed provided certain underlying hedge criteria were met. While the issues paper has no status as authoritative literature, it has influenced practice and the ensuing debate.

The EITF also considered hedge accounting for forecasted foreign exchange transactions that are hedged with options.[43] By analogizing to Statement 80, the EITF reached the consensus that it is appropriate to use hedge accounting for hedges of identified forecasted foreign currency risks in certain circumstances. In March 1992, while the EITF was considering the accounting for hedges with *complex option strategies,*[44] the staff of the SEC formally objected to allowing deferrals of realized or unrealized gains and losses arising from complex options and similar transactions that are designated as hedges of forecasted, but not firmly committed, foreign currency transactions.

FASB's Tentative Conclusions

In July 1993, the FASB issued tentative conclusions on some, but not all, of the hedge accounting issues. If included in a final statement, these conclusions would change hedge accounting as follows:

Encompass all hedges in which the hedging instruments are financial derivatives.[45]

Permit hedge accounting for cross-currency or proxy hedges.

Limit deferral of gains and losses based on the effectiveness of a hedge.[46]

Eliminate the requirement to assess correlation on an ongoing basis and discontinue hedge accounting if the correlation became less than "high."

Clarify that hedging means reducing the risk of adverse consequences—losses—with risk reduction to be assessed at the enterprise or business unit level on an ongoing basis.

As 1993 came to an end, FASB had not resolved the key issue: whether to permit or prohibit hedge accounting for hedges for forecasted transactions.

Taxation[47]

We have saved the most complex issue for last. (Perhaps we were subconsciously thinking that if we put it off long enough, we might not have to discuss it.) In the following, we will give you a short tour of the issues and the important decisions. However, if your interests in the tax treatment of hedging move beyond a casual, academic interest, you would be well-advised to seek the opinion of your tax counsel.

As we understand it, the central issue is whether the gains and losses on a hedge will be treated as "ordinary" or "capital" for tax purposes. The problem appears when the underlying business activity increases in value. In this instance, the hedge itself will lose value—a loss. But if the hedge loss is treated as a capital loss, the taxpayer can deduct the loss against income only if the firm has sufficient capital gains. So, the issue really boils down to asymmetric tax treatment:

> If gains/losses on the hedge are treated as capital gains/losses, instances can arise where the underlying gain is taxed but the taxpayer is unable to deduct the loss on the hedge.

If this occurs, the economic cost of hedging rises.

1936: The IRS's Policy Is Announced

In General Counsel Memorandum (GCM) 17322, the IRS declared that using futures contracts "to insure against the risks inherent in the taxpayer's business" generates *ordinary* business income or loss.

1955: The Policy Is Confirmed

A maize consumer purchased futures contracts to fix the cost of purchases and subsequently booked the profits from the contracts as capital gains, rather than ordinary income. In *Corn Products,* the Supreme Court supported the IRS and ruled that profits and losses "arising from the everyday operation of a business [known as *the business motive test*] be considered ordinary income."

Observers generally interpret *Corn Products* as focusing on the original purpose of derivative transactions: if transactions are undertaken for investment/speculation, gains or losses will be treated as capital; if they are intended to hedge ordinary expenses or income, gains or losses will be treated as ordinary.

1988: The Policy Is Reversed

In *Arkansas Best Corp v. Commissioner*[48] the Supreme Court removed the business motive test and rules that the question of ordinary/capital treatment of transactions depends on the precise wording of the Internal Revenue Code. The code defines a capital asset as "a property held by the taxpayer" and permits only five exceptions. One of these exceptions is "property of a kind which would properly be included in the inventory of the taxpayer"; another is surrogates or substitutes for inventory.

1992: The New Policy Is Applied . . . and Disputed

The IRS disputes the Federal National Mortgage Association's (Fannie Mae) ordinary treatment of losses, which arose from short-selling futures and buying options on futures in 1984 and 1985. Using the *Arkansas Best* decision, the IRS insists they be classed as capital losses. This would have obliged Fannie Mae to pay an additional tax of $131 million.

Fannie Mae argued that its interest rate transactions gave rise to ordinary gains and losses because they were "true hedges." Fannie Mae based this claim on the fact that its hedging transactions reduced the business risk arising from its commitment to purchase mortgages and its issuance of debt, and that a "true hedge" is one that offsets or reduces an existing risk.

Fannie Mae claimed that the ordinary treatment of gains and losses arising from true hedges never depended on *Corn Products*, but instead on GCM 17322. When *Arkansas Best* overturned the broad *Corn Products* doctrine, it says, the court didn't object to the pre–*Corn Products* ordinary treatment of true hedging transactions under the business insurance doctrine. Because the Supreme Court cited and discussed GCM 17322 without any indication of disapproval while hearing *Arkansas Best*, Fannie Mae held that its transactions should be characterized as ordinary under pre–*Corn Products* law.

Fannie Mae also submitted that its hedging losses on its interest rate transactions were in effect a substitute for interest expenses (nonstatutory substitution doctrine permits an item of income, expense, gain, or loss that substitutes for another such item to receive similar tax treatment). Using this line of argument, Fannie Mae concluded that, under *Arkansas Best,* hedging transactions that are an integral part of a business's acquisition and holding of noncapital assets should be treated as generating ordinary gains and losses.

1993: The Tax Court Rules . . . and IRS Announces Its New, New Policy

In June, the Tax Court issued its decision in favor of Fannie Mae, holding that FNMA could treat its losses on certain hedges as ordinary loses rather than as capital losses.

In October, the IRS published in the *Federal Register* both Temporary Regulations and Proposed Regulations on Hedging Transactions.[49]

The Temporary Regulations provide "that most business hedges give rise to ordinary gain or loss." However, *most* is not *all.* In his cover letter to Congress, Secretary Lloyd Bentsen noted that "hedges of an *ordinary* stream of income . . . that flows from a *capital* asset (such as an airline hedging its supply of jet fuel, or an insurance company hedging the interest income it earns on a bond it holds as an investment) will generate capital gain or loss." Secretary Bentsen indicated that the temporary regulations would apply immediately and retroactively, and will "permit *hundreds* of cases to be settled."

The Proposed Regulations would define a "hedging transaction" as one entered into in the normal course of business that would reduce interest rate, foreign exchange rate, or commodity price risk. Generally, hedging transactions so defined would give rise to ordinary gains or losses, irrespective of whether the instrument being used as the hedge would otherwise be regarded as a capital asset.

Notes

1. A similar "spike" in the implied volatility of the DM–US$ exchange rate occurred when sterling joined the European Monetary System in 1989.
2. This section draws liberally from an ambitious and useful study by Eli Romolona, "The Recent Growth of Financial Derivatives Markets," *Quarterly Review* (Federal Reserve Bank of New York, Winter 1992–93), pp. 28–43.
3. These contracts are used by commercial banks to hedge their interest rate swaps portfolios.
4. Virtually all the new net growth of the period 1986–92 came, moreover, from exchanges outside the United States, most of them newly established. As Remolona observes, since 1985 at least 18 new derivatives exchanges have been started around the world. (For a listing, see Remolona, Table 1, p. 33)
5. Such a phenomenal growth rate may reflect in part the newness of the instruments—increases on a small base result in larger percentage increases.
6. These new contracts were developed in 1990, precisely when the volatility of the Japanese market began to rise sharply.
7. Remolona, p. 28.
8. Business International Corporation, "The 1989 Treasury Survey: New Directions in Financial Risk Management," 1989.
9. Financial Executives Research Foundation and The Globecon Group, LTD., "Financial Products for Medium-Sized Companies," 1989.
10. "Which Derivatives do CFOs Really Use?" CFO Forum, *Institutional Investor*, April 1992.
11. "The Way it Is," *Treasury*, Spring 1993.
12. *Yield Curves Provide Problems—and Promises*, Greenwich Reports, North American Treasury Services 1992.
13. Among corporations, industrial and transportation companies have the largest proportion of users, 50 percent and 43 percent, while wholesale and retail trade and utilities have the lowest. Among financial institutions, large banks and finance companies are the most active, with 78 percent and 70 percent users, respectively; insurance companies remain the least active, at 34 percent. Finally, the Greenwich survey indicated that, while only 38 percent of money managers now use risk management products, another 23 percent said they expected to start using them.
14. Walter Dolde, "Use and Effectiveness of Foreign Exchange and Interest Rate Risk Management in Large Firms," University of Connecticut working paper, June 1993.
15. "Dell Computer at War with Analyst Critical of Its Currency Trades, *The Wall Street Journal*, November 30, 1992.
16. David Fiedler, the director of foreign exchange planning at the Eastman Kodak Company, quoted in "Companies Learn to Live with Dollar's Volatility," *The New York Times*, August 11, 1992.
17. "Learning to Dance with a Bouncy Dollar," *The New York Times*, September 8, 1991.
18. "Credit Implications for Firms that Use Derivatives," Moody's Special Comment, November 1991. To avoid criticism for quoting out of context, we must remind you that the next sentence in this report was a warning about using derivatives inappropriately: "Poor controls, inadequate analysis, and weak counterparty creditworthiness—to name but a few problems—can not only eliminate the benefits of derivatives, but can also create difficulties that did not exist before."
19. Indeed, some highly rated corporations are deploying capital to run swap books—especially in the energy area.
20. This section draws heavily on the Report of the Global Derivatives Project sponsored by the Group of Thirty, July 1993.
21. This list of SPVs was current as of the first quarter of 1994. These SPVs will be described in Chapter 17.
22. It is important to note that these risks are not unique to derivatives. These risks are the same risks that

financial institutions face with their "traditional" products.

23. This section is adapted from "Credit Implications for Firms that Use Derivatives," Moody's Special Comment, November 1991.
24. "UBS Profiting from Derivatives," *American Banker*, December 15, 1992.
25. June 9, 1993
26. The article in *American Banker* also included Republic New York as a newcomer. Since Republic New York shows in Table 3–9 as the 20th largest interest rate option dealer (and would rank 28th on the swap list and 30th on the FX forward list), we would be hard pressed to call it a newcomer. Moreover, NationsBank is really not that much of a newcomer—were we to extend Table 3–9, NationsBank would rank 23rd in interest rate options and 38th in swaps.
27. This is an interesting contrast to the approach of Credit Suisse, which set up its own derivatives unit—Credit Suisse Financial Products.
28. "Corrigan Warns Banks to Gauge Hidden Risks," *American Banker,* January 31, 1992.
29. *Recent Developments in International Interbank Relations,* Report prepared by a Working Group established by the Central Banks of the Group of Ten countries, Bank for International Settlements, Basle, October 1992.
30. AP Datastream Business News Wire, Thursday, December 17, 1992.
31. Ibid.
32. Speed to the ISDA Annual Meeting, Hong Kong, March 11, 1992.
33. Moreover, estimates provided by the Federal Reserve System suggest that the netting of offsetting interest rate and currency contracts among dealers would reduce these credit exposures by roughly 50 percent relative to gross replacement costs. See Letter from Alan Greenspan, chairman, Board of Governors of the Federal Reserve System, to Senator Donald Riegle, Jr., September 11, 1992.
34. "OTC Derivative Markets and Their Regulation," The Report of the Commodity Futures Trading Commission, October 1993.
35. Derivative Product Activities of Commercial Banks, Joint Study Conducted in Response to Questions Posed by Senator Riegle on Derivative Products, Board of Governors of the Federal Reserve System, Federal Deposit Insurance Corporation, Office of Comptroller of the Currency, January 27, 1993.
36. "Stop Swapping?" *The Economist*, March 13, 1993, p. 94.
37. *Derivatives: Practices and Principles*, Global Derivatives Study Group, Group of Thirty, Washington, D.C., July 1993.
38. *Congressional Record,* June 18, 1993, H 3322.
39. "Clinton Asks Regulators to Coordinate on Swaps," *American Banker*, January 11, 1994.
40. This discussion is taken from two publications of the Financial Accounting Standards Board: "An Analysis of Issues Related to Recognition and Measurement of Financial Instruments," Financial Accounting Series, Discussion Memorandum No. 109-A, November 18, 1991 and "A Report on Deliberations, Including Tentative Conclusions on Certain Issues Related to Accounting for Hedging and Other Risk-Adjusting Activities," June 1993. Special thanks is due to Halsey Bullen for his comments on this section.
41. FASB Concepts Statement No. 5, *Recognition and Measurement in Financial Statements of Business Enterprises,* paragraphs 66–70, discusses the existing mixed attribute system.
42. Statement 80 distinguishes between firm commitments and anticipated transactions and refers to anticipated transactions in paragraph 9 as "transactions—an enterprise expects, but is not obligated, to carry out in the normal course of business."
43. EITF Issue No. 90-17, "Hedging Foreign Currency Risks with Purchased Options," and EITF Issue No. 91–4, "Hedging Foreign Currency Risks with Complex Options and Similar Transactions."
44. These *complex options* included things like *break* and *range forwards*—structures that we will examine in Chapter 15.
45. Present standards permit hedge accounting only for futures contracts and for foreign currency transactions that hedge a foreign currency commitment; all other hedge accounting practices have been developed by analogy.
46. Any "excess" hedging gain or loss would be recognized annually in earnings.
47. Much of this section is adapted from "Court in the Act" by William Falloon which appeared in *Risk* in *May 1993*
48. 485 U.S. 212 (1988) Interestingly enough, this case, which caused such an uproar in the derivatives market, did not involve derivatives.
49. 26 CFR Part 1, October 18, 1993.

CHAPTER

4

How Risk Management Can Increase the Value of the Firm*

If a firm manages its financial price risk, it follows that the volatility of the value of the firm or of the firm's real cash flows will decline. This general relation is illustrated in Figure 4–1.

FIGURE 4–1 The Impact of Risk Management Hedging Is to Reduce the Variance in the Distribution of Firm Value

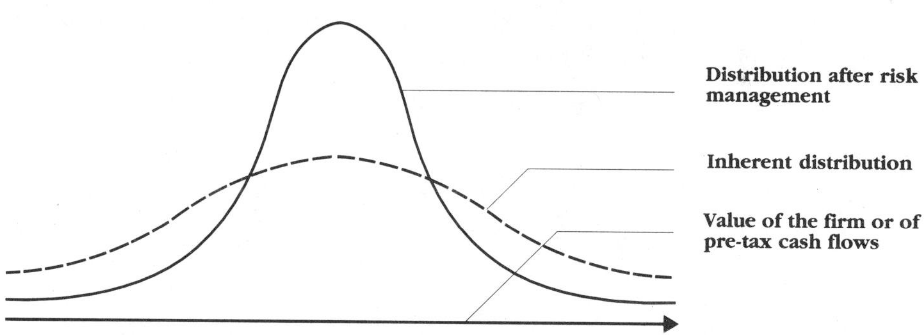

Since the value of a firm is sensitive to movements in interest rates, foreign exchange rates, or commodity prices, a tantalizing conclusion is that the value of the firm will necessarily rise if this exposure is managed. But however appealing, this conclusion does not follow directly. That a firm is confronted with strategic

*This chapter is adapted from Rawls and Smithson (1990).

risk is a *necessary* condition for the firm to manage that risk. The *sufficient* condition for a firm to manage risk is that the strategy increase the present value of the expected net cash flows, $E(NCF_{jt})$, where r_{jt}, is the discounted rate.

$$V_j = \sum^{t} \frac{E(NCF_{jt})}{(1 + r_{jt})}.$$

This equation provides the insight that if the market value of the firm is to increase, the gain must result from either an increase in expected net cash flows or a decrease in the discount rate.

Whether risk management will have an impact on the discount rate—the firm's cost of capital—is an issue we defer until Chapter 19. One special case should be mentioned now, however. For firms in which the owners do not hold well-diversified portfolios (such as proprietorships, partnerships, and closely held corporations) the risk aversion of the firm's owners can provide an important risk management incentive. At this point, we want to focus on how risk management could increase the value of the firm by increasing the firm's expected net cash flows. Hence, the question that must be answered is, how can hedging, or any other financial policy, have any impact on the real cash flows of the organization?

The relation between the firm's real cash flows and its financial policies was established by Franco Modigliani and Merton Miller in 1958 in what has come to be called the M&M proposition. The M&M proposition would imply that in a world with no taxes, no transaction costs, and a fixed investment policy, investors can create their own "homemade" risk management by holding diversified portfolios.[1] However, the message of the M&M proposition for practitioners becomes evident only when the argument is turned upside down:

> *If* financial policies matter . . . if risk management policies are going to have an impact on the value of the firm,
>
> *then* risk management must have an impact on the firm's taxes, transaction costs, or investment decisions.

Risk Management Can Add Value by Decreasing Taxes

For risk management to produce tax benefits, the firm's effective tax schedule must be *convex*. As illustrated in Figure 4–2, a convex tax schedule is one in which the firm's average effective tax rate rises as pretax (financial statement) income rises. If the firm's effective tax function is convex and if the firm is subject to financial price-induced volatility in its pretax income, it is a mathematical certainty that hedging will reduce the firm's expected taxes.[2] However, instead of resorting to a mathematical proof, we think that this point is demonstrated in the following illustration.

FIGURE 4–2 Convexity in the Tax Function

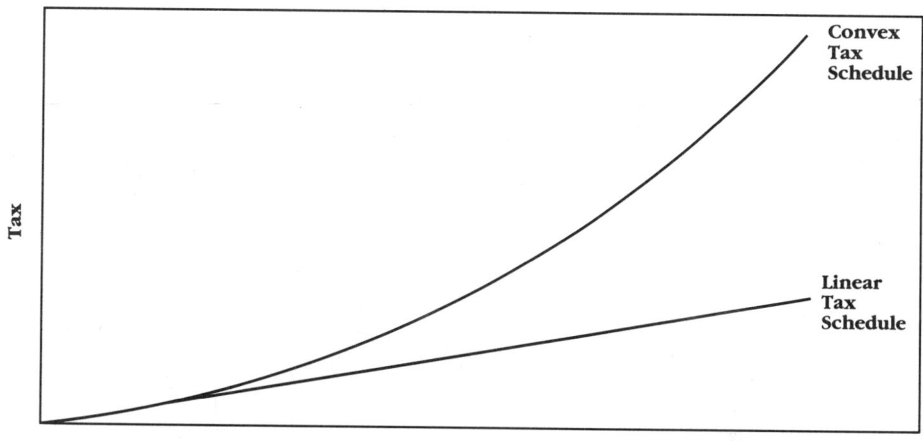

Illustration 4–1

Reducing Taxes with Risk Management

Consider a firm that is exposed to financial price risk; its pretax income is related to interest rates, foreign exchange rates, or some commodity price. Suppose that if the firm does not hedge, the distribution of its pretax income will be as shown below: for any given year, the firm's pretax income might be low or high, either with a probability of 50 percent.

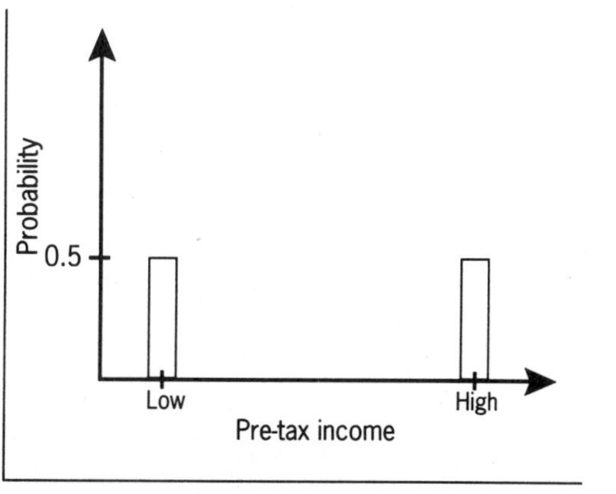

Reducing Taxes with Risk Management continued

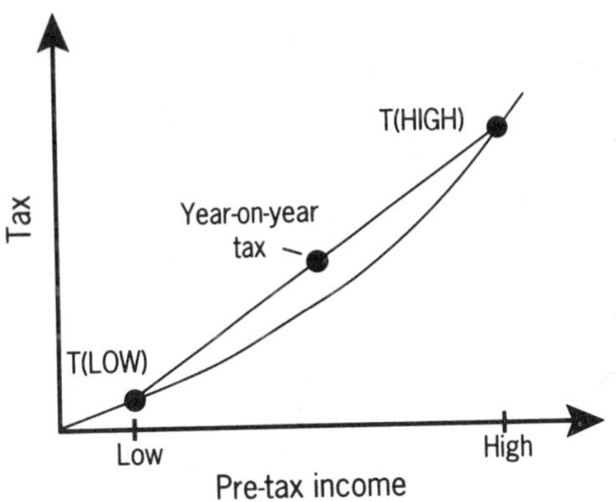

If the firm has the low pretax income, it will pay tax *T*(*LOW*); if the firm's pretax income is high, the tax will be *T*(*HIGH*). Hence if the firm does not hedge, its expected tax will be the average of these two taxes. In other words, the firm's year-on-year taxes would be on the straight line connecting *T*(*LOW*) and *T*(*HIGH*), halfway between *T*(*LOW*) and *T*(*HIGH*).

And as the next illustration shows, the firm will pay a tax that is strictly less if it hedges than if it does not hedge.

If the firm implements an effective risk management program, the volatility in its pretax income will decline. In the context of our simple distribution, a reduction in volatility means that the pretax income *LOW* and pretax income *HIGH* will both move toward the mean. For purposes of illustration, suppose that the firm hedges completely; in such a case the distribution of the firm's pretax income would be a single point, *MEAN*.

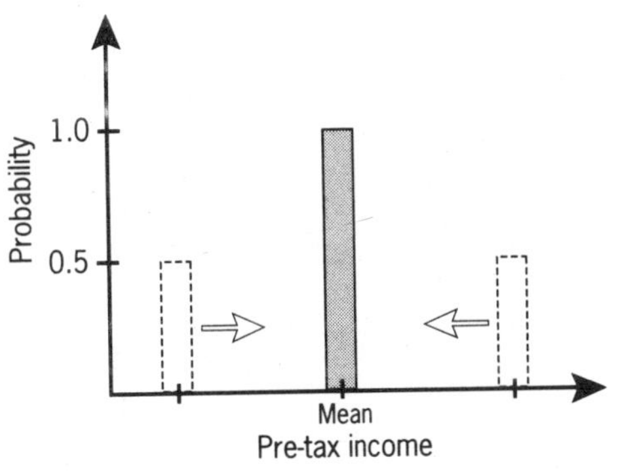

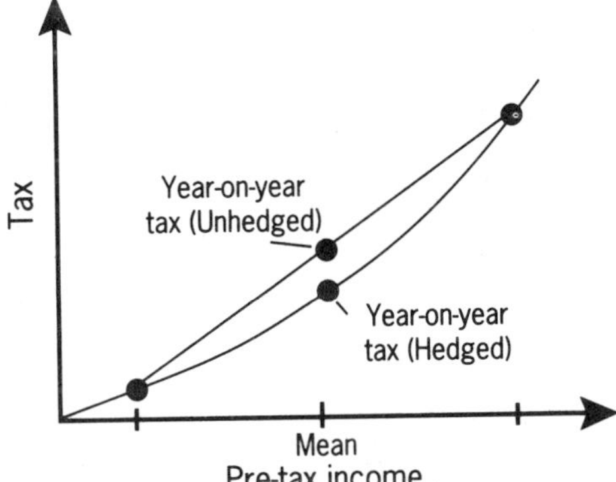

If the firm's effective tax function is convex, risk management can reduce the firm's expected taxes. And the more convex the tax schedule is, the greater the tax benefits are. The obvious question then is, why would my firm's effective tax function be convex?

The obvious factor that would make a tax schedule convex is *progressivity*, a tax schedule in which the statutory tax rate rises as income rises. Greater progressivity results in a more convex tax schedule. However, since the range of progressivity for corporate income taxes in the United States is relatively small, this factor would not be a significant source of convexity for most large, public industrial corporations.

Another cause of convexity in the effective tax function is *the existence of tax preference items*—for example, tax loss carryforwards and investment tax credits (ITC). Since a firm will always be induced to use the most valuable tax preference items first, these tax shields will result in the firm's effective tax function being convex.[3]

Finally, in the United States, firms that are subject to the alternate minimum tax (AMT) provision face convex effective tax functions. The AMT gives the tax authorities a claim that is similar to a call option on the pretax income of the firm, so the AMT puts a "kink" in the effective tax function, making it convex.

While the impact of hedging on the firm's taxes is driven by a mathematical relation—the convexity of the effective tax function—the underlying logic is simple, perhaps easiest to see in the case of the tax preference items. If the firm does not hedge, there will be some years in which the firm's income is too low to use (or use completely) the tax preference items, so the firm would lose a benefit. By reducing volatility in pretax income, hedging reduces the probability that the firm will not be able to take advantage of its tax preference items. In a similar fashion, hedging reduces the probability that the firm pays the higher tax rates specified under a progressive tax schedule or AMT provision.

Risk Management Can Add Value by Decreasing Transaction Costs

As illustrated in Figure 4–1, risk management reduces the volatility of the value of the firm. Figure 4–3 goes further to show that by reducing volatility, risk management reduces the probability of the firm's encountering financial distress and the consequent costs.

How much risk management can reduce these costs depends on two obvious factors: the probability of encountering distress if the firm does not hedge and the costs if distress occurs. The greater the probability of distress or distress-induced costs, the greater the firm's benefit from risk management through the reduction in these expected cost.

Default results when a firm's income is insufficient to cover its fixed claims. The probability of financial distress and subsequent default, therefore, is determined by two factors: *fixed-claims coverage* (because the probability of default rises as the coverage of fixed claims declines) and *income volatility* (because the probability of default rises as the firm's income becomes more volatile).

FIGURE 4–3 Hedging and Financial Distress

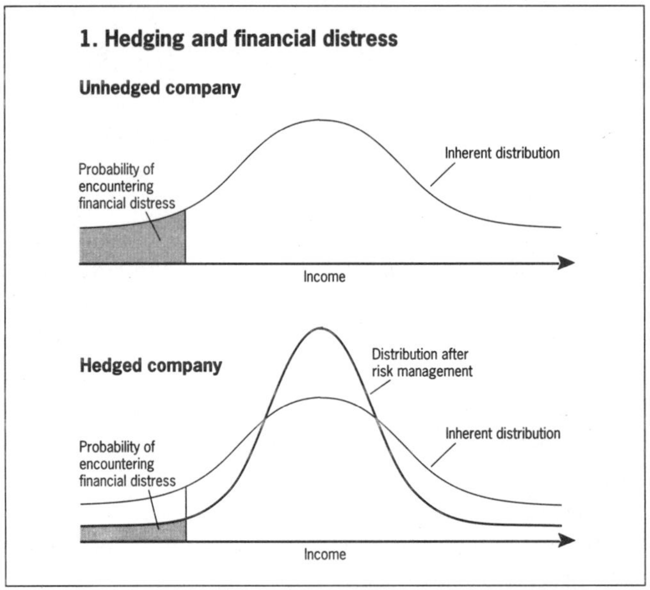

The cost of financial distress has two major components. The first is the direct expense of dealing with a default, bankruptcy, reorganization, or liquidation. The second is the indirect costs arising from the changes in incentives of the firm's various claim holders. For example, if the firm files for bankruptcy and attempts to reorganize its business under Chapter 11, the bankruptcy court judge overseeing the case is unlikely to approve nonroutine expenditures. The judge receives little credit if the activities turn out well, but is criticized by creditors with impaired claims if the efforts turn out badly. Thus, firms undergoing reorganizations are likely to pass up positive net-present-value projects systematically because of the nature of the oversight by the bankruptcy court.

But even short of bankruptcy, financial distress can impose substantial indirect costs on the firm.[4] These indirect costs include higher costs to the firm in contracting with its customers, employees, and suppliers.

The impact of financial distress on the cost of contracting with customers is perhaps the easiest to observe. Firms that provide service agreements or warranties make long-term contracts with their customers. As illustrated in the following example, if the firm is less viable, consumers place less value on the service agreements and warranties and are more likely to turn to a competitor.

If the firm can convince potential consumers that the likelihood of financial distress has been reduced, the firm can increase consumers' valuation of its service agreements and warranties. And this perceived increase in value will be reflected in

Illustration 4–2

The Impact of Financial Risk on Sales: The Case of Wang*

As reported in *The Wall Street Journal*, "The biggest challenge any marketer can face [is] selling the products of a company that is on the ropes."

For purchasers of computers, manufacturers' guarantees and warranties (both explicit and implicit) are extremely important. As the *Journal* put it, "Customers . . . want to be sure that their suppliers . . . will be around to fix bugs and upgrade computers for years to come." Not surprisingly, when Wang's leverage got to the point that earnings volatility could put the firm into financial distress, sales turned down. A potential Wang customer put it best when she noted that "before the really bad news, we were looking at Wang fairly seriously [but] their present financial condition means that I'd have a hard time convincing the vice president in charge of purchasing. . . . At some point we'd have to ask 'How do we know that in three years you won't be in Chapter 11?' "

*This illustration is from Bulkeley (1989).

the cash flows to the firm and in the price the consumers will be willing to pay for the product. These potential benefits of risk management are likely to be greater for firms that produce "credence goods" and firms whose future existence is more uncertain.

A credence good is one wherein quality is important but is difficult (and in some cases impossible) to determine prior to consumption. A good example is airline travel: quality is crucial, but until the trip is complete and baggage is recovered, there is no way for the consumer to judge the quality level. (In contrast, when firms purchase materials—for example, refined copper—they can determine the quality prior to use by assaying a sample.) Thus, firms that produce credence goods would receive a larger benefit from hedging and being able to assure potential customers that they will not depreciate quality.

Consumers are aware that firms approaching financial distress are more likely to cheat on quality than financially healthy firms. So the benefit from hedging would be larger for firms that have a higher probability of encountering financial distress.

Risk Management Can Add Value by Avoiding Investment Decision Errors

The M&M proposition implies that if hedging policy increases firm value, it does so by reducing contracting costs, by reducing taxes, or by controlling investment incentives. We now turn to this last general motive for corporate hedging—dysfunctional investment incentives.

Incentives to turn down positive net present value projects also can arise in firms that avoid bankruptcy. These incentives arise because of the conflict between the bondholders and the shareholders resulting from differences in the kind of claims each hold.[5] Bondholders hold fixed claims, while shareholders hold claims that are equivalent to a call option on the value of the firm. The conflict results in a constraint on the debt capacity of the firm (or in the firm's having to pay a higher coupon on its debt).

The severity of the conflict between the shareholders and bondholders is determined primarily by the debt-equity ratio. As debt level in the capital structure rises, the conflict becomes more significant. But other factors, such as the range of investment projects available to the firm, also affect the severity of the bondholder–shareholder conflict. As with any other option, the value of shareholders' equity rises as the variance in the returns to the underlying asset increases. If shareholders switch from low-variance investment projects to high-variance projects, they could transfer wealth from the bondholders to themselves.[6]

Basically, bondholders, or rather, potential bondholders, are concerned about the probability that they will be left holding the bag, that the value of the firm's assets will be insufficient to cover the promised payments in the indenture. In addition to concerns about future market conditions, potential bondholders are concerned about opportunistic behavior on the part of shareholders who might declare a liquidating dividend, burden the firm with extra debt, or select risky investments. Potential bondholders, however, recognize the possibility of opportunistic behavior and protect themselves by lowering the price they are willing to pay for the firm's bonds.

To convince potential bondholders to pay more for bonds, shareholders must assure them that wealth transfers will not occur. These assurances frequently have been given by attaching restrictive covenants to debt issues (restrictions on dividends and debt coverage ratios), issuing a mortgage bond (to preclude asset substitution), making the debt convertible (to align the interest of bondholders with those of the shareholders), and issuing preferred stock instead of debt (to reduce the probability that future market conditions will lead to default).

The shareholder–bondholder conflict can also be reduced through risk management. Figure 4–2 shows that risk management reduces the probability of default, so potential bondholders will be willing to pay more for the bond. Hence, risk management can increase the debt capacity of the firm. Likewise, risk management can decrease the coupon the firm will have to pay on its debt.

In addition to increasing the financing cost for investment projects undertaken, volatility in the firm's earnings can even cause the firm to pass up positive net-present-value projects. Textbook "underinvestment" occurs when the firm is highly levered and the value of the firm's assets is volatile: shareholders may opt not to undertake a positive NPV project because the gains accrue to the bondholders.[7] Perhaps the simplest way to understand this rather complex theoretical argument is with an example.

Illustration 4–3

The Impact of Volatility on Debt Capacity*

As *Corporate Finance* reported, a number of firms realize that "hedging techniques can stabilize a company's net worth and keep it from tripping into technical default . . . " and by doing so, the firm can increase its debt capacity. As a case in point, "Kaiser has effectively increased its debt-carrying capacity by removing volatility from its cost and revenue stream. . . . "

*This illustration is based on "Kaiser and Union Carbide Hedge Their Bets With Their Banks," which appeared in the June 1991 issue of *Corporate Finance*.

Illustration 4–4

Cutting Rate Risk on Buyout Debt: Reducing Shareholder-Debtholder Conflict on the RJR Nabisco Deal*

When Kohlberg, Kravis, Roberts and Co. got ready to issue the senior bank debt for the RJR Nabisco deal, they ran into the shareholder–debtholder conflict head-on. But by using risk management, they were able to reduce the conflict and increase their debt capacity.

The market was concerned about the interest rate risk such a large amount of debt would entail. If the debt carried a floating-rate coupon, and if rates rose substantially, the probability of default would rise dramatically. Therefore, to reduce the shareholder–debtholder conflict, KKR was required to purchase interest-rate insurance. As the vice chairman of Chase Manhattan explained, before committing any money to finance a corporate takeover, Chase insists that steps be taken to reduce the interest rate risk.

Consequently, KKR agreed to keep interest rate protection (in the form of swaps or caps) on half the outstanding balance of its bank debt. In this way, KKR was able to borrow $13 billion. Without the rate insurance, the amount the banks would have been willing to lend would have been substantially less.

*Based on Quint (1989).

Illustration 4–5

Controlling Underinvestment with Hedging*

Let's consider a 100 percent equity firm whose value is positively related to oil prices—a small oil producer, for example. The value of the firm in the initial period, Period 1, will be higher if oil prices are high than if they are low. For simplicity, let's suppose that there are only two outcomes, each with a 50 percent probability.†

Outcome	*Probability*	*Value of Firm in Period 1*
Price of oil high	.5	1000
Price of oil low	.5	200

While this initial value belongs completely to the shareholders—our simple firm begins as all equity—suppose that the shareholders plan to issue, in Period 1, bonds with *face value* of $500. All the proceeds of the debt issue will be passed directly to the shareholders.

Now suppose that the shareholders of the firm are presented with a riskless investment opportunity: if the shareholders make an outlay of $600 in Period 1 (before the issue of the debt), the investment project will result in an income to the firm of $800 in Period 2 *with certainty*. Logic would suggest that shareholders will always accept a riskless opportunity with a return above the riskless rate, but that's not necessarily how it will work.

As shown in Table 4–1, if the price of oil is low, the shareholders of this firm will pass up this positive NPV project. In other words, if the value of the firm in Period 1 is $200, the shareholders will not undertake the riskless investment project.

The reason for this surprising result is that the volatility in the value of the firm, coupled with a large debt-equity ratio, could transfer wealth from the shareholders to the bondholders if the shareholders elect to undertake the positive NPV project.

The total value of the shareholders' wealth position is the sum of their equity value in the firm at Period 2 plus the monies they receive from the debt issue. Note that while the *face* value of the debt is $500, the *market* value of the debt—what the potential bondholders will actually pay the shareholders for the debt—is equal to the expected value of the debt,

$$1/2(\$500) + 1/2(\$200) = \$350.$$

The expected value of the shareholder's equity in the firm is 1/2($700) + 1/2(0) = $350; the total value of the shareholders' holdings—the value of shareholders' equity in the firm plus the monies they received from the debt issue, is $350 + $350 = $700.

Now let's look at the impact of risk management on this situation. Suppose the shareholders of the firm hedged its exposure to the price of oil by entering into a simplified commodity swap agreement:

Price of oil high: This firm pays $400.

Price of oil low: This firm receives $400.

Now the value of the firm is hedged against oil price fluctuations. No matter what happens to oil prices, the value of the firm is $600.

As Table 4–2 indicates, with the value of the firm hedged against oil price fluctuations, the positive NPV project will always be undertaken.

Controlling Underinvestment with Hedging continued

TABLE 4–1

Period 1		Period 2			
Value of Firm		*Value of Firm*	*Value of Debt*	*Value of Equity*	*Will the Positive NPV Project Be Undertaken?*
$1,000	Undertake project	$1200	$500	$700	Yes
	Do not undertake project	1000	500	500	
$200	Undertake project	400*	500†	−100‡	No
	Do not undertake project	200	200	0	

*If the firm is worth only $200 initially, the shareholders would have to put up another $400 to get the $600 necessary to invest in the riskless project. In Period 2, the firm's treasury would contain the $800 proceeds from the investment project; but, $400 of these dollars would be earmarked for return to the shareholders.

†Even though the firm would be worth only $400, the treasury would contain the $800 proceeds from the investment (see * note above). Since the bondholders would have the senior claim, they can take the full $500 face value of the bond from the treasury.

‡The treasury would "owe" $400 to the shareholders (see * note above); but, after the bondholders took their $500 from the treasury, only $300 is left.

TABLE 4–2

Period 1		Period 2			
Value of Firm		*Value of Firm*	*Value of Debt*	*Value of Equity*	*Will the Positive NPV Project Be Undertaken?*
$600	Undertake project	$800	$500	$300	Yes
	Do not undertake project	600	500	100	

Controlling Underinvestment with Hedging continued

With the hedge against oil prices, the total value of the shareholders' wealth is $500 (the proceeds of the debt issue), plus $300 (the value of their equity at Period 2) to give them a total of $800. By hedging, the shareholders would increase the value of their wealth by $100.

---

*This illustration is based on Mayers and Smith (1987).

†For tractability, we have created this example with no transactions costs and no taxes and a risk-free interest rate equal to zero. These simplifying assumptions in no way influence the qualitative outcome of the example; but they make the exposition immensely more simple.

An instance in which risk management can avoid this type of underinvestment problem occurs in the long-term debt market. As we have noted, if a firm issues long-term debt, its shareholders have the incentive to pass up positive net-present-value projects or to shift from low-risk to high-risk projects. Recognizing this incentive, bondholders demand a large premium on long-term debt. However, this "opportunistic-behavior premium" is lower for firms with higher bond ratings, presumably because higher-rated firms have established reputations. Lower-rated firms can avoid this premium by issuing short-term debt. But short-term debt could expose the firm to interest rate risk. If, however, the firm issues short-term debt and then swaps the debt into a fixed-rate, the lower-rated firm can control the agency problem while avoiding interest rate risk.[8]

Illustration 4–6

The Impact of Earnings Volatility on Investment: The Case of Merck*

Since Merck's earnings are denominated in U.S. dollars, its pretax income fluctuates with the value of the dollar. If the dollar is weak, the dollar value of net income received from foreign operations will be high; if the dollar is strong, Merck's dollar income will be low.

Looking at its behavior in the past, Merck discovered that this volatility in earnings had impacted its investment decision. When the dollar was strong and pretax income was low, Merck had cut back the rate of growth of R&D spending.

---

*This illustration is based on Lewent and Kearney (1990).

But even without excessive leverage, volatility in earnings can lead to a form of underinvestment.

Since there is a well-established relation between R&D activity and value for pharmaceutical firms, there was a clear reason Merck would want to manage its foreign exchange risk. However, this form of the underinvestment problem is one that a number of firms have encountered. And if risk management permits the firm to undertake positive NPV projects that would otherwise be deferred, its net cash flows will necessarily rise.

Notes

1. The original M&M proposition focused on the firm's debt-equity ratio [Modigliani and Miller (1958)]. The rationale is that, because (under their assumptions) leverage by an individual is a perfect substitute for corporate leverage, an investor will not pay the firm for corporate leverage. The M&M proposition was extended to dividends in Modigliani and Miller (1961), with the argument that "homemade" dividends can be created as the investor sells the firm's stock.
2. Indeed, the mathematical paradigm that makes this happens even has a name: *Jensen's Inequality*.
3. A substantial body of evidence demonstrates that tax preference items will result in the effective tax function being convex. For example, see Siegfried (1974), Zimmerman (1983), and Wilkie (1988).
4. The work of Jerry Warner suggests that the direct costs of bankruptcy are small in relation to the value of the firm (Warner 1977b). However, his evidence suggests that there are scale economies in this cost function, so avoiding these costs is potentially more important for smaller firms.
5. This conflict has been discussed under the rubric of agency problems. The agency problem refers to the conflicts of interest that occur in virtually all cooperative activities among self-interested individuals. The agency problem was introduced by Jensen and Meckling (1976).
6. The problem referred to as *asset substitution* is a case in point. A firm can increase the wealth of its shareholders at the expense of its bondholders by issuing debt with the promise of investing in low-risk projects and then investing the proceeds in high-risk projects.
7. Myers (1977).
8. Wall (1989).

CHAPTER

5

MEASURING A FIRM'S EXPOSURE TO FINANCIAL PRICE RISK

Chapter 1 makes it clear that the financial environment is riskier today than it was before 1972. The volatility of interest rates, foreign exchange rates, and commodity prices is greater today than it has been in the past. The second message of Chapter 1 is that this increased volatility has put some otherwise well-managed firms into financial distress.

While a firm's CEO or CFO might find this discussion of the altered financial environment intellectually appealing, managers tend to be more pragmatic, reacting with more specific questions:

> Is *my* firm one that can be put out of business by this increased volatility? To what degree is my firm exposed to interest rates? Foreign exchange rates? Commodity prices?

These are the questions this chapter addresses.

We begin this chapter with a description of a firm's *risk profile*—a vehicle for summarizing the impact of financial price risk on a firm. We then describe methods of measuring a firm's exposure. We first look at the ways in which financial price risk would be reflected in the firm's annual report. We then look at methods firms have used to obtain internal estimates of their exposures. We conclude by looking at external—market-price-based—measures of exposures.

Before we begin, let's put this in perspective by looking at the experience of one large multinational firm.

Risk Management in Practice

Risk Management at British Petroleum

R. K. Hinkley

The formation of BP Finance in 1985 raised the profile of financial risk management across the BP Group. Subsequently a risk management unit was created, with the aim of capitalizing on the company's experience using financial products to manage foreign exchange, interest rate, and commodity-price risks. BP had proven trading expertise in these areas but saw further opportunity in a more systematic approach to the management of its longer-term, structural exposures.

In essence the approach adopted was to define a set of "benchmarks" based on an understanding of the company's main exposures, and consistent with its strategic financial objectives. Authority was delegated to centers of expertise to take positions, within predefined limits, away from these benchmarks, with the aim of enhancing shareholder value. From the outset, the management of economic rather than accounting exposures had priority.

An example may make the approach clearer. Following a Group study, the strategy was adopted of managing the company to a U.S. dollar base, notwithstanding BP's sterling statutory accounts. Consistently with this approach, BP borrows mainly in U.S. dollars, and it hedges its major nondollar flows, notably its capital expenditure on North Sea exploration and production and the sterling dividend it pays. The Group treasurer has discretion in implementing these policies, but his performance is marked against the benchmark strategy. An equivalent framework is used for interest rate management.

Such approaches clearly beg the question of defining the underlying exposures. While the financial services sector has been very proficient in developing products to manage risk, it has not always been as helpful in giving treasurers the necessary understandings to use them efficiently. In BP, we sought to resolve such concerns by commissioning extensive research of our financial risks, using external help for specific aspects where our own expertise was limited.

At the heart of this study lay two empirical studies:

1. an analysis of BP's historical cash flows, testing their correlation with key financial variables.
2. an analysis of BP's historical share prices, also testing their correlation with key financial variables.

As well as providing insight into BP's long-term exposures, comparison of the two sets of results indicated whether the market's perceptions of risk matched those based on recent performance.

The issues surrounding statistical analysis of this kind are well aired (in the textbooks). For us, the problems were compounded by the significant changes to the Group's portfolio that had occurred. However, we were able to derive a number of key conclusions.

The cash flow analysis highlighted the expected exposure to crude oil and product prices, but it was weaker than expected. It confirmed the use of the U.S. dollar base, but the interest rate exposure was lower than we had anticipated. Two important aspects of risk management were brought out in this work.

1. Correlations among financial variables. While it may be possible to isolate, say, a pure exchange risk in the short run and hedge it in a straightforward way using a forward or option, over the long term the correlations, for example, between exchange rates and oil prices, must be taken into account. This has obvious implications for financial strategy and the design of risk management products.

2. The significance of tax regimes. A good part of BP's North Sea revenues is paid to the UK government as royalties and taxes. Much of the tax rate is directly related to the oil price. BP is more exposed to this regime than its competitors. The outcome is that BP's oil price exposure is lower than its relative asset mix might imply, reflecting the offset through the tax system.

The share price analysis was conducted using an estimation equation similar to that provided in the final section of this chapter. As anticipated, the UK stock market proved to be a strong driver of BP's share price behavior over the period tested, but oil and product prices, and the dollar–pound exchange rate, also had significant explanatory power. This suggests that the market is differentiating BP according to its exposure to these variables. In principle, this kind of information should help the design of investor relations programs.

A potential weakness of both studies is that they are backward looking. Markets and company portfolios are subject to change. One way to help overcome such difficulty is through the use of forward-looking simulation models that can be tested and improved in real time. We are currently investigating the feasibility of such techniques.

Overall, the work we have done puts BP's risk management onto a sounder foundation. We are conscious of the limitations of the research, but our experience suggests that complete accuracy, if such a thing even exists, is not necessary. Having stable policies that are broadly correct is enough.

R.K. Hinkley is manager, Corporate Finance and Deputy Group treasurer. Prior to that he served in a number of planning control and finance posts, including a spell as corporate treasurer for BP Australia during 1988–90 and, most recently, head of BP's Strategy Team. Prior to joining British Petroleum, Dr. Hinkley was a member of HM Treasury from 1972 to 1981.

The Risk Profile

In Chapter 1, we talked about U.S. savings and loan associations as classic examples of firms subject to and, indeed, ultimately damaged by interest rate risk.

> With assets that had long maturaties (e.g., 30-year fixed-rate mortgages) and liabilities that were repricing frequently (e.g., passbook deposits), the value of an S&L was inversely related to interest rates: as the interest rate rose—as the term structure shifted upward—the value of an S&L's assets declined significantly, while the value of its liabilities changed little.

The resulting relation between interest rates and the value of the S&L is portrayed graphically in Figure 5–1. As interest rates rise, ($\Delta r > 0$; that is, as actual interest rates, r, rise above the expected rates, r^e) the value of the firm declines ($\Delta V < 0$). The *risk profile* summarizes this relation.[1]

For an S&L, the exposure to interest rates is apparent in the firm's balance sheet; the exposure results from a mismatch of maturities for assets and liabilities. However, firms can have *economic exposures* that are not reflected in their balance sheets. For example, a forest products firm is exposed to interest rates:

> Increases in interest rates decrease the demand for housing, thereby decreasing the demand for lumber, and as the cash inflows decline, the value of the forest-products firm declines.

FIGURE 5–1 The Risk Profile for a U.S. S&L

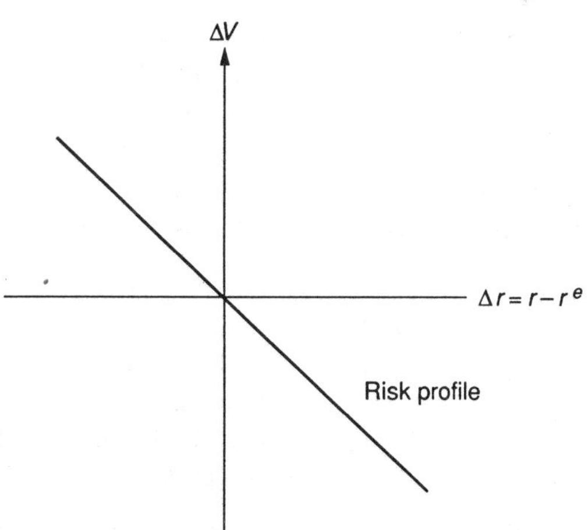

As actual interest rates, r, rise above the expected rate, r_e ($\Delta r > 0$) the value of the S & L's assets declines relative to the value of its liabilities; thus the value of the firm declines ($\Delta V < 0$).

FIGURE 5–2 The Risk Profile for a Forest Products Firm

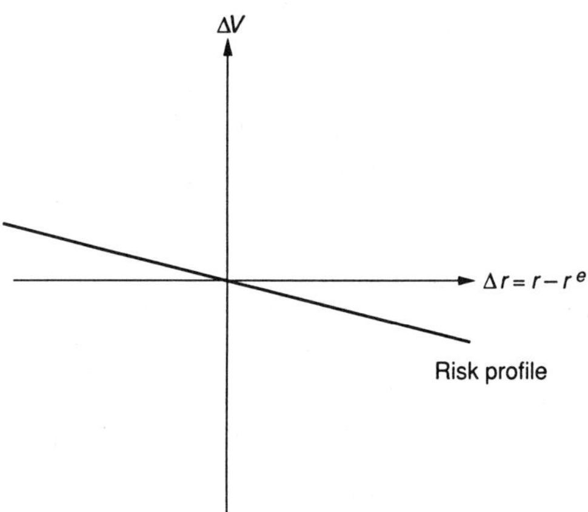

As actual interest rates, r, rise relative to the rate expected, r^e ($\Delta r>0$) the demand for housing declines. Consequently, housing starts decline and the demand for lumber drops. As cash inflows to the forest products firm decrease, the value of the firm decreases ($\Delta V<0$).

But this economic exposure—illustrated in Figure 5–2—will not appear on the firm's balance sheet.

We observe the same kind of relations in the case of foreign exchange risk. In the instances of translation and transaction exposures, the foreign exchange risk is apparent. Translation exposures result when a firm has to "translate" the local currency value of overseas assets and liabilities into a company's domestic currency for accounting purposes. Indeed, as we will see in Chapter 10, it was this kind of exposure that led to the development of swaps.

> In the early 1970s, the prevailing accounting treatment of foreign-denominated assets and liabilities (SFAS 8) required that foreign-exchange-induced changes in the value of foreign assets be reflected in the firm's net income. Consequently, when the Bretton Woods agreement collapsed, the resultant increase in foreign exchange volatility produced massive swings in reported earnings. In some instances, changes in exchange rates had a greater impact on reported earnings than the firm's operating results.

In addition to translation exposures, firms with international operations face transaction exposures that result when a firm purchases inputs or sells products in a foreign currency.

> A U.S. importer orders product from Germany, paying in deutsche marks (DM) when the products are delivered in 90 days. If, during that 90 days, the price of a DM rises—

FIGURE 5–3 The Risk Profile for a U.S. Importer

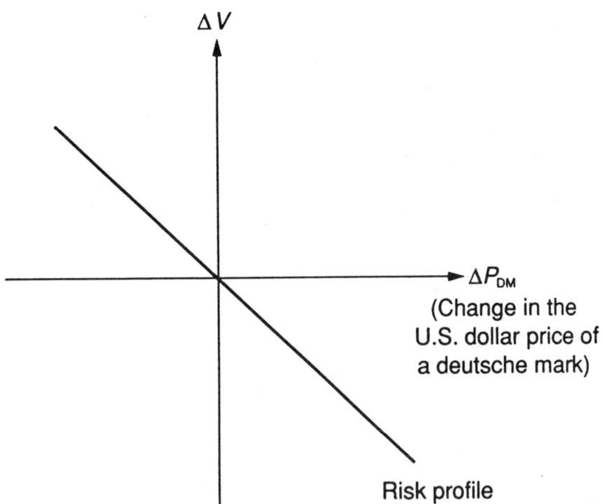

As the price of a deutsche mark rises, ($\Delta P_{DM} > 0$) the dollar cost of the importer's order rises. With rising cost, the importer's net cash flows decline, thereby reducing the value of the firm ($\Delta V < 0$).

the value of the dollar declines—the U.S. importer will have to pay more for the product. In this case—illustrated in Figure 5–3—an increase in the price of the foreign currency leads to a decrease in the value of the importer.

A more subtle problem is the recognition of a firm's economic exposure to foreign exchange rates—also referred to as competitive exposures. As we describe in Chapter 1, this effect was apparent in 1993 as the U.S. dollar reached postwar lows against the yen.

> The *New York Times* reported that the increase in the value of the yen came as a harsh blow to Japanese exporters like Toyota and Sharp, by making their products more expensive relative to products produced in other countries. In this case—illustrated in Figure 5–4—an increase in the price of the yen leads to a decrease in the value of a Japanese industrial corporation.[2]

And, not surprisingly, the same kind of relations appear with respect to commodity-price risk. As the price of oil rises and revenues to oil producers rise,[3] the value of an oil producer rises (see panel A of Figure 5–5).[4] But rising oil prices mean rising costs for an airline, so rising oil prices are linked to falling firm values (see panel B of Figure 5–5 on page 121).

For any financial price risk—interest rate risk, foreign exchange risk, or commodity-price risk—the *risk profile* is a useful means of summarizing the

FIGURE 5–4 Risk Profile for a Japanese Industrial Corporation

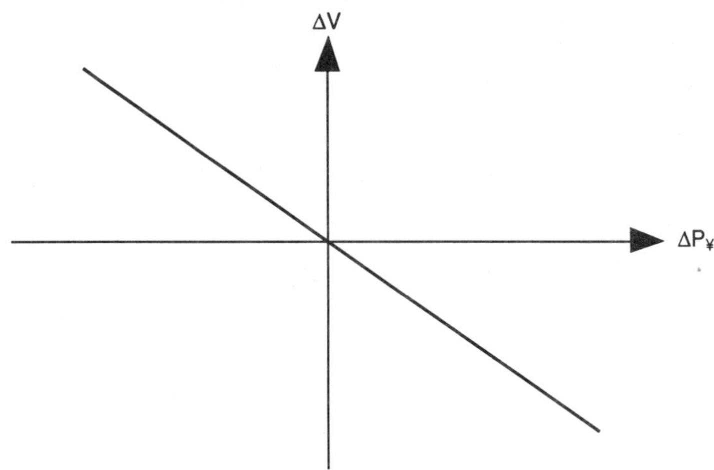

As the price of yen rises ($\Delta P_{¥}>0$), products produced in other countries are more able to compete against products produced in Japan and so, the value of the Japanese industrial corporation declines ($\Delta V<0$).

exposure of the firm. But the question that should concern you is, "How was the slope of the risk profile—$\Delta V/\Delta P$—determined? How do you estimate how much the value of the firm changes for a given change in the financial price?" It is this question to which the remainder of this chapter is devoted.

Financial Price Risk Reflected in the Firm's Financial Statements

Perhaps the first place to examine the impact of volatility in interest rates, commodity prices, and foreign exchange rates on a firm is in the firm's financial statements. In this section, we describe some of the ways in which financial price risk is reflected in the firm's balance sheet, statement of consolidated income, and statement of changes in financial position. We also note the one place the firm's annual report might reflect the firm's economic exposure.

The Balance Sheet

The balance sheet (including the notes) provides insight into a number of questions.

What Is the Firm's Liquidity? Some indicators of liquidity are the *current ratio* (current assets divided by current liabilities), which measures the ability of the firm to cover its bills within one year, and the *quick ratio* (cash, short-term investments,

FIGURE 5–5 (a) The Risk Profile for an Oil Producer (b) The Risk Profile for an Oil User

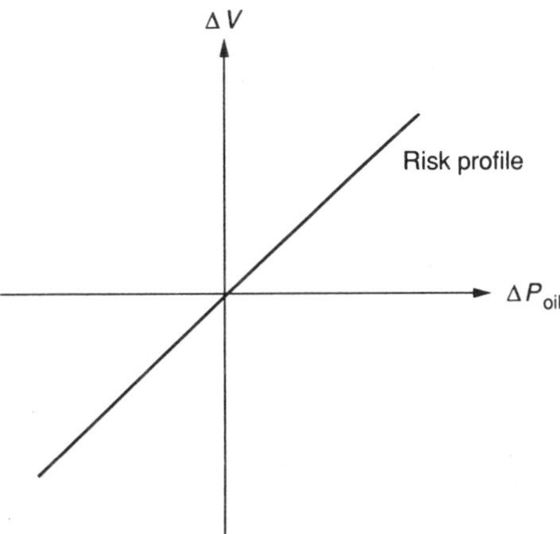

For an oil producer, rising oil prices ($\Delta P_{oil} > 0$) and rising revenues lead to an increase in the value of the firm ($\Delta V > 0$).

(a)

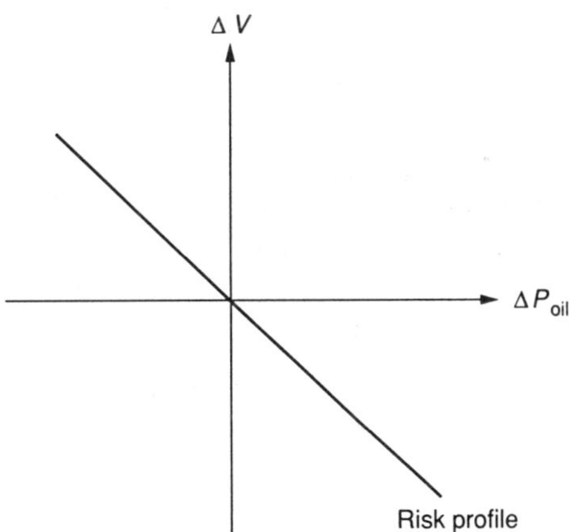

For an oil user, rising oil prices ($\Delta P_{oil} > 0$) mean increasing costs; so the value of the firm declines ($\Delta V > 0$).

(b)

and net receivables divided by current liabilities), which measures the firm's ability to cover its bills immediately.

Liquidity can substitute for risk management. Some firms—notably German industrial corporations—have so much liquidity that the impact of volatility in their cash flows induced by financial prices can be cushioned. This was the case for Japanese firms as well until the dramatic decline in Japanese equity values absorbed this liquidity. U.S. firms tend to have a much smaller liquidity cushion.

How Highly Leveraged Is the Firm? How much debt exists? How is the debt structured—for example, what percentage is fixed rate, floating rate, convertible, or some other form? Indicators of leverage include the firm's debt-equity ratio or the ratio of debt to debt plus current assets. Note also that some firms have material levels of off-balance-sheet leverage through leases that are reported in footnotes to the financial statement.

Does the Company Have Foreign Exchange Translation Exposures? The indicator of a translation exposure is the existence of foreign subsidiaries or foreign operations.

Does the Company Have Foreign Exchange Transaction Exposures? The balance sheet (or the notes) may indicate receivables or payables whose value will change if the foreign exchange changes. Transaction exposures generally occur when there is a mismatch between currency received and the currency being paid out. Companies often think that as long as they can adjust their selling price for adverse changes in exchange rate fluctuations, they have no exposure. But companies often are exposed because they are not able to react quickly enough. Many corporations use a bulletin system for posting their prices. By the time they get around to making a change in the printed prices, a year may have passed. During this period, competitors may have entered the firm's domestic market, pricing their products lower because exchange rates move in their favor.

Does the Company Have a Long-Term Foreign Exchange Exposure? A firm may wish to repatriate profits made through its overseas operations in the form of dividends, royalties, or intercompany transfers. The case for such repatriation is especially strong in countries where the company forecasts a continuing decline in the value of the local currency. And while U.S. companies traditionally hedge only those profits remitted to the parent, they should consider hedging the portion they do not. The argument for doing so is especially compelling for highly leveraged companies facing a potential ratings downgrade and those thinking of using stock in making future acquisitions, either at home or abroad.

Is the Company Exposed to Interest Rate Risk? The first place to look is at the firm's debt. If the firm has floating-rate debt, changes in short-term interest rates will result in changes in the firm's expenses. However, changes in interest rates will also change the cash flows received from (or the value of) the firm's investments. More generally, interest rate risk results if the firm has an asset–liability "gap."

Illustration 5–1

Using Financial Statement Data to Quantify the Impact of Interest Rate Changes on a Bank's Net Interest Income: The "Gap" Methodology

Most financial institutions still use the maturity gap approach to measure their exposure to interest rate changes.* The approach gets its name because it measures the "gap" between the dollar amounts of rate sensitive assets and rate sensitive liabilities (i.e., assets and liabilities that will reprice during the gapping period).

$$\text{Gap} = \text{RSA} - \text{RSL}$$

Changes in interest rates affect a financial institution by changing the institution's net interest income (NII). Once the gap is known, the impact on the firm of changes in the interest rate is given by

$$\Delta\text{NII} = (\text{Gap}) * (\Delta r)$$

To see how this works, consider the two hypothetical banks presented below. Bank 1 is a "standard bank." Its assets are primarily business and mortgage loans with maturities of one year and longer, while the bank's liabilities are primarily demand and savings deposits with maturities less than a year. Within the one-year gapping period, the assets that are rate sensitive—assets that will reprice—are the 3-month assets ($100), the 6-month assets ($100) and the 12-month assets ($400), so RSA = $600. Within the one-year gapping period, the liabilities that are rate sensitive are the 3-month liabilities ($400), the 6-month liabilities ($300) and the 12-month liabilities ($200); so, RSL = $900. Hence Bank 1 has a negative gap of −$300 million:

$$\begin{aligned}\text{Bank 1: Gap} &= \text{RSA} - \text{RSL}\\ &= \$600 - \$900 = -\$300.\end{aligned}$$

Bank 2 has precisely the same distribution of assets; but, this bank has concentrated on funding itself with one-year and longer CDs.

Bank 1 (All Values in $ Millions)

Assets		*Liabilities*	
3 month or less	100	3 month or less	400
6 month	100	6 month	300
12 month	400	12 month	200
Over 12 month	400	Over 12 month	100
	1,000		1,000

Bank 2 (All Values in $ Millions)

Assets		*Liabilities*	
3 month or less	100	3 month or less	100
6 month	100	6 month	100
12 month	400	12 month	300
Over 12 month	400	Over 12 month	500
	1,000		1,000

Using Financial Statement Data to Quantify the Impact of Interest Rate Changes on a Bank's Net Interest Income: The "Gap" Methodology continued

Consequently, the RSA for this bank remain at $600; but the liabilities that are rate sensitive during the one-year gapping period decline to $500—$100 in 3-month liabilities, $100 in 6-month liabilities, and $300 in 12-month liabilities. Hence, Bank 2 has a positive gap of $100 million,

$$\begin{aligned}\text{Bank 2: Gap} &= \text{RSA} - \text{RSL}\\ &= \$600 - \$500 = \$100\end{aligned}$$

Once the gap is known, the impact of changes in the interest can be calculated directly using the relation between NII, gap, and the change in interest rate specified above. For instance, if interest rates increase by 1 percent (100 basis points), the NII for Bank 1 will decrease by $3 million,

$$\text{Bank 1}$$
$$\Delta r = 0.01 \rightarrow \Delta\text{NII} = (-300) * (0.01) = -3,$$

while the NII for Bank 2 increases by $1 million

$$\text{Bank 2}$$
$$\Delta r = 0.01 \rightarrow \Delta\text{NII} = (+100) * (0.01) = +1.$$

Conversely, if interest rates decrease by 1 percent, the NII for Bank 1 will increase by $3 million while the NII for Bank 2 will decrease by $1 million.

These changes in NII for Banks 1 and 2 can be displayed in a *gap diagram* that shows the changes in NII that will occur for particular changes in interest rates (e.g., up 1 percent or down 1 percent) for various asset–liability structures (e.g., a negative gap of $300 or a positive gap of $100).

The *risk profile* we illustrated earlier shows the changes in the value of the bank with respect to changes in interest rates *for a given asset–liability structure*. In essence, the risk profile is like a "slice" of the gap diagram. For example, "slice" the gap diagram at the −$300 gap position: a 100-basis-point

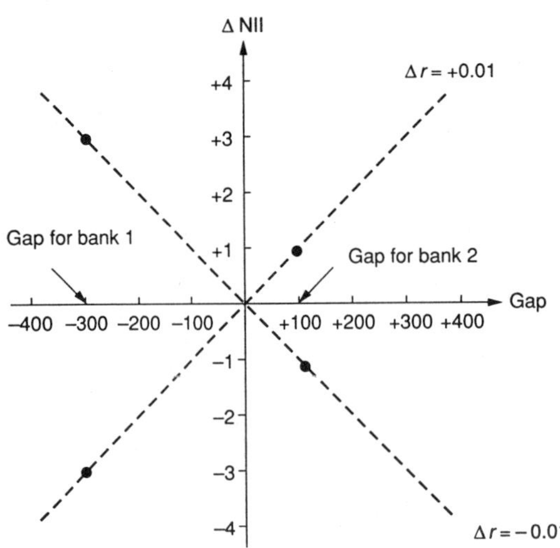

Using Financial Statement Data to Quantify the Impact of Interest Rate Changes on a Bank's Net Interest Income: The "Gap" Methodology continued

increase in the interest rate will decrease NII by $3; a 100-basis-point decrease in the interest rate will increase NII by $3. This "slice" of the gap diagram—the interest rate risk profile for Bank 1—is illustrated below.

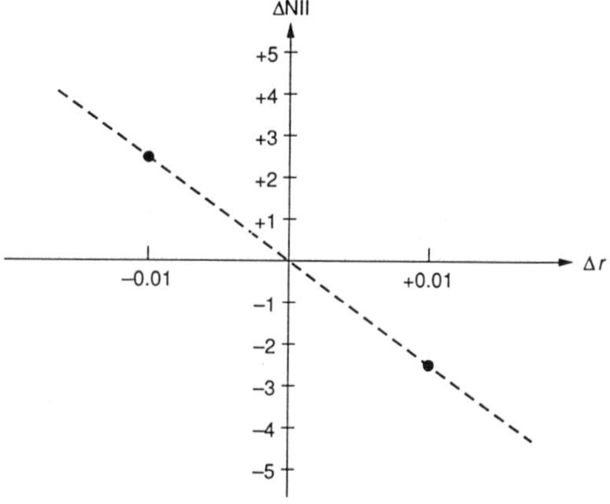

*Our discussion of the maturity gap model is taken from Alden Toevs (1984). In this discussion, we consider only the basic model. See Toevs for extensions to the periodic gap model or simulation models.

Illustration 5–2

Looking for Financial Price Risk in the Firm's Balance Sheet

On page 126 is a balance sheet for a hypothetical corporation that is a composite of a number of balance sheets from U.S. industrial corporations to illustrate how financial price risks might appear. The balance sheet itself tells us something about liquidity and leverage.

Looking for Financial Price Risk in the Firm's Balance Sheet continued

XYZ Corporation: Consolidated Balance Sheet

(In Millions) November 30, 1988

Assets		*Liabilities & Shareholders' equity*	
Current assets		Current liabilities	
Cash and short-term investment	$213	Accounts payable	$686
Receivables, net	314	Notes payable	493
Prepaid expenses	136	Accrued liabilities	650
Deferred income tax benefit	67	Other current liabilities	236
Inventories	452		
		Total current liabilities	2,065
Total current assets	1,182		
		Long-term debt	1,115
Property, buildings and equipment			
Property	937	Deferred income taxes	388
Buildings	1,363		
Equipment	3,052	Other liabilities	374
Construction in progress	166		
Total prop, bldgs, equip at cost	5,518		
less accumulated depreciation	(1,876)	Shareholders' equity	
		Preferred stock	234
Total net prop, bldgs, equip	3,642	Common stock	788
		Retained earnings	1,434
Other noncurrent assets	189	Less com. stock in treasury	(394)
		Cumulative foreign Currency adjustment	(8)
Other assets			
Intangible assets	65		
Investments in affiliates (foreign & domestic)	629	Total shareholders' equity	2,054
Miscellaneous assets	289		
Total other assets	983		
Total assets	$5,996	Total liabilities and shareholders' equity	$5,996

Quick ratio $\frac{213 + 314}{2,065}$

Current ratio $\frac{1,182}{2,065}$

Debt-Equity Ratio $\frac{2,065 + 1,115 + 374}{2,054}$

FX translation Exposure?

Liquidity

XYZ's balance sheet indicates some liquidity concerns. Its "current ratio" (current assets divided by current liabilities) is just 0.57, which means it can pay back roughly half of what it owes currently. (A less risky ratio would be 1.5–2.0). Its "quick ratio" (cash and short-term investments and net receivables divided by current liabilities), a measure of the firm's ability to cover its bills now if it had to, is just 0.25. (A more desirable ratio would fall somewhere between 0.75 and 1.0.)

Leverage

For XYZ, the ratio of debt to equity assets

$$\frac{2,065 + 1115 + 374}{2,054} = 1.73$$

Looking for Financial Price Risk in the Firm's Balance Sheet continued

is high enough to raise the eyebrows of ratings agencies.

In the case of XYZ, the notes to the balance sheet tell us even more than does the balance sheet itself:

Notes to the Consolidated Financial Statement

Significant Accounting Policies

Possible A/L "gap" Exposures

A. **Principals of Consolidation—**The consolidated financial statement includes the accounts of XYZ Corporation, a holding company, and its domestic and foreign subsidiaries at the close of our fiscal year which occurred on 11/30/88. Due to the dissimilar nature of its operations, **XYZ's wholly owned finance subsidiary** is included here on the equity basis. Hereafter XYZ Corporation will be known as "Parent Company," . . .

Commodity Price Exposure

C. **Inventories—**The LIFO method is used to value all inventories. Copper, a primary component for the maufacture of the latest design . . . and is among inventory . . .

F. **Income Taxes—**The provision for income taxes is based on pretax financial income which differs from taxable income. Differences generally arise because certain items, such as depreciation and write-downs of certain assets, are reflected in different time periods for financial and tax purposes. At XYZ Corporation, we chose to use the flow-through method of accounting for investment tax credits. This method enables a firm to recognize investment tax credits as a reduction of income tax expense in the year the qualified investments were made. The statutory Federal income tax rate for 1987 and 1988 was reduced by the Tax Reform Act of 1986. However, the effective income tax rate for 1987 actually increased due to the repeal of the investment tax credit (although some credits were allowed in 1986 under the transition rules) and a higher capital gains tax rate.

G. **Property, Plant & Equipment—**Recorded at cost . . .

FX Exposures

J. **Foreign Currency Transition—The local currency of the foreign subsidiary is the functional currency.** The rate of exchange in effect on the balance sheet is used to translate the value of the assets and liabilities. Operating results are converted to U.S. dollars by averaging the prevailing exchange rates during the period. Gains or losses due to currency translations over the period have been captured in a special equity retained account.

L. **Research & Development—**New product development . . .

Foreign Operations

FX Exposures

Sales from consolidated foreign operations were 15.5% of the total sales for 1988. Net income of consolidated foreign companies totaled $106MM in 1988. Net foreign assets consist of manufacturing facilities in Ireland, Spain, Italy and Taiwan.

Commitments, Contingent Liabilities and Restrictions on Assets

On November 30, 1988 commitments for capital expenditures in progress were approximately . . .

Discontinued Operations

During the second quarter of 1988, our southwestern manufacturing operations were discontinued. The net assets of these operations have been consolidated in this balance sheet. Additional after tax charges from these discontinued operations have been recorded.

The adjustments are the result of the anticipated effects of the 1986 Tax Reform Act, additional estimated tax costs and some other minor adjustments to reserves.

Supplemental Disclosures to Statements of Cash Flow

Interest and taxes have been classified . . .

Cash and Short-Term Investments

Interest Rate Exposure

Figures for cash and short-term investments consist of commercial paper, loan participations, certificates of deposits, and bankers' acceptance. All short-term investments are considered cash equivalents for purposes of disclosure in this balance sheet. The wholly owned finance subsidiary, XYZ Finance, purchases nearly all notes receivable resulting from domestic operations. **Foreign subsidiaries sell certain receivables to a non-affiliated finance company.**

Looking for Financial Price Risk in the Firm's Balance Sheet continued

Legal Proceedings

The matters cited below . . .

Preferred Shares of Stock

In 1985, the Parent Company issues 2,340,000 shares of **Adjustable Rate Cumulative Preferred Stock,** at face value of $100 per share. The annualized dividend rate for the initial dividend periods ended January 15, 1986, and April 15, 1986, was 10%. Thereafter, dividends have been set quarterly at an annualized rate of 1.85% less than the highest of the U.S. Treasury three-month, 10-year or 20-year maturity rates, which rate may not be less than 6.75% nor greater than 14.0%. The preferred stock is redeemable, in part or in whole, at the option of the Parent Company.

Foreign-Exchange Exposures

XYZ's balance sheet suggests the company may face significant foreign exchange translation exposures. The notes tell us that XYZ's net asset translation exposures consist of manufacturing facilities in Ireland, Spain, Italy, and Taiwan.

Because foreign sales make up only 15.5 percent of the company's total, XYZ may be less concerned about foreign exchange transaction exposures. Nevertheless, exchange rate fluctuations may affect the company's ability to compete against foreign manufacturers.

Interest Rate Exposures

Investments—XYZ's current assets include $123 million in cash and short-term investments, which include commercial paper, loan participations, certificates of deposit and bankers' acceptances. The company should consider the yield erosion that would occur on these instruments if rates decline.

Gap—Because the finance subsidiary purchases receivables from domestic operations, it must fund those purchases, presumably through long-term debt. The result is an interest rate funding/lending gap.

Commodity-Price Exposures

The notes to XYZ's balance sheet indicates the company is exposed to changing copper prices, referring to "copper [as] a primary component for the manufacturing component of the latest design."

XYZ has a hidden interest rate exposures in the capital structure. In 1985, XYZ issued 2.34 million shares of adjustable rate preferred stock that pays a dividend tied to an interest rate index. Consequently, XYZ has an interest rate exposure. Moreover this preferred is "dividend-constrained," guaranteeing that the preferred dividend payouts will be within a specified range—between 6.75 percent and 14 percent. The net result is that, by issuing this form of preferred stock, XYZ has sold an interest rate collar.

Are there investment tax credits and tax loss carryforwards that can be accessed via risk management instruments? Leveraged companies such as XYZ should be doing everything possible to reduce their tax burden and preserve cash, and one way to do that is via tax planning. It is essential for XYZ to use its investment tax credits (ITCs) and tax loss carryforwards (TLCFs). XYZ's balance sheet suggests the company might take advantage of both ITCs and TLCFs.

Is the Firm Exposed to Commodity-Price Changes? In addition to reflecting the firm's exposures to financial price risk, the balance sheet sometimes provides insights into the firm's rationale for using risk management. For example, the balance sheet will show whether the firm has investment tax credits or tax loss carry-forwards whose value could be increased through risk management instruments. As we note in Chapter 4, if the firm's pretax income is volatile because of changes in exchange rates, interest rates, or commodity prices, the firm can increase its value by hedging.

Statement of Consolidated Income and Statement of Changes in Financial Position

A balance sheet is limited in what it reveals about financial price risk. It is like a snapshot: it shows only what the firm's financial status was at one point in time. The balance sheet does not indicate whether the financial health of the firm is improving, getting worse, or developing a condition that could put the firm in distress.

To evaluate financial changes over time and the impact they have on a firm's risk profile, additional information is necessary, information that portrays the firm's financial health as both a snapshot and a movie (in financial jargon, both *flows* and *stocks*). That leads us to the firm's statement of consolidated income and statement of changes in financial position.

Statement of Consolidated Income. This account provides data on the state of the core business—the demand for the firm's products and the pattern of costs—and facilitates analysis of the firm's current financial health. From this baseline, one can identify the financial risks that could jeopardize or enhance the firm's position. This checklist indicates some of the questions analysts would ask and the line items they would examine:

What Is the State of the Market for This Firm's Output? Is the core business expanding or eroding? Some of the indicators are change in net sales and the inventory-turnover ratio.

Are the Company's Costs Changing Relative to Income? Indicators include cost of goods sold; selling, administrative, and general costs; and gross margin.

Are There Foreign Exchange Exposures? The income statement will provide information about currencies in which the firm buys or sells, and the analyst will want to look at transactional foreign exchange gains or losses.

How Well Is the Firm Carrying Its Debt? And are there year-to-year changes in the levels or the sensitivities of that debt? The indicators to focus on are times-interest-earned and debt-coverage ratios.

Illustration 5–3

Looking for Financial Price Risk in the Firm's Statement of Consolidated Income

Applying the preceding questions to the statement of consolidated income for XYZ Corporation yields some interesting results.

XYZ Corporation: Statement of Consolidated Income (in millions of U.S. dollars, except per share data)

	Fiscal Year Ended	
	11/30/88	*11/30/87*
Net sales	12,595	10,313
Costs and expenses:		
Costs of goods sold	7,808	5,672
Selling, administrative & general costs	3,230	3,106
Interest expense	463	403
Pension expense	80	69
Foreign currency expense	232	206
Depreciation	113	103
Total costs and expenses	11,926	9,559
Income from continuing operations before taxes	669	754
Income taxes (U.S. & foreign)	122	176
Income from continuing operations	547	578
Income per share—continuing operations	$8.29	$8.76
Discontinued operations after taxes	34	—
Net income	581	578
Net income per share	$8.81	$8.76
Average number of common shares	66	66

Net Sales are up by 22%

Selling costs have risen by only 4%

But.. Cost of goods sold increased dramatically

Interest and FX expenses are both up dramatically.

The income statement indicates that Sales and administration are doing well:

- XYZ's products are selling well. Net sales reflect an increase in revenues of about 22 percent. And, even after adjusting for the 4.8 percent inflation rate in 1988, XYZ has experienced a real increase in sales growth of roughly 17.2 percent.
- With such an increase in sales, many firms have had troubles keeping their people motivated: with sales increasing, the staff often begins to take life too easy. But the income statement indicates that no one at XYZ is living "high on the hog." Selling, administrative and general costs have risen by only 4 percent, a much smaller percentage than the increase in sales, indicating the sales representatives continue to fly coach and stay in Motel 6, while the office staff watches the paper clips.

But something is wrong in production and in finance:

- Costs of goods sold increased dramatically, rising from 55 percent of net sales in 1987 to 62 percent in 1988. A footnote to the financial statements addressed this, noting that most of this increase was attributable to a rise in the price of copper, a primary input in the production of XYZ's output. (In light of this copper price change, the performance of both side and S&A expenses should be reinterpreted; neither is particularly spectacular.)
- Interest expense is up. (The source of this increase will be discussed when we look at the statement of changes in financial position.) With this increase in interest expense,

Looking for Financial Price Risk in the Firm's Statement of Consolidated Income continued

Costs of Goods Sold.
In 1988, the average price of electrolytic copper rose to 122.66¢ per lb. from 84.80¢ per lb. in 1987. Since copper is a primary input in producing XYZ's products, this 45% increase in copper prices had a significant impact on cost of goods sold.

service on the firm's debt is becoming increasingly troublesome: times interest earned has declined from 1.88 times in 1987 to 1.51 times in 1988.

• As the value of the dollar continued its decline in 1988, XYZ's foreign currency expense increased markedly. The chief executive officer of XYZ mentioned this problem explicitly in his letter to the shareholders, as he complained about the monetary policies of the G-7 and about U.S. trade policies . . .

. . . and a significant portion of our problems can be laid at Washington's doorstep. Over the past three years, the dollar lost almost one-fourth of its value relative to the yen as the dollar fell from 168 yen per dollar in 1986 to 144 yen in 1987 and 128 yen in 1988. Since XYZ sources a significant amount of components from Asia, this decline in the value of the dollar has hit us hard . . . Furthermore, Washington's failure to negotiate down Japan's (and others') protective tariffs has severely limited our ability to recoup the high expense with export revenues . . .

And the result is reduced performance at XYZ.

• XYZ's net profit margin fell from 6 percent in 1987 to 4 percent in 1988.

Statement of Changes in Financial Position. More subjective evaluations of this statement are required. Fewer accounting ratios can be used as a basis for objective evaluations. Nevertheless, two issues tend to be stressed:

Quality of Earnings. An analyst looks beyond the funds a firm may be accumulating. After all, it can be doing so while going out of business. The more relevant question: Do the firm's earnings result from ongoing operations or do the earnings reflect short-term fixes?

Pension Fund Policies. Who manages the pension fund? What are the policy guidelines? What is in the portfolio? Are there substantial unfunded liabilities?

Illustration 5–4

Looking for Financial Price Risk in the Firm's Statement of Changes in Financial Position

Applying these general guidelines to XYZ, several conclusions are obvious.

XYZ Corporation: Statement of Changes in Financial Position
(in millions of U.S. dollars)

	Fiscal Year Ended	
	11/30/88	*11/30/87*
Funds provided (used) by operations:		
Net income	581	578
Depreciation	113	103
Deferred income tax	67	58
Accounts and notes receivable	(56)	(40)
Deferred pension plan costs	50	40
Accounts payable—trade	38	29
Funds provided by operating activities	793	768
Funds provided by discontinued operations	9	—
Funds provided by extraordinary items	3	—
Total funds provided by continuing operations	805	768
Funds provided (used) by investment activities: special pension funding	(37)	(25)
Total funds provided by investment activities	(37)	(25)
Funds provided (used) by financing activities:		
Short-term debt incurred	51	19
Short-term debt paid	(149)	(82)
Long-term debt paid	(220)	(142)
Dividend paid	(122)	(120)
Total funds provided by financing activities	(440)	(325)
Increase in cash and short-term investments	(6)	8
Net increase (decrease)	322	426

Net Income increased.

But all of the increase is offset by one-time transactions

The firm is adding short-term debt.

The firm is less liquid.

The quality of XYZ's earnings has declined:

- Comparing the 1988 financials with those for 1987, XYZ posted increases both in net income (from $578 million to $581 million) and in total funds provided by continuing operations (from $768 million to $805 million). Unfortunately, these aggregate figures disguise the fact that the "quality" of XYZ's earnings declined in 1988.
- The gain in total funds is overstated by two one-time, non-operation transactions: as recorded in the footnotes to the financial statements, XYZ benefited from the sale of a facility.

Discontinued Operations.

During the second quarter of 1988, XYZ sold its Ohio assembly operation to reduce operating costs and eliminate duplicated work responsibilities. Funds provided by this discontinued operation after taxes amounted to $9 million.

Looking for Financial Price Risk in the Firm's Statement of Changes in Financial Position continued

And from the settlement of a lawsuit.

> *Extraordinary Items.*
> *A favorable judgment for XYZ Corp. was found after several years of dispute over a matter of unfair competition. The suit was initiated by XYZ against ABC Corp. in 1986. An award in the amount of $3 million was granted by the Appellate Court to XYZ during the first quarter of this year...*

• Even more telling, net income represents a smaller percentage of total funds provided by continuing operations in 1988 than it did in 1987, falling from 75 percent to 72 percent.

There are problems in the investment division:

• According to a footnote, a special pension funding was required in 1988.

> *Retirement Benefits.*
> *XYZ Corp. increased funds allocated to the special pension account to offset losses in the internally managed fixed-income portfolio. The special pension fund is protected by internal policy which determines the funding limits...*

Losses in the fixed-income portfolio were the result of rising interest rates.

The structure of XYZ's financing has changed:

• As indicated in the funds provided (used) by financing activities section, XYZ incurred almost three times more short-term debt in 1988 than it did in 1987. Because the market value of its shares declined in 1988 and it issued no new shares in 1988, this increase in debt means that XYZ's debt–equity ratio has risen.

• The footnotes indicate that most of XYZ's debt is short-term, floating-rate debt.

> *Cash, Short-Term Investments.*
> *During the third and fourth quarters of fiscal year 1988, the management at XYZ saw it necessary to add $24.9 million in floating rate, short-term debt to the total debt outstanding... Total floating rate, short-term debt for the year amounted to $38.5 million while total fixed-rate debt equalled $12.50 million.*

XYZ is less liquid.

• Apparently, as XYZ has increased its marketing effort, it has had more trouble collecting its receivables from customers: accounts and notes receivable rose by 40 percent, about twice the increase in sales.

Looking for Financial Price Risk in the Firm's Statement of Changes in Financial Position continued

- Increase in cash and short-term investments shows XYZ decreased its holding of short-term financial assets in 1988.

Not surprisingly, these same problems have been noted by the rating agencies. Early in 1989, XYZ Corporation appeared in Standard & Poor's *CreditWeek* in a way it would have liked to avoid.

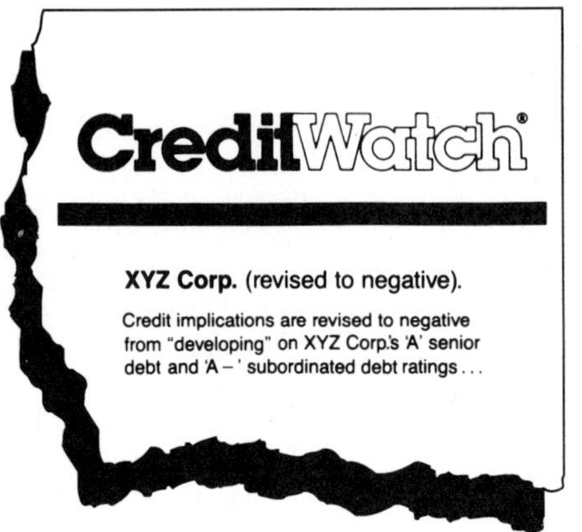

CreditWatch®
XYZ Corp. (revised to negative).
Credit implications are revised to negative from "developing" on XYZ Corp.'s 'A' senior debt and 'A–' subordinated debt ratings...

The Letter to the Shareholders in the Annual Report

So far, we have illustrated how changes in exchange rates, interest rates, or commodity prices can affect the value of the firm or the company's net income through changes in the value of assets or liabilities (known as *translation exposures*) or through firm commitment *transaction exposures*.

But changes in financial prices can also have an impact on the value of a firm through transactions not yet booked, so the firm must also consider what we call *contingent exposures*. Changes in exchange rates, interest rates, or commodity prices can influence a firm's sales and market share, so it's worthwhile for treasury executives to consider their competitive exposures as well.

As we illustrated earlier, anyone wishing to identify and quantify a firm's translation and transaction exposures will find plenty of helpful information in the firm's financial statements. The annual report, its income statement, and statement of changes in financial position all contain valuable information that can be used to measure risk.

It is somewhat difficult, but certainly not impossible, to find information about a firm's strategic exposures. A company's letter to shareholders in its annual report often contains clues. (See Illustration 5–5)

Internal Measures of Financial Price Risk

The internal measures of financial price risk are concerned with flows: how sensitive are revenues and expenses to changes in interest rates, foreign exchange

Illustration 5–5

Looking for Financial Price Risk in the Letter to the Shareholders

The letter to the shareholders from the president of XYZ Corporation reiterates some of the exposures identified in its accounting statements, but it also mentions some contingent and competitive exposures.

XYZ Corporation: Letter to shareholders

Pursuing total quality in everything we do is the key to creating value—value for our shareholders, for our customers, and for our employees.

This year's results

The year's results met the challenging goal of maintaining the Corporation's record of growth with an increase of sales of 22%. Our products showed excellent improvements in sales worldwide.

Corporate earnings, however, declined to an unsatisfactory level due greatly to unexpectedly sharp increases in the cost of copper and fierce competition which inhibited recovery of these costs. In addition to this raw materials price increase, we have continued to see price increases on intermediate products; and a significant portion of our problems can be laid at Washington's doorstep. Over the past three years the dollar lost almost one-fourth of its value relative to the yen as the dollar fell from 168 yen per dollar in 1986 to 144 yen in 1987 and 128 yen in 1988. Since XYZ sources a significant number of components from Asia, this decline in the value of the dollar has hit us hard.

Commodity Price Exposure

FX Exposure

In response to the severe foreign currency moves seen over the past several years, we have stepped up efforts to increase productivity and cut costs.

Tempered optimism

Our longer-term outlook, while optimistic, is tempered by the knowledge that we face substantial challenges: the need to increase our investment in product and facility improvements, higher customer expectations, competitive pressures on margins and substantial marketing costs. Furthermore, Washington's failure to negotiate down Japan's (and others') protective tariffs has severely limited our ability to recoup the high expense with export revenues.
Only the strongest performers will survive in the highly competitive years ahead, and we intend to be one of them. To do so, we must provide high-quality products that exceed our customers' expectations, instill a people-oriented culture throughout the company and implement the most cost-efficient operating and business processes possible.

If we focus on these priorities, and if we apply ourselves diligently to the basics of running the business, we will maintain our momentum and will continue to perform strongly in the years ahead.

John B. Doe
For the Board of Directors
Chairman and Chief Executive Officer

Looking for Financial Price Risk in the Letter to the Shareholders continued

Commodity-Price Exposure

XYZ's exposure to copper prices, which appeared in the "cost of goods sold" footnote to the statement of consolidated income, is highlighted in the letter to the shareholders.

Foreign-Exchange Exposures

It's not unusual to see poor earnings blamed on foreign exchange: Caterpillar, for example, said in its 1982 annual report that "the strong dollar is a prime factor in Caterpillar's reduced sales and earnings. . . . " Like Caterpillar, XYZ also faces transaction and contingent exposures: a weak dollar has made its input costs more expensive—and they may become even more expensive in the future.

rates, and/or commodity prices? Over the past several years, we have worked with a number of firms to quantify their exposures to financial prices. Our experience is that firms use one of two methods to obtain an internal measure of financial price risk.

Statistical Analysis of Revenues and Expenses

For many firms, the likely first step is to look at the behavior of accounting data—revenue and expense data. This is accomplished by using regression to estimate the historical relation between the relevant financial prices and important internal data on revenues and expenses (as well as more disaggregated items such as and capital expenditures). Using historical accounting data, managers can estimate models of the following form:

$$\text{Revenue}_t = a_0 + \sum a_i(\text{Financial price})_{it} + e_{rt}$$

$$\text{Expense}_t = b_0 + \sum b_i(\text{Financial price})_{it} + e_{rt}$$

Regression analysis is by definition an historical measure of a firm's sensitivity to financial prices. Although relatively simple to implement, the value of the results depends on historical relations holding true in the future. Therefore, for a firm entering new markets, these estimates of historical sensitivities are less informative than for a firm planning to maintain its current market position. In addition, accounting data will not necessarily reflect the true economic relations underlying the firm's financial price exposures. For example, accounting data typically do not reflect opportunity costs.

Simulation Analyses

An alternative to the regression approach is Monte Carlo simulation. The method of Monte Carlo simulation is intended to provide a forward-looking assessment of the firm's exposure to financial and commodity prices. Reports in the trade press suggest that some firms have begun using simulation models to examine the responsiveness of pretax income to changes in interest rates, exchange rates, and commodity prices.

Figure 5–6 illustrates how a Monte Carlo simulation would be used to measure the firm's exposure to a financial price. The first step is to model the firm's revenue and expense. Drawing on both the management team's knowledge of the firm's production processes and the markets in which the firm operates and on empirical analyses, we construct a mathematical model of the firm that relates financial prices to sales, product prices, and costs—panel A. We then randomly select a level for the financial price. Using this financial price in the model of the firm, we will generate a forecast for net income—panel B. If we select another level for the financial price, we will get another forecast for net income—panel C. We keep doing this until we have subjected the model to a large number of scenarios. (As long as the firm's environment is expected to be stable, these scenarios can be generated based on the historical volatility and correlations between the relevant financial prices.) The result is a distribution describing the likely distribution of values of net income.

Although more difficult to implement than a regression analysis, a Monte Carlo model has several advantages. Constructing the initial mathematical model requires rich understanding of the firm's expected exposure (as opposed to its historical exposure). Furthermore, a model allows a fuller set of assumptions to be explored, since it is not tied to historical relations.

External Measures of Financial Price Risk

Since "external" measures of financial price risk rely on values obtained in the market, they could also be called "market-based measures." To give you some idea of how different external measures of risk fit together, we can look at the external measures as different factor models.

We can write a general linear factor model as

$$R_{it} = \sum_{j} b_{ij} F_{jt} + e_{it} \tag{5–1}$$

where R_i is the rate of return on financial instrument i—it could be a bond or a deposit or a share of stock—F_j is the jth "factor," b_{ij} is the weighting coefficient for the jth factor, and e_i is the residual variation. In the sense of a risk measure, the

FIGURE 5–6 Monte Carlo Simulation

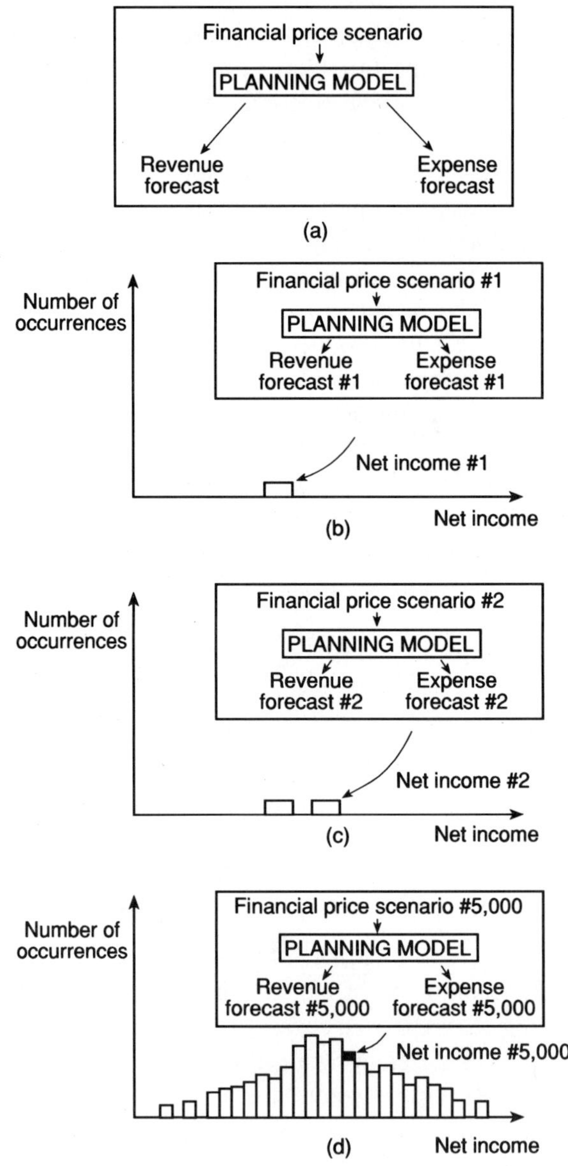

coefficient b_{ij} measures the financial instrument's sensitivity to—exposure to—the jth factor.

Duration

While factor models are normally associated with the equity market, the first factor model used in finance appeared in the bond market—the duration model.

Duration was "discovered" almost simultaneously by both Federich MacCaulay (1938) and Sir John Hicks (1939). However, these two gentlemen had very different objectives. MacCaulay's goal was to define a measure by which two bonds with common maturity but divergent payment structures could be compared. In the MacCaulay sense, duration measures when, on average, the value of the bond is received. Hicks attempted to measure interest rate sensitivity for any particular bond. In the tradition of Hicks, duration provides a measure of the exposure of the bond to interest rate risk.

In the context of a factor model, duration provides a measure of the relation between the rate of return on bond i and the percentage change in $(1 + r)$—the discount factor,[5]

$$R_{it} = b_i\left[\frac{\Delta r_t}{(1 + r_t)}\right] + e_{it} \qquad (5\text{–}2)$$

In the preceding factor model, the coefficient b_i is the "duration" of bond i.[6] Rearranging the terms of Equation 5–2,

$$b_i = \text{Duration} = R_{it}/[\Delta r_t/(1 + r_t)] \qquad (5\text{–}3)$$

and, since the rate of return on the bond, R, is simply the percentage change in the value of the bond ($\Delta V/V$), we can express duration in more familiar terms:

$$\text{Duration} = \frac{\text{Percentage change in value of the bond}}{\text{Percentage change in } (1 + r)} \qquad (5\text{–}4)$$

To make the concept of duration a little more concrete, let's consider Illustration 5-6.

Illustration 5–6

Using Market Data to Quantify the Impact of Interest Rate Changes on the Value of a Bank's Portfolio or Equity*

Consider a stylized bank balance sheet.

Assets		*Liabilities*	
Cash	100	1-year CD	600
Business loans	400	5-year CD	300
Mortgage loans	500	Equity	100
	1,000		1,000

Let's calculate the duration of the five-year CD and the business loan. The cash flows for these two instruments are illustrated below.

The CD

The CD is simple. Since it is a zero-coupon instrument, in a MacCaulay sense all of the value is received at maturity. Hence, the duration of the five-year CD is five years.

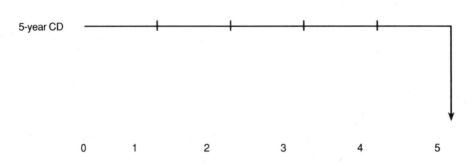

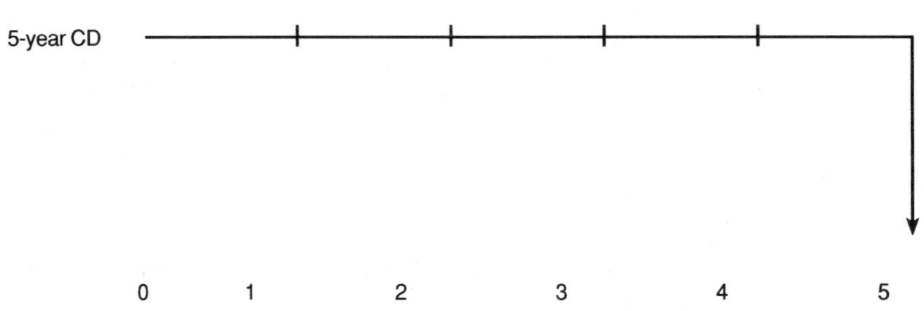

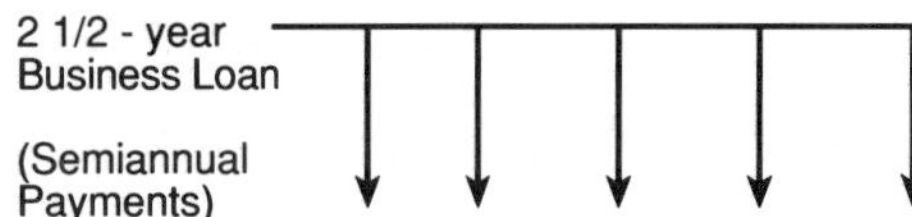

The Business Loan

Suppose that the business loan has a maturity of 2.5 years and is amortizing (has a sinking fund). As the cash flows presented above illustrate, value is received prior to maturity, so the duration of the instrument must be less than 2.5 years. To find out how much less, we need to ask, "When on average is the present value received?" The following table provides the answer.

Columns 1–4 provide the value of the bond. Column 1 gives time that the cash flows in column 2 are paid. Using the discount rates† in column 3, the present values are determined—column 4—and the sum of these present values yield the $400 value of

Using Market Data to Quantify the Impact of Interest Rate Changes on the Value of a Bank's Portfolio or Equity continued

(1) Time to Receipt (years)	*(2)* Cash Flow	*(3)* Discount Rate	*(4)* PV	*(5)* Weight	*(6)* Weight × Time
0.5	90	7.75%	88.70	0.22	0.11
1.0	90	8.00	83.33	0.21	0.21
1.5	90	8.25	79.91	0.20	0.31
2.0	90	8.35	76.66	0.19	0.38
2.5	90	8.50	73.40	0.18	0.45
			400.00		1.45

this loan. To determine when, on average, the present value was received, we need to calculate the weighted average time of receipt. Column 5 provides the weights—for example, at time 0.5 years, \$88.70/400 = 0.22 of the total present value of the instrument was received. Multiplying these weights (column 5) by the times the cash flows are received (column 1) and summing gives the weighted average time of receipt—the duration of this business loan—as 1.45 years.**

As we noted earlier, duration provides a means of relating changes in interest rates to changes in the value of the security:

$$D = -\frac{\Delta V}{\Delta r} \times \frac{(1 + r)}{V}$$

where D is the duration of the security as calculated above, V is the market value of the security, and r is the interest rate. Rewriting this equation, we can express the percentage change in the value of the security in terms of the percentage change in the discount rate—$(1+r)$—and the duration of the security,

$$\frac{\Delta V}{V} = -\frac{\Delta(1 + r)}{(1 + r)} \times D$$

For example, if the discount rate increases by 1 percent—that is, if $\Delta(1+r)/(1+r) = 0.01$—the market value of the five-year CD will decrease by 5 percent:

$$\Delta V/V = -(0.01)\,(5.0) = -0.05.$$

However, the same increase in the discount rate would decrease the value of the 2.5 year business loan by only 1.45 percent:

$$\Delta V/V = -(0.01)\,(1.45) = -0.0145.$$

And, since duration is additive, the duration technique can be expanded to deal with the impact of changes in interest rates on the value of the entire firm. For a portfolio with n assets having market values V_i and durations D_i, the duration of the portfolio is

$$D_{portfolio} = \frac{\sum V_i D_i}{\sum V_i}$$

We can use this equation to examine the duration of the assets of the bank in question. We already know that the duration of the business loan is 1.45 years. Suppose that the duration of the mortgage loans was calculated as 6.84 years. And, by definition, the duration of the cash is zero. Hence, the duration of the assets is

Using Market Data to Quantify the Impact of Interest Rate Changes on the Value of a Bank's Portfolio or Equity continued

$$D_A = \frac{(100 \times 0.0) + (400 \times 1.45) + (500 \times 6.84)}{1{,}000} = 4.0$$

Likewise, we can examine the duration of the deposits. We have CDs with durations of one and five years, so

$$D_D = \frac{(600 \times 1.0) + (300 \times 5.0)}{900} = 2.33$$

Combining the preceding, we can calculate the duration of the equity—the sensitivity of the value of the firm to changes in the discount rate $(1 + r)$.

$$D_{equity} = \frac{(V_A \times D_A) - (V_D \times D_D)}{V_E}$$

$$= \frac{(1{,}000 \times 4.0) - (900 \times 2.33)}{100} = 19.03$$

Therefore, if the discount rate increases by 1 percent, the value of the equity of this bank will decline by 19.03 percent.

---

*Our discussion of duration is based on George G. Kaufman, "Measuring and Managing Interest Rate Risk: A Primer," *Economic Perspectives*, Federal Reserve Bank of Chicago.

†These discount rates are zero-coupon rates that include the risk premium appropriate for this instrument.

**In algebraic form, the duration, D, is calculated as

$$D = \sum_{t=1}^{T} \left(\frac{PV_t}{V}\right) \cdot t$$

where PV_t is the present value of the cash flow received in time period t and V is the market value of the instrument.

A Factor Model for Quantifying Financial Price Risk

By regressing the rate of return to a particular equity (R_i) against the return for a market portfolio (R_m)

$$R_{it} = \alpha_i + \beta_i R_{mt} + e_{it} \qquad (5\text{–}5)$$

one obtains estimates of beta (β)—a measure of the firm's market risk.[7]

Using a technique much like that by which analysts obtain the firm's beta, it is possible to measure the market's perception of the sensitivity of the value of the firm to changes in interest rates, foreign exchange rates, and commodity prices. Our task is to decompose the variation in the share price return and to determine how much of the variation is attributable to movements in a specific financial price. We do so by adding the financial prices to the market model.

Our approach follows the work of earlier researchers who added interest rates (bond prices) or foreign exchange rates to examine interest rate and foreign exchange exposures:

Mark Flannery and Christopher James (1984) added the rate of return from holding a constant-maturity, default-free bond (R_B) to the market model,[8]

$$R_{it} = \alpha_i + \beta_i R_{mt} + \gamma_{Bi} R_{Bt} + e_{it} \tag{5–6}$$

to examine the interest rate exposure reflected in equity prices for banks and S&Ls. In Equation 5–6, γ_{Bi} measures the bond price exposure (interest rate exposure) faced by financial institution *i*. Sweeney and Warga (1986) used much the same model, substituting the change in the interest rates (Δr) for the rate of return calculated from bond prices,

$$R_{it} = \alpha_i + \beta_i R_{mt} + \gamma_{ri}(\Delta r_t) + e_{it} \tag{5–7}$$

to examine the interest rate exposure reflected in equity prices for nonfinancial corporations—measured by γ_{ri}.

Jorion (1990) added the rate of change in a foreign exchange rate ($\Delta P_{FX}/P_{FX}$) to the market model,

$$R_{it} = \alpha_i + \beta_i R_{mt} + \gamma_{FXi}\left(\frac{\Delta P_{FX}}{P_{FX}}_t\right) + e_{it} \tag{5–8}$$

to examine the exchange rate exposure reflected in equity prices for U.S. multinationals. This exposure to foreign exchange rates is measured by γ_{FXi} in equation 5–8.

Since we are interested in the exposure of financial and nonfinancial firms to movements in interest rates, foreign exchange rates, and commodity prices, our model incorporates the Flannery–James and Jorion models by including both the rate of change in interest rates ($\Delta r/r$) and the rate of change of exchange rates ($\Delta P_{FX}/P_{FX}$) as independent variables. Moving one step further to provide estimates of the firm's exposure to commodity-price risk, we add the rate of change of commodity prices ($\Delta P_c/P_c$). Hence, the equation we consider is

$$R_{it} = \alpha_i + \beta_i R_{mt} + \gamma_{ri}\left(\frac{\Delta r}{r}\right)^t + \gamma_{FXi}\left(\frac{\Delta P_{FX}}{P_{FX}}\right)^t + \gamma_{Ci}\left(\frac{\Delta P_c}{P_c}\right)^t + e_{it} \tag{5–9}$$

where β reflects the firm's exposure to the market and γ_{ri}, γ_{FXi}, and γ_{ci} reflect the exposure of firm *i* to interest rate risk, foreign exchange risk, and commodity-price risk, respectively.

Moving toward a more concrete illustration, suppose we wished to determine the sensitivity of some firm to

- three-month LIBOR,
- the 10-year Treasury bond rate,
- the deutsche mark–dollar exchange rate,
- the pound sterling–dollar exchange rate,
- the yen–dollar exchange rate, and
- the price of oil.

Using Equation 5–9, this question could be addressed by estimating the regression equation

$$\begin{aligned} R_{it} = \alpha_i &+ \beta_i R_{mt} \\ &+ \gamma_{3M}(\Delta r_{3M}/r_{3M})_t + \gamma_{10Y}(\Delta r_{10Y}/r_{10Y})_t \\ &+ \gamma_{DM}(\Delta P_{DM}/P_{DM})_t + \gamma_{£}(\Delta P_{£}/P_{£})_t + \gamma_{¥}(\Delta P_{¥}/P_{¥})_t \\ &+ \gamma_{Oil}(\Delta P_{Oil}/P_{Oil})_t + e_t, \end{aligned} \tag{5–10}$$

where R_{it} is the rate of return for holding a share of the firm's stock, R_{mt} is the rate of return for holding the market portfolio, $\Delta r_{3M}/r_{3M}$ is the percentage change in three-month LIBOR and $\Delta r_{10Y}/r_{10Y}$ is the percentage change in the 10-year Treasury bond rate; $\Delta P_{DM}/P_{DM}$, $\Delta P/P_{£}$, and $\Delta P_{¥}/P_{¥}$ are the percentage changes in the dollar prices of the three foreign currencies; and $\Delta P_{Oil}/P_{Oil}$ is the percentage change in the price of crude oil. The estimate of γ_{3M} and γ_{10Y} provide measures of the sensitivity of the value of the firm to changes in interest rates; γ_{DM}, $\gamma_{£}$, and $\gamma_{¥}$ estimate the sensitivity to the exchange rates; and γ_{Oil} estimates the sensitivity to the oil price.

These coefficients actually measure elasticities. Further, had we used the percentage change in (1 + interest rate) instead of the percentage change in the interest rates themselves, the coefficients γ_{3M} and γ_{10y} could be interpreted as "duration" measures. Specifically, we could modify the estimation equation to provide a measure of "the duration of equity."

Another application of these techniques is to examine market-based measures of exposures for the firm's major competitors. This exercise can provide useful insight into the nature of the competition and the structure of the industry. Examining competitors' exposures can be especially valuable if the firm is private and thus lacks the return data to estimate its exposures directly. Finally, note that these approaches are not mutually exclusive. In fact, our experience suggests a comparison of the results from the different methods yields a much richer understanding of the firm's exposure.

Notes

1. In fact, the relation between the value of the firm and the interest rate is nonlinear. However, for simplicity of exposition we will presume—for the time being—that the relation is linear.
2. Sterngold (1993).
3. This presupposes that the demand for oil is price inelastic.
4. There is no doubt that the value of an oil-producing firm is positively related to the price of oil. However, we would be remiss if we failed to note the indications that this positive relation may be becoming weaker. See for example, Sullivan (1988).
5. This interpretation follows Hopewell and Kaufman (1973).
6. If we refer to the MacCaulay measure as "duration," the measure in Equation 5–3 would be referred to as "modified duration." For a development of the relation between duration and modified duration, see Kaufman, Bierwag, and Toevs (1983).
7. For our purposes, Equation 5–5 can best be viewed as a variance decomposition, with the parameter beta measuring the share of the total variation in the share return that is attributable to variation in returns to holding the market portfolio.
8. Note the relation between this specification and the definition of duration.

CHAPTER

6 FORWARD CONTRACTS

As indicated in Chapter 2, the forward contract can be considered a fundamental building block for derivative instruments. It is the basis for the risk management instruments, both conceptually and in their use in the financial markets. (This becomes more evident when we look at the techniques dealers use to hedge their derivative portfolios in Chapter 18.)

The Structure of a Forward Contract

Of the financial derivatives, forward contracts are the most familiar, appearing in transactions as common as buying a puppy: "I'll pay you \$*X* for that puppy with the spot on its right leg when it is weaned." A forward contract is a contract made today for the delivery of an asset in the future. *The buyer of the forward contract agrees to pay a specified amount at a specified date in the future to receive a specified amount of a currency, amount of a commodity, or coupon payment from the counterparty.* The specified future price (or rate) is the *exercise price* of the contract. The most notable forward market is the foreign exchange forward market, in which current volume is in excess of one third of a trillion dollars per day.[1] Forward contracts may require physical delivery of something physical, as in the case of the puppy or with most foreign exchange forwards. However, forward contracts can also be *cash-settled*, requiring only the exchange of the difference between the exercise price and the spot price prevailing at the future date.

Figure 6–1 helps make this definition of a forward contract more concrete. Panel A illustrates a foreign exchange forward in which a party has agreed to pay, at time T, \$$Y$ to receive £X. Panel B illustrates a commodity forward contract in

FIGURE 6–1 Some Illustrative Forward Contracts

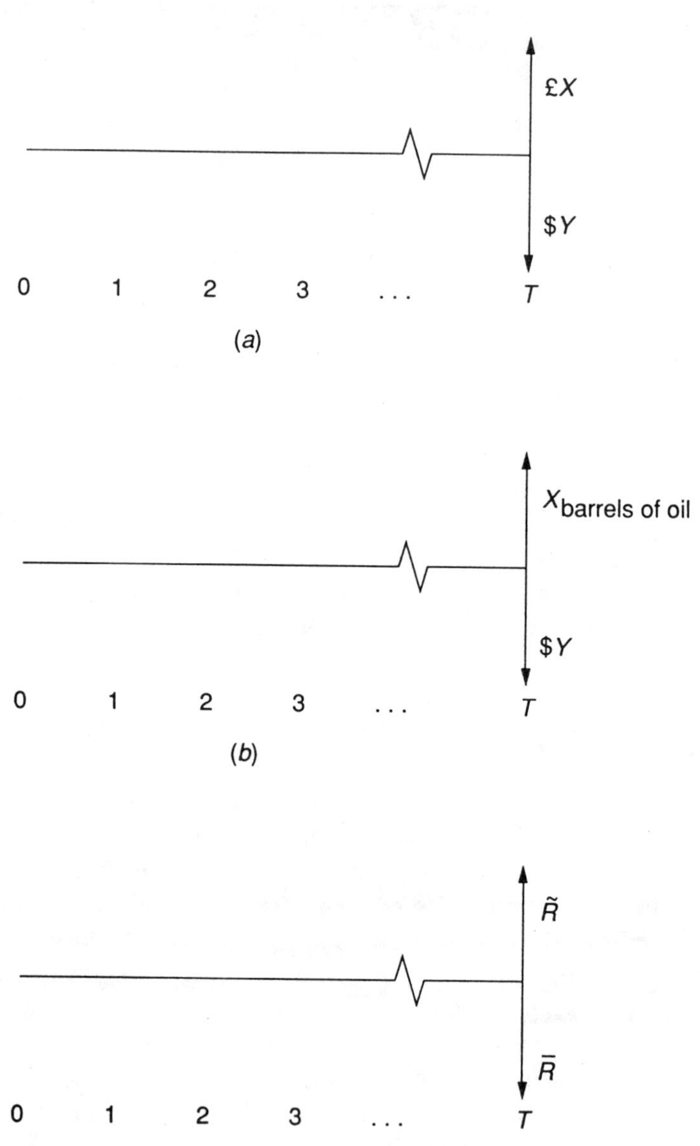

which a party has agreed to pay $Y to receive X barrels of oil at time T. Panel C illustrates a forward contract on interest rates, referred to in the market as a *forward-rate agreement (FRA)*. The parties to the contract have agreed on some *notional principal;* the party illustrated has agreed to pay a fixed-rate coupon on this notional principal, $\bar{R}_T$, at time T, in return for receiving a floating-rate coupon, $\tilde{R}$ (such as a six-month LIBOR).

At contract origination, the net present value of an *at-market* forward contract is zero. In an at-market forward, the exercise price of the contract is set at the expected future price (the *forward price*); neither the buyer nor the seller of the forward will obtain value unless the exchange rate, commodity price, or interest rate differ from expectations.

The payoff profile for forward contract positions is illustrated in Figure 6–2. Panel A provides the payoff profile for the buyer of the forward contract (the party who is long in the forward contract). At contract maturity, the buyer of the forward contract is obligated to buy the asset at the exercise price agreed to at contract origination, P_0^F. If the spot price at maturity, P_T, exceeds the exercise price, the forward contract owner will be able to buy the asset at the lower exercise price and sell at the higher spot price, making a profit of $P_T - P_0^F$ per unit. Hence, the profit

Aside

Notional Principal

Many risk management products (including forward-rate agreements and cash-settled forwards on commodities) specify a notional principal for the contract. The principal is notional in the sense that it is not paid or received at contract maturity but is instead used only to calculate the cash flows paid and received. An example may help to clarify this point:

Suppose you enter into an FRA to receive floating/pay fixed with the following terms:

Maturity: 1 year

Notional principal: \$1 million

Floating rate: one-year U.S. Treasury rate

Fixed rate (specified at contract origination): 5 percent

At contract maturity—in one year—the payment due to you is determined by the then current one-year Treasury rate and the notional principal of the contract. Suppose that one year from now the one-year Treasury rate is 6 percent; the payment due to you is

$$(0.06) \times \$1{,}000{,}000 = \$60{,}000.$$

The payment you are required to make is determined by the fixed-rate specified in the contract and the notional principal of the contract:

$$(0.05) \times \$1{,}000{,}000 = \$50{,}000.$$

Since FRAs are cash-settled, only the net payment is made. You receive a check for \$10,000.

for the owner of the forward contract is

$$\text{Profit} = (P_T - P_0{}^F)\ (\text{Number of units contracted}). \tag{6–1}$$

Conversely, the seller of the forward contract profits when the spot price at maturity is less than the exercise price; the seller of the forward can buy at the cheaper spot price and sell at the higher exercise price. Hence the profit for the seller of the forward contract is

$$\text{Profit} = (P_0{}^F - P_T)\ (\text{Number of units contracted}). \tag{6–2}$$

Since the net present value at origination of the at-market forward contract is zero, why do parties enter into forward contracts? The contract must certainly have value for both the buyer and the seller of the contract; otherwise they would not transact. This value might exist because one party expects the future spot price to be different from the forward price—the prevailing view of the market. Or the forward contract may be used to create a synthetic asset. (We will return to this topic in Chapter 15.)

In the main, however, most of the participants in the forward markets are reducing risk by fixing future transactions costs. For example, a car importer knows the cost of the car today in both the domestic and the foreign currency. He also may have a pretty clear idea about how much he can sell the car for in his domestic currency once the car is delivered to him. What the car importer is uncertain about is how much the car will cost him in his domestic currency when it arrives, since he

FIGURE 6–2 The Payoff for Forward Contract Positions

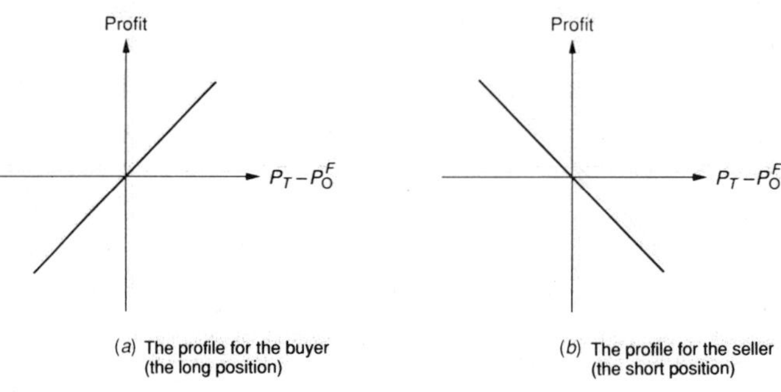

(*a*) The profile for the buyer (the long position)

(*b*) The profile for the seller (the short position)

must pay in a foreign currency at that time. To eliminate this uncertainty, he can use a forward contract today to lock in the exchange rate between domestic currency and foreign currency for this future date.

In the context of risk reduction, the number of potential users of forward contracts is consequently determined by the number of people and firms facing uncertainty about future prices. Since this description applies to so many people and firms, why isn't there a forward contracting agent on every street corner? As we will discuss next, the answer lies in the potential for default.

Forward Contracts and Default

So far we have ignored default and transactions costs. However, the forward contract exhibits both performance risk and transactions costs. Since transactions costs for a forward contract are usually small,[2] we concentrate on performance risk.

Forward contracts are by nature credit instruments. Consider a FX forward contract in which you contract to deliver a specified number of dollars per deutsche marks one year in the future for a specified number of dollars. Suppose that this contract implies a forward rate of 3.0 DM/$ (the dollar price of a DM is $0.33). If, at contract maturity, the exchange rate has risen to 4DM per dollar (the price of a DM has fallen to $0.25), you are now richer. You can buy the DM for $0.25 and then sell them for $0.33, a profit of 8 cents per DM. Conversely, your counterparty—the party who agreed to buy the DM—is now poorer by the same amount. Suppose the buyer of the forward contract—the loser on this contract—decides to abrogate the contract. You are out a sum of money, just as would be the case if your counterparty reneged on a loan. In this sense, a forward contract is a credit instrument.

The fact that forward contracts entail credit risk is important in determining who gets access to the forwards markets. Individuals, institutions, corporations, and governments that have access to credit lines are able to use forward contracts. Those for whom the costs of creating credit lines are high relative to the benefits of using the forward contract do not participate in the markets. Realistically, then, the forward market is less appropriate for the individual, the sole proprietorship, or the small corporation. It is a market for large corporations, governments, and other institutions—both financial and nonfinancial—that have access to credit lines as a daily part of their business.

Foreign Exchange Forwards

Foreign exchange forwards are traded in most major currencies, with bid-asked spreads quoted in standard maturities of 1, 2, 3, 6, 9, and 12 months.[3] Moreover, for the major currencies—sterling, yen, or deutsche mark—quotes for four months, five months or other intervals are also available. On a negotiated basis, forwards are available in major currencies for "odd dates" (also referred to as "broken dates") as well. The extent to which a currency forward is available depends on whether exchange controls exist, the depth of alternative markets, and a country's monetary policy. Because of regulatory differences among domestic markets, the reference market used to price a forward (set a forward rate for a currency) is usually the Euromarket.

The forward foreign exchange markets—like the spot FX markets—are liquid and efficient and are used by sophisticated participants. The behavior of these markets will therefore be largely regulated by the legal contract under which they operate and the enforceability of that contract.

The Contract

Since forward contracts entail performance risk, the foreign exchange forward contract is written to address that risk, making the FX forward contract similar to that for a loan or a line of credit. The contract defines responsibility in payment once the contract matures, ensuring that nonperformance is equivalent to not making a payment on a loan.

After the two parties agree on the forward price for the future exchange of the underlying currencies, the parties specify other terms of the contract: the amount of one currency to be exchanged for a stated amount of the other, as well as the date and location of the exchange.

If the contract is to be cash-settled, it specifies the spot rate at the maturity date as the average of the bid-ask prices quoted by a specified bank for the spot purchase and spot sale, respectively, of the contract currency in exchange for U.S. dollars at a prescribed location (usually New York, London, or Tokyo) at a prescribed time (usually 11:00 A.M. local time).

Forward contracting requires the counterparties to agree on the forward price and settlement date and to exchange written confirmations. The settlement date of a forward contract is the date at which a contract is actually payable. For example, if on March 1 we agree to a three-month forward, the maturity date would be June 3, with the settlement date two days later.[4] These dates, as well as the date of origination of the contract, are stipulated in a confirmation telex exchanged between the contracting parties. As in a loan agreement, if one party is late in delivery of funds on contract settlement, penalty interest is incurred on the outstanding balance.

Not surprisingly, most forward contract documentation involves credit issues; pricing and settlement issues are a minority. Events of default receive particular attention, thereby underscoring the credit nature of the contract.

For a forward contract, the maturity date is the only relevant date in calculating the amount one party will owe the other on settlement date. That is, the legal agreement stipulates that the settlement flows are based only on the deviation in contract price from the spot price *on the maturity date*. According to the contract (though not necessarily from the contractors' perspectives), the time path that the foreign exchange rate follows between the origination date and the maturity date (when the settlement payment is calculated) is of no consequence.

The Forward Foreign Exchange Rate

The pricing of a foreign exchange forward contract is equivalent to determining the *forward foreign exchange rate*. In a sense, the forward rate is the wholesale price for the forward contract. To this, the dealer adds the bid-ask spread, which will be discussed in the next section.

Since the expected net present value of an at-market forward contract must be zero at origination, the easiest way to obtain the forward foreign exchange rate contract is to determine the exchange rate that guarantees that the net present value of the contract is zero. This relation is called *interest-rate parity;* the technique used to do this is called *covered-interest arbitrage*.

Panel A of Figure 6–3 illustrates the cash flows for a forward foreign exchange contract for the party who has agreed to *buy* deutsche marks forward (or, conversely, *sell* dollars forward). The party illustrated must pay, at period *T*, a set number of dollars in return for a set number of deutsche marks. Panel B illustrates that

FIGURE 6–3 A Forward Contract as a Pair of Loans

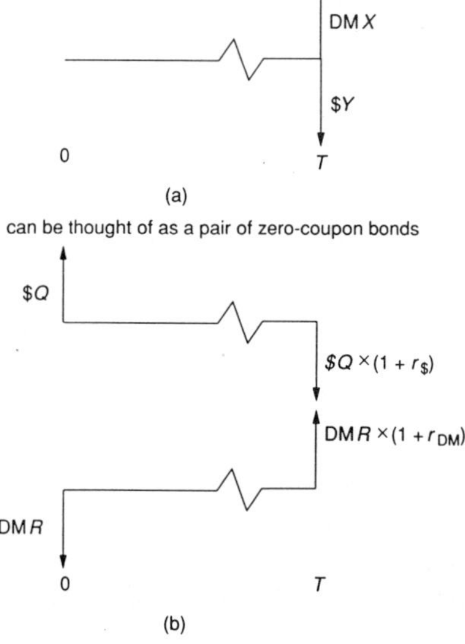

the cash flows in panel A could be replicated with a pair of zero-coupon loans (or notes). At contract origination (time zero), the party illustrated borrows Q dollars and simultaneously lends the equivalent amount in deutsche marks, R. That is, given the spot exchange rate between dollars and deutsche marks at time zero, S_0, Q dollars is equivalent to R deutsche marks—R DM = \$$Q \times S_0$. At maturity—at time T—the party illustrated will have to pay back $Q \times (i + r_{\$})$ dollars, where $r_{\$}$ is the U.S. dollar interest rate for maturity T, and will receive $R \times (1 + r_{DM})$ deutsche marks, where r_{DM} is the T-period rate for a deutsche mark borrowing. If the two cash flows diagrams illustrated in panel B were added together to obtain a single cash flow diagram, the result would be the forward contract illustrated in panel A, where

$$X\text{ DM} = R\,(1 + r_{DM})\text{ DM and } \$Y = \$Q\,(1 + r_{\$}). \tag{6–3}$$

Consequently, a forward contract for foreign exchange can be priced as if it were a pair of zero-coupon loans—the bullet repayments plus interest are netted against the future spot foreign exchange rate on the maturity date. Thus, from a purely mechanical pricing basis, the spot rate at origination, S_0, times the amount of the domestic currency, \$$Q$, fixes the amount of foreign currency to be lent. And with knowledge of the two relevant interest rates $r_{\$}$ and rDM, the amounts of the two cash flows to be exchanged at T are determined.

Therefore, the forward foreign exchange rate at contract origination, F_0, can be obtained by dividing the cash flows at T by one another:

$$F_0 = \frac{R \times (1 + r_{DM})}{Q \times (1 + r_{\$})}. \tag{6–4}$$

And since R deutsche marks equals \$$Q$ times the spot exchange rate at contract origination, $R = Q \times S_0$, it follows that the forward rate is

$$F_0 = S_0 \left[\frac{1 + r_{DM}}{1 + r_{\$}} \right] \tag{6–5}$$

Generalizing, we can express the forward exchange rate for currencies 1 and 2 at time t as

$$F_t = S_t \frac{(1 + r_2)}{(1 + r_1)}, \tag{6–6}$$

where the forward and the spot are defined at time t as the number of units of Country 2's currency per units of Country 1's currency. (For example, if Country 2 is Germany and Country 1 is the United States, $F(t)$ and $S(t)$ are defined in deutsche marks per dollar.)

Alternatively, Equation 6–6 can be written in the form often referred to as interest rate parity:

$$F_t/S_t = (1 + r_2)/(1 + r_1). \qquad (6\text{–}7)$$

That is, the ratio of forward rate to the spot is a reflection of the relation between the interest rates in the two countries.

If the interest rate in Country 2 is higher than in Country 1, then the forward rate is greater than the spot—or Country 2's currency is weaker in the forward market than Country 1's. Returning to dollars and deutsche marks, if the dollar interest rate is lower than the DM interest rate, the forward DM/$ rate is greater than the spot; an alternative way of saying the same thing is that the dollar would be selling at a *premium* to deutsche mark (or that DM is selling at a *discount* to today's spot rate).

Aside

Interest Rate Parity

The simplest way to illustrate the interest rate parity relation is to visualize the relation between currencies today and currencies in the future as a "box." In the following diagram we have continued using U.S. dollars and deutsche marks.

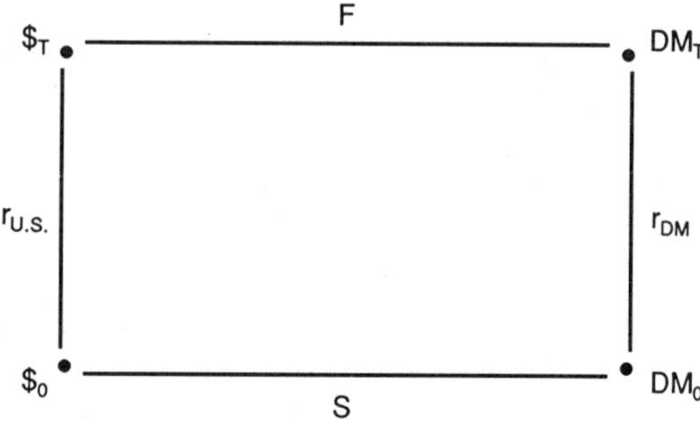

Dollars today ($\$_0$) are represented in the lower-left corner of the box; DM today are represented at the lower right. At the upper-left corner are future dollars ($\$_T$), and at the upper-right corner are future deutsche marks.

Four markets link these magnitudes:

1. Dollars today ($\$_0$) and dollars in the future ($\$_T$) are related by the U.S. credit market, which determines the domestic interest rate ($r_{U.S.}$).
2. German credit markets link deutsche marks today (DM_0) with future deutsche marks (DM_T), through the interest rate in Germany (r_{DM}).
3. Dollars today and DM today are linked by the spot currency market (S).

Interest Rate Parity concluded

4. Future DM and future dollars are linked through the forward/futures market (F).

We can get from future dollars to future DM via the forward currency market—across the top of the box. But we can also get from future dollars to future DM by going around the box the other way:

1. Borrow dollars today in the U.S. credit market.
2. Trade the current dollars received for current DM in the spot FX market.
3. Lend the DM today in the German credit market for future DM.

Since the same result can be achieved in two ways, arbitrage forces the price for DM in the future to be the same, regardless of the way we "move around the box." Therefore, the spot FX, forward FX, and credit market prices must be mutually consistent. The forward foreign exchange rate must be related to the spot rate via the domestic and foreign interest rates.

Illustration 6–1

Calculating a Forward Exchange Rate

On April 21, 1993, foreign exchange and interest rates were as follows:

Spot DM per dollars	1.6173
U.S. LIBOR (one-year)	0.03700
DM LIBOR (one-year)	0.06750

Using Equation 6–6, the one-year forward rate is

$$F = 1.6173 \times \left(\frac{1 + 0.06750}{1 + 0.03700}\right)$$
$$= 1.6649$$

The difference between the spot rate and the forward rate is called the *premium* if the difference is positive or the *discount* if the difference is negative. If the forward is less than spot, the DM is anticipated to be stronger in the future. If the forward is greater than spot, the DM is anticipated to be weaker in the future. In our example, the discount is 0.0476. Consequently, as of April 21, 1993, the DM is expected to be weaker against dollars in one year than it is at present.*

*The word "expected" might imply to some readers a theory of exchange rate determination, which is not the meaning intended here. Rather, we wish to convey that the forward rate is contracted in a way that, given existing market forces, implies a stronger future DM spot price.

Bid-Ask Spreads

In the preceding forward-rate calculations, we used what market participants normally refer to as *mid-rates*—the midpoint of the bid-ask spread. If buyers and sellers of FX forwards were to contract with each other directly, without having a dealer as an intermediary, the transactions would occur at this mid-rate. However, if a dealer is to provide immediacy—provide liquidity until the other side of the trade arrives—the dealer must earn a spread to cover the costs of creating the forward contract.

Since forwards are credit instruments, the dealers in the forward foreign exchange market are typically banks. The dealer (market maker) will quote one price to the buyer of FX forward and another price to the seller. In the spot and forward foreign exchange markets, prices are usually quoted in units of foreign

Illustration 6–2

Calculating a Forward Exchange Rate Again

On April 21, 1993, the relevant bid-ask spreads were:

Spot FX: DM per dollar	1.6168–1.6178
U.S. LIBOR (one-year)	0.03370–0.03500
DM LIBOR (one-year)	0.06750–0.06880

Utilizing Equation 6–6, we can calculate a bid-ask spread for the forward rate. To obtain the 12-month bid rate for the forward, we divide ($1 + r_{DM}$ bid) by ($1 + r_{US}$ ask) and then multiply by spot bid. The reverse is done to obtain the forward ask rate:

Forward rate
1.6676–1.6727

To understand the logic of this, let's construct the rate at which the dealer will buy DM in the future—the bid side on the forward rate. An alternative to buying the forward contract would be to borrow dollars, buy DM spot, and then invest the purchased DM for one year. Consequently, the relevant spot FX rate is the buy rate today—the bid spot rate—as our base. Since the dealer would be investing DM, the relevant DM interest rate is the deposit rate: the bid rate. Conversely, since the dealer would be borrowing dollars, he or she would have to pay the borrow rate—the ask rate. In our example the discount is 0.0508–0.0549.

Notice that the discount is quoted with the lower number first. Usually the foreign exchange forward market quotes the spot and then the forward premium or discount. If the currency is at a discount to the dollar as in this case (if DM interest rates are higher), then the lower figure is quoted first, which indicates that the numbers are added to the spot bid-ask spread.

currency per dollar.[5] Prices are quoted at the fourth decimal point for currencies such as deutsche marks, sterling, and Canadian dollars, and to the first or second decimal place for currencies such as Italian lira (trading at 1565.3 per dollar on March 2, 1993) or yen. The bid-ask spread on the major currencies in the spot market is very small. For example, on spot deutsche marks, the bid-ask spread is usually as low as 5 to 10 "pips," a pip being 1/10,000th of a DM. Thus, on April 21, 1993, at 10:30 A.M. EST, the Chase Manhattan Bank was showing a quote of DM/$ 1.6168/78 (DM/$ 1.6168 bid, 1.6178 offered).

The interest rate markets (the money markets) also operate on this bid-offer concept.[6] For example, on April 21 at 10:30 A.M. EST the 12-month Eurodollar deposit rate was 3.37–3.50, and the Euro–deutsche mark deposit rate was 6.75–6.88. Given this information, we can look again at the forward rate and the forward premium described in the previous example. But this time the exercise takes on a new twist: instead of mid-rates, we can calculate the relevant bid-ask forward rates.

To give you some idea how these prices actually appear in the market, we have in Figure 6–4 provided the spot and forward rates for some major currencies actually posted by the Chase Manhattan Bank on Reuters on April 21, 1993.[7]

FIGURE 6–4 Prices in the Foreign Exchange Market, Quoted on April 21, 1993
(Taken from Reuters Screens CMBX and CMBW)

Spot Prices

```
Apr 21 10:32 Reuters RDCDF Datafeed Service

0914 CHASE MANHATTAN BANK                                  CMBX
-GBP 1.5250/60       -XEU 1.2056/63       -SEK 7.5323/73
-DEM 1.6168/78       -FRF 5.4614/34       -NOK 6.8452/52
-JPY 112.41/51       -ITL 1547.57/37      -DKK 6.2065/85
-CHF 1.4790/00       -ESB 116.83/90       -FIM 5.5903/03
-AUD 0.7169/74       -NLG 1.8167/77       -THB
-CAD 1.2585/90       -BEF 32.459/74       -IDR
FIXING 11AM          FIXING 2PM           FIXING 2PM
GBP 1.5415/20        GBP 1.5415/20        GBPDEM 2.4679/95
                     LME 107/104          GBPJPY 171.33/47
```

Forward Prices (Discounts)

```
Apr 21 10:34 Reuters RDCDF Datafeed Service

CHASE MANHATTAN BANK LONDON - FORWARDS (SPOTS *CMBX*) CMBW
            GBP          DEM          JPY        CHF          XEU
WEEK                 16.2/16.6
 1M                  70/71                               61.5/60.5
 2M                  131/133                             119/117
 3M                  190/192                             171/169
```

FIGURE 6–4 ***(continued)***

Forward Prices (Discounts)
Apr 21 10:34 Reuters RDCDF Datafeed Service

CHASE MANHATTAN BANK LONDON - FORWARDS (SPOTS *CMBX*) CMBW

	GBP	DEM	JPY	CHF	XEU
6M		345/348			313/309
9M		456/461			420/410
12M		540/545			512/502

Key:

GBP = Pounds sterling
DEM = German marks
CHF = Swiss francs
FRF = French francs
BEF = Belgian francs
ITL = Italian lira
NLG = Dutch guilders
JPY = Japanese yen
AUD = Australian dollars
CAD = Canadian dollars
ESB = Spanish peseta
SEK = Swedish korna
NOK = Norwegian krone
DKK = Danish krone
FIM = Finnish marka
XEU = ECU

Note that currencies are quoted as units of foreign currency to dollars, except for sterling and ECU, which are quoted in dollars per unit of currency.

SOURCE: Reprinted by permission of Reuters.

Forward-Rate Agreements

Forward-rate agreements (FRAs) exist in various currencies, but the largest markets are in U.S. dollars, pounds sterling, deutsche marks, Swiss francs, and Japanese yen. Of these, the dollar and sterling interest FRA markets have the largest volume, because of the volatility of interest rates in these currencies. While the market is global, much of the business is done in London. Within the sterling and dollar markets, dealers will offer two-way quotes, with a bid-offer spread. This is, of course, similar to any actively traded securities market, and it closely parallels the forward foreign exchange market.

The Contract

Although each institution that deals in forward-rate agreements has its own "terms and conditions," the British Bankers Association (BBA) terms and conditions have become the industry standard.[8] Consequently, much of our discussion will refer to these terms and conditions.

Since a forward-rate agreement is a forward contract on interest rates and not a forward commitment to make a loan or take a deposit, the agreements under-score the notional-principal nature of the FRA—neither party has a commitment to lend or to borrow the contract amount. Furthermore, FRA contracts generally contain a "normal banking practice" clause that commits the parties to specific performance. If a party fails to perform, this clause makes the outstanding net cash value of the contract subject to the same conditions that would apply in the case of nonperformance on a loan. Such a clause highlights the fact that an FRA, like a foreign exchange forward, is a credit instrument. In a forward transaction, no value is conveyed at origin or over the life of the contract; all value is conveyed at maturity.

FRA transactions are normally done by phone or telex. Given the nature of the transaction, most firms require that phone conversations be taped. However, confirmation must be made in the form of a telex or registered letter.

This is the formula stated by the BBA for calculating the settlement of a forward contract:[9]

> Wherever two parties enter into an FRA the buyer will agree to pay to the seller on the settlement date (if the contract rate exceeds the BBA interest settlement rate), and the seller will agree to pay to the buyer on the settlement date (if the BBA interest settlement rate exceeds the contract rate) an amount calculated in accordance with the following formula:
>
> (a) when L is higher than R
>
> $$\frac{(L - R) \times D \times A}{(B \times 100) + (L \times D)},$$
>
> or
>
> (b) when R is higher than L
>
> $$\frac{(R - L) \times D \times A}{(B \times 100) + (L \times D)},$$
>
> where
>
> L = BBA interest settlement rate,
>
> R = contract rate,
>
> D = days in contract period,
>
> A = contract amount,
>
> B = 360 or 365 days, according to market custom.

The logic of the preceding formula is straightforward. The parties to the FRA agree on the forward interest rate (R). At the settlement date—in three months, in six months, or whatever—the actual rate (L) is observed in the market as the 11:00 A.M. London rate in the interbank market. The difference between L and R is now known. Depending if you were the buyer or seller, your gain or loss is this difference times the days in the contract period times the contract amount divided by the term $B \times 100$, which adjusts the days to the correct basis, plus the interest rate necessary to discount the original contract, $L \times D$.[10] To put some intuition into this rather dry formula, let's consider an illustration.

Illustration 6–3

An FRA Contract with Citicorp

Suppose a party entered into a FRA contract with Citicorp (CITI). The contracting party wants to be paid (to receive) income on a contract amount of USD 100 million if, in three months, the three-month USD LIBOR is more than the forward rate implied in today's yield curve (the three-month rate in three months). Let's suppose that the three-month forward rate is 10 percent. Neglecting for the moment the bid-ask spread, CITI would agree to pay if the settlement rate were above 10 percent and receive if the rate were below 10 percent.

Suppose that the contract is originated on March 15 with a June 15 spot date for determining the settlement rate, and actual transference of funds occurring two business days later—June 17 (the settlement date).

What happens if on June 15 the rate is exactly 10 percent? Nothing. Neither our contracting party nor CITI receives or pays. However, suppose that June 15 arrives and the three-month LIBOR rate determined by the reference bank in the contract is 11 percent. CITI must make a payment to the contracting party on June 17. How much does CITI pay? Before resorting to the formula, let's think it through logically. The notional amount is USD 100 million; the difference in settlement and contract rates is 1 percent; and the contract was for 92 days. First, we need to know how much the interest differential of 1 percent is worth for USD 100 million for 92 days (in a year with 360 days):

$$\$100{,}000{,}000\ (0.01)\ (92/360) = \$255{,}555.56.$$

This is the value after holding another three months, but the payments are going to be made at settlement, so the preceding amount must be discounted by the three-month LIBOR in effect:

$$\$255{,}555.56\ /\{1 + [.11\ \times (92/360)]\} = \$248{,}568.03.$$

We get precisely the same answer if we utilize the formula provided by the BBA:*

$$\frac{(L - R) \times D \times A}{(B \times 100) + (L \times D)}$$

$$= \frac{(11.00 - 10.00) \times 92 \times 100{,}000{,}000}{36{,}000 + [11.0 \times 92]}$$

$$= \frac{9{,}200{,}000{,}000}{37{,}012} = 248{,}568.03.$$

*Logically our intuitive approach could be written in this form:

$$\frac{A \times (L - R)/100 \times D/R\,,}{1 + [(L/100) \times (D/B)]}$$

which when manipulated algebraically exactly equals the BBA formula.

The Forward Interest Rate

In the previous discussion we took as given the contract rate—the forward interest rate. The fact is, however, that the forward interest rate, like the forward foreign exchange rate, can be derived from an arbitrage condition. To do so we will begin with an example, then generalize the arguments.

Illustration 6–4

Deriving a Forward Rate*

Suppose you have \$100 to invest for two years. Should you invest for one year, then reinvest the proceeds for another year, or should you invest for two years? Is there any difference?

In the first quarter of 1993, one-year investments were yielding approximately 4 percent, and two-year investments were yielding approximately 5 percent. Is the fact that the two-year rate exceeds the one-year rate sufficient information for you to make your decision?

No. To compare the two investments, you need to know not only the rates for one and two years but also the rate you would be able to invest for one year in one year's time—the *forward* rate.

In the same way that the foreign exchange forward rate must be that which eliminates arbitrage profit in the spot foreign exchange market and the interest rate markets for the currencies involved, the forward interest rate, f, must eliminate any potential arbitrage over time in a particular interest rate market. Borrowing (lending) for one year and then rolling the borrowing (lending) over for a second year,

$$[\$100\,(1 + .04)] \times [1 + f],$$

must be equivalent to the borrowing (lending) for two years,

$$\$100\,[1 + .05]^2.$$

Using this arbitrage relation,

$$[1 + f] = \frac{\$100\,[1 + 0.05]^2}{\$100\,[1 + 0.04]}.$$

So the one-year forward rate in one year must be 6.01 percent.†

The decision to invest in one year, then reinvest for the second year versus investing for the full two years can now be made. On the basis of the forward-rate calculation, the market's "expectation" for the one-year rate in one year is 6.01 percent. If you expect the one-year rate in one year to be higher than 6.01 percent, then invest for one year, planning to reinvest for a second year at the end of the first year. If, however, you expect the one-year rate in one year to be below 6.01 percent, the most appropriate strategy is to invest for two years today.

---

*Our discussion of these yield curve calculations is standard and is covered in many texts. For instance, see Brealey and Meyers (1988).

*Deriving a Forward Rate**

†Alternatively, we can look at the future values of the two strategies. If you invest for one year and roll over at the end of the first year, the future value is

$$FV = (1.04) \times 100 \times (1.0601) = 110.25.$$

If you invest for two years, the future value is

$$FV = (1.05)^2 \times 100 = 110.25.$$

The future value is the same from both strategies. Of course, if it were not, the forward rate we calculated would not be the arbitrage rate, and one strategy would dominate the other.

To generalize the formula for one-year investments, we recognize that the forward rate is implicit in the yield curve itself. For example, the one-year rate one year from today ($t = 0$), we solve the equation:

$$(1 + {}_0R_1)(1 + {}_1R_2) = (1 + {}_0R_2)^2, \tag{6–8}$$

where

${}_0R_1$ = the one-year interest rate today,

${}_0R_2$ = the two-year interest rate today,

${}_1R_2$ = the forward interest rate for one year in one year (i.e., the rate between years 1 and 2).

In general, the forward rate from year j to year k is given by ${}_jR_k$ in

$$(1 + {}_0R_j)^j (1 + {}_jR_k)^{k-j} = (1 + {}_0R_k)^k. \tag{6–9}$$

For periods less than one year, the equation must be modified. If we want to know the forward rate from month j to month k and if the interest rates are quoted as *simple rates*, we solve for ${}_jR_k$:

$$[1 + (j/12)\,{}_0R_j]\,[1 + ((k - j)/12)\,{}_jR_k] = [1 + (k/12){}_0R_k]. \tag{6–10}$$

If, however, the interest rates are quoted as compound rates, the appropriate formula is:

$$(1 + {}_0R_j)^{j/12} (1 + {}_jR_k)^{(k-j)/12} = (1 + {}_0R_k)^{k/12}.$$

Bid-Ask Spreads

In the same way that foreign exchange forwards evolved from parallel borrowing and depositing, FRAs evolved from *forward-forward contracts*. A forward-forward is an obligation in which one financial institution agrees to deposit money at another institution at a specified future date, at a specified interest rate (set at contract origination). Since physical deposits are to be made, the credit risk is obvious. The FRA evolved to separate the deposit risk from the interest rate risk. With an FRA, only the net interest flows need be exchanged, so the credit risk is reduced.

The language of the FRA market reflects this evolution; in the forward-forward market, the bid-offer spread is a deposit versus borrowing spread. Consequently, on a Reuters screen the FRA rate might be quoted, say, $3\frac{3}{4} - 3\frac{5}{8}$(i.e., you can *borrow* at $3\frac{3}{4}$ or *deposit* at $3\frac{5}{8}$). Of course, since FRAs are cash-settled forwards, there is no actual borrowing or deposit as would be the case with forward-forward contracts.

As with foreign exchange forwards, the bid-ask spread for an FRA is united by the actual cost associated with the physical depositing and borrowing that could occur instead of using the FRA. Indeed, since neither deposits nor borrowings occur, the bid-offer spread is more narrow for FRAs than for actual borrowings and deposits because the credit risk of the transaction has been reduced significantly. (There is, as pointed out earlier, still residual credit risk similar to that inherent in a forward foreign-exchange-rate contract.)

Figure 6–5 provides some insight into the bid-offer spreads for FRAs by reproducing a broker screen in Reuters. This screen presents quotes for three- and six-month UK sterling FRAs commencing in three months, four months, five months, and six months. Again, the jargon used in this market—3 V 6 for an FRA from month 3 to month 6 (a three-month rate in three months) and 5 V 11 for an FRA from month 6 to month 12 (a six-month rate in five months)—is a holdover from the forward-forward contract. Given the way forward interest rates are calculated, the indicative rates quoted reflect the forward rates from the zero-coupon sterling LIBOR curve.

FIGURE 6–5 Prices in the Forward Rate Agreement Market, Quoted on March 3, 1993 (Taken from Reuters Screen FRAS)

```
Mar 3 11:22   Reuters RDCDF Datafeed Service
1044 HILL SAMUEL LONDON TEL 071 606-1422 TLX 888471 FRAS
(FORWARD RATE AGREEMENTS) DEALING CODE - FRAS
                STG FRAS
3 V 6           5.50/45
4 V 7           5.40/35
5 V 8           5.35/30
6 V 9           5.30/25
9 V 12          5.33/28
3 V 9           5.45/40
4 V 10          5.39/34
5 V 11          5.37/32
6 V 12          5.35/30
RATES AT CLOSE TUES
```

Key:
The date 3M V 6M refers to a three-month FRA in three months; 4M V 7M refers to a three-month FRA in four months, and so on.

SOURCE: Reprinted by permission of Reuters.

Illustration 6–5

Booking an FRA

Suppose Banco Chase Manhattan of Brazil (BCM) wants to lock in its U.S. dollar LIBOR borrowing costs for three months, six months from now.

BCM's trader, having established that credit lines exist, calls Barclay's Bank in London. Since the yield curve is upward sloping, he knows that the quotes will be well above today's three-month LIBOR. (He has unraveled the yield curve to get the forward interest rate ${}_{3}r_{6}$.) But when he calls for a quote, he is not going to let Barclay's know whether he is going to deposit or borrow.

The Barclay's trader quotes 3.33–3.28 for "10 dollars" (a $10 million notional principal). Both understand that FRABBA terms apply (they have already exchanged master forward agreements). The BCM trader says no—his quote is for "12 dollars." The Barclay's trader requotes 3.33–3.28—exactly the same conditions. (For a very large amount of, say $100 million, the bid-offer spread could change.)

The Banco Chase Manhattan trader takes the 3.33 borrowing rate. BCM has now fixed its borrowing rate—though not the physical borrowing—for a three-month period in six months.

Notes

1. In "Central Bank Survey of Foreign Exchange Activity in April 1992," the Bank for International Settlements reported that forward foreign exchange volume (net of all double counting) was $384.4 billion per day in April 1992. (Daily spot FX volume was $393.7 billion.)
2. Transaction costs are small as a percentage of the forward contract size typically observed in the market. The cost of transacting has a high fixed-cost component, with very little marginal costs. Thus a $10,000 and a $10 million forward foreign exchange contract would have nearly the same transactions cost.
3. Longer-dated contracts do exist, in which case the bid-ask spreads are subject to negotiation.
4. Spot currency transactions are not actually dealt two days forward (with the exception of Canadian $/USD) and forwards are always quoted from spot. Thus, a March 1 spot quote is for March 3, so a three-month forward would be March 3 to June 3.
5. The exceptions to this rule are the pound sterling and the ECU, which are usually quoted as dollars per unit of sterling or ECU.
6. In this case we refer to the Euro markets; that is, the Eurodollar and Euro–deutsche mark markets.
7. Note in Figure 6–4 that the actual bid-ask spread for the forward premium for deutsche marks is smaller than the spread we calculated in our example—540/545 versus 508/549. The bid-ask spread in the forward market will likely be narrower than the arbitrage range spread because the credit risk inherent in the forward contract is less than that implied in the actual borrowing and deposit of funds that would be necessary to perform the arbitrage.
8. British Bankers Association (1985).
9. British Bankers Association (1985, Section D, p. 8).
10. For FRAs with a duration greater than 12 months, this formula is modified to create a series of one-year values for the contract, which are then discounted appropriately.

CHAPTER

7

Using Forwards to Manage Financial Price Risks

Forward contracts exist because they permit firms (as well as governments and some individuals) to separate financial price risk from the underlying business activity and transfer that price risk to another party. Forwards foster creativity. The creation of liquid forward foreign exchange markets, in various currencies, allows investors to develop customized investment strategies and firms to manage unavoidable business risks. In this chapter we will provide a few illustrations to show how forwards can be packaged to address the demands of financial institutions, industrial corporations, and portfolio managers.

The Choice between Forwards and On-Balance-Sheet Hedges

Consider, for example, a financial institution with a one-year exposure to the U.S. dollar–deutsche mark exchange rate. Suppose that, because the institution holds a significant portfolio of U.S. government bonds (denominated in U.S. dollars), the value of the financial institution is positively related to the value of the dollar. That is, if the value of the dollar rises in relation to the deutsche mark, the value of the financial institution will rise. Figure 7–1 shows this firm's risk profile.

The financial institution could manage this exposure by buying a forward contract on deutsche marks. Using the data from Chapter 6,

Spot DM per dollar = 1.6173

Dollar LIBOR (one-year) = 3.70 percent

DM LIBOR (one-year) = 6.75 percent

The financial institution could buy DM in one year at a rate of 1.6649 DM per dollar ($0.60 per DM). As illustrated in Figure 7–2, if the value of the dollar in one

FIGURE 7–1 An Illustrative Risk Profile

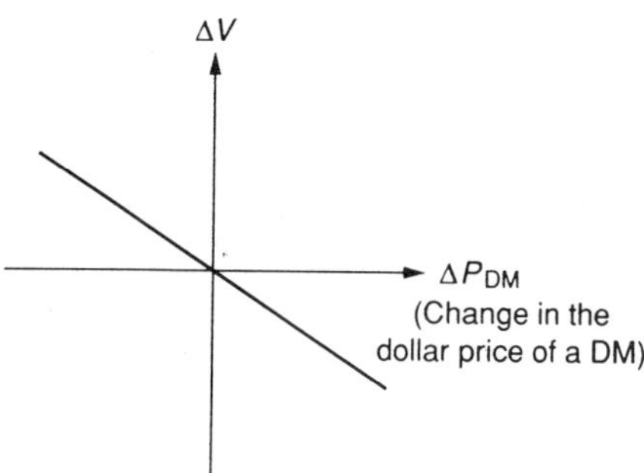

As the value of the dollar rises, P_{DM} falls and the value of the firm rises. As the value of the dollar falls, P_{DM} rises and the value of this firm falls.

year falls, the decline in the value of the investment portfolio will be offset by an increase in the value of the forward contract, and vice versa.

By using the forward contract, the financial institution transfers its foreign exchange risk to the seller of the forward contract. The financial institution that buys a forward contract on DM has neutralized its exposure to deutsche mark–U.S. dollar movements; as illustrated in Figure 7–3, the exposure now rests with the seller of the forward contract.

However, the financial institution could have achieved the same result using its balance sheet. As we described in Chapter 6, a long foreign exchange forward position can be created synthetically by borrowing dollars, buying DM (spot), and investing in a DM-denominated financial asset. In the context of the financial markets, the balance sheet of the financial institution would look as follows:

Assets	*Liabilities*
One-year Euro–deutsche mark deposit 10 million DM at 3.70 percent	One-year Eurodollar deposit \$6.183 million at 3.70 percent

Since firms have the alternative of using their balance sheet to manage risk, why would they use the forward market? One answer is default risk. A firm that uses its balance sheet must accept the credit risk of the institution or individual to whom it loans deutsche marks—with whom it makes the Euro–deutsche mark deposit. (By the same token, the individual placing the Eurodollar deposit with a financial institution has accepted that institution's credit risk.)

FIGURE 7–2 Hedging with a Forward Contract

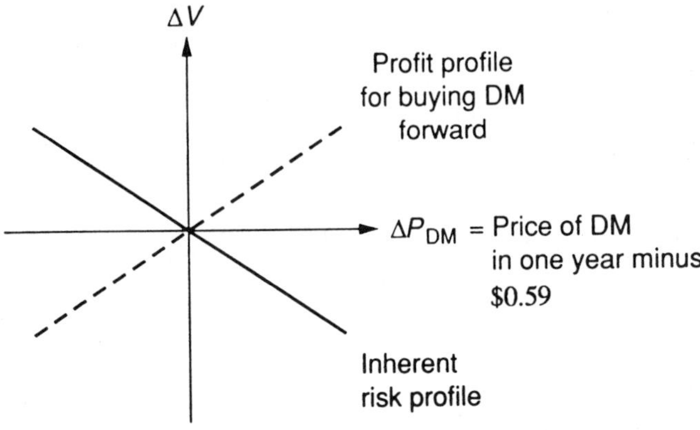

FIGURE 7–3 The Exposure of a Seller of a Forward Contract

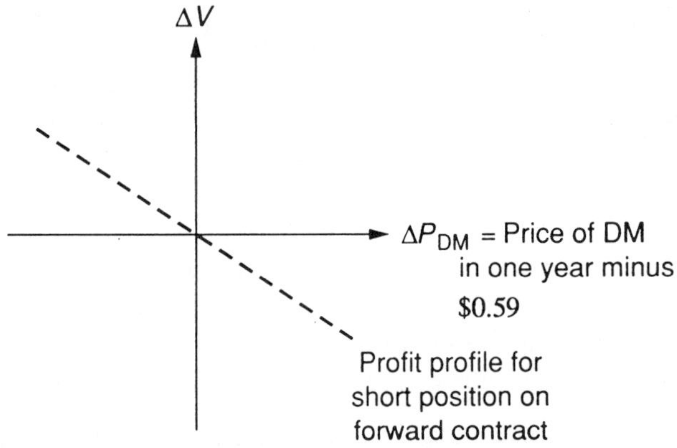

A forward contract does not *eliminate* the credit risk inherent in the on-balance-sheet hedge, but the risk is *reduced substantially,* since actual deposits are not created in the transaction. The amount at risk with a forward depends on the degree to which spot prices deviate from the forward price embedded in the forward contract. If spot prices behave as predicted by the forward prices at contract origination, the forward contract has no credit risk. As spot prices become more volatile and deviate further from the forward price, then the amount at risk is greater. Nonetheless, it is always less than the credit risk associated with the creation of offsetting positions on the balance sheet. Since credit risk is not costless (ease of transaction and regulatory issues aside), the forward market creates a less expensive alternative to making and taking deposits.

For many firms, transactions costs provide another reason to use forwards rather than the balance sheet. The transactions costs associated with the deposit arbitrage are high relative to transactions costs in the forward market.

However, regulation can be important in determining whether the firm hedges with forwards or through its balance sheet. For example, where exchange controls exist, offsetting back-to-back loans between parents and subsidiaries can sometimes be utilized to accomplish the task normally left to the forward market.

The Markets

In Chapter 6 we concentrated on the forward markets for foreign exchange and interest rates (FX forwards and FRAs), but forward markets also exist for commodities—gold, oil, and so forth. Some of these forward contracts have joined FX forwards and FRAs as part of the standard trading operations of large financial institutions.[1] Other forward contracts are traded outside traditional interbank markets. For example, forward contracts on North Sea crude oil (Brent) and forward contracts on primary metals are traded on the London Metal Exchange.

In the foreign exchange market, volume figures compiled by the Bank for International Settlements (Table 7–1) indicated that, by 1992, daily volume for forward foreign exchange contracts was $384 billion, about 64 percent of total volume in the foreign exchange market.[2] Trading continues to be dominated by DM/$, £/$, and Yen/$, followed by SF/$ and various nondollar to nondollar deals.

TABLE 7–1 Reported Foreign Exchange Market Turnover, by Market Segment: Daily Averages, April 1992

	Net-net Turnover*	
Market Segment	*In Billions of US Dollars*	*Percentage share*
Total Gross Turnover†	832.0	100
of which:		
Spot market	393.7	47
Forwards	384.4	46
of which:		
Outright	58.5	7
Swaps	324.3	39
Futures	9.5	1
Options	37.7	5

*Adjusted for both local and cross-border double-counting.

†Totals do not sum owing to incomplete reporting of market segment.

Trading in foreign exchange (excluding FX forwards) is concentrated in London, New York, Hong Kong, and Tokyo. But the market is truly global. Major dealing centers can be divided by time zones. Books are moved round-the-clock:

→London→New York→Tokyo→Hong Kong→

The major time zones can be divided into trading centers and subcenters, depending on currency:

Far East	*Middle East*	*Europe*	*Americas*
Tokyo	Bahrain	London	New York
Hong Kong		Paris	Chicago
Singapore		Zurich	Toronto
Sydney		Geneva	San Francisco
		Frankfurt	

Other centers, though on much smaller scales, include Brussels, Luxembourg, Madrid, Milan, Amsterdam, Munich, Hamburg, Kuwait, Kuala Lumpur, Los Angeles, Montréal, and Johannesburg.

Many currencies can be dealt either directly or indirectly in the FX forward markets. These foreign currencies are currently traded:

U.S. dollar	With ease
Pound sterling	
Deutsche mark	
Swiss franc	
French franc	
Canadian dollar	
Japanese yen	
Dutch guilder	
Danish krone	Less liquid but quotes are readily available
Irish punt	
Italian lira	
Finnish mark	
Belgian franc	
Spanish peseta	
Austrian schilling	
Australian dollar	
Singapore dollar	
Hong Kong dollar	
Kuwait dinar	
New Zealand dollar	
Malaysian ringit	
South African rand	
Portuguese escudo	
Thai baht	
Saudi riyal	
Swedish krone	
Norwegian krone	
ECU	
SDR	

The FRA market is also growing. Annual turnover in 1988 was estimated to be $300 to $500 billion, up from only $50 billion in 1985. Growth has been primarily in the interbank market, where FRAs are used as an effective tool for asset and liability management. But FRAs are becoming more widely used by corporate treasurers to manage interest rate risk. Though less than 10 percent of all FRA transactions now involve nonfinancial corporations, that percentage is expected to rise to 20 percent as the market becomes more developed.

Average sizes of forward-rate-agreement transactions are $5 million to $20 million, although contracts to $100 to $200 million are not unusual. The most liquid markets are in dollars and sterling, but deutsche marks are becoming more important; they threaten to overtake the leaders as the most traded currency.[3]

Most trading continues to be done in London with over 150 traders said to be trading FRAs. Considering the close relation between FRAs and interest rate swaps, which we described in Chapter 2, one might expect New York to dominate trading, at least in dollar FRAs, but this has not happened. Indeed, as with the forward foreign exchange market, London continues to dominate trading. Markets for both FRAs and FX forwards tend to be more liquid with finer bid-ask spreads in London trading hours.

Foreign Exchange Forward Trading

FX forwards are normally traded in conjunction with the spot foreign exchange desk and the deposit desk. As shown in illustration 7-1, this practice allows the risk to be broken apart and reassembled into different forms.

In this example, the trader used the "typical" way of synthetically creating a hedge for the forward position. There are others. For example, the trader could have closed the spot leg and left open the deposit by putting the dollars in an overnight account or, if it were more convenient, used a 3-month deposit with a 3- versus 12-month FRA. (Indeed, because of volatility of the spot rates, most traders are likely to close the spot leg first, then worry about the other prices of the transaction.)

What is important to remember is that FX forwards, deposits, and FRAs can be put together to create alternative ways to close or open positions. Traders must open and close legs in the most cost-efficient way in order to maximize the return on their positions.

FRA Trading

Like foreign exchange forward trading, FRA trading is driven by arbitrage—in this case, the arbitrage of taking and placing deposits for mismatched dates. Consequently, the FRA is a vehicle that permits the user to move up and down the yield curve, leaving the balance sheet intact.

Trading FRAs is best illustrated by another example. (See Illustration 7-2) This time we will begin with a user of FRAs and then turn our user into a trader.

Illustration 7–1

Laying off an FX Forward

George Brown trades FX forwards at the London branch of XYZ Bank of Hong Kong. He makes a market in DM/$ forwards and is responsible for managing the risk of his position. Available to him on the trading room floor are the related markets: spot foreign exchange, Eurodeposits, FRAs, and all the rest.

On July 5, 1988, he received a call from BHZ Co. of Birmingham, a firm he has talked to on a regular basis for several years. BHZ sells products it buys from a U.S. manufacturer in Germany. BHZ is long deutsche marks and short dollars.

BHZ: George, how's the dollar?
George: DM/$1.6800–1.6810, with the deutsche mark trading lower [weaker] in active trading.
BHZ: I am worried about a commitment we have in 12 months. If we get a bounce [if the deutsche mark gets stronger], let's cover for 50 dollars [$50 million] for 12 months outright.
George: Okay, the premium now for 12 months is 355/345, so the 12-month forward should be at DM/$1.6445–1.6465.
BHZ: Call me back in about an hour.

One hour and 20 minutes later and spot has moved against BHZ. The DM has weakened further and is now trading at DM/$1.6900/10 spot. George calls BHZ with the bad news.

BHZ: Hello, George? Okay! That's awful.
George: No sign of intervention in Frankfurt but the SNB [Swiss National Bank] has done a FX swap for $120 million against Swissie for three months.
BHZ: What's an FX swap?
George: This is a forward outright with a spot transaction. It's designed to push interest rate differentials and soak up francs simultaneously. The Swiss are trying to break the strength in the dollar. Odds are the Bundesbank will be in later, but I'm not sure the Fed is committed. We'll have to watch when New York opens.
BHZ: Okay, call me if the Fed comes in by 3:00 P.M.

George calls BHZ at 4:00 P.M.

George: BHZ? Okay, the Fed's in and the spot has retreated to DM/$1.6795–1.6805. I think you should cover now.

BHZ: Okay, I'll cover; I want to buy dollars, 12 months forward for a size equal to $50 million.

George: Fine, done at DM/$1.6460 for $50 million.

How then does George lay off this position? He may be lucky enough to find someone who will sell $50 million in 12 months at his ask price (DM/$ 1.6440), giving him a profit of $100,000.

However, if George can't find that forward seller of dollars, he can lay off the position in the cash markets. In July 1988, the

Laying off an FX Forward continued

12-month deposit rate for dollars was 8 percent, so equation 6–5 and the techniques in the example of pages 151-53 indicate that the "no-arbitrage" DM borrowing rate would be 5.78 percent. For the forward contract he just concluded with BHZ, George knows that in 12 months, he will receive DM 82.3 million and will have to pay $50 million. If he borrows DM 77,803,000 at 5.78 percent, converts the DM into $46,297,500 at today's spot rate (1.6805) and then deposits the dollars at 8.00 percent, George would just break even:

Today	*In 12 Months*
Borrow DM 77,803,000	Owe DM 82,300,000
Convert the borrowed DM at spot rate of 1.6805→$46,297,500	
Deposit $46,297,500	Deposit worth $50,000,000

However, George wants to do better than just break even. It might be the case that the DM money market trader at XYZ Bank of Hong Kong is particularly aggressive and is willing to lend at an attractive rate.* If, for instance, the DM money market desk is willing to lend him DM for 12 months at 10 basis points below the market rate (at 5.68 percent) George can earn a profit of $43,800.

Today	*In 12 Months*
Borrow DM 77,876,600	Owe DM 82,300,000
Convert the borrowed DM at spot rate of 1.6805→$46,341,300	
Deposit $46,297,500	Deposit worth $50,000,000
Profit of $43,800	

*A real-life George may have had access to an aggressive DM lending rate because the bank had unmatched DM yield curve positions being managed in its Frankfurt office.

In Illustration 7–2, Gobibank utilizes an FRA trader to manage the bank's own interest rate risk. In this case the trader is constantly adjusting the FRA book in response to the bank's funding position. The FRA trader will adjust bids and offers away from the midpoint, depending on the bank's inherent position as a taker or a

Illustration 7–2

Gobibank

Gobibank, located in the midwestern United States, has $5 billion in assets. Gobi deals with small corporations, and, as the area's premier consumer bank in its market, directly with the public.

Gobibank has just formed a syndication with the New York branch of a Swiss bank and a major U.S. investment bank. In this syndication Gobibank agreed to provide $200 million on a two-year fixed-rate basis.

Gobi's Asset and Liability Management Committee has been convened to discuss the bank's increased exposure to interest rates. Before the transaction, the bank had a "square" (matched-maturity) asset and liability position. With the addition of the syndication, Gobi has increased its assets by $200 million. This increase is currently being funded on an overnight basis in the Fed funds market. To replace the Fed funds borrowing, Gobi expects that it can increase its placings of six-month CDs with the state pension fund.* The A/L committee decides to issue the CDs—Gobi's cheapest form of funding. However, funding the two-year syndication with six-month CDs leaves Gobi with a mismatched maturity. (In terms of our maturity gap discussion in Chapter 5, Gobi has a "negative gap.")

Three months later the Asset and Liability Management Committee meets again: the CDs will be rolled over in another three months; the loans have one year and nine months to go, but the bank's management is worried that interest rates will rise. Indeed, Gobi's management is extremely concerned about a spike in rates just when Gobi will need to issue the new CDs. The managers of Gobi tell their treasurer to "get them through" the upcoming refunding.

The treasurer has a dilemma. Does she issue new CDs now and seek out additional assets? Does she issue new CDs now and place the proceeds in the Euromarket for three months? In either of these cases the treasurer would "blowup" (increase) Gobi's balance sheet by an extra $200 million for three months. Given capital-adequacy ratios,† the treasurer decides instead to manage Gobi's exposure off-balance-sheet.

She calls Gobi's interbank contact at DDF Bank in New York. After a short discussion, she decides to leave Gobi's position funded on a six-month basis but to use an FRA to lock in the bank's borrowing costs in three months' time. On the Reuters screen, three-month versus nine-month FRAs are being quoted as 3.44–3.38. That is, the implied six-month rate three months from now is about 3.41. With a bid-offer spread of 3 basis points around the midpoint, Gobi's treasurer will lock in a rate of 3.44 percent.

Having learned about this technique of managing the bank's interest rate risk, the treasurer decides that FRAs can be a better way to manage interest rate risk than actually taking and placing funds. Consequently, she hires an FRA trader to manage Gobi's risk. The trader will work closely with Gobi's funding desk to shift Gobi's risk profile—in other words, the maturity gap. The treasurer can now finance assets with the "cheapest"

Gobibank continued

source of funds relative to the market (the CD, in this case) and use FRAs to restructure Gobi's interest rate risk, depending on asset maturity mixes. No longer does the treasurer have to be as active in all different instruments on the liability side—from Fed funds to bonds—merely to shift interest rate risk.

*The pension fund buys the CDs in $100,000 amounts, getting a FDIC-guaranteed instrument at a higher rate than other government paper.

†The additional $200 million would require that this U.S. bank add an additional $14.86 million to its capital.

placer of funds of various maturities. Open positions will be covered in the funding book and vice versa. So, the FRA trader is an integral part of the bank's treasury operation.

However, FRAs need not be traded in conjunction with a natural position. While the trader can run a FRA book using only other FRAs to hedge risk, it is more likely that FRAs will be traded with other instruments—that is, by a swaps trader or a futures trader. FRA positions can be substituted (or hedged) in these other markets as well. As we will see in Chapter 18, integration of risk across markets and exploitation of natural positions are the keys to a company's success in FRA trades.

End Users

Managing Foreign Exchange Risk

A primary use of FX forwards is to hedge transactions exposures. The easiest way for us to describe the techniques and problems involved in this application is through an illustration.

While FX forwards have heretofore been used primarily by industrial corporations to hedge transaction exposures—FX positions they do not want—FX forwards can be and are used by portfolio managers to manage their exposures. Illustration 7-3 helps explain this point.

Illustration 7–3

Hedging Transaction Exposures

SSW of North America, Inc., a subsidiary of a major German firm, imports and distributes German-made SSW cars. SSW of North America entered the U.S. market in 1984 when the dollar averaged DM 2.84. At that exchange rate, SSW realized a 20 percent profit margin on each imported automobile it sold in the United States.

Recognizing that the SSW was in the U.S. market for the long haul, the firm brought capital into the United States and converted it into dollars. It contracted to hire Americans and distribute its autos through American-owned-and-operated outlets, with the autos priced in U.S. dollars. The key to its strategy was to sell *at least* 50,000 cars per year (a goal that seemed likely at 2.8 deutsche marks per dollar). If, however, SSW were to sell only 20,000 cars, it would suffer a loss (at the same price per car).

At the end of 1984, the U.S. dollar had strengthened to more than DM 3.0, so the dollar price of a German auto had fallen, and the profit outlook for SSW of North America was bright. Indeed, when the time came to import the cars for sale in 1985, the dollar was so strong against the DM that SSW would have a profit margin of 30 percent if it could achieve its sales goal of 50,000 units.

To lock in this windfall, SSW's CEO instructed the treasurer of SSW to hedge all the foreign exchange risk for 1985. Aware of the well-functioning market for foreign exchange forward contracts, the treasurer turned to this instrument to accomplish his task. But how much should he hedge, and how?

Within SSW of North America, dollars were coming in on each car (with a 30- to 60-day delay), and DM were going out. The lag from importation to sales was fairly predictable. The treasurer—knowing with reasonable certainty how much SSW of North America would receive for each car, how many cars would be imported per month during the year, and the latest forward foreign exchange rates—was ready to deal.

But how would he deal? Where would he deal? He started by calling his local banker, but the banker had no idea what the treasurer was talking about. "In this area we don't get too many requests for foreign exchange forwards," said the banker, who referred the treasurer to a money-center bank.

After listening to the treasurer's request, the money-center bank's account officer's response was immediate: "No problem." (The treasurer's years of experience, however, made him leery; whenever a banker says "no problem," there usually was one.)

The account officer passed the treasurer on to the dealing desk, where the problems began. The traders seemed to be speaking another language. When the treasurer asked for a price for the forward contract on DM/USD, they responded with: "Ten dollars at big figure 80/90." The account officer translated: 10 dollars? (10 million dollars.) Big figure? (The closest pfennig.)

And there were more questions: Did the treasurer want to hedge the DM purchase price in dollars on a monthly basis, weekly basis, yearly average, or what? Would the DM import price vary over the year?

Hedging Transaction Exposures continued

After resolving questions, the SSW treasurer elected to hedge DM 187,500,000 per month, with the first settlement in three months. But how would the treasurer implement the hedge? He knew that the next month and each month thereafter, he would have to come up with DM 187.5 million. But how?

The account officer said, "It is obvious. SSW will have to enter into a set of 12 forward contracts. The first contract is for one month, the second is for two months, and so forth on out to 12 months. Each contract is for the present value of 187.5 million DM." Relieved, the treasurer of SSW instructed the account officer to implement the hedge.

The treasurer thought the plan was set, but the account officer called back to say the 8-, 10-, and 11-month forwards were not "standard"; they would be a little more difficult and therefore more expensive to do. The treasurer, having gone so far, said, "Okay do it."

A week later the treasurer thought he could return to his job of managing lines of credit and investing excess corporate cash and finally forget about foreign exchange exposure for a while. But the account officer called again. "Sorry, but you have not signed a master foreign exchange forward agreement, so the back office at the bank rejected the forward order you placed yesterday." Too tired and busy to start over, the treasurer said to send out the document and he would have SSW's lawyers go over it.

By January 1985, the lawyers had spent two weeks looking over the document. The treasurer signed it and placed the order for 12 forward contracts (adjusting for the time lost during the discussions).

Yet the process was still not quite over. The account officer called back to say that SSW of North America had a low credit rating; it would have to provide collateral. Getting angry, the treasurer pointed out that SSW's debt was guaranteed by its AAA-rated German parent. Realizing that SSW was ready to do business elsewhere and acknowledging the parent's guarantee, the account officer backtracked and approached the credit chain of the bank for a foreign exchange credit line for SSW of North America.

Finally, the order was placed and executed. SSW was set for the year. The treasurer could see the CEO and report that everything was okay.

In the meantime, the dollar had strengthened even more and the treasurer was looking like a genius for taking so long to put on the hedge, thereby increasing the firm's profit margin. The CEO was happy. But just before the treasurer left for vacation, the CEO showed up with questions: "Which way do you think the dollar will go from here? Shouldn't we take our profit now?"

Illustration 7–4

Deutsche Marks, Pounds, Dollars, and Yield Curves

As the 1980s neared their end, Jim Davis, the manager of a U.S. dollar–based portfolio, had decided to go short dollars and long the mark. But he also liked longer-term instruments, since he was expecting long rates to fall globally. He wanted to be long DM bonds, but he wanted to pick up yield over the DM bond and have sterling–dollar FX risk.

In early 1988 he saw his opportunity: when Margaret Thatcher and Nigel Lawson had a public row over monetary policy and the lid came off the DM/£ exchange rate, Jim moved quickly by calling Diane Johnson, a trader at a major U.S. dealer in London:

Jim: I want to get long against DM but I don't want gilt risk. [Gilts are UK government bonds in sterling.]
Diane: Fine; how about this strategy? (1) Buy DM spot with dollars. (2) Purchase a 10-year DM bond yielding 6.04 percent p.a. (3) Do a one-year sterling forward against DM picking up the premium of another 6 percent. We run it two months and unwind. You make money if spot DM strengthens against dollars, if spot sterling strengthens against DM, or if DM bond interest rates fall. And you have a "yield-curve arbitrage tool."
Jim: What do you mean "yield-curve arbitrage tool?"
Diane: Look at the shapes of the three yield curves. The sterling yield curve is flat out to 10 years with 10-year gilts at about 10 percent (1-year was also about 10 percent), while 10-year DM bonds are at 6 percent, and the 1-year rate is 3.5.
Jim: Maybe I should change my mind about the sterling risk and just buy gilts?
Diane: No way! Gilt rates are three times as volatile as DM bond rates; besides, over the carry period you pick up yield over the gilt rate through the differently shaped yield curve.
Jim: Sketch me the position and fax it over.

Diane's fax arrives:

	Assets	Liabilities	
		Dollars	7.0%
6.5%	+£ −DM 1 year		
6.0%	DM bonds		

Jim: Diane? Good, do it for the equivalent of $25 million.
Diane: Okay, let's confirm: (1) Buy £ one-year forward against DM; (2) Convert USD spot to DM; (3) Buy DM bonds.
Jim: Right. Do it.
Diane: Fine. Your rates are. . . .

Epilogue. Jim did well. DM/£ went from 3.00 to 3.17. The dollar declined, with little change in DM bonds. Jim unwound on Diane's advice and was promoted.

Managing Interest Rate Risk

One of the most apparent and widely publicized examples of firms subject to interest rate risk is found in the experience of the U.S. savings and loan associations (S&Ls) during the late 1970s and early 1980s. Let's consider the asset and liability structure of a typical 1970s S&L. As illustrated in Figure 7–4, the S&Ls' liabilities were short-term deposits that would be repriced frequently—daily, monthly, or semiannually—while the S&Ls' assets were long-term mortgages. The difference between the interest paid on the government-insured, short-term deposit on

FIGURE 7–4 A Stylized Balance Sheet for a S&L in the Mid-1970s

Assets	*Liabilities*
Mortgages	Government-insured deposits
	Equity

the liability side and the interest earned on the more lucrative, long-term mortgage on the asset side was *net interest income (NII)*. In the mid-1970s, short-term deposit rates were in the neighborhood of 6 percent, while long-term mortgage rates were in the neighborhood of 10 percent. On assets of $100 million, net interest income would be $4 million. This yield-curve spread, or gapping (owning a long-term asset funded with short-term borrowings), was typical for S&Ls. Indeed, the managers of S&Ls were, at the time, considered conservative bankers.

However, when the yield curve started shifting in the very early 1980s, the position of the S&Ls changed dramatically. By 1982, long-term rates had risen 10 percent to about 11 percent, but average short-term deposit rates had made a dramatic leap: from 6 percent to 12 percent. Let's presume that the S&L stayed at the same size ($100 million) and that one fourth of its mortgage loans had matured and had been replaced with new mortgage loans at the new higher rates. Now interest earned was

$$10\% \times (\$75 \text{ million}) + 11\% \times (\$25 \text{ million}) = \$10.25 \text{ million.}$$

However, the S&L was still supported by short-term deposits, so interest paid was

$$12\% \times (\$100 \text{ million}) = \$12 \text{ million.}$$

Hence NII was a *negative* $1.75 million.

As a result of interest rate volatility, NII swung from a plus $4 million to a negative $1.75 million. If an instrument had been available to manage that interest rate risk, it would certainly have helped.[4] For the moment, let us assume that a market in interest rate forward contracts, such as forward-rate agreements (FRAs), had existed.

And instead of waiting around for the crash, let's suppose that in 1979 the manager of the S&L decided to use a forward-rate agreement to hedge interest rate risk. Given the balance sheet in Figure 7–4, the manager is aware of the need to adjust the S&L's cash flows to protect against a rise in the cost of funding in case short-term rates rise. Utilizing the forward market in interest rates, the manager can neutralize the costs of unanticipated changes in rates.

The risk profile for this S&L is illustrated in Figure 7–5: if interest rates rise, the firm could be forced into bankruptcy. Conversely, if rates fall, the S&L would make more profit. If rates remain as predicted by current forward rates, the expected profit is considered satisfactory. Consequently, the manager of the S&L decides to hedge, thereby neutralizing the effects of a volatile money market.

How do S&L managers create this hedge? They need the hedge to throw off a neutralizing cash flow with the same periodicity as the repricing of their liabilities, let's say every three months. To do so, they must construct a forward position such that if interest rates are greater than expected in the future, they will receive a payment, and if they are less they make a payment. But they must construct the position such that the cash flows are thrown off every three months. Thus, they must construct a set of FRAs, one expiring every three months for the next, say, three years.

As illustrated in Figure 7–6, the FRAs offset the cash flows on the $100 million short-term deposits. Here, the manager chooses a partial hedge; the notional

FIGURE 7–5 The Risk Profile for the S&L

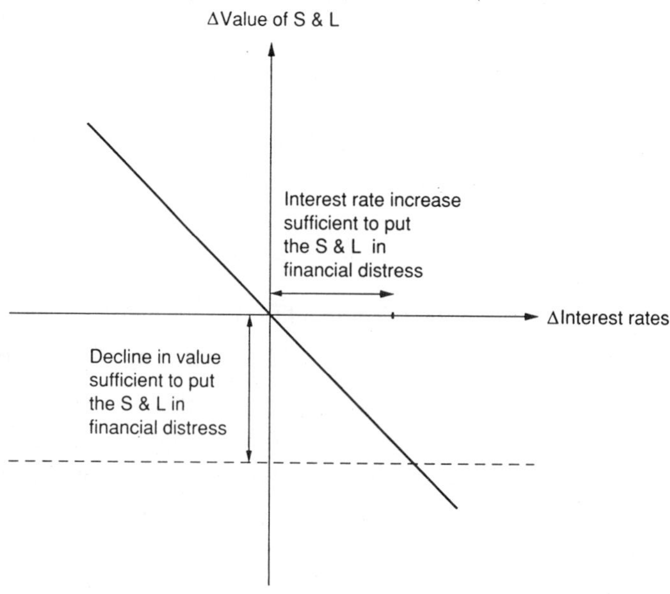

FIGURE 7–6 The Hedged S&L's Risk Profile

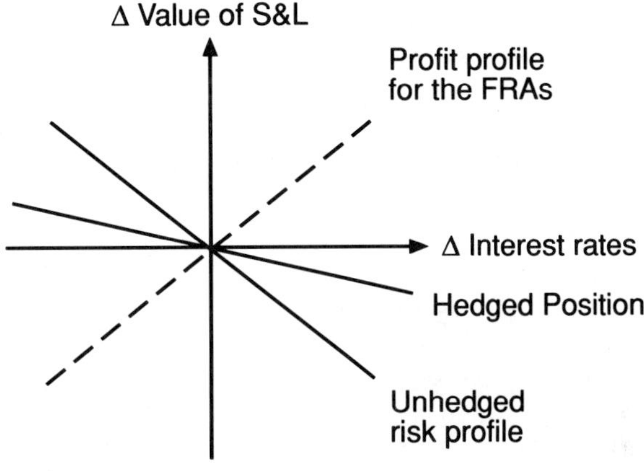

Illustration 7–5

Using FRAs in an Insurance Company*

George Demitri is the asset manager for ADS Insurance Company of New York. ADS writes life insurance policies in San Francisco, Los Angeles, and (through its Japanese subsidiary) Tokyo. As with any insurance company, the maturity profile of his portfolio is designed to match expected benefit payments (retirement, death, and so forth). In general these liabilities (payments) are of long-term duration. So are his assets, except for one portion concentrated in money market instruments, including T-bills.

Increasing maturity ↓	Assets	Liabilities
	2 billion	100 million
	19 billion	2 billion
		18.9 billion

Using FRAs in an Insurance Company continued

But George has a problem. His boss is demanding higher yield on the short-term portfolio. George is told to maintain liquidity but to increase yield. George knows that to maintain liquidity he must stay in very liquid, short-dated, low-yielding U.S. Treasuries. (Liquidating a billion dollars of paper to get cash in an emergency—when an earthquake hits San Francisco or Tokyo—is not all that easy if it is tied up in mortgage-backed securities or Australian bonds.)

George notes that the yield curve is upward sloping, so instruments of longer duration increase his yield. Three-month rates are around 3 1/4 percent, and the five-year rate is over 6 percent. If only he could invest long term while at the same time maintaining liquidity, he could pick up yield. And he can. He can keep his short-term portfolio in place but use an FRA to "synthetically" construct a longer-term instrument.†

George decides to try to "extend the maturity" of $100 million in six-month Eurodeposits to three years. His six-month deposits are yielding 3.6 percent. George wants to lock in the premium of the three-year yield relative to the 3.6 percent six-month yield. The way he will do this is with a series of FRAs.

Instead of starting at the beginning, let's look at the end. George wants to lock in a rate three years from now: in other words, in three years, he wants to pay six-month LIBOR and get some guaranteed rate. What is the six-month rate in three years? He must get banks to bid on an FRA of this duration.

While such a long forward interest rate—a six-month rate in three years—is not readily available on a Reuters screen, it can be calculated using the spot yield curve. The spot Eurodollar yield curve was as follows:

	Yield
6 month	3.60%
12 month	4.00
18 month	4.40
24 month	4.70
30 month	5.00
36 month	5.25
42 month	5.50

From this yield curve, George calculated the implied 6-month rate in 36 months, ${}_{36}R_{42}$:

$$(1 + {}_0R_{36})^3 (1 + {}_{36}R_{42})^{1/2} = (1 + {}_0R_{42})^{3.5}$$

$$(1.0525)^3 (1 + {}_{36}R_{42})^{1/2} = (1.055)^{3.5}$$

$$(1 + {}_{36}R_{42})^{1/2} = \frac{1.2061}{1.1659} = 1.0345$$

$${}_{36}R_{42} = (1.0345)^2 - 1 = 7.01\%$$

George then calls his bankers and has them bid on that forward contract—in the jargon of the FRA market, a 36 V 42. (George knows that this long-dated FRA was nonstandard, so he knows that he will likely have to give up 5 to 10 basis points to do the deal.) With this FRA, George can lock in the premium implied in the yield curve for the six-month instrument he owns in three years. He could lock in a premium for the other four repricings in the same way.

Hence, George needs an FRA for each of the six-month periods, a strip of FRAs, one for each rollover date:

6 months vs. 12 months
12 months vs. 18 months

Using FRAs in an Insurance Company continued

18 months vs. 24 months
24 months vs. 30 months
36 months vs. 42 months

In the same way that he has already calculated the forward six-month rate in three years, George must calculate the implied forward rate for each period, package it and get a bid on the "strip" of FRAs from his banks.**

George can now report victory to his boss. With this strip of FRAs in place, he has locked in the higher yield without sacrificing liquidity.

*This example was created using interest rates that prevailed in the first quarter of 1993.

†Is this risky for ADS? No. At present, the asset maturities are "too short" (because of the need to maintain liquidity) relative to the liabilities.

**George, like you, is probably wondering if there is another contract that will accomplish the same trick: something that will look like a "strip" of FRAs, but will not entail signing so many contracts. The answer is swaps, an instrument we will discuss in Chapters 10 and 11.

principal of each FRA is $80 million. The contract terms of the FRAs state that if a reference interest rate (say three-month LIBOR) is above what is expected (the forward interest rate at contract origination) then the S&L receives the difference in interest rates times the $80 million notional principal. Of course, as with all forwards, the reverse would also hold true. The only problem with such a hedge is that FRAs, like all forwards, are credit instruments. And 12 of these forward contracts, the longest of which has a maturity of three years, could use up all of this S&L's credit lines. (A three-year FRA is fairly risky, and even in 1979, this S&L is likely not a AAA risk.)

In addition to financial institutions, insurance companies have significant interest rate exposures that could be managed through FRAs. Since an insurance company must have liquidity to meet claims as they occur, it will keep much of its assets in the form of short-term, highly liquid money market or Treasury instruments. However, the insurance company often finds that, in doing so, it has mismatched its assets and liabilities. By using FRAs, the institution can continue to hold the liquid assets it needs, while synthetically moving the payoffs to its asset portfolio further out the yield curve to better "duration match" or "gap match" its liability structure.

Suppose a bank wants to create assets. Instead of simply buying only floating-rate notes or floating-rate bonds to match its floating-rate funding, it might find it useful to have a "synthetically created" floating-rate instrument through a set of FRAs. The point is that the existence of the FRA allows institutions to change interest rate exposures without huge cost. And portfolio managers may wish to shorten the duration of their fixed-income portfolios; FRA's are one tool available for doing so.

Notes

1. Of particular interest are gold forwards, which are vehicles for institutions holding gold to create active returns on previously sterile (noninterest-bearing) assets.
2. In Table 7–1, volume for forward contracts is subdivided into outright forwards and swaps. An outright forward is the contract we have been discussing throughout Chapters 6 and 7. A foreign exchange swap, on the other hand, is the simultaneous execution of an outright forward and an offsetting spot transaction with the same counterparty. Thus, if the forward leg of the swap is the purchase of DM, the spot leg will be the sale of DM.
3. Estimates are from Dickins (1988) and Grindal (1988). Volume figures are estimates, and disputes about which currencies are most liquid abound. Indeed, one set of survey results found that sterling FRAs had 60 percent of the London market in 1987. Moreover, the domestic French franc market has developed considerable steam and provides an alternative to the MATIF for risk management.
4. Indeed, many managers used an instrument introduced during this period: financial futures, which we will discuss in Chapter 8.

CHAPTER

8 FUTURES

The Futures Contract

As described in Chapter 2, a futures contract is a price-fixing mechanism that involves a legally binding commitment to buy or sell a specified quantity of a specified asset at a specified date in the future. Some futures contracts (notably agricultural futures) require physical delivery of the asset, so the buy/sell activities implied in the contracts are actually consummated. The price paid to take delivery or received to make delivery of a given asset on a given date is determined by the price at which that specific futures contract trades. Other futures contracts (notably stock index futures and Eurodollar futures) are cash-settled. In fact, few futures contracts are held to maturity and exercised; the majority of positions are closed through a reversing trade on the futures exchange.

Futures contracts are traded on organized exchanges; the oldest, the Chicago Board of Trade (CBOT), opened in 1842. The mechanism of futures trading is "open outcry" by buyers and sellers announcing their intentions in an open trading "pit."[1] Trading in futures contracts in the United States is regulated by the Commodity Futures Trading Commission (CFTC).

The range of available futures markets and contracts is extremely wide. Futures contracts are actively traded on 67 exchanges in 26 countries. See Table 8–1.

TABLE 8–1 Futures Exchanges

North America	*Europe*	*Far East and Australasia*
United States	*United Kingdom*	*Hong Kong*
Chicago Board of Trade	Baltic Futures Exchange	Hong Kong Futures Exchange
Chicago Mercantile Exchange	International Petroleum Exchange	
Coffee, Sugar & Cocoa Exchange	London Futures and Options Exchange	*Australia*
Kansas City Board of Trade	London International Financial Futures Exchange	Sydney Futures Exchange
MidAmerica Commodity Exchange*	London Metal Exchange	
Minneapolis Grain Exchange		*Japan*
New York Commodity Exchange (Comex)	*France*	Tokyo Stock Exchange
New York Cotton Exchange	Compagnie de Commissionnaires Agrées	
New York Futures Exchange	Lille Potato Market	*Malaysia*
Philadelphia Stock Exchange	MATIF	Kuala Lumpur Commodities Exchange
Canada	*Netherlands*	*New Zealand*
Toronto Futures Exchange	Amsterdam Pork and Potato Exchange	New Zealand Futures Exchange
Winnipeg Commodity Exchange		
		Phillipines
		Manila International Financial Futures Exchange
		Singapore
		Singapore International Monetary Exchange

*Merged with Chicago Board of Trade.

SOURCE: *Global Investor,* a *Euromoney* publication, March 1988. Used with permission.

In addition to the agricultural commodities for which the futures markets are best known—such as corn, oats, soybeans, pork bellies—futures contracts are traded on precious metals:

Gold   Silver   Platinum

And on industrial commodities:

Aluminum	Copper
Lead	Nickel
Heating oil	Natural gas
Gasoline	Crude oil

Futures contracts are also traded on a number of financial assets, including foreign exchange:

Swiss francs	Australian dollars
Deutsche marks	Canadian dollars
British pounds	Japanese yen
French francs	ECU

And interest-bearing securities:

- T-bills
- Gilts
- Eurodollar deposits
- Muni bond index
- T-notes and bonds
- Bank bills
- German government bonds
- Federal funds

And stock indexes:

- S&P 500 Index
- Major Market Index
- NYSE Composite Index
- National OTC Index
- Financial Times Index
- All Ordinaries Index
- Nikkei Index
- Value Line Index
- Institutional Index
- Russell Indices
- Toronto Stock Exchange Index
- Hang Seng Index
- Barclays Index

The first financial futures contracts, foreign currency futures, were introduced on the International Monetary Market of the Chicago Mercantile Exchange in 1972. Foreign currency futures were followed by GNMA futures in 1975, T-bill futures in 1976, T-bond futures in 1977, and so on. But as we have noted, futures contracts are not a recent development. As noted in Chapter 1, futures-like contracts were traded as early as the 17th century in Japan. Futures first appeared on the Chicago Board of Trade in 1865 and have been traded ever since.[2] (When the CBOT opened in 1842, the contract it traded was the forward rather than futures contract.)

Forwards enabled the CBOT to permit farmers and millers to fix the price of grain, but it is not hard to imagine the kind of defaults that occurred. If the price of grain rose over the period covered by the forward contract, farmers had incentives to default; when the time came to deliver the grain, the miller would be left "waiting at the warehouse" (not a much better place to wait than at the altar), while the farmer sold grain for a better price elsewhere. Conversely, if the price of grain fell over the period of the contract, it would be the miller who had incentives to default and the farmer would be the one "waiting at the warehouse."[3] (Unfortunately, we can't show you examples of the complaint letters that were written, since the Great Chicago Fire of 1871 took care of the files.) The CBOT's response to the complaints—a switch from forwards to futures—better controlled these incentives and thereby reduced the likelihood of default.

Institutional Features that Reduce Credit Risk

The futures contract is like a forward contract in the sense that the futures contract is also a means of contracting in advance of delivery. With either of the contracts, we contract to buy or sell at a future date at a price agreed today.

However, as noted in Chapter 6, forward contracts have the significant limitation of being pure credit instruments. In a sense, a futures contract is designed to deal directly with the credit (default) risk problem; the futures contract is structured and traded so as to reduce substantially the credit risk borne by the contracting parties.

Moreover, the institutional features of the futures market are designed to provide a liquid secondary market. In the discussion to follow, we will highlight those institutional features of the futures contract that reduce the credit risk. In the final section of this chapter we look at those features of the contract itself, and of the market, that provide liquidity.

But first we consider the three institutional features of the contract and of the market that interact to lower the credit risk for a futures contract: *daily settlement*, *margin requirements*, and the *clearinghouse*. At the end of this section we will also consider another feature of some futures markets, *price limits*, to see its impact on the credit risk of a futures contract.

Daily Settlement

With a forward contract, the performance period is the same as the maturity of the contract:

> On July 1, Party A enters into a forward contract with Party B such that Party A agrees to purchase 125,000 deutsche marks on September 21 at a price of 61 cents per deutsche mark ($0.6100).
>
> On July 2, the market price of September 21 deutsche marks—that is, deutsche marks for delivery on September 21—rises to $0.6150.
>
> Party A's position in the forward contract now has a positive value: Party A has the right to buy deutsche marks more cheaply than the prevailing market price. However, with this forward contract, Party A will not receive the value until contract maturity, in 82 days.

In the preceding example, Party A is exposed to the default risk of Party B (and vice versa). When the market price of the deutsche mark rises, Party B owes Party A, but this value will not be conveyed until contract maturity. Further, the risk of default increases as the performance period increases. For example, if the time to contract maturity in the preceding example were 120 days rather than 83 days, the risk of default would be greater. It follows then that reducing the performance period reduces the credit risk.

With a futures contract, the performance period is *one trading day*. Futures contracts are *marked-to-market* and *settled* at the end of every business day. To see the effect of daily resettlement, let's look at a simple example.

When the futures contract is marked-to-market and settled daily, the performance period is reduced to a single day. In Illustration 8–1, while the maturity of the contract is 83 days, the performance period is not 83 days but is instead one business day. With the reduced performance period, default risk declines accordingly.

Illustration 8–1

Implement Daily Settlement

On July 1, Party A agrees to buy from Party B 125,000 deutsche marks for delivery on September 21 at a price of \$0.6100 per deutsche mark.* At origination, both parties agree that \$0.6100 per deutsche mark is the prevailing price for September 21 deutsche marks, so the net present value of the contract is zero.

Suppose that on July 2, the price of September 21 deutsche marks rises to \$0.6150 per deutsche mark. Such a rise is the result of changes in the demand for and supply of deutsche marks, both in the spot and futures market. However, for our purposes, let's simplify the situation and propose that a third party, C, enters the market demanding September 21 deutsche marks.

Since Party A has agreed to buy for \$0.6100 per unit an asset that is now worth \$0.6150 per unit, the value of Party A's position has risen. Marking the contract to market, Party A's contract now has a net present value of \$625:

$$125{,}000\ (\$0.6150 - 0.6100) = \$625.$$

Conversely, the market value of the contract to Party B is a negative \$625.

The contract is settled by Party B making a payment to Party A in the amount of \$625. After the settlement, the net present value of the contract once again equals zero.

*Party A, by executing a "buy" trade, is "long" in the parlance of the futures market.

Moreover, the illustration demonstrates a point we alluded to in Chapter 2: in effect, a futures contract is like a bundle of forward contracts. Each day the forward contract originated on the previous day is settled and replaced with a new contract with a delivery price equal to the settlement price for the previous day's contract.[4]

In this vein, the futures contract described in Illustration 8–1 can be viewed as follows: on July 1 a forward contract was purchased with a maturity of 83 days and a delivery price of \$0.61 per deutsche mark. On July 2, the July 1 forward contract was settled at a price of \$0.6150 per deutsche mark and was replaced with a new forward contract that has a maturity of 82 days and delivery price of \$0.6150 per deutsche mark. Figure 8–1 depicts this view of a futures contract as a bundle of forward contracts.

Margin Requirements

Daily settlement reduces the performance period to one day, but for this one-day period the probability that the counterparty will default still exists. (In the context of our illustration, there is the possibility that on July 2 Party B would not make the necessary \$625 payment.)

FIGURE 8–1 A Futures Contract as a Bundle of Forward Contracts

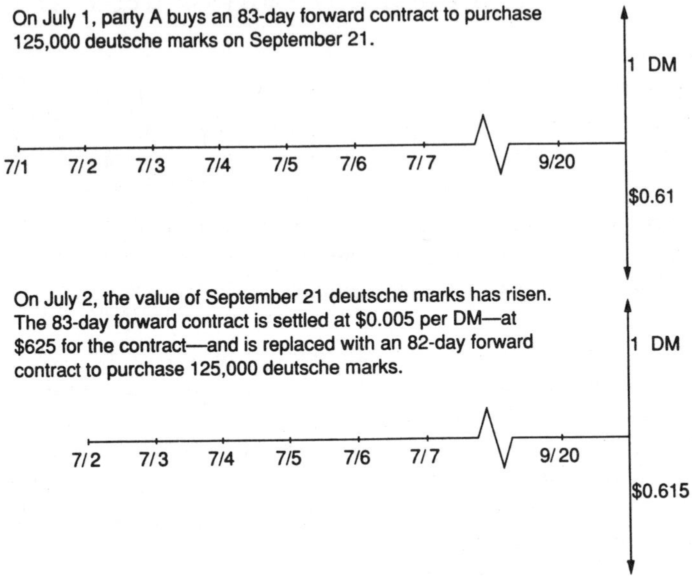

On July 1, party A buys an 83-day forward contract to purchase 125,000 deutsche marks on September 21.
1 DM
7/1 7/2 7/3 7/4 7/5 7/6 7/7 9/20
$0.61
On July 2, the value of September 21 deutsche marks has risen. The 83-day forward contract is settled at $0.005 per DM—at $625 for the contract—and is replaced with an 82-day forward contract to purchase 125,000 deutsche marks.
1 DM
7/2 7/3 7/4 7/5 7/6 7/7 9/20
$0.615

The surest way to deal with this interday credit risk is to require the contracting parties to post a *surety bond*, and that is precisely what is done. In the futures market, this bond is referred to as the *margin*. To buy or sell a futures contract, the individual must post a specified margin as bond to guarantee contract performance. The required margin is determined by the exchange itself for each contract.

At the time the contract is bought or sold, the trader posts the *initial margin*. The initial margin varies with the type of futures contract; it should be no surprise that the initial margin is related to the maximum expected daily price change for the contract in question. That is, the amount of the surety bond required is generally enough to cover the largest changes in the value of the contract that have occurred historically.

The range of initial margin requirements is wide. It can be as little as 0.04 percent for Treasury bills (e.g., the initial margin on a futures contract to purchase $1 million is $405) or as much as 6 percent for the S&P Index contract.[5] Margin requirements change frequently and have been as high as 15 percent for the S&P Index contract. However, for most contracts, this initial margin is 5 percent or less.[6]

In U.S. futures markets, margin can be posted in the form of cash, a bank letter of credit, or Treasury instruments. If margin is posted in the form of securities, the customer continues to earn the interest accrued while the security acts as margin.

On each trading day, gains are credited or losses debited to customer's margin account—in cash—as the futures position increases or decreases in value. In the context of our example, on July 2, $625 would be transferred from Party B's margin account to Party A's margin account; this $625 is referred to as the *variation margin*. If, as a result of the value of the customer's position declining, the balance in the margin account declines below a specified level—referred to as the *maintenance margin*—the customer is required to replenish the margin, returning it to its initial level. If a customer's margin account falls below the maintenance level and is not replenished, the position is closed.[7] To see how this works in practice, let's return to our illustration.

As is indicated by Illustration 8–2, if the contract is marked-to-market daily, and if the initial and maintenance margins are set appropriately, the probability of loss from a default is quite low. However, with less than 100 percent margin, it is not eliminated. For example, on October 19 and 20, 1987, many futures positions were defaulted. Clearly, the margin levels were not set high enough to foreclose default, given this unprecedented change in prices.

Illustration 8–2

Tracing Margin Balances

Suppose Parties A and B have agreed that the initial margin for a contract on 125,000 deutsche marks will be $2,025 and that the maintenance margin will $2,000.*

On July 1, the futures contract between Party A and Party B is originated; both parties will be required to post the initial margin of $2,025.

On July 2, the price of September 21 deutsche marks rises from $0.6100 to $0.6150. Consequently, at the close of business on July 2, $625 will be transferred from the margin account of Party B to Party A. Party A now has a margin account balance of $2,650, but Party B has a margin account balance of only $1,400.

Since Party B's margin account is now below the maintenance margin, Party B will be requested to replenish the margin account, returning the balance to the initial margin. This means adding $625 to the margin account to restore the balance to $2,025.

If Party B replenishes the margin account, the contract continues. If, on July 3, the price of September 21 deutsche marks again rises, funds again will be transferred from Party B's margin account to Party A's account, and if the price increase is great enough, Party B may once again be required to add margin. (The reverse is true if the price of September 21 deutsche marks falls on July 3.)

Tracing Margin Balances continued

If, however, Party B does not add the required $625 to the margin account, Party B's position is closed. Party B will no longer have the futures position and will be reimbursed the balance of $1,400 in the margin account. To continue to buy deutsche marks for a September 21 delivery, Party A must find another party to accept the sell position.†

---

*These were the actual margins for deutsche mark contracts on the International Monetary Market on February 17, 1993.

†In truth, Party A will not actually have to search for a counterparty. The clearinghouse performs this task.

The Clearinghouse

Although daily settlement and the margin requirement can reduce substantially default-induced losses in a futures contract, the costs associated with default are certainly not zero because two sources of costs resulting from credit risk remain.

First, as we have set up our illustration, Parties A and B would exchange funds directly with one another, so they would necessarily expend resources evaluating each other's credit risk. Thus, one remaining cost associated with default is the cost of evaluating the credit risk of the parties with whom you trade:

> Party A buys one September 21 futures contracts on 125,000 deutsche marks from Parties B and C and D. Party A would have to evaluate the credit risk of each of the three parties.

Second, if a party with whom you trade defaults, you are protected against direct losses, but you are subject to an opportunity loss in the sense that the contract is closed. The remaining cost associated with credit risk is the cost of replacing a contract if your counterparty defaults:

> Party A has purchased September 21 futures contracts on deutsche marks from Parties B, C, and D. If the price of September 21 deutsche marks rises and Party C drops out (by not replenishing the margin account) Party A will not lose directly. However, Party A either has to search for a replacement counterparty or live with one less deutsche mark futures contract.

The clearinghouse handles these two problems by breaking apart and depersonalizing agreements. The clearinghouse does not take a position in any trade, but the clearinghouse interposes itself between all parties to every transaction. Hence, the equity of the clearinghouse provides an additional bond for the parties contracting for futures contracts through the clearinghouse.

The manner in which the clearinghouse functions is illustrated in Figure 8–2. Panel A illustrates the futures contract we have described so far: Party A agrees to

FIGURE 8–2 Operation of the Clearinghouse

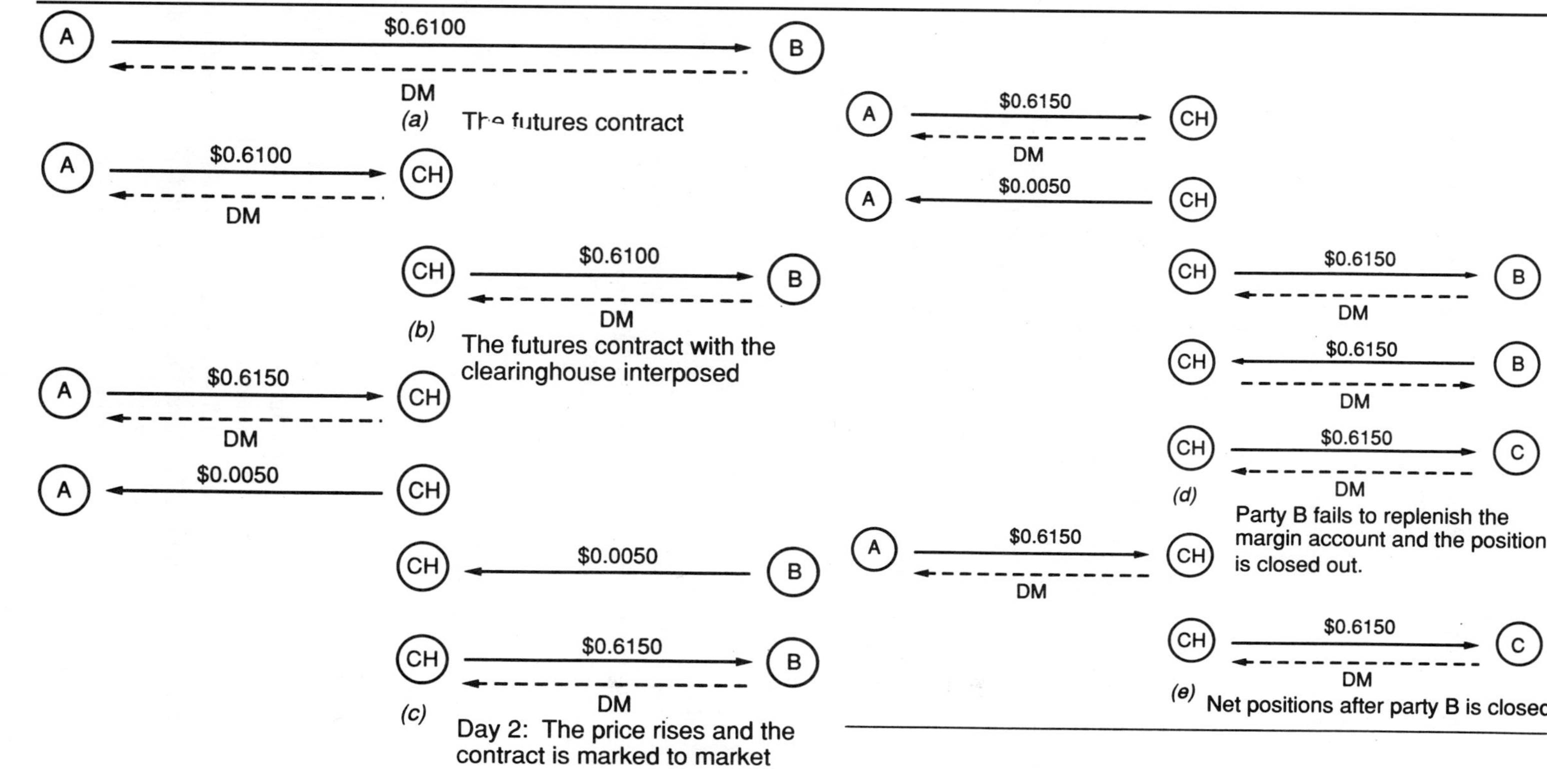

SOURCE: William F. Sharpe, *Investments,* 3e, © 1985, pp. 525–526. Adapted by permission of Prentice Hall, Inc., Englewood Cliffs, New Jersey.

(*a*) The Futures Contract. (*b*) The Futures Contract with the Clearinghouse Interposed. (*c*) Day 2: The Price Rises and the Contract is Marked to Market. (*d*) Party B Fails to Replenish the Margin Account, and the Position Is Closed Out. (*e*) Net Positions After Party B Is Closed Out.

buy 125,000 deutsche marks from Party B at a price of $0.6100 per deutsche mark. Panel B illustrates the same transaction, but with the clearinghouse interposed between the two parties: Party A agrees to buy 125,000 deutsche marks at $0.61 each from the clearinghouse. Party B agrees to sell 125,000 deutsche marks to the clearinghouse at $0.61 per DM. At this point, the *open interest* is 125,000 deutsche marks—or one contract.

Panel C illustrates what happens when the futures price of the DM rises and the contract is marked-to-market. Suppose that, as a result of changes in the demand for or supply of deutsche marks, the futures price of September 21 DM rises to $0.6150. This price change requires a payment of $0.0050 per DM ($0.0050 × 125,000 = $625) from Party B to the clearinghouse and the same payment from the clearinghouse to Party A.

Note that panel C again illustrates how a futures contract is like a bundle of forward contracts. On day 2, the 83-day forward contract is settled through a payment of $0.0050 per DM and is replaced with an 82-day forward contract with a price of $0.6150 per DM.

Panel C illustrates the marking-to-market. What if, as in our example, the marking-to-market requires that Party B replenish the margin account? If Party B returned the margin balance to the initial level, Figure 8–2 would reflect no change. However, if Party B failed to replenish the margin account, Party B's position would be closed.

Panel D of Figure 8–2 illustrates what happens when Party B fails to meet a margin call. When Party B is unable to restore the margin account to the initial level, the clearinghouse enters into a reversing trade with Party B—the clearinghouse contracts to sell 125,000 September 21 DM to Party B at a price of $0.6150 per DM—thereby netting out, or closing, the position.[8] However, Party A's position is still open; the clearinghouse is still obligated to deliver the September 21 DM. The clearinghouse covers this obligation by matching Party A with another contract, this one a contract to purchase September 21 DM from Party C at a price of $0.6150.

Panel E displays the effect of closing out Party B's contract. Note that the open interest is still only one contract.

Price Limits

In the aftermath of the "crash" of October 19, 1987, there has been considerable discussion of imposing price limits on financial futures contracts. More common for futures contracts on commodities than for financial futures, the concept of a price limit has considerable intuitive appeal: with daily resettlement and the margin account mechanisms in place, the problem of default risk would arise only when the futures price moves "too much" in a single day. Therefore, to "solve" this problem, we institute a rule that says that price can move only so much in a single trading day.

More specifically, the rule is such that if the futures price for a specified contract moves the limit during a trading day, trading is then halted on that contract for the remainder of the day. This idea of a price limit is certainly appealing, but this kind of reasoning has a serious flaw. William Sharpe (1985) provided the best exposition of the fallacy in his story of a farmer:

> Tired of the violent fluctuations in temperature that occur from one day to the next in the American Great Plains (and the consequences on his crops), this farmer decided to "eliminate" this problem by having his thermometer altered so that it could move no more than five degrees in either direction from the previous day's reading.

The point of this anecdote is that price limits cannot eliminate volatility in futures prices any more than altering the thermometer can eliminate volatility in temperatures. Changing the thermometer does nothing to change climatic or meteorological conditions; price limits do nothing to change the underlying economic factors that lead to the volatility in futures prices.

However, it has been argued that price limits could reduce the credit risk problem to the extent that the price limit substitutes for margin.[9] The reasoning behind this argument is that price limits *could* reduce the amount of information available to the traders in the futures market. To see how this would work, let's return to our example:

> Suppose that on July 2, world economic conditions were altered such that the value of the dollar would decline dramatically relative to the deutsche mark.

If there are no price limits on the DM/$ futures contract, the futures prices could fully reflect the altered conditions:

> On July 2, the futures price of September 21 deutsche marks rose from $0.6100 to close at $0.6325.

With such a dramatic move, credit problems and "reneging" would be likely:

> Marking the contract to market, Party B owes $2,812.50 (and Party A is owed the same amount). However, Party B's margin account balance is only $2,025. Party B will face a margin call of $2,812.50 (to leave the margin account balance at $2,025).
>
> Given the $0.0225 one-day change in the price of a DM—a change of 3.6 percent in one day—Party B is unwilling to meet the margin call. Party B reneges on the futures contract. The contract will be closed out, but Party B's broker—or the clearinghouse[10]—will suffer a loss of $2,812.50 − $2,025 = $787.50.

Suppose however that a price limit were in effect for the DM/$ futures contract. Let's suppose that the daily price limit for the DM/$ futures had been set at $0.0100 per DM—in other words, if the price of DM rises or falls by as much as one cent, trading is suspended for that day. Such a rule would limit the amount that could be lost on a DM/$ futures contract to $1,250 per day:

> On July 2, the price of September 21 deutsche marks immediately begins to rise from $0.6100; with the price limit, it can rise no higher than $0.6200.

> Party B's contract must be marked to market at the end of the trading day. Consequently, Party B has lost \$1,250 and his margin account balance has dropped below the maintenance margin to \$775. Party B faces a margin call of \$1,250.

With this limit on how much Party B could lose in a day, the ability of the futures market to convey information to the traders is reduced. Hence, the probability that the party will renege on the contract is altered:

> Party B knows that the \$0.6200 is not an equilibrium price. Party B knows that the equilibrium price is higher than \$0.6200 but not how much higher. If Party B thinks the equilibrium price is only a little above this level, say at \$0.6210, Party B might be willing to meet the margin call of \$1,250 to restore the position's margin account balance to \$2,025.

The price limits might alter the amount of information available to the trader, but again the price limit does not alter the underlying economic conditions:

> On July 3, the market opens and immediately moves the limit: the price of September 21 deutsche marks rises to \$0.6300 and trading is suspended.
>
> After losing another \$1,250, Party B's margin account balance is down to \$775. Again faced with a \$1,250 margin call, Party B might make this margin call or might renege. Let's suppose the latter.
>
> On July 5, equilibrium is finally reached. The market opens and the price of September 21 deutsche marks immediately goes to its equilibrium price, \$0.6325. Party B's broker closes the contract. The loss on the contract on July 5 is \$312.50, which is subtracted from Party B's margin account, leaving a balance of \$775 − \$312.50 = \$462.50, which is returned to Party B.

In the preceding example, the price limit reduced the credit risk to the broker and the exchange: without the price limit, the broker/exchange lost \$787.50; with the price limit, the broker/exchange lost nothing. However, this change was solely the result of the customer's getting "tricked"; with the price limit in place, the customer's perception of what the equilibrium price would be was different from what the market-determined equilibrium price turned out to be. If the customer cannot be tricked, the effect disappears. The example implies that the futures price is the customer's only source of information. To the extent customers have alternative sources of information about the equilibrium price, the ability to trick them—the effectiveness of the price limit—declines. Thus, price limits are more frequently observed in agricultural futures markets, where there are few alternate sources of price information. Price limits are rarely observed in financial futures markets, where other related financial markets provide rich alternate sources of price information.

Institutional Features That Promote Liquidity

In addition to the three features that reduce default risk, two features of the futures contract and market enhance the liquidity of the market: *standardized contracts* and the *organized exchange*.

Standardized Contracts

For a market to be liquid, the commodity/asset being traded in the market must be homogeneous. To attain this homogeneity, contracts traded in the futures market are standardized. The contract specifies a standardized asset and a standardized maturity date.

> Consider again the deutsche mark futures contract. On the International Monetary Market (IMM) of the Chicago Mercantile Exchange (CME) the DM contract specifies a contract size of 125,000 deutsche marks with maturities occurring on the third Wednesdays of March, June, September, or December.

Moreover, in a futures contract, the mechanism for delivery is commonly standardized.[11] For example, on the IMM the T-bill future requires the delivery of T-bills with a total face value of $1 million and a time to maturity of 90 days at the expiration of the futures contract. The T-bond futures contract permits latitude with respect to the specific bonds to be delivered—the contract specifies the delivery of $100,000's worth of T-bonds that have at least 15 years remaining until maturity or to their first call date.[12]

Furthermore, the price of the futures contract is also standardized to the extent that the minimum price movement—the "tick size"—is also specified. For example, the tick size for the deutsche mark contract we have been following is $0.0001 per DM (or $12.50 per contract).

Organized Exchanges

To bring together buyers and sellers, the futures market is organized into exchanges, each exchange trading particular futures contracts. This is in marked contrast to a forward market, in which the contracts are negotiated on a one-off basis in a decentralized market.

Most of futures exchanges are organized like the Chicago Board of Trade. Membership on the CBOT is by individuals and entitles members to the right to trade on the exchange and to have a voice in its operation. (While only individuals can be members, brokers like Merrill Lynch are permitted to trade on the exchange.) Memberships are traded like any other asset and can be purchased or leased from the current owner.

While the CBOT has at times been likened to a "club"—a nonprofit organization of its members—it is probably more fruitful to think of the futures exchanges as for-profit "partnerships." The members of these exchanges have strong individual incentives to form stringent rules for running the exchange that maximize the value of their memberships.[13] An anecdote might help to illustrate this point: when a trade is made in the "pit," there is always the possibility of an error. The buyer and the seller might write down different amounts or different prices, for instance. On the Chicago Mercantile Exchange and other exchanges, the rule for settling such errors is that if direct methods of correcting the error have been unsuccessful, the two parties split the loss. Traders will be unlikely to buy or sell contracts from a colleague with an unusually high error rate. Because the traders want to maximize their own profit, each has the incentive to maximize accuracy.

The upshot is that rules on the futures exchanges work to maximize the value of a membership on the exchange and simultaneously to maximize the liquidity on the exchange.

Futures Prices

At maturity—on the delivery date for the futures contract—arbitrage between the underlying asset and futures markets force the price of the futures and the cash price of the asset to be the same. Prior to maturity, the cash price and the futures price need not be the same. But because the futures price must converge to the cash price at maturity, we know some systematic relation between the two prices must exist. We examine this relation in the next section.

Futures Prices and the Cost of Carry

To examine the relation between cash and futures prices, let's look at some illustrative prices. Figure 8–3 provides data on the cash prices—the spot prices—of some grains and feeds on Tuesday, February 16, 1993. Figure 8–4 provides data on corresponding futures prices on the same day.

FIGURE 8–3 Cash Prices

CASH PRICES

Tuesday, February 16, 1993.
(Closing Market Quotations)
GRAINS AND FEEDS

	Tues	Fri	Yr.Ago
Barley, top-quality Mpls., bu	2.35	2.25-.40	2.52½
Bran, wheat middlings, KC ton	62.00	59.-62.0	74.00
Corn, No. 2 yel. Cent-Ill. bu	bp2.06½	2.05	2.56
Corn Gluten Feed, Midwest, ton ..	85.-108.	85.-108.	101.00
Cottonseed Meal,			
Clksdle,Miss. ton	147.50	147.50	140.00
Hominy Feed,Cent-Ill. ton	52.00	52.00	87.00
Meat-Bonemeal, 50% pro. Ill. ton.	220.00	n.a.	207.50
Oats, No. 2 milling, Mpls., bu	n1.61-.67	1.68¼	1.73
Sorghum, (Milo) No. 2 Gulf cwt ...	4.28	4.28	5.30
Soybean Meal,			
Centr. Ill., 44% protein - ton ..	165.-167.	165½-170½	173.25
Soybean Meal,			
Centr. Ill., 48% protein - ton ..	177.-180.	177½-180½	184.00
Soybeans, No. 1 yel Cent.-Ill. bu ..	bp5.60	5.59	5.67
Wheat,			
Spring 14%-pro Mpls. bu	3.98½	4.00	4.44¼
Wheat, No. 2 sft red, St.Lou. bu ...	bp3.74½	3.76½	3.74½
Wheat, No. 2 hard KC, bu	3.67¼	3.68½	4.35¾
Wheat, No. 1 sft wht, del Port Ore	4.06	4.06	4.79

bp-Country elevator bids to producers.

SOURCE: Reprinted by permission of *The Wall Street Journal*,

FIGURE 8–4 Futures Prices

	Open	High	Low	Settle	Change	Lifetime High	Lifetime Low	Open Interest
GRAINS AND OILSEEDS								
CORN (CBT) 5,000 bu.; cents per bu.								
Mar	212¼	212¾	211¾	212	– ¼	281¼	211	75,458
May	220	220¾	219¾	220	– ¼	284¾	219	64,600
July	227½	228	227	227½	....	286	226	80,397
Sept	233½	234¼	233½	233½	– ½	271½	230½	14,071
Dec	240½	240¾	240¼	240¼	....	268½	233¾	27,510
Mr94	246¾	247	246¾	247	+ ¼	254¾	240½	1,730
May	251	251	251	251	....	257½	249½	338
July	254½	255	254½	255	....	327	254½	165
Est vol 20,000; vol Fri 20,287; open int 264,312, –33.								
OATS (CBT) 5,000 bu.; cents per bu.								
Mar	139¾	139¾	137	139	– 1¼	195¼	122	3,025
May	139	139½	136½	138¼	– 2	177¼	126	3,253
July	139¼	139¼	136¼	138	– 1¾	163½	129½	826
Sept	....	....	....	138	– 1¾	156	138¼	112
Dec	142	142	140	140½	– 2¼	159	141½	589
Est vol 1,200; vol Fri 562; open int 7,818, –33.								
SOYBEANS (CBT) 5,000 bu.; cents per bu.								
Mar	570	572¼	568	571	+ ½	664	538¾	40,913
May	573	575	570½	573½	+ ¾	668½	546	31,824
July	577	579¾	575½	578¾	+ ¾	671	551	35,294
Aug	579½	580¾	577½	580½	+ 1½	655	551	4,395
Sept	581	581¼	579	580¾	+ ¾	630	554	2,467
Nov	585¾	588	584½	587	+ 1	620	555½	13,527
Ja94	595	595	593¼	594¾	+ 1½	608½	576½	1,163
Nov	591	592	591	592	+ 1½	607	588	195
Est vol 26,000; vol Fri 18,556; open int 129,877, +771.								
SOYREAN MEAL (CBT) 100 tons; $ per ton.								
Mar	177.50	177.80	176.70	177.20	– .20	210.00	176.80	22,235
May	178.60	179.10	177.90	178.60	....	210.00	177.90	20,692
July	180.70	180.90	180.00	180.50	....	208.00	179.80	17,907
Aug	181.50	181.80	181.10	181.40	+ .10	193.50	180.90	3,501
Sept	182.50	182.50	182.10	182.40	+ .30	193.50	181.60	2,060
Oct	183.10	183.40	183.10	183.20	– .10	194.50	182.60	1,170
Dec	185.00	185.30	184.70	185.20	– .10	194.00	184.50	2,083
Ja94		....	....	185.30	– .30	189.50	185.50	182
Est vol 10,000; vol Fri 6,329; open int 69,830, +381.								
SOYBEAN OIL (CBT) 60,000 lbs.; cents per lb.								
Mar	20.78	20.98	20.63	20.96	+ .16	23.20	18.55	21,170
May	21.15	21.24	20.89	21.23	+ .17	23.50	18.85	22,252
July	21.38	21.44	21.13	21.44	+ .16	23.20	19.15	14,975
Aug	21.38	21.54	21.25	21.53	+ .19	23.25	19.29	2,705
Sept	21.45	21.50	21.43	21.55	+ .20	23.25	19.40	2,141
Oct		....	....	21.61	+ .21	22.35	19.55	1,264
Dec	21.65	21.70	21.45	21.70	+ .10	23.45	19.76	4,212
Ja94	21.60	[illegible]	21.60	21.70	+ .03	22.20	21.11	189
Est vol 12,000; vol Fri 11,501; open int 68,948, +795.								
WHEAT (CBT) 5,000 bu.; cents per bu.								
Mar	363½	363½	358¼	361½	– 3¼	440	319½	18,622
May	340	341	336	339¾	– 1½	375	318	9,974
July	322¾	322¾	319½	321½	– 2½	373	302¼	15,323
Sept	325½	327	323½	325½	– 2½	353	307½	2,321
Dec	334½	335	331½	332¾	– 3¼	360	317½	1,255
Est vol 12,000; vol Fri 6,956; open int 47,537, –792.								
WHEAT (KC) 5,000 bu.; cents per bu.								
Mar	346½	346¾	342¾	346	– 1	410	309¾	16,796
May	328½	328½	323¾	327	– 2	350	310¾	3,895
July	319½	319½	316	318	– 2¾	359	300½	8,923
Sept	322	322	319¾	321½	– 2½	339	309¾	1,102
Dec	330¼	330¼	330	330	– 2	341½	324	101
Est vol 6,582; vol Fri 4,191; open int 30,817, –798.								
WHEAT (MPLS) 5,000 bu.; cents per bu.								
Mar	334¼	334¼	329	333½	– 1½	384	306	9,649
May	328¼	328¼	324	327¼	– 2	372½	310	5,214
July	326	326¼	323¾	324	– 2½	350½	306½	1,394
Sept	319	319	319	321	– 1¾	336	314	580
Est vol 3,268; vol Fri 2,550; open int 16,912, +29.								
BARLEY (WPG) 20 metric tons; Can. $ per ton								
Mar	90.00	90.50	89.80	90.00	– .40	101.10	89.10	2,377
May	90.70	91.40	90.70	91.00	– .10	100.50	90.50	1,327
Jly	93.30	93.30	93.10	93.10	– .40	100.70	92.70	516
Oct	94.90	94.90	94.70	94.70	....	102.40	92.40	1,428
Dec		....	....	96.20	+ .30	96.00	95.30	1,466
Est vol 340; vol Mon 117; open int 7,114, +8.								
FLAXSEED (WPG) 20 metric tons; Can. $ per ton								
Mar	255.00	256.50	253.90	255.30	+ 2.80	295.50	227.80	2,351
May	260.00	262.50	259.80	262.00	+ 2.00	299.00	251.10	2,323
July	264.50	266.50	264.10	265.70	+ 2.20	298.90	255.00	776
Oct	270.90	273.00	270.50	273.00	+ 2.70	301.80	260.00	1,668
Dec	274.50	276.20	273.50	276.20	+ 2.70	300.50	265.40	887
Est vol 895; vol Mon 2,770; open int 37,285, –55.								
CANOLA (WPG) 20 metric tons; Can. $ per ton								
Mar	337.00	338.00	330.00	333.30	– 3.20	348.70	273.10	4,671
June	341.00	341.00	331.50	336.20	– 2.90	352.20	278.50	15,707
Sept	315.10	315.10	307.80	311.30	– 2.40	323.40	283.00	3,487
Nov	311.50	311.50	304.20	307.10	– 4.20	320.40	281.00	9,839
Ja94	309.00	311.90	308.50	311.50	– 3.50	325.50	305.00	2,985
Mar		....	....	313.00	– 5.00	323.70	315.30	596
Est vol 3,600; vol Mon 2,770; open int 37,285, –59.								
WHEAT (WPG) 20 metric tons; Can. $ per ton								
Mar	91.50	91.50	91.00	91.20	– .70	115.00	90.40	2,095
May	91.70	92.50	91.70	92.50	+ .50	115.50	90.50	3,173
July	93.70	94.50	93.70	94.50	+ .50	103.50	92.30	2,276
Oct	98.40	98.60	98.10	98.50	+ .40	108.00	96.50	2,420
Dec	100.00	100.20	100.00	100.20	+ .30	100.50	98.50	1,736
Est vol 550; vol Mon 74; open int 11,700, –38.								

CBT: Chicago Board of Trade
KC: Kansas City Board of Trade
MPLS: Minneapolis Grain Exchange
WPG: Winnipeg Commodity Exchange

Look, for instance, at corn prices. The spot price of yellow corn is $2.065 per bushel in central Illinois. But the price on a futures contract on the Chicago Board of Trade that is deliverable in corn and will mature in only 29 days—on the third Wednesday in March—is 212 cents ($2.12) per bushel. And as Figure 8–4 indicates, the futures price of corn in May is higher than that in March; the futures price of corn in July is higher than that in May, and so on. Hence, the data on corn prices illustrate two frequently observed characteristics of futures prices: the futures price of a commodity or asset, F, is greater than the spot price, P,[14] and the futures price, F, rises as the time to maturity increases.[15]

These characteristics reflect the *cost of carry* for a futures contract and illustrate a critical arbitrage relation. To see how this works, an illustration is useful.

Illustration 8–3*

Cash and Carry Limits on Wheat Futures Prices

Suppose the spot price of No. 2 Red Wheat in a Chicago warehouse is 300 cents per bushel, the yield on a one-month T-bill is 6 percent, and the cost of storing and insuring one bushel of wheat is 4 cents per month.

Given these data, what can be said about the price today for a one-month futures contract—that is, the price of a futures contract that has one month to maturity?

Instead of buying a futures contract on wheat, I could buy wheat today and store it for one month. In one month, the total cost of this transaction to me is the cost of using the money for one month (the forgone interest) and the cost of storing and insuring the wheat:

$$300.0[1 + (30/360)0.06] + 4.0 = 305.5.$$

Hence, 305.5 cents per bushel is the maximum the one-month futures contract could cost. If the futures contract is priced at 306, I can sell futures contracts, buy wheat today, and store it for one month and make a riskless profit—an *arbitrage* profit.

*This illustration is adapted from Sharpe (1985).

Illustration 8–3 points out that the futures price must be related to the spot price through the *cost of carry*, *c*, for the futures contract in question. The illustration shows that, for commodity contracts, arbitrage guarantees that the futures price will be less than or equal to the spot price plus the cost of carry:

$$F < P + c. \qquad 8\text{–}1$$

With respect to Equation 8–1, we saw in the illustration that if $F > P + c$, a trader could make a riskless profit by taking a long position in the asset and a short position in the futures contract. If $F < P + c$, the arbitrage strategy would be to buy the futures and sell the commodity short, but short sales of a physical commodity are difficult. (However, if one had a large inventory of wheat, the strategy could be accomplished by reducing inventory—selling wheat on the spot market—and buying futures.)

However, we are more concerned with futures on financial assets, and short selling *is* possible for financial assets. In this case, if $F < P + c$, a trader could make an arbitrage profit. Hence, with the financial futures, the principle of no arbitrage requires that Equation 8–1 be a strict equality:

$$F = P + c. \qquad 8\text{–}2$$

FIGURE 8–5 Futures Prices

FUTURES PRICES

Tuesday, February 16, 1993

Open Interest Reflects Previous Trading Day.

	Open	High	Low	Settle	Change	Lifetime High	Lifetime Low	Open Interest
JAPAN YEN (CME)–12.5 million yen; $ per yen (.00)								
Mar	.8254	.8360	.8230	.8330	+ .0041	.8372	.7445	69,832
June	.8332	.8362	.8327	.8332	+ .0041	.8362	.7745	2,282
Sept	.8343	.8360	.8340	.8340	+ .0041	.8360	.7945	1,013
Dec	.8360	.8380	.8358	.8352	+ .0041	.8380	.7970	1,522
Est vol 15,176; vol Fri 18,499; open int 74,649, –680.								
DEUTSCHEMARK (CME)–125,000 marks; $ per mark								
Mar	.5999	.6115	.5999	.6100	+ .0111	.7025	.5724	124,421
June	.5970	.6042	.5964	.6028	+ .0110	.6920	.5890	20,965
Sept	.5968	.5985	.5968	.5974	+ .0109	.6720	.5867	3,113
Est vol 53,619; vol Fri 51,091; open int 148,520, –1,975.								
CANADIAN DOLLAR (CME)–100,000 dlrs.; $ per Can $								
Mar	.7950	.7971	.7928	.7933	– .0017	.8712	.7610	21,860
June	.7914	.7917	.7872	.7877	– .0017	.8360	.7532	2,191
Sept	.7859	.7859	.7820	.7824	– .0017	.8335	.7515	855
Dec	....	....	....	.7775	– .0017	.8310	.7470	580
Est vol 4,660; vol Fri 3,783; open int 25,515, +186.								
BRITISH POUND (CME)–62,500 pds.; $ per pound								
Mar	1.4140	1.4466	1.4140	1.4416	+ .0298	1.9400	1.4050	42,908
June	1.4200	1.4368	1.4200	1.4320	+ .0290	1.9100	1.4020	1,647
Sept	1.4200	1.4310	1.4170	1.4254	+ .0284	1.5580	1.3980	142
Est vol 15,162; vol Fri 14,391; open int 44,703, +625.								
SWISS FRANC (CME)–125,000 francs; $ per franc								
Mar	.6451	.6644	.6451	.6620	+ .0157	.8140	.6451	47,483
June	.6516	.6605	.6503	.6584	+ .0153	.8070	.6423	2,482
Sept	.6493	.6570	.6493	.6559	+ .0148	.7100	.6407	391
Est vol 23,130; vol Fri 18,695; open int 50,356, +450.								
AUSTRALIAN DOLLAR (CME)–100,000 dlrs.; $ per A.$								
Mar	.6799	.6868	.6799	.6844	+ .0071	.7450	.6611	3,781
Est vol 576; vol Fri 280; open int 3,817, +6.								
U.S. DOLLAR INDEX (FINEX)–1,000 times USDX								
Mar	95.40	95.40	93.50	93.74	– 1.65	95.96	81.45	9,047
June	95.79	95.79	94.90	95.13	– 1.63	97.20	82.55	1,094
Est vol 3,675; vol Mon 2,787; open int 10,145, +1,117.								
The index: High 94.45; Low 93.05; Close 93.24 –1.21								
EURODOLLAR (LIFFE)–$1 million; pts of 100%								
Mar	96.68	96.70	96.68	96.71	+ .03	96.99	91.45	11,172
June	96.51	96.56	96.51	96.54	+ .06	96.66	91.50	6,984
Sept	96.22	96.23	96.22	96.24	+ .07	96.29	92.50	2,104
Dec	95.69	95.72	95.69	95.71	+ .07	95.72	92.24	1,281
Mr94	95.44	95.44	95.44	95.48	+ .07	95.44	92.20	338
June	....	....	....	95.08	+ .07	94.95	94.15	185
Est vol 2,019; vol Mon 2,018; open int 22,092, +301.								
STERLING (LIFFE)–£500,000; pts of 100%								
Mar	94.07	94.10	94.01	94.04	– .03	94.50	87.50	62,931
June	94.61	94.65	94.56	94.57	– .04	94.88	87.58	58,028
Sept	94.70	94.75	94.68	94.68	– .03	94.94	87.20	59,842
Dec	94.63	94.67	94.60	94.60	– .03	94.81	88.95	40,974
Mr94	94.32	94.34	94.30	94.31	+ .04	96.41	89.87	26,384

	Open	High	Low	Settle	Change	Lifetime High	Lifetime Low	Open Interest
TREASURY BONDS (CBT)–$100,000; pts. 32nds of 100%								
Mar	108-02	108-20	107-22	107-27	– 4	7.251	+ .011	287,463
June	106-26	107-12	106-14	106-19	– 4	7.365	+ .012	55,751
Sept	105-23	106-05	105-07	105-12	– 4	7.478	+ .012	6,373
Dec	104-22	104-28	104-02	104-06	– 5	7.590	+ .015	7,605
Mr94	103-11	103-15	103-04	103-04	– 6	7.691	+ .018	3,397
June	102-29	102-29	102-04	102-04	– 7	7.789	+ .022	308
Sept	....	....	....	101-07	– 7	7.878	+ .022	83
Est vol 380,000; vol Fri 390,825; op int 361,279, +3,738.								
TREASURY BONDS (MCE)–$50,000; pts. 32nds of 100%								
Mar	108-12	108-20	107-22	107-26	– 6	7.254	+ .014	12,227
Est vol 5,900; vol Fri 3,363; open int 12,307, –94.								
TREASURY NOTES (CBT)–$100,000; pts. 32nds of 100%								
Mar	110-04	110-14	110-00	110-02	+ 3	6.609	– .012	184,572
June	108-23	109-02	108-22	108-23	+ 3	6.785	– .012	14,116
Sept	107-21	107-22	107-13	107-13	+ 3	6.960	– .012	150
Est vol 60,000; vol Fri 54,803; open int 198,859, +103.								
5 YR TREAS NOTES (CBT)–$100,000; pts. 32nds of 100%								
Mar	09-235	110-04	109-23	109-29	+ 8	5.695	– .055	139,052
June	08-255	09-035	08-255	108-29	+ 8	5.916	– .056	11,861
Est vol 41,200; vol Fri 20,384; open int 150,943, +1,598.								
2 YR TREAS NOTES (CBT)–$200,000, pts. 32nds of 100%								
Mar	06-132	106-18	06-132	106-15	+ 2¾	4.578	– .044	16,433
June	105-29	06-017	105-29	05-315	+ 3½	4.825	– .056	1,494
Est vol 500; vol Fri 1,995; open int 17,927, +154.								
30-DAY FEDERAL FUNDS (CBT)–$5 million; pts. of 100%								
Feb	96.94	96.95	96.93	96.94	....	3.06	....	2,532
Mar	96.94	96.94	96.94	96.94	– .01	3.06	+ .01	2,582
Apr	96.96	96.96	96.96	96.96	+ .01	3.04	– .01	2,265
May	96.94	96.94	96.93	96.93	....	3.07	....	1,859
June	96.87	96.88	97.87	96.87	+ .01	3.13	– .01	1,766
July	96.83	96.83	96.82	96.82	+ .01	3.18	– .01	958
Est vol 333; vol Fri 353; open int 12,056, +134.								
TREASURY BILLS (CME)–$1 mil.; pts. of 100%								
Mar	97.06	97.08	97.04	97.05	+ .01	2.95	– .01	19,425
Jun	96.89	96.95	96.88	96.90	+ .02	3.10	– .02	16,422
Sep	96.60	96.67	96.60	96.63	+ .04	3.37	– .05	1,667
Dec	....	....	....	96.28	+ .08	3.72	– .08	258
Est vol 3,741; vol Fri 2,679; open int 37,772, +177.								
LIBOR-1 MO. (CME)–$3,000,000; points of 100%								
Mar	96.77	96.78	96.75	96.75	....	3.25	....	9,306
Apr	96.78	96.79	96.77	96.77	+ .01	3.23	– .01	6,505
May	96.73	96.74	96.71	96.72	+ .02	3.28	– .02	3,057
Jun	96.69	96.70	96.67	96.66	+ .02	3.34	– .02	2,038
Jly	96.62	96.62	96.60	96.59	+ .02	3.41	– .02	1,034
Est vol 2,332; vol Fri 4,766; open int 32,116, +1,215.								
MUNI BOND INDEX (CBT)–$1,000; times Bond Buyer MBI								
Mar	99-[illegible]	99-[illegible]	99-14	99-17	+ 3	99-[illegible]	98-02	20,345
June	98-[illegible]	98-[illegible]	98-19	98-22	+ 5	98-30	91-16	396
Est vol 2,[illegible]; vol Fri 2,741; open int 20,741, –12.								
The index: Close 99-04; Yield 6.15.								

Contract delivery months that are currently traded

Prices represent the open, high, low, and settlement (or closing) price for the previous day

One day's change in the settlement price

EURODOLLAR (CME)–$1 million; pts of 100%

	Open	High	Low	Settle	Chg	Yield Settle	Yield Chg	Open Interest
Mr93	96.68	96.72	96.68	96.68	....	3.32	....	278,563
June	96.49	96.56	96.49	96.51	+ .02	3.49	– .02	287,365
Sept	96.23	96.27	96.20	96.21	+ .03	3.79	– .03	221,871
Dec	95.70	95.76	95.68	95.69	+ .05	4.31	– .05	147,736
Mr94	95.46	95.52	95.45	95.46	+ .06	4.54	– .06	121,016
June	95.06	95.14	95.06	95.07	+ .06	4.93	– .06	97,261
Sept	94.73	94.81	94.73	94.75	+ .06	5.25	– .06	84,071
Dec	94.32	94.40	94.32	94.33	+ .06	5.67	– .06	60,300
Mr95	94.20	94.31	94.19	94.23	+ .06	5.77	– .06	58,780
June	93.94	94.05	93.94	93.97	+ .06	6.03	– .06	43,959
Sept	93.73	93.84	93.73	93.77	+ .07	6.23	– .07	34,691
Dec	93.43	93.53	93.42	93.46	+ .07	6.54	– .07	31,565
Mr96	93.38	93.45	93.38	93.41	+ .06	6.59	– .06	29,276
June	93.19	93.25	93.19	93.21	+ .06	6.79	– .06	19,951
Sept	93.05	93.12	93.05	93.08	+ .06	6.92	– .06	16,615
Dec	92.81	92.88	92.81	92.84	+ .06	7.16	– .06	13,952
Mr97	92.82	92.89	92.82	92.85	+ .06	7.15	– .06	10,567
June	92.67	92.72	92.67	92.70	+ .06	7.30	– .06	10,303
Sept	92.60	92.65	92.60	92.63	+ .06	7.37	– .06	8,854
Dec	92.45	92.49	92.44	92.47	+ .06	7.53	– .06	6,093

Est vol 254,171; vol Fri 224,310; open int 1,582,904, +3,009.

The number of contracts still in effect at the end of the previous day's trading session. Each unit represents a buyer *and* a seller who still have a contract position

One day's change in the futures' interest rate – equal and opposite to change in the settlement price

The interest rate implied by the settlement price, e.g., 100 – 93.18 = 6.28

The total of the right column, and the change from the prior trading day

IMM: International Monetary Market
LIFFE: London International Financial Futures Exchange
CTN: New York Cotton Exchange
NYFE: New York Futures Exchange
CBT: Chicago Board of Trade
MCE: MidAmerica Commodity Exchange

SOURCE: Reprinted by permission of *The Wall Street Journal,*

In Figure 8–5 we provide data on financial futures for Tuesday, February 16, 1993, the same date that we used to illustrate futures prices for commodities. We also have annotated Eurodollar futures contracts data to show how they can be read.

The arbitrage underlying the cost-of-carry relation holds for financial assets as it does for commodities. The only difference is in the elements of the cost of carry. For commodities, the cost of carry includes the cost of storing and insuring the commodity. For financial assets, the cost of carry is limited to the *net* financing costs (coupon income minus financing costs). Put another way, the cost of carry is the difference between the opportunity cost of holding the asset (the short-term interest rate, the financing cost) and the yield earned from holding the financial asset (such as the coupon payments investors receive when holding bonds).

Equation 8–2 is useful for considering what is referred to as *basis* in a futures contract. Basis is defined as the difference between the futures price and the spot price:

$$\text{Basis} = F - P. \qquad 8\text{–}3$$

From Equation 8–2 it follows that some movements in the basis for a particular asset are predictable movements, based on the cost of carry of the asset.

The first of these predictable movements is the convergence of the futures price to the price implied by the cost-of-carry relation. We must keep in mind that the cost-of-carry model is an equilibrium model. If the futures price strays from the price implied by Equation 8–2, the arbitrage forces we have described above act to bring the futures price back to that predicted by the cost-of-carry model; over the life of the futures contract, futures prices will tend to converge toward that price implied by the cost-of-carry relation.

The second predictable movement is the convergence of the futures price to the cash price at expiration of the futures contract. As the time to delivery becomes shorter, the cost of carry declines. Storage and insurance costs are lower as there is less time to store the commodity, and the shorter the holding period, the smaller the opportunity cost for holding an asset. As specified by Equation 8–2, as the time to delivery becomes shorter and the cost of carry, c, becomes smaller, the futures price, F, converges to the cash price, P.

Futures Prices and Expected Future Spot Prices

So far we have seen that the price today for a futures contract specifying delivery at period T is related to the *prevailing* spot price through the cost of carry. However, a more important question is how the price today for a futures contract specifying delivery at period T is related to the *expected* spot price at period T.

The expectations model proposes that the current futures price is equal to the market's expected value of the spot price at period T:

$$F_t = E(P_T). \qquad 8\text{–}4$$

If this expectations model is correct, a speculator can expect neither to win nor to lose from a position in the futures market; expected profits are zero:

$$E(\text{Profit}) = E(P_T) - F_t = 0. \qquad 8\text{–}5$$

Put another way, if the expectations model is correct, the speculator can anticipate earning only the riskless rate of return. Illustration 8–4 explains this somewhat counterintuitive idea.

Proponents of the expectations model argue that, in a market with rational traders, the expectations model simply has to work. The argument behind this position goes something like this:

> If most traders expect the spot price at maturity to be above the prevailing futures price, they will buy futures, thereby forcing up the futures price. Conversely, if these rational traders expected the spot price in the future to be below the current futures price, they sell futures, lowering the futures price. Hence, the only price that will give an equilibrium is for the futures price to equal the expected spot price at maturity.

Cost of Carry versus Expectations

So far, we have presented two views of the way in which futures prices are formed. Suppose the expected future price does not change over the maturity of the futures

Illustration 8–4

Speculation and the Expectations Model

Suppose that, at time period 0, a speculator purchases a futures contract at a price of F_0 and posts 100 percent margin in the form of riskless securities. At contract maturity at time T, the value of the margin account will have grown to

$$F_0(1 + r_f),$$

where r_f is the risk-free rate of return for a period equal to that of the maturity of the futures contract. At maturity, the value of the futures contract itself will be

$$P_T - F_0.$$

The actual return the speculator will earn is

$$\text{r} = \frac{(1 + r_f)F_0 + (P_T - F_0)}{F_0} - 1$$
$$= r_f + \frac{(P_T - F_0)}{F_0}$$

The expected return the speculator will earn is

$$E(r) = r_f + \frac{(E(P_T) - F_0)}{F_0}$$

Hence if the expectations model is correct, the expected return is

$$E(P_T) = F_0 \rightarrow E(r) = r_f$$

contract; suppose price expectations are constant. The expectations model would yield a constant futures price, as illustrated by the horizontal line in Figure 8–6.

John Maynard Keynes (1930) was among the first to take exception to such a model. In his *Treatise on Money*, he looked at commodity futures and argued that futures provide a mechanism to transfer risk from the hedgers (the commodity producers who have natural long positions in the commodity) to speculators. To accomplish this transfer of risk, the equilibrium in the futures market would be such that hedgers would be (on net) short commodity futures contracts (to offset their natural long positions), while speculators would be long commodity futures contracts. Consequently, to get the speculators to buy the commodity futures contracts—to hold the long positions in futures—the expected rate of return for holding futures would have to exceed the risk-free rate. For the expected rate of return on the futures position to exceed the risk-free rate, the futures price would have to be less than the expected spot price and rise as the contract maturity approaches. This relation, referred to by Keynes as *normal backwardation*, is illustrated as the rising line in Figure 8–6.

Conversely, if hedgers are the ones who were on net long futures contracts (that is, if hedgers are the users of the commodity), the speculators would have to be enticed to sell futures contracts. In this case the futures price would begin above the expected spot price and fall as contract maturity approaches. Referred to by Keynes as *normal contango*, this relation is illustrated by the falling line in Figure 8–6. Illustration 8–5 elaborates on both backwardation and contango.

FIGURE 8–6 Futures Prices over Time with Constant Future Price Expectations

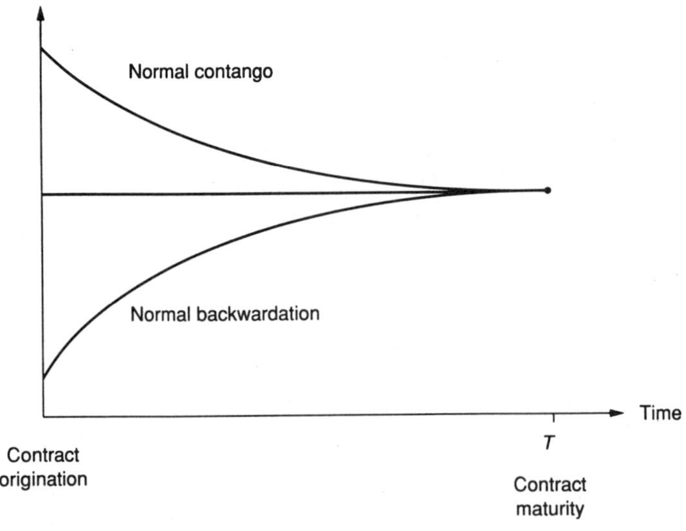

Illustration 8–5

Backwardation and Contango in Bond Futures

Consider again construction of a synthetic futures position, this time a futures position on bonds: I borrow (at the short-term rate) and use the proceeds to purchase bonds (yielding the long-term rate).

The cost of this synthetic bond futures contract is the rate I have to pay on my short-term borrowing minus the rate I earn from the coupons I receive on the long-term bonds. And through arbitrage, the futures price in a standard futures contract must be equal to the cost of this synthetic futures.

If the yield curve is positively sloped, the cost of this synthetic futures is negative—the long-term yield I receive exceeds the short-term yield I pay. Hence, the expected return to the holder of the long futures position is positive. This is a case of *normal backwardation*; the futures price is less than the expected future spot price and futures prices are lower for futures contracts whose delivery dates are further in the future. Look again at Figure 8–5, specifically at the Treasury bond futures traded on the Chicago Board of Trade. The further in the future is the delivery date, the lower the futures price is:

March	107–27
June	106–19
September	105–12
December	104–06
March '94	103–04
June '94	102–04
September '94	101–07

If the yield curve had been inverted—negatively sloped—the reverse would be true. The cost of the synthetic futures would have been positive, so bond futures prices would have exhibited *normal contango*.

Stephen Figlewski (1986) takes issue with Keynes; Figlewski holds that it is the cost-of-carry model, rather than the expectations model, that explains the manner in which futures prices are determined. He argues that the expectations model fails to take into account arbitrage. His reasoning can be paraphrased as follows:

> If individuals are holding Treasury bonds that can be delivered against a Treasury bond futures contract, and if the futures price equals these individuals' expectations of the future spot price of Treasury bonds, arbitrage is possible. The bondholders sell futures against their cash positions, thereby eliminating all the risk in the positions but still earning the same return expected had the risky bond positions remained unhedged. This means that the expected returns the bondholders are earning exceed the risk-free rate; the bondholders earn a risk premium without bearing the risk.
>
> Such a situation attracts other investors. As more people try to buy bonds and sell futures, the cash price is bid up and the futures price is bid down, until the cost-of-carry relation in Equation 8–2 is reestablished.

Figlewski's argument does not mean that the cost-of-carry relation ignores expectations. The market's expectation of the future spot price of the asset is reflected in the current spot price. In an efficient market—and everything we have seen suggests that these financial markets are efficient—the price today impounds all available information, including information about what the asset will be worth in the future. Following Figlewski (1986), "The point of the cost of carry model is that given the current cash price [which impounds a forecast for future spot prices], expectations about the cash price at expiration should not have any *independent* effect on futures prices."

Futures Prices and the Cost of Hedging: Basis

Given what we have said about hedging in general, it follows that, as long as financial futures are priced according to the cost-of-carry relation, the total return to the holder of a fully hedged position should be the risk-free rate of return. The cash position in the underlying asset is a risky position, so the market return to holding this position would be made up of the risk-free rate of return plus a risk premium. By selling a futures contract against the underlying exposure, the hedger has transferred the riskiness of the asset to the buyer of the futures contract; the buyer of the futures contract should earn the risk premium. Hence, an individual who holds the asset and has hedged completely by selling a futures contract against the asset is left with the riskless rate of return.

The problem is that the underlying cash position may not be fully hedged; the return to the futures contract may not be exactly equal to the risk premium on the underlying asset. The hedger has a long position in the asset and a short position in the futures contract and has consequently invested in the difference between these two assets. Hence, the return to the hedged portfolio is determined by what happens to the difference between the spot and the futures prices, which is what we defined earlier as the *basis*:

$$\text{Basis} = F - P.$$

The hedger, the person with the long position in the asset and the short position in the futures contract, profits if the basis gets smaller and loses if the basis gets larger. The reverse is true for the speculator.

Hence, the hedger has not eliminated all risk but has instead replaced price risk with basis risk. Hedgers use the futures market because basis risk is potentially more manageable than price risk. But managing the basis risk requires us first to understand the sources of this risk.

Basis risk goes to zero if the hedge is maintained until the maturity date of the futures contract. However, for shorter holding periods, basis risk results from unpredictable movements in the basis—unpredictable differences between the futures price and the spot price.[16] While these unpredictable movements in the basis arise from various sources, there are four primary sources of basis risk:

1. Changes in the convergence of the futures price to the cash price.
2. Changes in factors that affect the cost of carry.
3. Mismatches between the exposure being hedged and the futures contract being used as the hedge.
4. Random deviations from the cost-of-carry relation.

The Convergence of the Futures Price to the Cash Price. Figure 8–7 depicts a "normal" pattern of convergence of the futures price to the cash price: panel A illustrates the spot and futures prices themselves; panel B illustrates the basis—the difference between these two prices. At contract maturity, the futures price and the cash price coincide, so for a hedge in which the futures contract is held to maturity, the return on the futures position will be equal to the return on the asset itself. However, if the futures position is unwound prior to contract maturity, the return from the futures position could be different from the return on the asset itself because of the basis risk. And as is obvious in Figure 8–7, the basis is in large part determined by the speed of and the path of convergence of the futures price to the spot price. Moreover, the convergence determines the behavior of the margin account. For the case illustrated, the futures price rises smoothly over time. Thus, there would be a gradual flow of margin from the account of the party who sold the futures contract to the account of the buyer of the futures contract.

Suppose the path of convergence was different from that in Figure 8–7. On one hand, if the futures price converged more rapidly than Figure 8–7 suggests, the basis would decline toward zero more quickly and would consequently be smaller at any point in time. In this case, the flow of margin from the futures seller to the futures buyer would occur more rapidly than indicated in Figure 8–7.[17]

Alternatively, consider the situation illustrated in Figure 8–8, in which the futures price overshoots its equilibrium. In this situation, the basis is negative for a time. Also, margin first moves from the seller of the futures contract to the buyer, then from the buyer to the seller, then from the seller to the buyer.[18]

Changes in Factors That Affect the Cost of Carry. Clearly, as the cost of carry changes, the basis on a futures position changes. For commodity futures, the cost of carry includes storage and insurance costs; changes in either of these would cause the basis to change. However, the most significant determinant of the cost of carry is the interest rate. As the interest rate increases, the opportunity cost of holding the asset rises, so the cost of carry and, therefore, the basis rise.

FIGURE 8–7 Convergence of the Futures Price

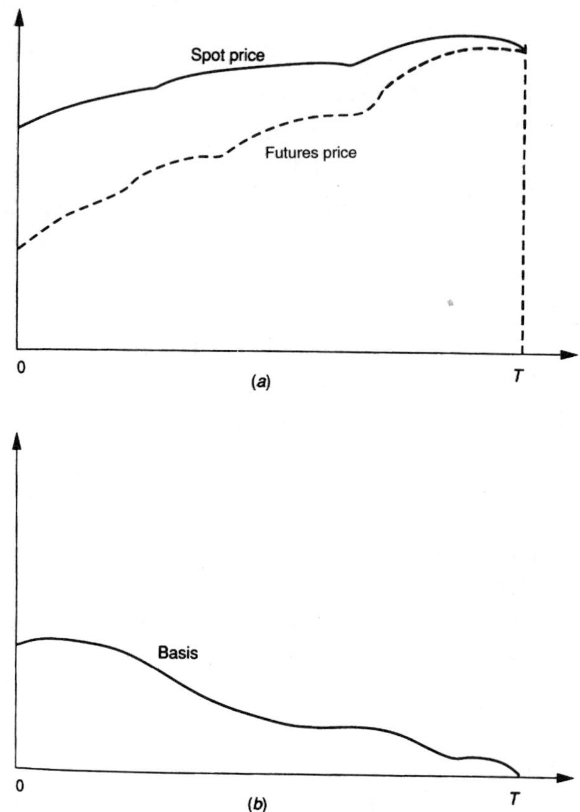

Mismatches between the Exposure Being Hedged and the Futures Contract Being Used as the Hedge. So far, we have examined situations in which the exposure being hedged is the same as the futures contract, such as hedging an exposure to a movement in the deutsche mark-dollar exchange rate with a deutsche mark futures contract or hedging an exposure to the U.S. Treasury bill interest rate with Treasury bill futures. However, in some situations the position being hedged is not the same as the deliverable for any futures contract, and the hedger will have to rely on a *cross-hedge*.[19] For example, a deutsche mark futures contract might be used as a cross hedge for an exposure in Swedish krona,[20] or a Treasury bill futures contract might be used as a cross-hedge against an exposure to the U.S. commercial paper rate.

A cross-hedging situation entails an additional source of basis risk. Basis results not only from differences between the futures price and the prevailing spot

FIGURE 8–8 Convergence of the Futures Price

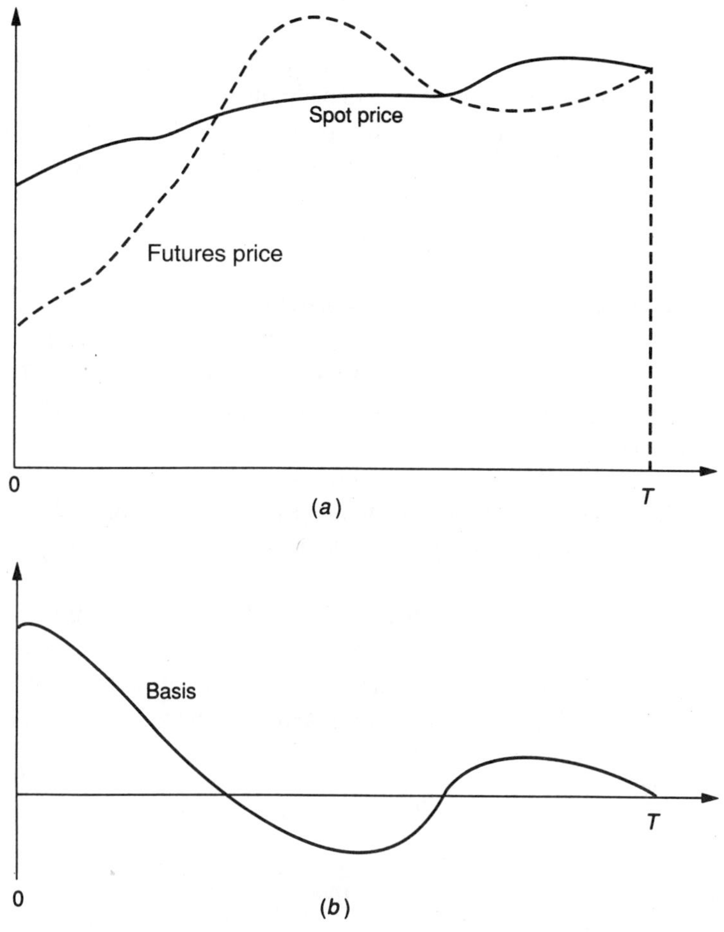

price of the deliverable asset but also from differences between the spot prices of the deliverable asset and the exposure being hedged:

$$\text{Basis}_{\text{cross-hedge } x \text{ for } y} = (F_x - P_x) + (P_x - P_y).$$

For example, if I hedge an exposure to the U.S. commercial paper rate with a Treasury bill futures contract, basis could result either from differences in the futures and spot prices of Treasury bills or from differences in the spot Treasury-bill and commercial paper interest rates. We can define the latter contribution to basis risk—differences in the spot Treasury-bill and commercial paper interest rates—as the *cross-hedge basis*. In Chapter 9 we will look at how typical cross-hedge basis can be determined by the correlation between the spot price of the asset being hedged and the spot price of the deliverable in the futures contract being used as the hedge.

Figlewski (1986) has argued that there are three important factors responsible for variation in the basis for a cross-hedge:

1. *Maturity mismatch.* The maturity of the underlying instrument for the futures contract may be different from the maturity of the asset underlying the exposure. For example, an S&L facing exposure to 30-year mortgage interest rates can construct a hedge using Treasury-bond futures, for which the underlying instrument has a maturity of 15 years.[21]

2. *Liquidity differences.* Suppose that the asset being hedged is traded in a market that is illiquid in comparison to the market for the deliverable asset in the futures contract. In such an instance, the price fluctuations for the asset being hedged would be likely to be large relative to the fluctuations in the price of the deliverable asset, implying that basis would increase. Hence, the basis is inversely related to the liquidity for the asset being hedged.

3. *Credit risk differences.* An example provided by Figlewski is the use of Treasury bond futures to hedge a portfolio of corporate bonds. Put another way, changes in the quality spread show up in the basis for a cross-hedge.

Random Deviations from the Cost-of-Carry Relation. This final source of basis risk is the catchall component. Day to day and minute to minute, the basis on a futures position will change for reasons not understood, but over longer periods this random, white-noise component of basis risk will cancel itself out.

Notes

1. This open outcry auction stands in marked contrast to the specialist system for trading equities.
2. Chicago Board of Trade (1988) presents a concise history of the futures markets in the United States.
3. The Chicago Board of Trade (1988) notes, "Many merchants were not fulfilling their forward commitments, causing bitter disputes between buyers and sellers."
4. This statement is adapted from Sharpe (1985). There are subtle, theoretical differences between a futures contract and a bundle of forward contracts, as French (1983) notes. However, as French concludes, the most important differences between forwards and futures lie in the structure of the contracts rather than the pricing.
5. Chicago Mercantile Exchange SPAN© Minimum Performance Bond Requirements, February 9, 1993.
6. The relatively small magnitude of the margin for futures contracts versus the margin requirement for stocks and the fact that initial margin for futures are set by the exchange rather than the Federal Reserve elicited considerable attention following the events of October 19, 1987. It should be noted, however, that the maintenance margin is set by the exchange in both cases. NYSE sets its maintenance margin for the entire exchange; thus, the margin for stocks should be related to the maximum price change for the most volatile stock on the exchange. The futures exchanges set the margin for each contract. Thus, since the volatility of the S&P Index is significantly less than that of individual stocks, the appropriate margin is correspondingly lower.

7. In the discussion so far we have pretended that Party A contracts directly with Party B. However, in the futures markets, the parties are anonymous. The contracting process actually goes through a broker—a futures commission merchant—who then executes the trade on the futures exchange. Consequently, credit risk is further reduced by the fact that the broker endorses the contract, thereby accepting performance risk.
8. In the example at hand, the reversing trade locks in Party B's loss of $625 from July 1 to July 2, a loss that has already been paid from the margin account. The remainder of the margin account would be returned to Party B.
9. This discussion is adapted from Brennan (1986).
10. As Ira Kawaller points out, the loss would accrue to the clearing member before it accrued to the clearinghouse itself.
11. This delivery specification is particularly important for commodity futures. For example, in the case of wheat futures on the Chicago Board of Trade only certain kinds of wheat are acceptable for delivery (No. 2 Soft Red, No. 2 Hard Red Winter, No. 2 Dark Northern Spring, or No. 1 Northern Spring) and delivery may be accomplished only through warehouse receipts issued by warehouses approved by the exchange.
12. The deliverable bonds have a wide range of coupons and maturities. Consequently, there will be a range of prices for the deliverable bond; at any point in time there will be one bond that is cheapest to deliver.

    To avoid problems with sellers' of the futures contracts all wanting to deliver this one cheapest bond, and the consequent market corners or squeezes, the Chicago Board of Trade uses a conversion factor that adjusts the delivery values of the different bonds to reduce the effects of the differing coupons and maturities. The conversion factor is determined by the value of the specific deliverable bond having an X percent coupon and Y years to maturity relative to a "normal bond" having an 8 percent coupon and 20 years to maturity.
13. While the rules of operation are set by the exchange, they are subject to the approval of the Commodity Futures Trading Commission.
14. In our corn example, this will be true even after we adjust for the transportation cost differential between St. Louis and Chicago.
15. In this we will ignore any seasonality like that evident in the futures price of oats.
16. Predictable movements in basis, like the convergence of the basis toward the cost of carry during the life of the futures contract and the convergence of the basis to zero at contract maturity, discussed earlier in this chapter, are incorporated into the expected return on the hedged position.
17. Regardless of the speed of convergence, the total amount of margin that moves from the seller of the contract to the buyer of the contract is the same; the only difference is in the timing of the cash flows. The slower the futures price converges to the spot price, the slower are the transfers of the margin. Consider an extreme situation in which the spot price moves as before, but the futures price does not move at all until just before maturity.

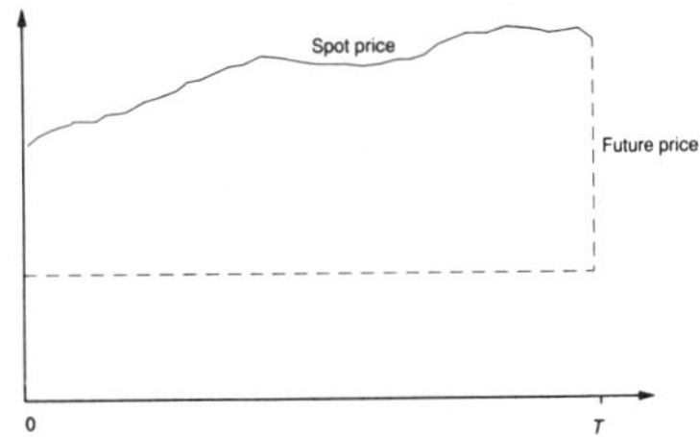

    With the convergence as illustrated, no funds are transferred from the contract seller to the contract buyer until just before contract maturity. In such a case the futures contract behaves essentially like a forward contract.
18. However, since the starting and ending points for the futures price are the same, the undiscounted sum of margin payments that change hands remains the same.
19. In Chapter 9, we will spend considerable time examining the way a cross-hedge is constructed and managed.
20. This so-called proxy hedging was common in hedging European foreign-exchange exposures until September 1992, when the relation between the deutsche mark and the other European currencies broke down.
21. As noted earlier, to be delivered against a T-bond futures contract the bond must have at least 15 years remaining to maturity.

CHAPTER

9

Using Futures to Manage Financial Price Risks

As we noted in Chapter 1, futures contracts on financial assets are a recent addition to the financial engineer's tool box that appeared only with the introduction of foreign exchange futures in 1972. Nonetheless, financial futures have come to be widely used to hedge exposures to foreign exchange, interest rate, and commodity-price risk. Table 9–1 and Figure 9–1 illustrate the expanding use of futures by tracing the trading volume of some familiar futures contracts: the U.S. Treasury bond futures traded on the Chicago Board of Trade, the deutsche mark and Eurodollar futures traded on the Chicago Mercantile Exchange, and futures on crude oil traded on the New York Mercantile Exchange.

The logic of using futures to hedge an underlying exposure is apparent in Figure 9–2. If the firm has an inherent short position in a financial asset—if increases in the price of the asset will decrease the value of the firm—the hedge will be constructed by buying the appropriate number of the appropriate futures contracts for the appropriate expiration month. Combining the inherent position with the hedge, the exposure is neutralized. Ira Kawaller of the Chicago Mercantile Exchange provides an example.

For the firm with an inherent long position, the hedge is constructed by selling the appropriate number of the appropriate futures contract for the appropriate expiration month. The problem for the hedger is, of course, to determine those appropriates: the appropriate futures contract with the appropriate expiration month and the appropriate number of contracts. An example helps demonstrate how the hedger determines these *appropriates*. The following discussion concerns a firm with an interest rate exposure, but the logic is the same for foreign exchange and commodity exposures.

FIGURE 9–1 Yearly Futures Contract Volumes

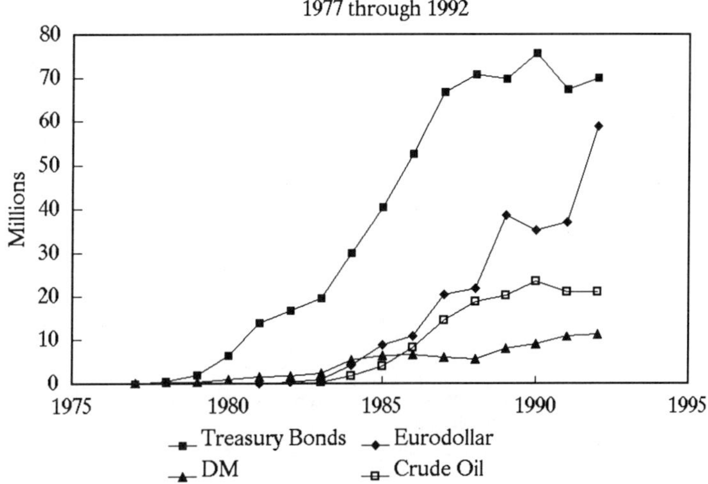

TABLE 9–1 Futures Contract Volumes, 1977–92: Contracts Traded

	*Treasury Bonds**	*Eurodollar*†	*Deutsche Mark*†	*Crude Oil***
1977	32,101	—	134,368	—
1978	555,350	—	400,569	—
1979	2,059,594	—	450,856	—
1980	6,489,555	—	922,608	—
1981	13,907,988	15,171	1,654,891	—
1982	16,739,695	323,619	1,792,901	—
1983	19,550,535	891,066	2,423,508	323,153
1984	29,963,280	4,192,952	5,508,308	1,840,342
1985	40,448,357	8,900,528	6,449,384	3,980,867
1986	52,598,811	10,824,914	6,582,145	8,313,529
1987	66,841,474	20,416,216	6,037,048	14,581,614
1988	70,793,284	21,747,446	5,708,728	18,860,770
1989	69,854,033	38,637,265	8,087,735	20,260,249
1990	75,566,341	35,203,448	9,169,222	23,479,997
1991	67,374,655	39,916,728	10,795,815	21,082,735
1992	69,983,763	58,843,870	11,340,667	21,027,380

*Chicago Board of Trade.
†Chicago Mercantile Exchange.
**New York Mercantile Exchange.
SOURCE: "Volume of Futures Trading," Futures Industry Association, Washington, DC.

FIGURE 9–2 The Logic of the Futures Hedge *(a)* **A Long Hedge** *(b)* **A Short Hedge**

If the firm has an inherent short position

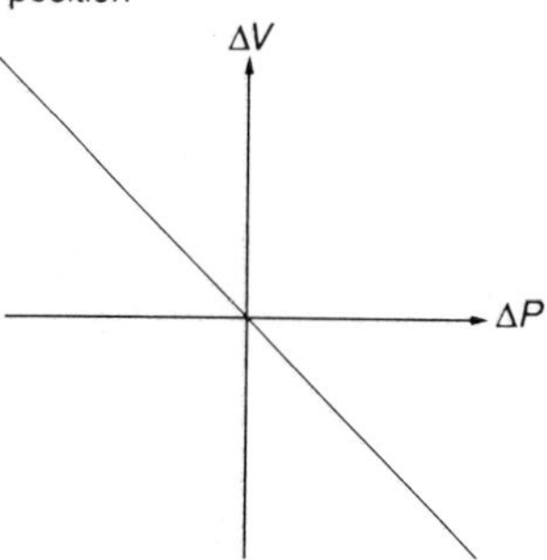

the hedge will be created by buying the appropriate number of the appropriate futures contract

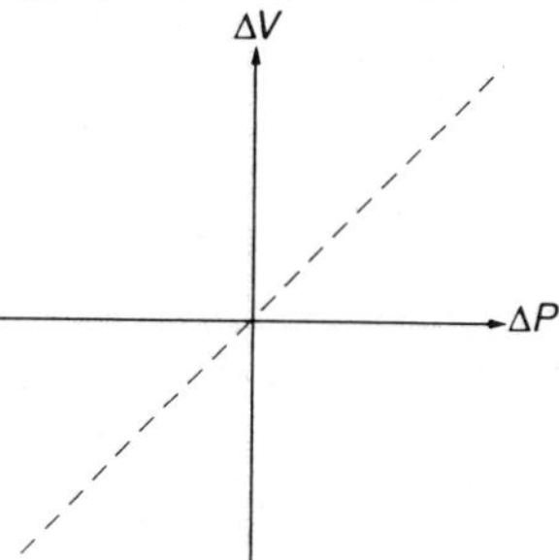

to neutralize the exposure.

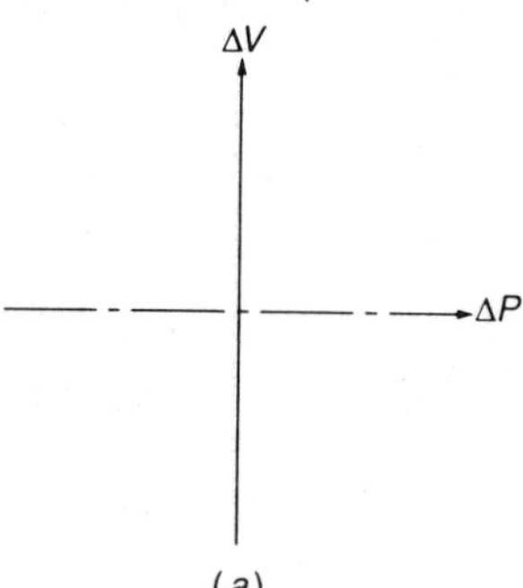

(*a*)

If the firm has an inherent long position

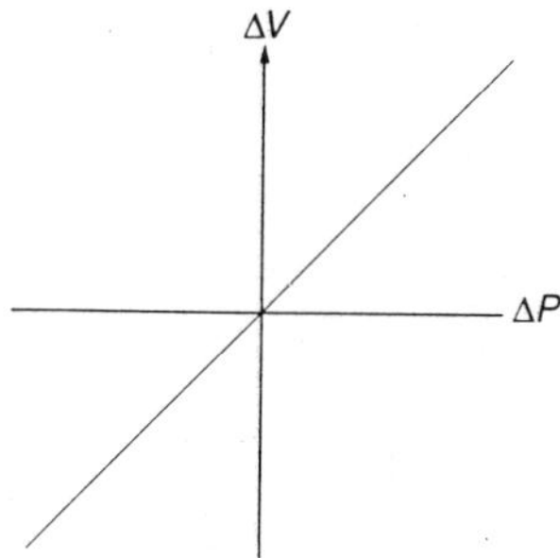

the hedge will be created by buying the appropriate number of the appropriate futures contract

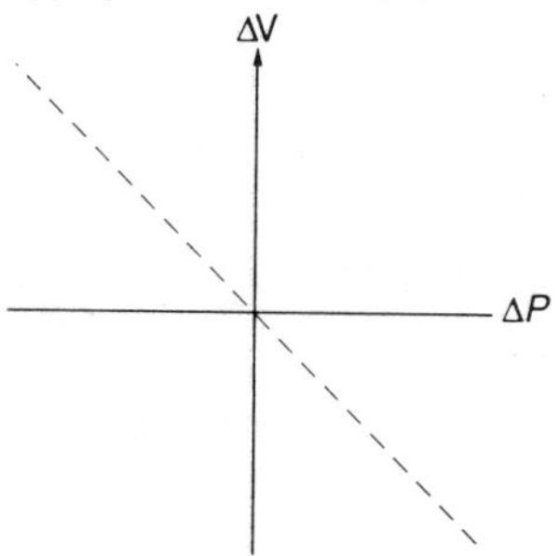

to neutralize the exposure.

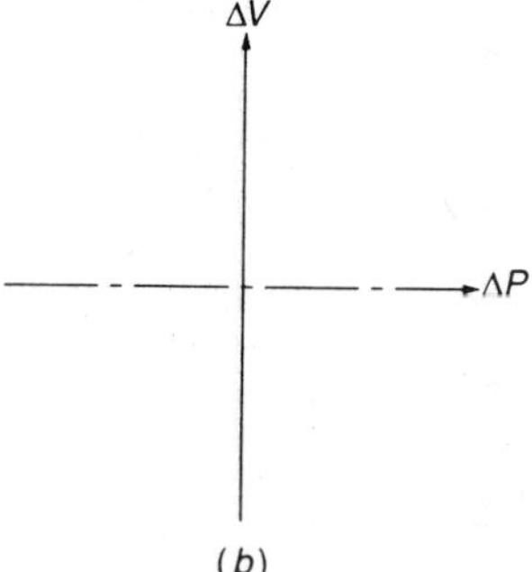

(*b*)

Risk Management in Practice

To Hedge or Not to Hedge*

Ira G. Kawaller

Edwin Charles, the treasurer of Benzoe Corp.,[†] plans to take down a $10 million loan within the next quarter. The loan rate will be set at the time of the takedown, at three-month LIBOR plus 100 basis points. This rate will be reset each quarter on balances remaining outstanding. Clearly, if interest rates rise before the takedown, Benzoe's interest expenses will rise commensurately, but if rates fall, lower interest expenses will result. How can Edwin protect himself against the unknown at the lowest possible cost?

Strategy 1: Do nothing. This choice would be most appropriate if Edwin thinks that the likelihood that interest rates will rise is limited or negligible. He, of course, must be comfortable living with the consequences if his assessment turns out to be wrong.

Strategy 2: Lock in an interest rate today. This may be accomplished by selling Eurodollar futures contracts timed to expire at about the same time as the loan rate is to be set. Any expiration mismatch will foster some uncertainty or "basis risk," but less risk than the prevailing market interest rate exposure itself. The rate that Edwin can secure would be 100 basis points above the rate implied by the futures contract (that is, 100 minus the futures price). The additional 100 basis points reflect the bank's spread over LIBOR.

Before the takedown, it is uncertain which strategy will generate the lower cost of funds. Each alternative hedge strategy should be assessed in light of its cost versus its potential benefits or consequences. For example, a consequence of using futures is forgoing the benefit of lower spot market interest rates.

Suppose, for example, that today three-month LIBOR is at 7 percent and that the Eurodollar futures contract is at 92.90 (in other words, at a rate of 7.10 percent). In the accompanying table, I consider two scenarios—one in which three-month LIBOR rises to 8 percent and the other in which three-month LIBOR falls to 6 percent.

To Hedge or Not to Hedge continued

Outcomes of Alternate Hedging Strategies

Hedge Strategies	*1) Do Nothing*	*2) Sell Futures*
Scenario I: Spot LIBOR Rises to 8 Percent.		
Interest paid to bank (based on 9 percent interest)	$225,000	$225,000
P&L on hedge (10 contracts + price change of hedge vehicle)		22,500
Net interest	225,000	202,500
Effective rate	9 percent	8.10 percent
Scenario II: Spot LIBOR Falls to 6 Percent.		
Interest paid to bank (based on 7 percent interest)	$175,000	$175,000
P&L on hedge (10 contracts × price change of hedge vehicle)		(27,500)
Net interest	175,000	202,500
Effective rate	7 percent	8.10 percent

If Charles does nothing, the cost of funds will simply be equal to spot LIBOR plus 100 basis points—7 percent or 9 percent. If Charles sells futures, he locks in a rate of 100 basis points above the initial futures rate—8.10 percent.

Ira G. Kawaller is vice president and director of the New York office for the Chicago Mercantile Exchange. After receiving a Ph.D. from Purdue University, he served at the Federal Reserve Board in Washington. He subsequently worked for the AT&T Company and J. Aron Company, Inc. Kawaller currently serves on the board of directors of the National Option and Futures Society and the board of advisors for the International Association of Financial Engineers. He is the author of Financial Futures and Options.

*This example was adapted from material in *Treasury and Risk Management* magazine, Fall 1991, and is reprinted with permission. © 1991 CFO Publishing Corp.

†The people and companies presented here are fictional.

Using Futures to Hedge an Underlying Exposure

To illustrate how a futures contract can be used as a hedge, it is probably best to begin with the simplest case.[1]

The construction of the hedge in Illustration 9–1 is simple because everything matched. The underlying exposure is to three-month LIBOR, the same as the deliverable for the futures contract. The end of the exposure matches exactly the deliv-

Illustration 9–1

No Basis Risk

At the beginning of 1994, the treasurer of Ajax Enterprises knows that because of seasonal variations in sales and in the production of inventory for Christmas sales, the firm will require a three-month, $1 million bank loan on June 13. The treasurer knows that the contractual rate Ajax will have to pay on the loan will be the three-month Eurodollar rate (LIBOR) plus 1 percent. Hence, the treasurer is concerned about increases in three-month LIBOR, since every 1 percent (100 basis point) increase in LIBOR increases Ajax's borrowing costs by $2,500.

Using the Eurodollar futures contract traded on the Chicago Mercantile Exchange, the treasurer can achieve a perfect hedge. The treasurer can lock in the Eurodollar borrowing rate given by the implied forward LIBOR rate by selling one June Eurodollar futures contract.

Suppose that on January 2, the three-month LIBOR rate is 3.75 percent. Suppose further that the implied forward LIBOR rate from the June Eurodollar futures contract is 4.25 percent.* Given that Eurodollar futures are quoted as 100 minus the interest rate, this means that the price of the June Eurodollar futures contract on January 2 is

$$100 - 4.25 = 95.75.$$

The treasurer of Ajax sells one June futures contract at 95.75 to lock in a three-month rate of 4.25 percent.

Suppose that the treasurer's fears are realized and that by the time he needs to borrow, the three-month LIBOR is up. While extreme, let's suppose that, precisely on June 13, the three-month LIBOR rate rises from 3.75 percent to 5.50 percent. This 175-basis-point increase in LIBOR means that Ajax's borrowing costs have increased by $1.75 \times \$2{,}500 = \$4{,}375$. Conversely, the increase in the interest rate means that Ajax has earned monies on the futures position that can be used to offset some of this increase in the borrowing cost. In 1994, June 13 will be the last day for trading and delivery of June Eurodollar futures contract. Thus, on June 13 as the futures contract expires, the futures rate and the spot rate must coincide, so the price of the June forward contract on June 13 must be

$$100 - 5.50 = 94.50.$$

Hence, the price of the futures contract has declined by 1.25, or 125 "ticks." The price movement per tick is $25, so Ajax's profit on the futures contract is $125 \times \$25 = \$3{,}125$.

Combining the preceding, Ajax's net increase in its borrowing cost is $1,250,

$$\$4{,}375 - \$3{,}125 = \$1{,}250,$$

which is equivalent to an increase in the three-month Eurodollar rate of 50 basis points. That is, the effect of the hedge is to lock in a three-month LIBOR rate of 4.25 percent, precisely the implied forward three-month LIBOR rate that existed when the hedge was established.

*These were the interest rates implied in futures market as of April 1993.

ery date for the futures contract. The magnitude of the exposure equals the amount of the futures contract.

Moreover, the price movement in Illustration 9–1 is such that no funds are transferred into or out of the margin account during the life of the contract. Consequently, Ajax neither earns additional interest income (in its margin account) nor forgoes interest on funds paid out of its margin account.

However, in the real world, the exposure being hedged typically does not match the characteristics of the futures contract exactly. Generally, the futures contract is liquidated before expiration, and as noted in Chapter 8, the convergence obtained in Ira Kawaller's example is not guaranteed. What is virtually assured is that price changes will not all occur on the final day of the futures contract. The remainder of this section demonstrates the impact these factors have on how the futures hedge would be constructed.

Mismatches on Maturities: Basis Risk

In Illustration 9–1, there is no basis risk; the period of the exposure matches precisely the period covered by the futures contract. Consequently, the futures price and the spot price are the same when the futures hedge is lifted. Were this not the case, basis risk would result.

The situation in Illustration 9–2 is typical; because of basis, the hedge can be more or less than 100 percent effective. Since the hedger can do nothing about the underlying causes of basis that we discuss in Chapter 8, the only other approach to try is to line up exposure dates—in the preceding example, loan pricing dates—with the maturity dates for the futures contract.

Illustration 9–2

Basis Risk

Suppose that Ajax would require the $1 million loan not on June 13 but on June 1, about two weeks before maturity for the futures contract. The treasurer of Ajax would still hedge the exposure by selling one June futures contract on January 2 at 95.75 in an attempt to lock in a three-month Eurodollar rate of 4.25 percent.

To keep the numbers simple, let's suppose that on June 1, three-month LIBOR rises to 5.50 percent (as it did on June 13 in the preceding example).* So, as before, the

Basis Risk continued

increased borrowing cost for Ajax will be $4,375. With this increase in the spot interest rate, the futures interest rate will also rise, so the price of the futures contract will fall. But since June 1 is not the expiration date for the contract, there is no guarantee that on June 1 the futures and spot rates will coincide. Let's suppose that they do not, and that on June 1 the futures price falls not to 94.50 but only to 94.75. The futures price has moved 100 ticks; Ajax's profit on the futures position is 100 × $25 = $2,500.

The result is that Ajax's net increase in its borrowing cost is

$$\$4,375 - \$2,500 = \$1,875,$$

an amount equivalent to a 75-basis-point increase in the three-month LIBOR rate. Hence, the treasurer ends up not with the desired 4.25 percent rate but instead with a rate of 4.50 percent. The 25-basis-point difference is the result of the basis of 25 basis points that exists when the futures contract is closed.†

In this case, the basis goes against the treasurer, and the hedge is less than 100 percent effective. However, the basis could favor the hedger. If the price of the futures contract on June 1 were 94.25, the rate Ajax would end with would be 4 percent, and we would have said that the hedge was more than 100 percent effective.

---

*For now, we continue to suppose that the price change occurs only on June 1; LIBOR remains at 3.75 percent from January 2 to May 31, so the margin account is unaffected.

†When the futures contract is closed, the spot interest rate is 5.50 percent. The rate implied by the futures price is

$$100 - 94.75 = 5.25 \text{ percent.}$$

Hence, the basis is 25 basis points.

Mismatches on Maturities: Strip and Rolling Hedges

So far, we have considered a single exposure in which the maturity for the exposure fits a single futures contract. However, a hedger might have more than one maturity to hedge.

The strategy in Illustration 9–3 works well as long as there is sufficient liquidity in the more distant futures contracts. However, if the more distant futures contracts do not have sufficient liquidity—or if the maturity of the exposure exceeds the term of the most distant traded futures contract—the hedger can resort to a rolling hedge. A rolling hedge can achieve the same result as the strip hedge.

While a rolling hedge can, in some instances, achieve the same results as a strip hedge (as in Illustration 9–4), in other instances a rolling hedge can also accom-

Illustration 9–3

A Strip Hedge

The treasurer of Beta Manufacturing also faces uncertainty about future borrowing costs. Like Ajax, Beta uses three-month borrowing for which it pays a rate linked to three-month LIBOR, but unlike Ajax, Beta borrows not simply once per year but rather throughout the year. On January 2, the treasurer of Beta expects the following borrowing pattern over 1994:

March 1	$15 million
June 1	45 million
September 1	20 million
December 1	10 million

To hedge the resulting exposure to the three-month Eurodollar rate, the treasurer of Beta would "sell a strip of futures." On January 2, she would sell 15 March Eurodollar futures contracts, 45 June contracts, 20 September contracts, and 10 December contracts.

On March 1, Beta would close out the hedge on its first borrowing by buying 15 March contracts. Likewise, on June 1, Beta would buy 45 June contracts; on September 1, Beta would buy 20 September contracts; and on December 1, Beta would buy 10 December contracts. As Illustration 9–2 showed, the effectiveness of the hedge would depend on the basis existing on the dates at which the contracts are closed.

Illustration 9–4

A Rolling Hedge

If the treasurer of Beta is concerned about the liquidity of more distant futures contracts, she can hedge the exposure to the three-month Eurodollar rate by rolling the hedge:

January 2	Sell 90 March Eurodollar contracts
March 1	Buy 90 March Eurodollar contracts
	Sell 75 June Eurodollar contracts
June 1	Buy 75 June Eurodollar contracts
	Sell 30 September Eurodollar contracts
September 1	Buy 30 September Eurodollar contracts
	Sell 10 December Eurodollar contracts
December 1	Buy 10 December Eurodollar contracts

By doing this, the treasurer takes advantage of the liquidity in nearby contracts.

Illustration 9–5

A Rolling Hedge Again

At the beginning of 1994, the treasurer of Beta continues to have the same expectations about borrowings in 1994:

March 1	$15 million
June 1	45 million
September 1	20 million
December 1	10 million

So, on January 2, she implements the rolling hedge detailed in Illustration 9–4:

January 2 Sell 90 March Eurodollar futures contracts

However, suppose that by March 1, the treasurer has developed her forecast for Beta's borrowing needs for March 1, 1995, as $20 million. To hedge this revised borrowing schedule, the transactions done by Beta on March 1 are as follows:

March 1 Buy 90 March Eurodollar futures contracts
Sell 95 June Eurodollar futures contracts

In Illustration 9–4, Beta's remaining planned borrowings total $75 million. Now, with an additional $20 million of borrowing forecast in March 1995, Beta's planned borrowings—the amount it wants to hedge—are $95 million, so Beta will sell 95 rather than 75 June futures contracts.

Continuing in the same manner, suppose that by June 1 the treasurer is forecasting borrowing $60 million for June 1, 1995. Hence:

June 1 Buy 95 June Eurodollar futures contracts
Sell 110 September Eurodollar futures contracts

By buying the 95 June contracts, Beta is closing out the hedge for its June 1994 borrowing.* At the same time, it sells 110 contracts to hedge its September 1994 borrowing (20 contracts), its December 1994 borrowing (10 contracts), its March 1995 borrowing (20 contracts), and its June 1995 borrowing (60 contracts).

The treasurer can continue this system indefinitely. On September 1, she closes out the hedge for the September borrowing by buying the 110 September contracts and sells December '94, March '95, June '95, and September '95 contracts sufficient to hedge her anticipated borrowing needs in December 1994, March 1995, June 1995, and September 1995. On December 1, she buys December contracts to close out the hedge for the December borrowing and sells March 95, June 95, September 95, and December 95 contracts to hedge borrowing needs in March, June, September, and December 1995. On March 1, 1995. . . .

*The effectiveness of this strategy again depends on the basis between the spot three-month LIBOR rate and the implied rate from the futures price on June 1.

plish a hedge that was not possible with a strip hedge. By "stacking" the contracts, futures contracts can be used to hedge an exposure that extends beyond the end of the longest available contract. However, this stacking approach does have drawbacks.[2] First, more contracts must be bought and sold as the hedge is rolled forward, thereby increasing the transaction costs of the hedge. Second, the prices for futures contracts not yet traded are uncertain, creating an additional source of basis risk.

Mismatches in the Asset: Cross-Hedging

To this point, we have considered only cases in which the underlying exposure is to the same financial price that determines the price of the futures contract. In our examples so far, the firm is exposed to three-month LIBOR, precisely the same financial price that determines the price of the Eurodollar futures contract. Often, however, a traded futures contract does not match the hedger's exposure exactly. In such cases, the hedger must resort to a *cross-hedge*. This requires answering two questions: (1) What futures contract should be used to hedge the exposure? (2) How many contracts are required to hedge the exposure?

The short answer to the first question is simple. To establish the "best" cross-hedge, use the futures contract that is most closely correlated with the underlying exposure. To see how this works, let's look again at Ajax.

As Illustration 9–6A shows, the appropriate futures contract for instituting a cross-hedge is normally the futures contract that is most highly correlated with the underlying exposure. However, this simple decision rule may need to be modified if it leads to the selection of a futures contract that has insufficient liquidity. In an illiquid market, the bid-asked spread will usually be large, leading to an increase in the all-in cost of the hedge. Moreover, if the futures contract is illiquid, a large order can have a discernable effect on the price. To the extent that the hedger's buy order triggers a price increase and sell order triggers a price decrease, the cost of constructing a hedge increases. Consequently, concerns about the liquidity of a particular futures contract could result in the hedger's shifting to a contract that has higher liquidity but a lower correlation.

Once the appropriate futures contract is selected, the hedger must answer the second question: How many contracts are required to hedge the exposure? The answer is itself made up of two parts. The hedger must first consider the relation between movements in the underlying exposure and the price of the futures contract used in the hedge. Since the financial price used in the hedge is not the same as the financial price responsible for the firm's underlying exposure, there is no guarantee that there will be one-for-one movements in the two financial prices. The hedger must determine how these two prices move. For example, in the case of interest rate risk, if the rate in the hedge changes by X basis points, how much

Illustration 9–6A

A Cross-Hedge: Selecting the Appropriate Futures Contract

At the beginning of 1994, the treasurer of Ajax Enterprises again expects Ajax will need to borrow on June 1. However, let's change the parameters of this expected borrowing. First, instead of $1 million, let's suppose the forecasted borrowing is $36 million. Second, instead of a three-month bank borrowing tied to LIBOR, let's suppose that the treasurer has decided to issue one-month commercial paper.

Nonetheless, the treasurer remains concerned about rising interest rates and wishes to hedge his interest rate exposure. But there is no futures contract in one-month commercial paper. To select the "best" contract to hedge the exposure to commercial paper rates, the treasurer looks at the correlations between the one-month commercial paper (CP) rate and several interest rates for which there are traded futures contracts available.

Futures Contract	*Interest Rate*	*Correlation with One-Month CP Rate**
U.S. T-bills	90-day T-bill rate	0.987
Eurodollars	90-day LIBOR	0.991
U.S. T-bonds	15-year T-bond rate	0.856

The high correlation between the 90-day LIBOR rate and the one-month commercial paper rate, shown below, leads the treasurer to select the Eurodollar contract as the most appropriate futures contract.

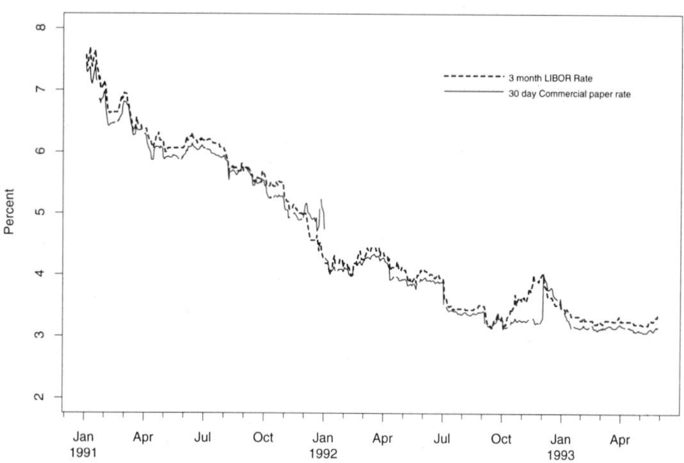

*The correlation coefficients displayed were calculated using data for the nearby futures contract for the period January 2, 1991, through May 28, 1993.

will the rate to which the firm is exposed change? While there are many ways to answer this question, the simplest and most straightforward is to use a linear regression. The analyst regresses the financial price to which the firm is exposed, P_{exposure}, on the financial price embedded in the futures contract being used as the hedge, P_{futures},

$$P_{\text{exposure}} = a + bP_{\text{futures}}.$$

Or, in the case at hand in which the financial prices are interest rates, the regression equation would be

$$r_{\text{exposure}} = a + b(r_{\text{futures}}),$$

where r_{exposure} is the interest rate to which the firm is exposed, and r_{futures} is the interest rate embedded in the futures contract. The estimate of b tells how the interest rate to which the firm is exposed moves in relation to the interest rate embedded in the futures contract. For example, if the estimate of b is 0.5, the rate to which the firm is exposed moves only half as much as the rate in the futures contract, so all other things equal, only half as many futures contracts are required to hedge the exposure. Conversely, if the estimate of b is 2, the rate to which the firm is exposed moves twice as much as the rate in the futures contract, and, all other things equal, twice as many futures contracts are required to hedge the exposure.

In determining the number of futures contracts needed to hedge an exposure, the second thing the hedger must consider is the effect of a one-unit change in the

Illustration 9–6B

A Cross-Hedge: Selecting the Appropriate Number of Contracts, Part 1

The treasurer of Ajax has decided to hedge his June 1 exposure to the one-month commercial paper rate with June Eurodollar futures contracts, priced off three-month LIBOR. To determine how these two rates move in relation to one another, he uses monthly data for 1991–93 to estimate the relation

$$r_{\text{exposure}} = a + b(r_{\text{futures}}).$$

The estimate of b he obtains is 0.75. The treasurer, *considering only the relation between the one-month commercial paper rate and the three-month LIBOR rate*, knows that to hedge his \$36 million exposure, he must sell $36 \times 0.75 = 27$ June Eurodollar contracts.

financial price on the underlying exposure versus the effect of this one-unit change in the financial price on the value of the futures contract. For the case at hand, an increase in the interest rate need not have the same effect on the underlying exposure as it does on the value of the futures contract. If a given change in the interest rate has a larger impact on the underlying exposure than on the value of the futures contract, fewer futures contracts are required to hedge the position, and vice versa.

Putting the preceding together, the construction of a cross-hedge requires that the hedger do the following:

1. *Determine the appropriate futures contract to use as the hedge.* In general, the appropriate futures contract is the one that is most closely correlated with the underlying exposure. However, an alternate futures contract may be selected if there is insufficient liquidity in the preferred contract.

2. *Determine the appropriate number of futures contracts.* The appropriate number of futures contracts is determined by (a) the relation between movements in the underlying exposure and the price of the futures contract used in the hedge and (b) the effect of a one-unit change in the financial price on the underlying expo-

Illustration 9–6C

A Cross-Hedge: Selecting the Appropriate Number of Contracts, Part 2

As we know, the treasurer of Ajax has decided to hedge a $36 million June 1 one-month commercial-paper borrowing with June Eurodollar futures—that is, with three-month LIBOR.

However, a one-basis-point movement in the interest rate does not have the same impact on a one-month borrowing as it does on the three-month futures contract. A one-basis-point movement changes the value of a one-month $1 million borrowing by

$$\$1{,}000{,}000 \times 0.0001 \times 30/360 = \$8.33.$$

But as we have already seen, a one-basis-point movement changes the value of the $1 million futures contract by

$$\$1{,}000{,}000 \times 0.0001 \times 90/360 = \$25.$$

The response of the futures contract is three times that of the underlying exposure, the one-month borrowing.

Hence, *considering only the difference in the way the borrowing and the futures contract respond to a given change in the interest rate*, the treasurer of Ajax knows that he requires only one third as many futures contracts to hedge the exposure; to hedge a $36 million one-month exposure, he must sell 12 rather than 36 three-month futures contracts.

sure versus the effect of this one-unit change in the financial price on the value of the futures contract.

To see how this is accomplished, let's put our example together in Illustration 9–6D.

Once the cross-hedge is implemented, the degree to which it will actually hedge the underlying exposure is determined, as before, by the basis. However, in the case of the cross-hedge, the hedger is using a futures contract in financial price *X* to hedge an exposure to financial price *Y*, so there are two distinct sources of basis risk. First, the cross-hedge is subject to the normal basis; when the hedge is removed, the spot price for *X* need not be equal to the futures price of *X*.[3] The second source of basis risk is in deviations between the spot price of *X* and the spot price of *Y*.[4] To see how this occurs, let's examine how our cross-hedge worked.

Illustration 9–6D

A Cross-Hedge

At the beginning of 1994, the treasurer of Ajax Enterprises expects that it will be necessary for Ajax to borrow $36 million on June 1 by an issue of one-month commercial paper. Concerned about rising interest rates, the treasurer wishes to hedge his interest rate exposure. Since there is no futures contract in one-month commercial paper, he looks for the best contract to hedge the exposure by identifying the futures contract interest rate that has the highest correlation with the one-month commercial paper rate, which turns out to be three-month LIBOR. Hence the appropriate futures contract is the June Eurodollar futures contract.

To determine the appropriate number of June Eurodollar futures to hedge the $36 million one-month commercial paper exposure, the treasurer first uses monthly data for 1991–93 to estimate the relation

$$r_{\text{exposure}} = a + b(r_{\text{futures}}).$$

The estimate of *b* he obtains is 0.75. Secondly, the treasurer notes that a one-basis-point movement changes the value of a one-month $1 million borrowing by $8.33, but a one-basis-point movement changes the value of the $1 million futures contract by $25. Hence, the response of the futures contract is three times that of the underlying exposure, the one-month borrowing. Putting this together, the number of contracts necessary to hedge the exposure is

$$36 \times 0.75 \times 0.33 = 9.$$

Consequently, on January 2, the treasurer of Ajax sells nine June Eurodollar futures contracts.

Illustration 9–6E

The Results of the Cross-Hedge

Let's continue to suppose that on January 2 three-month LIBOR is 3.75 percent and the price of June Eurodollar futures is 95.75, implying a June futures LIBOR rate of 4.25 percent. Let's further suppose that on January 2 the spread between the spot LIBOR rate and the commercial paper rate is 60 basis points, so the one-month commercial paper rate is 4.35 percent.

In preceding cases, Ajax hopes to lock in the futures rate of 4.25 percent, an increase in three-month LIBOR of 50 basis points. In Illustration 9–6B, the treasurer of Ajax estimates the relation between changes in three-month LIBOR and changes in the one-month commercial paper rate to be 0.75. So an expectation of a 50-basis-point increase in three-month LIBOR results in an expectation of a $0.75 \times 50 = 37.5$ basis-point increase in the one-month commercial paper rate. Hence, the one-month commercial paper rate Ajax is trying to lock in is 4.35 percent + 37.5 basis points = 4.725 percent.

As before, let's suppose that precisely on June 1 the three-month LIBOR rate rises to 5.50 percent* and the price of June futures falls to 94.75. As we saw in Illustration 9–2, Ajax's profit on each futures contract is $2,500, so the profit on the nine contracts is $22,500.

If the estimated relation between three-month LIBOR and one-month commercial paper holds, the 175-basis-point increase in three-month LIBOR (5.50 percent − 3.75 percent) should result in a $0.75 \times 175 =$ 131.25 basis-point increase in the one-month commercial paper rate. Hence the one-month rate the treasurer expects is 4.35 percent + 131.25 basis points = 5.6625 percent. However, let's suppose that on June 1 the one-month commercial paper rate rises to 5.75 percent. The increase in Ajax's borrowing costs resulting from the increase in the commercial paper rate is

$$\$36{,}000{,}000 \times (0.0575 - 0.0435) \times 30/360 = \$42{,}000.$$

Combining the increase in the borrowing cost with the profit on the hedge position, Ajax's net increase in its borrowing cost is

$$\$42{,}000 - \$22{,}500 = \$19{,}500.$$

An increase in the borrowing cost of $19,500 is equivalent to an increase in the one-month rate of 65 basis points. Hence Ajax's final one-month borrowing rate is 4.35 percent + 65 basis points = 5 percent.

The difference between this final rate Ajax pays on its borrowing, 5 percent, and the rate the treasurer tries to lock in, 4.725 percent, is 27.5 basis points. The difference is again the result of basis risk, but in this case there are two sources of the basis:

1. On June 1, the spot LIBOR rate of 5.50 percent differs from the LIBOR rate implied by the futures price, 100 − 94.75 = 5.25 percent, by 25 basis points. Since the estimated relation between the three-month LIBOR rate and the one-month commercial paper rate is 0.75, the basis of 25 basis points

The Results of the Cross-Hedge continued

for three-month LIBOR will translate to a basis of $0.75 \times 25 = 18.75$ basis points for one-month commercial paper.

2. On June 1, the expected one-month commercial paper rate is 5.6625 percent, but the actual commercial paper rate is 5.75 percent. This difference results in a basis for the one-month commercial paper hedge of 5.75 percent − 5.6625 percent = 8.75 basis points.

Combining the two sources of basis,

$$18.75 + 8.75 = 27.5 \text{ basis points,}$$

we obtain the total basis for this one-month commercial paper hedge.

*We are still presuming that the price change occurs only on June 1; from January 2 through May 31, LIBOR remains at 3.75 percent.

Adjusting for the Margin Account: "Tailing" the Hedge

So far, in looking at the construction of a hedge we have considered only the gain or loss on the futures position at the end, when the hedge is removed. However, as you know from Chapter 8, profits and losses accrue to a futures contract over the life of the contract as funds are transferred into or out of the hedger's margin account. Since the funds in the margin account earn interest, funds that flow in early are more valuable than those that flow in later. (Conversely, the value of the hedger's position is higher if funds flow out of the margin account late rather than early.)

For purposes of illustration, suppose a firm sells a futures contract to hedge an underlying position. Gains on the hedge will be used to offset losses on the underlying position. Figure 9–3 illustrates the effect of the timing of cash flows and of the margin account. In all three panels, the gain to the hedger independent of the margin account is equal to the difference in the beginning and ending futures prices times the size of the futures contract $(F_0 - F_T)FC$. However, the accrued interest for the margin account is very different for the three cases displayed in panels A through C. First, compare panels A and B. Panel A is much like the situation we have considered so far—the futures price remains constant until the end of the hedge period—while in panel B funds are flowing into the hedger's margin account smoothly over the duration of the hedge. In the situation illustrated by panel A, there is essentially no interest earned, while for that illustrated by panel B, the hedger earns interest on the increases in the margin account. Consequently, if the futures price behaves like panel B rather than panel A, the number of futures contracts necessary to hedge a given position is

FIGURE 9–3 The Effect of the Timing of Cash Flows into the Margin Account

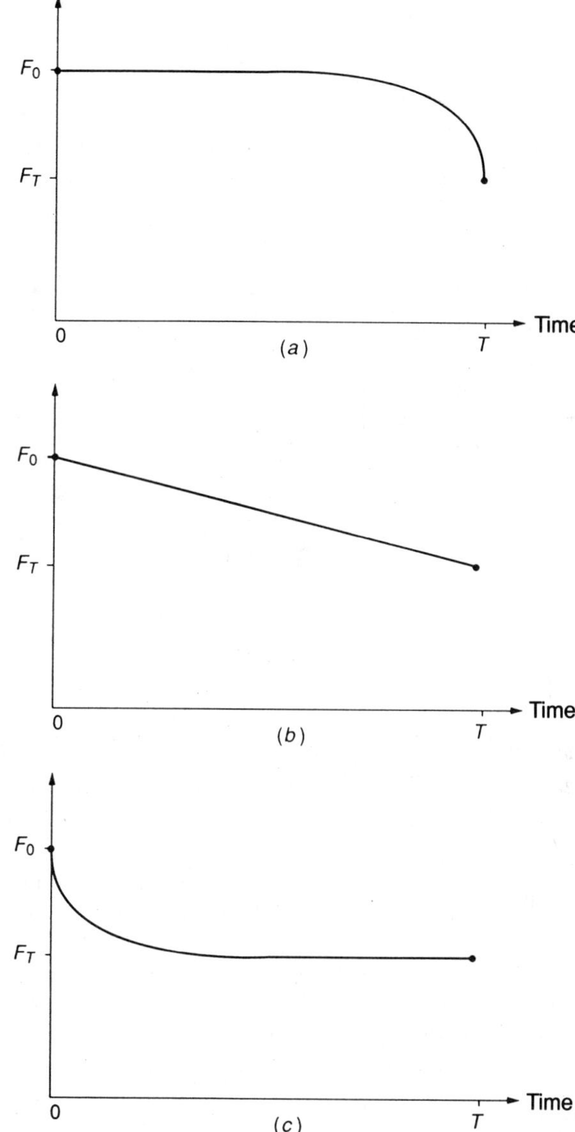

smaller. And if futures prices behave like the situation illustrated in panel C, the hedge position can be even smaller, since more of the funds flow in early during the hedge period.[5]

The upshot of all this is that the number of futures contracts needed to hedge an exposure must be adjusted for the effect of the daily resettlement of the margin account. Profits today are magnified by the interest earned if reinvested. This effect, if not accounted for properly, causes overhedging. Although the effect turns out to be small for short hedging periods and low interest rates, it can by corrected by a technique known in futures market jargon as "tailing" the hedge. The "tail" adjusts the number of futures contracts so that the *present value* of the hedge equals the underlying exposure. Hence, if ignoring the effect of daily resettlement of the margin account, the number of contracts to be sold to hedge a given exposure is N, then the "tailed" hedge is

$$Ne^{-rT},$$

where T is the maturity of the hedge and r is the appropriate riskless interest rate.

Illustration 9–7

A "Tailed" Hedge

Cassa Manufacturing, like Ajax, expects to have to issue one-month commercial paper in the future. However, Cassa expects to issue $400 million in 15 months.

The treasurer of Cassa wants to hedge this exposure using futures contracts. Using what we have seen in Illustration 9–6, it would appear that the appropriate futures contract is the Eurodollar, and, ignoring the effect of the margin account, the appropriate number of contracts to sell would be

$$400 \times 0.75 \times 0.33 = 100.$$

However, if daily resettlement of the margin account is taken into account—if the hedge is "tailed"—the number of Eurodollar futures contract she should sell is

$$100e^{-rt}.$$

where T is 15 months. If we suppose that the corresponding riskless interest rate is 8.2 percent, the treasurer of Cassa will sell 90 Eurodollar futures contracts,

$$100e^{-(0.082)(15/12)} = 90.25.$$

Moreover, the hedger needs to monitor the rate at which funds are moving into or out of the margin account. If funds are flowing into or out of the margin account at a rate different from that expected when the hedge was established, the tailing factor for the hedge must be adjusted accordingly.

Finally, and most importantly, hedgers will have to monitor basis risk. After all, by using the futures contract, a hedger has

A "Tailed" Hedge

accepted basis risk in place of price risk and should manage this basis risk as much as possible. Hence the hedge should be rebalanced occasionally if the relation between the prices of the assets being hedged and the assets underlying the futures contract changes. Change in the relation between the spot and futures prices also may require rebalancing the hedge.

The illustrations in this chapter rely on interest rate hedging to show how futures can be used. Futures, however, are equally well-suited to hedging commodity and foreign exchange exposures. Ira Kawaller demonstrates how a foreign exchange hedge works.

Risk Management in Practice

Waging War against Currency Exposure

Ira G. Kawaller

It was mid-December in 1990. An outbreak of hostilities between the United States and Iraq was imminent. As General Norman Schwartzkopf pondered ways to safeguard his troops, Treasurer Joanna Knobler pondered ways to safeguard the Trilobyte Corporation from potential swings in foreign exchange rates.

The computer manufacturer had just scored a tandem success. Aggressive bargaining clinched a deal to secure computer boards from Japan at a particularly attractive price of ¥125 million. Another campaign won a large contract to supply a German wholesaler with computers for DM1.25 million.

But if the coalition forces attacked Iraq, the gains Trilobyte had made could be wiped out by movements in foreign exchange rates. Knobler sought a way to safeguard Trilobyte's exposure to the wild currency swings that would inevitably accompany an army's march into the desert.

Because of the difference in timing between Trilobyte's needing to buy the ¥125 million in March and receiving the DM1.25 million in late May, Knobler found the uncertainty meant too much risk. Trilobyte would be vulnerable if the dollar weakened against the yen before March 1991 or if it strengthened against the deutsche mark before late May.

Waging War Against Currency Exposure continued

If the dollar behaved as it had during periods of international tension, it would weaken on the outbreak of war, which would drive up Trilobyte's cost of buying yen. If fighting was prolonged, the company's German deal would benefit from a weakened dollar. But what if the war was over quickly and the dollar soared?

Knobler decided to hedge her bets, as well as her exposure. She hedged all of Trilobyte's yen requirements. But because the deutsche mark deal would be more profitable if the dollar weakened, she hedged only 50 percent of that exposure up front. If the dollar dropped significantly, she could lock in the other half of the deutsche mark exposure at lower levels. On the other hand, if she saw signs of a longer-term strengthening of the dollar, she would move quickly to hedge the rest of the deutsche mark exposure.

- On December 14, 1990, she bought 10 yen futures contracts for March delivery—each contract covered ¥12.5 million for coverage of the ¥125 million exposure.
- She also sold short five June deutsche mark futures contracts, each for DM125,000 to cover half her exposure on the German contract.

On January 17, the Middle East battle began. Knobler took the opportunity to capture some of the consequent weakness in the value of the dollar by short selling another five deutsche mark futures contracts worth DM625,000, locking in a more favorable exchange rate.

The hedge positions and the results on May 20 are summarized in the following table.

The Yen Hedge

Dec 14	Bought 10 March ¥ Futures at $.(00)7508/¥
March 18	Cover 10 March ¥ Futures at $.(00)7225/¥
	Buy ¥125 million at 138.41 = $903,114

Effective Rate for Yen:

$$\frac{\frac{\text{¥ 125 million}}{\text{¥138.41/\$}} - 10(7225 - 7508) \times \$12.50}{\text{¥125 million}} = \$.(00)7508 \text{ or } ¥133.19/\$$$

Effective cost of ¥ 125 million at 133.19 = $938,509
Opportunity cost of yen hedge = $ 35,395*
Commissions would bring the rate to $.(00)7509 or $.(00)7510

*Knobler would have done better by not hedging the yen.

Waging War Against Currency Exposure continued

The Deutsche Mark Hedge

Dec 14	Sold 5 June DM futures at \$.6671/DM
Jan 17	Sold 5 June DM futures at \$.6712/DM
May 20	Cover 10 June DM at .5762/DM
	Sell DM1.25 million at DM1.7325/\$

Effective Rate for Deutsche Mark:

$$\frac{\dfrac{\text{DM1.25 million}}{\text{DM1.7325}} + 5(6671 - 5762) + (6712 - 5762) \times \$12.50}{\text{DM1.25 million}} = \$.6702/\text{DM} \text{ or DM1.4922/\$}$$

Sale of DM1.25 million at 1.7325 = \$721,500
Sale of DM1.25 million at hedge rate 1.4922 = \$837,689
Benefit of deutsche mark hedge: \$116,189*
Commissions bring the effective rate to \$.6700 or .6701/DM.

---

*Knobler's deutsche mark hedge worked out well, saving her \$116,189.

As it happened, Knobler's yen exposure coincided with the quarterly delivery cycle of currency futures traded on the International Monetary Market of the Chicago Mercantile Exchange. But for the deutsche marks, the nearest she could get to her May 20 date was the June contract, scheduled to expire three weeks later.

Although Knobler wanted to lock in a DM–USD exchange rate for May 20, the nearest futures contracts she could use actually reflected the forward rate for June 20, four weeks later. A firm hedging with futures contracts can be assured of realizing the futures rate only if the hedge is held to the futures expiration date, as was the case with the yen hedge but not with the deutsche mark hedge. By unwinding the hedge before expiration, the nonconvergence of spot and futures prices upon hedge liquidation results in an exchange rate that generally conforms to the desired forward date (May 20 here), as opposed to the futures value date (June 20). Knobler could have locked in the exact dates by hedging in the interbank market. But she might have less flexibility to exercise the hedge and—as a smaller company—would have to pay retail prices for her foreign exchange cover. In contrast, futures markets essentially offer wholesale prices to all customers; no one gets preferential treatment.

The amount of risk a treasurer is willing to take determines how much exposure to offset at any time. Thus, futures can be progressively applied or selectively unwound as rates swing to and fro. Knobler set criteria beforehand, based

Waging War Against Currency Exposure continued

on her expectation of the future. She didn't, therefore, chase the market with hedges to cover every short-term trend in rates.

Adjustable hedges with trigger points take a great deal more self-discipline and confidence to manage than a "fire and forget" application of futures. The initial decision to hedge is critical: treasurers should understand from the beginning exactly what they hope to achieve. If the goal is to eliminate risk by locking in a currency rate, a hedge will do that—even if in hindsight it would have been more profitable not to hedge the risk. It's worth remembering that the maximum exposure occurs when people have no hedge at all.

Ira G. Kawaller's biography appears earlier in this chapter. This example was adapted from material in *Treasury and Risk Management* magazine, Fall 1992, and is reprinted with permission.

Managing a Futures Hedge

Once the hedge has been established, it is essential that it be monitored. As observers of the futures market note, placing a hedge and then forgetting it amounts to imprudent hedging.[6]

Margin calls and the daily marking-to-market demand a hedger's attention. In many cases, the funds required to meet the margin calls must be obtained from sources other than the underlying position itself. For this reason, a successful hedging program must include a source of these funds. Clearly, hedgers do not want to have too small a source of funds to meet margin calls; if the funds are not available, the hedge will be closed. But hedgers do not want to keep too large a pool of liquid funds available for meeting margin calls, since they forgo interest that could otherwise be earned.[7]

Notes

1. This case and some of those that follow have been adapted from *Using Interest Rate Futures and Options*, a publication of the Chicago Mercantile Exchange.
2. Drabenstott and McDonley (1984).
3. Again, the spot price and futures prices are guaranteed to be equal only at expiration of the futures contract.
4. As Ira Kawaller points out, this second source of risk is the risk that the *ex post* relation between X and Y (the parameter b in our equation) turns out to be equal to the *ex ante* estimate of the relation from the regression equation.
5. For purposes of illustration, we have presumed that funds flow only one direction during the duration of a

hedge. This is certainly not necessary. As illustrated below, funds could first flow out of the margin account from period 0 to period t_1,

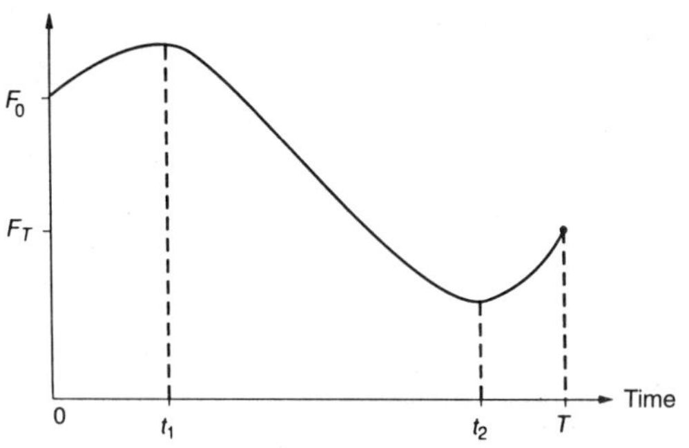

then flow into the margin account from period t_1 to t_2, and then flow out of the margin account again from period t_2 to T.

6. Drabenstott and McDonley (1984).
7. Figlewski (1986, Chapter 8) provides a method for determining the optimal pool of liquid funds available to meet margin calls.

CHAPTER

10 SWAPS*

Swaps are the newest of the risk management products. When we traced the evolution of such products in Chapter 1, we noted that forwards were used at least as early as the 12th century, that futures existed as early as the 16th century, and that option contracts were used as early as the 17th century. However, the origins of the swap are generally dated from the public announcement of the currency swap between IBM and the World Bank in 1981.

As we noted in Chapter 3, the swap market has grown dramatically since 1981. This dramatic growth, however, is one of the few aspects of the swap market upon which market participants agree. The market's rapid growth contributed to much confusion, misinformation, and folklore about the hows and whys of swaps.

In this chapter, we hope to clear up some of this confusion. We describe how the swap contract first appeared and how it evolved over time. We examine the development and subsequent growth of the swap market and discuss how swaps are priced and valued.

Evolution of the Swap Contract

When swaps were introduced in the 1980s, the conventional wisdom was that swaps somehow "appeared"—as if by magic—in the markets. (Indeed, we have

*We are particularly indebted to Lee Macdonald Wakeman for the development of our discussion of swaps. Much of the material we used is taken from three papers we coauthored with Lee: Smith, Smithson, Wakeman (1986), (1987), and (1988). Moreover, much of our thinking—indeed, much of the thinking of the swaps market in general—on pricing and hedging swaps is based on Lee's work on the zero-coupon yield curve and hedging a portfolio of swaps.

often said that it sounded as if swaps were something handed down on stone tablets on some mountain top.) The truth is swaps did not just appear; they evolved from existing financial products. And from these first swaps—which now seem simple in retrospect—increasingly complex swap structures have evolved.

From Parallel Loans to Currency Swaps

As we described in Chapter 1, the breakdown of the Bretton Woods accord in 1973 brought increased foreign exchange risk to multinational companies. With elimination of fixed exchange rates, the volatility of foreign exchange rates increased dramatically. Coupled with the prevailing accounting treatment of foreign-denominated assets and liabilities (Statement 8), the increase in foreign exchange volatility produced massive swings in reported earnings.

In some instances, changes in exchange rates had a greater impact on the reported earnings of the firm than did changes resulting from operations. For firms with significant overseas operations, the effects of financial changes were swamping the effects of real changes.

For example, if the pound became more valuable (in other words, if the dollar price of a pound rose), the dollar value of the assets held by a UK subsidiary of a U.S. firm would rise; its U.S. parent would be better off, and vice versa. (See Figure 10–1.)

FIGURE 10–1 Risk Profile for a U.S. Company with a UK Subsidiary

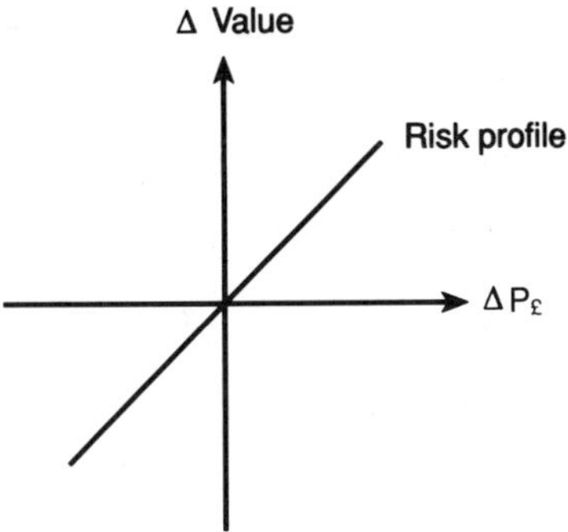

If a U.S. parent has assets in the United Kingdom, it faces risks resulting from movements in the price of the pound. If the dollar price of a pound ($P_£$) rises, the value of the assets in the United Kingdom rises. This increases the value of the U.S. parent through the increased reported earnings.

Before the introduction of currency swaps, these foreign exchange exposures could have been hedged using *parallel loan agreements* (also known as back-to-back loans).

Parallel loan structure worked and became popular with many U.S. firms as a means of hedging the currency exposures created by U.S. accounting practices. However, the use of parallel loans involves two major problems:

1. *Default risk.* The loans are independent instruments, so default by one party does not release the counterparty from contractually obligated payments.
2. *Balance sheet impact.* If the balance sheets of the parent and its subsidiary must be consolidated, the parallel loans inflate the balance sheet, which

Illustration 10–1

Hedging a U.S. Parent/UK Subsidiary with a Parallel Loan

The U.S. company and its UK subsidiary would be matched with a UK company that had a U.S. subsidiary. The U.S. company would make a dollar-denominated loan to the U.S. subsidiary of the UK company. Simultaneously, the UK company would make a pound-denominated loan of equal current value to the UK subsidiary of the U.S. firm.*

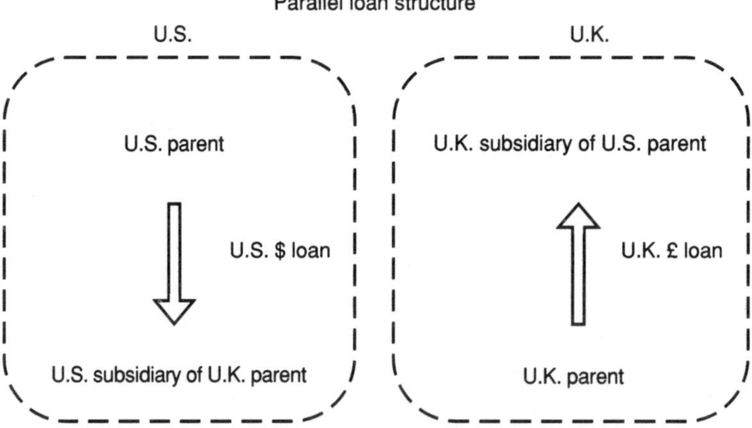

The loans have parallel interest and principal repayment schedules, as illustrated by the following.

Hedging a U.S. Parent/UK Subsidiary with a Parallel Loan continued

Cash Flows from a Parallel Loan Agreement.

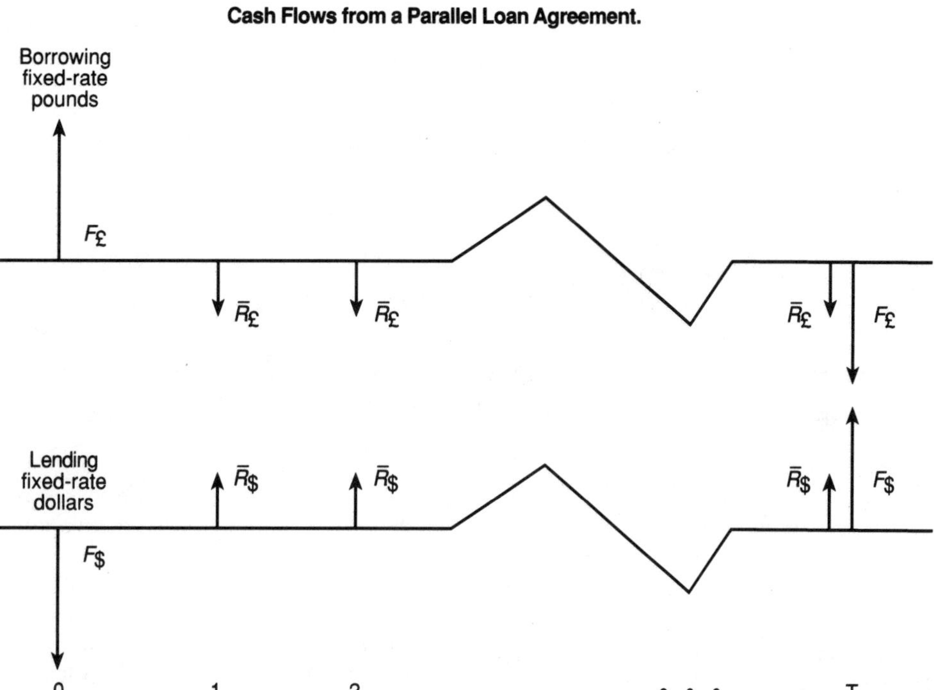

In this figure, inflows are denoted by upward arrows and outflows by downward arrows. The magnitude of the cash flow is indicated by the arrow's length.

At time 0, the U.S. firm, through its UK subsidiary, borrows pounds ($F_£$) at the prevailing T-period pound rate. At the same time, the U.S. firm makes a loan to the U.S. subsidiary of the UK firm—at the prevailing T-period dollar rate—in an amount in dollars that is equivalent (at the current exchange rate) to the sterling principal it borrowed ($F_\$$).

During the term of the loan, the U.S. firm makes interest payments in pounds ($R_£$) to the UK firm, which in turn makes interest payments in dollars ($R_\$$) to the U.S. firm. At maturity (time T) the two firms make their final interest payments and return the principals; the U.S. firm returns pounds and the UK firm returns dollars.

As illustrated on page 238, this parallel loan structure would hedge the U.S. parent's exposure to dollar–pound movements.

Hedging a U.S. Parent/UK Subsidiary with a Parallel Loan continued

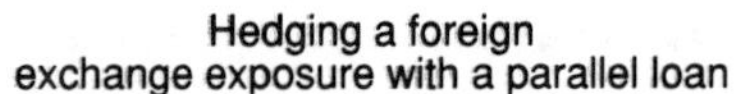

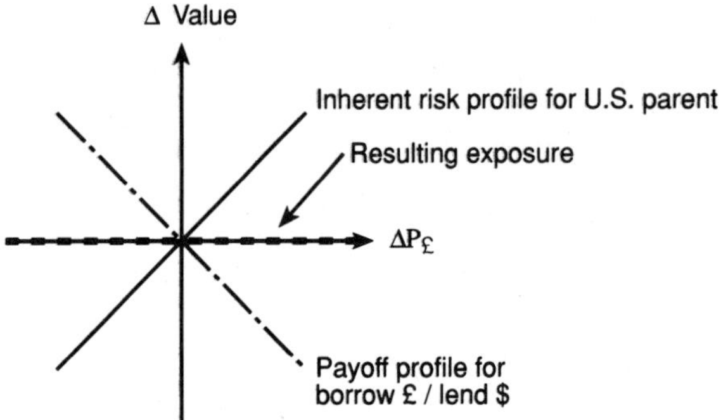

If the value of the pound rises (falls), the U.S. parent would suffer a loss (profit) on the parallel loan. Hence, the change in the value of the parallel loan would offset the firm's inherent position. If the U.S. parent matched the size of the parallel loan to the size of the inherent exposure, its U.S. dollar, UK pound exposure could be eliminated.

---

*The motivation for the U.S. firm to enter into this parallel loan agreement would have been to reduce the volatility of reported income (under SFAS 8). The UK firm would have been attracted to this transaction because the British government had (as had other governments) imposed controls on capital movements, in effect taxing the export of capital. These capital controls would have made it difficult for the UK parent to fund expansions in its U.S. subsidiary. By entering into the parallel loan agreement, the UK parent would have been able to bypass the capital controls and provide funds to its U.S. subsidiary.

can lead to problems with financial covenants. Although the two loans effectively cancel each other out, they remain on the balance sheets for accounting and regulatory purposes.

Default risk can be managed by establishing cross-default provisions between the two loans, or the problem can be handled by combining the two independent instruments into a single instrument. Put another way, we can "staple the two contracts together." As a result, the two sets of cash flows for a parallel loan become the single set of cash flows illustrated in Figure 10–2. The resulting instrument is a *currency swap*.

FIGURE 10–2 Making a Parallel Loan Agreement into a Single Instrument: Creating a Currency Swap

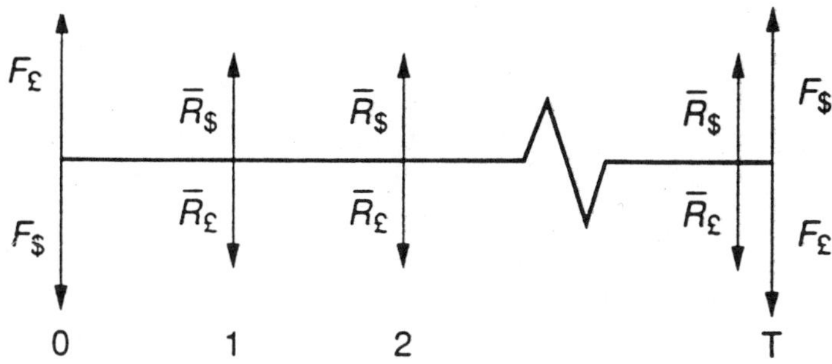

As Figure 10–2 indicates, the counterparties to the swap contract have agreed to exchange, or swap, cash flows. To determine the magnitude of the cash flows, the counterparties define some *notional principal*. The principal is "notional" in the sense that neither party owes it to the other—as would be the case in a loan.

The party illustrated in Figure 10–2 agrees to pay a series of cash flows based on the notional principal of the swap (in sterling) and the fixed sterling interest rate that is appropriate for the maturity of the swap:

$$\bar{R}_£ = (\bar{r}_£)\,(NP_£)$$

This party receives a series of cash flows determined by the U.S. dollar notional principal of the swap and a fixed U.S. dollar interest rate that is appropriate for the maturity of the swap:

$$\bar{R}_\$ = (\bar{r}_\$)\,(NP_\$)$$

The counterparty takes the reverse position.

By combining the parallel loans into a single legal document called a swap, the default risk has been reduced substantially. Default risk can be reduced further by *netting* the payments: at each of the *settlement dates* 1,2, . . . ,T, it is not necessary for the party illustrated in Figure 10–2 to pay $\bar{R}_£$ and receive $\bar{R}_\$$. Instead, the two parties can exchange a *difference check*. If the value of sterling rises, the party illustrated in Figure 10–2 pays a difference check to the counterparty; if the value of sterling falls, the party illustrated in Figure 10–2 receives a difference check.

The second problem with parallel loans, their impact on balance sheets, disappears when the parallel loans are stapled together to form the currency swap: current accounting and regulatory practices treat swaps as off-balance-sheet instruments. So the swap will not inflate the firm's balance sheet.

Aside

Currency Swaps versus FX Swaps

If swaps were not confusing enough, it turns out that the name "swap" is used to describe two different transactions in the foreign exchange market. One is the "currency swap" defined above; the other is the "FX swap" familiar to traders in the foreign exchange spot and forward markets.

An FX swap involves the simultaneous sale and purchase of FX forward contracts of different maturities. For example, suppose a firm currently will receive yen in 60 days but will not have to make a corresponding yen payment for 90 days. The firm might then do an FX swap where it sells a 60-day forward contract on yen and simultaneously buys a 90-day forward on yen.

In Chapter 2 we stressed that swaps—currency swaps—can be viewed as a portfolio of forward contracts with different maturities but, within the portfolio, all either long or short. As you can see from the preceding, the FX swap can also be viewed as a package of forward contracts with different maturities, one long and the other short.

From Currency Swaps to Interest Rate, Commodity, and Equity Swaps

From the currency swap evolved other kinds of swaps. As we have seen, the currency swap involves the exchange of fixed-rate cash flows in one currency for fixed-rate cash flows in another. As shown in Figure 10–3, replacing one of the fixed-rate cash flows with a floating-rate cash flow is a simple matter. The resulting instrument is a *currency-coupon swap*. (This construction is sometimes called a cross-currency interest rate swap.)

A special case of a currency-coupon swap occurs when the two currencies are the same. This special case, an *interest rate swap*, is illustrated in Figure 10–4. As with currency swaps, initial principal exchange is not necessary in an interest rate swap. However, in contrast to standard currency swaps, interest rate swaps do *not* require the reexchange of principal at maturity, because all the principal amounts of an interest rate swap are expressed in the same currency units. Therefore, we can illustrate the interest rate swap as in Figure 10–5.

In an interest rate swap, the cash flows are determined by one fixed interest rate and one floating interest rate (both in the same currency). In a *basis-rate swap*, both interest rates are floating (again, both are in the same currency). Thus, the basis-rate swap permits a borrower (or investor) to exchange a stream of payments determined by one floating interest rate for a payment stream determined by another floating interest rate. For example, a basis-rate swap would permit firms to convert from six-month LIBOR to one-month U.S. commercial paper rates.

FIGURE 10–3 Currency Swap Converted to a Currency-Coupon Swap

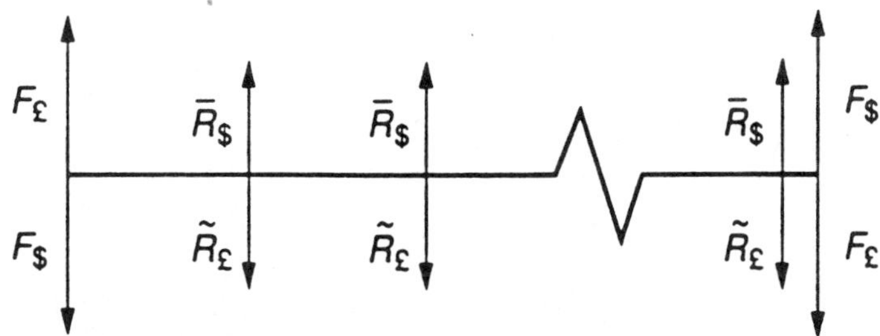

A swap of a fixed-rate cash flow ($\bar{R}_\$$) in one currency for a floating-rate cash flow ($\tilde{R}_£$) in another currency is called a *currency coupon swap*.

FIGURE 10–4 A Currency-Coupon Swap Converted to an Interest Rate Swap

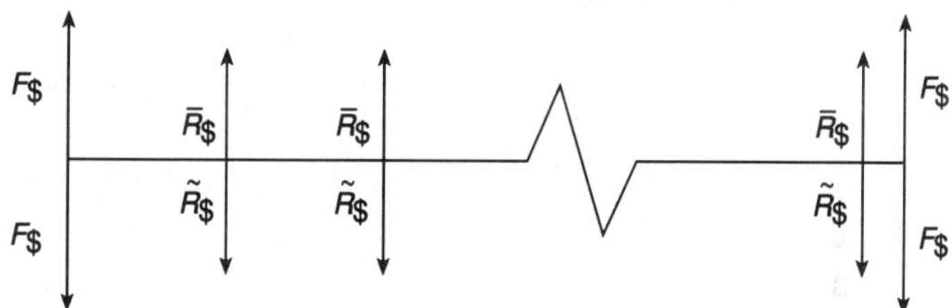

If all the cash flows in currency coupon swap are paid in the same currency, the result is an interest-rate swap.

Figure 10–6 illustrates such a swap. As this figure suggests, a basis-rate swap is equivalent to a combination of two simple interest rate swaps. The flows are converted from floating to fixed, and then converted from fixed to floating (but on a different basis).

Swaps that are defined in prices other than interest rates and foreign exchange rates also have appeared. Once a principal amount is determined and that principal is contractually converted to a flow, any set of prices can be used to calculate the cash flows.

In 1986, the first *oil swap* was transacted (intermediated by the Chase Manhattan Bank). As in the other swaps we have described, the parties agree on a notional principal, but in this case the notional principal is expressed in barrels of oil rather than in dollars. Then in a manner analogous to the fixed and floating pay-

FIGURE 10–5 An Interest Rate Swap: Cash Flows for a Floating-Rate Payor

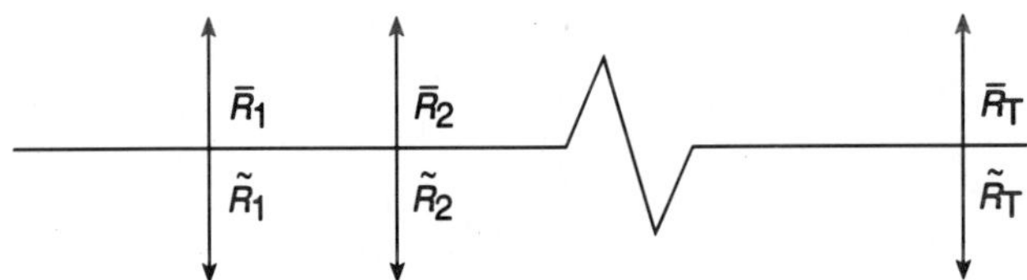

The counterparty illustrated receives a series of cash flows determined by the T-period fixed interest rate ($\bar{R}$t) at origination, in return paying a series of cash flows ($\tilde{R}$t) determined by the relevant floating-interest rate, reset at the beginning of every period.

FIGURE 10–6 A Basis Swap: LIBOR to U.S. Commercial Paper

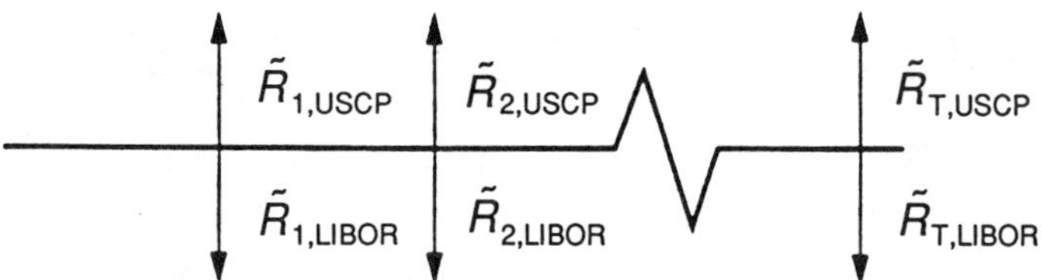

The party illustrated receives semiannual cash flows based on the compounded one-month U.S. commercial paper rates, while paying cash flows determined by six-month LIBOR rates.

ments in an interest rate swap, regular settlements are made on the basis of fixed and floating oil prices. Figure 10–7 illustrates the cash flows for a party who receives cash flows based on a fixed price per barrel and pays cash flows determined by the floating (spot) price of oil. In contrast to currency and interest rate swaps, the floating price used in an oil swap is not normally a single spot price but rather the average price of oil over a specified period.

While the cash flows are expressed in terms of oil, no physical quantities of oil need be involved. At the settlement date, the difference check paid or received simply reflects the price of oil. If oil prices have risen since contract origination, the party illustrated in Figure 10–7 pays a net difference check; if oil prices have fallen, this party receives the check.

FIGURE 10–7 **An Oil Swap**

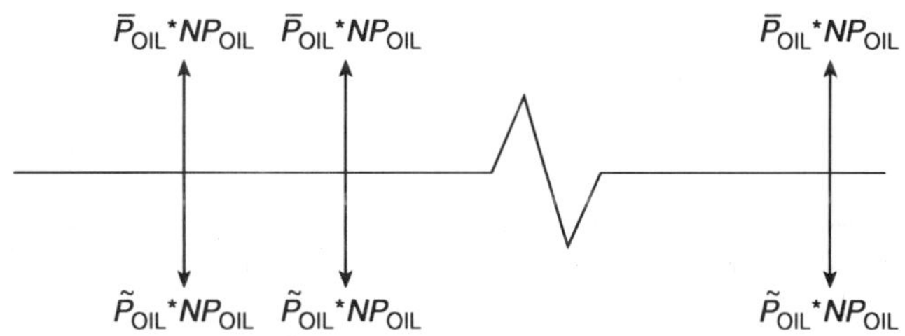

The party illustrated receives a cash flow based on an oil price which is fixed at origination ($\bar{P}_{OIL}$) and pays a cash flow based on the average spot price over the period ($\tilde{P}_{OIL}$). The notional principal (NP_{OIL}) is expressed in barrels of oil.

Note also that the oil swap, like all other swaps, can be decomposed into long and short positions in loans (that is, lending and borrowing). For example, the oil swap illustrated in Figure 10–7 can be decomposed into lending with standard fixed-rate coupon payments and simultaneously borrowing the same amount where the coupon payments are expressed in terms of barrels of oil.

As Chapter 1 noted, the early development of the commodity swap market was chilled by regulatory action by the Commodity Futures Trading Commission. However, since the CFTC established "safe harbors" for commodity swaps, the market for OTC derivatives on commodities has developed rapidly. Table 10–1 provides a perspective on the size and composition of the commodity swaps market.

The next type of swap to appear was the *equity-index swap*. In an equity-index swap, the parties pay and receive on the basis of the rate of return on a specified equity index. Figure 10–8 illustrates cash flows for a equity-index swap for the counterparty who receives cash flows based on the rate of return to the Tokyo Stock Price Index (TOPIX) and makes payments determined by U.S. dollar LIBOR. However, equity-index swaps can be structured so that the party makes payments on the basis of one equity index (such as the S&P 500) and receives payments on the basis of another. And, most recently, *single equity swaps* have begun to appear. In this structure, one side of the cash flows would be determined by the rate of return for a single equity rather than an equity index.

In contrast to the commodity swaps, no regulatory problems have been experienced with equity swaps. Under the agreement known as the Shad-Johnson Accord, equity swaps are regulated by the Securities and Exchange Commission (SEC) instead of the CFTC. Equity swap volumes for 1992 are provided in Table 10–2.

TABLE 10–1 Commodity Swaps Outstanding at Year-End 1992 (Notional Principal in Billions of U.S. Dollars)

	Energy	*Metals*	*Total*
Transactions between dealers	5	—	5
Transactions with end users	10	3	13
Total outstanding	15	3	18

SOURCE: International Swaps and Derivatives Association.

FIGURE 10–8 An Equity Index Swap

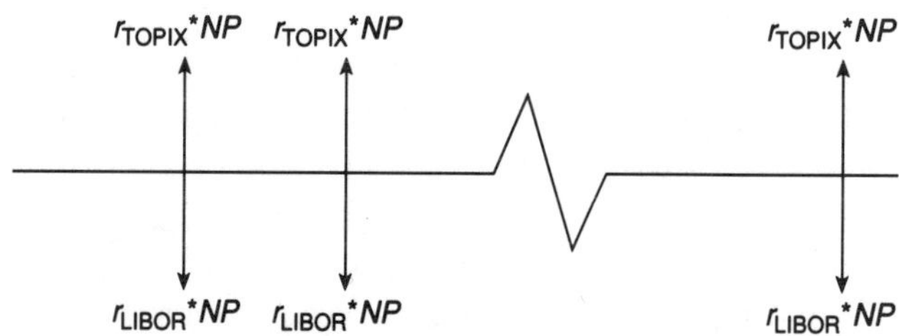

At settlement t (t=1,2...,T), the party receives a cash flow determined by the rate of return on the TOPIX between t-1 and t (minus or plus a spread) and pays a cash flow determined by U.S. LIBOR (minus) or plus a spread)

TABLE 10–2 Equity Swaps Outstanding at Year-End 1992 (Notional Principal in Billions of U.S. Dollars)

	Transactions between Dealers	*Transactions with End Users*	*Total Outstanding*
Indices (by index country)			
Japan	3	3	6
U.S.	1	1	2
Other	—	1	1
Baskets and individual stocks	—	1	1
Total	4	6	10

SOURCE: International Swaps and Derivatives Association.

Risk Management in Practice

Observations on the Shad-Johnson Accord and SEC-CFTC Jurisdictional Disputes

Kenneth Lehn

The dramatic growth in the market for derivatives and hybrid financial products (which combine attributes of derivatives and securities) in the 1980s revealed great inadequacies in the structure of U.S. financial regulation. Concurrent with the growth in these markets, the Securities and Exchange Commission (SEC) and the Commodity Futures Trading Commission (CFTC) engaged in a costly turf battle over which agency should be the dominant regulator of these new evolving markets.

Jurisdictional disputes between the two agencies have been common ever since the CFTC's inception in 1975. In the 1974 amendments to the Commodity Exchange Act (CEA), which created the CFTC, Congress gave the CFTC exclusive jurisdiction over financial products that have elements of a futures contract. The SEC and CFTC soon were embroiled in a controversy over the regulation of Ginnie Mae options. Were these products futures or were they securities? By the early 1980s, there was great uncertainty about which agency had regulatory authority over options generally and stock index futures.

In 1982 the chairmen of the SEC and CFTC (John Shad and Phillip Johnson, respectively) negotiated the Shad-Johnson agreement, which attempted to revolve this jurisdictional dispute. Under Shad-Johnson, the SEC has exclusive jurisdiction over options on securities and stock index options, and the CFTC has exclusive jurisdiction over all futures contracts (including stock index futures) and all options on futures (including options on stock index futures).

In some respects, the Shad-Johnson agreement has served investors well. Perhaps most importantly, this agreement saved stock index futures from excessive regulation by the SEC. As the SEC revealed after the 1987 stock market crash and the 1989 mini-crash, it has unwarranted hostility toward stock index futures. Undoubtedly, the SEC would have overregulated the stock index futures market and reduced the efficiency of this product as a risk management tool if Shad-Johnson had given the SEC jurisdiction over stock index futures.

Although the Shad-Johnson agreement sensibly divided jurisdiction over well-defined futures, options, and securities, it did not anticipate the proliferation of hybrid financial products that has occurred since 1982. As a result, it did not establish a framework for allocating jurisdiction over hybrids between the two agencies. This has resulted in substantial costs as the SEC and CFTC continue to engage in jurisdictional disputes over hybrids.

The most glaring illustration of the costs associated with these jurisdictional battles concerns the SEC's approval of a new product, index participations (IPs), in 1989. IPs

Risk Management in Practice continued

are financial instruments that are priced off an index of stocks, such as Standard & Poor's (S&P) 500. IPs have features of both futures contracts (holders can cash out on a quarterly basis at prices equal to the index values on these settlement dates) and securities (they pay dividends and have indefinite lives). In 1989, the SEC approved proposals from the Philadelphia Stock Exchange, American Stock Exchange, and Chicago Board Options Exchange to trade IPs. Literally within hours, futures exchanges sued the SEC on grounds that these products were futures contracts that, under the CEA, only the CFTC could regulate.

Later in 1989, Judge Easterbrook of the U.S. Seventh Circuit Court of Appeals ruled in favor of the futures exchanges and ordered that trading in IPs be ceased until the CFTC approved the trading of this product on registered futures exchanges. Judge Easterbrook acknowledged that IPs had features of both futures and securities and equated the court's task to deciding "whether tetrahedrons belong in square or round holes." However, the exclusivity clause of the CEA compelled the court to rule as it did, and it resulted in the cessation of trading of a product for which there was demand.

A more sensible alternative to Shad-Johnson would be to allow any product that has elements of a security to trade on a securities exchange and any product that has elements of a future contract to trade on a futures exchange. This would enable any exchange to register new hybrid products as either securities, subject to SEC regulation, or as futures, subject to CFTC regulation. This rule would create healthy competition between the two agencies, as exchanges would opt in to whichever body of regulation is most suitable for the trading of these products. This would remove existing, anticompetitive, regulatory impediments to the development on new hybrid instruments that serve the interests of both investors and issuers.

Kenneth M. Lehn is professor of business administration in the Katz Graduate School of Business Administration at the University of Pittsburgh. Previously, he served as chief economist at the U.S. Securities Exchange Commission (1987–1991). Professor Lehn has published extensively, not only in the leading academic journals (*Journal of Financial Economics, Journal of Finance, Journal of Political Economy*, and *Journal of Law and Economics*), but also in more popular publications (*The Wall Street Journal* and *National Law Journal*). He is the editor of *Modernizing U.S. Securities Regulation: Economic and Legal Perspectives*. Professor Lehn received his Ph.D. in economics from Washington University in 1981.

Development of the Swap Market

The historical development of the swap market is evident in both the evolution of the products and changes in the market's participants. Both tell the same story. We first examine the products.

Currency swaps, as we noted, came first. The earliest swaps were done on a one-off basis, which involved a search for matching counterparties, matching not only in the currencies but also in the principal amounts and timing desired. These early swaps were custom-tailored products. Because the deals were all one-off, they involved a lot of work by the financial institution arranging the swap. But (and this point is crucial) they involved virtually no direct exposure for the broker. In the language of the market participants, the early swaps required "creative problem solving" rather than capital commitment from the intermediary.

As interest rate swaps emerged, the movement toward a more standardized product began. There were fewer areas in which counterparties might not match with the U.S. dollar interest rate swaps than had been the case for currency swaps. The product had become more homogeneous, and so the demand for one-off deals declined. Instead of looking for one exactly matching counterparty, the intermediary could look for a number of counterparties that together matched the notional principal.

With the move toward homogeneity and the reduced reliance on an identifiable counterparty, markets for swaps—in particular, interest rate swaps—began to look more and more like markets for commodities. Increased competition forced down the spreads. And with the increased competition, an extensive search for a counterparty or group of counterparties was unprofitable for the intermediary. Instead, the intermediaries began to accept swap contracts without having a matching counterparty. Intermediaries took the interest rate risk into their own books and hedged the residual risk with interest rate futures or U.S. Treasuries. (We will return to this idea in Chapter 18 when we describe the way a dealer hedges a portfolio of derivative transactions.)

Thus, the evolution of the products offered in the swap market paralleled that of most markets. Swaps evolved from a customized, client-specific product into a standardized product. With the customized product, the role of the intermediary had been one of problem solving. As the product became more standardized, the role of the intermediary changed considerably, with less emphasis on arranging the deal and more on transactional efficiency and capital commitment.

Among participants in the swap market, the dominant intermediaries in the early stage of development were investment banks. As the market evolved, the entrants into this market were more highly capitalized firms, in particular commercial banks. The evolution of the role of the intermediary mirrors the change in the products. In the early stages the emphasis was on the intermediary's arranging the transaction rather than accepting risk from the transaction; investment banks were the natural intermediaries. But as swaps became more standardized, it became essential for the intermediary to be willing to accept a potential transaction into its books. Hence, commercial banks, with their greater capitalization and comparative advantage in managing high-volume, standardized transactions, became a more significant factor.

The dominance of commercial banks in the swap market is illustrated by looking at the largest swap dealers. Table 10–3 provides a listing of the largest 20 swap dealers in 1993, ranked according to notional principal outstanding.[1]

Standardization has been in large part behind the growth in swaps. One market observer put it well by noting that "swaps have become a high-volume, lower margin business, rather than the personalized, corporate financial deal of the past."[2]

TABLE 10–3 Largest Swap Dealers: Interest Rate and Currency Swaps

Rank	*Firm*	*Amount ($M)*
1	JP Morgan	453,080
2	Compagnie Financiere de Paribas	431,728
3	Chemical Banking	411,782
4	Bankers Trust New York	315,879
5	Merrill Lynch	308,000
6	Credit Lyonnais	302,885
7	Citicorp	254,596
8	Chase Manhattan	237,773
9	BankAmerica	214,817
10	Banque Indosuez	184,924
11	Westpac	173,160
12	Royal Bank of Canada	134,844
13	Credit Commercial de France	110,495
14	Canadian Imperial Bank of Commerce	102,332
15	Bank of Nova Scotia	90,029
16	First Chicago	84,535
17	American International Group	82,874
18	General Re Corporation	63,914
19	Nomura Securities	61,768
20	Toronto-Dominion Bank	58,621

This data is from Swaps Monitor Publications, New York (*World's Major Derivatives Dealers,* 1993 Edition). The ranking is only of those firms which publish audited data on their interest rate option outstandings.

The growth of the swap market also has corresponded to the expanding liquidity available through the secondary market. Swap positions can be traded (that is, the swap contract can be assigned to a third party), and this market is growing. However, much of the secondary market in swaps involves the reversing (unwinding) of a position. The simplest way to unwind a swap involves the cancellation of the agreement, with a final difference check determined by the remaining value of the contract. Alternatively, the swap could be unwound by writing a *mirror swap* to cancel the original. Most market observers indicate that the secondary market is sufficiently deep to decrease risks in the primary market, particularly for short-term swaps.

Growth of the Swap Market

In the early stages of the development of the swaps market, analysts ascribed the growth to some kind of "arbitrage opportunity" through swaps. Robin Leigh-Pemberton, then a governor of the Bank of England, articulated this view when he argued that swaps enabled borrowers to "arbitrage" the credit markets, allowing "a good credit rating in one part of the currency/maturity matrix to be translated into relatively cheap borrowing in another."[3]

An example of this "credit arbitrage" that was widely cited in the 1980s is the case of an interest rate swap between an AAA-rated borrower and a borrower with a BBB rating.[4] As illustrated in Table 10–4, a borrower rated AAA would be expected to be able to borrow more cheaply than one rated BBB in either fixed or floating. However, note in Table 10–5 that the credit spread between the AAA and the BBB is higher for fixed than for floating.

The assertion is that the swap "arbitrages the credit spread differential" of 120 − 50 = 70 basis points. As illustrated in Table 10–6, suppose the AAA borrows fixed and the BBB borrows floating. Then, if the two firms enter into an interest rate swap, both firms can end up with lower borrowing costs. Indeed, in the preceding case where there was no financial intermediary, the firms ended up splitting the credit-spread differential.

TABLE 10–4 Illustrative Borrowing Costs for AAA and BBB Borrowers

	AAA	*BBB*
Borrow fixed	10.8%	12.0%
Borrow floating	LIBOR + 1/4%	LIBOR + 3/4%

TABLE 10–5 Illustrative Credit Spreads

BBB − AAA Borrowing Rates		
Fixed	12.0% − 10.8%	= 120 basis points
Floating	(LIBOR + 3/4%) − (LIBOR + 1/4%)	= 50 basis points

TABLE 10–6 The "Savings" from a Swap

	AAA	*BBB*
AAA borrows fixed	(10.8%)	
BBB borrows floating		(LIBOR + 3/4%)
AAA receives	10.9%	
Pays floating	(LIBOR)	
BBB receives floating		LIBOR
Pays fixed		(10.9%)
All-in cost of funding	LIBOR − 1/10%	11.65%
Savings	0.35%	0.35%

This illustration is entirely consistent with the available data:

1. There exist quality differentials between fixed and floating borrowing, referred to as the *quality spread*, and these quality spreads are generally observed to increase with maturity.[5]
2. The fixed-rate payer in a swap is generally the less creditworthy party.
3. Firms have been able to lower their nominal funding costs by using swaps in conjunction with these quality spreads.

However, it is less clear that this kind of evidence has anything to do with classic financial arbitrage. First, financial arbitrage should lead to decreasing, not increasing, swap volumes. As the quality spread is arbitraged, the rate differences would be eliminated, and this rationale for interest rate swaps should disappear. Second, this simplistic "credit arbitrage" story ignores the underlying reason for the quality spread.

Comparative Advantage

In the 1980s, we heard many market participants assert that quality spreads result from firms' having a "comparative advantage" in one of the credit markets. According to this view, the AAA-rated company borrows in the fixed-rate market where it has a comparative advantage. The BBB-rated company borrows in the floating-rate market where it has a comparative advantage. Then the firms use an interest rate swap to exploit their comparative advantages and produce interest rate savings.

While this comparative-advantage argument is appealing, it neglects arbitrage. With no barriers to capital flows, the comparative-advantage argument from elementary trade theory cannot hold. Arbitrage eliminates any comparative advantage.

Aside

Comparative Advantage

International trade theory relies on the concept of comparative advantage to explain why countries trade. As you should remember from your economics courses, this concept was based on *factor immobility*: the United States has a comparative advantage in wheat because the United States has wheat-producing acreage not available in Japan. If land could be moved—if land in Kansas could be relocated outside Tokyo—the comparative advantage would disappear.

For the concept of comparative advantage to make sense as a rationale for swaps, immobility would have to be a characteristic of the financial markets. It is not. Integrated capital markets provide the BBB access to fixed-rate markets, either directly or indirectly by AAA-rated firms borrowing fixed and relending to BBB-rated firms.

Given the weakness in this comparative-advantage rationale, several alternative explanations have been proposed.

Underpriced Credit Risk (Risk-Shifting)

Some have suggested that the quality spread results from the difference in pricing credit risk in the market for fixed-rate funding the market for floating-rate funding. Specifically, analysts have argued that credit risk is underpriced in floating-rate loans.[6] Underpriced credit risk for floating-rate loans would certainly explain the growth of the interest rate-swap market; the gain from the swap would be at the expense of the party who is underpricing credit risk in the floating-rate debt market. But the expansion of the swap market effectively increases the demand for floating-rate debt by lower-rated companies and the demand for fixed-rate debt by higher-rated companies, thereby eliminating the supposed differential pricing. So like the comparative-advantage argument, this rationale is self-defeating; it does not explain the continuing growth of the swap market.

Along a similar line, Jan Loeys (1985) has suggested that the quality spread is the result of the shifting of risk from the lenders to the shareholders. To the extent that lenders have the right to refuse to roll over debt, more default risk is shifted from the lender to the shareholders as the maturity of the debt decreases. With this explanation, the "gains" from a swap would instead be transfers from the shareholders of the lower-rated firm to the shareholders of the higher-rated firm.

Differential Cash Flow Packages

The differences in nominal (stated) borrowing cost obtained through a swap can also be explained by considering options available to the borrower. Most fixed-rate debt includes a prepayment option. If interest rates decline, the borrower can put the loan back to the lender and obtain lower-cost financing by paying the prepayment fee and the origination fees on the new financing. Indeed, in standard corporate bond issues, this is simply the *call provision.*

In contrast, interest rate swaps contain no such prepayment option. According to the standards proposed by the International Swap Dealers Association (1986), early termination of a swap agreement requires that the remaining contract be marked-to-market and paid in full.

Hence, the positions of the firm that has borrowed fixed directly and the one that has borrowed floating and swapped-to-fixed are quite different. The former owns a put option on interest rates; the latter does not.

In this context, the transaction between the AAA-rated firm and the firm rated BBB looks less like financial arbitrage and more like an option transaction. The BBB-rated firm can borrow at a fixed rate more cheaply by swapping from floating because the borrow-floating/swap-to-fixed alternative does not include the

Illustration 10–2

Embedded Interest Rate Options

Consider the BBB-rated firm described above. It can obtain fixed-rate funding in two ways. It can either:

1. borrow fixed directly at 12 percent, or
2. borrow floating and swap to fixed at 11.65 percent.

If capital markets are efficient, and the available evidence says they are, the fact that 1 costs more than 2 implies that 1 has something 2 does not. Included in that something may well be the right to repay the loan early. When would the firm want to exercise this right? Clearly the firm would want to exercise the right if rates fell.

If rates fall, the firm could pay off this loan and refinance at the lower rate; the further rates fall, the more valuable this right becomes.

The illustration of the value of the right to repay early is the payoff profile for owning an interest rate option, specifically a put option on interest rates. Hence it is not surprising that 1 costs more than 2, since 1 contains an option that 2 lacks.

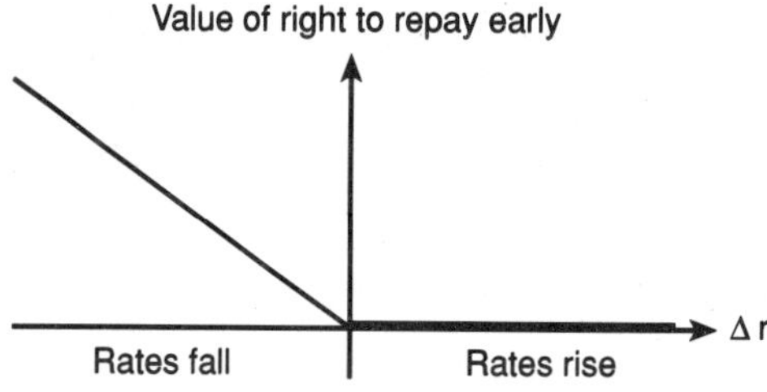

interest rate option contained in the borrow-fixed alternative. The BBB firm in effect has sold an interest rate option. The funding cost "savings" obtained by the BBB firm (as well as the cost savings gained by the AAA firm) simply reflect the premium on this option.

More generally, for the differences in cash flows in Table 10–6 to represent arbitrage opportunities, the resulting cash flow characteristics must be equivalent. Here, this is not the case. Since the BBB company borrowed short term, the credit risk premium on the loan varies over the life of the swap; it is not fixed as it is with the long-term borrowing. (To fix the credit spread, one would have to examine a swap plus a floating-rate loan of the same term with the fixed-rate borrowing.)

Information Asymmetries

Why does a firm choose to issue short-term floating-rate debt and then swap this floating-rate payment into a fixed-rate payment rather than one of the alternatives: keeping the short-term debt unswapped, issuing long-term fixed-rate debt, or issuing long-term floating-rate debt? Marcelle Arak, Arturo Estrella, Laurie Goodman, and Andrew Silver (1988) have argued that the "issue short-term/swap-to-fixed" combination would be preferred if the firm is in one of these circumstances:

- The firm has information causing it to expect that its own credit spread will be lower than the market expects in the future.
- The firm is less risk-averse than the market to changes in its credit spread.
- It expects higher risk-free interest rates than does the market.
- It is more risk-averse to changes in the risk-free rate than is the market.

For example, suppose the firm desired fixed-rate funding for a project but the company had inside information indicating that its credit rating would improve in the future. By issuing short-term debt, the firm would be able to exploit its information asymmetry, and by swapping the debt into fixed-rate, the firm would be able to eliminate its exposure to interest rate risk.

As Arak *et al.* point out, firms that are pessimistic about future risk-free rates but optimistic about their own credit standings are drawn to the swaps market; they issue short-term debt to take advantage of the information asymmetry and then swap the debt to a fixed rate to protect the firm against future interest rate increases. The expected savings will be divided between this firm and the counterparty based on prevailing demand and supply conditions.

Tax and Regulatory Arbitrage

In contrast to the classic arbitrage considered above (in which the firm would earn a riskless profit by exploiting pricing differences for the same instrument), tax and regulatory arbitrage enables the firm to earn a risk-free profit by exploiting differences in tax and/or regulatory environments.

A firm issuing dollar-denominated, fixed-rate bonds in the U.S. capital markets must comply with the requirements of the U.S. Securities and Exchange Commission. In the less-regulated Eurobond market, the costs of issue could be considerably lower—as much as 80 basis points less (Loeys (1985)). However, not all firms have direct access to the Eurobond market. The swap contract gives firms access to the Eurobond market and enables more of them to take advantage of this regulatory arbitrage.

Moreover, firms that issue in the U.S. capital markets, as well as the security purchasers, generally face the provisions of the U.S. tax code. The introduction of the swap market has allowed an "unbundling," in effect, of currency and interest rate exposure from the tax rules in some very creative ways. For example, with the introduction of swaps, a U.S. firm could issue a yen-denominated debt in the Eurobond market, structure the issue to receive favorable tax treatment under the Japanese tax code, avoid much of the U.S. securities regulation, and yet still manage the firm's currency exposure by swapping the transaction back into dollars. Unlike the classic financial arbitrage described above, there is no reason for opportunities for tax or regulatory arbitrage to disappear (barring changes, of course, in the various tax and regulatory codes).

To illustrate the manner in which tax and regulatory arbitrage induces swaps, consider the way one U.S. firm used swaps to exploit special tax and regulatory conditions in Japan. (See Illustration 10-3)

The arbitrage opportunity in the preceding example disappeared when the Japanese tax authorities changed their ruling on yen zeros. However, other tax and regulatory opportunities have been available, and some still are. For example, in many European countries the purchasers of a zero-coupon bond do not escape taxes (as was the case in our example), but the tax is deferred until the maturity of the bond, and the tax rate paid is the lower capital gains rate. Sometimes there are also regulatory barriers limiting entry of potential issuers and thereby reducing the cost of borrowing in that market.

Exposure Management

Since swaps can be used to manage a corporation's exposure to interest rate, foreign exchange, and commodity-price risk, part of the growth in interest rate swaps simply reflects general corporate hedging activities. As we demonstrated in Chapter 3, corresponding to the growth in the swaps market, market data suggest that the use of the other off-balance-sheet hedging instruments is also increasing. So another way of asking why swaps have grown so dramatically is to consider why more and more firms have decided to manage their exposures to financial prices—that is, to exchange rates, interest rates, and commodity prices.

Synthetic Instruments

Still another reason for the growth of the swap market is the usefulness of swaps in the creation of "synthetic" financial instruments. For example, consider long-dated interest rate forward contracts, historically a very illiquid market. Since interest rate swaps can be viewed as portfolios of forward interest rate contracts, long-term swaps have been stripped to create synthetic long-dated forwards and thereby increase liquidity in the market for long-dated forward-rate agreements.

Less obvious is the manner in which currency and interest rate swaps have been used to fill gaps in the international financial markets. In Chapter 11, we

Illustration 10–3

Arbitraging Japan's Tax and Regulatory Authorities

In 1984, *Business Week* reported that U.S. firms had discovered a way to make "free money."* As it turns out, this "free money" was being given away by the Japanese tax authorities. In 1984, zero-coupon bonds received particularly favorable tax treatment in Japan. The income earned from holding the zero-coupon bond (the difference between the face value of the bond and the price at which the bond was purchased) was treated as a capital gain; since capital gains were untaxed, the effect was to make the interest income on the zero-coupon bond nontaxable for the Japanese investor. The result was that a zero-coupon bond sold to Japanese investors would carry a below-market interest rate.

In contrast, the U.S. tax authorities regarded zeros as they did any other debt instrument. Any U.S. firm issuing such a bond was permitted to deduct the imputed interest payments from income, thereby maintaining its tax shield.

Hence, a tax-arbitrage opportunity arose. The two tax authorities treated the same instrument differently. Not surprisingly, a number of U.S. firms—Exxon and General Mills among them—issued zero-coupon yen bonds, illustrated below.

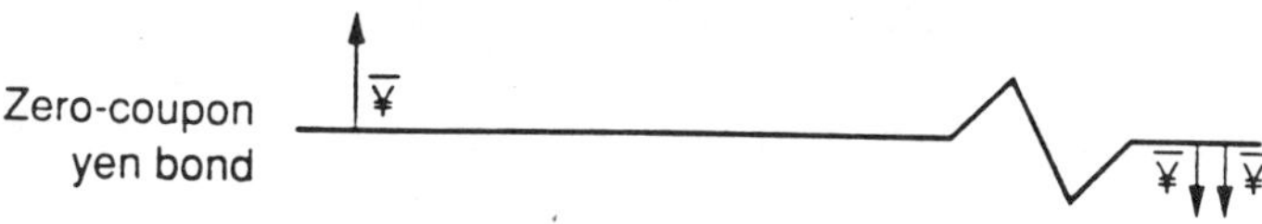

The U.S. firm issuing the zero-coupon bond was no doubt pleased with the savings it achieved in interest expense. However, most U.S. issuers were much less pleased with the yen exposure that came with this yen zero.

Therefore, the assignment to the merchant/investment bank was relatively straightforward: eliminate the yen exposure while keeping as much of the savings in interest expense as possible.

As should be clear, the exposure profile for this U.S. issuer of a zero-coupon yen bond is as illustrated below. Such an exposure could be managed through a forward yen–dollar contract. But the maturity of these bonds, 5 to 10 years, eliminated forward contracts as a possibility, since the bid-offer spread on a 10-year forward contract was unacceptably high.

Futures contracts were also eliminated as a means of managing this exposure, since 5- and 10-year futures contracts were not available. (Five- and 10-year strips of futures are still not available. The longest available futures contract on foreign exchange is about 12 months.)

Hence, the best available financial instrument for neutralizing this yen exposure was (and still is) a swap. To minimize the cost of the swap—the bid-offer spread—we would want to use a standard, at-market-rate cur-

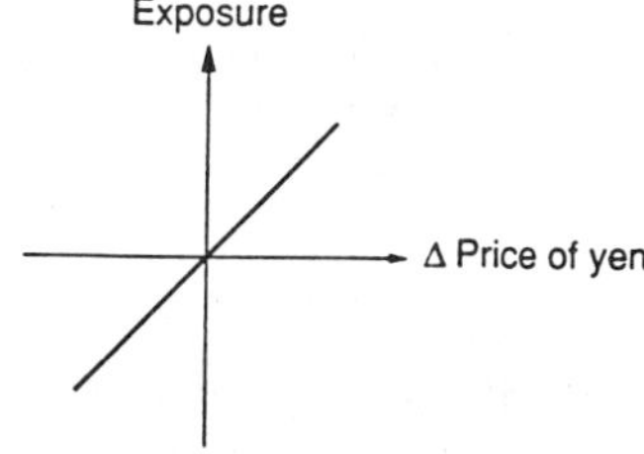

Illustration 10–3 continued

rency swap. However, when we combine such a currency swap with our zero-coupon bond, we see in the following that our task is not yet complete; there are still some yen cash flows.

The remaining yen cash flows could be eliminated by adding a simple loan with a sinking fund. As the bottom figure illustrates, the amortizing yen loan would eliminate the

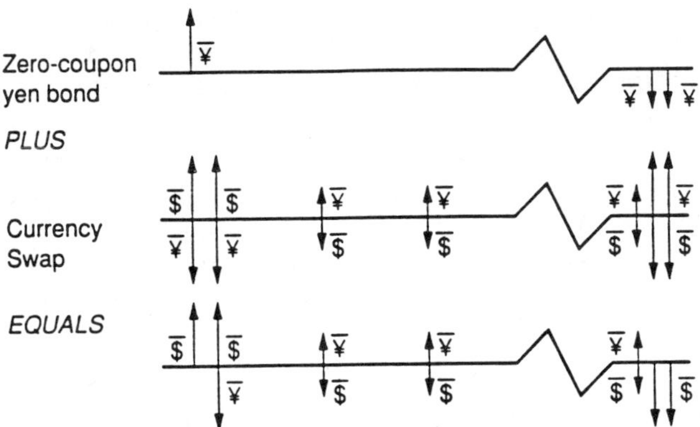

remaining yen cash flows, and the U.S. issuer would end up with a set of cash flows identical to those for a dollar bond with below-market coupons.

However, it turned out that there was a way to structure the package that would result in a still lower realized interest rate for the U.S. issuer. In addition to the tax arbi-

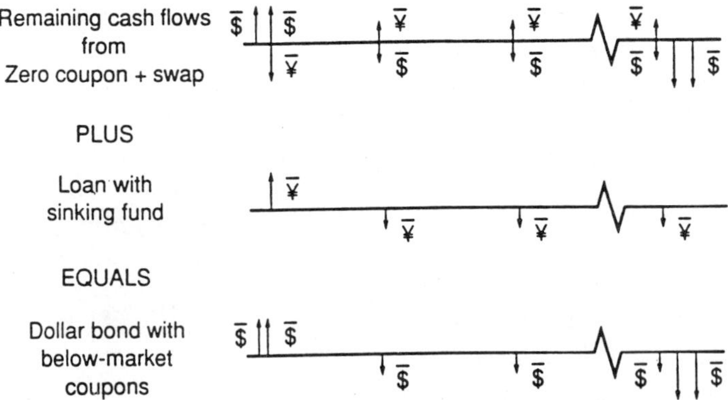

trage, a regulatory arbitrage was available: the Ministry of Finance limited the amount a Japanese pension fund could invest in non-yen-dominated bonds issued by foreign corporations to at most 10 percent of their portfolio. However, the Ministry of Finance ruled that dual-currency bonds qualified as a yen issue for purposes of the 10 percent rule, even

Illustration 10–3 continued

though the dual-currency bond has embedded within it a dollar-denominated zero. By issuing the dual-currency bond, the U.S. firm was able to capitalize on the desire of Japanese pension funds to diversify their portfolios internationally, while at the same time adhering to the regulation imposed by the Ministry of Finance.

Therefore, the remaining yen cash flows from the yen zero would be absorbed not by the amortizing loan but rather by the combination of a dual-currency bond and a spot currency transaction, as illustrated below. Moreover, this figure illustrates that the resulting cash flows are like those for a deep-discount dollar bond with below-market coupons.

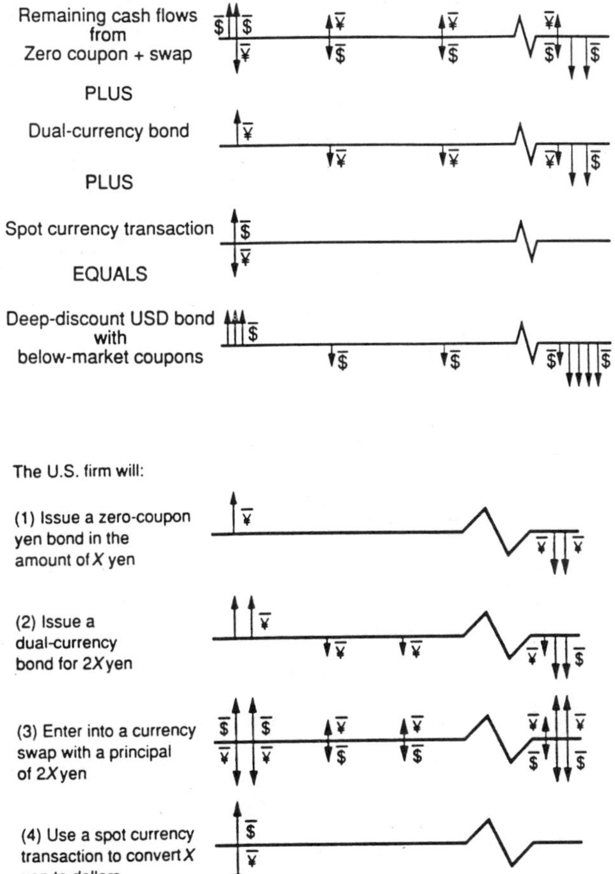

Illustration 10–3 continued

The entire process can be summarized as follows: the U.S. firm will:

1. issue a zero-coupon yen bond in the amount of *X* yen,
2. issue a dual-currency bond in the amount of 2*X* yen,
3. enter into a currency swap with a principal of 2*X* yen, and
4. use a spot currency transaction to convert *X* yen to dollars.

The result of these transactions is a set of cash flows that are like a deep-discount dollar bond with below-market coupons.

The chief financial officer of this firm is happy because the firm obtains below-market funding. The merchant/investment banker is happy because the bank earns a nice fee. And *The Wall Street Journal* and *Financial Times* are both happy because the papers receive the advertising revenue for running the three tombstones.

**Business Week* (1984).

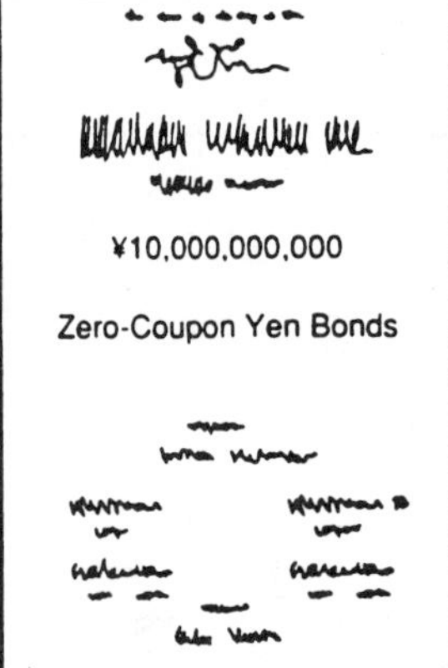

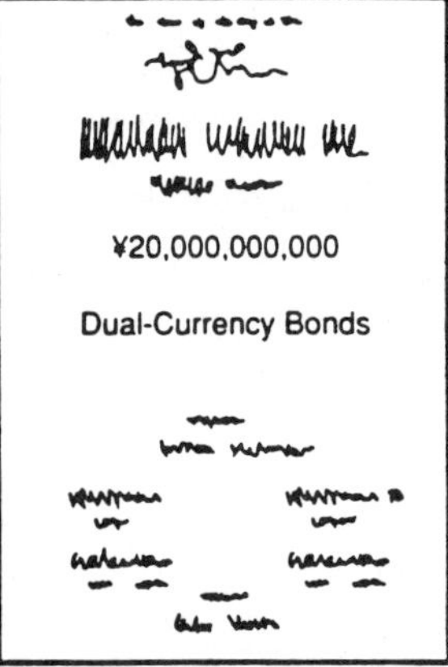

will provide an illustration of the way in which swaps have been used to create other instruments.

Further, swaps can be combined with existing products to create new financial instruments. As will be described in Chapter 16, the combination of a conventional fixed-rate loan and an interest rate swap in which the party pays fixed results in a "reverse-floating-rate loan."

Liquidity

A final factor explaining the observed growth in this market is the substantial reduction in bid-ask spreads. In 1982, the bid-ask spread for interest rate swaps exceeded 200 basis points. As we will note later in this chapter, in September 1993, the bid-ask spread for a three-year interest rate swap in the interbank market was only four basis points. Even a 10-year swap had a bid-ask of only six basis points. Thus, the dramatic increase in volume has been accompanied by an equally dramatic increase in the liquidity of the swaps market.

Pricing and Valuing Swaps

We have demonstrated that a swap can be decomposed into either a portfolio of loans or a portfolio of forward contracts. In Chapter 17, we will make use of the concept of a swap as a portfolio of forwards to gain insights into the default risk of a swap. Here we use the concept of a swap as a portfolio of loans to provide insights into the pricing of a swap.

Pricing an At-Market Swap

Figure 10–9 again illustrates the equivalence between an interest rate swap and a pair of loans. The implication of this figure is that if you can value (price) loans, you should be able to value (price) a swap contract. Put another way, if you know the mechanics of pricing loans, you should be able to determine the appropriate fixed rate in the swap illustrated in Figure 10–9. And that is indeed the case.

The loans are both zero-expected net present value (NPV) projects.[7] Consequently, since the swap is nothing more than a long and a short position in loans, the expected NPV of the swap must also be zero; if you can determine the actual or expected floating-rate payments at time periods 1, 2, . . . , T and if you know the term structure of interest rates, you can set the NPV of the swap equal to zero and solve for the fixed rate. Perhaps the best way to explain this is to go directly to an example. (See Illustration 10-4)

As our example illustrates, pricing an interest rate swap requires that the cash flows be identified and then discounted by the zero-coupon—spot—interest rate.

FIGURE 10–9 Decomposition of an Interest Rate Swap into a Portfolio of Loans

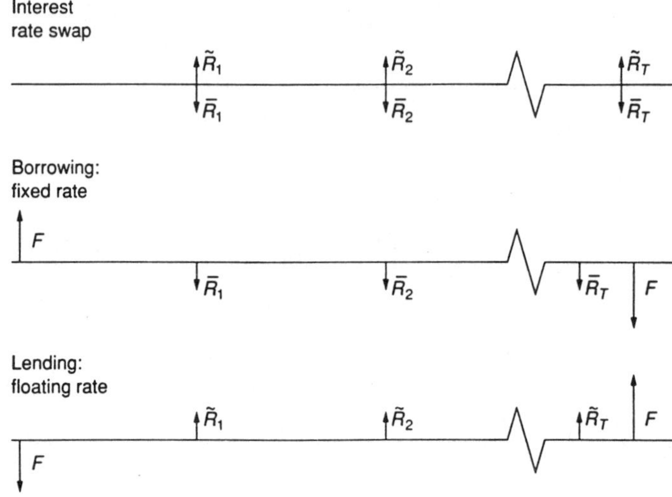

The cash flows from an interest rate swap where the party pays fixed is equivalent to the cash flows of a portfolio of two loan contracts, where borrowing is at a *T*-period fixed rate ($\bar{R}_t$), lending is at a floating rate ($\tilde{R}_t$), and *F* is the face value of the loan.

To obtain the expected cash flows for the floating payments, it is necessary to obtain the forward interest rates from the forward yield curve. And finally, in the case of this simple at-market swap, the appropriate fixed rate was simply the par rate. Hence, to price an interest rate swap, we ended up using three yield curves: the zero-coupon yield curve, the forward yield curve, and the par yield curve.

Swap Pricing Conventions

The swap described in Illustration 10-4 and illustrated in Figure 10–9 is referred to (almost condescendingly) as a *plain vanilla* interest rate swap. For this simple, one-year swap, we ended up with a quote of

Six-month LIBOR (the spot rate)
against
One-year par rate.

The market convention has come to be to price these plain vanilla swaps as LIBOR *flat* (i.e., no spread) against the U.S. Treasury [par] rate *plus* a spread. An illustration of market-style quotations for such a swap is provided in Figure 10–10.

Illustration 10–4

Pricing an Interest-Rate Swap

Galactic Industries (GI) wishes to enter into a swap in which GI will pay cash flows based on a floating rate and receive cash flows based on a fixed rate. In the jargon of the swap market, Galactic—the floating-rate payer—is referred to as the seller of the swap (or as short the swap).

Market convention is to quote the terms of interest rate swaps as the floating-rate index (normally LIBOR) flat against some fixed rate; Galactic will pay cash flows based on the floating rate flat and will receive cash flows based on a fixed rate of *X* percent. The question is, "What is the appropriate fixed rate; what is *X*?"

To keep our calculations at a minimum, suppose GI requested a quote from the Dead Solid Perfect Bank (DSPB) on the following simple swap:

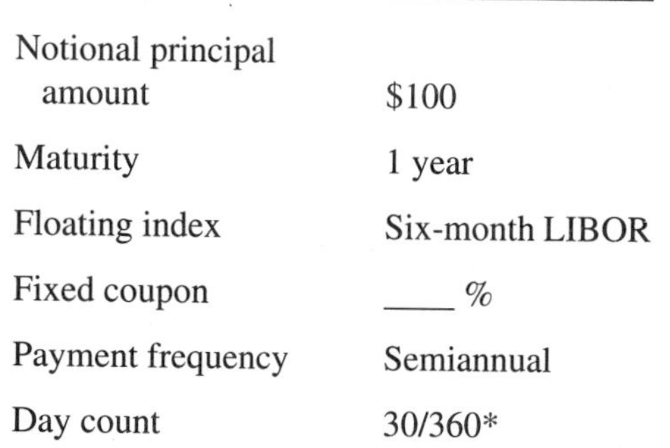

Notional principal amount	$100
Maturity	1 year
Floating index	Six-month LIBOR
Fixed coupon	____ %
Payment frequency	Semiannual
Day count	30/360*

From these terms, we know what Galactic will pay: at the six-month settlement, GI pays a "coupon" determined by the 6-month LIBOR rate in effect at contract origination. At the 12-month settlement GI's "coupon" payment is determined by the six-month LIBOR rate prevailing at month 6. What is missing is the fixed interest rate that will determine the payments Galactic will receive from DSPB.

Suppose that the LIBOR yield curve—the spot yield curve—prevailing at origination of this swap is the simplified yield curve shown below:

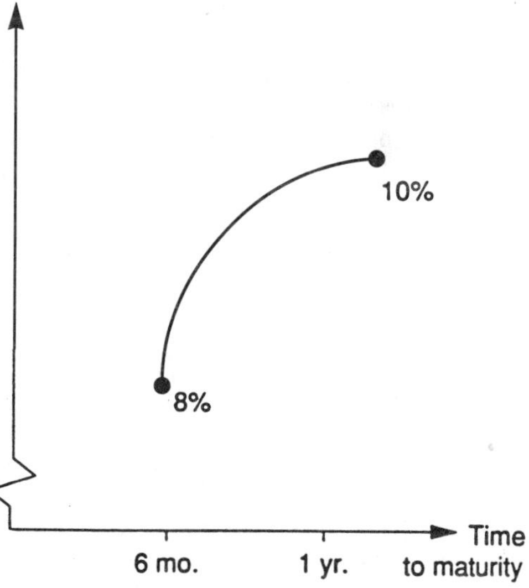

Pricing an Interest-Rate Swap continued

To determine the appropriate fixed rate, the managers of DSPB must consider the contractual/expected cash flows from this swap:

$\uparrow\ \tilde{R}_1 \qquad \uparrow\ \tilde{R}_2$

$\downarrow\ \bar{R}_1 \qquad \downarrow\ \bar{R}_2$

6 mo. 1 yr.

The first floating-rate inflow—$\tilde{R}_1$—is the easy one. The floating-rate cash flow DSPB will receive at the first settlement date is determined by the six-month rate in effect at contract origination, 8 percent. Hence at the six-month settlement, DSPB expects to receive

$$\tilde{R}_1 = \$100\,[(180/360)0.08] = \$100\,(1/2)\,0.08 = \$4.00.$$

Note that in this calculation and all that will follow, we use the bond method for calculating interest payments.†

To obtain the expected floating-rate inflow at the one-year settlement, we need to know the six-month rate in six months. This rate, the rate from $t = 6$ months to $t = 1$ year, is the *forward rate*. Arbitrage guarantees that**

$$(1 + r_{12}) = [1 + (1/2)\, r_6] \times [1 + (1/2)\, {}_6r_{12}],$$

where r_{12} and r_6 are, respectively, the current one-year (12 month) and six-month *zero* (spot) rates. Using this arbitrage condition, the six-month and one-year rates of 8 percent and 10 percent, respectively, require that the forward rate ${}_6r_{12}$—that is, the six-month rate in six months—be 11.5 percent. Therefore,

$$\tilde{R}_2 = \$100 \times (1/2) \times 0.115 = \$5.75.$$

Hence, the contractual/expected floating-rate inflows to DSPB are as illustrated below:

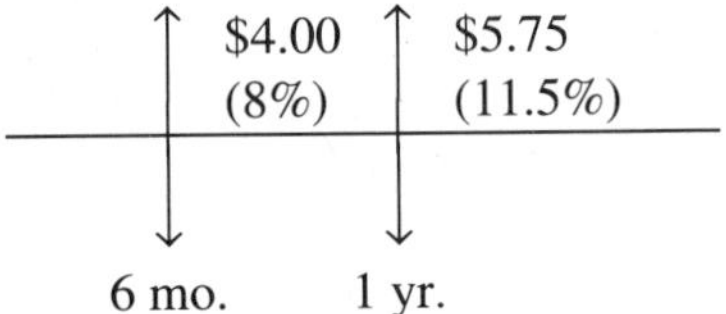

What DSPB needs to determine is the outflows, the appropriate fixed-rate payments. At origination, the expected net present value of this at-market swap is zero. That is,

$$\frac{(\$4.00 - \bar{R}_1)}{[1 + (1/2)0.08]} + \frac{(\$5.75 - \bar{R}_2)}{(1.10)} = 0,$$

where $\bar{R}_1 = \bar{R}_2$. Solving this equation, $\bar{R}_1 = \bar{R}_2 = \$4.85$. Hence, the appropriate fixed rate is 9.70 percent.

At first blush, if you look at the term structure of interest rates, it might seem that the appropriate fixed, one-year interest rate would be 10 percent, so the fixed-rate outflows would be

$$\bar{R}_1 = \bar{R}_2 = \$100(1/2)0.10 = \$5.00.$$

However, if $\bar{R}_1 = \bar{R}_2 = \$5.00$:

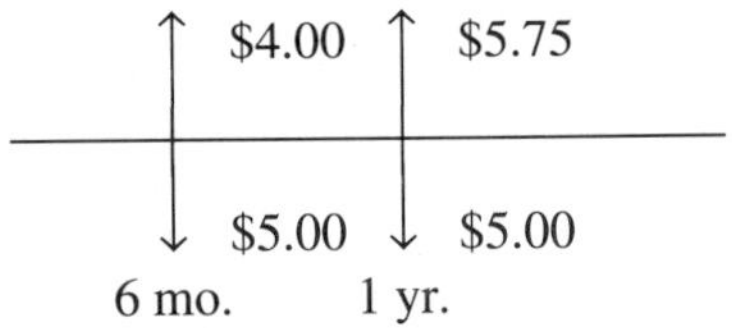

The present value of the swap to DSPB would be negative,

$$\frac{-1.00}{1 + 1/2(0.08)} + \frac{0.75}{1.10} = -0.28$$

Pricing an Interest-Rate Swap continued

The problem is that 10 percent is a zero-coupon rate. As should be clear from Figure 10–9, $\bar{R}$ is associated with a coupon-bearing instrument (loan). What we need is the market coupon-interest rate, the *par* rate. The par rate is that coupon rate that would have the bond trade at par. In our case that means the compounded annualized par rate $r_{1yr.}$ is given by

$$100 = \frac{(1/2)\,(\bar{r})100}{[1 + (1/2)0.08]} + \frac{(1/2)(\bar{r})100}{(1.10)} + \frac{100.}{(1.10)}$$

Solving the preceding equation, the one-year par rate, $r_{1yr.}$, is 9.70 percent, precisely the rate we solved for earlier.

Hence, in the case of this simple, at-market swap, the appropriate fixed rate is the one-year par rate, 9.70 percent. The terms of this swap can now be completed

Notional principal amount	$100
Maturity	1 year
Floating index	Six-month LIBOR
Fixed coupon	9.70%
Payment frequency	Semiannual
Day count	30/360

The expected cash flows for DSPB are as illustrated below.

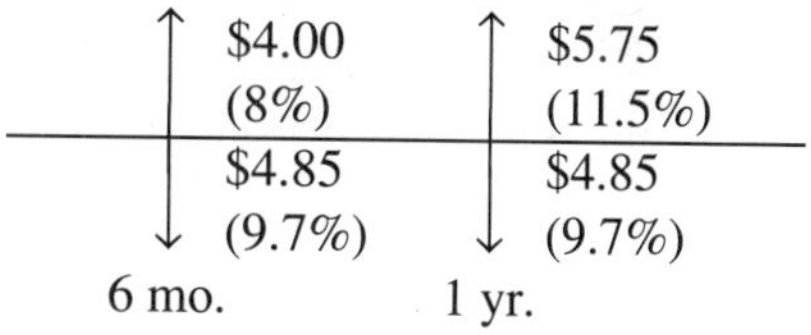

	6 mo.	1 yr.
↑ Receive	$4.00 (8%)	$5.75 (11.5%)
↓ Pay	$4.85 (9.7%)	$4.85 (9.7%)

*We use this 30/360 convention for convenience in our example. In truth, the day count convention for LIBOR is Actual/360, as are commercial paper and banker's acceptances.

†For maturities less than one year, prevailing market practice is to quote interest rates such that compounding is already imbedded in the quoted rate. If the annualized six-month rate is 8 percent, the amount that will be received at the end of six months on an investment of $100 can be calculated simply as

$$(\$100) \times (180/360) \times 0.08 = \$4.00,$$

where the convention is that compounding occurs annually but the periodicity of the rate is monthly.

In contrast, the convention used by most finance textbooks is to treat the interest rate as *subject to compounding*. The most common method of compounding is *discrete compounding*. Using this method, if the annualized six-month rate is 8 percent, the amount that will be received at the end of six months on the $100 investment is

$$(\$100) \times (1.08)^{180/360} - \$100 = \$3.92,$$

where the periodicity is again monthly, but the rate is now compounded monthly. Put another way, to yield the $4 at the end of six months, the stated interest rate using the method of discrete monthly compounding would be 8.16 percent:

$$(\$100) \times (1.0816)^{180/360} - \$100 = \$4.00.$$

While the different conventions are sometimes confusing, they cause no problem as long as the user is sure which convention is being used.

**In the preceding footnote, we noted the various ways interest rates can be quoted and the coupons calculated. Had the interest rates been quoted subject to monthly compounding, the arbitrage condition would have had to take the compounding into consideration. If we denote the annualized rate subject to compounding as r, the arbitrage condition would become

$$(1 + r_{12}) = (1 + r_6)^{1/2}\,(1 + {}_6r_{12})^{1/2}.$$

FIGURE 10–10 U.S. Dollar Interest Rate Swap Quotes: Treasury–LIBOR

```
1046 PREBON YAMANE (UK) LTD
NEW YORK 212-952-2676
     YAMANE TANSHI
      US TREAS    US AMM
      ACT/365     ACT/360
2 YRS T+   15-11   3.95-91
3 YRS T+   23-19   4.33-29
4 YRS C+   25-21   4.64-60
5 YRS T+   22-18   4.91-87
7 YRS T+   38-34   5.30-26
10YRS T+   36-32   5.69-65
```

SOURCE: Reuters Datafeed Service (October 4, 1993).

As Figure 10–10 indicates, on Monday, September 12, 1993, the market was pricing a three-year interest rate swap such that . . .

. . . if you want to receive the fixed rate, you will pay LIBOR and receive the three-year Treasury par rate + 19 basis points.

. . . if you want to pay the fixed rate you will receive LIBOR and pay the three-year Treasury par rate + 23 basis points.

The difference between the receive Treasuries and pay Treasuries—four basis points—was the bid-asked spread.

Valuing a Swap (Marking the Swap to Market)

This market convention of LIBOR versus Treasuries + spread works well if all you want to do is price at-market swaps at origination. However, this par-rate convention does not work well if you want to value a swap after origination or if you want to value (price) an off-market swap.

After origination, the only way to value a swap is to employ the zero-coupon yield curve. Once the swap has been contracted, its value depends on what happens to the market price on which the swap is based. The value of a dollar–sterling currency swap to the party paying dollars rises (falls) as the value of sterling rises (falls). The value of a commodity swap varies with the market price of the commodity. And as we illustrate in the continuation of our example, the value of an interest rate swap depends on what happens to market interest rates.

In the following example, we *marked the swap to market*. And if we calculate the value of the swap for different shifts in the yield curve, we can obtain a payoff profile for the swap. For example, if we look at the value of the following swap for shifts in the Treasury zero curve of +2 percent, +3 percent, −1 percent, −2 per-

Illustration 10–5

Valuing an Interest-Rate Swap

Galactic Industries and the Dead Solid Perfect Bank contracted to the interest rate swap outlined in the preceding example on the afternoon of July 23.

On the morning of July 24, the LIBOR yield curve (zero-coupon curve) shifts up by 1 percent, as illustrated below.

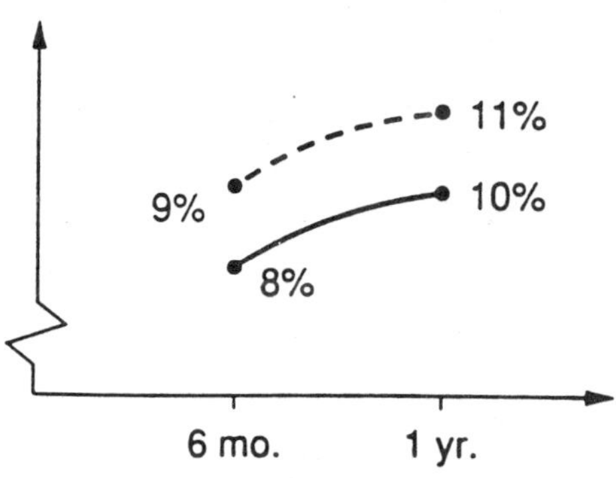

The terms of the swap contract specifies that DSPB will pay at an annual rate of 9.70 percent. DSPB's first floating-rate receipt was determined at origination, so the $4 DSPB will receive in six months is also unchanged. For this one-year swap, the only cash flow that will be changed is the expected floating-rate inflow at one year. With the new term structure the forward rate ${}_6r_{12}$ is 12.4 percent,

$$(1 + 0.11) = [1 + (1/2)0.09] \times [1 + (1/2)_6r_{12}],$$

so the expected floating-rate inflow in one year is

$$\tilde{R}_2 = \$100 \times (1/2) \times 0.124 = \$6.22,$$

and DSPB's expected cash flows are as illustrated below:

	6 mo.	1 yr.
↑ Receive	$4.00 (8%)	$6.22 (12.4%)
↓ Pay	$4.85 (9.7%)	$4.85 (9.7%)

Calculating DSPB's expected net cash inflows,

$$\frac{6\text{ mo.}}{-\$0.85} + \frac{1\text{ yr.}}{\$1.37}$$

and discounting these expected net cash inflows by the corresponding zero rates from the *current* zero-coupon yield curve,

$$\frac{6\text{ mo.}}{9\%} + \frac{1\text{ yr.}}{11\%}$$

the value of the swap to DSPB has risen from zero at origination to 42 cents,

$$\frac{-\$0.85}{[1 + (1/2)0.09]} + \frac{\$1.37}{(1.11)} = \$0.42.$$

cent, and −3 percent, the average change in the value of the swap contract per 1 percent change in the yield curve—(Δ value of swap)/ Δ r—is 42 cents. We can sketch the payoff profile for this swap as in Figure 10–11.[8]

FIGURE 10–11 Value of Swap to DSPB

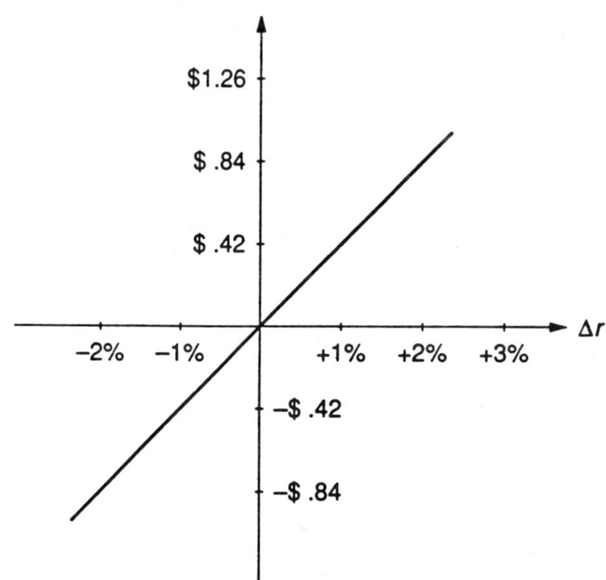

The lesson in all this is simple. To price an at-market interest rate swap, you can use the par yield curve. But to value a swap after origination, it is necessary to use the zero-coupon yield curve, not the par yield curve.

Notes

1. This table repeats a portion of Table 3–8 from Chapter 3.
2. Schuyler (1985).
3. Stevenson (1987).
4. The specific example we use is adapted from Bankers Trust Company (1985). However, the arguments in this example were used widely in the swaps market in the 1980s.
5. For a discussion of the quality spread in the context of swaps, see Wall and Pringle (1988a, 1988b).
6. For example, Ramaswamy and Sundaresan look at the market for floating-rate loans and argue that the default premiums for floating-rate loans are lower than would be predicted.
7. We presume here again that the capital markets are efficient.
8. Although the value of a swap does exhibit some nonlinearity with respect to interest rates, we continue to use a linear approximation. In Chapter 18, we will consider the nonlinearity—also known as convexity or "gamma"—inherent in a swap.

CHAPTER

11

USING SWAPS TO MANAGE FINANCIAL PRICE RISKS*

In Chapter 3 we noted that the end users of swaps (as well as the other OTC derivatives) include industrial corporations, financial institutions, governments, and institutional investors. Firms use swaps to modify the nature of either balance sheet items or cash flows (income or expenses).

Swaps have been used widely to change the nature of assets and liabilities that appear on the firm's balance sheet. When end users employ swaps to modify their debt, they normally are trying to reduce their funding costs or increase their debt capacity. When end users employ swaps to modify assets, they are usually trying to enhance yield, as well as to protect the portfolio from interest rate and equity price risk. On both the asset and liability sides, end users make use of swaps to create synthetic instruments.

Swaps are also widely used to modify the exposure of the firm's cash flows to volatility in foreign exchange rates, interest rates, and/or commodity prices. In some cases, the hedge is a hedge on income (for example, some firms hedge the foreign exchange exposure of the income they earn in other countries and remit to the parent). In other cases, the hedge is a hedge on cost (for example, cruise ship operators or transportation companies may hedge their exposure to fuel prices). In still other cases, the hedge is more macro, involving both revenues and expenses. Perhaps the most straightforward example of a macro hedge is the asset-liability management done by financial institutions in which they hedge net interest income (or the value of the equity) against changes in interest rates.

---

*The authors wish to acknowledge the assistance of Gregory Greiff in assembling the first draft of this chapter.

Using Swaps to Reduce Funding Costs

Over the years, we have heard a lot of conversations about using swaps to reduce the cost of funding the firm. Once we boiled these conversations down, we concluded that the ways swaps are used to reduce funding costs can be grouped under three broad headings—acting on a view, arbitraging markets, and reducing transactions costs.

In the next few pages we will examine some of the ways in which swaps can be used to reduce funding costs. But as with so many other things, the best way to show you how it is done may well be with an example. We are fortunate to have an extraordinary example provided by Tony Pearl and Frank Hankus that illustrates how McDonald's has used swaps to reduce its funding costs.

Acting on a View

Swaps can be used to take a view on the *level* of interest rates. If the managers of the firm believe that an interest rate (or the entire term structure) is going to fall, then they will want to enter into a swap in which it pays a floating rate. If rates do fall, the firm's interest expense will decline. In the example to follow, Pearl and Hankus discuss how McDonald's took such a view on UK interest rates in 1992.

Instead of a view on the level of rates, the firm might take a view on the *shape* of the term structure. A firm might take the view that, in the future, the term structure will be steeper than the current yield curve. In the cash market, such a view would be implemented by borrowing at the short end of the yield curve and investing the proceeds at the long end.

However, this view could be implemented in the swap market by "spreading" longer-term swaps against shorter-term swaps. If I expect the yield curve to steepen, I will want to receive at the long end of the yield curve and pay at the short end. Entering into a swap where I receive a floating rate indexed to a long-term rate (for example, the 10-year Treasury bond rate) and simultaneously entering into a swap where I pay a floating rate indexed to a short-term rate (for example, the six-month Treasury bill rate) is a way of implementing this view.

The spreads in the swap market contain information about how the market "expects" the term structure to behave. If the floating rate is indexed to a longer-term rate, the spread on the fixed-rate (Treasury + spread) is typically wider than the spread for a swap with the floating rate indexed to a shorter-term interest rate. When the spreads for swaps indexed to shorter-term rates widen relative to those indexed to longer-term rates, the market is reflecting increased uncertainty about the future shape of the yield curve.

In late 1990, 1992, the U.S. dollar yield curve steepened dramatically—the spread between the 30-year Treasury bond rate and the three-month Treasury bill rate increased from about 50 basis points to about 300 basis points. In the summer of 1991, we witnessed a reversal in the swap spreads: two-year swap spreads became wider than the five-year spreads. The swap market was predicting that the yield curve flatten out.

Instead of entering into two swaps, a firm could act on a view about the shape of the term structure via a *yield curve swap*.[1] Similar to the *basis swap* described in Chapter 10, a yield curve swap involves the exchange of two floating rate cash flows (in the same currency). However, instead of floating rates from two different yield curves (for example, LIBOR versus commerical paper), the floating rates are from two different points on the yield curve—one of the floating-rate cash flows is determined by a short-term interest rate and the other is determined by a longer-term rate.

Suppose I want to act on the view that the yield curve is going to steepen. I could enter into a yield curve swap where I receive a floating rate indexed to the 10-year Treasury bond rate and pay a floating rate indexed to the six-month Treasury bill rate.

A still more subtle way of taking a view is by taking a view about the relation between the forecasts of future spot rates implied by the yield curve—the forward rates embedded in the term structure—and actual future spot rates. As we demonstrated in Chapter 10, swaps are priced on the basis of the forward yield curve. So the question is whether interest rates will behave as indicated by the prevaiing forward yield curve.

Risk Management in Practice

Do Forward Rates Predict Future Interest Rates?*

Gregory S. Hayt

The ability of forward premia in interest rates to predict subsequent spot interest rates has been of interest to academics for decades. It is of particular relevance for participants in the derivatives market given the very steep yield curves of recent years.

Under the "pure expectations" hypothesis the variation in forward premia is directly attributable to expected changes in the spot rate. However, early tests of this hypothesis found the slope of the term structure contained very little information about subsequent changes in spot rates.

One explanation for the failure of early studies is that forward premia, in addition to containing a forecast of the expected spot rate, also contain information about the risk premium for holding multiperiod bills. Variation in expected risk premia would tend to obscure the ability of the forward rate to

Do Forward Rates Predict Future Interest Rates? continued

predict the spot rate. Taking variation in risk premia into account, a study by Eugene Fama[†] found that high forward premia on U.S. Treasury bills consistently preceded a rise in spot rates. Spot rates, however, did not change by as much as would have been predicted based on the forward curve. In other words, forward rates were found to be biased predictors of future spot rates.

Fama also found that variation in forward premia did not explain much of the fluctuation in subsequent spot rates. In a statistical analysis, forward premia could account for no more than 29 percent of the variation in the one-month spot rate one month ahead between 1959 and 1982. The ability of forward rates to explain variation in more distant spot rates was considerably lower.

Gregory Hayt is a second vice president in the Global Risk Management sector of The Chase Manhattan Bank. Mr. Hayt assists Chase's corporate and institutional customers in the analysis of financial price risk and the development of hedging strategies.

*This originally appeared in *Financial Risk Management*, a newsletter published by the Risk Management Research Center of The Chase Manhattan Bank.

[†]Eugene Fama, "The Information in the Term Structure," *Journal of Financial Economics* 13 (1984).

As indicated by the accompanying box, some academic research suggests that forward rates "overforecast" future spot interest rates. If the yield curve is very steep, the firm might then take the view that future interest rates will not be as high as are implied in the yield curve (and, indeed, priced into an interest rate swap).

> In 1992 and 1993, a number of firms—including McDonald's—implemented such a strategy. Since interest rates were at historic lows, the firms elected to issue long-term debt—20-year, 30-year, 40-year, and even 100-year debt. However, because the yield curve was so steeply sloped, the firms believed that future spot rates would be lower than the rates implied by the forward yield curve. The firm implemented this view by entering into a one- to five-year swap in which the firm would pay a floating rate. The firm ended up with financing in which the firm paid a floating rate in the early years and fixed rate in the later years.

"Arbitraging" the Markets

In Chapter 10 we noted that the term "arbitrage" has been used widely in connection with the swap market. As we said there, we find little evidence of any sort of textbook arbitrage—simultaneously buying and selling to earn a riskless profit. Rather, the "arbitrage" accessed by the use of swaps is generally the result of asymmetric tax treatments or government regulation.

Sometimes the "arbitrage" is the result of some barrier to entry to a particular debt market. If an effective barrier exists, the supply of fixed-income securities in that market will be restricted; so, the price for securities will be higher than would be the market-determined price. Correspondingly, these securites would carry below-market coupons. The end users who are able to access such an "arbitrage" are usually sovereigns who have special access (for example, the World Bank) or extraordinary corporates (for example, the "supranational" corporates).

At other times, the "arbitrage" is the result of tax provisions that treat a debt issue different in one market and another.

> Such an arbitrage occurred in 1990. As Tony Pearl and Frank Hankus describe in their example, McDonald's—and a number of other corporations—were able to borrow at below-market rates by issuing debt in New Zealand and swapping it back into U.S. dollars. The source of this arbitrage was asymmetric tax treatment.

Reducing Transaction Costs

One of the most important (but probably least discussed) ways in which swaps can reduce the cost of funding is by reducing the transaction costs that are a natural consequence of raising funds. Avoiding transaction costs may become one of the most important uses of swaps as markets get more efficient. Transaction costs include not only the bid-ask spread, but also such things as the costs of acquiring information and liquidity costs.

Swaps may help end users in highly regulated markets avoid some business costs. In such markets, substituting swaps for on-balance-sheet instruments may reduce associated costs to the firm, such as capital requirements.

For an international corporation, borrowing needs in a particular country or countries may be too small to be funded cost-effectively through the local capital markets. The firm may find it cost-effective, however, to borrow more than needed in its own capital markets and swap excess debt into the other needed currencies. In their example, Pearl and Hankus show how McDonald's exploited this strategy to fund their Danish and Spanish activities.

Risk Management in Practice

Using Swaps at McDonald's Corporation

Carleton Pearl and Frank Hankus

As a global company, McDonald's has financing needs that carry multiple risks in the foreign exchange and interest rate arenas. Swaps are some of the tools used to manage these debt portfolio risks and to implement our financing strategies.

Using Swaps at McDonald's Corporation continued

Interest Rate Swaps

We use interest rate swaps to manage the interest rate exposures of our portfolio. As of mid-1993, the swap portfolio included 45 interest rate swaps in eight currencies.

As a general rule, because of the long-term nature of our business assets and our desire to lock in occupancy costs, our debt portfolio consists primarily of long-term fixed-rate debt. Depending on our upcoming funding needs and our view of interest rate trends, the overall percentage of consolidated fixed-rate debt generally ranges from 60 to 80 percent.

We use interest rate swaps in three ways—to change the mix of our fixed- and floating-rate debt, to position the company for an expected change in interest rate levels, and to adjust the average maturity of the portfolio.

In July 1993, we secured historically low fixed-rate U.S. dollar funding when we issued $200 million of 40-year bonds domestically. So as not to sacrifice the entire benefit of low U.S. floating rates over the near term, we swapped $100 million of it into five-year floating-rate debt and the second $100 million into seven-year floating-rate debt. The swaps reduce the interest cost on the bond by an average of over 200 basis points.

Internationally, we have also reduced our interest costs by positioning our portfolio for expected changes in interest rates.

In September 1992, for example, we felt that UK interest rates were going to be declining. In four transactions, we swapped 60 million of fixed-rate pound sterling liabilities into three- and five-year floating-rate liabilities on which we receive about 9 percent fixed. Interest rates have declined and we are currently paying about 6 percent floating after having paid over 9 percent on the initial three- or six-month terms. The fixed rates we are receiving average more than 2 percent above current market rates, which, of course, means that the debt could be refixed at 2 percent below its original fixed rate.

Because of its huge size, the swap market is flexible, readily accessible, efficient, and cost-effective—much more so than alternatives for managing our interest rate risks, and that's important because views on interest rates and the needs of the company can change.

We can choose the effective date for a swap, which can be two days from transaction or farther into the future on a forward start basis. We can also easily initiate and close out positions, and prompt execution permits us to lock in the terms of the deal immediately. The alternative method for adjusting our fixed- to floating-rate debt is to issue new floating-rate debt and use the proceeds to call or repurchase one of our fixed-rate bonds or to purchase fixed-rate government securities; however, these alternatives are much more costly and time-consuming, and impractical in many instances.

Using Swaps at McDonald's Corporation continued

Currency Swaps

The advantages of interest rate swaps carry over into currency swaps, which we use to manage the currency mix of our debt portfolio. As of mid-1993, we had 51 currency swaps in our portfolio, denominated in 12 different currencies.

In line with our overall financing philosophy, currency swaps create foreign currency liabilities and cash outflows that match assets and cash inflows in those currencies. Currencies received in swap transactions of McDonald's are often onlent to foreign subsidiaries.

The subsidiary balance sheet reflects an intercompany liability in a currency that matches the land, buildings, and equipment on the asset side. The subsidiary income statement reflects interest expense in the same currency as revenues generated from product sales and licensee fees.

McDonald's, as a borrower of foreign currency in the swap and as lender of the same currency to the international market, also has a matched asset and liability and a matched stream of interest income and interest expense.

In addition to this hedging of intercompany loans, the matching of foreign currency liabilities and cash flows helps us to manage the parent company's exposures that arise from its international investments. The parent company balance sheet reflects a liability in a currency that matches the international investment, and its income statement reflects interest payments in the same currency as cash receipts, such as royalties and dividends, generated by that investment.

Ideally, we would like to create foreign currency obligations by borrowing the needed currencies in the domestic or Euro public markets, or the private placement or loan markets of specialized investors or banks. However, in terms of timing, amounts and terms needed, flexibility, and cost-effective pricing, what we want is not always what is available.

The swap market is often the only source of long-term fixed-rate foreign currency for certain of our international markets, whose borrowing needs are just too small to be funded through the capital markets. Local bank lines are most likely available, but they are generally more expensive by at least 150 basis points.

Here are some examples of small borrowings that could not have been done in the capital markets.

> In June, 1992, we swapped $16 million of commercial paper into 100 million Danish kroner and repaid more expensive local Danish bank lines. The swap market's ready access permitted us to complete the deal just before the Danish vote on the Maastricht treaty and to avoid the interest rate increase that occurred after the vote. Even if size was not an issue, a bond or any long-term borrowing in Danish kroner would have been difficult if not impossible at that time.
>
> In June 1993, we swapped $40 million of commercial paper into 5 billion Spanish pesetas and repaid more expensive local Spanish bank lines. The flexibility of the swap market afforded us

Using Swaps at McDonald's Corporation continued

the chance to do half the deal just prior to Spanish parliamentary elections as a hedge against possible interest rate increases, and to do the other half after the elections had passed and interest rates had actually fallen.

Up until recent months, the swap market has provided foreign currencies at more cost-effective terms than the public debt markets. For most of the past year or two, our debt market interest rates have been higher than those of the swap market by at least 20 to 40 basis points.

During 1992 and the first two quarters of 1993, McDonald's converted $950 million into nine foreign currencies through 30 swaps. The 20–40 basis-point benefit in pricing means $1.9 to $3.8 million in annual interest savings.

In some instances, currency swaps help us achieve economies of scale by deriving more than one currency from an attractively priced larger borrowing.

In July 1991, McDonald's borrowed 50 million deutsche marks for five years through a private placement and onlent 30 million of the total to our German subsidiary, where more expensive local bank lines were repaid. The remaining 20 million deutsche marks were not needed in Germany and were swapped into fixed-rate Swiss francs for use in our Swiss operation—pricing on the swap was 180 basis points better than local fixed-rate funding available to Switzerland.

In other instances, currency swaps help us capitalize on arbitrage between the debt and swap markets, which can exist because of the different basis for pricing in each.

In February 1990, we issued a 100-million New Zealand dollar bond at attractive rates. Twenty-five million New Zealand dollars were onlent to our New Zealand subsidiary to repay more expensive local bank lines and 50 million New Zealand dollars were ultimately swapped into U.S. dollars. Because of the arbitrage, we were able to get 11 basis points below our commercial paper cost. The remaining 25 million New Zealand dollars were simply converted to U.S. dollars, creating a long-term hedge, and the proceeds were used to pay down outstanding commercial paper.

Since we first entered the swap market in 1983, the transactions have proven invaluable in allowing us to secure cost-effective financing in a timely fashion and to properly manage the foreign exchange and interest rate risks that naturally arise in our business. Swaps do carry risks that other financing alternatives do not, but the risks are certainly manageable and they are definitely outweighed by the benefits provided.

Carleton Day Pearl is vice president and treasurer for McDonald's Corporation. He was appointed vice president in 1982 and treasurer in 1987. Mr. Pearl joined McDonald's in 1978 as director of International Finance, a position he held until February 1981, when he was promoted to assistant vice president and managing director of International Finance. Prior to McDonald's,

Using Swaps at McDonald's Corporation continued

Mr. Pearl worked for Bankers Trust Company, New York, where he held positions in both the domestic and international lending areas. He also was general manager of Bankers Trust (International) Midwest Corp., the Chicago Edge Act Corporation for Bankers Trust. A 1967 graduate of New York University, Mr. Pearl received a B.A. from Colgate University in Hamilton, New York, and an M.B.A. in Finance and International Business from NewYork University.

Frank Hankus is the director of Financial Markets for McDonald's Corporation. He joined the company in September 1975 as a member of Administrative Accounting. Before assuming his financial markets responsibilities in January 1992, he had been the director of Worldwide Income Tax Accounting since July 1987. Prior to joining the company, Mr. Hankus spent seven years working in and managing the restaurant operations of a McDonald's franchise. While working in restaurant operations, he received his Bachelor of Science in accounting from Walton School of Commerce, Chicago, Illinois, and earned his CPA certificate in May 1975.

Using Swaps to Increase Debt Capacity (or Gain Access to Debt Markets)

One of the primary themes of this book has been (and will continue to be) that, if used appropriately, swaps—and other financial derivatives—reduce the risk of a firm. And if a firm is less risky, it should be able to support more debt.

Greg Millman made this point more concretely when he reported that, by stabilizing the company's net worth and keeping it from tripping technical default triggers, swaps and other hedging techniques have permitted companies like Kaiser Aluminum and Union Carbide to carry more debt.[2]

Indeed, at Kaiser, comprehensive financial price risk management was apparently one of the cornerstones of the firm's drive to stabilize performance and thereby sustain a heavy debt burden. Kaiser's lenders were well aware that Kaiser was subject to external price risks from energy and aluminum. By managing these financial price risks, Kaiser increased its debt capacity by removing volatility from its cost and revenue stream.

Turning the preceding argument around: *the more financial price risk the firm faces, the less debt it can carry.* Taking this argument to its limit, there could be cases where the financial price risk is so great that the firm is effectively denied access to the debt markets. In such a case, swaps could be used to provide access to the debt markets. This is precisely the point of the following illustration, which demonstrates a highly innovative use of a commodity swap.

Mexicana de Cobre (Mexcobre) is the copper-exporting subsidiary of Grupo Mexico, a large Mexican mining group. In the late 1980s, Mexcobre would have been barred access to international capital markets because of credit risk concerns within the banking community. However, in 1989 Mexcobre was able to borrow $210 million for 38 months from a consortium of 10 banks, led by Paribas. Let's look at the way in which the Mexcobre loan was structured to minimize the political and commodity-price risks inherent in the transaction.

Illustration 11–1

Mexicana de Cobre*

The 10 banks lent Mexcobre $210 million for 38 months at a fixed rate of 11.48 percent. This replaced borrowings from the Mexican government at 23 percent that Mexcobre had previously been paying.

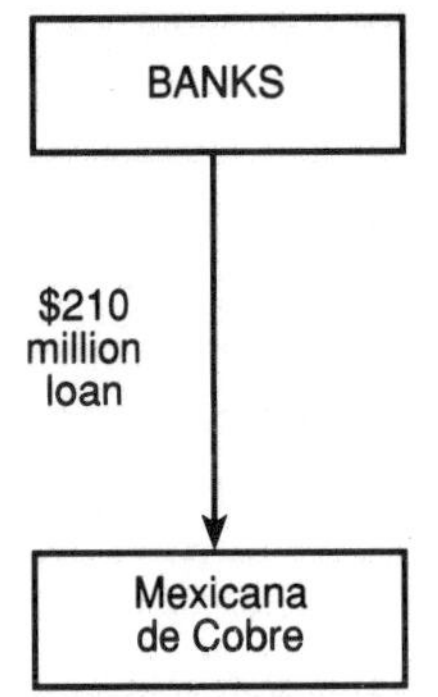

To reduce political risk, a forward sale was incorporated into the transaction. A Belgian company, Sogem, agreed to buy from Mexcobre 3,700 tons of copper per month at the prevailing spot price for the copper—determined by the LME price of copper. The payments from Sogem went not to Mexcobre but instead into an escrow account in New York. Funds in the escrow account were then used to service the debt (and any residual was returned to Mexcobre).

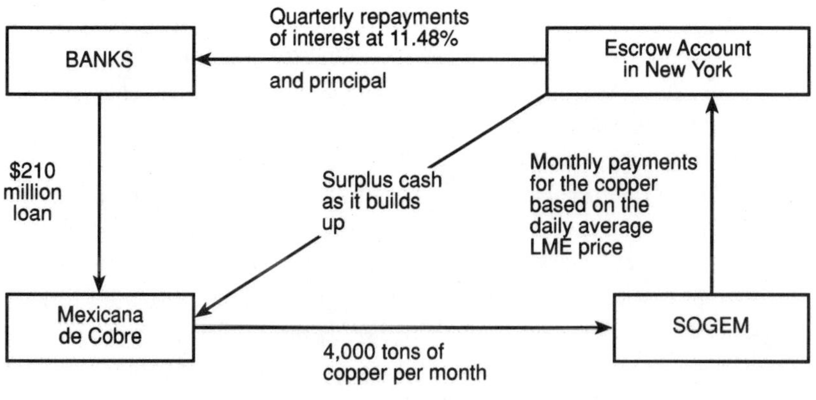

Mexicana de Cobre continued

While the New York escrow account dealt with the political risk, it did nothing about the copper price risk. Were the price of copper to fall, there could be a shortfall in the escrow account. To eliminate this price risk, Paribas arranged a copper swap *with the escrow account* in which the payments received based on a floating copper price were converted to payments based on a fixed price of copper.

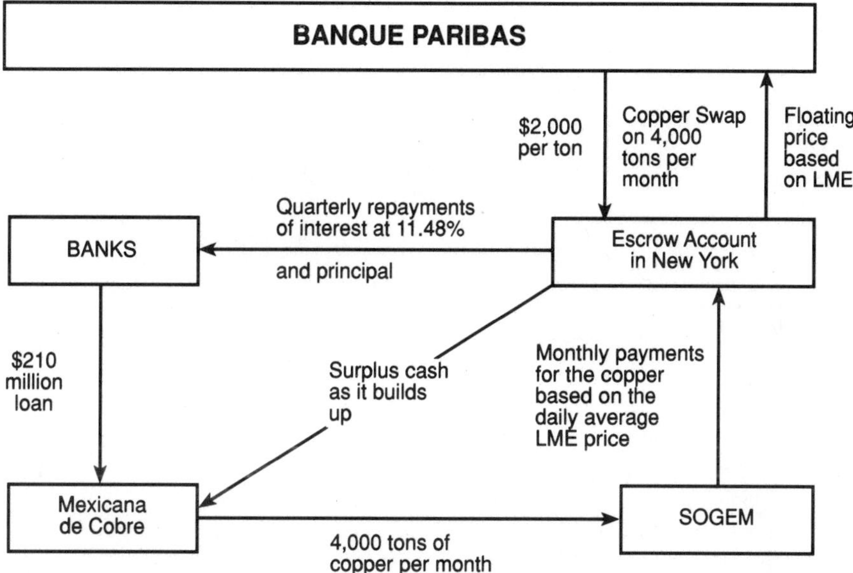

As a result of the swap, the payments into the escrow account were fixed at a level 10 percent above what was needed to service the bank debt.

There was a final step. The loan to Mexcobre was a fixed-rate loan; but the banks in the syndicate wanted a floating-rate asset. Paribas arranged another swap—this time an interest rate swap with the banks—to convert the cash flows from fixed rate to floating rate.

Mexicana de Cobre continued

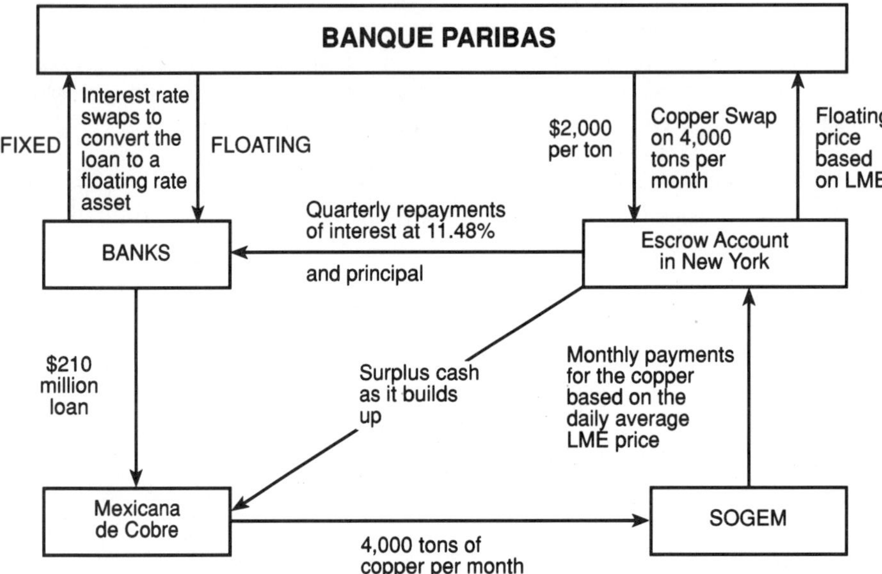

Mexcobre's net position is of owing fixed-rate payments on its debt and receiving fixed-rate payments for its copper, where the fixed-rate payments on its copper production are in excess of what it needs to service its debt. The end result was that Mexcobre was able to borrow a larger amount for a longer-term than would otherwise have been the case. The deal, which was agreed to in July 1989, was the first voluntary foreign currency borrowing for a private sector Mexican company since the debt crisis began in 1982. Without the copper swap, it is unlikely that money would have been lent.

*This discussion is based on Paul B. Spraos, "The Anatomy of A Copper Swap," *Corporate Risk Management*, and on "Mexcobre Loan Deal Repays Debt," *Corporate Finance*, August 1989.

Using Swaps to Hedge the Firm

In Chapter 4 we talked about why a firm would *want* to hedge. In Chapter 19 we will provide some evidence about the way that the market reacts *when* the firm hedges. At this point, we want to spend a little time talking about *how* a firm hedges, providing some examples of the ways in which firms have implemented hedging strategies using swaps.

Hedging Interest Rate Risk

The available evidence suggests that management of interest rate risk is the most common use for swaps. In Chapter 3, we noted that the market for interest rate swaps is far and away the largest of the markets for OTC derivatives.

The general perception of market participants is that interest rate swaps have been used most extensively to hedge liablities—the firm's debt. However, swaps are not used exclusively for liabilities. Swaps can be used to manage the interest rate risk associated with the value of a firm's assets. Corporate treasurers are increasingly taking account of the interest rate sensitivity of both assets and liabilities in designing hedges. Interest rate swaps can be used to adjust the average maturity or interest rate sensitivity of a company's debt portfolio so that it more closely matches the interest rate sensitivity of the asset side of the balance sheet. This reduces the exposure of the company's net worth or market value to interest rate risk.

The trade press has reported that Kraft, the U.S.-based food giant, takes an active approach to interest rate risk management.[3]

> Kraft's debt grew from $600,000 in 1985 to $1.6 billion in 1987, making interest rate risk a serious concern to management. Viewing its balance sheet as a portfolio, Kraft's treasury has used the techniques we described in Chapter 5 to assign a duration to all its assets and liabilities. Given its estimate of asset duration, Kraft uses interest rate swaps to adjust the duration of its debt to keep the balance sheet hedged.

Hedging Foreign Exchange Rate Risk

The evidence we have seen suggests that the dominant use of currency swaps is to modify the nature of a debt issue. A firm will borrow in one currency and use a swap to transform the cash flows to another currency. (Look again at the McDonald's example.) However, currency swaps have been used to hedge the firm's foreign exchange rate risk—primarly transaction exposures.

For example, a U.S. manufacturing firm might contract to provide product to a distributor in Germany at a fixed deutsche mark price. As long as the deutsche mark value of the dollar remains stable or declines, the U.S. manufacturing firm is happy; the worry is, of course, that the value of the dollar will rise. To protect against adverse foreign exchange rate movements, the U.S. manufacturing firm could enter into a currency swap in which it pays a fixed deutsche mark cash flow and receives a fixed U.S. dollar cash flow from its counterparty. The swap contract changes the deutsche mark receipts into dollar receipts—thereby eliminating the foreign exchange exposure.

Hedging Commodity-Price Risk

As we described in Chapter 3, the most common type of commodity swap is one indexed to energy prices. A firm that is a user of energy—such as a chemical manufacturer, a utility firm, or an airline—faces two types of risk. First, the energy user is exposed to delivery risk—the firm must be sure that it will receive the oil or natural gas or jet fuel when and where they need it. To assure itself of a reliable supply of the commodity, the energy user might enter into a long-term agreement with an energy producer calling for the delivery of a specified amount of the product at a specified date but with the price determined by the spot market. The second risk—price risk—is not mitigated by the long-term agreement. To eliminate this remaining price risk, the energy user could enter into an energy swap in which the energy user will pay cash flows determined by a fixed energy price and will receive cash flows determined by the spot price of the energy product.

Firms also use swaps to hedge commodity exposures other than energy.

> FMC is a diversified manufacturer of everything from chemicals and defense equipment to food, petroleum, and material-handling equipment. It sells in 85 countries and manufactures in 14 of them. Sales in 1989 totaled $3.5 billion.
>
> By entering into a long-term contract with the U.S. Army to build the Bradley Fighting Vehicle at an essentially fixed price, FMC accepted long-term exposures to the price of metals.[4] Traditionally, metals purchasers had relied on forward contracts to hedge their exposures; but FMC discovered that, because the credit risk for swaps is smaller than that for forwards, long-term hedges using swaps were cheaper than long-term hedges comprising forward contracts. Consequently, FMC turned increasingly to commodity swaps to hedge its exposure to metal price volatility—by 1991, 30 percent of FMC metals hedges were commodity swaps.

Investor Uses of Swaps

The earliest use of swaps by institutional investors involved asset swaps, in which the cash flows from a particular asset are swapped for other cash flows, possibly denominated in another currency or based on a different interest rate. The goal was for the "swapped asset" to have a higher yield than the original asset.

Increasingly, banks, insurance companies, or large investors are using interest rate swaps to reduce the interest rate risk inherent in their portfolios. Most institutional investors have a mismatch between the duration of their assets and liabilities. Consider, for instance, an investor who holds short-term liabilities and long-term assets. The investor could swap out some portion of the cash flows based on its long-term assets at a fixed rate and receive a short-term floating rate. This would offset losses if short-term rates were to rise relative to long-term rates.

Most recently, institutional investors are using equity swaps to protect the value of their portfolios.

Uses of Swaps by Governments

Governmental entities, including national governments, local governments, state-owned or -sponsored entities, and supranationals use derivatives for much the same reasons as nonfinancial corporations. They use derivatives in financing activities, to diversify their sources of funds, and to achieve cost savings through the issuance of structured securities. Derivatives are also used for debt management purposes, especially by those governments borrowing in many different currencies.

The use of swaps by supranational entities such as the World Bank is long-standing.[6] At the federal level in the United States, government-sponsored enterprises such as the Federal National Mortgage Association and the Student Loan Marketing Association are significant users of the derivatives markets for risk management and as hedges related to structured financings.

The use of swaps by governments is not limited to interest rate and currency swaps. Recently, some governmental entities have turned to commodity derivatives to manage oil price risk.

Aside

Finland[5]

Finland is a highly rated sovereign and an active borrower in the international capital markets. The government of Finland, through the Ministry of Finance, has actively used swaps to lower its effective cost of debt, to manage the currency composition of its foreign liabilities, and to hedge its foreign exchange risks. During the period 1987 to 1990, Finland entered into approximately 50 swaps with a notional principal equivalent to U.S. $50–200 million at a time. Roughly 30 percent of the government's total outstanding foreign debt was swapped, with most swaps being related to newly issued debt. Swaps were used in 1990 to achieve funding costs of 30–50 basis points below LIBOR. They were also used to configure the currency composition of Finland's foreign liabilities in the direction of its official currency basket. The Finnish mark was pegged to the value of the currency basket. The ministry used currency swaps to access the lowest-cost offshore debt markets and then translated the currency composition of the debt portfolio to the desired mix. Substantial changes in the debt composition were achieved through swaps. For example, although the actual share of the Japanese yen in the external debt was 23 percent in 1989, currency swaps were used to reduce the effective share to 12 percent in 1989 and 5 percent in 1990.

Aside

Hedging Fuel Costs with Commodity Swaps[7]

By mid-1991, numerous municipal governments and authorities, including Atlanta, Boston, San Francisco, and Washington, D.C., were using derivatives to lock in fuel costs as a way of controlling their energy budgets. For example, the Metropolitan Atlanta Rapid Transit Authority (MARTA) entered into a one-year commodity swap in May 1991 to lock in a fuel price for its budget. The swap contract guaranteed MARTA a price of 53.3 cents per gallon for No. 2 heating oil on 9 million gallons of fuel purchased during the 1991–92 fiscal year. The transaction is estimated to have saved MARTA more than $1.5 million over actual market prices.

Using Swaps to Create Synthetic Instruments

We have already seen that one of the most common uses of swaps is to transform one form of debt to another:

Fixed-rate debt
plus
pay-floating / receive-fixed interest rate swap
results in
synthetic floating-rate debt

In the same way, by combining a pay-fixed swap with floating-rate debt, a firm creates synthetic fixed-rate debt.[8]

Going a step further, as we will describe in Chapter 16, a pay-fixed swap can be combined with floating-rate debt to create an *inverse floating-rate note*.[9] An inverse floating rate note pays a prespecified (fixed) interest rate *minus* LIBOR, for example, 8 percent − LIBOR might be the yield for a three-year inverse floater.

Synthesizing financial instruments—financial engineering—is a topic that more and more treasurers are becoming familiar with. (And a topic to which we will return in Chapters 15 and 16.) In this text, we will stress simplicity—we talk a lot about assembling building blocks. However, as the following discussion illustrates, the people who actually put financial engineering to work at industrial corporations sometimes have to do a little more engineering to get the theory into practice.

Risk Management in Practice

Using Interest Rate Swaps to Synthesize a Long-Dated Foreign Exchange Forward

Jacques Tierny

In Chapter 6, Smithson, Smith, and Wilford showed how a foreign exchange forward could be created—read that *synthesized:*

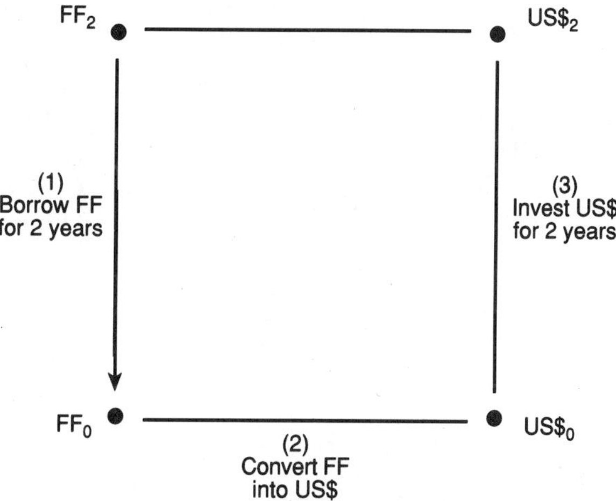

The preceding figure indicates that I could synthesize a two-year French franc–U.S. dollar forward by (1) borrowing French francs for two years, (2) converting the French francs I borrowed to U.S. dollars via a spot foreign exchange transaction, and (3) depositing the U.S. dollars for two years.

In this simple exposition, the authors gloss over the fact that the two-year borrowing and two-year deposit necessary to synthesize the foreign exchange forward must be a zero-coupon loans and deposits. An industrial corporation might be able to do a zero coupon deposit (e.g., certificate of deposit, or CD). However, we do not have ready access to zero-coupon borrowings. Instead we rely on LIBOR-based borrowings, loans on which we make annual interest payments.

So, before I could actually synthesize that two-year French franc–U.S. dollar forward, I must first synthesize a two-year zero coupon borrowing. Interest

Using Interest Rate Swaps to Synthesize a Long-Dated Foreign Exchange Forward continued

rate swaps permit me to do precisely that—I can use a combination of standard LIBOR borrowings and interest rate swaps to synthesize a zero-coupon borrowing.

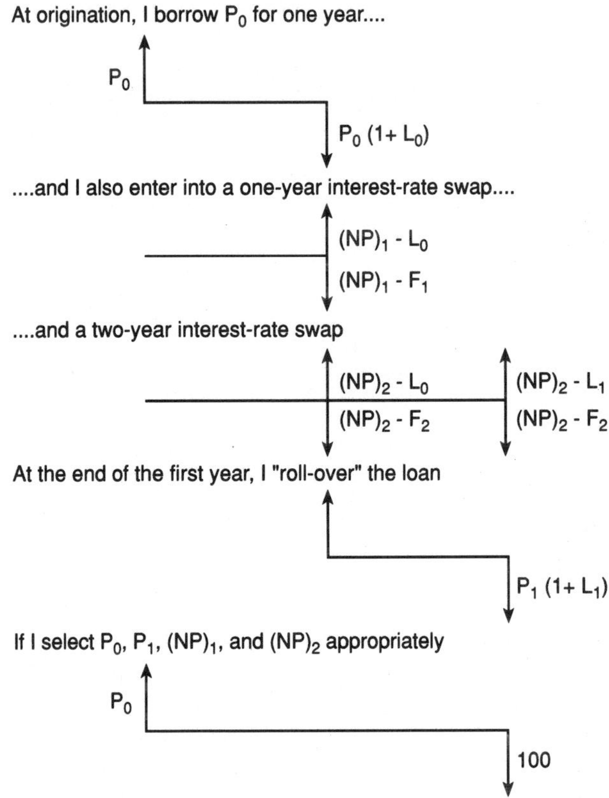
At origination, I borrow P0 for one year....
P0
P0 (1+ L0)
....and I also enter into a one-year interest-rate swap....
(NP)1 - L0
(NP)1 - F1
....and a two-year interest-rate swap
(NP)2 - L0
(NP)2 - F2
(NP)2 - L1
(NP)2 - F2
At the end of the first year, I "roll-over" the loan
P1 (1+ L1)
If I select P0, P1, (NP)1, and (NP)2 appropriately
P0
100

The way that this is accomplished is illustrated in the accompanying figure: Initially, I need to do three transactions:

I borrow P_0 for one year. At maturity of this transaction, I will owe $P_0 \times (1 + L_0)$ where L_0 is the one-year LIBOR rate known at the time I originate the set of transaction

I enter into a standard, one-year interest rate swap with a notional principal of $(NP)_1$ in which I receive an annual cash flow determined by one-year LIBOR and make an annual payment determined by the one-year swap rate, F_1 (which is specified at origination)

Using Interest Rate Swaps to Synthesize a Long-Dated Foreign Exchange Forward continued

I also enter into a standard, two-year interest rate swap with a notional principal of $(NP)_2$ in which I receive annual cash flows determined by one-year LIBOR and make annual payments determined by the two-year swap rate, F_2 (which is specified at origination)

At the end of the first year, I need to roll over the loan:

I borrow P_1 for one year. At maturity of this transaction—at year 2—I will owe $P_1 \times (1 + L_1)$ where L_1 is the one-year LIBOR rate in one year—at the time I roll over the loan

I have four parameters. Two are loan principals—the principal of the original loan, P_0, and the principal of the rollover, P_1. The other two are the notional principals of the swaps—the one-year swap, $(NP)_1$, and the two-year swap, $(NP)_2$. If I set these parameters "appropriately," I can end up with a (par) zero-coupon borrowing with a principal repayment of 100.

And, it turns out that finding the "appropriate" values is not as hard as it might first appear.

Begin with the year 2 cash flows. The face value of the zero-coupon loan (FVZCL), 100, must be equal to the repayment of the rollover, $P_1 \times (1 + L_1)$, plus the fixed-rate payment on the two-year interest rate swap, $(NP)_2 \times F_2$, minus the floating-rate receipt on the two-year interest rate swap, $(NP)_2 \times L_1$.

$$\text{FVZCL} = 100 = P_1 \times (1 + L_1) + (NP)_2 \times F_2 - (NP)_2 \times L_1 \qquad 11\text{–}1$$

Moreover, I know that the face value of the zero-coupon loan is invariant to changes in LIBOR:

$$\frac{d(\text{FVZCL})}{dL_1} = P_1 - (NP)_2 = 0 \qquad 11\text{–}2$$

Using Equation 11–2 in Equation 11–1, the unknown one-year LIBOR rate at year one drops out and we can solve for P_1 and $(NP)_2$.

$$P_1 = (NP)_2 = \frac{100}{1 + F_2} \qquad 11\text{–}3$$

Using these values, we iterate back to solve for P_0 and $(NP)_1$. As illustrated in the accompanying figure, the principal of the rollover, P_1, must be equal to the amount due from the original loan, $P_0 \times (1 + L_0)$, plus the fixed-rate payments on both the one- and two-year interest rate swaps, $(NP)_1 \times F_1 + (NP)_2 \times F_2$, minus the floating-rate receipts for the one- and two-year interest rate swaps, $(NP)_1 \times L_0 + (NP)_2 \times L_0$.

$$\begin{aligned} P_1 = P_0 \times (1 + L_0) &+ (NP)_1 \times F_1 + (NP)_2 \times F_2 \\ &- (NP)_1 \times L_0 - (NP)_2 \times L_0 \end{aligned} \qquad 11\text{–}4$$

Using Interest Rate Swaps to Synthesize a Long-Dated Foreign Exchange Forward continued

And, similar to Equation 11–2 for the face value of the zero-coupon loan, the principal of this rollover loan is invariant to changes in the one-year LIBOR in effect when the transaction is begun.

$$\frac{dP_1}{dL_1} = P_0 - (NP)_1 - (NP)_2 = 0 \qquad 11\text{–}5$$

Since we already know P_1 and $(NP)_2$ and since L_0 is known, Equations 11–4 and 11–5 represent two equations with two unknowns; so, we can solve for P_0 and $(NP)_1$.

Precisely the same method can be used to construct zero-coupon loans with maturities of three years or more.

Once the zero-coupon loan is synthesized, I can then create the synthetic foreign exchange forward.* But the question you may be asking yourself is, why? Why would a treasurer go to all of this trouble to synthesize FX forwards, since FX forwards are available in the market?

The answer is that the synthetic forwards can cost less. The bid-ask spread for long-dated FX forwards can be large. In contrast, the bid-ask spreads for LIBOR borrowings, for standard interest rates swaps, and for spot FX transactions are tiny. If I build my own FX forwards, I have found that I can cut by one half to two thirds the bid-ask spreads for long-dated FX forwards.

*To reduce the involvement of the company's balance sheet, the deposit and loan can be combined via the "FX swap" described in the first part of Chapter 10: In the spot market, I sell the U.S. dollar deposit against the French franc. Simultaneously, I buy it back in the one-year forward market.

Jacques Tierny is responsible for group treasury in a multinational company, a position he has held for the past 12 years. He manages the company's financial exposures and has centralized and netted the company's foreign exchange exposures. Moreover, he has put in place several arbitrage and opportunity-driven financing structures. Jacques Tierny is a graduate of H.E.C. in France.

Notes

1. This discussion is adapted from "Yield Curve Applications of Swap Products" by Rupert Brotherton-Ratcliffe and Ben Iben, in *Advanced Strategies in Financial Risk Management*, Robert J. Schwartz and Clifford W. Smith, Jr., eds., (New York Institute of Finance, 1993).
2. Gregory J. Millman, "Kaiser and Union Carbide Hedge Their Bets with Their Banks," *Corporate Finance*, June 1991.
3. "Kraft: The Well-Processed Spreadsheet," *Corporate Finance*, September 1990.
4. This discussion is taken from "FMC Uses Metals Swaps to Lock in Margins," *Corporate Risk Management*, January 1991.
5. See "Government Use of Cross Currency Swaps," in *Cross Currency Swaps*, Carl Beidleman, ed., (Homewood, Ill.: Business One Irwin, 1992).

6. Remember that the swap market is dated from the 1981 currency swap transaction between IBM and the World Bank.
7. This example is taken from the Report of the Derivatives Study Group, Group of Thirty, Washington, D.C., July 1993.
8. Remember, however, that the synthetic fixed-rate debt is not precisely like the "normal" fixed-rate debt—e.g., the synthetic fixed-rate debt has no call provision.
9. We will show in Chapter 16 that an inverse floating-rate note is composed of a floating-rate note and an interest rate swap with a notional principal twice that of the original floating-rate note. The floating-rate note has a principal P and coupon payment of $\tilde{R}$. If this *FRN* is combined with an interest-rate swap with notional principal $2P$, the resulting coupon payment is $2\bar{R} - \tilde{R}$—if interest rates rise, the coupon payment falls.

CHAPTER

12 A PRIMER ON OPTIONS

In contrast to forward, futures, and swaps contracts, which impose *obligations* on the counterparties, an option contract conveys from one contracting party to another a *right*. Where a forward, futures, or swap contract *obliges* one party to buy a specified asset at a specified price on a specified date and *obliges* the other party to make the corresponding sale, an option gives its purchaser the *right* to buy or to sell a specified asset at a specified price on (or before) a specified date. To flesh out this definition, let's look more closely at the option contract and the contracting parties.

The Option Contract

The Contracting Parties

In an option contract, one party grants to the other the right to buy from or sell an asset. The party granting the right is referred to as the *option seller* (or the *option writer* or the *option maker*). The counterparty, the party purchasing the right, is referred to as the *option buyer*. Alternatively, the option buyer is said to be long the option position. It follows that the option seller is said to have a *short* position in the option.

The Right to Buy or to Sell

An option to buy an asset at a specified price is a *call* option on the asset. The call buyer has the *right* to purchase the asset. On the other side of the transaction, the call option seller has the *obligation* to sell. An option to sell an asset at a specified price is a *put* option on the asset. The put buyer has the *right* to sell; the put seller has the *obligation* to buy.

The Specified Asset

Options are available on a wide range of assets: equities, equity indices, interest rates (or bond prices), foreign-exchange rates, and commodities. Since our objective is to provide a general understanding of how options work, we begin with those options about which the most has been written—options on shares of stock. In Chapter 13, we will expand the discussion to the other assets.

The Specified Price and Date

The price at which the option buyer can buy or sell the asset is called the *exercise* or *strike* price.

The final date on which the option owner can buy or sell the asset is known as the *expiration* or *maturity* date. An option that can be exercised only on the expiration date is referred to as a *European* option. An *American* option can be exercised on or before the expiration date.[1]

The Graphics of Options

As with the other financial derivatives, the simplest way to understand how options work is with a picture. Let's begin by considering the value at expiration of a European call option for a share of stock. For options, we use the following notation:[2]

S = the share price, the price of the asset;

X = the exercise price for the option;[3]

C = the value of the call option;

P = the value of the put option.

If, at expiration, the share price is less than the exercise price ($S < X$), the option to purchase the asset for the exercise price is worthless ($C = 0$). In this case, since the share could be purchased in the cash market for less than X, the right to buy it for X has no value. However, if the share price is greater than the exercise price at expiration of the option ($S > X$), the value of the right to buy the share at the exercise price is equal to the difference between the share price and the exercise price ($C = S - X$). If $S > X$ at expiration, the call owner could purchase the share for X and then sell it in the cash market at S, pocketing $S - X$ as profit. The value of a call option at expiration is summarized in the mathematical expression

$$C = \text{Max}[0, (S - X)] \tag{12–1}$$

and is summarized graphically in Figure 12–1. As illustrated, if at expiration the share price is higher than the exercise price, the owner of the call option benefits at

Illustration 12–1

Reading the Options Quotes

We have reproduced a portion of the quotes on equity options as they appeared in *The Wall Street Journal* on Monday, July 26, 1993. These quotes are for the close of business on the preceding trading day—in this case, on Friday, July 23.

C16 THE WALL STREET JOURNAL MONDAY, JULY 26, 1993

LISTED OPTIONS QUOTATIONS

Friday, July 23, 1993

Volume, close, net change and open interest of the 1,400 most active equity and 100 most active long-term contracts. Volume figures are unofficial. Open interest is total outstanding for all exchanges and reflects previous trading day. **CB**-Chicago Board Options Exchange. **AM**-American Stock Exchange. **PB**-Philadelphia Stock Exchange. **PC**-Pacific Stock Exchange. **NY**-New York Stock Exchange. **a**-Underlying stock on primary market. **c**-Call. **p**-Put.

MOST ACTIVE CONTRACTS

Option/Strike				Vol	Exch	Last	Net Chg	a-Close	Open Int
TelMex	Aug	50		6,614	CB	1¼	+ ¾	49⅛	22,466
TelMex	Aug	45	p	5,177	CB	¼	− 1	49⅛	13,093
EleArt	Sep	30		4,101	CB	1¾	...	28⅛	637
I B M	Aug	40	p	3,934	CB	1⅛	+ 5/16	42¼	11,587
I B M	Aug	45		3,232	CB	15/16	− 3/16	42¼	9,718
Citicp	Oct	30	p	2,767	CB	1⅛	− 1/16	31¾	10,918
Micsft	Oct	85		2,697	PC	2⅞	− ¼	77⅝	1,383
TelMex	Aug	50		2,537	AM	1¼	+ 13/16	49⅛	22,466
I B M	Aug	45	p	2,271	CB	3¾	+ 13/16	42¼	13,871
Disney	Oct	35	p	2,161	AM	11/16	− 9/16	39¼	3,374
Disney	Sep	40		2,065	AM	1½	+ 1	39¼	177
Intel	Aug	55		1,981	AM	⅞	+ ¼	51¾	10,450
TelMex	Sep	45	p	1,833	CB	⅞	− ⅞	49⅛	392
TelMex	Nov	45	p	1,822	CB	1⅝	− 15/16	49⅛	4,722
Compaq	Aug	50	p	1,693	PC	2 1/16	− 15/16	50⅜	3,444
Disney	Aug	40		1,628	AM	13/16	+ 7/16	39¼	5,539
Compaq	Aug	50		1,528	PC	2⅜	+ ½	50⅜	6,598
I B M	Aug	50		1,487	CB	⅛	− 1/16	42¼	15,941
Caterp	Aug	80		1,383	AM	2	+ ⅛	80¼	1,211
MedcoC	Aug	30		1,352	PC	1¾	+ 13/16	29	1,914
I B M	Oct	45		1,315	CB	1 15/16	− 5/16	42¼	7,231
I B M	Oct	40	p	1,264	CB	1 15/16	+ 7/16	42¼	6,569
G M	Aug	50		1,213	CB	7/16	− 3/16	46¾	6,199
I B M	Oct	50		1,168	CB	¾	− ⅛	42¼	13,654
Caterp	Aug	75		1,166	AM	5⅛	+ 1¼	80¼	761

EQUITY OPTIONS

-A-B-C-

Option/Strike				Vol	Exch	Last	Net Chg	a-Close	Open Int
A Hess	Aug	50		60	PB	¾	+ ⅛	49⅝	396
A Hess	Aug	50	p	100	PB	1⅜	− 1½	49⅝	251
A M D	Aug	22½	p	114	PC	9/16	+ 1/16	24⅜	1,846
A M R	Aug	60		55	AM	6¼	+ ¼	65⅝	1,160
A M R	Aug	60	p	60	AM	7/16	− ⅛	65⅝	2,278
A M R	Aug	65		114	AM	2 5/16	+ 3/16	65⅝	3,156
A M R	Aug	65	p	131	AM	1⅞	+ ⅜	65⅝	2,146
A M R	Aug	70		93	AM	⅝	+ 1/16	65⅝	5,761
A S A	Aug	50		79	AM	9/16	− ⅛	46	3,926
ABrrck	Jan	25		103	AM	3	+ ¼	24⅛	4,312
ABrrck	Aug	25		66	AM	11/16	− ⅛	24⅛	2,657
ADT	Aug	5		50	CB	3⅝	...	8⅝	...
ADT	Aug	7½	p	75	CB	⅛	...	8⅝	...
ADT	Aug	7½	p	75	NY	⅛	...	8⅝	...
AlnGrp	Aug	130		50	CB	9	+ 1½	138⅝	561
ALC Cm	Aug	20		80	AM	3¼	+ 11/16	23½	218
ALC Cm	Aug	22½		65	AM	1⅜	+ 7/16	23½	181
AMedHI	Aug	12½		80	PB	½	− ⅛	12⅜	92
APwrCv	Aug	35		373	CB	6	+ 1⅛	40¾	462
APwrCv	Sep	35		85	CB	7	+ ¾	40¾	638
APwrCv	Sep	35	p	110	CB	1 3/16	− ½	40¾	692
APwrCv	Aug	40		204	CB	2½	+ ⅝	40¾	1,046
APwrCv	Aug	40	p	53	CB	2¼	− ⅝	40¾	472
APwrCv	Sep	40		101	CB	3⅞	+ ⅝	40¾	1,368
APwrCv	Sep	40	p	163	CB	3¼	− ⅞	40¾	31
APwrCv	Sep	45		86	CB	1¾	+ ⅛	40¾	236
AST Rs	Aug	17½		100	AM	⅜	+ ⅛	15½	1,222
AT&T	Oct	55	p	76	CB	¼	...	63⅝	3,334
AT&T	Aug	60	p	156	CB	⅜	+ ⅛	63⅝	1,741
AT&T	Oct	60		125	CB	4¾	− ⅜	63⅝	4,795
AT&T	Oct	60	p	278	CB	1	+ ¼	63⅝	2,327
AT&T	Jan	65		352	CB	2 13/16	− 7/16	63⅝	3,919
AT&T	Aug	65		447	CB	13/16	− 1/16	63⅝	5,029
AT&T	Sep	65		80	CB	1¼	− ⅜	63⅝	142
AT&T	Oct	65		118	CB	1¾	− ⅛	63⅝	5,476
AT&T	Sep	70		212	CB	¼	− 1/16	63⅝	54
AT&T	Oct	70		168	CB	½	− 1/16	63⅝	189
Abbt L	Feb	25	p	65	PB	1⅝	− ⅜	25⅞	156
Abbt L	Nov	30		78	PB	⅜	+ 1/16	25⅞	2,232
…claim	Aug	30	p	65	CB	1 13/16	+ 5/16	31⅛	213
	Aug	20		144	AM	4	+ 1 3/16	23⅞	232
			p	50	AM	¼	− 9/16	23⅞	321
						2	+ ¾	23⅞	970

Option/Strike				Vol	Exch	Last	Net Chg	a-Close	Open Int
Caterp	Aug	75		1,166	AM	5⅛	+ 1¼	80¼	761
Caterp	Aug	75	p	83	AM	½	− 1⅛	80¼	747
Caterp	Sep	75		205	AM	4½	− ⅞	80¼	4
Caterp	Sep	75	p	728	AM	1⅜	− ⅞	80¼	149
Caterp	Aug	80		1,383	AM	2	+ ⅛	80¼	1,211
Caterp	Aug	80	p	257	AM	2⅛	− 1¾	80¼	305
CellPro	Aug	22½		50	CB	¾	+ 3/16	20¼	78
ChamDv	Jan	5	p	62	CB	⅞	+ 1/16	4¾	100
ChamDv	Sep	5		80	CB	7/16	+ 3/16	4¾	65
Chase	Aug	30		120	AM	2⅛	− ⅛	32⅛	739
Chase	Sep	30		157	AM	2⅜	...	32⅛	5,7[illegible]6
Chase	Sep	30	p	500	AM	11/16	+ 1/16	32⅛	13,659
Chase	Dec	30	p	55	AM	1½	...	32⅛	3,230
Checkp	Aug	10	p	115	PC	¾	− ½	10¼	45
Checkp	Nov	12½		100	PC	9/16	− 7/16	10¼	235
ChemBk	Aug	40		229	AM	1¼	...	40¼	1,932
ChemBk	Aug	40	p	100	AM	1	− ¼	40¼	944
ChemBk	Dec	40		100	AM	2⅞	− ¼	40¼	1,203
ChemBk	Dec	40	p	70	AM	2⅝	− ⅛	40¼	862
Chevrn	Aug	85	p	50	AM	1⅛	− ⅜	87⅝	1,516
Chevrn	Sep	85		229	AM	3½	+ ¾	87⅝	2,205
Chevrn	Sep	85	p	204	AM	1½	− ⅝	87⅝	667
Chevrn	Aug	90		380	AM	9/16	+ 1/16	87⅝	1,657
Chevrn	Dec	90		83	AM	2⅜	+ ¼	87⅝	682
Chevrn	Dec	95		108	AM	1⅛	+ ½	87⅝	80
Chiron	Oct	45		120	AM	21	+ 2¼	65	189
Chiron	Jan	50		85	AM	18½	+ 1⅝	65	43
Chiron	Aug	55	p	105	AM	5/16	+ 1/16	65	339
Chiron	Jan	60	p	66	AM	5⅛	+ ⅜	65	117
Chiron	Aug	60		507	AM	6⅝	− 1⅜	65	832
Chiron	Aug	60		92	CB	7½	− ⅝	65	832
Chiron	Aug	60	p	313	AM	1	+ 1/16	65	215
Chiron	Sep	60	p	80	AM	2 3/16	+ 5/16	65	34
Chiron	Aug	65		454	AM	3¼	− 1	65	1,683
Chiron	Aug	65		166	CB	3	− ⅝	65	1,683
Chiron	Aug	65	p	298	AM	3	+ ⅞	65	187
Chiron	Aug	65	p	125	CB	3	...	65	187
Chiron	Aug	65	p	50	PC	2½	+ 5/16	65	187
Chiron	Sep	65		55	AM	4⅜	− ¼	65	32
Chiron	Aug	70		665	AM	1¼	− ½	65	413
Chiron	Aug	70		60	PC	1	− 1/16	65	413
Chryslr	Jan	40		62	CB	8	− ⅜	45	1,203
Chryslr	Aug	40		572	CB	5½	+ ⅜	45	2,450
Chryslr	Aug	40	p	195	CB	⅜	...	45	781
Chryslr	Sep	40	p	212	CB	11/16	...	45	131
Chryslr	Oct	40		117	CB	6⅝	+ ⅛	45	5,401
Chryslr	Jan	45		102	CB	5	...	45	2,707
Chryslr	Aug	45		393	CB	1⅞	+ 1/16	45	6,702
Chryslr	Aug	45	p	105	CB	1⅝	− ¼	45	7,296
Chryslr	Oct	45		99	CB	3¼	− ⅜	45	5,113
Chryslr	Aug	50		198	CB	⅜	− 1/16	45	8,642
Chryslr	Oct	50		226	CB	1½	− ¼	45	4,290
CinMil	Aug	22½	p	70	PB	1¼	...	22	29
CirCty	Aug	30		47	PC	¾	+ ⅛	28⅛	190
Circus	Aug	50	p	52	AM	1¼	+ ⅛	52⅜	69
Circus	Aug	55		101	AM	1⅜	+ ⅛	52⅜	433
Cirrus	Sep	15	p	50	CB	½	− ⅝	19	53
Cirrus	Dec	15	p	100	PC	1¼	...	19	20
Cirrus	Dec	15	p	100	CB	1¼	− ⅜	19	20
Cirrus	Aug	17½		125	CB	2½	+ ½	19	625
Cirrus	Aug	17½	p	201	CB	15/16	− 3/16	19	269
Cirrus	Aug	20		50	NY	1 3/16	+ 3/16	19	338
Cirrus	Aug	20		188	CB	1¼	+ 7/16	19	338
Cirrus	Aug	20		285	PC	1¼	+ 5/16	19	338
Cirrus	Aug	20	p	206	CB	2	− ⅜	19	50
Cirrus	Sep	20		116	CB	2	+ ½	19	524
Cirrus	Sep	22½		47	CB	1	+ 1/16	19	183
Cisco	Aug	45		50	PC	8½	+ 1¾	52⅞	1,27…
Cisco	Aug	45		166	CB	8¾	+ 2¼	52⅞	
Cisco	Aug	50		1,114	CB	5¼	+ 1⅜		
Cisco	Aug	50	p	86	CB	1 13/16	− 17…		
Cisco	Oct	50		154	CB	7…			
Cisco	Aug	55		102	PC				
Cisco	Aug	55		745	CB				
Cisco	Sep	55		47	C…				
Cisco	Aug	60		184					
Cisco	Aug	60	p	10…					
Cisco	Sep	60							
Cisco	Oct	60							
Citicp	Jan	20	r						
Citicp	Jan	25							
Citicp	Jan	2…							
Citicp	Oct								
Citicp	Jan								
Citicp	J…								
Citicp									
Citicp									
C…									

Option/Strike				Vol	Exch	Last	Net Chg
F N M	Sep	75	p	109	PB	9/16	−
F N M	Aug	85		50	PB	⅞	+
F N M	Aug	85	p	60	PB	3⅜	−
F N M	Sep	85		101	PB	1 15/16	+
F N M	Sep	90		300	PB	9/16	+
FHLB	Jan	60		90	AM	1½	
FIntste	Aug	65	p	50	CB	2⅛	−
FM Cop	Mar	22½	p	100	PB	2 3/16	+
FM Cop	Mar	25		129	PB	2⅛	
FM Cop	Sep	25		212	PB	9/16	−
FM Cop	Dec	25		100	PB	1⅝	−
FM Cop	Dec	30		115	PB	7/16	−
FUnion	Aug	45	p	160	PC	1⅜	+
FedDSt	Sep	22½	p	50	CB	1¼	+
FedExp	Jan	55		45	CB	5	−
FedExp	Oct	55		96	CB	3⅛	+
FleetC	Aug	30		142	CB	1½	
FleetC	Sep	30		61	CB	2½	
FleetC	Aug	35		82	CB	½	
FleetC	Nov	35		94	CB	13/	
Ford	Aug	50		793	CB	2	
Ford	Aug	50	p	419	CB		
Ford	Sep	50		53	CB		
Ford	Sep	50	p	138	CB		
Ford	Dec	50		102	CB		
Ford	Aug	55		66	CB		
Ford	Sep	55		112	CB		
ForstL	Sep	40	p	60	CB		
FostWh	Oct	30		93	PC		
FounHI	Aug	25	p	110	AM		
FounHI	Aug	30		80	AM		
FounHI	Aug	30	p	125	AM		
FounHI	Aug	35		233	AM		
FounHI	Aug	40		82	AM		
FounHI	Sep	40		62	AM		
FrMcRP	Aug	20		51	AM		
FrMcRP	Sep	20		91	AM		
FrMcRP	Dec	20		135	AM		
FruitL	Aug	25	p	54	NY		
FruitL	Aug	30	p	1,165	NY		
FruitL	Sep	30		103	NY		
FruitL	Aug	35		50	NY		
FruitL	Aug	35	p	162	NY		
FruitL	Aug	40		260	NY		
FshSci	Oct	25		300	C…		
FshSci	Oct	25	p	300	C…		
FtPcNt	Aug	15	p	210	P…		

-G-

Option/Strike				Vol
G M	Aug	40	p	55
G M	Sep	40		260
G M	Sep	40	p	300
G M	Dec	40		4…
G M	Mar	45		2…
G M	Aug	45		
G M	Aug	45	p	
G M	Sep	45		
G M	Sep	45		
G M	Dec	45		
G M	Aug	5…		
G M	Aug			
G M	Se…			
G M				
G T E				
G T E				
G…				

For reasons that are probably apparent, Charles's attention usually first goes to quotes on options on shares of Chase stock; so, let's use Chase as an illustration.

Columns 1 through 4 plus column 6 identify the option: *the underlying equity, the maturity month, the exercise price, whether the option is a call (no designation)*

Reading the Options Quotes concluded

or a put (denoted "p"), and the exchange on which the option is traded. The *Journal* indicates that while other options on Chase may be listed on the American Stock Exchange, trading activity on July 23 was focused on four options, all of which have an exercise price of \$30—an August call, September puts and calls, and a December put.

Column 9 provides the closing price for the underlying share. Note that on July 23, Chase shares closed at 32 1/8; so, the calls are all in-the-money calls.

Columns 5, 7, 8, and 10 tell us about the market activity for the option in question. Look, for instance, at the September call: 157 contracts were traded on July 23 (in contrast to 500 contracts on the September put). The closing price for the September call was 2 3/8, which was unchanged from the previous day (in contrast to the August call, which fell in price by 1/8). And as of July 22, there were 5,736 September calls outstanding.

the expense of the seller of the call option: the payoff to the option owner is $S - X$, the payoff (expense) to the seller of the option (the option "writer") is the reverse, $X - S$. If, however, the share price at expiration is less than the exercise price, the call option is worthless; the payoff to both parties is zero.

Given the preceding development of the value of the call option, the valuation at expiration of a put option on a share of stock follows directly. The put option—the right to sell the share of stock at a price of X—is worthless ($P = 0$) when the price of the share in the asset market is greater than the exercise price ($S > X$). (Why exercise the option and sell the asset for a price of X when it could be sold in the cash market for more than that?) If, however, the price of the share at expiration is less than the exercise price, the right to sell the share at a price of X is valuable: the value of the option is the difference between the price the share can be sold at by exercising the option and the price it could be sold for in the asset market directly, $X - S$.[4] Hence the value of the put option at expiration can be summarized mathematically as,

$$P = \text{Max}[0, (X - S)] \tag{12–2}$$

or graphically as in Figure 12–2. As illustrated, value is conveyed from the seller of the put option to the buyer of the put option only if at expiration the price of the share in the asset market is less than the exercise price.

FIGURE 12–1 The Value at Expiration of a European-Style Call Option (*a*) The Payoff Profile for the Call Buyer (*b*) The Payoff Profile for the Call Seller

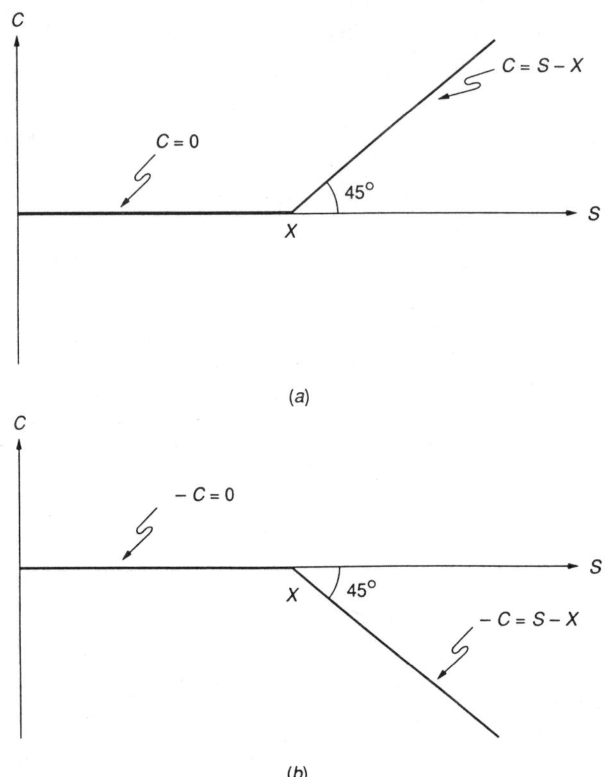

To the reader with any experience in markets, Figures 12–1 and 12–2 should provoke a question: Since the writer of the option can only lose, why would anyone write an option? Clearly the answer to this question is something not included in these payoff profiles—the *option premium.* At origination, the buyer of the option pays the option premium to the writer of the option. As illustrated in Figure 12–3 for the call option, the option premium shifts the payoff profile for the option buyer down and that for the option writer up. Precisely the same is true for the put option.

Hence, we know that both at origination and during the life of the option, the option has some value—the premium that would be required to purchase the option. But how can we determine this value? It is to this question we turn.

FIGURE 12–2 The Value at Expiration of a European-Style Put Option (*a*) The Payoff Profile for the Put Buyer (*b*) The Payoff Profile for the Put Seller

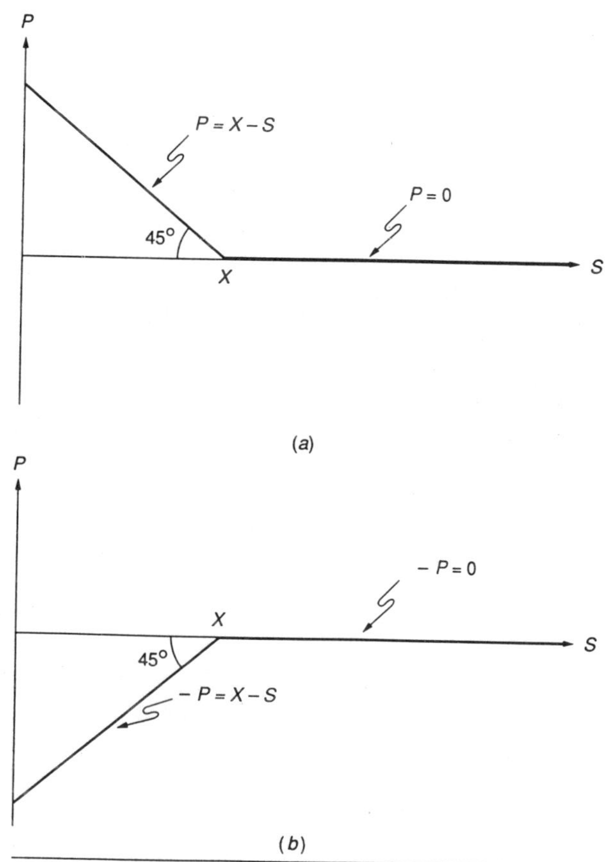

Option Valuation

Put-Call Parity

The preceding discussion suggests that we will have to derive two option premiums—the premium for calls and the premium for puts. Luckily, there is a relation between European puts and calls that requires us to derive only one of the premiums. If we know the premium for a call, we can solve for the premium for a put and vice versa. This useful relation is referred to as *put-call parity*.

FIGURE 12–3 The Value at Expiration of a European-Style Call Option, Including the Option Premium (*a*) The Profit Profile for the Call Buyer (*b*) The Profit Profile for the Call Seller

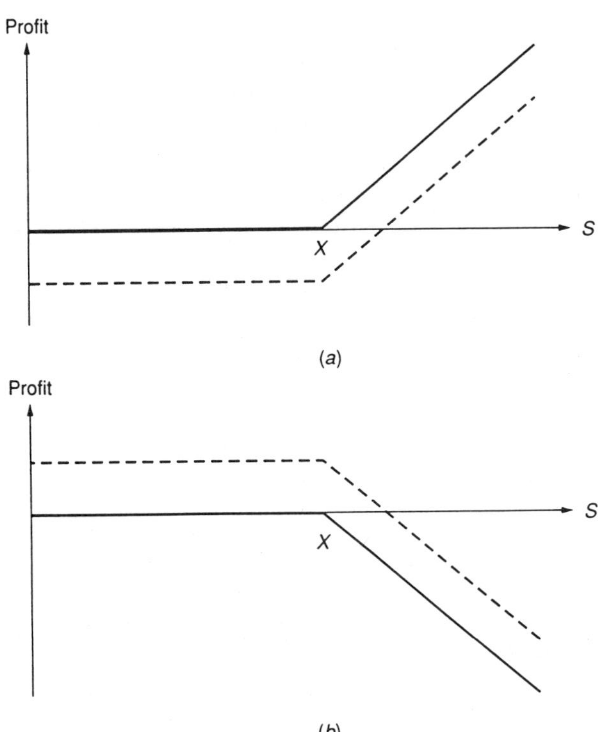

To see how this relation works, consider two portfolios: Portfolio 1 is made up of a European call option on a share of stock and the discounted exercise price for this option. (Remember that the option can be exercised only at maturity—in T days.) Hence, today I don't need to hold the exercise price, X, but instead need to hold only the discounted value of the exercise price XD. The discount factor, D, is a function of the time to maturity, T, and the prevailing Treasury bill rate for that maturity, r.[5]

$$\text{Portfolio 1: } C + XD$$

The second portfolio is made up of a European put option on the share of stock that has the same exercise price and time to maturity as the call option in portfolio 1 and a share of the stock.

Portfolio 2: $P + S$

For these two portfolios, let's consider the values at the maturity of the options (and let's denote these expiration values using an asterisk). As Table 12–1 indicates, we must consider two cases. If the share price at expiration is less than (or equal to) the exercise price for the options ($S^* \leq X$), the value of the call is zero but the value of the put is $X - S^*$. If, however, the share price at expiration is greater than the exercise price ($S^* > X$), the value of the put is zero but the value of the call is $S^* - X$. However, at expiration the two portfolios are guaranteed to have the same value: if $S^* \leq X$, the value of each portfolio is X and, if $S^* > X$, the value is S^*.

TABLE 12–1 The Arbitrage Relations for Put-Call Parity

	$S^* \leq X$	$S^* > X$
Portfolio 1: $V_1 = C + XD$	$0 + X$	$(S^* - X) + X$
Portfolio 2: $V_2 = P + S$	$(X - S^*) + S^*$	$0 + S^*$
	$V_1^* = V_2^*$	$V_1^* = V_2^*$

Since the value of the two portfolios is guaranteed to be the same at expiration, arbitrage guarantees that the two portfolios will have the same value at origination. Hence, it follows that

$$C + XD = P + S \tag{12–3}$$

or, after rearranging some terms,

$$P = C - (S - XD). \tag{12–4}$$

That is, as long as I know the value of the call (the call premium), the value of the share, and the discounted value of the exercise price, I can solve for the value of the put.

However, $S - XD$ is the value of a forward contract on a share with an exercise price of X.[6] Hence, put-call parity is normally remembered as the relation among calls, puts, and forwards:[7]

> The combination of long a call and short a put is equivalent to being long a forward position,
>
> $$C - P = F.$$
>
> The combination of long a put and short a call is equivalent to being short a forward position,
>
> $$P - C = -F.$$

These relations are illustrated graphically in Figure 12–4.[8]

FIGURE 12–4 Put-Call Parity Relations (*a*) Long a Call + Short a Put = Long a Forward (*b*) Long a Put + Short a Call = Short a Forward

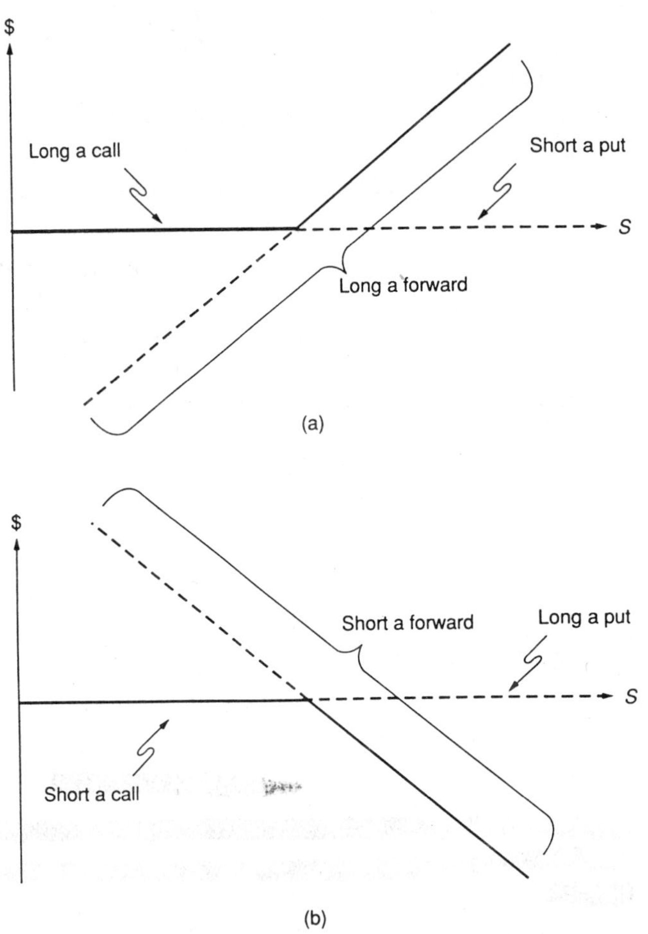

Bounding the Value of the Option[9]

Given the put-call parity, we need only to consider one type of European option; if we know the value of a European call, we can solve for the value of a European put and vice versa. Using T to denote the time remaining until expiration of the option, we know that for $T = 0$ (in other words, at expiration), the value of the call option is

$$C^* = \text{Max}[0, (S^* - X)]. \tag{12–5}$$

However, what is most important to the buyer and seller of the option is not how much the option will be worth in the future (at expiration) but how much the option is worth today.

Before we take up the explicit valuation of this call, let's build some intuition by looking at the bounds on the value of a call option.

To bound the value of an option, we rely on the fact that markets price assets so that no asset is "dominated."

> For asset A to "dominate" asset B over some period, the rate of return to A must be at least as great as the rate of return to B for all possible outcomes and the rate of return to A must be strictly greater than the rate of return to B for some outcomes.

In a well-functioning market, dominated securities will not exist or, at least, will not exist very long. Since no one would want to hold a dominated security, its price would be bid down until the domination is eliminated.

The value of a call cannot be negative. From the definition of a call option, exercise is voluntary. Since exercise will only be undertaken when in the best interests of the option holder:

$$C(S, T; X) \geq 0 \quad \text{[European call]}, \tag{12–6}$$

$$C_A(S, T; X) \geq 0 \quad \text{[American call]}. \tag{12–7}$$

At any date prior to the maturity date, an American call must sell for at least the difference between the stock price and the exercise price. An American call can be exercised at any time before the expiration date, therefore:

$$C_A(S, T; X) \geq \text{Max}[O, S - X]. \tag{12–8}$$

If two call options differ only with respect to the expiration date, the one with the longer term to maturity, T_1, must sell for no less than that of the shorter term to maturity, T_2. At the expiration date of the shorter option, its price will be equal to the maximum of zero and the difference between the stock price and the exercise price (from Equation 12–5), and this is the minimum price of the longer option by Equation 12–8. Thus, to prevent dominance:

$$C(S, T_1; X) \geq C(S, T_2; X), \tag{12–9}$$

where $T_1 > T_2$.

If two call options differ only in exercise price, then the option with the lower exercise price must sell for a price that is no less than the option with the higher exercise price. This can be demonstrated by constructing and comparing the payoffs to two portfolios: portfolio A contains one European call with exercise price X_2, $C(S, T; X_2)$, and portfolio B contains one European call with exercise price X_1, $C(S, T; X_1)$, where $X_1 > X_2$. As illustrated in Table 12–2, if, at maturity, the stock price is above the lower exercise price, X_2, the terminal value of portfolio A, V^*_a, is greater than that of portfolio B, V^*_b. If the current prices of the two portfolios were equal, then the rate of return to portfolio A would exceed the rate of return for portfolio B whenever the stock price exceeded X_2 and portfolio B would be a dominated portfolio. Thus, if $X_1 > X_2$, the current price of portfolio A must be no less than the current price of portfolio B:

$$C(S, T; X_1) \leq C(S, T; X_2), \tag{12–10}$$

TABLE 12–2 A Call with a Lower Exercise Price, X_2, Will Have Dollar Payoffs Greater than or Equal to a Call with a Higher Exercise Price, X_1

$X_1 > X_2$

		Stock Price at t*		
Portfolio	*Current Value*	$S^* \leq X_2$	$X_2 < S^* \leq X_1$	$X_1 < S^*$
A	$c(S,T;X_2)$	0	$S^* - X_2$	$S^* - X_2$
B	$c(S,T;X_1)$	0	0	$S^* - X_1$
		$V_a^* = V_b^*$	$V_a^* > V_b^*$	$V_a^* > V_b^*$

An American call must be priced no lower than an identical European call. Since an American call confers all the rights of the European call plus the privilege of early exercise, then

$$C_A(S, T; X) \geq C(S, T; X). \tag{12–11}$$

The value of the call option cannot exceed the value of the underlying stock. More specifically, the underlying stock is at least as valuable as a perpetual call ($T = \infty$) with a zero exercise price. From equations 12–8, 12–9, and 12–10, it follows that

$$S \geq C(S, \infty; O) \geq C(S, T; X) \tag{12–12}$$

[S may exceed $C(S, \infty; O)$ because of dividends, voting rights, etc.].

A call on a non-dividend-paying stock must sell for at least the stock price minus the discounted exercise price. Let $D(T)$ be the discount factor for payments received T periods from now (alternately, it is the price of a risk-free, pure discount bond that pays \$1 T years from now). Now consider two portfolios: portfolio A contains one European call, $c(S, T; X)$ and X bonds, which have a current value of $XD(T)$; portfolio B contains the stock, S. Table 12–3 demonstrates that the terminal value of portfolio A, V^*_a, is not less than that for portfolio B, V^*_b. Therefore, the current value of portfolio A, V_a, must be greater than or equal to the current value of portfolio B to avoid dominance. This restriction can be rearranged to yield

$$c(S, T; X) \geq \text{Max}[O, S - XD(T)] \tag{12–13}$$

TABLE 12–3 A Call Plus Discount Bonds with a Face Value of X Yield a Terminal Value Greater than or Equal to That of the Respective Stock if the Stock Pays No Dividends

		Stock Price at t*	
Portfolio	*Current Value*	$S^* \leq X$	$X < S^*$
A	C(S,T;X) + XB(T)	0 + X	(S* − X) + X
B	S	S*	S*
		$V_a^* > V_b^*$	$V_a^* = V_b^*$

Figure 12–5 summarizes the preceding boundary restrictions on the value of call options. Equation 12–6 requires that the value of the call be no less than zero; Equation 12–12 requires that it be no greater than the stock price; and Equation 12–13 requires that it be no less than the stock price minus the discounted exercise price.

FIGURE 12–5 Bounds on the Price of a Call Option

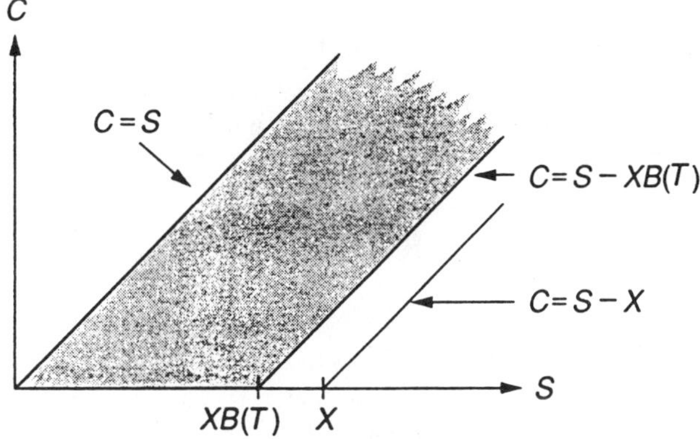

A Simplified Approach to Option Valuation

So far, we have specified the value of an option *at maturity*. However, the real question facing the buyer and the seller of the option is not the value at maturity but rather the value *today*. In the next chapter, we will examine the range of option-pricing models that have been developed to value different types of options on the various underlying assets. But first let's look at a simplified approach to option pricing provided by William F. Sharpe (1978) and expanded by John C. Cox, Stephen A. Ross, and Mark Rubinstein (1979). This approach is referred to as the *binomial option-pricing model,* or—given its authors—the Cox, Ross, Rubinstein (C-R-R) approach. While the binomial pricing model is most widely used in the valuation of interest rate options, for simplicity we begin by looking at the pricing of a European option on a share of stock. (We return to other applications of the binomial model in Chapter 15.)

In this simplified approach to option pricing, we are going to envision our continuous-process world as a series of snapshots. Let's suppose that today, on day 0, the price of a particular share of stock is \$100. Let's suppose further that tomorrow it could rise or fall by 5 percent:

Day 0	*Day 1*	
100	105	Up by 5 percent
	95	Down by 5 percent

Let's consider the value of a one-day call option on this share of stock. For simplicity, set the exercise price of this one-day call option at \$100. The value of the call option *at maturity—at day 1*—is as shown below:

Illustration 12–2

A Realistic Approach?

At first blush, the preceding lattice looks too simplistic to have any connection to the real world. However, it is simple only because we have let the share price move only once per day. What if we let the share price move up or down by 5 percent every 12 hours?

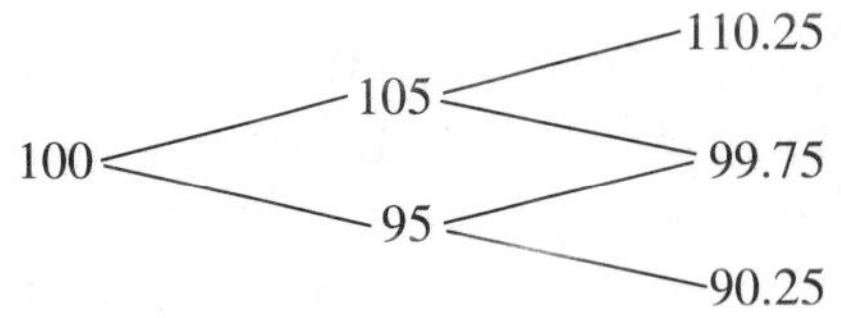

or every six hours . . . or . . . ?

If we make the intervals shorter, this simple binomial model becomes more realistic, in much the same way that a movie approximates continuous movements although it is a series of still pictures.

Share Price at Expiration	*Value of Call at Expiration*
\$105	\$5
95	0

However, if I am thinking about selling (or buying) this call option, I am not as interested in its value at maturity as I am in its value *today*. A number of very smart people have tried to find this value directly . . . and failed.[10] The approach we are going to follow is modeled on the approach of Fischer Black and Myron Scholes: instead of trying to value the option separately, we will value the option by valuing an *arbitrage portfolio* that contains the option.

An arbitrage portfolio is one that earns a riskless return. Let's form such a portfolio out of the two risky assets—the share of stock and the call option on the share of stock. That is, let's form a portfolio in which the gains made on one of the assets would be exactly offset by losses on the other. As the following table indicates, for the case in point, such a portfolio could be formed by creating a portfolio in which we are *long* one share of stock and *short* two call options:

S	*C*	*2C*	*S-2C*
105	5	10	95
95	0	0	95

As indicated, the value of this portfolio—S-2*C*—will be \$95 regardless of the value of the share of stock. Hence, we have formed a portfolio that has no risk. (See illustration 12-3)

In the remainder of this discussion, we will refer to the *hedge ratio* (Δ) as the *inverse* of the number of calls necessary to form the arbitrage portfolio,

$$\Delta = 1/N. \tag{12–14}$$

Hence, for the case in point, the hedge ratio is $\Delta = 1/2$.

On day 0, the value of the share is \$100; the value of the arbitrage portfolio, $S - 2C$, is $100 - 2C$, which reinforces the fact that the value of the call option on day 0 is so far unknown. We do know, however, that on day 1, the value of the portfolio is 95. Hence, we know that

$$(100 - 2C)_{\text{day 0}} > (95)_{\text{day 1}}.$$

To turn the preceding into an equality—and therefore to be able to solve for *C*, the value of the call option on day 0—it is necessary to discount day 1 values to day 0 values or to inflate day 0 values to day 1 values. The convention is to discount rather than to inflate; so, we can express the present value of the \$95 to be received in one day as

Illustration 12–3

Calculating the Hedge Ratio

In the preceding, it was pretty easy to see that two calls would exactly hedge the movement in one share of stock.* However, we will need a more general rule when we encounter more complex situations. Not surprisingly, it's nothing more than a little algebra. For the case in point, we want to find the number of call options that will make the value of the portfolio when the share price is 105,

$$105 - (N \times 5),$$

equal to the value of the portfolio when the share price is 95,

$$95 - (N \times 0).$$

Hence, if

$$105 - (N \times 5) = 95 - (N \times 0),$$

it follows that $N \times 5 = 10$; so, $N = 2$.

Generalizing, let's define the share price if the price change is up as *SU* and the share price if the price change is down as *SD*. Likewise, define the value of the call option when the share price is up as *CU* and the value of the call when the share price is down as *CD*. Then the number of calls necessary to form the arbitrage portfolio (*N*) is

$$N = (SU - SD)/(CU - CD).$$

*The share price could change by \$10; the value of the call could change by \$5; so, it would take two calls to cover the possible change in the value of the share.

$$100 - 2C = 95/(1 + r),$$

where r is a one-day interest rate. Since the arbitrage portfolio is riskless, the interest rate used is the *risk-free interest rate*. Continuing our example, if the annualized one-day risk-free rate—the Treasury bill rate for one-day bills—is 7.5 percent, the rate for one day is $(1/365) \times 0.075 = 0.0002$, and the preceding equation becomes

$$100 - 2C = 95/(1.0002).$$

Hence, for our example, the value of the one-day call option on day 0 is \$2.51. (See Figure 12–6.)

At this point some of you may be saying that this is all very well and good . . . but not very relevant, since it is not very likely that we will encounter many one-day option contracts. So let's see what happens when we let the option run for two days.

Continuing to assume that the share price can move up or down by 5 percent every day, the distribution of share prices over the three days—and the resulting values of the call option—are as follows:

FIGURE 12–6 Valuing a One-Day Option

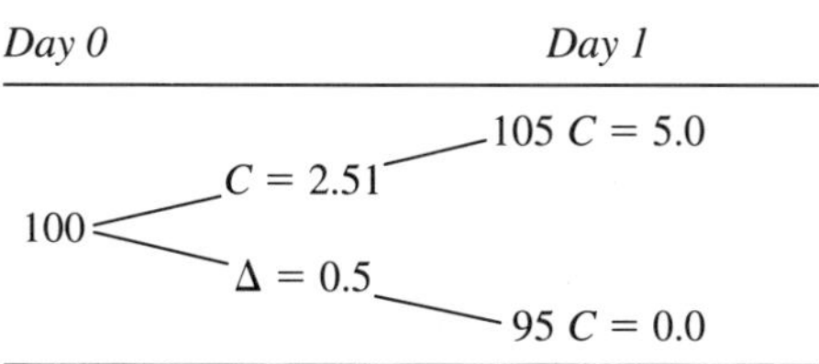

Illustration 12–4

An Option Payoff Diagram

The tree diagram in Figure 12–6 provides the value of the call of a particular share price on day 0—in this instance, a share price of $100. To transform this tree diagram to a more familiar option diagram, we need to think about the value of the call on day 0 for *various* share prices.

To accomplish this, we need the general expression for the value of this one-period call option as provided by Cox, Ross, and Rubinstein*

$$C = \frac{\left\{\dfrac{(1+r) - {}^{SD}/_{S}}{(SU - SD)/S}\right\} CU + \left\{\dfrac{{}^{SU}/_{S} - (1+r)}{(SU - SD)/S}\right\} CD}{(1+r)}$$

where SU, SD, CU, and CD are as defined earlier, and S is the initial stock price. Using this general equation, consider three cases:†

1. *If on day 0, the share price is less than or equal to X/(SU/S)*, the value of the call option is zero. For the case in point, if the share price on day 0 is less than or equal to 100/(105/100) = 95.23, the value of the call is zero.
2. *If on day 0, the share price is greater than or equal to X/(SU/S), the value of the call option is S − X/(1 + r)*. For the case in point, if the share price on day 0 is greater than or equal to 100/(95/100) = 105.26, the value of the call is $S - 99.98$.
3. *If on day 0, the share price is greater than X/(SU/S), but less than X/(SD/S), the value of the call option is*

$$\left\{\frac{(1 + \mathrm{r}) - {}^{SD}/_{S}}{(SU - SD)/S}\right\}\left\{\frac{SU - X}{(1+r)}\right\}.$$

For the one-period option we have been looking at

An Option Payoff Diagram continued

Share Price on Day 0	*Value of Call*
101	3.04
100	2.51
99	1.98

The payoff diagram for the specific option we have been examining can then be drawn as follows:

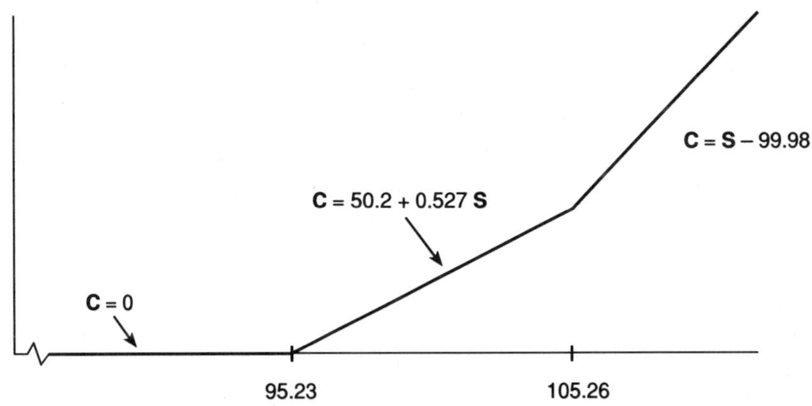

Or, more generally, the payoff diagram for a one-period option can be illustrated as

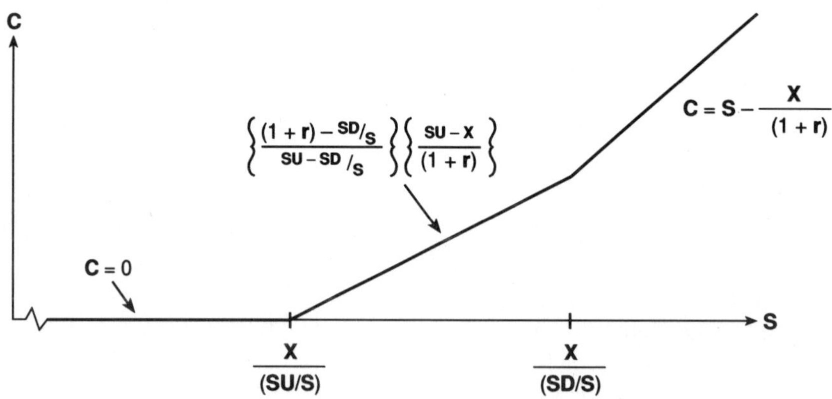

*Cox, Ross, and Rubinstein (1979).

†This material is taken from Cox and Rubinstein (1985).

Day 0	*Day 1*	*Day 2*	
		110.25	$C = 10.25$
	105		
100		99.75	$C = 0$
	95		
		90.25	$C = 0$

If we want to derive the value of the call option at day 0, we first must determine the values of the option for the share prices that could exist on day 1 (that is, 95 and 105) and then use these values to determine what the option will be worth on day 0.

On day 1, if the value of the share is 105, the arbitrage portfolio would be $S - (1.025)C$. That is, the number of call options necessary to hedge one share of stock would be

$$\begin{aligned} N &= (110.25 - 99.75)/(10.25 - 0) \\ &= 10.50/10.25 \\ &= 1.025. \end{aligned}$$

(Alternatively, the hedge ratio is $1/N = 0.976$.) So,

$$(105 - 1.025C)_{\text{day 1}} > (99.75)_{\text{day 2}}.$$

Therefore,

$$(105 - 1.025C) = (99.75)/(1.0002),$$

so *the value of the call would be $5.14.*

On day 1, if the value of the share is 95, the value of the call would be zero, since the value of the call will be zero regardless of whether the value of the share rises to $99.75 or falls to $90.25.[11]

On day 0, the relevant lattice has become

	105	$C = 5.14$
100		
	95	$C = 0$

Hence, the number of call options necessary to hedge one share of stock is

$$\begin{aligned} N &= (105 - 95)/(5.14 - 0) \\ &= 10/5.14 \\ &= 1.95. \end{aligned}$$

(Or, the hedge ratio is 0.514.) Thus, the arbitrage portfolio is $S - 1.95C$:

$$(100 - 1.95C)_{\text{day 0}} > (95)_{\text{day 1}}.$$

Therefore, continuing to use 7.5 percent as the relevant annualized rate for a one-day Treasury bill,

$$(100 - 1.95C) = (95)/(1.0002),$$

so *the value of the call option would be 2.579—that is, $2.58.*

This valuation is summarized in Figure 12–7.

If we can value a two-day option, we can value a three-day or four-day or *n*-day option: the logic is exactly the same—we solve iteratively from expiration to time period 0; the only thing that changes is the size of the problem.

The purpose of this pricing discussion is twofold. The first purpose is obvious: to demonstrate that the pricing of an option is not as difficult as it might otherwise seem. The second objective is much more subtle: to highlight the five variables that determine the value of an option. Look again at the examples. We employed the following five variables to value the option:

The prevailing share price, *S*. In our example the share price on day 0, the date of origination of the option contract, was $100.

The exercise price of the option, *X*. In our example we used $100 as the exercise price.

The time to expiration of the option, *T*. We considered both one day and two days.

The risk-free interest rate corresponding to the time remaining on the option, *r*. In our example, the annualized rate for a one-day T-bill was 7.5 percent; the one-day interest rate was 0.0002 percent.

The volatility in the share price, σ. In the context of the binomial pricing model we have been using, the value of the call option was determined in

FIGURE 12–7 Valuing a Two-Day Option

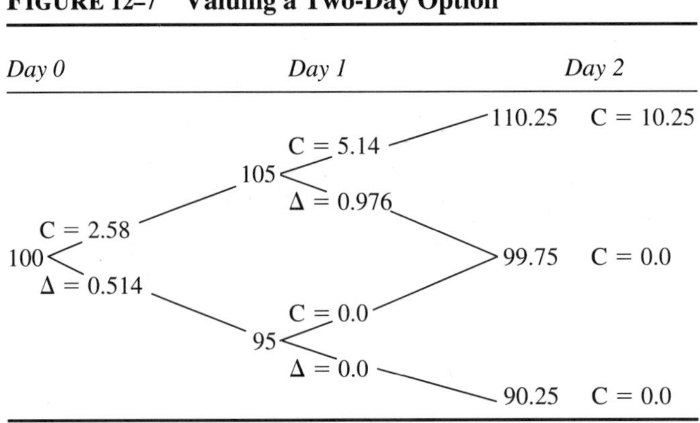

part by the magnitude of the movements in the share price. In our example, we used price movements of 5 percent up or down per day. This magnitude of the movements in the share price could be summarized by the variance in the distribution of share prices. (Normally the variance is denoted as σ^2—and the standard deviation as σ.)

Hence, we could write an implicit function for the value of a call option as

$$C = C(S, X, T, r, \sigma). \tag{12–15}$$

The discussion also provides insight about the manner in which the option value changes as these five variables—determinants—change.

Increases in the share price increase the value of the call option. For example, if we increase the original share price by $10 in our example,

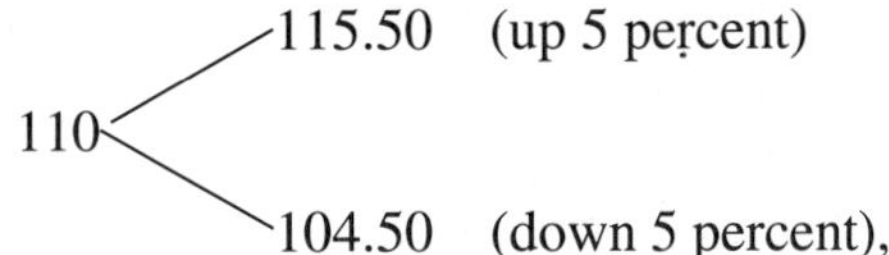

while leaving the exercise price at $100 and the other determinants unchanged, the value of the call option will rise from $2.51 to $5.52.

Increases in the exercise price decrease the value of the call option. If we increase the exercise price rise from $100 to $101, the value of the one-day call option would fall from $2.51 to $2.01.

Increases in the time to expiration increase the value of the call option. As noted, increasing the time to maturity from one to two days increased the value of the call option from $2.51 to $2.58.

Increases in the risk-free interest rate increase the value of the call option. If the annualized rate on a one day T-bill rose from 7.5 percent to 15 percent, the daily risk-free interest rate would rise from 0.0002 to 0.0004 and the value of the one-day call option would rise from $2.51 to $2.52.

Increases in the volatility of share price increase the value of the call option. Suppose that instead of 5 percent up or down each day, share prices could move up or down by 10 percent each day

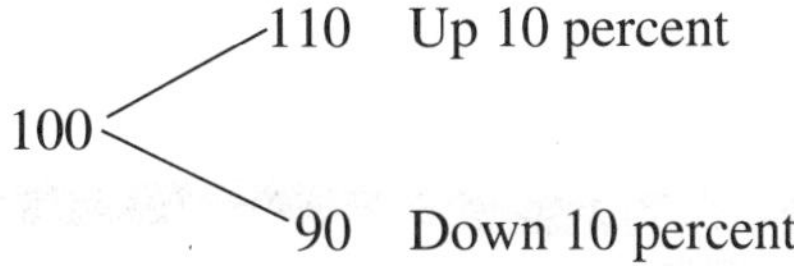

With no other changes in the determinants of the option value, the value of our one-day call option would rise from $2.51 to $5.01.

The preceding relations between the value of a European call and the five determinants can be summarized as

$$\overset{}{C} = C(\overset{+}{S}, \overset{-}{X}, \overset{+}{T}, \overset{+}{r}, \overset{+}{\sigma}). \tag{12–16}$$

The definition of a put option makes it clear that the right to sell an asset at a predetermined price X becomes more valuable as the market price of the asset (S) falls or the exercise price (X) rises. Using the put-call parity relations defined in Equation 12–4, the value of a European put can be expressed as

$$P = C(\overset{+}{S}, \overset{-}{X}, \overset{+}{T}, \overset{+}{r}, \overset{+}{\sigma}) - S + XD(\overset{-}{r}, \overset{-}{T}). \tag{12–17}$$

From the put-call parity relation, the effect of both T and r on the value of a put are indeterminate because both increase the value of the call (C) but decrease the discounted exercise price (XD); the offsetting effects may lead to a net increase, a net decrease, or no change in the value of the put.[12] Finally, since an increase in volatility (σ) increases C but has no effect on S or XD, it follows that an increase in volatility will increase the value of the put option. These relations can be summarized as follows:

$$P = C(\overset{-}{S}, \overset{+}{X}, \overset{?}{T}, \overset{?}{r}, \overset{+}{\sigma}) \tag{12–18}$$

A Note on American Options

An American option gives its owner all the rights in a European option plus something extra: the American option also gives its owner the right to early exercise; the owner of the American option has the right to exercise the option before its maturity. It follows then that the value of the American option is always at least that of the European option. Whether the American option is worth more than the European option depends on whether or not the option would ever be exercised early.

Hence, the question of the value of an American option depends on yet another question: Will an American option ever be exercised early? And, as with so many other things, the answer is "it depends."

American Calls

If the share of stock pays no dividend, it is never optimal to exercise the American call early. To understand why, suppose that at some time prior to expiration, the American call is in the money; that is, the prevailing share price (S) is greater than the exercise price for the call option (X). If the option is *exercised*, the owner will receive a gain equal to the difference between the prevailing share price and the exercise price for the option receipt from early exercise, $S - X$. However, if instead the owner of the option *sells* the option, the market value of the option will not be less than the difference between the prevailing share price and the *discounted exercise price*; so, the receipt from sale will not be smaller than $S - XD$. The strategies are detailed in Table 12–4.

As long as there is any time remaining to maturity of the option, $D < 1$; it follows that $(S - XD) > (S - X)$ and

$$S - XD + \textit{Time value} > S - X \tag{12–19}$$

Hence, for a non-dividend-paying stock, early exercise of an American call option will never occur. Therefore, in this case, the value of an American call option is identical to that for a European call option.

For an American call option on a dividend-paying share of stock, early exercise will be optimal if the dividend is sufficiently large, and, if at all, early exercise will occur immediately before the stock goes ex-dividend. Since shares purchased on or after the ex-dividend day do not receive the next dividend, the share price will fall on the ex-dividend day by an amount approximately equal to the dividend. It is this drop in price that provides the incentive for early exercise of the American call option: if I exercise the option just before the ex-dividend date, I receive a dividend payment that I would not receive if I do not exercise the option. Hence, the issue is whether the amount I receive if I exercise the option,

$$S_x - X + \text{Dividend},$$

(where S_x is the ex-dividend stock price) is greater or less than the value of the call option if I were to continue to hold it:

$$C(S_x, X, T).$$

It follows that the American call would be exercised early if

$$\text{Dividend} > C(S_x, X, T) - (S_x - X) \tag{12–20}$$

And to value the American call, the value of this early exercise provision would have to be evaluated for each of the ex-dividend dates that occur during the life of the option. This early exercise provision of American calls is most valuable when

TABLE 12–4 Strategies for Realizing an In-the-Money American Option

Strategy	*Gain*
Exercise the option early	$S - X$
Sell the option	$S - XD$ + Time value

the dividend is large, the time to maturity is short, and the call is significantly in the money.

American Puts

Early exercise of an American put option will be optimal if the price of the stock falls sufficiently below the exercise price. This rather complex concept is best explained with an example. Let's consider an American put option with these characteristics: $X = \$100$; $T = 1$ year; and $r = 20$ percent.

Suppose the price of the share has fallen to \$10. If I exercise the option early, I will receive $X - S = \$100 - \$10 = \$90$ today. If I hold that \$90 in a T-bill, I will have at maturity $\$90 \times (1.2) = \$108$. Instead, if I hold the option to maturity, the most the option will be worth is \$100, and this only if the share price falls to zero. In this case, since $\$108 > \$100$, it is clear that the American put option will be exercised early.

If, however, the share price has fallen only to \$20, the situation is more complex. If I exercise the option early, I will receive \$80 today and will have $\$80 \times (1.2) = \$96$ at the end of one year. As before, the option could be worth at maturity as much as \$100; it may not be optimal to exercise early. But the option is worth \$100 only if the value of the share drops to zero. If instead the share price were \$5 at expiration, the value of the option would be \$95, and it would have been better to exercise the option early. Hence, in this case, it may or may not be optimal to exercise the American put option early, depending on the probability distribution of share prices.

The point of the preceding is that to determine the value of an American put option on a non-dividend-paying stock, it is necessary to determine whether it would be optimal to exercise the option early on any of the days prior to expiration. Since there exists no simple formula that provides the solution, this involves an iterative, numerical approximation problem—not unlike the binomial lattice we have just considered: we first check to see if early exercise could be optimal on the day prior to expiration, then on the day before that, then on the day before that, and so on.

Interestingly, while dividends make it more difficult to value American call options (because dividends make it possible that early exercise is optimal), the existence of dividends makes it easier to value American put options. As we have noted, American puts are exercised early only if there is a sufficiently large drop in the share price. And as indicated above, for non-dividend-paying stocks, we would have to check this relation for each trading day prior to expiration. However, for dividend-paying stocks, the predictable share price fall on an ex-dividend date makes the probability of optimal early exercise highest on ex-dividend dates. Hence, for American puts on dividend-paying stocks, the correct value can be closely approximated by considering early exercise only for the finite number of remaining ex-dividend dates.

Notes

1. Note that the terms European and American refer only to the style of the option—whether or not it can be exercised before the expiration date. The fact that an option is European or American says nothing about where the option is traded; e.g., options traded on the Amsterdam Exchange are American, not European, options. In Chapter 15, we will describe other options with geographic names—"Asian" and "Bermuda" options.
2. To keep things simple, we ignore transactions costs and taxes.
3. In other sources, you may find the symbol K used to denote the exercise price.
4. Put another way, if $S < X$, the owner of the put option could purchase the share for S and sell it at X, thereby profiting in the amount of $X - S$.
5. If we employ discrete discounting, the discount factor is

$$D_{\text{DISCRETE}} = 1/(1 + r)^T.$$

If we were to use continuous discounting, the discount factor would be

$$D_{\text{CONTINUOUS}} = e^{-rT}.$$

In either case, increases in the time to maturity, T, or the interest rate, r, would decrease the discount factor, D,
6. Applying the logic of Chapter 6, since the forward contract calls for no payments prior to maturity, the price of a forward on a non-dividend-paying stock is simply the current stock price minus the discounted exercise price of the forward.
7. We have distinguished between forwards as commitments and options as rights, but now that we have derived put-call parity we can make the relation more precise. Because the forward can be decomposed into a long call and a short put, the forward is a package containing both a right if it matures in the money and a commitment if it matures out of the money.
8. In Figure 12–4 we do not illustrate the option premium. However, since the option premiums would cancel out, this exclusion does not affect the conclusions drawn from the figure.
9. The bounds for the value of an option were first discussed by Robert Merton (1973).
10. Bachelier (1900), Bierman (1967), Boness (1964), Hausman and White (1968), Samuelson and Merton (1969) and Thorpe and Kassouf (1967).
11. Put another way, since the number of shares necessary to hedge one share of stock is, in the limit, a positive infinity,

$$N = (99.75 - 90.25)/(0 - 0)$$
$$= 9.50/0 > \infty,$$

the value of the call option must approach zero as a limit.
12. On first inspection of Equation 12–7, the reader might also think that the effects of changes in S and X on the value of a put are indeterminant:

$$\delta P/\delta S = \overset{+}{\delta C/\delta S} + \overset{-}{(-1)}$$

$$\delta P/\delta X = \overset{-}{\delta C/\delta X} + \overset{+}{D(r, T)}$$

However, a little more investigation clears up the confusion. Since the value of the call does not rise as rapidly as the share price, $\delta C/\delta S < 1$, so $\delta P/\delta S < 0$. And the change in the value of a call for a change in the exercise price, $\delta C/\delta X$, is bounded by the negative $D(r, T)$; so, higher exercise prices are associated with higher put prices—$\delta P/\delta X > 0$.

CHAPTER

13 A TAXONOMY OF OPTION-PRICING MODELS*

In 1973, Fischer Black and Myron Scholes published the first general equilibrium solution for the valuation of options. Recognizing that shares and calls could be combined to construct a riskless portfolio, they developed an analytical model that provides a no-arbitrage value for European-style call options on shares as a function of the share price, the exercise price of the option, the time to maturity of the option, the risk-free interest rate, and the variance of the stock price. As the benchmark around which trades could occur, the Black-Scholes model provided the breakthrough that permitted the rapid growth of the options market.

The Black-Scholes model is often regarded as either the *end* or the *beginning* of the story. In truth, it is *both*. It is the end of the story in the sense that it solved a problem that economists had wrestled with for at least three quarters of a century. It is the beginning of the story in the sense that it spawned a number of generalizations or extensions.

Indeed, it is most helpful to consider the Black-Scholes model in the context of a *family tree of option-pricing models*. Using this family tree analogy, it is possible to identify three major *tribes* within the family of option pricing models: analytical, numerical, and analytic approximation.

The Black-Scholes option-pricing model is itself an analytical model. So, before we begin our examination of the "geneology," let us take some time to examine the Black-Scholes model itself.

---

*This chapter is the most analytical in this book. While we have attempted to hold the mathematics to a minimum, we recommend that readers who find themselves bogged down by the math skim this chapter and then move on to Chapter 14. This chapter is based on "Wonderful Life" by Charles Smithson which appeared in *Risk* in 1991 and on "Option Pricing: A Review" by Clifford Smith, which appeared in the *Journal of Financial Economics* in 1976.

The Black-Scholes Option Pricing Model

The paradigm that makes the Black-Scholes model work is the concept of the *arbitrage portfolio*—you can combine options and shares to form a portfolio that is *riskless*. Black and Scholes were the first to note that a riskless hedge can be created out of positions in the option and shares of underlying stock. Because the hedge is (instantaneously) riskless, arbitrage ensures that the return to the hedge must be the riskless rate. By combining this equilibrium condition with the appropriate boundary conditions, Black and Scholes were able to derive a specific option-pricing model.

The Black-Scholes model was developed to value European-style options on shares of stock. It is crucial to remember that the Black-Scholes model is based on a number of assumptions. These assumptions are summarized in Table 13–1.

Most of these assumptions are straightforward. However, the *continuous Ito process* probably needs a little explanation.

TABLE 13–1 Assumptions Embedded in the Black-Scholes Model

1. The share pays no dividends.
2. Transactions cost and taxes are zero.
3. Interest rates are constant.
4. There are no penalties for short sales of stock.
5. The market operates continuously and the share prices follows a *continuous Ito process*.
6. The distribution of terminal stock prices (returns) is lognormal

Aside

A Continuous Ito Process

In various mathematics texts, an Ito process is defined simply as "a Markov process in continuous time." For our purposes, a little more detail is in order.

A *Markov process* is one where the observation in time period t depends only on the preceding observation. For example, if the stock price follows a Markov process, the stock price S in period t could be defined as

$$S_t = X(S_{t-1}) + E_t$$

where X is a constant and E_t is a random error term.

A process is *continuous* if it can be drawn without picking the pen up from the paper.

On the basis of the preceding definitions, Figure 13–1 provides an illustrative path of a random variable, *S,* which follows a continuous Ito process through time.

When we examined the simplified approach to option pricing in Chapter 12, we noted that the crucial concept is the hedge portfolio—the arbitrage portfolio—which is formed by combining both stock and call options. The value of the hedge portfolio, V_H, can be expressed as:

$$V_H = Q_s S + Q_c C \tag{13–1}$$

where S is the price of a share of the stock, C is the price of a European call option to purchase one share of the stock, Q_s is the quantity of stock in the hedge, and Q_c is the quantity of call options in the hedge.

The change in the value of the hedge, the derivative of the value of the hedge, dV_H, is simply

$$dV_H = Q_s dS + Q_c dC \tag{13–2}$$

Note in Equation 13–2 that, since the quantities of options and stock are given at a point in time, the change in the value of the hedge results simply from the change in the prices of the assets, dS and dC.

As noted in Table 13–1, the stock price is assumed to follow a continuous Ito process; so, there exists a specific mathematical expression for dS. We know that the call price is a function of the stock price and the time remaining to expiration of the option. What we need is a mathematical expression for dC. This is provided by *Ito's Lemma*. As indicated on the next page, Ito's Lemma provides an expression for the differential of functions of variables that follow Ito processes.

A crucial insight of Ito's Lemma is that the change in the call price, dC, can be expressed as the sum of two terms, one related to the change in the stock price and the other related to the change in the time to maturity,

FIGURE 13–1 A Continuous Ito Process

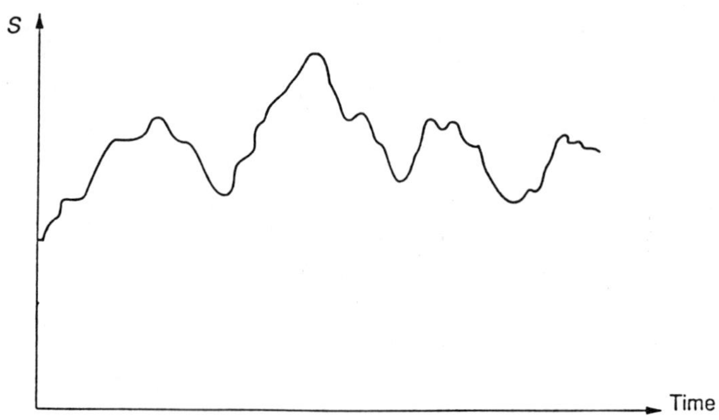

Aside

Ito's Lemma

Ito's Lemma is a differentiation rule for random variables whose movement can be described as an Ito process. If stock price follows a simple Ito process, the returns to the stock can be represented by

$$\frac{dS}{S} = \mu dt + \sigma dZ$$

Where μ and σ are constants, dt is the change in time and dZ is a normally distributed random variable with a mean of zero and a variance dt. Multiplying both sides of the equation by S, it follows that

$$dS = \mu S dt + \sigma S dZ.$$

The expected value and variance of dS are

$$E[dS] = \mu S dt \qquad \text{Var}[dS] = \sigma^2 S^2 dt$$

As noted above, the value of a call option written on the stock is a function of the stock price and the time remaining to expiration of the option:

$$C = C(S, t).$$

What we want to know is the effect of incremental changes in S and t on the value of the call option, i.e., $C(S + \Delta S, t + \Delta t) - C(S, t)$. To obtain $C(S + \Delta S,\ t + \Delta t)$, we use a second-order Taylor series approximation:

$$C(S + \Delta S, t + \Delta t) = C(S, t) + \frac{\partial C}{\partial t}\Delta t + \frac{\partial C}{\partial S}\Delta S + \frac{1}{2}\frac{\partial^2 C}{\partial S^2}(\Delta S)^2.$$

Then:

$$dC = C(S + \Delta S, t + \Delta t) - C(S, t)$$
$$+ \frac{\partial C}{\partial t}\Delta t + \frac{\partial C}{\partial S}\Delta S + \frac{1}{2}\frac{\partial^2 C}{\partial S^2}(\Delta S)^2$$

and, interpreting $(\Delta S)^2$ as the variance of dS:

$$dC = \frac{\partial C}{\partial S} dS + \left(\frac{\partial C}{\partial t} + \frac{1}{2}\frac{\partial^2 C}{\partial S^2} S^2\sigma^2\right) dt.$$

$$dC = \frac{\partial C}{\partial S} dS + \left(\frac{\partial C}{\partial t} + \frac{1}{2}\frac{\partial^2 C}{\partial S^2} S^2\sigma^2\right) dt \qquad (13\text{–}3)$$

It is helpful to look at this decomposition of the change in the call price graphically. Figure 13–2 illustrates the first term in Equation 13–3. For small changes in the stock price, dS, the associated change in the call price is given by the slope of the tangent, $\partial C/\partial S$, times the stock price change, dS. The second term in Equation 13–3, the component related to the change in the time to maturity, is illustrated in Figure 13–3. Given the prevailing stock price, S_0, a decrease in the time to maturity decreases the present value of the exercise price. Thus, from Equation 13–3, decreasing the time remaining to maturity decreases the value of the call. Note that on the right hand side of Equation 13–3 only the first term, $(\partial C/\partial S)dS$, is stochastic; the rest of the terms are deterministic.

FIGURE 13–2 The Change in the Call Price, dC, from a Change in the Stock Price, dS, is the Slope of the Tangent $\partial C/\partial S$, Times the Stock Price Change, dS

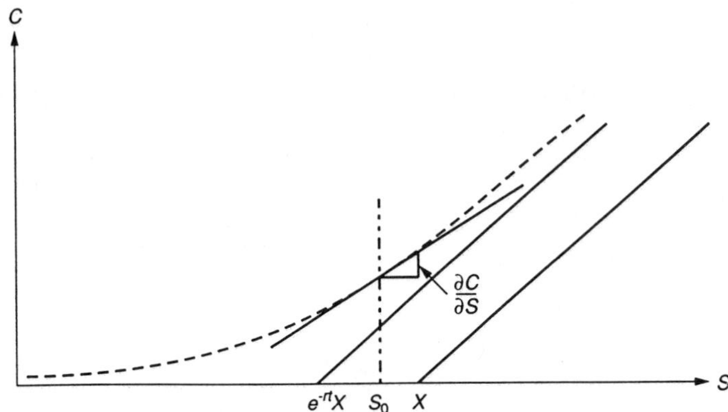

FIGURE 13–3 The Change in the Value of the Call, dC, from a Change in the Time to Maturity, dt, is the Shift in the Curve When the Present Value of the Exercise Price Changes from $e^{-rt}X$ to $e^{-rt'}X$

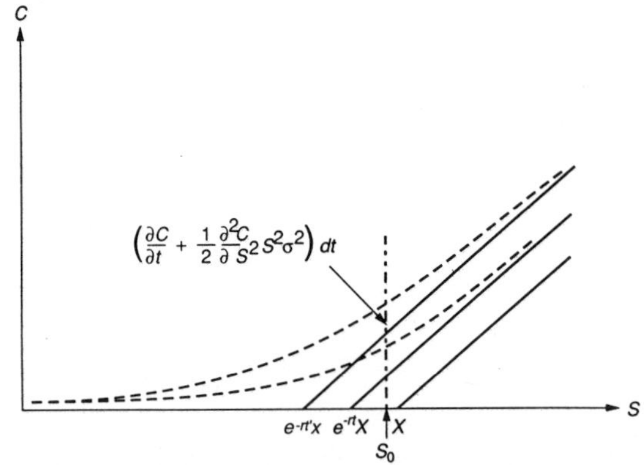

If Equation 13–3 is substituted into Equation 13–2, we obtain the following expression for the change in the value of the hedge portfolio:

$$dV_H = Q_S dS + Q_c\left[\frac{\partial C}{\partial S}dS + \left(\frac{\partial C}{\partial t} + \frac{1}{2}\frac{\partial^2 C}{\partial S^2}S^2\sigma^2\right)dt\right] \tag{13–4}$$

If the quantities of stock and of call options in the hedge portfolio are chosen so that Q_s/Q_c equals $-(\partial C/\partial S)$, the first two terms on the right hand side of Equation

13–4 sum to zero. And, since these are the only stochastic terms, it follows that if Q_s/Q_c is equal to $-(\partial C/\partial S)$, the change in the value of the hedge becomes deterministic—that is, the hedge portfolio becomes riskless.

What this means is that, with the appropriate long position in the stock and short position in the call, an increase in the price of the stock will be offset by the decrease in the value of the short position in the call, and vice versa.[1] This can be illustrated graphically by returning to Figures 13–2 and 13–3. By setting Q_s/Q_c equal to $-\partial C/\partial S$, the unanticipated change in the call price because of a stock price change (illustrated in Figure 13–2) is hedged by the stock price change itself so that the predictable change in the call price from the reduction in the time to maturity illustrated in Figure 13–3 is all that remains.

Hence, the insight provided by Black and Scholes is that if the quantities of the stock and of the call option in the hedge portfolio are continuously adjusted in the appropriate manner as asset prices change over time, then the return to the portfolio becomes riskless. Setting $Q_c = -1$ and $Q_s = (\partial C/\partial S)$ in Equation 13–4 yields

$$dV_H = -\left[\frac{\partial C}{\partial t} + \frac{1}{2}\frac{\partial^2 C}{\partial S^2}S^2\sigma^2\right]dt \tag{13–5}$$

Therefore, mathematically we have eliminated all the stochastic terms (since dt is deterministic, dV_H is deterministic); so, this hedge portfolio is riskless. Hence, the return to the hedge portfolio must equal the riskless rate

$$\frac{dV_H}{V_H} = (r)dt \tag{13–6}$$

We are now ready to do some arithmetic to derive an explicit expression for the change in the call price. Imposing $Q_c = -1$ and $Q_s = (\partial C/\partial S)$ on Equation 13–1,

$$V_H = \left(\frac{\partial C}{\partial S}\right)S - C \tag{13–7}$$

Then, using Equation 13–7 in Equation 13–6:

$$dV_H = r\frac{\partial C}{\partial S}S\,dt - (rC)\,dt \tag{13–8}$$

And, setting the right-hand sides of Equation 13–5 and Equation 13–8 equal to one another, we obtain

$$\frac{\partial C}{\partial t} = rC - r\frac{\partial C}{\partial S}S - \frac{1}{2}\frac{\partial^2 C}{\partial S^2}(S^2\sigma^2) \tag{13–9}$$

Thus, we are close to our objective: we want an expression for the value of the call. What we have in Equation 13–9 is an expression for the change in the value of the call over time—what mathematicians call a differential equation. What we need to do is get from the differential equation to an equation for the value of the call—that is, given the differential equation in Equation 13–9, we want to solve for the value of the call.

As noted in the following, to derive an expression for the call value we must have a boundary condition, something to tie down our expression for the change in call value. The required boundary condition for the solution of this differential equation is the condition we outlined in Chapter 12: at expiration of the option, the option value must equal the maximum of either the difference between the stock price and the exercise price, $S^* - X$, or zero,[2]

$$C^* = \text{Max}\,[S^* - X, 0] \qquad (13\text{–}10)$$

Thus, the value of the call option will be obtained by solving Equation 13–9 subject to Equation 13–10.

Before proceeding, note that, whatever the form of the solution, it must be a function only of six variables—the stock price, S; the exercise price, X; the variance rate, σ^2; time, t; and the riskless interest rate, r—because these are the only variables that appear in the problem.

Aside

Differential Equations

A differential equation is simply an equation that contains derivatives. If there is a single independent variable, the derivatives are ordinary derivatives and the equation is an ordinary differential equation. For example an ordinary differential equation would be $dy/dx = 0.8$. If there are two or more independent variables, the derivatives are partial derivatives and the equation is called a partial differential equation. Note that Equation 13–9 is a partial differential equation because it involves both $\partial C/\partial S$ and $\partial C/\partial t$.

To provide some intuition, consider the simple ordinary differential equation above, $dy/dx = 0.8$. Since the differential equation is equal to a constant, 0.8, the equation is telling us that the slope of y plotted against x would be a constant 0.8. In other words, this differential equation implies that the function linking y and x is a straight line with a slope of 0.8. But there are an infinite number of straight lines with a slope of 0.8—which one is the correct one? To identify one line, we also need a "boundary condition," a fixed point to tie down the function. Hence, also knowing that if $x = 0$, $y = 2$ tells us that the unique solution we seek is $y = 2 + 0.8x$.

To obtain the solution to the differential equation Black-Scholes noted that Equation 13–9 could be transformed into an equation that is familar to physicists—the "*heat-exchange equation*." However, since we would anticipate that few of you are familiar with this particular equation, a more intuitive solution technique is likely to be more useful and informative.[3]

Note that when we described the equilibrium return to the hedge portfolio, the only assumption we made about the preferences of the market participants is that two assets that are perfect substitutes must earn the same rate of return—because the hedge portfolio has no risk, it must earn the riskless rate of return. Hence, since no assumptions involving the risk preferences of the economic agents have been made, the pricing model implied by Equation 13–9 must be invariant to risk preferences. It follows then that if we can find a solution to the problem for a particular preference structure, it must also be the solution to the differential equation for any other preference structure that permits a solution.

Therefore, to solve Equation 13–9, we choose the preference structure that simplifies the mathematics: we assume a preference structure in which all agents are risk-neutral. In a risk-neutral world, the expected rate of return on all assets would be equal. Hence, the current call price is the present value of the expected call price at expiration of the contract, $E[C^*]$ discounted the marketwide discount rate, r. That is,

$$C = e^{-rT}E[C^*] \tag{13–11}$$

where T is the amount of time remaining until expiration. If we assume further that the distribution of stock prices at any future date will be lognormal, Equation 13–11 can be expressed as

$$C = e^{-rT} \int_X^{\infty} (S^* - X)L'(S^*)dS^* \tag{13–12}$$

where $L'(S^*)$ is the lognormal density function.

Equation 13–12 is integrated using a theorem developed by Cliff Smith (1976). The result of this integration is the Black-Scholes solution to the European call pricing problem:

$$C = S * N\left\{\frac{ln(\frac{S}{X}) + (r + \frac{\sigma^2}{2})T}{\sigma\sqrt{T}}\right\} - e^{-rT}X * N\left\{\frac{ln(\frac{S}{X}) + (r - \frac{\sigma^2}{2})T}{\sigma\sqrt{T}}\right\} \tag{13–13}$$

where $N\{\cdot\}$ is the cumulative normal distribution function.

As we would have anticipated given the results in Chapter 12, the Black-Scholes option-pricing model involves only five variables,

$$C = C(\overset{+}{S}, \overset{-}{X}, \overset{+}{T}, \overset{+}{r}, \overset{+}{\sigma})$$

where the signs above the variables represent their partial derivatives. The partial effects again have intuitive interpretations.

- As the stock price increases, the expected payoff of the option increases.
- With a higher exercise price, the expected payoff decreases.
- With a longer time to maturity, the present value of the exercise payment is lower, thus increasing the value of the option.
- With a higher interest rate, the present value of the exercise payment is lower thus increasing the value of the option.
- With a larger variance for the underlying stock price (or with a longer time to maturity), the probability of a large stock price change during the life of the option is greater. Since the call price cannot be negative, a larger range of possible stock prices increase the maximum value of the option without lowering the minimum value.

Figure 13–4 illustrates graphically the relation between the Black-Scholes valuation of the call and the stock price (holding the exercise price, time to maturity, and the riskless rate constant).

Additional understanding of the Black-Scholes model is obtained by going a little deeper into the risk-neutral pricing.

FIGURE 13–4 Black-Scholes Call Option Price for Different Stock Prices, with a Given Interest Rate, Variance Rate, and Time to Maturity

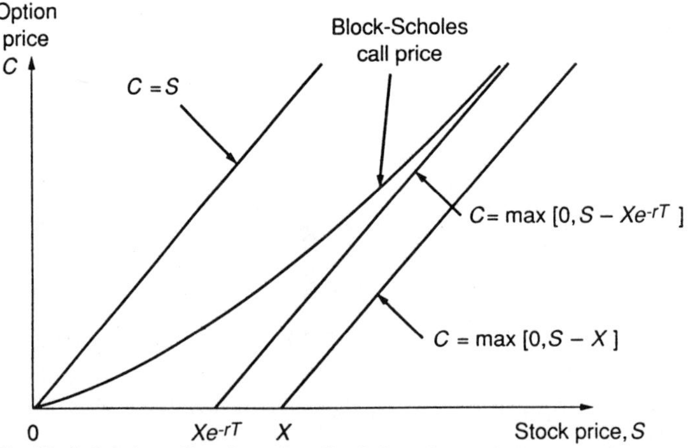

The Black-Scholes call option prices lies below the maximum possible value, $C = S$ (except where $S = 0$), and above the minimum value, $C = \max[0, S - X e^{-rT}]$. Note that the curve relating to the Black-Scholes call price to the stock price asymptotically approaches the $C = \max[0, S - X e^{-rT}]$ line.

Aside

Interpreting the Black-Scholes Formula

We can rewrite Equation 13–12 to express the value of the call in terms of conditional expected value,[4]

$$C = e^{-rT}E(S^* > X)\,\text{Prob}(S^* > X) - e^{-rT}X\,\text{Prob}(S^* > X)$$

The first term is the product of

- discounted expected value of the stock at maturity, conditional on the stock price at maturity exceeding the exercise price and
- probability that, at maturity, the stock price is greater than the exercise price.

The second term is the product of

- discounted exercise price and
- probability that, at maturity, the stock price is greater than the exercise price.

The Black-Scholes value for a call option varies from zero (for way out-of-the-money calls) to the difference between the share price and the discounted exercise price (for way in-the-money calls). To see this, consider two extreme cases:

An extremely out-of-the-money call ($S^* << X$): The ratio of stock price to exercise price is much less than 1—$S/X << 1$. The logarithm of that ratio is negative—$ln(S/X) << 0$)—so, the area under a normal distribution from negative infinity to that point is very small, $N(ln(S/X))$ ⁻0. Therefore, the value of this extremely out-of-the-money call is approximately zero.

An extremely in-the-money call ($S^* >> X$): The ratio of stock to exercise price is much greater than 1—$S/X >> 1$. The logarithm of that ratio is positive—$ln(S/X) > 0$—so, the area under a normal distribution from negative infinity to that point is close to one, $N(ln(S/X)) \rightarrow 1$. Therefore, the value of this extremely in-the-money call is approximately $S \rightarrow e^{-rT}X$.

The Analytical Models

In the same way that we can distinguish among the analytical, numerical, and analytic approximation *tribes*, we can subdivide the analytical tribe itself into two distinct *lineages—generalizations* to the Black-Scholes model and *extensions* of the Black-Scholes model. In the discussion of these lines, we will, to as great an extent as possible, highlight the similarities and differences of the members of these lines by showing how they relate to the Black-Scholes model—that is, by showing how Equation 13–13 would be modified to obtain the option valuation model in question.

Generalizations of the Black-Scholes Model

As Table 13–1 highlights, the Black-Scholes model is based on a number of assumptions. The decade following the publication of the Black-Scholes model saw the development of models that relaxed the assumptions. The "geneology" of this line of the analytical tribe is illustrated in Figure 13–5. In addition to the "geneology," we can also summarize these models in the *generalization* line by relating the various members of this line to the assumption that was relaxed. Table 13–2 provides these relations.

In 1973, Robert Merton considered European-style options on dividend-paying shares. The inclusion of dividends changes the Black-Scholes formula as follows:

$$C = S * N\left\{\frac{ln(\frac{S}{X}) + (r + \frac{\sigma^2}{2})T}{\sigma\sqrt{T}}\right\} - e^{-rT}X * N\left\{\frac{ln(\frac{S}{X}) + (r - \frac{\sigma^2}{2})T}{\sigma\sqrt{T}}\right\} \quad (13–14)$$

where δ is the constant dividend yield. As Equation 13–14 demonstrates, the dividend reduces the value of the share to the holder of the option by the present value of the forgone dividend and reduces the cost of holding a share by the dividend stream that would be received.

FIGURE 13–5 The Analytical Models

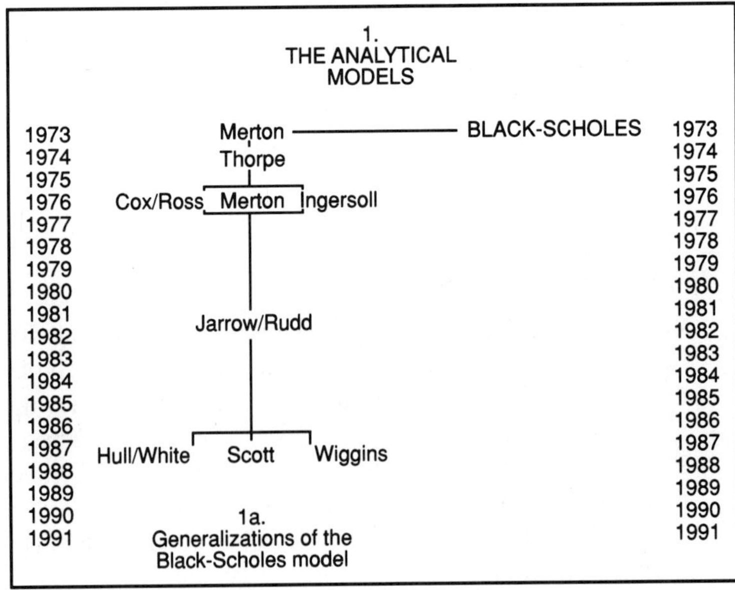

TABLE 13–2 Models That Relaxed the Black-Scholes Assumptions

Assumption	*Relaxed by*
No dividends	Merton (1973)
No taxes or transaction costs	Ingersoll (1976)
Constant interest rates	Merton (1973)
No penalties for short sales	Thorpe (1973)
Market operates continuously and share price is continuous	Merton (1976)
	Cox/Ross (1976)
Terminal stock price (returns) distribution is lognormal	Jarrow/Rudd (1982)

In 1975, Jonathan Ingersoll took Merton's inclusion of dividends one step further to consider a world where dividends are taxed at rate τ, while capital gains are untaxed.

$$C = \overset{e^{-\delta(1-\tau)T}}{\cancel{}} S * N\left\{\frac{ln(\frac{S}{X}) + (\overset{(r-\delta)(1-\tau)}{\cancel{r}} + \frac{\sigma^2}{2})T}{\sigma\sqrt{T}}\right\} - e^{-\overset{r(1-\tau)}{\cancel{r}}T} X * N\left\{\frac{ln(\frac{S}{X}) + (\overset{(r-\delta)(1-\tau)}{\cancel{r}} - \frac{\sigma^2}{2})T}{\sigma\sqrt{T}}\right\} \quad (13\text{–}15)$$

In the 1973 paper in which he considered dividends, Robert Merton also considered variable interest rates, a generalization that alters the Black-Scholes formula to

$$C = S * N\left\{\frac{ln(\frac{S}{X}) + \overset{-lnB(T) + (\hat{\sigma}^2/2)T}{\cancel{(r + \frac{\sigma^2}{2})T}}}{\underset{\hat{\sigma}}{\cancel{\sigma}}\sqrt{T}}\right\} - \overset{B(T)}{\cancel{e^{-rT}}} X * N\left\{\frac{ln(\frac{S}{X}) + \overset{-lnB(T) + (\hat{\sigma}^2/2)T}{\cancel{(r - \frac{\sigma^2}{2})T}}}{\underset{\hat{\sigma}}{\cancel{\sigma}}\sqrt{T}}\right\} \quad (13\text{–}16)$$

where $B(T)$ is the value of a default-risk-free discount bond with a maturity equal to the maturity of the option and $\hat{\sigma}$ is a variance measure that incorporates not only the variance of the stock but also the variance in the value of the discount bond (interest rate).

In the Black-Scholes model, prices follow a pure diffusion process—price moves continuously from one value to the next. The consequence of this pure diffusion process is that the terminal distribution of share prices is lognormal. The idea that prices do not move continuously but rather jump from one point to another was first considered by John Cox and Stephen Ross (1976)—an idea subsequently expanded in the Cox-Ross-Rubinstein binomial model discussed in Chapter 12.

Robert Merton (1976) went a step further by proposing the combination of a jump process and a diffusion process—after each jump, price again follows a diffusion process. If we constrain the jump process by assuming that the size of the jumps are distributed lognormally, this jump-diffusion model can be illustrated as a modification to the Black-Scholes formula:[5]

$$C = \sum_{n=0}^{\infty} \frac{e^{-\lambda(1+k)T}[\lambda(1+k)T]^n}{n!} \left[S * N\left\{\frac{ln(\frac{S}{X}) + (\hat{r} + \frac{\hat{\sigma}^2}{2})T}{\hat{\sigma}\sqrt{T}}\right\} - e^{-\hat{r}T}X * N\left\{\frac{ln(\frac{S}{X}) + (\hat{r} - \frac{\hat{\sigma}^2}{2})T}{\hat{\sigma}\sqrt{T}}\right\} \right] \quad (13\text{–}17)$$

where λ is the rate at which jumps occur, k is the average jump size as a proportional increase in the share price, r is $r - \lambda k + \{n[ln(1 + k)]\}/T$ and $\hat{\sigma}^2$ is $\hat{\sigma}^2 + n\,\sigma_j^2/T$, with σ_j^2 being the variance in the distribution of jumps.

In 1982, Robert Jarrow and Andrew Rudd examined the case in which prices follow a diffusion process, but not necessarily a process that generates a lognormal distribution. They examined the effect on the valuation of an option as the variance, skewness, and kurtosis of the actual distribution differ from a lognormal distribution. In general, as the tails of the resulting distribution are "fatter" or "thinner" than those of the lognormal distribution, the Black-Scholes formula will undervalue or overvalue the option. Jarrow and Rudd provided an adjustment to the Black-Scholes model that takes into account the discrepancies between the moments of the lognormal distribution and the true distribution.

In 1987, all three of the dominant academic finance journals published papers that dealt with the same generalization of the Black-Scholes model. The option pricing models proposed by John Hull and Alan White, Louis Scott, and James Wiggins all allowed volatility to itself be a stochastic process.

Extensions to the Black-Scholes Model

As we noted at the outset, the Black-Scholes model was designed to value European-style options on individual shares of stock. Not surprisingly, subsequent research was aimed at valuing options on underlying assets other than stock and on valuing American-style options. The family tree of option valuation models, with the addition of this *extension* line of the analytical tribe, is illustrated in Figure 13–6.

Options on Futures. In 1976, Fischer Black extended the model he developed with Myron Scholes to incorporate options on futures contracts

$$C = e^{-rT}F * N\left\{\frac{ln(\frac{F}{X}) + (\frac{\sigma^2}{2})T}{\sigma\sqrt{T}}\right\} - e^{-rT}X * N\left\{\frac{ln(\frac{F}{X}) - (\frac{\sigma^2}{2})T}{\sigma\sqrt{T}}\right\} \quad (13\text{–}18)$$

where F is the forward (futures) price.

Options on Currencies. In 1983, Mark Garman and Steven Kohlhagen provided an analytic valuation model for European options on currencies using an approach similar to that used by Merton for European options on dividend-paying stocks:

FIGURE 13–6 Extensions to the Analytical Models

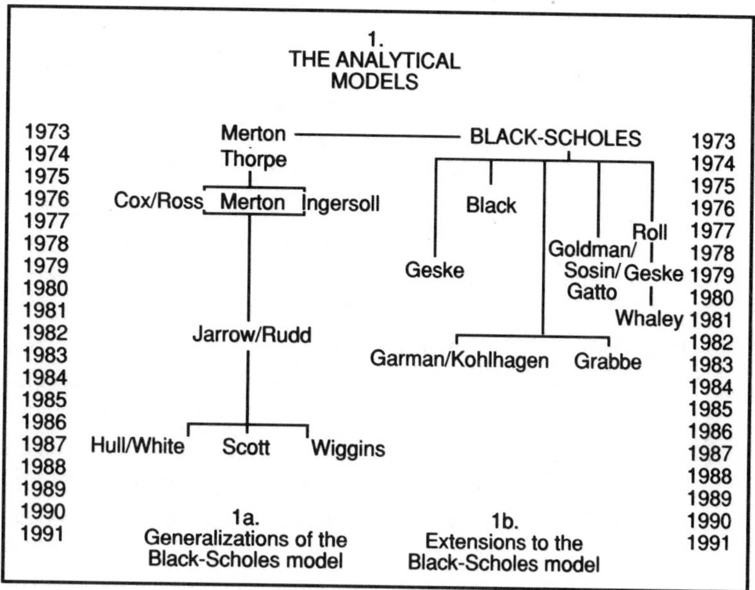

$$C = S * N\left\{\frac{ln(\frac{S}{X}) + (r + \frac{\sigma^2}{2})T}{\sigma\sqrt{T}}\right\} - e^{-rT}X * N\left\{\frac{ln(\frac{S}{X}) + (r - \frac{\sigma^2}{2})T}{\sigma\sqrt{T}}\right\} \quad (13\text{–}19)$$

where r_D is the interest rate on the domestic currency and r_F is the interest rate in the foreign currency. Note that in Equation 13–19, the interest rate on the foreign currency has the same function as did the dividend rate on the share in Equation 13–14.

In the same year—indeed, in the same issue of the same journal—Orlin Grabbe provided an alternative specification for the value of European options on currencies using an approach similar to that used by Black for futures,

$$C = S * N\left\{\frac{ln(\frac{S}{X}) + (r + \frac{\sigma^2}{2})T}{\sigma\sqrt{T}}\right\} - e^{-rT}X * N\left\{\frac{ln(\frac{S}{X}) + (r - \frac{\sigma^2}{2})T}{\sigma\sqrt{T}}\right\} \quad (13\text{–}20)$$

where $B(T)$ is the price of a *domestic* currency discount bond, F is the forward price of the foreign currency, and σ_F is determined by the variance of the forward foreign exchange rate.

Note that Equations 13–19 and 13–20 are mirror images of each other. Using interest rate parity, we can value an option either using the spot rate and the foreign interest rate (Garman-Kohlhagen) or using the forward rate (Grabbe).

Compound Options. That an option on a firm's equity is actually a compound option was recognized by Black and Scholes. They noted that the equity for any firm that issues debt is like a call option on the value of the assets; so, an option on equity is an option on an option on the value of the firm's assets. An analytic model for the valuation of compound options was provided by Robert Geske in 1979. Geske noted that the fundamental problem in using the Black-Scholes formula for the valuation of compound options is that Black-Scholes assumes that the variance is constant, while in the case of options on shares variance depends on the level of the share price (or more fundamentally on the value of the firm). When compared with the Black-Scholes model, the compound option model delivers higher values for deep-out-of-the-money options and near-maturity options and lower values for deep-in-the-money options.

Path-Dependent Options. In 1979, Barry Goldman, Howard Sosin, and Mary Ann Gatto examined the pricing of a European call option in which the exercise price is the minimum price of the share over the life of the option—an option now referred to as a "lookback" option. As we will describe in Chapter 15, a number of option-pricing models have been developed to consider not only "lookback" options but also other options for which the path the price takes is important in valuation—options on the average price and barrier options ("up-and-in," "down-and-out," and the like). Many of the models used to value path-dependent options are regarded as proprietary, so there is less about these models in the public record.[6]

American-Style Options. The analytic valuation model for an American-style share option was developed by Richard Roll (1977), Robert Geske (1979), and Robert Whaley (1981). As illustrated by Equation 13–21, an analytic solution which provides for early exercise requires that the Black/Sholes formula be expanded to include not only the cumulative standard normal distribution $N\{.\}$, but also a cumulative bivariate normal distribution $M\{.,.,.\}$. Following John Hull,[7] the model developed by Roll, Geske, and Whaley can be written as

$$C = S * N\left\{\frac{\ln(\frac{S}{X}) + (r + \frac{\sigma^2}{2})T}{\sigma\sqrt{T}}\right\} - e^{-rT} X * N\left\{\frac{\ln(\frac{S}{X}) + (r - \frac{\sigma^2}{2})T}{\sigma\sqrt{T}}\right\} \quad (13\text{–}21)$$

$$+ M\left\{\frac{\ln(\frac{S - e^{-rT_D}D}{X}) + (r + \frac{\sigma^2}{2})T}{\sigma\sqrt{T}}, \frac{\ln(\frac{S - e^{-rT_D}D}{\mathcal{S}}) + (r + \frac{\sigma^2}{2})T_D}{\sigma\sqrt{T_D}}, \sqrt{\frac{T_D}{T}}\right\}$$

$$+ XM\left\{\frac{\ln(\frac{S - e^{-rT_D}D}{X}) + (r - \frac{\sigma^2}{2})T}{\sigma\sqrt{T}}, \frac{\ln(\frac{S - e^{-rT_D}D}{\mathcal{S}}) + (r - \frac{\sigma^2}{2})T_D}{\sigma\sqrt{T_D}}, \sqrt{\frac{T_D}{T}}\right\}$$

where D is the final dividend prior to option expiration, T_D is the time until the final dividend, and $\mathcal{S}$ is the solution to $C(\mathcal{S}, T) = \mathcal{S} + D - X$. Given the complexity of an analytic valuation, it is not surprising that most users turn to the binomial models and analytic approximation models (also discussed in this chapter) for valuation of American-style options.

This listing is by no means a complete catalogue of the analytical option pricing models that have been developed and are currently in use. Other examples include the model developed by William Margrabe in 1978, which values the option to exchange one asset for another, and the model developed by René Stulz in 1982 to value an option on the minimum or the maximum of two risky assets.

The Numerical Models

Within the tribe of the numerical models, there are three lineages. The best known is the binomial model line; the other two are the finite difference models and the Monte Carlo simulation models.

The Binomial Models

We introduced you to the binomial approach to option valuation in Chapter 12. This approach—also known as the lattice approach—was first suggested by William Sharpe in 1978. However, this methodology is normally associated with the paper John Cox, Stephen Ross, and Mark Rubinstein published in 1979. As illustrated in Figure 13–7, development of the binomial models has continued.

As proposed by Cox-Ross-Rubinstein, this approach divides the time until option maturity into discrete intervals and presumes that, during each of these intervals, the price of the asset—for example, the stock price—follows a binomial process moving from its initial value, S, to Su (with probability p) or Sd (with probability $1 - p$). As illustrated in Figure 13–8, this process yields a "tree" (or lattice) of stock prices. Given this set of share prices, the call can be valued by working backwards from maturity. If we begin with one of the terminal share values, we can obtain the corresponding terminal value of a call option directly. Then, using Black and Scholes's insight that shares and calls can be combined to create a riskless portfolio, we can work our way back down the tree from time period T to time period $T - 1$, discounting portfolio values in period T to period $T - 1$ values using the risk-free interest rate. We continue the process from $T - 1$ to $T - 2$ and so on until we obtain the value of the call at contract origination.

The power of the binomial model is that it can deal with a range of different assets or options or market conditions. Consequently, it has been widely used to value American-style options and to value more complex options.

One of the most widely discussed uses of the binomial option-pricing model is in the valuation of interest rate options. Early on, either the Black-Scholes

FIGURE 13–7 The Numerical Models

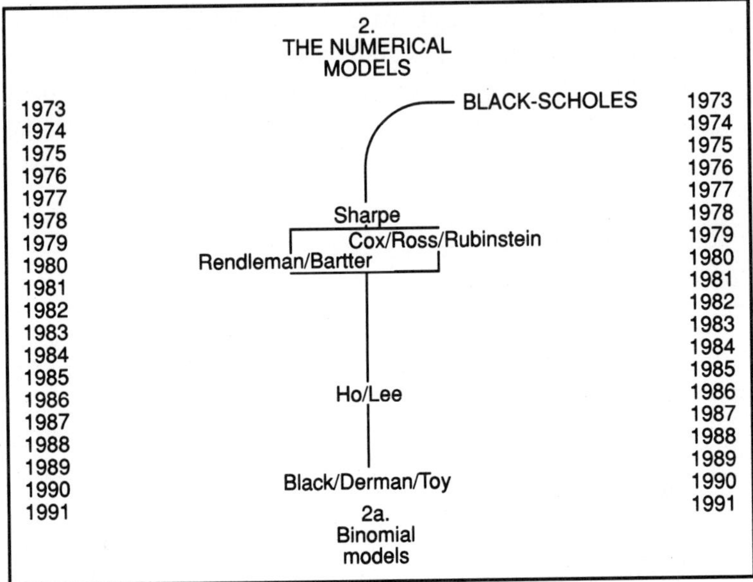

FIGURE 13–8 Lattice of Stock Prices

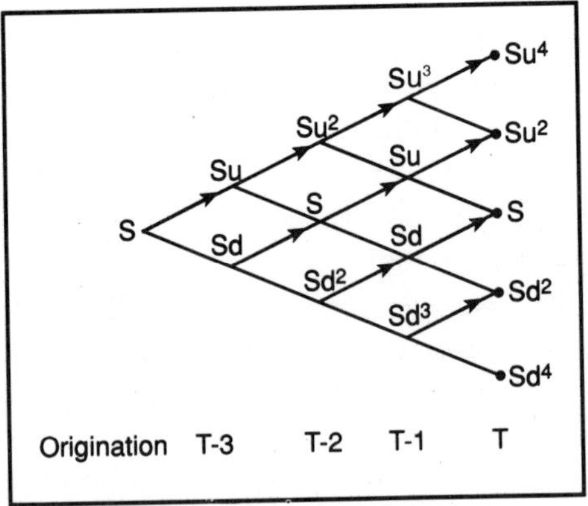

model or Black's futures model were used to value bond options. The users recognized that there are two problems with using these models: (1) the Black-Scholes and Black models assume that interest rates are constant, an assumption clearly at variance with pricing an option on bond prices; (2) the Black-Scholes and Black models assume that volatility is constant; but, for interest rates, volatility declines as maturity increases—as the bond approaches maturity, volatility tends toward zero.

The first binomial pricing model designed to deal with interest rate options was that proposed by Richard Rendleman and Brit Bartter in 1979. They use a single-parameter model to describe the term structure, a model that assumes that the risk-free rate grows at a constant rate and has a constant volatility.

In 1986, Thomas Ho and Sang-Bin Lee provided a model that considers changes in the whole term structure rather than just changes in an interest rate.[8] In the Ho-Lee model each node represents a set of discount bond prices and the tree is constructed so that it reflects bond prices observed in the market. However, like the Rendleman-Bartter model it requires that all interest rates have the same volatility—all spot interest rates and all forward interest rates are equally variable.

The model proposed by Fischer Black, Emanuel Derman, and William Toy in 1990 expanded on the Ho-Lee model by specifying a time-varying structure for volatility—that is, $\sigma(t)$. And, since the Black-Derman-Toy model uses a declining volatility curve, it incorporates mean reversion.[9]

The Finite Difference Methodology

This approach was first suggested by Eduardo Schwartz in 1977 and was extended by Georges Courtadon in 1982.

This methodology is based on finding a numerical solution to the differential equation that the option valuation must satisfy—that is, the differential equation is converted into a set of difference equations and the difference equations are solved iteratively. However, it is probably useful to employ the insight provided by Michael Brennan and Eduardo Schwartz and think of this methodology as a *trinomial lattice* approach. In 1990, John Hull and Alan White provided a modification that insures that the trinomial lattice methodology converges to the solution of the underlying differential equation.

Monte Carlo Simulations

The problem faced in option pricing is that the value of an option is determined by the *expected value* of the underlying asset at expiration of the option. So far, we have reviewed three different ways of dealing with this expected value: analytical models like the Black-Scholes model and the models that followed were based on specifying and solving a stochastic differential equation. The lattice models avoided the requirement to solve a stochastic differential equation by specifying a particular

Aside

Evolution of Models to Value Interest Rate Options

The evolution from analytical models to binomial models to finite difference models (a.k.a. trinomial models) is perhaps most relevant for interest rate options.

Not all that long ago, most of the market makers for OTC interest rate options used a Black-Scholes model to value interest rate options. However, most of the houses quickly changed to a Black model, since the relevant underlying interest rate is a forward rate, not a spot rate.

But, the Black model still presumes that interest rates are fixed—a presumption at odds with the facts if one is valuing options on interest rates. Some market makers adopted models like the Rendleman-Bartter model. Others made two "evolutionary jumps" at the same time and moved to models like the Ho-Lee model, which incorporates an explicit term structure.

Once the term structure was incorporated, the next step in the evolutionary chain was to incorporate volatility—either in a term structure of volatility like that in the Black-Derman-Toy model or models that permit the future volatilities of short rates to be set independently from those for long rates.

A graphical representation of this evolution of interest rate option pricing models is provided.

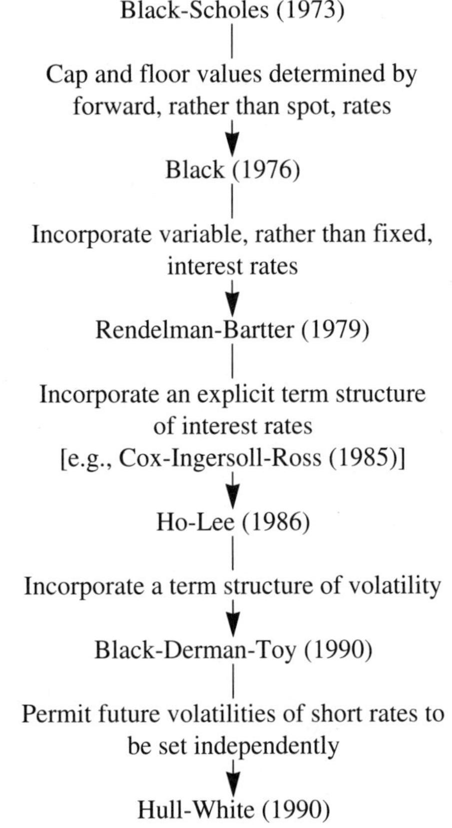
Black-Scholes (1973)
Cap and floor values determined by forward, rather than spot, rates
Black (1976)
Incorporate variable, rather than fixed, interest rates
Rendelman-Bartter (1979)
Incorporate an explicit term structure of interest rates [e.g., Cox-Ingersoll-Ross (1985)]
Ho-Lee (1986)
Incorporate a term structure of volatility
Black-Derman-Toy (1990)
Permit future volatilities of short rates to be set independently
Hull-White (1990)

process for the underlying asset price (a binomial process) and then using an iterative approach to solve for the value of the option. The finite difference methodology involves replacing the differential equation with a series of difference equations.

In 1977, Phelim Boyle proposed a simulation methodology. This method uses the fact that the distribution of asset values at option expiration is determined by the process that generates future movements in the value of the asset. If this process can be specified, it can be simulated on a computer. Each time this simulation is done, a terminal asset value is generated. If this simulation process is done several times—make that several thousand times—the result is a distribution of terminal asset values from which one can directly extract the expected asset value at option expiration.

The finite difference method and the Monte Carlo simulation lines complete the numerical models *tribe*. The complete geneology for this tribe is illustrated in Figure 13–9.

FIGURE 13–9 The Numerical Models

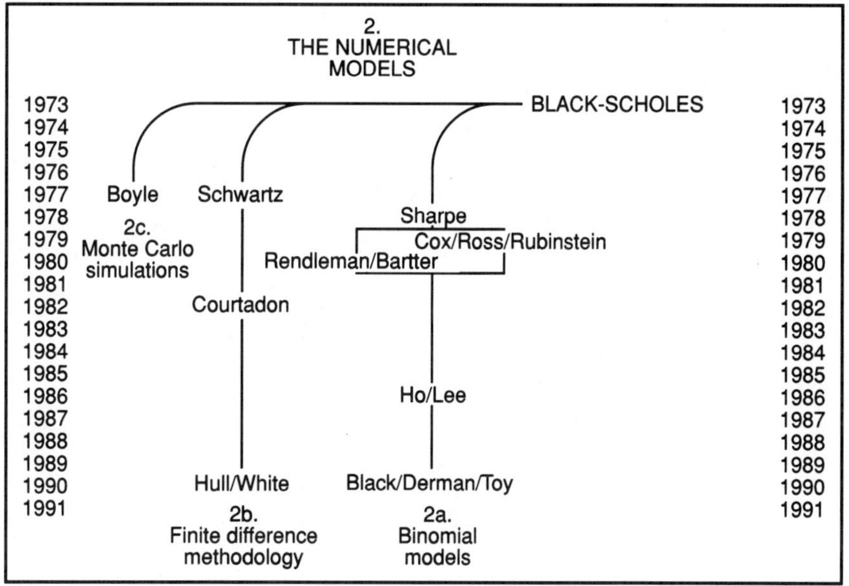

The Analytic Approximation Models

Stretching the analogy of a family tree one more time, we might say that this tribe represents a reunification of the other two tribes. The analytic approximation technique involves estimating the premium for early exercise (using a numerical technique) and then adding this premium to the price of a European option (obtained from an analytical model).

Lionel Macmillan originally suggested valuing options using a quadratic approximation approach in 1986. The approach was implemented by Giovanni Barone-Adesi and Robert Whaley in 1987. This approach has been used to value American calls and puts on stocks, stock indices, currencies, and futures contracts.

The Family Tree

We have talked about a lot of option-pricing models. However, there is yet one more group of models we should point out to you. As we alluded to as we began this chapter, there were some *precursors* to the Black-Scholes model.

Aside

Precursors to the Black-Scholes Model

The earliest attempt we know of to provide an analytical valuation for options was in Louis Bachelier's doctoral dissertation at the Sorbonne in 1900. Bachelier posited that share prices follow an arithmetic (rather than geometric) Brownian Motion process leading to a normal distribution of share returns. While Bachelier was on the right track, the process Bachelier used to generate share prices would permit both negative security prices and option prices that exceed the price of the underlying asset, the formulation required risk neutrality, and no time value of money was included.

Case Sprenkle dealt with two of the problems in Bachelier's formulation. He assumed that stock prices are lognormally distributed and allowed drift in the random walk (thereby ruling out negative security prices and permitting risk aversion). To give you some idea how close Sprenkle came, following is Sprenkle's model written as a modification of the Black-Scholes model:

$$C = S * N\left\{\frac{\ln(\frac{S}{X}) + (r + \frac{\sigma^2}{2})T}{\sigma\sqrt{T}}\right\} - e^{-rT}X * N\left\{\frac{\ln(\frac{S}{X}) + (r - \frac{\sigma^2}{2})T}{\sigma\sqrt{T}}\right\}$$

where ρ is the average rate of growth of the share price and z is the degree of risk aversion.[10]

James Boness went a step beyond Sprenkle by including the time value of money—i.e., he discounted the expected terminal stock price back to the present using the expected rate of return to the stock.

Paul Samuelson extended Boness's model by permitting the option to have a different level of risk than does the stock. To show how close these precursors to Black-Scholes had come, we can write this specification as a modification of the Black-Scholes equation,

$$C = S*N\left\{\frac{\ln(\frac{S}{X}) + (r + \frac{\sigma^2}{2})T}{\sigma\sqrt{T}}\right\} - e^{-rT}X * N\left\{\frac{\ln(\frac{S}{X}) + (r - \frac{\sigma^2}{2})T}{\sigma\sqrt{T}}\right\}$$

where ρ is the average rate of growth of the share price and w is the average rate of growth in the value of the call.

If we combine Figures 13–6 and 13–9 and then add the "geneologies" for the analytic approximation models and the precursors, we get the family tree illustrated in Figure 13–10. This family tree illustrates graphically what we said at the outset—the Black-Scholes model is neither the beginning nor the end of the story.

However, even this complex family tree is incomplete. We noted earlier that we did not include Margrabe's model for the valuation of the option to exchange one asset for another and Stulz's valuation model for an option on the minimum or the maximum of two risky assets. The 1990s have witnessed expansion in the use of these options—the so-called multifactor options. We will return to a consideration of these options in Chapter 15.

FIGURE 13–10 The Family Tree of Option-Pricing Models

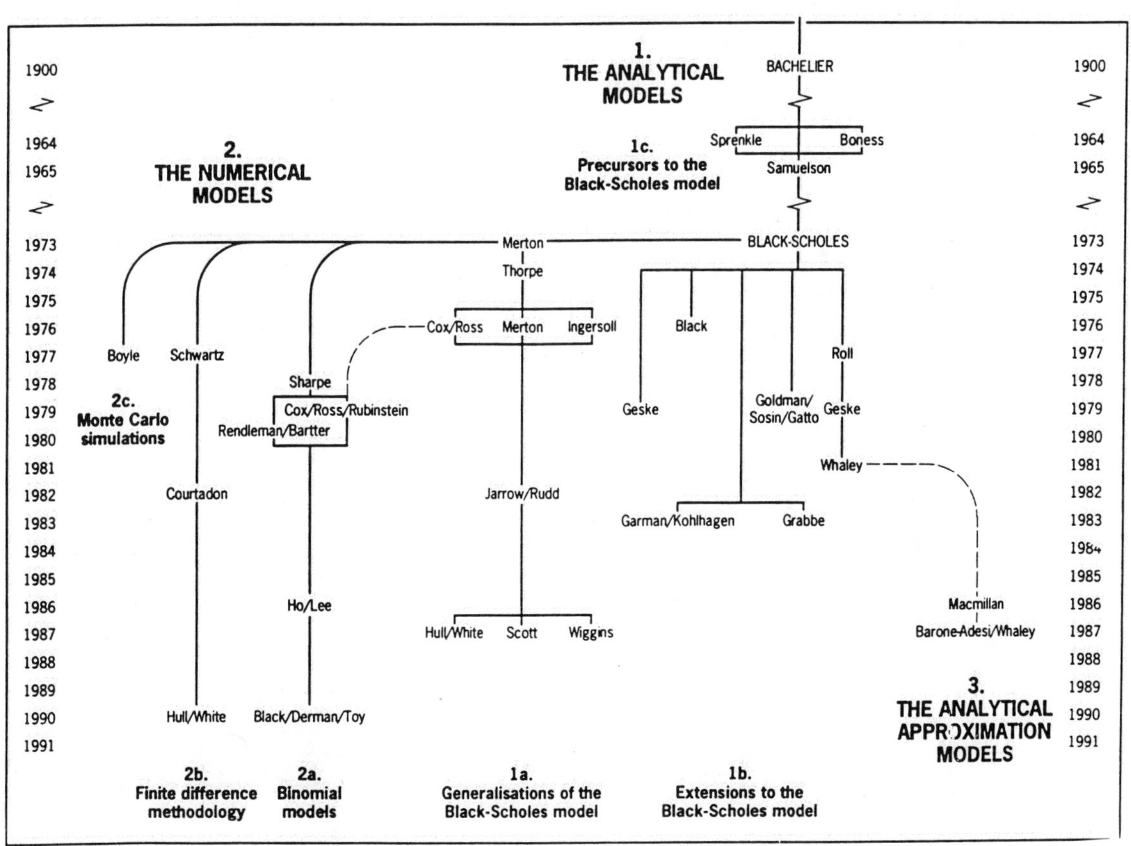

Notes

1. The riskless hedge could also be created with a short position in the stock and a long position in the call. Note that the above restriction is placed on the ratio Q_s/Q_c; it makes no difference which asset is short.
2. In general, for the solution of a partial differential equation (a differential equation that is a function of more than one variable) one boundary equation is required for each dimension. Equation 13–10 is the boundary condition in the time dimension. In the stock price dimension, the boundary condition is that the call price is zero if the stock price is zero. However, because it is explicitly assumed that the call price is lognormally distributed, the stock price cannot be zero, the boundary condition will never be binding, and therefore in this special case can be ignored.
3. See Friedman (1975), especially page 148, for a mathematical proof of the solution technique.
4. As long as individuals are risk-neutral.
5. This description of the jump diffusion model is adapted from Hull (1989) at pages 312–13 and 323–24.
6. There are some exceptions. Mark Garman provided a valuation model for "lookback" options in an issue of *Risk* (1988). A.G.Z. Kemna and A.C.F Vorst (1990) provided a model for options on geometric averages in "A Pricing Method for Options Based on Average Asset Values," *Journal of Banking and Finance* 14 (March 1990), 113–124. (October 1988, pp. 16–19). And, while some techniques for valuing options on arithmetic averages are regarded as proprietary, Stewart Turnbull and Lee Wakeman (1991) provided a methodology for pricing European-style average rate options.
7. Hull (1989), pp. 131–33.
8. Ho and Lee incorporated a model of the term structure that permitted nonconstant volatilities and thereby processes like mean reversion. The models of the term structure of interest rates might be viewed as another *family*—one distinct from the family of option-pricing models but one on which most of the recent interest rate option valuation models are based. Prominent members of this family of term structure models (as identified by their authors) include Pye (1966), Vasicek (1977), Brennan and Schwartz (1979), Cox, Ingersoll, and Ross (1985), and Heath, Jarrow, and Morton (1990).
9. In the same year, John Hull and Alan White (1990) suggested a model that goes one step further to incorporate not only a time varying structure for volatility—$\sigma(t)$—but also another time varying function—$\phi(t)$—which permits the future variability of short interest rates to be set independently of other data. This model was in the context of the finite difference methodology to be discussed following.
10. Indeed, Fischer Black mentioned to Charles that he and Myron Scholes used Sprenkle's paper to get the solution to their system of equations.

CHAPTER

14

USING OPTIONS TO MANAGE FINANCIAL PRICE RISKS*

A firm may elect to purchase an option instead of using forwards, futures, or swaps for several reasons. First, the most that can ever be lost is the price paid for the option, but increases in the underlying financial price will be reflected in the value of the option. Consequently, many firms choose options because they wish to remain in a position to benefit if the financial price goes their way. Second, options are highly flexible tools for designing hedges or targeting investment objectives. With options, it is easy to buy the protection you need and sell off coverage you do not need. And because such tailored hedges can be constructed by combining relatively standardized products, the hedge usually can be reconfigured if information about the size or timing of the underlying exposure changes or if changes in the company's risk management policy require more or less coverage. Third, options can be purchased either on an exchange or over-the-counter, so the end user has considerable flexibility in the choice of marketplace.

Users sell options as well as purchase them. Selling calls generates a premium that can be kept in the event that the underlying instrument declines or remains unchanged. A firm might choose to sell a call option as an alternative to selling a forward contract or a futures or to entering into a swap. However, if I sell a call option, I face unlimited potential risk—in the same way as I do if I use forwards, futures, or swaps—but my gain is limited to the price received for the option—unlike forwards, futures, or swaps.

---

*The authors wish to acknowledge the assistance of Gregory Greiff in assembling the first draft of this chapter.

In this chapter, we examine several ways that options are being used. We look at using options to hedge the firm, using options to take a view, selling embedded options to reduce funding costs, and using options as a competitive tool.

Using Options to Hedge the Firm

So far, we have seen how financial price risk can be managed using forwards, futures, or swaps. Options are another important weapon in the risk manager's arsenal. But, unlike forwards, futures, or swaps, options provide the end user with protection against adverse movements in a financial price without forgoing completely the advantages from a favorable movement in the financial price.

Hedging Interest Rate Risk

A firm funded with floating-rate debt is usually concerned about the possibility of rising interest rates. To protect against this, the firm could buy a call option on the relevant interest rate—an *interest rate cap*.[1] If rates rise, gains on the cap would offset the increased costs of borrowing. If, instead, rates fall, the firm would still be able to take advantage of the lower borrowing costs. The price of this protection is the premium paid for the cap. Often, the choice between locking in a rate via a swap and "insuring" against future rate increases is made on the basis of the firm's view about the level of rates.[2]

> By 1989, Falcon Cable had grown to be the 15th largest multiple system cable operator, with 800,000 subscriptions serving 500 small to medium-sized communities. To continue its aggressive expansion, Falcon had expanded its borrowings—between 1989 and 1990, total borrowings increased 41 percent. Consequently, interest rate risk became an important concern.
>
> Falcon fixes a substantial portion of its debt through interest rate swaps. It manages its remaining interest rate risk with caps and collars.
>
> In 1990, the company evaluated the relative benefits of using swaps or caps to hedge \$35 million of a \$70 million variable-rate loan. At the time, the yield curve was positively sloped—three-year Treasury rates were 8.75 percent and five-year rates were 9.02 percent. A three-year swap would have left Falcon with a 12.60 percent fixed rate at a time when its borrowing rates were 11 percent.
>
> The company's view was that rates were relatively high. So, Falcon chose to "insure against" further increases in interest rate risk with a cap—and pay the up-front premium—rather than to enter into a swap—and lock in what the firm viewed as a high fixed rate.

While most firms have a continuous interest rate exposure, some retailers have more seasonal borrowing needs. These firms go from net borrowers in the spring and summer to net investors after the peak Christmas selling season. An option strategy can be constructed that caps such a firm's short exposure in the spring and, if desired, puts a floor on the firm's long position in January. One of the most widely cited such transactions was the seasonal hedge constructed for L.L. Bean.[3]

> L.L. Bean, the clothing and outdoor equipment retailer based in Freeport, Maine, is a seasonal borrower. As do other retailers like Sears, F.W. Woolworth, and Mattel Toys, L.L. Bean relies on borrowings to expand inventories before the critical fourth quarter. Consequently, L.L. Bean faces the risk that interest rates will rise in spring or summer, when they need capital most.
>
> L.L. Bean constructed a three-year seasonal interest rate cap on its annual borrowing costs. The hedge was designed specifically to be seasonal because the company only wanted to hedge interest expense during its peak borrowing season—the summer, when it builds up inventory for the Christmas ordering season.

Interest rate floors—put options on interest rates—can be used to hedge natural long exposures to interest rates. A company that holds a floating-rate asset has just such an exposure to interest rates. If short-term rates fall, then the income received from this asset will also fall. As the following example illustrates, the company could hedge this exposure with an interest rate floor.[4]

> First Union Bank, a regional bank in the southeastern United States, uses derivatives to actively manage the interest rate risk inherent in its investments.
>
> In 1991, First Union bought a five-year interest rate floor giving it the right to receive 6.5 percent minus three-month LIBOR on a notional principal of $1 billion. First Union paid a $3 million premium for the floor. The floor protected the earnings on First Union Bank's assets from a decline in interest rates.
>
> By February 1992, in fact, interest rates had fallen so far that the value of First Union's floor was $30 million. The floor offset, in part, the reduced earnings on its investments over the life of the floor.

Caps and floors can be sold as well as purchased. Interest rate options might be sold and the premium received used to reduce the cost of funding the firm or to increase the yield on an investment.

For example, a firm with a floating-rate asset might choose to sell an interest rate cap to boost yield. The asset owner collects a premium from the sale of the cap, but in return effectively agrees to "cap" the interest rate it receives on the floating-rate asset. If the floating interest rate remains unchanged or falls, the premium received on the sale of the cap acts as a "supplement" to the asset owner's interest income. However, if the floating rate rises above the cap rate, the asset owner forgoes interest income that "might have been."

Resuming an example he began in Chapter 9, Ira Kawaller takes us through the process a treasurer might use to decide whether to hedge the interest rate risk of a prospective borrowing by selling a futures contract or buying an interest rate cap—or selling an interest rate floor.

Risk Management in Practice

To Hedge or Not to Hedge: Part 2

Ira G. Kawaller

In Chapter 9, I introduced Edwin Charles, treasurer of Benzoe Corp.,* who is planning to take down a $10 million loan within the next quarter. (The loan rate will be set the time of the takedown, at three-month LIBOR plus 100 basis points.) In that earlier example, I considered two strategies:

Strategy 1: Do nothing.

Strategy 2: Lock in an interest rate today by selling Eurodollar futures contracts timed to expire at about the same time as the loan rate is to be set.

Edwin has a third course of action.

Strategy 3: Insure against rising rates.

Buying an interest rate cap or buying puts on Eurodollar futures will accomplish this end. Doing either involves an initial cash outlay, which will vary depending on the level of the cap rate (or strike price), the length of time for which the insurance is required, and the market's collective assessment of prospective volatility. But ultimately, if the market rate for LIBOR is higher than the cap rate (or the futures price is lower than the strike price of the put option), the final value of the cap will compensate for the market rate being higher than the ceiling rate. This strategy may sound like the most attractive one—until Edwin goes to write the check for the desired protection.

As before, the strategy that performs best depends on the state of the environment; each alternative hedge strategy should be assessed in light of its cost versus its potential benefits or consequences. Using futures means forgoing the benefit of lower spot market interest rates. The consequence of purchases of options is the forgone premium when interest rates decline.

To evaluate the three strategies, I again consider the environment I used in Chapter 9: suppose, for example, that today three-month LIBOR is at 7.00 percent and that the Eurodollar futures contract is currently priced at 92.90 (that is, at a rate of 7.10 percent). Now, suppose that the price of a put option on Eurodollar futures with a strike price of 93.00 (7.00 percent) is 0.40. In the following table, I have considered two scenarios—one in which three-month LIBOR rises to 8 percent and the other in which three-month LIBOR falls to 6 percent.

To Hedge or Not to Hedge: Part 2 continued

Hedge Strategies	*1. Do Nothing*	*2. Sell Futures*	*3. Buy Puts*
Scenario I: Spot LIBOR rises to 8.00%			
Interest paid to banker (based on 9.00%)	$225,000	$225,000	$225,000
P&L on hedge	NA	22,500	15,000
10 contracts × price change of hedge vehicle			
Net interest	225,000	202,500	210,000
Effective rate	9.00%	8.10%	8.40%
Scenario II: Spot LIBOR falls to 6.00%			
Interest paid to banker (based on 7.00%)	$175,000	$175,000	$175,000
P&L on hedge	NA	(27,500)	(10,000)
10 contracts × price change of hedge vehicle			
Net interest	175,000	202,500	185,000
Effective rate	7.00%	8.10%	7.40%

If Mr. Charles does nothing, the cost of funds will simply be equal to spot LIBOR plus 100 basis points—7.00 percent or 9.00 percent. If Mr. Charles sells futures, he locks in a rate of 100 basis points above the initial futures rate—8.10 percent. (Note again that this example assumes perfect convergence of spot and futures rates at the time the hedge is liquidated.) Buying puts guarantees a worst case of 8.40 percent in this example (100.00 percent − 93.00 percent + 1.00 percent + .40 percent), with the potential benefit of lower costs if interest rates decline.

Note however that Mr. Charles could create his own "middle ground" by combining bits and pieces of the different alternatives. Edwin could deal with the expense of buying insurance protection by "selling off" some of his potential benefits. For example, he could buy a cap that protects against LIBOR rising above, say, 7 percent and simultaneously sell a cap that protects against LIBOR rising above 8 percent. That is, once rates exceed the higher cap level (8 percent), Edwin is again exposed. By doing this combination, the receipts from selling the second cap offset the initial cost—at least partially—of the first cap.

Another common way of mitigating the expense of protection is to sell a floor against a cap. For example, buying a 7 percent cap and selling a 6 percent floor covers Edwin from the risk of rates rising above 7 percent but forces him

To Hedge or Not to Hedge: Part 2 continued

to forgo the benefit if rates drop below 6 percent. His up-front cost would then be the cost of the cap minus the price of the floor.

So what should Edwin do? Strictly speaking, there isn't a "correct" choice, only reasonable actions. Frankly, any treasurer's decision will reflect his or her operating style and corporate investment policies. In a few instances, however, I would recommend the "do nothing" approach. Consistently taking this posture strikes me as shrinking from responsibility because it leaves a firm chronically exposed to interest rate risk. I don't think this approach is reasonable.

From the perspective of hedging with derivative instruments, at a minimum, I think Edwin should either use futures to lock in some portion of his interest rate exposure or buy puts—also on a fractional basis. The choice would largely depend on the implied volatility conditions for the put options at the time of hedging initiation. Most commercial bankers and any institutional broker could give Edwin a reading on the volatility conditions. With low implied volatilities, Edwin should probably opt for puts; with high implied volatilities, he might be better served by selling futures. In the midrange, he should think about buying puts and selling at least some alternative options. If he feels that interest rates probably won't rise very much, he should sell cheaper puts, such as a second cap with a higher ceiling rate than the original cap. If he thinks it more likely that interest rates will go up, he should sell calls.

---

*The people and companies presented here are fictional.

Ira G. Kawaller is vice president–director of the New York office for the Chicago Mercantile Exchange. After receiving a Ph.D. from Purdue University, Mr. Kawaller served at the Federal Reserve Board in Washington. He subsequently worked for the AT&T Company and J. Aron Company, Inc. Mr. Kawaller currently serves on the board of directors of the National Option & Futures Society and the board of advisors for the International Association of Financial Engineers. Mr. Kawaller is the author of *Financial Futures & Options* (Probus).

This example reprinted with permission from the Fall 1992 issue of *Treasury and Risk Management.* © 1992 CFO Publishing Corp.

Buying and selling caps and floors are the four basic interest-rate-option hedging strategies. However, instead of using a single instrument, many firms use combinations of these to achieve specific hedging objectives.

Consider a firm using floating-rate lines of credit to fund operations. The firm might want to cap its exposure to higher rates but views the premium for the cap as "too expensive." By simultaneously selling a floor, the firm collects a premium to offset the cost of the cap.

As we will discuss in more detail in Chapter 15, such a combination of buying a cap and simultaneously selling a floor is called a *collar*. Collars effectively lock in a range for the firm's borrowing costs: the cap sets a maximum possible borrowing rate for the life of the contract, protecting the firm against higher interest rates, while the floor establishes a minimum rate for the firm's borrowing costs.[5]

> Muzak, the well-known provider of office music, used a two-year collar when it refinanced term floating-rate debt in 1990. Muzak was looking for insurance against sharply higher rates. However, in order to reduce the cost of the interest rate cap, Muzak sold a floor at the same time. Muzak's interest costs can still vary through several hundred basis points up or down, but the firm is protected from catastrophic rate increases.

In Chapter 12 you saw that in-the-money options cost more than out-of-the-money options. In the OTC market, interest rate options can be bought or sold at any strike price. Because of this flexibility, a popular hedging strategy is to create a so-called costless collar.

A costless collar is created by varying the strike prices of the cap purchased and the floor sold so that the income received from the sale of the floor exactly matches the cost of the call. Costless collars are popular because they provide the firm with interest rate protection at no out-of-pocket expense.

There may be instances in which relying on bank credit facilities is more cost-efficient than issuing equity capital or public debt. The availability of interest rate options makes it easier for firms to take advantage of bank debt when the form and structure of borrowing needs is of concern to the firm. Bank debt is most often floating-rate debt; but by utilizing "zero cost" interest rate collars, the firm can effectively limit the maximum interest rate and cost of the debt.[6]

> Revolving credit lines are part of the everyday mix of funding sources for a corporation. These credit lines typically allow a corporation to borrow up to a fixed limit at a floating interest rate.
>
> In 1991, Applied Power, Inc., used its $200 million revolving credit facility to finance an acquisition, consolidate outstanding liabilities, and refinance existing long-term fixed-rate debt. Not wanting to remain exposed to floating interest rates, Applied Power then hedged its resulting exposure with zero-cost interest rate collars.
>
> Borrowings under the line of credit were priced at a floating rate equal to either the bank's reference rate or to LIBOR plus 1 percent. After drawing on its credit facility, Applied Power hedged $120 million of the debt with interest rate collars—it bought interest rate caps with an average cap rate of 9.5 percent and sold interest rate floors with an average floor rate of 7.75 percent. When it subsequently reduced its borrowings, Applied power sold back some of its interest rate collars to keep its hedge in line with its falling debt level.

The decision whether to use a cap or collar often depends on prevailing market conditions as well as the company's specific hedging objectives. Caps—call options on forward interest rates—get more expensive as the yield curve steepens (that is, as the forward rates rise) and as the volatility of the underlying interest rate increases. Market conditions may lead the company to want to change the extent or structure of its hedge. The flexibility afforded by options gives the hedger the ability to modify an existing hedge with subsequent options trades. A company that originally purchased a cap for protection can create a collar by selling a floor sometime in the future when market conditions are more favorable.[7]

Aside

Hartmarx Corporation

Hartmarx Corporation is the nation's largest manufacturer and retailer of men's tailored clothing. The Chicago-based company manufactures some three million suits a year under such well-known lines as Hart Schaffner and Marx, Kuppenheimer, Pierre Cardin, and Austin Reed.

In the late 1980s, Hartmarx began expanding operations through mergers and acquisitions and by opening new retail stores, financing new inventory with short-term borrowings. As a result, its bank loans rose from $57 million in 1987 to $267 million in 1989, leading Hartmarx to become concerned about its exposure to interest rate risk.

The company considered several options. It could, for instance, replace its current short-term debt with long-term borrowings. Alternatively, it could enter into a pay-fixed/receive-floating swap, effectively locking in a fixed rate. The third alternative was an interest rate cap or collar.

Several concerns entered into the decision about which was the best hedging strategy to pursue. First, both the long-term borrowing and the swap would lock the company into a long-term rate that the company believed to be unattractive. Second, the firm expected its borrowing needs to decline over time and did not want to lock itself into a long-term rate, only to later decide it had overborrowed. These factors led Hartmarx to conclude that a flexible hedging strategy, using caps, floors, and collars, was the most appropriate mechanism to serve its needs.

Early in 1989, Hartmarx bought a $50 million interest rate cap. This was meant to serve as a straightforward "insurance policy" in light of rising interest rates. By October 1989, the yield curve inverted—short-term rates were higher than long-term rates. Because of this, the price of interest rate floor contracts rose. Hartmarx was able to receive a higher premium for the sale of an interest rate floor than it would have received in the beginning of the year when it first established the hedge.

Having thus bought a cap and sold a floor—although at different times—Hartmarx had created a "costless" collar. Its borrowing costs were capped at the then-current rate of 8.75 percent and an interest rate floor was established at 7.5 percent. As a result, Hartmarx had no upside exposure on the hedged amount and would benefit from any fall in rates down to 7.5 percent.

Hartmarx established five such collar transactions for a total hedge of $125 million, about half of its total short-term borrowings. Because of its advantageous timing, the 8.75 percent ceiling was about 125 basis points lower than it would have had to pay on a long-term borrowing.

Going the other way, a firm with a collar can buy back the floor to leave it with a cap only. It might decide to do this, for instance, if it wishes to regain the opportunity to benefit from subsequent declines in interest rates.

Further, as Satyajit Das and John Martin demonstrate, even after the decision to purchase an option is made, the treasurer may still face other decisions.

Risk Management in Practice

Protective Strategies

Satyajit Das and John Martin

When three-month LIBOR was 8 percent and the two-year swap rate was 8.5 percent, Company C purchased a two-year, $100 million interest rate cap on three-month LIBOR to hedge its portfolio of floating-rate U.S. dollar borrowings. For a 9 percent cap, the firm paid 0.44 percent.

The cap protects Company C against interest rate increases above 9.24 percent a year (the strike rate on the cap plus the premium paid amortized over the life of the cap). At the settlement dates, if three-month LIBOR exceeds 9.24 percent, Company C benefits from a lower cost of funds. The following table summarizes the payoff for the interest rate cap and contrasts it with that of an interest rate swap of the same maturity.

Interest Rate Cap Payoffs (% pa)

	Gain (Loss) Under:		**Company C Interest Cost**	
Average 3-month Libor	*2-year Interest Rate Swap*	*2-year Interest Rate Cap*	*2-year Interest Rate Swap*	*2-year Interest Rate Cap*
6	(2.50)	(0.24)	8.50	6.24
7	(1.50)	(0.24)	8.50	7.24
8	(0.50)	(0.24)	8.50	8.24
9	0.50	(0.24)	8.50	9.24
10	1.50	0.76	8.50	9.24
11	2.50	1.76	8.50	9.24

Suppose that over the next three months, three-month LIBOR rose to 11 percent and the 1.75-year swap rate rose to 10 percent. As a result of the

Protective Strategies continued

increase in interest rates, the interest rate cap position will have an unrealized gain. The Treasurer of Company C can choose to manage its existing interest cap position to preserve its unrealized gain, using some of the following strategies.

Sell a Cap

Company C could choose to liquidate its interest rate cap by selling the position. With the increase in interest rates, the cap (now with a maturity of 1.75 years) can be sold for 2.31 percent a year (flat). This represents a gain of 1.87 percent, or $1.87 million on the transaction.

If the cap is sold, Company C reverts to a floating-rate dollar borrowing at three-month LIBOR less 1.18 percent a year. This margin represents the gain on the sale of the cap amortized over the remaining life of the original transaction. If the cap is sold, Company C benefits when three-month LIBOR averages less than 10.18 percent a year over the remaining 1.75 years of the transaction.

Enter into an Interest Rate Swap

Instead of selling the cap, the firm could lock in the gain on its cap by entering into a $100 million interest rate swap to receive the fixed rate (current market rate 10 percent) and pay three-month LIBOR. The swap locks in a gain of 1 percent a year (the difference between the swap and cap rates) on each of the remaining seven quarterly periods. This equates to a present value benefit of 1.59 percent flat, which adjusted for the premium paid for the cap is equivalent to 1.15 percent.

If interest rates decline, this interest swap would have the effect of leveraging the returns to the company. This is because receiving fixed under an interest rate swap is the equivalent of selling a series of interest rate caps and simultaneously purchasing a series of interest rate floors. However, Company C would have no protection were interest rates to increase from current levels.

In this transaction, the *"sell a call option on interest rates"* position embedded in the swap is offset by the interest rate cap that Company C had purchased. Company C's net position is then *"long a put option on interest rates"*—Company C owns an interest rate floor that increases in value if interest rates decline. The payoffs from this particular strategy are summarized in the following table.

Protective Strategies continued

Reversal of Cap with Interest Rate Swap (% pa)

Gain (Loss) Under:

Average 3-month Libor	*Interest Rate Cap*	*Interest Rate Swap*	*Total*	*Company C Total Interest Rate Cost*
7	(0.24)	3.0	2.76	4.24
8	(0.24)	2.0	1.76	5.24
9	(0.24)	1.0	0.76	8.24
10	0.76	0.0	0.76	9.24
11	1.76	(1.0)	0.76	10.24
12	2.76	(2.0)	0.76	11.24

The use of the swap to reverse the interest rate cap position is particularly useful in instances in which the interest rate cap cannot be sold at or near its true economic value.

Buy a Floor

Company C could seek to lock in its gain, without sacrificing protection against further interest rate increases, by purchasing a floor for a term of 1.75 years at a strike price of 10 percent for a premium of 0.51 percent (flat) or 0.32 percent a year. The next table indicates that Company C remains protected against further increases in interest rates, albeit at a slightly higher level, but continues to benefit from future declines in interest rates.

Hedging Cap with Purchased Floor (% pa)

Gain (Loss) Under:

Average 3-month Libor	*Interest Rate Cap*	*Interest Rate Floor*	*Total*	*Company C Total Interest Rate Cost*
8	(0.24)	1.68	1.44	6.56
9	(0.24)	0.68	0.44	8.56
10	0.76	(0.32)	0.44	9.56
11	1.76	(0.32)	1.44	9.56
12	2.76	(0.32)	2.44	9.56

To Hedge or Not to Hedge: Part 2 continued

Sell a Floor

Company C could protect its gain by writing a floor (at a strike rate of 9 percent and a premium equivalent to 0.13 percent per annum). This combined with the purchased interest rate cap equates to an interest rate swap where Company C pays a fixed rate and received three-month LIBOR.

If rates are expected to remain steady or increase, the premium resulting from the sold floor would decrease the cost of borrowing, partially offsetting the previously incurred cost of purchasing the interest rate cap. The payoffs for this strategy follow.

Hedging Cap with Sold Floor (% pa)

Gain (Loss) Under:

Average 3-month Libor	*Purchased Interest Rate Cap @ 9%*	*Sold Interest Rate Floor @ 9%*	*Total*	*Company C Total Interest Rate Cost*
7	(0.24)	(1.87)	(2.11)	9.11
8	(0.24)	(0.87)	(1.11)	9.11
9	(0.24)	0.13	(0.11)	9.11
10	0.76	0.13	0.89	9.11
11	1.76	0.13	1.89	9.11
12	2.76	0.13	2.89	9.11

The alternatives identified are all predicated on the willingness of Company C to switch between fixed and floating-rate borrowings. Each strategy, however, has different risk profiles. For example, if interest rates are expected to continue to increase, the sold-floor alternative would be the preferred method. However, if interest rates are expected to decline, then the sale of the cap, entry into a receive-fixed interest rate swap, or the purchase of the floor, would be the preferred methods for managing the interest rate cap's value.

Satyajit Das is treasurer and John Martin was formerly manager, treasury planning, at TNT Group. The views and opinions expressed are those of the authors and do not reflect those of TNT. The concepts are based on material from a chapter of *The Global Swap Market*, Satyajit Das, ed. (London: IFR Publishing, 1991).

Hedging Foreign Exchange Rate Risk

Most corporate hedging of foreign exchange risk is of "firm commitments"—both the timing and the amount to be hedged are known. A company that contracts to deliver goods overseas on particular delivery dates for a specified amount of foreign currency is just such an example. If this company decides to hedge with options, it could use the strategies described above. There is no "right answer" as to which of these three strategies the company should choose to hedge. Each offers a different level of protection at a different cost.

Illustration 14–1

Constructing a Currency Hedge*

Suppose that a U.S. food products firm contracted to sell DM 19 million worth of goods to a German supermarket chain over the next year. Delivery of the goods and payment in deutsche marks will take place on the 15th of March, June, September, and December.

If the current exchange rate is $0.59 per DM, this firm knows it has roughly $2.8 million worth of receivables coming to it each quarter for the next year. If it does nothing and the mark weakens, then the revenue from the contract, once translated into dollars, may fall enough to make the deal unprofitable.

Consider the following three strategies:

1. The firm can buy at-the-money puts with a strike price of $.59 per DM. This will hedge the firm completely, but is the most expensive hedge.
2. The firm can buy out-of-the-money puts—for example, with a strike price of $.57 per DM. This will cost the company less, but will leave the company exposed to possible losses in the range of a dollar appreciation between $.59 and $.57 per DM.
3. The company could lock in a range over which the currency is allowed to fluctuate, but outside which the firm is fully hedged. For example, the firm could buy a put with a strike price of $.58 and sell a call with a strike price of $.60.†

Each quarter the company receives (DM 19 million)/4—or DM 4.75 million. Because the identical transaction will take place four times on four distinct dates, let's examine how the company might manage the foreign exchange exposure of the first transaction. Subsequent transactions could be hedged identically or by another strategy.

The company could hedge by matching the amount of foreign currency it will receive with the size of the option contract. For instance, if the firm uses the currency option contract traded on the Philadelphia Stock Exchange that delivers into DM 62,500, the hedge would be DM 4.75 million/DM 62,500 = 76 contracts.

Strategy 1 involves purchasing 76 at-the-money put option contracts at the Philadel-

Constructing a Currency Hedge concluded*

phia Stock Exchange with a strike price of \$.59. The cost of this option is, say, \$.0188 per unit of currency, making the total cost of the hedge

$$76 \times .0188 \times 62{,}500 = \$89{,}300.$$

Strategy 2 involves purchasing 76 out-of-the-money puts with a strike price of \$.57. This option might cost roughly .0090 per unit of currency, so the total cost of the hedge would be

$$76 \times .0090 \times 62{,}500 = \$42{,}750.$$

In strategy 3, we buy a somewhat out-of-the-money put with a strike price of \$.58 and sell an out-of-the-money call with a strike price of \$.60. The price of these options would be about .0135 and .0072 per unit of currency, respectively. So, the total cost of the hedge is

Cost of put	$76 \times .0135 \times 62{,}500$	= \$64,125
Less price of call	$76 \times .0072 \times 62{,}500$	= \$34,200
Total cost of hedge		= \$29,925.

*This example was constructed by Gregory Greiff.

†As we will note in Chapter 15, such a structure is called a *range forward.*

Moreover, the company is not limited to just these three strategies. The company can choose any strike price it wants; each strike price offers the company a different level of protection at a different cost.

The company could also choose different combinations of options; for instance, the company could buy an at-the-money put and sell an out-of-the-money put. This would give the firm protection down to a certain level (the level at which the lower strike was sold), but no more, so if the currency went below the lower strike, the company would not be protected against further falls.

Another strategy is for the company to scale down its protection by buying options at different strike prices. For instance, instead of buying all 76 options at one strike price (at-the-money options), the firm could instead buy 19 puts with a strike price of \$.59, 19 puts with a strike price of \$.585, 19 puts with a strike price of \$.58, and 19 puts with a strike price of \$.575. This strategy would give a kind of "intermediate" protection when compared with the strategy of buying all at-the-money options versus all out-of-the-money options. The cost of the hedge would be intermediate too. (Note that the company could sell calls in much the same way in strategy three; this would generate less revenue but more potential for upside gain than the strategy detailed above.)

The great advantage of options is that they allow this type of flexibility, giving the firm the opportunity to choose the level of protection it needs at a cost it is willing to pay.

So far we have confined ourselves to hedging transaction exposures. As we noted in earlier chapters, foreign exchange risk often takes on strategic dimensions, impacting on the firm's ability to compete effectively with overseas rivals. Hence, the firm's risk management policies should be directly related to its sales and marketing policies.

Options give corporations the added flexibility to manage risk in a way that makes it easier to pursue broader strategic considerations.[8]

> Applied Biosystems, a California-based manufacturer of instruments and chemicals for life sciences research, believes that pricing goods in local currency is part of keeping international customers satisfied. Applied Biosystems is rather unusual in that few companies of its size—annual sales totaled just $163.9 million in 1991—deal with management of foreign exchange risk in order to pursue this "dual-currency" pricing strategy. Central is the idea that providing stable, long-term pricing is key to keeping customers in highly competitive markets and to building shareholder value.
>
> Initially, Applied Biosystem's foreign exchange risk management program was designed to protect its balance sheet, using forwards to lock in the dollar value of its receivables. As the company became more concerned about the strengthening dollar, however, it began to use options to hedge, and it began to revise its risk management policies. Risk management moved beyond hedging specific items related to the long-term delivery of product, either to or from the company, to a broader strategy of protecting operating margins. The company uses options to hedge projected sales volume, based on a long history of sales in these countries. The idea is to lock in a floor so that no matter how far the dollar strengthens, the company's operating margin was protected.
>
> To do this, the company first determined its risk tolerance levels—that is, the point above which the dollar's strengthening would be unacceptable. Then the company purchases out-of-the-money options. Applied Biosystems considered anything beyond a 5 percent currency change to be detrimental to its operating margin. Thus, it purchased options that were 5 percent out-of-the-money. Purchasing out-of-the-money options also reduced its premium costs to no more than 0.5 percent of international sales.

Hedging Commodity-Price Risk

The concerns that motivate firms to manage interest rate and foreign exchange rate risk also exist for commodity-price exposures. Energy and metals represent some of the basic inputs to manufacturing and service industries. Uncertainties in the prices of these basic inputs can interfere with management's ability to price and market finished goods. Fluctuations in costs can also lead to undesirable fluctuations in a company's cash flow and profitability over time, which can in turn lead to additional problems, such as higher costs of credit.

Consider a company with a long-term contract to supply a finished product at a fixed price. Rising input costs would cut into the firm's margin. By locking in the cost of its production inputs, the firm is in a better position to protect this margin. If the firm could not lock in its costs in this way, it might be unwilling to enter into a long-term supply relationship. This could prevent the company from capturing profitable business if customers—who are also looking to fix their costs—prefer long-term arrangements to minimize their risks. Even if customers did not have such strong preferences, the willingness to enter into such a contract might prove to be a competitive advantage in competition with other firms.

Tour operators in the UK, who started hedging their exposures to fuel costs, are finding that they can use this situation to their advantage, both in marketing their services and in competing with other firms.[9]

> The negative publicity that resulted when tour operators imposed surcharges to cover unexpected increases in fuel prices (not to mention pressure from UK regulators) led some of Europe's largest airlines and tour operators to begin taking a more active approach to hedging their jet fuel exposure. Thomson, a tour operator and airline owner, offered its customers a no-surcharge guarantee on holidays booked for the next year. Thomson hedged its exposure through a series of jet fuel cap agreements covering its entire fuel requirement.
>
> International Leisure Group and Sitmar, a cruise company, also entered the oil derivatives market through a series of swaps and caps.

Many firms use options to lock in a margin between operating costs and selling prices. Small firms, or those in financial distress, may be required to hedge some or all of their exposures by their banks or other creditors. As you saw in Chapter 4, decreasing the probability of bankruptcy and its incumbent costs increases the value of the firm. Thus, the firm that hedges away such exposures can be expected to have access to capital at lower costs. Even financially healthy firms can benefit in this way by hedging away unnecessary risks.

All of the option strategies available for hedging interest and foreign exchange rate risk apply equally well to hedging commodity-price risk. Firms might simply buy puts or calls or they might use strategies involving combinations of options.[10] The firm might decide to "spread" options—for example, a firm might decide to buy a call option at one strike and then sell the a call at a higher strike, a "call spread." Option spreads have several possible advantages:

1. Spreads allow the company to target a range for protection and to precisely tailor the hedge to the underlying exposure or to the company's expectations for movement in the underlying instrument.
2. Spreads allow the company to target the cost of protection. By selling off the right to profit from gains over favorable ranges of price movement, the company can reduce or eliminate the cost of protecting against unfavorable price movements.

3. Spreads allow the company to match its hedging needs with its outlook on the underlying volatility of the market.

Collars, especially zero-cost collars, are a popular strategy. Firms that use collars are often more concerned with reducing the uncertainty associated with volatility in the markets in which they buy and sell than with positioning themselves to take advantage of windfall gains in the event that market prices move favorably. As with any hedging decision, there is no "right answer" as to whether a firm should collar a risk rather than, say, cap it—that will depend on the firm's hedging objectives, market circumstances, and other considerations. But many firms find that collaring a risk enables the company to achieve other objectives laid out in a business plan.

The following two examples illustrate how firms use options for these kinds of business purposes. A firm can use options to keep on track with the objectives laid out in a business plan.[11]

> Qualex, the nation's largest photofinisher, recovers silver as a by-product of its photofinishing operations; more than 100,000 ounces of 99 percent pure silver are collected each month and sold to refiners at the spot market price. Because receipts from silver sales are credited to the firm's cost of goods sold, the company's gross profit is sensitive to fluctuations in silver prices. Qualex thus believes that fixing the price of silver is important to gain control over its business planning.
>
> Qualex uses commodity collars to set a lower limit on the revenue it will receive for its silver. The company originally intended to buy floors. However, since Qualex requires a floor level close to the prevailing market price (to meet its business plan), the premium for such a near-the-money floor was prohibitive. To reduce this cost, the company sold a ceiling at the same time it bought the floor. This means the firm would have to forgo potential windfall profits if silver prices ran up sharply; but the company's primary interest was in protecting its business plan, not speculating on the price of silver.
>
> Moreover, the collar was custom-tailored to meet the seasonal patterns in Qualex's recovery of silver. Because there are peak periods—after Christmas and the summer vacation season—the number of ounces specified in the collar agreement varies from month to month.

Alternatively, a firm can hedge with options to send a signal to prospective investors that it has costs under control.[12]

> The Paducah & Louisville (P&L) Railroad transports coal, chemicals, and aggregates, including stone and clay, on 300 miles of track in western Kentucky. The railroad uses approximately 500,000 gallons of fuel monthly. When the cost of diesel fuel averages around 50 cents a gallon, as it did prior to the invasion of Kuwait, diesel fuel expense makes up about 10 percent of most railroads' operating expenses. Severe cold weather can double fuel expense, as it did in December 1989, when a sudden cold snap boosted fuel oil prices to more than $1 a gallon.

> In August 1990, when P&L was preparing to talk to the investment community about plans to raise new equity capital through a public offering, it decided to hedge its exposure to oil price volatility. The Iraqi invasion of Kuwait had sent crude oil prices soaring, and the company wanted to assure public investors that it would not be vulnerable to further increases in diesel fuel prices.
>
> The company hedged its exposure by purchasing a cap on 250,000 gallons per month, about half its normal consumption (the rest of the company's exposure is protected by cost-escalation clauses in contracts with customers).[13] Before selecting a commodity cap, P&L considered using a swap or collar. In the end, the company viewed the cap as cheap insurance; in addition, it feared that if it sold a floor or swapped into a fixed price, it might put the company at a competitive disadvantage if fuel costs dropped.

State and local governments face risks with respect to their costs and revenues just as much as corporations. Government entities, however, often have less flexibility to respond when they experience a shortfall in revenues or an increase in costs.

Legislatures are understandably reluctant to pass retroactive tax increases when revenues do not meet budgeted levels. Although some entities may go into deficit spending in such circumstances, many are restricted by constitutional or other legal prohibitions requiring a balanced budget.

Other governmental bodies, such as transit authorities, may not be able to raise fares to make up for unexpected cost increases. These agencies are generally charged with providing a long-term, stable price and have little or no room to adjust fares or prices in the short term.

Faced with risks on both the revenue and cost side and with restricted ability to respond by changing price or reducing output (such as temporarily reducing services, such as schools, police and fire protection, etc.), it would seem that governments and governmental agencies would be quite frequent users of risk management products. It turns out that this is not yet true.

Not unexpectedly, the biggest constraint to government use of hedging tools is also political: it is difficult to communicate to constituents the objectives of even the most conservative hedging programs or to convince them that use of derivatives is not some kind of "gambling." Most private firms report that convincing a board of directors about the importance of a risk management program is an uphill climb. The task of communicating and informing the public at large—the ultimate board of directors in the political arena—is all the more difficult.

Nonetheless, a number of states and other governmental agencies are testing the waters in this area—cognizant of the advantages of improved planning at the budgeting stage that a sound risk management program can help provide. Massachusetts, New Mexico, New York, Ohio, and Oklahoma all have legislation pending that would allow them to manage their risks. Even the federal Department of Energy is considering using derivatives to manage the nation's strategic oil reserves. In addition, many transit authorities, which are large consumers of fuel, are using, or considering using, derivatives to manage their risks. The following example describes Texas's initial foray into using derivatives to manage the risk that revenues from a 4.6 percent severance tax on every barrel of oil produced will not meet budgeted levels because of fluctuations in the price of oil.[14]

> In Texas, a plunge in the price of oil can lead to shortfalls in oil tax revenues, and thus can contribute to unexpected budget deficits and the political crises that accompany them (as it did in 1986–87). Thus, the state has begun to recognize its interests in protecting its income and in stabilizing revenues so as to make the budgeting process less uncertain.
>
> Texas's limited hedging program involves purchasing out-of-the-money puts three months out. The state views this as cheap insurance. The state is also considering OTC alternatives such as swaps and collars.
>
> One option strategy under study in 1992 was a "straddled zero-cost collar." A standard zero-cost collar combines a long out-of-the-money put with a short out-of-the-money call; so, if the price of oil were $22 per barrel, the state could buy a put with a strike price of $20 and sell a call with a strike price of $23.50; the cost of the call would offset the price of the put, and the state would have locked in a range at no out-of-pocket cost.
>
> In a straddled zero-cost collar, the state buys a deep out-of-the-money call on top of the collar to allow it to participate if oil prices undergo a "Texas rally." So, for instance, it could buy a call with a strike price of $25, which would offset the lower $23.50 strike call if prices rise that high. In order to keep the hedge at zero out-of-pocket cost, the state must lower the strike price of the put it buys, say to $19. This would give the state a little less protection on the downside, but it could save it from the political risks if oil prices rise dramatically and the hedge prevents the state from enjoying the benefits.

States that are consumers of energy are also using derivatives to hedge their purchasing costs. States that are exclusively energy consuming, such as Delaware, and municipal transit authorities in Washington, D.C., and Pennsylvania, are already using energy derivatives to manage their budgets. Other states and transit authorities are considering following suit. In many cases, fuel is the single largest purchase made annually. Hedging these costs can aid substantially in the planning process.

Using Options to Reduce Funding Costs

To reduce funding costs a firm might elect to sell rather than buy options. Earlier in this chapter we noted that firms funded with floating-rate debt might buy interest rate caps to protect them from rising rates. Alternatively, a firm funded with floating-rate debt might sell an interest rate floor to reduce its funding costs. The premium it receives "lowers" its funding cost.

Suppose a firm that would normally pay a rate of LIBOR + 50 on three-year debt sells a three-year, 4 percent interest rate floor. Suppose further that the value of the interest rate floor, amortized over three years, is 35 basis points. If LIBOR is 4 percent or above, the firm will pay LIBOR + 50 − 35 = LIBOR + 15; but, if LIBOR drops below 4 percent, the firm will pay a flat 4.15 percent.[15] If LIBOR rises, the coupon the firm must pay will rise. However, the firm will receive the benefit of a declining LIBOR only to the floor rate; below the floor rate, the firm will not benefit from a further lowering of rates.

As we describe in detail in Chapter 16, corporations can reduce their funding costs by issuing "hybrid debt." One example of hybrid debt is a debt package that contains an option. The most familar of this kind of structure is a bond with an equity warrant. This debt instrument can be thought of as containing two components: (1) a standard debt instrument and (2) a call option on the value of the equity of the firm. Purchasers of the debt compensate the firm for this attached option by paying a higher price for the package—which reduces the coupon on the debt. We have also seen options on assets other than the firm's equity attached to a bond. Indexed bonds, as this debt is sometimes called, have been issued that contain options on many different underlying assets; commodities (such as gold) and international stock market indices (for example, the S&P 500 index).

Further, firms sell "embedded options" to reduce their funding costs. Although "embedded options" have all the features of "standard" options, they are not separate instruments but are part and parcel of the larger contract. In many cases the option embedded in the contract has the same, or similar, payoff characteristics as other options traded on an exchange or over-the-counter. When this is the case, the holder of the option can sell the liquid exchange or OTC counterpart to generate revenue or reduce funding costs.

Many everyday business transactions contain embedded options. The right to opt out of a contract—for example, the right to prepay a mortgage—is just such an embedded option.

Callable corporate debt is another example of an contract that contains an embedded option. From the issuing firm's perspective, callable fixed-rate debt can be thought of as two things combined into one contract: (1) standard fixed-rate debt and (2) an out-of-the-money interest rate option. The callable debt gives the issuer the right to purchase the debt at a fixed price at a specified time in the future (and so, it has the same payoff profile as a put option on interest rates). If interest rates decline after the debt is issued, the firm can buy back the debt at a fixed price once the call waiting period has elapsed. This serves as the firm's hedge against a decline in interest rates after it issues debt. There is some evidence that, in the past, investors undervalued the embedded interest rate option. Some firms took advantage of this underpricing by selling a put on interest rates after issuing the bond. Amortizing the premium for the put option sold by the issuing firm resulted in below-market fixed-rate debt.[16]

Using Options as a Competitive Tool

When a firm makes an overseas bid, it is confronted with both a high degree of uncertainty about success and, most likely, a need to establish costs and revenues in local currency. The following example shows how a defense firm turned this problem into a competitive advantage by purchasing a cleverly designed over-the-counter option:[17]

> A U.S. defense manufacturer was submitting a bid to sell scientific equipment to a Scandinavian firm. A complicating factor was that payment was to be made in unequal disbursements at six irregularly spaced dates over two years.
>
> The principal competition was a French firm. The U.S. company was confident that it had the superior technology and lower cost. But it was concerned about presenting a bid denominated only in U.S. dollars, since the French firm's bid was in Norwegian kroner.
>
> The manufacturer turned to its bank, which provided a multiple option facility. This facility permitted the Scandinavian customer to choose to pay in U.S. dollars, deutsche marks, French francs, Finnish markka, or Norwegian kroner. The deal was structured so that the customer could choose its preferred currency of payment on each successive payment date.
>
> In essence, what the bank sold to the U.S. company was a two-year American-style call option on the dollar, with puts against each of the four nondollar currencies. The strike prices for the options were set at the spot levels of June 1990, when the deal was struck.[18] These strike levels give the Scandinavian customer a ceiling on the amount of foreign currency it will have to pay at any time, while guaranteeing that the U.S. firm will always receive the full dollar price.
>
> > The first payment was for the amount of $2.5 million.
> >
> > Suppose that the dollar had weakened so that spot rates on the payment date were below the strike prices for the nondollar currencies and that the customer decided to make the first payment in deutsche marks, at a prevailing market rate of DM 1.5/dollar. The customer pays 3.75 million deutsche marks to the U.S. company, which, in turn, sells the Deutsche marks in the spot market and pockets the $2.5 million. In this case the U.S. company does not need to exercise its put.
> >
> > Suppose instead that the dollar had strengthened to, say, 2.0 marks per dollar. At the spot rate, the customer would pay DM 5 million to cover its obligation. But with the option in place, it pays only the ceiling amount of DM 4.25 million. The U.S. company, in turn, exercises its put at the strike price of DM 1.7 to get the full $2.5 million.
>
> The strike levels thus represent the worst-case scenarios for the customer. Over the life of the contract, the customer knows it will never be required to pay more than a specific maximum amount in any particular currency. Thus, this gives the customer the ability to directly compare these worst-case scenarios with the terms of any other competing offers denominated in the same foreign currency.
>
> The total cost to the U.S. customer for this customized option was about $400,000; it was passed on to the customer in the total purchase price.[19]

By offering its customer five different currencies in which to pay, the U.S. firm gave the customer the opportunity to reduce its costs by paying a lower price if one of the five currencies depreciated relative to the Norwegian kroner. Although this option may not have itself sealed the deal, it may have provided an edge over the French firm competing for the same contract with a deal that allowed payment in only one currency.

The versatility of options permits corporations to create or market products more finely attuned to the needs of particular buyers. Burns & McBride, a small, family owned heating oil distributor in Wilmington, Delaware, recognized the interests and concerns of customers and responded through the use of options.[20]

> In 1990, Burns & McBride offered their customers protection from unexpected increases in heating oil prices during the winter months. The firm offered a guaranteed price, in effect, selling a call option on heating oil prices to their customers. The firm protects itself by hedging 60 percent of its fuel requirements with the heating oil futures (New York Mercantile Exchange). The firm buys over-the-counter call options to protect itself on the remaining 40 percent of its requirements. Out-of-the-money put options are also used to allow the firm to benefit from any sharp price drops.
>
> When they offered this price protection, Burns & McBride experienced a substantial increase in its customer base—even though the option premiums add several cents per gallon to the price charged to customers.

In this case Burns & McBride offered its customers something they probably could not get on their own—few residential customers buy enough heating oil to justify purchasing their own hedge. Burns & McBride was able to bring a kind of efficiency of scale by aggregating the collective hedging needs of many residential consumers.

More common are examples of financial firms using options to segment and target their customer base. Banks and insurance companies are familiar with options and so are able to design attractive products with embedded options.

One of the most widely cited such product was the S&P indexed CD first introduced by the Chase Manhattan Bank in 1987. This FDIC-insured CD guaranteed the depositor the better of a fixed interest rate or a rate indexed to the performance of the S&P 500 index. Decomposed, this product is simply a standard CD plus a call option on the S&P 500 index. However, the package provided depositors with a lower-cost access than was available otherwise.

Banks and insurance company have made use of options to craft financial products designed to appeal to different customer bases. These products could not be offered unless there were an underlying derivatives market in which the company could manage its risk. But with the strategic use of options to help tailor the company's menu of investment choices, customers are given a wider variety of products from which to choose. This extends the range of prospective customers to the firm and enables the firm to serve the needs of existing customers more fully.

Notes

1. Options on debt instruments can be based on different conventions: on *bond prices* or on the *interest rates* implied by the bond prices. A call on interest rates is the same thing as a put on bond prices. Thus, a cap could also be defined as a put on the price of the debt instrument. To avoid confusion, we will use the convention of discussing options on interest rates.
2. Adapted from "Falcon Cable Foils Risk," *Corporate Risk Management*, November 1990.
3. This discussion is adapted from "Hedging Seasonal Borrowing," *Corporate Risk Management*, September 1989.
4. This example is adapted from work by Robert Mackay, director, Center for Study of Futures and Options Market, Virginia Tech. The transaction was described in *United States Banker*, August 1992.
5. "How Muzak Stays in Tune with Interest Rates," *Corporate Cashflow*, March 1990.
6. "Applied Power Hedges a Strategic Acquisition," *Corporate Cashflow*, August 1991.
7. "Hartmarx Buttons Down an Interest Rate Collar," *Corporate Cashflow*, November 1990.
8. "Biosystems Is Ready for the Dollar's Rebound," *Corporate Finance*, September 1992.
9. "Chocks Away for New Market in Oil Hedging," *Corporate Finance*, November, 1988.
10. Some of these strategies, including the use of straddles and strangles, will be discussed in Chapter 15.
11. "Qualex Protects Its Silver Lining," *Corporate Cashflow*, September 1990.
12. "The P&L Railroad Keeps Its Fuel Costs on Track," *Corporate Cashflow*, March 1991.
13. The company faces some basis risk on the hedge because the reference price on the cap is tied to the price of heating oil rather than diesel fuel.
14. "Texas Parries," *Risk*, September 1992.
15. The 4 percent floor plus the 15-basis-point spread.
16. We will return to this topic in Chapter 15 when we discuss swaptions.
17. "Corporate Risk Management's 'Done Deals,' " *Corporate Risk Management*, January 1991.
18. The strike prices were 1.7 deutsche marks, 5.7 French francs, 6.5 Finnish markka, and 4.0 Norwegian kroner.
19. The currency that contributed the most to the price of the facility was the Norwegian kroner. On a larger deal, the thin market in kroner options and the high volatility of the currency would make inclusion prohibitively expensive. But this deal was small enough that the company wanted to include the kroner to increase the flexibility of the structure.
20. "Burns & McBride Hedges a White Christmas," *Corporate Risk Management*, December 1990.

CHAPTER

15 ENGINEERING "NEW" RISK MANAGEMENT PRODUCTS*

In the five years since the first edition of this book was published, "financial engineering" has come into the vocabulary of the corporate treasurer. Banks and the other dealers of financial derivatives have engineered a dazzling array of new tools for hedging financial risks. To the casual observer of the markets for financial derivatives, it often seems that the dealers are constantly developing *new* instruments. Indeed, one of the largest worries of the regulators in the early 1990s was that dealers were inventing "exotic" new products that no one knew how to manage.

However, many of the new instruments are not really new. Indeed, the best definition we have heard of a "new" product is one that creates a risk for the dealer to manage that previously did not exist.[1] In Chapter 18, when we describe how a dealer actually manages the market risks inherent in a portfolio of derivatives, we will talk about managing delta risk, gamma risk, vega risk, yield curve twist risk, and all the rest. If a "new" product is simply a different "package" of these same risks, it is not really new.

If a dealer creates new products by combining or restructuring existing instruments, the warehouse may have more or less of a particular kind of risk, but the process doesn't create new kinds of risk. So, while these products may well fit the needs of the end users better, these new products are really not all that new.

And, when a dealer creates futures on pollution rights or copper swaps or options on the debt of less-developed countries, there are new risks to be managed. But these are risks with which the dealer is familiar—the dealer already knows

*This chapter was originally drafted by Eileen Smith, director of product development, Chicago Board Options Exchange and Deborah Whang, director, financial markets and trading programs, Illinois Institute of Technology.

about managing warehouses that contain futures on agricultural and industrial products or swaps on oil or options on U.S. Treasury bonds and options on equity.

There are, however, some new instruments that do create risks that previously did not exist. The ones we will describe in this chapter are "multifactor" swaps and options that produce *correlation risk.*[2] Once the multifactor instruments—"rainbow options," "diff swaps," "quanto options," and "basket options"—are added to the portfolio, the dealer must now not only manage delta, gamma, vega, yield curve twist, and the rest for each of the individual factors but must now manage the *risk that correlations between the various factors will change.*

Combining Building Blocks to Produce "New" Instruments

In Chapter 2, we introduced our "building-block" theme, identifying forwards, futures, swaps, and options as the risk management building blocks. In subsequent chapters, we have shown how the individual risk management building blocks can be used. One way—in many respects the simplest way—that new risk management products are engineered is by combining two or more of the building blocks to construct a customized product.

Combining Forwards with Swaps

Combining a forward and a swap into a single instrument—specifically, offering a forward contract on a swap—results in an instrument normally referred to as a *forward* or *delayed-start swap.* (See Figure 15–1.)

Although the swap payments do not begin until the specified future date, the forward swap is identical to a regular swap once the start date is reached. A forward swap is often used by a treasurer who expects to issue floating-rate debt in the future and wants to lock in existing rates. For example, if XYZ Corporation intends to issue floating-rate notes in nine months but wants to lock in today's fixed rate, it can enter into a nine-month forward swap with the notional principal and maturity of the swap set equal to that of the expected debt offering. In nine months, the payments on the swap will begin: XYZ will pay a fixed rate, which was known at origination of the forward swap, and will receive cash flows based on LIBOR (which XYZ will in turn use to make the payments on the floating-rate debt).

Combining Options with Forwards

The forward-swap combination eliminates the potential for unfavorable outcomes but also eliminates potential favorable outcomes. The combination of options with forward contracts allows managers to hedge against potential unfavorable situations while participating in gains if rates move in the user's favor.

FIGURE 15–1 Creating a Forward Swap

Creating a Forward Swap.

Pay fixed, receive floating for periods 1 through T

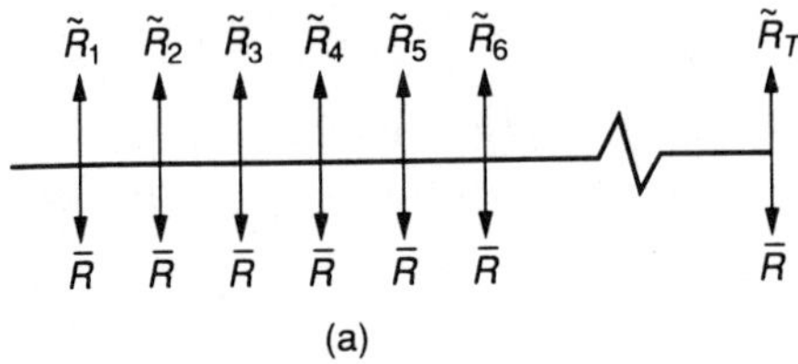

(a)

Plus Pay floating, receive fixed for periods 1 through 4

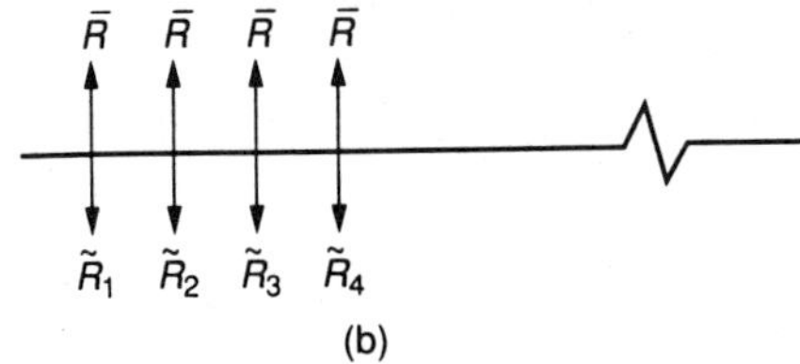

(b)

Equals A four-period forward contract on a pay fixed, receive floating swap

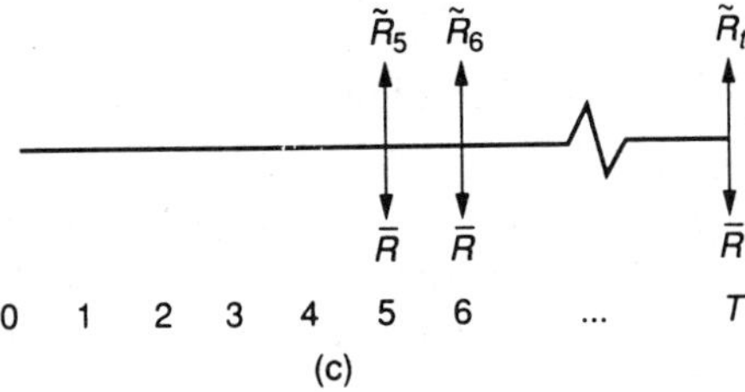

(c)

Forward-option combinations are normally referred to as types of forwards—*break, range,* and *participating forwards*. While not limited to FX, these constructions have been more common in the foreign exchange markets.

In Figure 15–2, we have illustrated a situation in which the contract rate of a standard sterling forward contract is \$1.50. Alternatively, the risk manager can buy a break forward contract that is constructed with a contract rate of \$1.55 and that permits the holder to break—unwind—the forward contract at a price of \$1.50.

Note that the payoff of this modified forward is equivalent to a long call on sterling—the right to buy sterling at a price of \$1.50. If the dollar value of sterling rises, at expiration the manager will earn the then prevailing spot price minus \$1.55. On

FIGURE 15–2 Break Forward

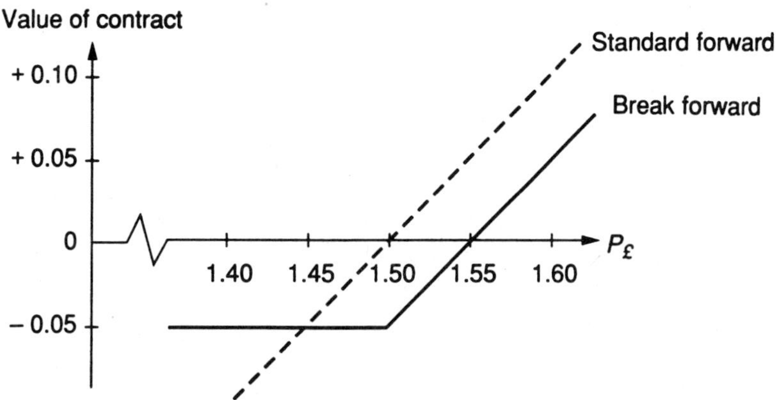

the other hand, if the value of sterling declines, the holder of the break forward will unwind the contract at $1.50. The $0.05 difference in the contract rates for the standard forward contract versus the break forward represents the implicit premium paid for the option structure.

Aside

Why Break Forwards?

At this point, many of you ought to be wondering why break forwards ever appeared. After all, a break forward is simply an option with a different way of expressing the premium. The reason lies in the accounting treatment of the two building blocks. Under FASB Statement No. 52, forward foreign exchange contracts would be eligible for hedge accounting treatment—gains or losses in the forward could be deferred until the hedged transaction was recognized. However, options that were sold would have to be marked-to-market. In the late 1980s and early 1990s, break forwards (and other "complex forwards") were accounted for as forwards rather than as options. This practice was discontinued in March 1992 when the staff of the Securities and Exchange Commission objected to this practice.

FIGURE 15–3 Range Forward

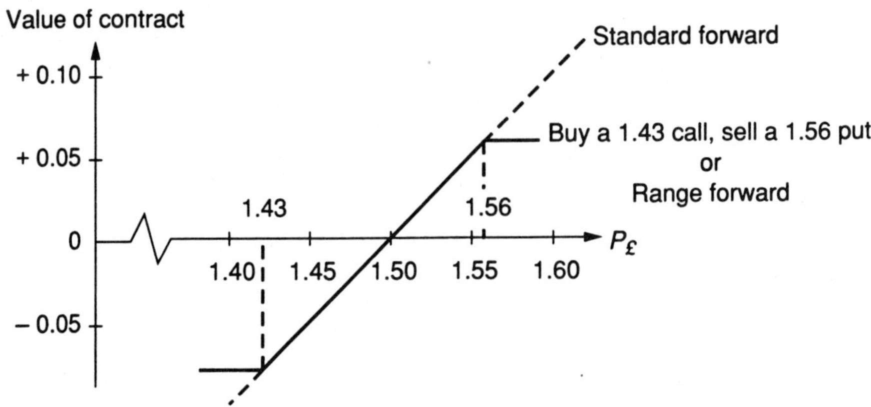

A range forward takes the forward and option combination one step further, adding a second option position. As we saw in Chapter 14, a common option strategy involves the sale of a put in order to fund the call option premium. Figure 15–3 provides an example of a range forward: The standard forward contract has a contract rate of $1.50. In Figure 15–3, the premium for a put option on sterling with an exercise price of $1.56 is equal to the premium for a call with an exercise price of $1.43. A range forward contract would allow the holder of the contract to purchase sterling at $1.50 at maturity while allowing him to unwind the contract if sterling falls below $1.43. But, it also allows the seller of the range forward the right to unwind the contract if sterling rises beyond $1.56.[3] In this range forward, the implicit premium for the right to unwind the forward contract is covered by the short put position so that the risk manager has eliminated the out-of-pocket cost for the option construction.[4]

With the break forward, the option premium is reflected in an "off-market" contract rate for the forward contract; the range forward reduces—or eliminates—the premium by having the holder of the complex forward position sell an option to finance the one he wants to purchase. A *participating forward* (or *participation*) eliminates the up-front premium in a different manner.

As is illustrated in panel (a) of Figure 15–4, buying an out-of-the-money call can provide a floor on the financial price risk. The cost of the "insurance" is the option premium. In the range forward, the option premium for the purchased call would be offset by the option premium for selling an out-of-the-money put. However, the risk manager need not sell an out-of-the-money put. Another alternative is to sell a put at the same strike as the desired call. This put would be in-the-money; and, as panel (b) of Figure 15–4 illustrates, the premium for this in-the-money put

FIGURE 15–4 Participating Forward

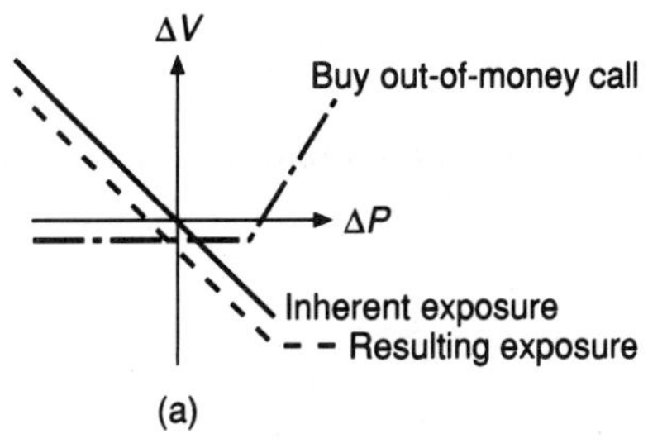

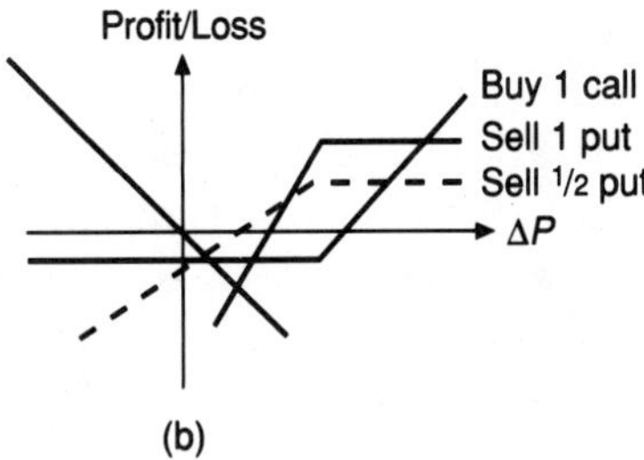

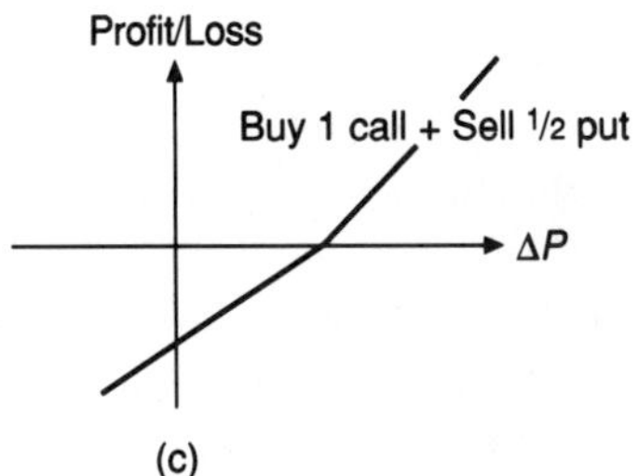

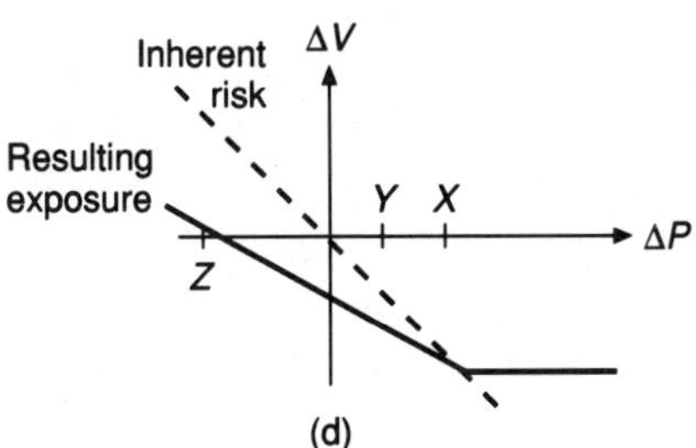

would exceed the premium for the out-of-the-money call. So, instead of selling a put with the same notional value as the call, the risk manager would only have to sell a fraction of the put to finance the cost of the call. In panel (b) of Figure 15–4 we illustrate a situation in which the risk manager would have to sell in-the-money puts for only 1/2 of the notional principal of the forward. Panel (c) of Figure 15–4 illustrates the complete construction: No up-front premium is paid—the contract rate for the participating forward is the same as that for a standard forward. As panel D illustrates, the protection is paid for only if the final asset price is below the strike price *X*. As the final asset price declines, the cost of the protection increases. The provider of the floor is paid with a portion of the potential profits—the seller of this structure "participates" in upside gains.

Combining Options with Swaps

Cancelable swaps—also referred to as *collapsible swaps*—embed an interest rate option in the swap contract.[5] The firm enters into a swap but has the right to cancel the transaction. For example, the treasurer, if receiving LIBOR in the swap, would like to cancel the swap if interest rates decline; a cancelable swap gives the treasurer that right—that option. The treasurer pays for the option to cancel by paying a fixed rate on the swap that is higher than prevailing fixed rates.

In a cancelable swap, changes in interest rates trigger a change in the *nature* of interest payments or receipts; for example, if the interest rate falls, the treasurer has the right to switch from paying a fixed-rate coupon to paying a floating-rate coupon. In an *indexed-principal swap* (*IPS*), changes in interest rates trigger a change in the *level* of the underlying notional principal on which interest-rate-determined flows are paid or received.

For example, in an indexed-principal swap, the fixed-rate payer has the right—the option—to amortize the notional principal of the swap if interest rates fall. This is implemented by having the notional principal of the swap tied to the future movement of an interest rate—usually LIBOR. The notional principal will decline according to a preestablished schedule if rates decline.[6] To pay for the embedded interest rate option in an indexed-principal swap, the fixed-rate paid is higher than the rate for a standard swap.

Indexed-principal swaps could be used to express a view on the future path of interest rates; for example, if I expect a period of low rate volatility, I might enter into an indexed-principal swap as a fixed-rate receiver, locking in a higher-than-market fixed rate. However, the principal advantage of an indexed-principal swap is that it exhibits positive convexity.[7] Such an instrument can be used to mitigate the negative convexity exhibited by many mortgage-backed securities, that is, pools of mortgages characterized by high prepayment when interest rates decline.

Combining Options with Other Options

In the same way we can create new payoff profiles by combining options with forwards and swaps, we can create still more new payoff profiles by combining options with other options. One big difference is that option combinations generally have more colorful names—-like straddles, strangles, butterflies—than do the combinations of options with forwards and swaps. Figure 15–5 illustrates some of these combinations.

Straddles and strangles are option strategies that allow the buyer of the combination to make money when the price of the underlying asset moves—regardless of whether the price increases or decreases. Hence, in these strategies, the buyer of

FIGURE 15–5 Combinations of Options

Buying a call...

and buying a put at the same exercise price...

results in buying a *straddle*

V X P

V X P

V X P

(a) Straddle

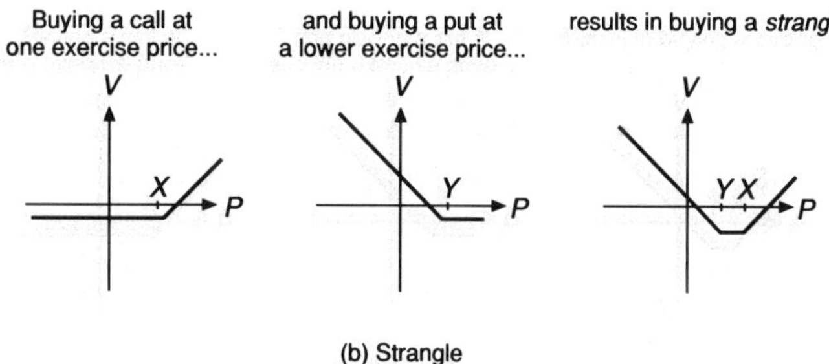
Buying a call at
one exercise price...
and buying a put at
a lower exercise price...
results in buying a *strangle*
V
X
P
V
Y
P
V
YX
P

(b) Strangle

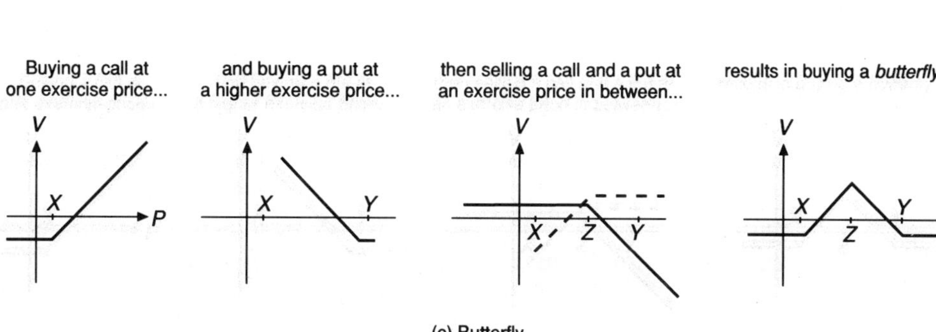
Buying a call at
one exercise price...
and buying a put at
a higher exercise price...
then selling a call and a put at
an exercise price in between...
results in buying a *butterfly*
V
X
P
V
X
Y
V
X
Z
Y
V
X
Y
Z

(c) Butterfly

the combination is in essence "buying volatility" and the seller of the combination is "selling volatility."

A long straddle position is created by buying a call and a put with the same strike price (as well as the same time to expiration). If the stock price increases, the call ends in-the-money; if the stock price decreases, the put ends in-the-money. This strategy can be quite expensive because the buyer must pay premiums for the two options; but, if the underlying financial price is volatile enough, the call or the put will finish in-the-money by enough to offset the cost of the two options. Panel (a) of Figure 15–5 shows the payout of a long straddle.

A strangle is similar to the straddle, but the call and the put are both purchased out-of-the-money. In comparison to the straddle, this substantially reduces the cost of the strategy, but the holder can lose both premiums if the underlying closes between the two strikes; the break-even price move for a strangle is higher than that for the straddle. Panel (b) of Figure 15–5 shows the payout of the long strangle.

Straddles and strangles involve combinations of two options; a butterfly involves the combination of four options. Panel (c) of Figure 15–5 shows the payoff of the long butterfly constructed by buying a call with a strike at *X*, buying a put with a strike of *Y*, and selling both a call and a put at strike *Z*. However, there are three other ways that this butterfly could be constructed:

1. Buy a call at strike *X*, sell two calls at strike *Z*, and buy a call at strike *Y*.
2. Buy a put at strike *X*, sell two puts at strike *Z*, and buy a put at strike *Y*.
3. Buy a put at strike *X*, sell a put and a call at strike *Z*, and buy a call at strike *Y*.

In contrast to straddles and strangles, which pay off when the underlying financial price changes, butterflies are used when the underlying asset is expected to stay within a certain range.

And this list by no means exhausts the possibilities of option combinations—or the colorful names for these combinations. For example, in the same way that a straddle can change into a strangle by moving the strike prices apart, a butterfly can change into a "condor."

Restructuring Building Blocks to Produce "New" Instruments

Instead of creating "new" instruments via the combination of standard building blocks, we have also seen "new" instruments created by *restructuring* the standard building blocks. In some instances, it is difficult to differentiate between combinations and restructurings.

> Should a participating forward be viewed as a combination of options or a restructured forward?

And, while some of this restructuring has dealt with swaps—notably "delayed-reset" swaps—most of the focus of the restructuring has been on options.

Restructured Swaps

As we saw in Chapter 10, in a standard swap, the floating-rate payment made at one settlement is determined by the floating rate that was in effect when the last settlement was made. A *delayed-reset swap*—also referred to as an *in-arrears* or *back-end-set swap*—restructures the cash flows such that the floating-rate payment is determined by the floating rate in effect at the settlement date.

Figure 15–6 illustrates the cash flow differences between the standard and delayed-reset structures for a swap where the floating rate is six-month LIBOR. For the standard swap, the floating-rate payment at the first settlement date—month 6—is determined by six-month LIBOR at origination; the payment at the second settlement date—month 12—is determined by six-month LIBOR at month 6, and so on. The delayed-reset swap advances the date for computing the floating-rate cash flows by six months. The first payment, made at month 6, is determined by the six-month LIBOR rate in effect at month 6; the second floating-rate payment, made at month 12, is determined by the six-month LIBOR rate in effect at month 12.[8]

FIGURE 15–6 A Restructured Swap

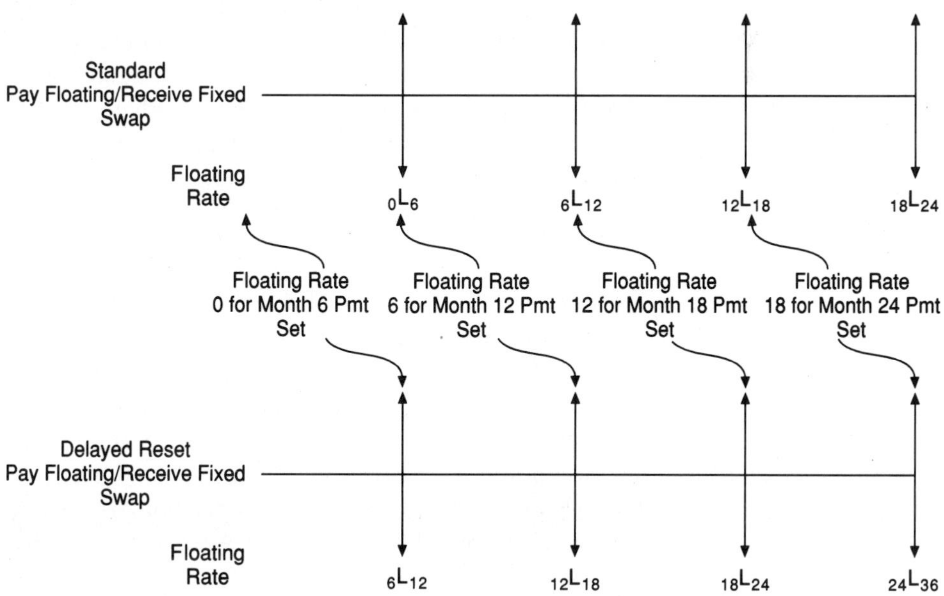

With a standard swap both parties know the amount of the floating-rate payment six months in advance. With the delayed-reset swap neither party knows for certain what the floating rate payment will be until the payment is due.

In Chapter 10 we showed you how the forward rates determine the fixed rate in a standard swap. The fixed rate in a delayed-reset swap is determined in the same way; but the relevant forward rates are one period further out for a delayed-reset swap. Hence, the difference between the fixed rate in a standard swap and a delayed-reset swap is as a result of the difference in the forward rates.

If the yield curve is upward sloping, the fixed rate for a delayed-reset swap is higher than that for a standard swap—because the forward rates used to price the delayed-reset swap will be higher. And, the more steeply upward sloping the yield curve is, the higher the fixed rate in a delayed-reset swap relative to that in a standard swap. Consequently, when the yield curve is steeply upward sloping, pay-floating/receive-fixed delayed-reset swaps are particularly attractive because the fixed rate is so high.

However, there is no "free lunch" here. The counterparties who enter into these trades are implicitly taking a view that the future spot rates will be lower than the rates implied by the forward yield curve.

Options on Forwards, Futures, Swaps, or Other Options

Options on Futures. In our description of the evolution of the risk management products in Chapter 1, we noted that options on futures contracts on financial prices first appeared in the early 1980s. Options on futures trade on most of the major futures exchanges in the world and are available on a wide range of financial prices—commodity prices, foreign exchange rates, and interest rates.

Given the relations we have established between futures and forwards and futures and swaps, you probably suspect that the introduction of options on forwards and options on swaps would have followed close on the heels of the options on futures. However, options on forwards—in particular, options on forward rate agreements—and options on swaps—referred to as swaptions—appeared only at the end of the 1980s.

Options on Swaps: Swaptions. The holder of a swaption has the right to enter into an interest rate swap in the future.[9] Swaptions can be "European style," meaning that the holder of the swaption can enter into the swap only on a specified date (the expiration date of the swaption); or they can be "American style," meaning that the holder of the swaption can enter into the swap at any time prior to the expiration date of the swaption. Instead of using the jargon of puts and calls, the swaption market refers to *payer swaptions,* which give the holders the right to enter into a swap in which they will pay the fixed rate, and *receiver swaptions,* which give the right to enter into a swap to receive the fixed rate.

Illustration 15–1

A Delayed LIBOR Reset Swap

In Chapter 10 we considered a one-year interest-rate swap between Galactic Industries and the Dead Solid Perfect Bank when the spot LIBOR yield curve is as follows:

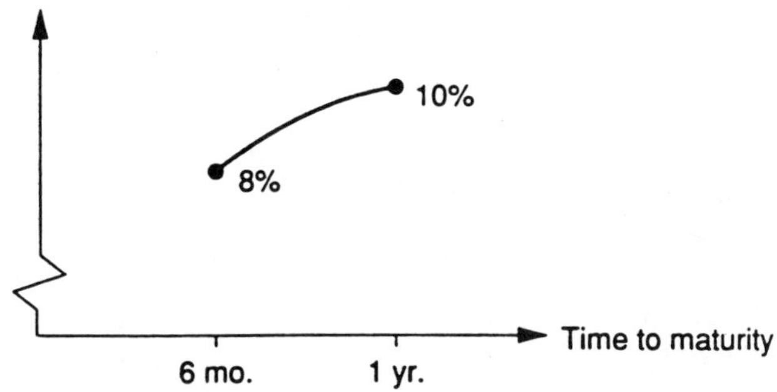

We saw in Chapter 10, that for a standard (plain vanilla) swap, the fixed rate Galactic would receive was 9.70%. Let's change our swap between Galactic Industries and the Dead Solid Perfect Bank to a delayed LIBOR reset swap. With this structure, at origination, the rate DSPB *expects* to receive at month 6 is not the six-month spot rate at origination, 8 percent, but is instead the forward rate—the six-month rate in six months—11.5 percent. Hence:

$$\tilde{R}_1 = \$100\,(1/2)0.115 = \$5.75.$$

Likewise, in an in-arrears swap the rate DSPB expects to receive at month 6 is not the six-month rate in six months but the six-month rate in *12 months*. Let's suppose this forward rate is 13 percent and

$$\tilde{R}_2 = \$100\,(1/2)0.13 = \$6.50.$$

DSPB's expected outflows are as illustrated below.

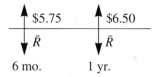

6 mo.	1 yr.
↑ \$5.75	↑ \$6.50
↓ $\bar{R}$	↓ $\bar{R}$

To determine the appropriate fixed rate for DSPB to pay, we know that the expected net present value of the swap at origination must be zero, so

$$\frac{5.75 - \bar{R}}{1 + \frac{1}{2}(0.08)} + \frac{6.50 - \bar{R}}{1.10} = 0$$

Solving the preceding equation, $\bar{R} = \$6.11$. Hence in the case of this off-market swap, the appropriate fixed rate for Galactic to receive is 12.22 percent, not the par rate of 9.70 percent.

The buyer of a "payer swaption" holds the functional equivalent of a call option on interest rates—the buyer will exercise the right to enter into a pay-fixed swap if the floating rate rises. Conversely, the buyer of a "receiver swaption" holds the equivalent of a put option on interest rates—the buyer benefits from a drop in interest rates by exercising into a receive-fixed swap if the floating rate declines.

For swaptions, corporate hedgers may opt for physical settlement: The parties actually enter into the swap agreement upon exercise. However, in order to minimize the credit risk associated with a swaption, the market is increasingly moving toward cash settlement: At exercise, the underlying swap is marked-to-market and the value is conveyed to the owner of the swaption in cash.

Most swaptions permit the buyer of the swaption to specify the settlement dates for the underlying swap when the swaption is exercised rather than upon origination of the swaption. Therefore, to avoid nonstandard coupon exchange dates, these swaptions tend to be European-style.[10]

As illustrated in Table 15–1, since introduction in the late 1980s, the swaption market has grown dramatically—even faster than the market for the underlying interest rate swaps. While the U.S.-dollar-based contracts still account for the majority of deals outstanding, swaptions in other currencies, particularly the deutsche mark, are rapidly outstripping the volume in U.S. dollar-denominated swaptions.[11]

The swaption market got a "kick start" early on when many firms realized that swaptions could be used to "monetize" the value of the interest rate option embedded in the call provision of bonds issued in the U.S. capital market. A case in point is Ford Motor Credit Corporation.[12]

> Ford Motor Credit Corporation issued 10-year fixed-rate notes callable after five years. Since FMCC had the option to call the notes, they had a put option on interest rates. The firm then entered into a standard "pay-floating/receive-fixed" interest rate swap, turning the fixed-rate liability into a floating-rate liability. However, at the same time, FMCC also sold through its underwriter the right to terminate the swap after five years; that is, FMCC sold a swaption. In effect, the buyer of the swaption purchased the right to pay floating and receive the fixed rate specified today for years 5 through 10. Clearly, this right is valuable (would be exercised) only if rates fall; that is, the buyer of this swaption has bought the put option on interest rates that Ford Motor Credit

TABLE 15–1 Swaptions Outstanding (Notational Principal in Billions of U.S. Dollars)

	1989	*1990*	*1991*	*1992*
U.S. dollars	51	63	57	31
Other currencies	21	31	52	96
Total	72	94	109	127

SOURCE: International Swaps and Derivatives Association, Inc.

owned as a result of the call provision on its notes. According to *Investment Dealers' Digest*, this structure "was rumored to have cut Ford's borrowing costs by roughly 20 basis points." Put another way, the put option on interest rates sold by Ford had a value equivalent to 20 basis points on the $250 million borrowing.

Deals like the preceding worked because the swaption market valued the embedded interest rate options higher than the bond investor. Issuers could lower financing costs by "selling the call" to the swaption dealer, earning an up-front premium. If interest rates rise, the swaption expires worthless and the issuer need not call the bonds—the issuer continues to pay the fixed rate obtained at issue. However, if interest rates fall sufficiently, the purchaser of the swaption will exercise: The purchaser of the swaption will elect to receive the fixed rate and pay the now lower floating rate for the maturity of the swap contract. This will likely require the issuer to call the bonds, but the benefit of the lower interest rate goes to the purchaser of the swaption rather than the issuer.[13]

For this "monetizing calls" strategy to work, the swaption dealer must place a higher value on the interest rate options than do the purchasers of the callable bonds (the sellers of the interest rate options to the bond issuer). The available evidence suggests that the difference between these values narrowed dramatically during the early 1990s. As you would expect, access to this market increased the efficiency of the pricing and reduced the impetus for corporations to sell swaptions.

Instead, corporations are increasingly purchasing swaptions as components of their interest rate risk management. Long swaption positions can be employed to hedge an anticipated or uncertain exposure. For example, a corporation bidding on a project may want to take advantage of current low financing rates without being locked into a long-term swap if the transaction is not executed. A long payer swaption position enables the corporation the opportunity to pay the fixed and receive the floating rates if interest rate rise prior to expiration.

Note however that instead of the swaption, an interest rate cap could be used to hedge a potential future liability.

Risk Management in Practice

Protective Strategies: Part 2

Satyajit Das and John Martin

In Chapter 14, we considered the situation in which an increase in interest rates resulted in an unrealized gain to the purchaser of an interest rate cap and exam-

Protective Strategies: Part 2 continued

ined how the treasurer could use interest rate options to preserve the unrealized gain. We now look at a similar example to see how swaptions might be used to preserve the value in a swap.

Company A has on its books an interest rate swap that had been booked six months earlier to convert part of the company's floating-rate borrowings into a fixed-rate liability. Under this $100 million swap, Company A was paying a fixed rate of 9 percent (semiannual) and receives six-month LIBOR. The initial maturity of the swap was five years.

Six months earlier, when the swap was originated, six-month U.S. dollar LIBOR was 8 percent. Since then, U.S. dollar interest rates had risen rapidly across the maturity spectrum, taking six-month LIBOR to 13 percent and the 4.5-year swap rate to 11 percent.

As a result of the increase in interest rates, the existing swap position had an unrealized gain (in present value terms) of approximately $7 million.*

As long as Company A (1) is willing and has the capacity to convert part of its portfolio from fixed to floating rate† and (2) is willing to manage actively the fixed/floating mix of the portfolio within preestablished risk/reward parameters to minimize interest costs, the treasurer of Company A could choose to manage its position to preserve its unrealized gain. Several strategies are available:

Swap Cancelation

The treasurer of Company A could choose to reverse or cancel the existing swap. This would generate an up-front gain equivalent to $7 million, which is equivalent to 2 percent a year over the remaining 4.5 years of the transaction. The reversal of the swap would have had the following impact on Company A's position:

1. Company A's interest cost would immediately rise to the level of current six-month LIBOR—13 percent (an increase of 4 percent from the existing fixed level). *The up-front gain (together with interest earnings thereon), provides a degree of protection against the immediate rise in interest cost—a "cushion" equivalent to 2 percent a year over the remaining life of the transaction.*
2. As a result of unwinding its swap, Company A would have no protection against interest rate increases above current market levels or an inversion of the yield curve. *Company A would still benefit if six-month LIBOR averages less than 11 percent a year over the next 4.5 years.*

Protective Strategies: Part 2 continued

Cap/Floor Swaption Strategies

Paying fixed and receiving floating rates under an interest rate swap can be characterized as buying a cap and simultaneously selling a floor with a strike price equivalent to the fixed rate under the swap**—in this case, 9 percent.

Using this construct, the treasurer of Company A can manage the existing position by entering into a series of interest rate option transactions—writing caps, buying floors or writing caps and buying floors (selling collars)—or can use a swaption. These strategies provide protection of the value derived from the original swap against unfavorable interest rate movements—via purchased options—or provide additional income—through the sale of options.

Purchased Options

1. The treasurer of Company A can purchase a six-month swaption that would permit Company A to elect to receive the fixed rate (at 11 percent) against payment of six-month LIBOR. The swaption affords protection from a decline in swap rates over the six-month period. If swap rates decline, then the value of the swaption increases, offsetting the loss of value in the underlying swap position.

2. The treasurer of Company A can purchase floors whereby the company would benefit if six-month LIBOR fell below the strike level (say 11 percent over the term of the floor). Using this strategy, in return for the payment of an up-front premium, Company A repurchases the sold floor component of the swap. The purchase allows A to switch back to floating-rate funding if six-month LIBOR falls below the strike yield level.

Assume the current market rates are as follows:

Swaption	*Interest Rate Floor*
Type: Purchase of option on swap (swaption) to receive fixed rate and pay floating rate under an interest rate swap	*Type:* Interest rate floor agreement (call options)
Strike rate: 11% a year (semiannually)	*Floating-rate index:* 6-month LIBOR
Floating-rate index: 6-month LIBOR	*Strike level:* 11% a year
Option expiry: 6 months	*Term:* 4.5 years
Premium: 0.87% (flat)	*Settlement:* 6-monthly in arrears against spot 6-month LIBOR
	Premium: 2% (flat)

The swaption allows Company A to reverse its swap in six months if swap rates decline. Exercise of the swaption will reverse the original swap for an

Protective Strategies: Part 2 continued

up-front gain of $5.5 million. This gain is lower than an immediate cancelation of the swap because the present value of interest flows has declined with the elapse of six months and the $870,000 swaption premium. For this strategy to be preferred, the decline in swap rates has to occur during the term of the swaption.

The floor also protects Company A from an interest rate decline. However, the payoff profile differs from that under the swaption. Under the floor, A receives a net payment if six-month LIBOR falls below 11 percent over the remaining term of the swap (4.5 years). Company A continues to pay fixed rates under the swap and maintains its protection against interest rate increases. The cost of the floor increases the effective swap rate by 0.58 percent a year (the amortized premium of the floor) to 9.58 percent.

The use of floors and swaptions to manage the existing swap position entails an element of yield curve risk. The yield curve could twist—swap rates might fall back to 9 percent while LIBOR does not fall below 12 percent (the strike level of the floor). In this case, the swap gain is extinguished but is *not* offset by a gain on the floor transaction.

On the other hand, while a swap reversal through the exercise of the swaption exposes Company A to future increases in interest rates, the combination of the swap and floor affords protection from an upward move in interest rates but allows it to benefit from a fall in short-term rates.

In essence, the combined position is a type of "cross-yield-curve" cap. Put-call parity suggests that a bought call (the floor) and a "short" underlying position (the swap) gives us a bought put (an interest rate cap). It is a "cross-yield-curve" cap because Company A is protected from an upward movement in interest rates (both swap rates and LIBOR) but only benefits from falling rates if LIBOR declines.

The effectiveness of realizing the gain in this way depends on the shape of the yield curve. The maximum gain is achieved if short-term rates fall further than swap rates (that is, the yield curve moves to a positive shape). A lesser gain is realized on the swap reversal if swap rates decline by more than LIBOR (that is, the yield curve becomes more inverted).

Another interesting aspect of the strategy of using a floor is that it can be purchased over a shorter period, say one year, effectively buying back the call option component of the original swap for only part of the remaining term.

Sold Options

Instead of purchasing options to manage its existing swap position, the treasurer of Company A could sell options (interest rate caps or swaptions). The

Protective Strategies: Part 2 continued

sale of options has a radically different risk profile, as it leaves the company exposed to any upward movement in interest rates and provides a small benefit from a fall in rates.

Assume the following market rates:

Swaption	*Interest Rate Cap*
Type: Sale of option on swap (swaption) to receive fixed rate and pay floating rate under an interest rate swap *Strike rate:* 11% a year (semiannually) *Floating-rate index:* 6-month LIBOR *Option expiry:* 6 months *Premium:* 0.6% (flat)	*Type:* Interest rate cap agreement (put options) *Floating-rate index:* 6-month LIBOR *Strike level:* 11% a year *Term:* 4.5 years *Settlement:* 6 monthly in arrears against spot 6-month LIBOR *Premium:* 1.5% (flat)

1. The treasurer can sell the swaption. The company will receive premium equivalent to 0.6 percent, which is equivalent to 0.17 percent a year and subsidizes A's borrowing costs.

If swap rates continue to increase, the swaption will be exercised. Exercise of the swaption will result in cancelation of the swap, realizing a gain of $6.3 million ($6.9 million inclusive of the swaption premium). However, there is an opportunity loss, as Company A could have closed down the swap at a higher effective gain. In addition, on cancelation of the swap, Company A would have no further protection from increases in interest rates as it has effectively reverted to a floating-rate borrowing.

If swap rates decline, the swaption will not be exercised. However, the fall in swap rates will erode value in the existing swap position, which will only be partially offset by the premium received.

2. The treasurer could "securitize" the fixed-rate component of the swap through the sale of the cap. This strategy would have the following impact:

Company A receives premium equivalent to 1.5 percent of the contract value at the start of the transaction. This is equivalent to an annualized amount of 0.43 percent, which has the effect of subsidizing A's borrowing costs. If six-month LIBOR rates fall, the cap is not exercised. The premium received lowers the effective fixed rate under the swap, but there is an opportunity loss to Company A if rates average less than 8.57 percent a year for the remainder of the life of the swap transaction. If rates rise above the strike level, 11 percent a year, the cap is exercised and Company A must make payments to the cap purchaser that effectively transform its borrowing into a

Protective Strategies: Part 2 continued

floating-rate liability at a rate equivalent to six-month LIBOR less 0.43 percent a year (the amortized premium). Consequently, A has no protection against increases in six-month LIBOR rates if these average more than 11.43 percent a year for the next 4.5 years.

The sale-of-options strategy seeks to exploit the potential for further gains within the swap instead of "locking in" the existing gain resulting from market interest rate movements to date.

The sale of these interest rate options effectively prevents the company from benefiting from any further rises in interest rates. The company forgoes its protection in return for the receipt of a premium.

In these cases, Company A's maximum benefit is realized if interest rates remain at or about current levels for the term of the option, as it continues to receive the interest cost saving generated by the original swap and to benefit from the premium received from the sale of options.

Comparison of Alternatives

Each of the alternatives available to manage an existing swap position implies an inherently different risk/reward profile. The choice between alternatives is complex. The following graph sets out a comparison of the various strategies outlined under different interest rate scenarios.

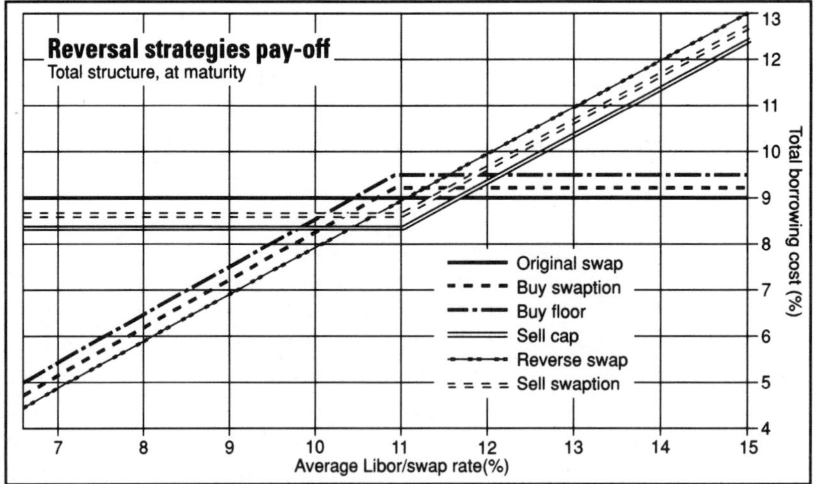

Protective Strategies: Part 2 continued

The choice between alternatives is driven substantially by the treasurer's expectation of future interest rate movements, including the expected shape of the yield curve:

1. If interest rates are expected to decline across the yield curve, the maximum benefit is realized by reversing the existing interest rate swap today.
2. If, however, the interest rate decline is expected to take some time, an alternative may be to reverse part of the swap by entering into a forward swap to reverse, say, the last two or three years of the existing five-year swap. This would leave A protected for the first two to three years but would convert it into a floating-rate borrower for future periods when interest rates are expected to be lower.
3. If interest rates are expected to decline but there is considerable uncertainty as to the timing or degree of the decline, then the purchase of the floor or swaption are the preferred alternatives. The selection between the floor and swaption will be dictated by expectations of the future shape of the yield curve.
4. If rates are expected to increase, no action needs to be taken, although a floor or swaption may be purchased to protect against the failure of these expectations to be realized.
5. If rates are expected to remain relatively static at or around current levels, the sale of caps/swaptions is the economically superior alternative.

The alternatives for managing the interest rate swap portfolio considered above relate to a situation where an increase in interest rates creates an unrealized gain in the existing swap portfolio. Similar management techniques are applicable when, because of a fall in interest rates, the existing swap position shows an opportunity loss.[§]

---

*The gain on the swap results from the fact that Company A can enter into a swap whereby it receives 11 percent a year (the current swap rate), thereby locking in a margin of 2 percent relative to the existing swap, where it pays 9 percent a year; the floating-rate (six-month LIBOR) legs under the swap would offset. Typically, the original swap would be canceled or "bought out" with the counterparty making a payment to A representing the present-valued equivalent of the margin of 2 percent a year.

[†]This presumes that Company A's portfolio is large enough for a change from fixed to floating of $100 million to have no significant strategic impact on its compet-

Protective Strategies: Part 2 concluded

itive position, and that its assets and revenue flows are sensitive to and correlated with interest rate movements.

**See the discussion of *put-call parity* in Chapter 12.

§Satyajit, Das, "Swap Strategies in the New Climate," *Corporate Finance,* August 1989, pp. 12–13.

Satyajit Das is treasurer and John Martin was formerly manager, treasury planning, at TNT Group. The views and opinions expressed are those of the authors and do not reflect those of TNT. The concepts in this article are based on material from a chapter from *The Global Swap Market*, Satyajit Das, ed. (London: IFR Publishing, 1991).

As Das and Martin illustrate, the choice between interest rate caps/floors and swaptions depends on the users' expectations about future interest rates. In order to have equivalent terms, the cap would be structured as a series of calls that cover the life of the swaption plus the life of the underlying swap. The cap offers multiple settlement dates and thus multiple opportunities to gain from favorable rate movements. Therefore, the premium on a swaption is less than that of a comparable cap; this provides greater leverage and requires less capital tied up in the hedge during the period of uncertainty.[14]

Options on Options: Compound Options. An option that gives its purchaser the right to buy a specified option at some time in the future for a premium that is specified today is one member of the family of compound options we introduced in Chapter 13. In Chapter 13, we concentrated on the pricing difficulties encountered by the dealer—the price of an option on an option depends not only on the volatility of the underlying asset but also on the volatility of the value of an option. Here we will concentrate on the user's perspective, noting that options on options can make sense to an end user because it is cheaper to purchase an option on an option than to purchase the option itself.

The first time we encountered applications of compound options was in the foreign exchange markets—options on foreign exchange options. An engineering or construction firm that was bidding on a project in a foreign country faced a dilemma. If it won the contract, it would have a foreign exchange exposure that it would want to cover—and the cost of that cover needed to be included in the bid. However, knowing that it might not be awarded the contract, the firm did not want to be locked into a forward contract nor did it want to pay a large premium for an option it might not need. The option on an option worked for this firm. If it won the contract, the firm would exercise its right to purchase an option—at a price specified at the time it made its bid. If it lost the contract, the "insurance premium" was as small as possible.

In addition to foreign exchange, compound options have been used in both the interest rate and equity markets. Indeed, to date, the widest acceptance of compound options may well be in the interest rate markets: options on caps and floors, or captions and floortions.[15]

A caption gives its holder the right to buy a specified cap at a specific price on (or, if the caption is American-style) before a given date. The captions contract specifies not only the cap rate and the maturity for the underlying cap but also the premium that will be paid for the cap if the caption is exercised—the strike price for the caption—and the time to expiration for the caption.[16]

For example, consider a two-year cap that currently has a premium of 100 basis points. An at-the-money, six-month caption—an option to purchase the cap in six months for 100 basis points—could currently be purchased for 10 basis points. If, at the caption's expiration, the cap has a value of 125 basis points, the holder of the caption exercised the option to buy the cap for 100 basis points. A caption will increase the current premium of the cap—the total cost to the buyer is 110 basis points (the premium for the underlying cap plus the cost of the caption); however, it will lock in the ability to hedge at a later date.

Path-Dependent Options

The terminal value of a standard European-style option depends only on the spot price of the underlying asset *at expiration of the option—it only matters where the price is at expiration; it doesn't matter how the price got there*. In contrast, the value of a path-dependent option depends on the path that the price of the underlying asset follows during the life of the option. The family of path-dependent options includes a number of members—options on averages, barrier options, and contingent premium options.

Options on Averages. Several members of the path-dependent option family use average prices over some period of the option's lifetime rather than spot prices at expiration in determining the final payoff.

The most widely observed of this type is the average rate option—also known as an Asian option.[17] For an average rate option, the payoff at expiration is based on the difference between the strike and the average spot rates observed over some designated period during the contract's life:

$$\text{Average rate call payoff} = \max\,[S_{AVG} - X, 0],$$

where S_{AVG} is the average spot price. The number and timing of spot price observations is determined in advance and may start at the beginning or near the end of the life of the option. Observations may also be weighted in favor of prices observed on designated dates. Because the volatility of an average price is always less than the volatility of the price series that makes up the average, the premium for an average rate option is below that of the corresponding standard option.

Aside

Prices: Average Rate versus Standard Options

When we tell them that average rate options are cheaper than standard options, the reaction is predictable: "How much?"

And, it should come as no surprise that our response is equally predictable: "It depends."

Specifically, the relation between the prices of standard and average rate options depends on the relation between the exercise price and the forward price and that between the volatility of the spot prices and the volatility of the average price.

However, to give you some idea about the relation between these prices, we have included a pricing example Maria Nordone prepared during the summer of 1993.*

Beginning in June 1993, Company USA has a nine-month contract to import goods from a UK firm. Since Company USA has to pay for the goods at the end of each month in UK pounds, it is worried that the dollar will weaken. Company USA decided to use an out-of-the-money call option strategy to protect against a strengthening of the pound; but it needs to decide whether to use a strip of European-style calls or an average rate call.

In June, the U.S. dollar price of the pound was \$1.55. Following is a comparison of the two structures. Both have an exercise price of \$1.70 per pound, and all of the premiums are expressed as percent of the U.S. dollar amount of the option.

Strip of European Style Calls			**Average Rate Call**
Month	*Premium*		
June	0.01%	Total cost 0.48%	0.27%
July	0.08		
August	0.20		
September	0.34		
October	0.46		
November	0.60		
December	0.74		
January	0.87		
February	0.99		

In this example, the cost of the average rate option approached 50 percent of the cost of the individual options.

*Maria Nordone is with Goldman Sachs. Previously, she was a vice president of the Chase Manhattan Bank, responsible for marketing FX options. This example originally appeared in the July 1993 issue of *Financial Risk Management,* a newsletter published by the Risk Management Research Center of the Chase Manhattan Bank.

Average rate options are becoming more widely used in the currency markets. The exposure of many multinational corporations is more likely to be an exposure to foreign exchange rates over some period—over a quarter, over the next six months, over a year—rather than an exposure to a foreign exchange rate on some specific date in the future. Hence, an option on the average exchange rate over the period is more appropriate than is a standard foreign exchange rate option.

Average rate options are the norm in the commodity markets. The following example shows how Phelps Dodge, the world's second-largest copper producer, used "average cost" options to hedge the price of its principal product, copper cathode.[18]

> Phelps Dodge used options where the average spot price was defined as the 1991 annual average price. At a time when the spot price of copper was near $1.30 per pound, Phelps Dodge bought puts on 258 million pounds of copper cathode (about 25 percent of its expected 1991 mine production) at a strike price of $1 a pound and simultaneously sold calls on 86 million pounds at a strike price of $1.23 per pound to help finance the put purchase.[19]
>
> Phelps Dodge purchased out-of-the-money puts and sold in-the-money calls. By using in-the-money calls, the company was able to finance more out-of-money puts than it would have been able to using a more traditional out-of-money call in the collar. The company choose this combination because it was bullish on copper prices and so did not want to lock itself out of the opportunity to gain if copper prices rallied.[20]
>
> One third of the resulting hedge was a collar (a result of the combination of the long put and short call); the other two thirds was straightforward put protection. The total cost of this hedge was less than 10 percent of the margin on the firm's copper sales. Phelps Dodge's cost of copper at the time the hedge was implemented was about 60¢ per pound. In the worst-case scenario of a selling price of $1 per pound, the firm's margin is 40¢; thus, the hedging strategy cost only about 4¢ per pound.

Average strike options are also available but are somewhat less common. In the average *rate* option, the spot price is the average of observed spot prices, and the strike price is set at origination. For the average *strike* option, the spot price is the observed spot price at maturity, and the strike price is the average of observed spot prices over a specified period. For example, the payoff at expiration for an average strike call option is as follows:

$$\text{Average strike call payoff} = \max\,[S - X_{\text{AVG}}, 0],$$

where the exercise price of the option, X_{AVG}, is the average price of the underlying asset. For the average *rate* option, the payoff depends on the relation between an average of prices for the underlying and a strike rate specified at origination. For the average *strike* option, the payoff depends on the relation between the average of the underlying financial price and the spot price at expiration.

Another path-dependent option based on average prices is the cumulative option. Perhaps the most widely used of this type is the cumulative interest rate cap.[21] The cumulative interest rate cap pays off if interest rates have moved over the year in such a way that the firm's annual interest expense exceeds the specified cap level—that is, if the average of the interest rates observed at the rollover dates for the firm's underlying financing exceeds some specified rate. This allows a treasurer to hedge interest rate expense against short-term changes in interest rates over a year.

Barrier Options. In addition to the strike price and the maturity, the user of a barrier option also specifies a "trigger price." Depending on the type of barrier option being used, when the spot price of the underlying asset hits this "trigger price," the option will either appear (be "knocked in") or disappear (be "knocked out").

Knockout options are the most common type of barrier option. If the trigger price is above the spot price at origination, the option would be an "up-and-out." If the trigger price is below the spot price at origination, the option would be a "down-and-out."

The payoff of a knockout is the same as a standard option unless the underlying price touches the trigger price. If, however, the underlying price touches the trigger price, the option disappears. Because there could exist situations in which the option would disappear, the premium of the knockout option is generally less than that of the standard option because of the chance of early expiration. Therefore, the knockout option can be written upon high-volatility underlying instruments for which the standard option premium would be prohibitively high.

Consider a call option on the Nikkei 225 stock price index. In the early 1990s, a fund manager might have found the premium on a standard six-month call on the Nikkei 225 to have been prohibitively expensive—the volatility was in excess of 30 percent. However, if the fund manager is relatively confident that the market is not ready for a market correction in the near term, she could purchase a six-month down-and-out call with a trigger set at 10 percent below the current at-the-money strike price.

Figure 15–7 illustrates possible outcomes based on alternative paths for the index over the six-month life of the option. If the index remains above the trigger price, the fund manager's returns on the knockout will exceed those for purchasing a standard call by the amount of the premium "savings." However, if the index dips below the trigger, even temporarily, the option disappears. After hitting the trigger, if the index subsequently rises, the fund manager will forgo all future profits because the knockout option would no longer exist. The closer the trigger is set to the prevailing price, the greater the cost savings relative to the standard option but also the less likely that the instrument will survive the daily price fluctuations.

Up-and-out puts have been used by multinational corporations to reduce the cost of hedging a foreign exchange exposure. This strategy works only as long as

FIGURE 15–7 Payout of a Down-and-Out Call

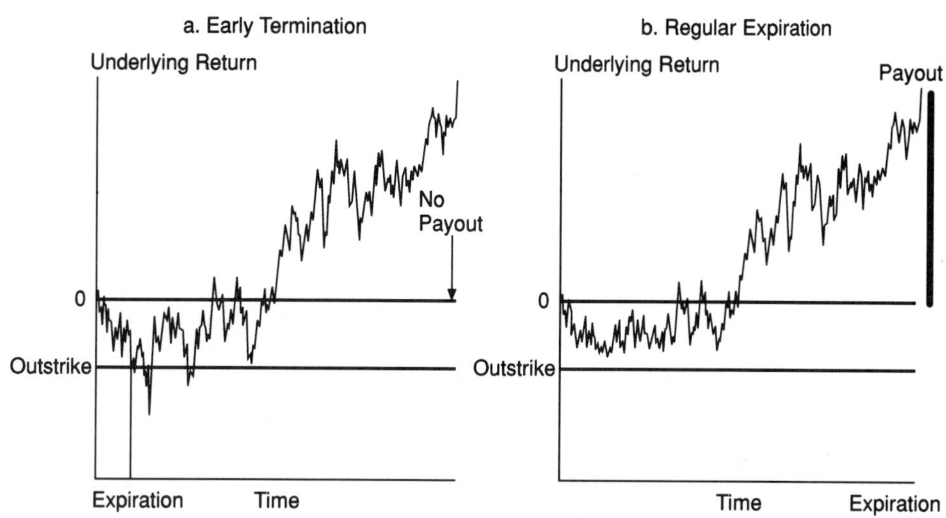

the management of the firm is willing to forgo the hedge if the underlying value moves sufficiently in the firm's favor.

The lower costs of down-and-out calls and up-and-out puts may be viewed as the premium reduction that reflects the potential for the protection to disappear. The reduced cost of other forms of barrier options might better be viewed as reflecting the limited profit potential. Up-and-out calls and down-and-out puts are automatically exercised when the underlying financial price reaches the trigger price—when the options are sufficiently in-the-money.[22]

Knock-in options are the form of the barrier option in which the option appears only when the trigger price is reached. Up-and-in calls and down-and-in puts are activated when the trigger is reached, producing a standard contract.

For instance, the down-and-in S&P 500 put can be constructed to activate if the index falls by 10 percent over the contract life. Its holder enjoys portfolio protection if declines go beyond the trigger level, but not until that point.

Roll-up puts and roll-down calls are cousins of the knock out options. These are contracts that become barrier options if the underlying financial price moves through a certain price, termed the roll-up (-down) strike. In the case of the roll-up put, if and when the roll-up strike is breached, the standard put becomes an up-and-out put with the roll-up strike serving as the new, more favorable strike price. The roll-up put affords the manager a higher level of protection unless the trigger is reached, causing it to expire. This type of product may be used for hedging stocks or fixed-income portfolios when the manager anticipates a moderate short-term rise in value and wants to lock in or reset the put to incorporate the new market conditions. The price for a roll-up (-down) option is typically close to that for the corresponding standard options with the same original strike.

Lookback Options. The lookback option is a path-dependent option that allows the holder to exercise the option against the most favorable price of the underlying asset that has occurred during the contract's life. For example, if I hold a lookback call option on an equity index, the value of my call at expiration would be the difference between the strike price specified at origination and the highest price the equity index reached during the lifetime of the contract.

$$\text{Lookback call payoff} = \max\,[S_{HIGH} - X, 0]$$

The lookback option can be used for any of the financial prices, but so far it has been applied primarily to foreign exchange, in addition to equities.

The holder of the lookback option has all the rights associated with an American-style option—plus one. In an American-style option, I have the right to early exercise on any day prior to option expiration; in a lookback option, I get to look at all of the data before I make my decision. Thus, the value of the lookback option at expiration will be greater than or equal to that of the American-style option; so, it will have a higher premium at the outset.[23] The higher the underlying volatility, the more valuable the lookback feature and hence the greater the difference in premium between the lookback and the standard contract.

A variation of the lookback is the more general reset option, such as the ladder or step-lock option, which provides either specific thresholds or set times for reevaluation of the strike price applicable upon exercise. Sparked by recent volatility, these structures are becoming increasingly common in the European equity and currency markets.

Contingent Premium Option. The final form of path-dependent option we will examine is the contingent premium option—sometimes referred to simply as a contingent option. In a contingent option, the premium is set at contract origination but is paid only if the contract expires in-the-money. If the option is out-of-the-money at expiration, the seller receives nothing. And, since there will be cases in which the option seller receives no premium, the contingent premium is substantially higher than that of a standard option.[24]

Figure 15–8 provides a comparison of the at-expiration payoff for at-the-money options, one a contingent premium option and the other a standard option. At expiration, if the price of the underlying asset has declined, the purchaser of the contingent premium option pays nothing. If, however, the price of the underlying asset has remained constant or increased, the contingent premium option is automatically exercised, and the holder receives the difference between the spot and

FIGURE 15–8 Payoff of a Contingent Premium and Standard Call Option

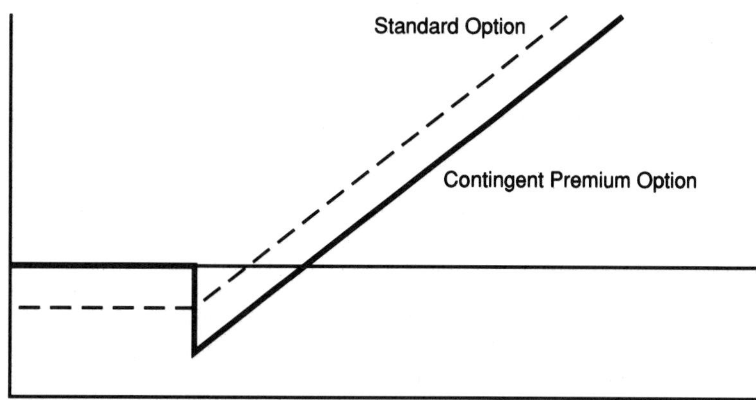

strike prices, less the larger premium amount. Obviously, it takes a much larger movement in the index to recover the contingent premium, but the benefit is that no up-front premium is paid.

The trade press suggests that contingent premium options have been used in the equity, foreign exchange, and interest rate markets as a form of "disaster insurance" in periods of high volatility. For example, the uncertainty about the cross-rates in the ERM during the early 1990s induced some fund managers who desired protection against massive devaluations to use contingent premium puts to provide "disaster insurance" with no premium outlay if the unfavorable movement failed to materialize.[25]

Binary Options

Once the strike price is reached, the payoff for a standard option rises continuously with the price of the underlying. In contrast, the payoff for a binary option is discontinuous. As illustrated in Figure 15–9, a binary option pays a *fixed* amount if the strike price is reached. The payoff amount of a binary option is a predetermined fixed amount that is not related to the amount by which the underlying financial price is above or below the strike.

Like standard options, binary options can be either calls or puts. A binary call option would pay a predetermined amount if the underlying financial price closed above a certain level, while a binary put would pay off a predetermined amount if the underlying closed below a certain level. For example, a binary call option on the value of XYZ shares with a payoff of $5 and a strike price of $80 would pay $5 if XYZ closed above $80 at expiration. If the price of XYZ shares was below $80 at expiration, the holder would receive nothing.

FIGURE 15–9 A Binary Option

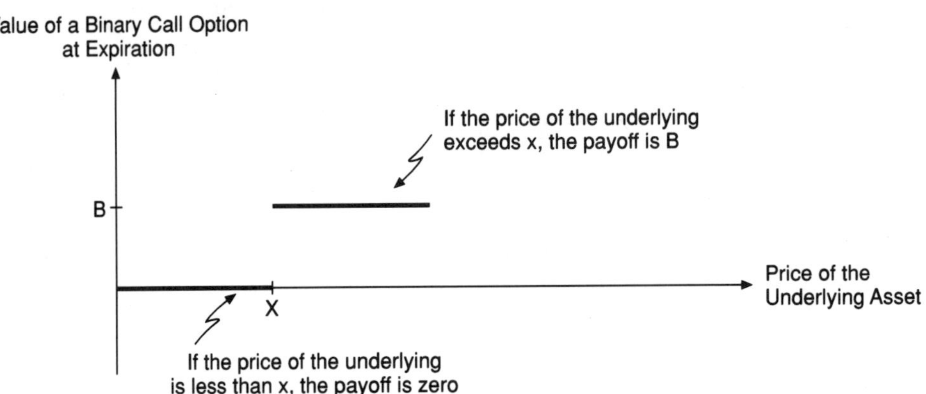

So far we have described binary options that resemble standard European-style options: "All-or-nothing options" pay off if the price of the underlying is above (for a call) or below (for a put) the strike price *at expiration*. However, binary options can be path-dependent: "One-touch options" pay off if the price of the underlying reaches a specified trigger price at any time during the life of the option.

The price of a binary option depends on two factors: (1) the likelihood that the underlying will touch (in the case of a one-touch option) or close above or below (in the case of an all-or-nothing option) a certain price and (2) the present value of the payoff amount.

Binary options are often used in conjunction with other instruments to create structured products. Indeed, the contingent premium option discussed earlier is constructed as the sum of a long standard option and a short binary option with the same strike.

Another example of a structured product created using a binary option is the semifixed swap. As illustrated in Figure 15–10, a semifixed interest rate swap has two fixed rates—one below and the other above the current market swap rate. The trigger that will determine which rate applies could be the current interest rate.

> In May 1993, three-month LIBOR was 3.25 percent and the three-year swap rate was 4.65 percent. Suppose that a treasurer believes that three-month LIBOR will stay below 6.0 percent for the next three years.
>
> By acting on that view, the treasurer can save 50 basis points on the swap rate via a semifixed swap structured so that the firm will pay
>
> 7.15% if 3-month LIBOR is above 6 percent
>
> 4.15% as long as 3-month LIBOR remains at or below 6 percent.

FIGURE 15–10 Semi-Fixed Swap

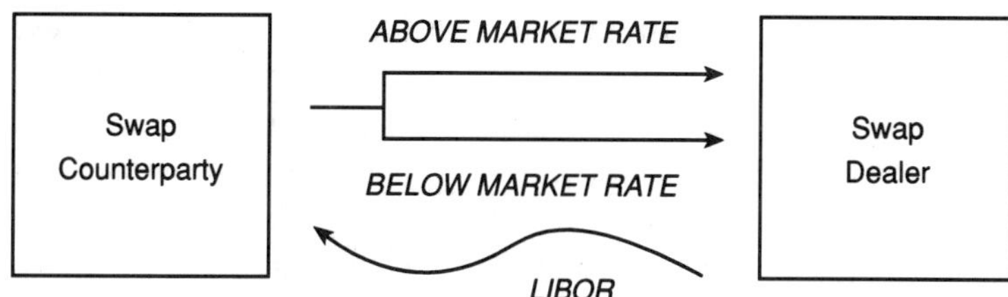

> And, these rates are entirely adjustable. The treasurer might want to save more than 50 basis points—the lower rate to be below 4.15 percent. To obtain this larger saving from the prevailing swap rate, she would have to agree to either a higher upper rate (higher than 7.15 percent) or a lower exercise price for the binary option (lower than 6 percent).

The trigger for the semifixed swap need not be an interest rate; it could as easily be another financial price. Indeed, a firm that relies heavily on oil or oil products as inputs might wish to enter into a semifixed swap with oil prices as the trigger: If the price of oil is high, the oil-user pays a below-market interest rate; if the price of oil is low, the oil-user pays an above-market interest rate.

Bermuda Options

A European-style option can be exercised only at maturity. An American-style option can be exercised on any date on or prior to maturity of the option. A quick look at a globe implies that a Bermuda option must lie somewhere between the two—and this is precisely the case. A *Bermuda option*—also referred to as a *mid-Atlantic, quasi-American*, or *limited exercise option*—can be exercised only at specific dates on or prior to expiration of the option.

Bermuda options are often found embedded in callable or puttable corporate bonds. For example, a corporation may issue a five-year callable bond with a refunding provision. This issue can be called at any coupon date (limited exercise dates) and replaced with a new issue at a lower rate.

Not surprisingly, the price of a Bermuda option also lies between the prices of American and European options. Since the American option may be exercised at any time, it is more expensive than the Bermuda option. Similarly, the Bermuda option is more expensive than the European option, since it can be exercised more frequently than the European option.

Applying the Building Blocks to New Underlying Markets to Produce "New" Instruments

In some instances, financial engineering has led to the development of new products that are nothing more than the standard building blocks applied to new underlying markets. Today, derivative exchanges are in a frenzy to develop standardized contracts based on previously untapped underlying markets. Further, dealers are anxious to write or buy derivatives on any underlying index or security that will solve customers' risk management problems. This section explores these new derivative markets, both on and off the exchange floors.

Exchange-Traded Products

Recently several new exchange-traded futures and options products have been listed (or proposed) that represent the use of existing building blocks for new underlying markets. These include the Chicago Board of Trade's proposed clean-air futures, insurance futures, and the Chicago Mercantile Exhange's options and futures on the Goldman Sachs Commodity Index.

The 1990 Clean Air Act requires utilities to reduce sulfur dioxide (SO_2) emissions. To that end, the Environmental Protection Agency (EPA) began a program that allots a certain number of credits to each utility. If a utility requires more or less than its allotment, the credits may be traded. The CBT is proposing to trade futures on these credits to allow users to hedge the future costs of acquiring additional credits.

The CBT currently offers three catastrophe insurance futures and futures options products based on national as well as eastern and midwest property/casualty insurance claims. Each contract represents the ratio of quarterly catastrophe losses to earned premiums. The eastern essentially monitors hurricanes, while the midwestern contract focuses on tornadoes.

The catastrophe contracts are geared both toward insurance companies wishing to hedge the risk of a catastrophe and speculators willing to bet that a catastrophe will occur. The CBT began trading the eastern and national contracts in 1992; the midwestern contract began in May 1993. In the first seven months of 1993 options and futures on the three contracts traded a total of only about 8,500 contracts.

The Chicago Mercantile Exchange listed options and futures on the Goldman Sachs Commodity Index in mid-1992. These products allow trading in a liquid group of nonfinancial commodities with a single trade. The GSCI is a market-value-weighted index that represents the sum of each commodity's U.S. dollar value of world production. The index includes grains and oilseeds, livestock, metals, energy, and food and fiber. The underlying futures contracts for each of these commodities is used to determine the dollar value of world production. This index is unique because it is the first derivative product based on an index of futures prices. In the first seven months of 1993 the GSCI futures and options traded approximately 90,000 contracts.

New OTC Swaps and Options

The OTC market has also witnessed a movement toward the application of existing derivative structures to new underlying markets. One important recent development has been the over-the-counter market for commodity derivatives such as swaps, caps, and floors on commodities ranging from orange juice to natural gas. Listed commodities futures and futures options offer physical settlement, standardized terms, and generally liquid and transparent markets. In contrast, the OTC products have expanded the number of tools available for hedging risk by offering longer maturities, greater position size, cash settlement, and overall better customized payoffs.

Volatilities in the natural gas[26] and soft commodity markets, such as orange juice, coffee, cotton, and wheat, have created interest in hedging price risk using the OTC swap market. To date, maturities have usually been limited to less than five years. These deals are primarily driven by the producers in the energy market and users in the soft commodities markets. Where a natural two-sided market does not appear, the dealer lays off risk in the listed markets if sufficient liquidity is available. While it is difficult to measure the impact of the OTC market on the listed market, exchange volume provides some indication—for example, the volume of natural gas futures traded on NYMEX more than tripled in 1991, in large part because of the growth of the OTC business.

LDC Debt Derivatives. Derivatives on the debt of less-developed countries (in Latin America, Eastern Europe, and Asia) are beginning to appear. While forwards are traded, the most common are options on the debt—for example, a put option on a Venezuelan Brady bond. While the underlying cash market remains small relative to other, more established markets, high volatility in the prices of these securities has stimulated demand for hedging by the purchasers of the underlying debt,[27] as well as some speculative activity. The market downturn in late 1991, coupled with historic lows in U.S. interest rates, have fueled the growth of trading of forwards and options on LDC debt. One example of their usage, for instance, is a U.S. fund manager who desires a higher yield than U.S. instruments are carrying. He may move from U.S. bonds into Mexican or Venezuelan Brady bonds and purchase insurance in the form of short-term put options. Currently, only the largest dealers are participating in LDC debt-derivative market making, but this market is likely to develop as cash-market trading grows.

Which underlying markets are likely to attract derivative interest next? The real estate market looms as a possible target because of its size and volatility, which fund managers are certain to want to hedge away. Early in 1993, Morgan Stanley executed what is believed to be the first real-estate swap deal done for a U.S. fund manager. The deal was a two-part, five-year, \$20 million swap in which the fund, with sizable real-estate holdings, pays a floating rate based on the level of the Frank Russell National Council of Real Estate Investment Fiduciaries (NCREIF) Index. The fund pays the dealer a floating, LIBOR-based rate but also swaps out of LIBOR into the return on an index of foreign stocks. Thus, the fund was able to shift its exposure from real estate to foreign equities without having to liquidate its position in the cash markets.

Instruments That Produce New Types of Risk

The final group of new derivatives we will examine is the group that involves a new form of risk—correlation risk. So, in the sense of the definition of new products with which we began this chapter, this group of derivatives is *truly new*.

This group of derivatives is generally referred to as multifactor derivatives. The value of the derivatives we have discussed so far is determined by the behavior of one financial price; the value of a multifactor derivative is determined by the behavior of two or more financial prices.

Rainbow Options

The value of a *rainbow option*—also known as a "better of" option—is determined by the relative performance of two or more underlying assets. There are different kinds of rainbow options.

Rainbow options can differ according to the number of underlying assets. A rainbow option based on the performance of *n* assets is referrd to as a *n*-color rainbow option.

And, rainbow options can differ according to their payoff structures. The most common type of rainbow option pays off on the basis of the better performance of two or more assets. These "better of" options are used in the equity, interest rate, and currency markets.

Rainbow options might involve assets from the same asset class. Rainbow options have been used widely in the equity markets, permitting investors to obtain the return associated with the better performing of some number of equity indices. For example, an investor might be debating between holding a position in the German equity index—the Deutsche Aktienindex (DAX)—and a position in UK equities—the Financial Times Stock Exchange Index (FTSE). This investor could purchase a "two-color" rainbow option that would pay off according to the better performing of the FTSE or the DAX. If the FTSE increased by 13 percent and the

DAX decreased by 6 percent, the holder of the rainbow option would receive a return based on the 13 percent increase in the FTSE—the better performance of the two underlying assets.

Alternatively, rainbow options might involve assets from different asset classes. A combination that was popular in the early 1990s was a two-color rainbow option based on the performance of a stock market index and a bond market index. An investor who is unsure whether to invest in stocks or bonds could buy an outperformance option that, over the time period of the option, has a pay off determined by the better performance of stocks or bonds. If at expiration, the stock market had increased by 10 percent while the bond market had increased by 5 percent, the payoff to the holder of the rainbow option holder would be based on the 10 percent performance of the equity index.

And rainbow options can differ according to their payoff structures. In addition to the "better of" the performance of two assets, the payoff for a two-color rainbow could be determined by the worse performing of two assets. Rainbow options can also depend on the sum of or difference between the performance of the two assets. For example, a spread rainbow option allows the holder to receive the difference between the performance of two assets. For example, an investor holding a position in the DAX who wants to switch his exposure to FTSE could purchase a rainbow spread option. This option would pay off according to the difference in returns of the two indices—but only if the FTSE outperformed the DAX. If the FTSE increased by 13 percent and the DAX decreased by 6 percent, the holder would receive a return based on the 7 percent difference in the returns. When this type of option is held in conjunction with the DAX portfolio, the investor essentially receives the return of the FTSE, excluding the cost of the option. Such an option could be advantageous to the investor who cannot, for structural reasons, sell the portfolio that is currently being held.

Diffs and Quantos

Diff Swaps. *Differential ("diff") swaps*—a.k.a. *cross-indexed* or *quanto swaps*—are swaps that permit users to take advantage of differences between rates in different markets, without exposing themselves to foreign exchange rate risk. Perhaps an example might be the most effective way to introduce this structure.[28]

As illustrated in Figure 15–11, in the spring of 1992, U.S. dollar interest rates were significantly lower than German interest rates—six-month USD LIBOR was 4.25 percent, while six-month DM LIBOR was 9.63 percent. Moreover, the U.S. yield curve was steeply upward sloping while the German yield curve was inverted. A common diff swap structure required the holder to pay cash flows determined by six-month USD LIBOR and a USD notional principal and receive cash flows determined by six-month DM LIBOR *but a USD notional principal.*

FIGURE 15–11 Implied Forward Six-Month LIBOR Rates (Semiannual, Actual/360 Basis)

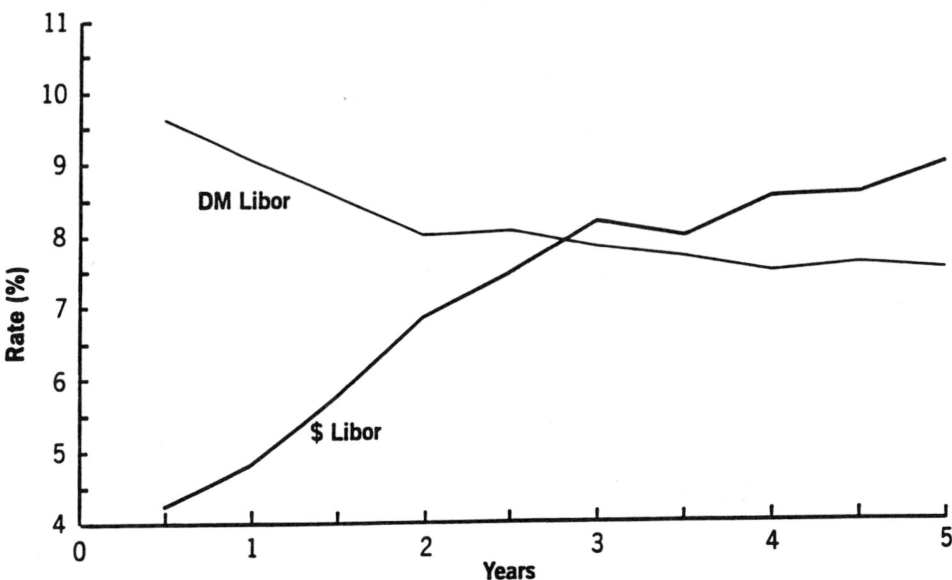

SOURCE: William Falloon, "Curves and the Fuller Figure," *Risk* 5, no. 5 (May 1992).

	Receive	*Pay*
Diff swap	$r_{6mUSDLIBOR}*NP_{USD}$	$r_{6mDMLIBOR}*NP_{USD}$

This swap is portrayed graphically in Figure 15–12. The parties entering into such a swap were implicitly taking the position that U.S. rates would not rise as rapidly as implied by the forward yield curve and/or that German rates would not fall as rapidly as implied by the forward yield curve.

A diff swap looks deceptively similar to the other structures. When we first heard about diff swaps, it seemed like a diff swap "should be" made up of some combination of interest rate and currency coupon swaps:

Interest rate swap—USD	$r_{6mUSDLIBOR}*NP_{USD}$	$r_{FIXED}*NP_{USD}$
Interest rate swap—DM	$r_{6mDMLIBOR}*NP_{DM}$	$r_{FIXED}*NP_{DM}$
Currency coupon swap	$r_{6mUSDLIBOR}*NP_{USD}$	$r_{6mDMLIBOR}*NP_{DM}$

FIGURE 15–12 A Diff Swap

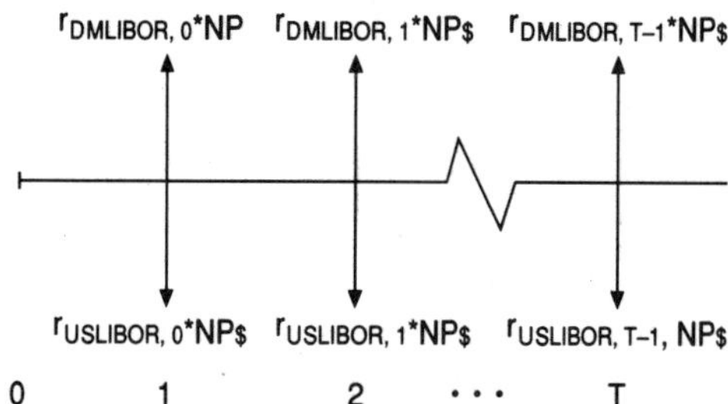

At period t (t = 1, 2, ..., T) the party receives (pays) a cashflow determined by the *difference* in the *nominal* DM and US LIBOR rates in effect at period t–1. That is the payment is

$$(r_{DMLIBOR,\,t-1} - r_{USLIBOR,\,T-1})\ {}^{*}NP_{\$}$$

If the payment is positive (negative) the party illustrated receives (makes) a payment.

But, regardless how you combine these swap structures, USD notional principals will always be associated with USD interest rates. It is impossible to put together the preceding swaps to end up with a USD notional principal multiplied by a DM interest rate.

> In order to hedge or deconstruct a differential swap, it is necessary for the seller of the differential swap to hedge USD denominated DM interest rate risk using DM denominated instruments. Although the prevailing exchange rate will determine the initial quantum of the hedge, ongoing changes in the exchange rates will vary the size of the hedge required. In order to calculate the cost associated with this hedge rebalancing, the seller of the differential swap must make assumptions about the correlation—covariance—between DM LIBOR and $/DM exchange rate.
>
> $$\text{Cov}\,(r_{6\text{mDMLIBOR}},\ S_{\$/\text{DM}})$$
>
> And, if the dealer overestimates this covariance, he will lose money.

This is the additional risk faced by a dealer when he offers diff swaps and the other multifactor derivatives.[29]

Quanto Options. Quanto options are options that eliminate the exchange rate risk inherent when I purchase an asset denominated in a currency other than my own. As with diff swaps, perhaps the easiest way to explain a quanto option is via an example, as on page 396.

Risk Management in Practice

Cross-Currency Caps

Martin Cooper and Matthew Hunt

Cross-currency caps are options on the spread between two interest reference rates, typically two LIBOR rates. They are denominated in a single currency and can be thought of as bearing the same relationship to a differential swap as a cap or floor does to a standard interest rate swap.

In return for a premium, the seller of a cross-currency cap pays the purchaser a rate of interest equal to the LIBOR of one currency minus the LIBOR of a second currency minus a strike, when such a rate exceeds zero. The notional principal to which the calculated interest rate is applied can be denominated in either of the reference currencies or a third unrelated currency.

The cross-currency cap is a natural evolution of the differential swap and now enables counterparties to buy or sell volatility on interest differentials as well as taking outright positions. Concerns about the European Monetary Union have focused attention on interest differentials and the need for more sophisticated instruments for positioning or to hedge European interest rate convergence/divergence.

The cross-currency cap is particularly important because no other instruments can be packaged together to provide the same risk profile. A combination of a cap and floor in the appropriate currencies, for example, would provide a hedge against an interest differential but can result in the purchaser paying a lot extra for effectively unwanted protection. If the correlation between two interest rates is very high, the volatility of the spread between them will be much lower relative to the volatilities of the individual currency interest rates. In such circumstances the cross-currency cap will be significantly cheaper than the combination of cap and floor.

Similarly, a corporate treasurer seeking to subsidize funding costs by selling volatility on an interest differential to which he is indifferent would be forced to take exposure to the absolute level of rates if he were to sell caps and floors.

Cross-currency caps appeal widely to both investors and liability managers. A typical scenario for the liability manager might be a corporate treasurer, paying LIBOR on deutsche mark funding, who has a strong expectation of a convergence of Italian lira and DM interest rates, and believes the current ERM turmoil has resulted in volatility being overpriced. As illustrated below the treasurer can subsidize funding costs by selling a three-year DM-denominated cross-currency cap on six-month lira LIBOR/six-month DM LIBOR with a

Cross-Currency Caps continued

strike of 2.5 percent compared to the current LIBOR differential of 2.25 percent. This cross-currency cap will give an effective subsidy of 80 basis points per annum, reducing his funding cost to DM LIBOR minus 80 bp with the cap currently out-of-the-money.

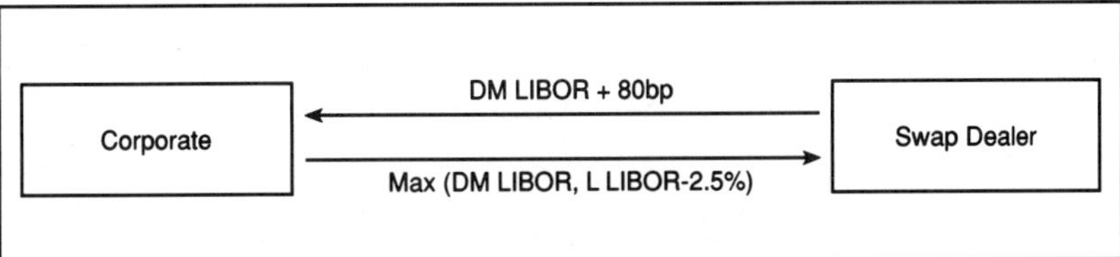

Another favored application is to use a cross-currency cap in conjunction with a differential swap to ensure a limited downside on the risk profile. Structured medium-term notes that incorporate a (sometimes leveraged) differential swap typically also include a cross-currency cap to ensure a nonnegative coupon. As illustrated below, an investor might wish to enter a U.S.-dollar-denominated differential swap to take a position on sterling and DM interest rates but wishes to put a floor on the overall downside of the transaction. The differential swap would provide for the investor to receive DM LIBOR and pay sterling LIBOR minus 30 basis points for three years, giving an initial premium of 130 bp. He could then cap the differential of sterling LIBOR minus DM LIBOR at a strike of 1 percent for a cost of 86 basis points a year. In this way, the maximum loss is restricted to 156 basis points, but the transaction is still worth 44 bp for the initial setting.

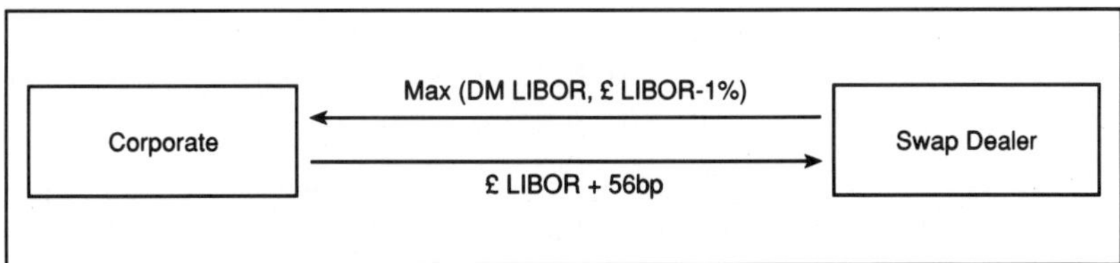

One of the problems that houses offering the cross-currency cap have had to solve is the pricing of the implicit correlations. Risk traders categorize correlation risk into either first order or second order, according to the impact it has on the price of the structure. The correlation risk between interest rates and foreign exchange rates, which is key to the pricing of all quanto products, has a relatively small impact on price and is accordingly categorized as second-

Cross-Currency Caps concluded

order correlation. Cross-currency caps have this second-order correlation risk. But the biggest impact on the price is the correlation between the two interest rates, which is an example of a first-order correlation risk and is common to all spread options or two-asset option structures.

Neither the first- or second-order correlations can be directly hedged, which places a high dependence on the modeling and evaluation of correlation coefficients and the dynamic hedging techniques required. Market makers trading volatility in several currencies accordingly benefit from a pricing advantage.

Martin Cooper is chief dealer on the Treasury New Products Desk of Chase London. He holds an MA from Oxford University and is also a qualified Chartered Accountant.

Matthew Hunt is a second vice president and works on the Treasury New Products Desk of Chase London. He holds a BSc from Bristol University.

Suppose that I buy a European-style option giving me the right to buy some DM-demoninated asset (e.g., the DAX). At maturity, the USD value of this option,

$$S_T * \text{Max}\ (0, V_{\text{DM}} - X),$$

depends on the spot USD–DM exchange rate at option maturity (S_T). Instead, I would like to have an option that eliminates the foreign exchange rate risk. This is accomplished by fixing the exchange rate on the date when the option is issued (S_0). At maturity, the USD value of such an option—a quanto option—would be

$$S_0 * \text{Max}\ (0, V_{\text{DM}} - X)$$

Thus, the investor is not exposed to the risk that the currency in which the underlying asset is denominated will outperform the investor's home currency. Conversely, the investor will not benefit from the investor's home currency outperforming the index base currency.

As with diff swaps, the additional risk faced by a dealer when he offers quanto options is a correlation risk. It is necessary for the seller of the quanto option to make some assumptions about the covariance between the value of the asset and the exchange rate and to hedge the portfolio against potential changes in this covariance.

Basket Options

A basket option pays off on the basis of the aggregate value of a specified "basket" of financial assets rather than on the value of the individual assets. As Fred Stambaugh illustrates in the following box, the basket option is an application of portfolio theory: As long as the financial prices that make up the basket are not perfectly positively correlated, the option on the basket will be less expensive than buying individual options on each of the assets.

For example, an exporter of goods to Germany and Japan needs protection against the dollar rising relative to the deutsche mark and the yen. He could purchase put options on both the DM and the yen separately or he could purchase a basket option on the DM and yen. Since the DM and yen are not perfectly correlated, the basket option will be cheaper than the corresponding two options. This is essentially the same as creating an index on which to base the option and has the same effect as lowering the volatility.

Risk Management in Practice

Basket Options

Fred Stambaugh

A *basket option* is a simple, inexpensive way to collect a set of identifiable foreign exchange exposures and hedge them with a single transaction. The basket option creates an index that represents the dollar (or other home currency) value of a portfolio of FX positions. The hedger can then buy a single option to ensure that the dollar value of the portfolio does not fall below a certain level.

The premium of such an option reflects the probability that the index will change in value rather than the probability that the individual currencies will change. (There could be an instance where the value of one portion of the portfolio increases while the rest of it decreases by the same amount; so, the index itself will not change.)

The basket option makes use of portfolio theory. Consider a portfolio with just two currency positions of equal dollar value.

> If the two currencies are perfectly positively correlated, the percentage change in the portfolio's value will be the same as the percentage change of the dollar against either currency. Its price volatility will be equal to that of the dollar against either currency.
>
> If the two currencies are perfectly negatively correlated, the value of the portfolio will never change: every move by one currency will be neutralized by an offsetting move in the other. The price volatility of the portfolio would be zero.
>
> If the currencies are not perfectly correlated, the price volatility of the portfolio will be a fraction of the sum of the volatilities of the individual currency components.

Basket options continued

In real life the correlations between currencies covers a wide range: DEM and NLG exhibit about 99 percent correlation, AUD and DEM exhibit only about 8 percent correlation. Clearly, the volatility of a given portfolio's value depends upon the currency makeup of the portfolio and the relative weightings of the currency components.

Suppose a dollar-based investor has the bond positions in the following table:

Position	*Spot Rate*	*3-Month-Forward Outright*
DEM 50,000,000	1.6900	1.7054
JPY 3,000,000,000	101.00	100.92
FRF 120,000,000	5.9500	6.0194
CHF 45,000,000	1.5000	1.5053
GBP 25,000,000	$1.4900	$1.4805
ITL 48,000,000,000	1600.00	1624.54
NLG 60,000,000	1.9000	1.9154
AUD 30,000,000	$.6775	$.6728

Converting all these dollar amounts at their current forward rates produces a portfolio value of $226,910,000. A package of eight options on the individual currency positions, all struck at the forward outright, would cost $5,574,750. A basket option to protect the value of the portfolio at that level would cost $4,402,000—nearly $1,175,000 less than the package of standard options. The reason for this difference lies in the currency correlations. While all the currencies in the portfolio have current three-month volatilities against the dollar of 10.6–13.1 percent, the volatility of the portfolio as a whole against the dollar is only 9.84 percent. Because of relatively low correlations among the currencies, changes in the dollar value of the individual components of the portfolio will have a certain tendency to be self-hedging; this reduces the risk of the portfolio and therefore the cost of protection. If, at the end of three months, the conversion of these currency amounts at the spot rate prevailing at that time resulted in an amount less than $226,910,000, the buyer of the option would be due a cash payment from the dealer to make up the difference. Thus, the minimum value of the portfolio after three months will be ($226,910,000 – 4,402,000) = $222,508,000. The maximum value, of course, is theoretically unlimited and dependent upon the degree to which the currencies as an aggregate appreciate against the dollar.

There are several advantages to covering a portfolio such as this with a basket option:

Basket options continued

First, it is administratively simple. The risk manager has only one option to execute, easing paperwork and operational hassle both at inception of the trade and at exercise. (When a basket option is exercised, the dealer notifies the customer of both the exercise and the exercise payment. Frantic last-minute calls to exercise a barely in-the-money option are largely avoided.)

Second, basket options are flexible. They can accommodate virtually any number of currencies (as long as liquid markets and enough data to establish correlations exist), in any position size. What is more, if a portfolio manager should decide to alter the composition of his portfolio, the basket option can be rejigged to reflect the new weightings (this may entail an incremental payment of premium—or receipt of premium—to reflect the change in portfolio values versus the basket strike price). On the other hand, if the portfolio manager chooses not to alter the composition of the basket option to match the new weightings in his portfolio, his hedge can continue to reflect the weightings of a given benchmark portfolio, thus helping to isolate the local market effect of his allocation decision from the exchange effect.

Third, a basket option costs less. The premium of the basket option can be, depending on the composition of the portfolio, as much as 20 percent less than the combined premiums of individual options.

Inevitably, one gives up some opportunity for profit in exchange for the lower premium. Owning a set of individual options could be worth more at maturity than the single basket option. In the context of our example, suppose JPY appreciated radically while the others weakened. With individual options, those currencies that weakened would be covered, while the yen portion would exhibit substantially higher valuation. The portfolio would reflect a profit (before taking into account the premiums paid). With the basket option, the portfolio as a whole may decline slightly in value because of the heavy weighting in weakening currencies. The basket option portfolio would protect the inception value of the portfolio (before taking into account the premium paid).

The degree to which the yen appreciates will determine whether the individually hedged portfolio generates superior returns despite the higher total premiums. A closing spot rate of 97.00 would make up the $1,175,000 premium difference.

The price advantage of a basket option increases notably when the basket is diversified to include currencies that are not highly correlated. Events in the European FX market in 1992 and 1993 served to diminish the correlation among currencies that only a few months earlier seemed headed for correlations of 100 percent. As a result, the diversity of risk in European portfolios has increased. While that has reduced the concentration of risk, it has also increased

Basket options continued

the complications of dealing with the risk. Basket options represent a way of responding that is simple, user friendly, and attractively priced.

Mr. Stambaugh is vice president, head of Sales and Marketing, Global FX Options for Chase Manhattan Bank. He has been in the FX markets since 1981, when he joined the corporate FX desk at First Chicago in Chicago.

Mr. Stambaugh holds a bachelor's degree from Miami University, and master's degrees from the University of Chicago (MA, International Relations) and The American Graduate School of International Management (Thunderbird School—Master's of International Management).

Concluding Remarks

We have introduced many new product concepts that have come into being within the last few years. We hope that you have seen that many of the "new" instruments are actually not new but rather are simply combinations of the basic building blocks or extensions of the building blocks to cover different underlying financial prices. This should give you some comfort that the building-block approach will facilitate your understanding of new exotic derivatives as they are created. We have outlined the fundamentals of the truly new product concepts—those structures based on multiple cash markets.

While the concept of financial engineering may be new to most corporate risk managers, it is likely to grow in scope and importance in the decades to come.

The building-block approach will facilitate your understanding of new exotic derivatives. But, it may or may not help when it comes to accounting for the new derivatives.

Risk Management in Practice

The Creation and Management of Exotic Options

Steven H. Bloom

When exotic options first became prevalent, we were skeptical of the utility of these new complex tools—perhaps they were merely the result of "idle hands

The Creation and Management of Exotic Options continued

in the quants' workshop," Upon further exploration however, it became clear that exotics can be precise and cost-effective hedges for unique hedging problems. Instruments such as average rate, barrier, and basket options often provide optimal solutions for diverse risk management questions.

At Susquehanna, we view derivative securities as risk transfer instruments that allow market participants to buy or sell risk. Options are particularly useful in that they provide users the ability to buy and sell specific parts of their risk profile to create the profile they ultimately desire. Therefore, the increased demand for exotic options is a natural evolution—as derivatives' expertise in the marketplace has expanded in the past several years, users have sought more sophisticated products to provide specific hedges for their portfolios and cash flows. Exotic options enable end users to more accurately customize their exposure with regard to any number of risk-producing variables such as time, underlying price, volatility, etc. For example, a corporation that wants to hedge a series of regular cash flows may have, in the past, hedged with a strip of standard options. If that corporation is really interested in its average exposure over the life of those cash flows and has no real need to insure the value of each of its individual cash flows separately, an average rate option can be a less expensive and better hedge. Exotic options are also particularly useful in that they can be constructed to address a combination of risk factors. For example, a quanto option (an option on a foreign security where the final payout is denominated at a fixed domestic currency rate) addresses the combination of foreign security price and exchange rate risk.

In our role as an options market maker and dealer in FX and equity markets we must be able to accurately and quickly price exotic options, and manage the subsequent risk of the large portfolio of exotics that we accumulate in our trading book. The simplest way to perform both of these tasks is to decompose the exotic option into its component building blocks; that is, forwards, standard options, etc., and examine the pricing and risk of the portfolio of these synthetic pieces. In cases where this decomposition is impossible, we must then derive unique analytical models or run Monte Carlo simulations. Analytical solutions are preferable because of faster computation time and greater consistency of results—we have developed analytical solutions for almost all of the exotic option types that we trade.

Even though the risk management of a large exotic options book entails principles similar to those used in managing a portfolio of standard options, risk management of exotics requires a much greater appreciation for the complexities and subtleties of options. One must fully understand the effects of risk factors on pricing and risk management measures such as delta, gamma, theta, and rho because the effects of those factors are often magnified. Many

The Creation and Management of Exotic Options continued

of the simplifying assumptions of the Black-Scholes model—normal distribution of the underlying and volatility and interest rates that remain unchanged for the life of the option's contract—cannot be safely assumed when dealing with exotics because the effect on pricing and risk measures can often be significant. For example, a barrier option is a standard option that includes an additional provision that allows the option to either be extinguished or activated when the underlying reaches a predetermined barrier point. In order to value the entire barrier option it is important to accurately assess the probability of the underlying asset reaching the option's barrier point. This valuation must include the effects of time-dependent volatilities and interest rates, and jump processes if it is to be accurate. Another complexity that must be considered in many exotics is the multidimensional correlation matrix of assets and their risk variables, for example, volatilities. These covariances, and their stability through time, are especially critical when working with large portfolios and multiasset options.

Finally, from a practical sense, a complete understanding of exotic risk management is tremendously important because trading exotics is like performing acrobatics without a net. When trading standard options, the marketplace is your net, so to speak, in that you can rely upon competitive pricing information as a reference point for your own valuation judgment. Moreover, the marketplace provides liquidity and the ability to shed risk. Trading exotic options without adequate expertise or guidance can be risky because many contracts are unique. Because there is no liquid market in comparable instruments readily available, if you misjudge the value or risk in an exotic transaction, it may be some time before you are aware of your error. Be careful, it can be a long fall from the exotic high wire.

Steven H. Bloom is one of the founding managing directors of the Susquehanna Investment Group, a 200-person derivative securities trading firm. Mr. Bloom has been a market maker on the Chicago Board Options Exchange and Philadelphia Stock Exchange and has 10 years of trading and supervisory experience in foreign currency, equity and index derivative markets and has worked on developing many of Susquehanna's analytical and technical systems. He was responsible for foreign exchange derivative trading and product development and managing Susquehanna's Foreign Exchange business alliance with Chase Manhattan Bank. Steven H. Bloom has an undergraduate degree from the State University of New York at Binghamton and a master's degree from the University of Michigan.

Risk Management in Practice

Accounting for New Risk Management Products

Halsey G. Bullen

One of the more intriguing areas in financial accounting is applying the advances of financial engineering to the accounting for the results of that engineering. This book clearly demonstrates that assembling desired financial structures from building blocks—future cash flows, options, swaps, forwards—and decomposing complex financial structures into their building-block components are essential to efficient management of the risks faced by modern businesses. Accounting is intended to be the language of business. But so far, accounting principles for financial instruments have taken little heed of these advances in financial engineering.

For example, APB Opinion 14 requires that, while issuers should allocate the proceeds of bonds issued together with separable stock-purchase warrants between debt and equity accounts, bonds convertible into stock should be treated entirely as debt, which is its predominant characteristic. Many convertible issuers think that treatment reports overly high debt-equity ratios and low average interest cost ratios, which may be misleading some users of financial statement information. Opinion 14 reversed an earlier one that required allocating convertible proceeds between debt and equity. Complaints had arisen—perhaps because the higher interest expense reported after allocation reduced the attractiveness of convertibles—that it was too difficult to measure the relative values of the conversion option and the straight debt. Score one against the building-block approach!

A related issue arose in 1986 concerning debt instruments indexed, for example, to the S&P 500 index. In that issue (EITF 86-28), a task force decided that allocation was appropriate only if the index feature was separable from the straight debt, citing Opinion 14 in its reasoning. Score another one against the building blocks!

On the other hand, a FASB project on transfers of receivables with recourse did conclude in 1983 that a receivable could be treated as sold, even though the seller retained a recourse obligation should the receivables go unpaid, as long as that obligation could be reliably measured. Perhaps because of the advantages for the securitization transactions that were then at the early stages of what has become a trillion-dollar market, few complaints arose that it was too

Accounting for New Risk Management Products continued

difficult to measure the relative values of those components. Score one for the building blocks.

The 1991 FASB Discussion Memorandum, *Recognition and Measurement of Financial Instruments,* discussed the choice between two general rules, the predominant characteristics approach used in Opinion 14 and Issue 86-28 and the building-block approach used in Statement 77—and a third ad hoc approach. If a building-block approach is to be used, there are two main issues. The first is whether to display *all* components separately—a radical shift—or to separate only the equity component(s) from the net of all other components. The second is how to measure the components, especially if the whole appears to be worth more—or less—than the sum of its parts.

Some work is under way to aid in resolving these nontrivial issues in adopting a financial components or "building-block" approach to accounting for complex financial instruments. Barth, Landsman, and Rendleman's 1993 working paper, *Accounting for Financial Instruments: An Options Pricing-Based Approach to Measuring Corporate Debt,* has not only made some progress on the accounting measurement front but also highlighted some covariance-related problems in valuing instruments composed of several building blocks not previously considered in the financial engineering literature. More work along those lines by the FASB and other standard setters, their constituents, and others will be necessary to make this promising accounting approach workable.

Halsey Bullen has been a member of the Financial Accounting Standards Board's research and technical activities staff since 1983. He managed the FASB project on financial instruments and off-balance-sheet financing from its initial stages through the issuance of the 1987 disclosure exposure draft and has been working since then on financial instruments recognition and measurement issues, most recently in hedge accounting.

Mr. Bullen was principal author of the 1991 discussion memorandum on recognition and measurement. He also consults on other FASB work on financial instrument issues. Mr. Bullen has spoken and written frequently about accounting for financial instruments, including derivatives.

Mr. Bullen previously managed the FASB's cash flow reporting and recognition and measurement concepts projects. Before joining the FASB staff he was an audit manager at the San Francisco office of Deloitte Haskins and Sells (now Deloitte & Touche).

Mr. Bullen received his AB degree in economics from Dartmouth College and his MBA from Stanford University.

Notes

1. This way of defining new products was suggested to us by Jim Garnett, the market risk executive for Chase's Global Risk Management sector—the derivatives business at Chase.
2. In the context of the "fraternity row" description of risks—delta, gamma, and so on—which we will introduce in Chapter 18, this risk is often referred to as "omega."

3. The numbers in Figure 15–3 are only for purposes of illustration. To determine the exercise prices at which the values of the puts and calls are equal, one would have to use an option-pricing model.
4. In options terminology, the combination of long call, short put with an underlying position is known as a *collar*.
5. In fact, the option embedded is actually a "swaption"—a structure we will discuss in the next section of this chapter.
6. Most indexed-principal swaps have a "lockout period" at the beginning of the swap during which no amortization occurs. After the lockout period, if rates decline, the fixed-rate payer in effect exercises the option to reduce or cancel a portion of the remaining term of the swap.
7. Specifically, the fixed-rate-pay side of an indexed-principal swap has positive convexity.
8. Actually, the rate is set some number of days prior to the settlement date.
9. Note that this is different from the payoff of the forward swap. The forward swap parties are *obligated* to enter the swap at the specified future date while the swaption holder has the *right* to enter the swap on the future date. No "premium" is paid by the forward swap purchaser.
10. Reportedly, 90 percent of swaption transactions are European style. The remaining 10 percent that have American-style exercise are mostly reversible contracts—swaptions whose underlying swap terms are set at the inception of the contract. "Behind the Mirror," *Risk* 2, no. 2 (February 1989), pp. 17–23.
11. Recent credit issues have dampened the growth of the dollar market, compelling new deals to be cash settled with daily marking-to-market.
12. This illustration is adapted from "First Boston Snares Ford Credit with Swaption-Linked Deal," *Investment Dealers' Digest*, January 16, 1989, pp. 42–43.
13. Once the swaption is exercised, the issuer of the bond must begin paying the holder of the swaption a fixed-rate "coupon." Consequently, the bonds will likely be called and the debt refinanced on a floating-rate basis, so the floating rate that the bond issuer will receive on the swap can flow through to the holders of the bonds. After all this, the net effect is that the issuer of the bond is still paying a fixed rate—only now the fixed-rate payment is going to the holder of the swaption rather than the holders of the bonds.
14. For a more detailed discussion of the relative premiums, see Ed Rombach, "The Cost of Insurance," *Risk* 4, no. 5 (May 1991), p. 12.
15. To show you to the extent to which the jargon goes, there are some who speak of "collartions."
16. The tenor of the caption is generally less than that of the cap.
17. Early on in the option markets, the options traded on exchanges in the United States were what we now call American-style options. Likewise, the options traded on the European exchanges were, by and large, of the type we now call European-style options. To the best of our knowledge, there is no corresponding geographic origin for the "Asian" option. Instead, the term Asian option seems to have been one of those clever names that occur in the derivatives markets.
18. "Hedging during Market Backwardation," from "Corporate Risk Management's Done Deals," *Corporate Risk Management*, January 1991.
19. These are average prices. Phelps Dodge actually entered into several transactions with different financial institutions at different times and using different strike prices.
20. At the time these transactions were done, the copper market was in "backwardation"—futures prices were lower than spot market prices. Normally, futures prices are above spot prices reflecting such factors as storage fees and carrying costs. When the futures price falls below the cash price, it indicates either a short-term supply squeeze or bearish expectations from the market.
21. At Chase, we refer to this as a "Q cap."
22. The profit on exercise can be transferred immediately or deferred until the standard expiration date. These options are widely available in the OTC market. And, in 1991, the Chicago Board Options Exchange (CBOE) listed CAPS™—an exchange-traded form of up-and-out and down-and-out options—on the S&P 100 and S&P 500 indices.
23. Reportedly, the premium of the lookback may be at least twice that of a standard contract.
24. In the November 1991 issue of *Risk* Jim Durrant, head of research for Paribas Capital Markets, was quoted as saying that the premium for a contingent premium option was typically twice that for a standard European-style option. Armand Tatevossian, a vice president in the New Products unit of Fuji Cap-

ital Markets Corporation was quoted with the same price relation in the September 24, 1992, issue of *Derivatives Week*. More generally, the premium for a contingent premium option is approximated by the standard option premium divided by its delta.

25. "Buy Now, Pay Later," *Risk*, November 1991.
26. For more on the developing natural gas swaps market, see "Filling Up with Gas," *Risk*, March 1992.
27. The purchaser of the debt instrument from a developing country might buy "insurance" to put a floor on the value of the bond by buying a put on the bond.
28. This example is adapted from "Curves and the Fuller Figure," *Risk*, May 1992.
29. Earlier in this chapter, we noted that this risk is sometimes referred to as "omega." Carefully placing his tongue in his cheek, our colleague Lee Wakeman notes that it might be called the "Oh My Gosh" risk.

CHAPTER

16 Hybrid Securities*

Hybrids are most commonly associated with agricultural commodities such as corn or wheat. However, today a hybrid may also be a hybrid security. In the same way that a hybrid corn variety is created by combining two types of corn, a hybrid security is created by combining two types of securities: typically a standard debt or equity security and an OTC derivative—a forward contract, a swap, or an option.

Hybrid securities are not new. The market regularly trades hybrid securities created by adding equity derivatives (equity options) to standard debt to create convertible bonds (first issued by the Erie Railroad in the 1850s) and bonds with equity warrants (first issued by American Light & Power in 1911).[1] In the U.S. capital market, callable bonds are a form of hybrid securities that contain an interest rate option in addition to a standard debt issue.

Even hybrids created by adding commodity derivatives to debt are not new. Indeed, in Chapter 1 we noted the hybrid security issued by the Confederacy in 1863, a bond that was convertible into cotton. By the 1920s, commodity-linked hybrids were a feature of the U.S. capital markets. A case in point is the gold-indexed bond issued by Irving Fisher's Rand Kardex Corporation in 1925, in which the principal repayment of the bond was tied directly to gold prices.[2] The firm's funding costs could be lowered significantly by furnishing a scarce security desired by investors—in this case, a long-dated forward on gold prices. This innovation was imitated by a number of other U.S. companies during the 1920s, but like so many of the financial innovations of the 1920s, that wave of hybrid debt financings

---

*This chapter is adapted from "The Uses of Hybrid Debt in Managing Corporate Risk," a paper that Charles Smithson wrote with Donald H. Chew, Jr. for the *Journal of Applied Corporate Finance* (Winter 1992).

was ended with the regulatory reaction of the 1930s. Specifically, the "Gold Clause" virtually eliminated indexed debt by prohibiting "a lender to require of a borrower a different quantity or number of dollars from that loaned." It was not until Congress passed the Helms Amendment in October 1977 that the legal basis for commodity-indexed debt was restored.

The two and a half decades following enactment of the Helms Amendment have witnessed a dramatic expansion in the use of hybrid securities. Hybrids have been developed with payoffs indexed to interest rates, foreign exchange rates, commodity prices, and the behavior of the stock market. Hybrids have been developed to reduce the credit risk inherent in a debt issue. And everything that we can see indicates that the innovations will continue as long as volatility exists. For example, when the price of soybean futures soared after the flooding in the American Midwest in 1993, Goldman Sachs issued a security whose principal repayment was linked to the price of soybeans.[3]

In this chapter, we look at the expanded use of hybrids in three ways. First, we trace the time path of evolution. Second, we decompose the hybrid securities into their underlying building blocks. Third, we examine the economic rationale behind the issuance of hybrids.

The Evolution of Hybrid Securities

From the turn of the century until the 1970s, volatility was primarily associated with prices of individual equity securities. So it is not surprising that the most familiar hybrids are those that involve equity. However, the onset of volatility in foreign exchange rates, interest rates, and commodity prices in the 1970s provided the necessary condition for a new wave of hybrid securities.

Figure 16–1 provides a time line of the development of hybrid securities in the post–Bretton Woods environment. The recent wave of corporate hybrids began in 1973, when PEMEX, the state-owned Mexican oil producer, issued bonds that incorporated a *forward contract* on a commodity (in this case, oil). In 1980, Sunshine Mining Company went a step further by issuing bonds incorporating a commodity *option* (on silver). In 1988, Magma Copper made yet another advance by issuing a bond giving investors a *series of commodity options* (on copper)—in effect, one for every coupon payment.

As mentioned, other new hybrids have had their payoffs tied to interest rates, foreign exchange rates, and the behavior of the stock market. In 1981, Oppenheimer & Company, a securities brokerage firm, issued a security whose principal repayment is indexed to the volume of trading on the New York Stock Exchange. Notes indexed to the value of equity indices appeared in 1986, and inflation-indexed notes (tied to the Consumer Price Index, or CPI) were introduced in 1988.

FIGURE 16–1 Development of Hybrid Securities: 1973–1991

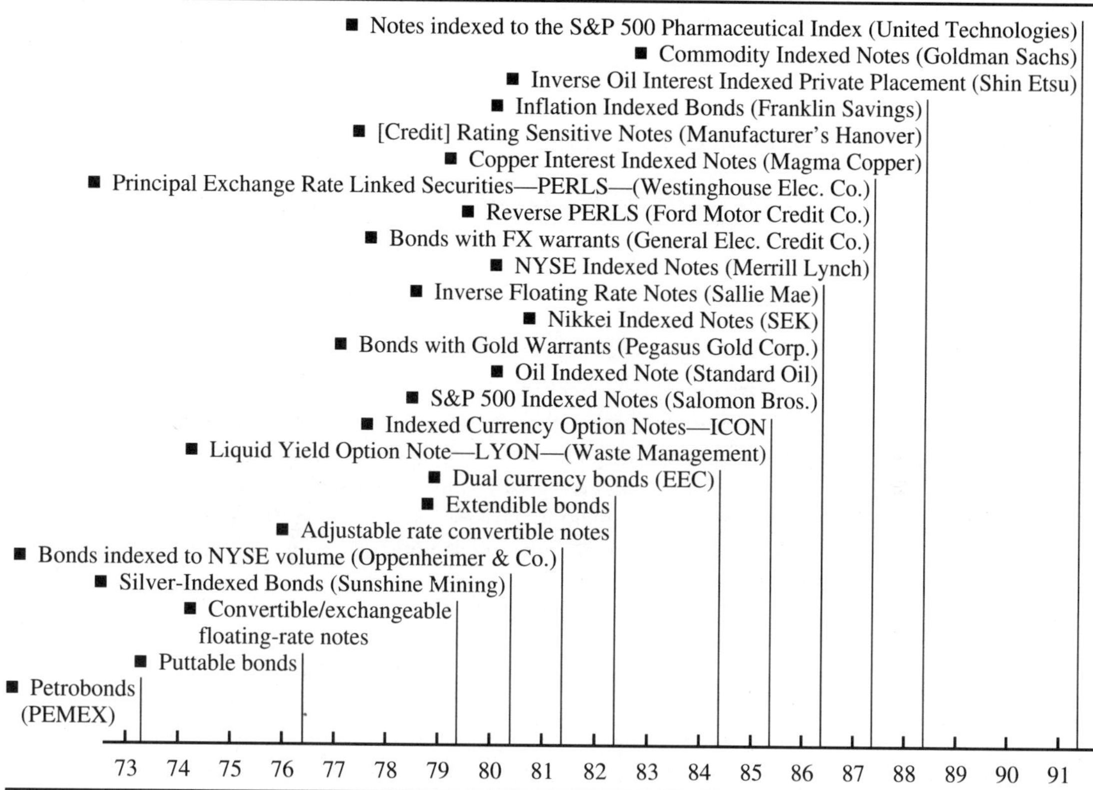

Hybrids with payoffs that, like those of convertibles, are tied to company-specific performance also emerged in the 1980s. For example, the Rating Sensitive Notes issued by Manufacturer's Hanover in 1988 provide for increased payments to investors if Mannie Hannie's creditworthiness declines. And the LYON[4] pioneered and underwritten by Merrill Lynch in 1985 grants investors not only the option to convert the debt into equity but also the right to "put" the security back to the firm.

Decomposition of Hybrids into Underlying Building Blocks

Since a hybrid security is the combination of a standard debt or equity security and a "derivative"—a forward contract, a swap, or an option—even seemingly complex hybrids should be able to be decomposed into these simpler, more understandable building blocks.

This decomposition is not unique. Indeed, many corporate treasuries decompose structures into their components—into their building blocks—to evaluate the structure.

Risk Management in Practice

Decomposing Hybrids to Assess Value

Walter D. Hosp

As a corporate finance manager in a large multinational organization, I spend much of my time evaluating the merits of various financial proposals. All such proposals have pricing elements, which also require evaluation. The simple question, "Are we receiving full value?" is usually asked several times throughout the decision-making process. My challenge has often been to deliver proposals for approval and to demonstrate why they are cost-effective. I have found the technique of decomposition to be very useful in meeting this challenge.

Decomposition is a term I use to describe the process in which a risk identified by a company is examined and unbundled into components. An example would be the purchase of computer equipment. Aside from the risk of loss or theft, there is also the risk of obsolescence. Property insurance can diversify or eliminate the risk of loss or theft but not the risk of obsolescence. However, leasing instead of purchasing the equipment can allow for the transference of this risk. By decomposing the risks associated with the purchase of computer equipment, separate solutions to each risk component can be found to address the total risk of purchasing this equipment.

How, then, can decomposition be used to show the cost-effectiveness of a given financial proposal? Two specific examples, the pricing of a convertible bond and the pricing of underwriting fees, should demonstrate the value of this technique.

A bond that is convertible into a set amount of equity shares is a hybrid instrument with two pricing components. The first component is a straight debt piece; the second component is a call option on the equity (it is a call option because the holder has the right, but not the obligation, to buy the equity shares through conversion at a set price over a predetermined time period). These two components can be valued separately and added together to verify the price of the convertible bond. If the sum of the parts is greater than the whole, then cost-effective pricing has been achieved. If the reverse is

Decomposing Hybrids to Assess Value concluded

true, then a corporate issuer must have some other overriding reason for issuing a convertible bond. At the very least, the cost of this overriding reason is quantified. Because the synthetic alternative to the convertible bond exists, a direct check of the pricing can be achieved with nearly identical terms and timing. This method is more precise than comparing to a similar, recently issued convertible bond.

In a similar fashion, underwriting fees can be broken down into two components. The first component is the service of selling a security. The advice of traders and the use of the distribution network of the investment bank are all part of this component. The second component is the pricing risk associated with underwriting securities. This is the risk that the price of the security will move lower before the investment bank can sell off the position it takes from underwriting. This is a short-term risk usually lasting from only several hours to a week. Noteworthy is the fact that there is upside potential as well as downside risk to the underwriter's position.

The two components of the underwriter's fee can now be priced separately. Most investment banks will readily quote a transaction under an "agented basis" versus a "fully underwritten" transaction. Under an agented arrangement no price guarantee is made to the issuer, and the security is sold on a "best efforts" basis. This pricing for the service of selling the security can be readily compared to other agented transactions of similar size and complexity. The underwriting risk can be synthetically priced by looking at the price of an interest rate hedge for a bond offering or the price of a short-dated put option for an equity offering. Again, if the sum of the pricing of the two components exceeds the full underwriting commission, then cost-effective pricing exists. If not, then the issuer has reason to negotiate further on pricing or accept only an agented transaction and obtain downside price protection elsewhere, if desired.

These are only two examples using the technique of decomposition to establish cost-effective pricing. Used creatively, the technique can at least serve as a verification of the pricing of some financial proposals. At best, it can offer different and more cost-effective alternatives.

Walter D. Hosp is the director of corporate finance for CIBA-GEIGY Corporation in Ardsley, New York. He is responsible for the treasury planning and analysis, banking and cash management, and investor relations functions. He holds MBA and BS degrees from New York University.

To examine how hybrids are constructed, we look first at hybrids constructed by adding derivatives to debt. We then consider hybrids constructed by adding derivatives to equity.

Hybrids Composed of Debt and Derivatives

It turns out that "standard debt" isn't all that standard; there are various types, reflecting the various ways in which the coupon and principal are paid. The coupon can be paid in three ways: traditional fixed-rate coupons, floating-rate coupons (which appeared in 1974), and zero coupons (which appeared in 1981).[5] The principal can be either amortized over the term of the debt or repaid at maturity (a coupon repaid at maturity is known as a *bullet*). These various types of debt have been combined with forwards, swaps, and options to create a range of hybrid debt securities.

Debt plus Forward Contract

Dual Currency Bond (1984). The combination of a fixed-rate, bullet-repayment bond and a long-dated forward contract on foreign exchange yields a dual currency bond. Figure 16–2 illustrates the decomposition of one of the early dual currency bonds, that issued by Phillip Morris Credit in 1985. In this issue, the coupon payments were made in Swiss francs while the principal was repaid in U.S. dollars. In the years since 1984, various combinations of currencies have been used.

New Issue | *This announcement appears as a matter of record only* | September 1985

PHILIP MORRIS CREDIT CORPORATION

Dual Currency Bonds Due 1993
U.S. $ 57,810,000

Interest Payable in SFr. at 7¼%
on the Aggregate Subscription price of
SFr. 123,000,000

FIGURE 16–2 A Dual Currency Bond

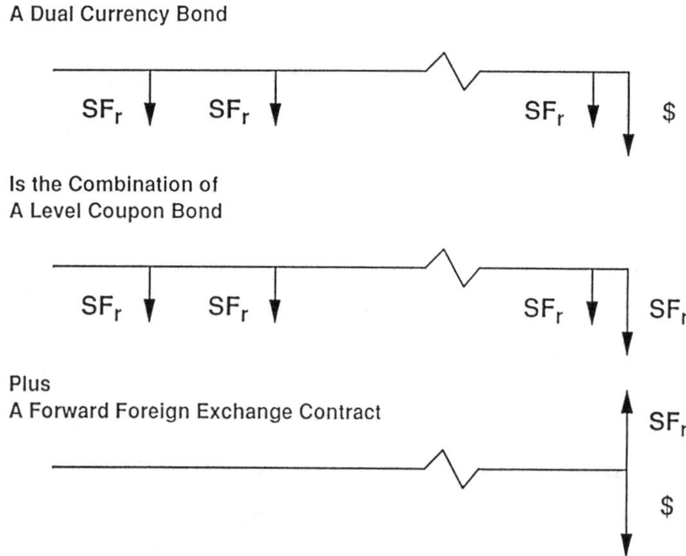

A variant of the dual currency structure is the *Principal Exchange Rate Linked Security* (*PERLS*). In 1987, Westinghouse Electric Company issued PERLs, wherein the bondholder received at maturity the U.S. dollar value of 70.13 million New Zealand dollars. The issuer's motive in this case was likely to reduce its funding costs by taking advantage of an unusual investor demand for long-dated currency forwards. Earlier in the same year, and presumably with a similar motive, Ford Motor Credit Company issued *Reverse PERLs*. In that issue, the principal repayment varied inversely with the value of the yen.[6]

Petrobonds (1973). The bonds issued by PEMEX in 1973 were very similar to dual currency bonds, except that the principal was indexed to oil prices rather than the price of some foreign exchange. Hence, the petrobonds could be viewed as the combination of straight debt and a forward contract on crude oil.

Debt plus Swap

Inverse Floating-Rate Note (1986). When inverse floating-rate notes were first issued in the public debt market, these hybrids were referred to as "yield curve notes."

As illustrated in Figure 16–3, an inverse floating-rate note is composed of a floating rate, bullet-repay note and an interest rate swap. Begin with a floating-rate note (FRN) with principal P and coupon payment of $\tilde{R}$. If this FRN is combined with an interest rate swap with notional principal P, the resulting coupon payment is the fixed coupon $\bar{R}$, so we would have constructed a synthetic fixed-rate note. How-

This announcement is neither an offer to sell nor a solicitation of an offer to buy any of these Securities. The offer is made only by the Offering Circular.

$150,000,000

SallieMae

Student Loan Marketing Association

Yield Curve Notes due 1990

Interest on the Yield Curve Notes Due 1990 will accrue from April 11, 1986 and is payable semi-annually in arrears on each April 11 and October 11, commensing October 11, 1986, at a rate for the Initial Interest Period of 3.50% per annum and thereafter at a floating rate of 15.10% per annum minus the arithmetic mean of the London interbank offered rates for six month Eurodollar deposits ("LIBOR") prevailing two Business Days before the beginning of each Interest Period. Interest will be computed on the basis of a 365 or 366 day year, as the case may be, and the actual number of days in the applicable Interest Period.

Copies of the Offering Circular may be obtained in any State from the undersigned in compliance with the securities laws of such State.

MORGAN STANLEY & CO.
Incorporated

April 7, 1986

ever, to construct a reverse floater, this FRN is combined with an interest rate swap with notional principal of $2P$, so the resulting coupon payment is $2\bar{R} - \tilde{R}$—if interest rates rise, the coupon payment falls.

Adjustable-Rate Convertible Notes (1982). Figure 16–4 illustrates that an adjustable rate convertible note can be viewed as the combination of a convertible floating-rate note with coupon payment $\tilde{R}$ and a swap wherein the bondholder pays $\tilde{R}$ and receives a rate tied to the dividend rate on the firm's common stock.

Debt Plus Option. There exists a wide range of hybrid securities that can be decomposed into a debt security and an option. For exposition, these hybrids have

FIGURE 16–3 An Inverse Floating-Rate Note

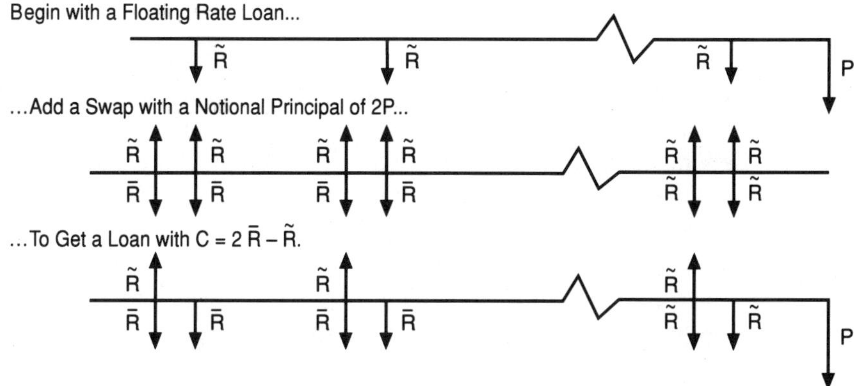

FIGURE 16–4 An Adjustable-Rate Convertible Note

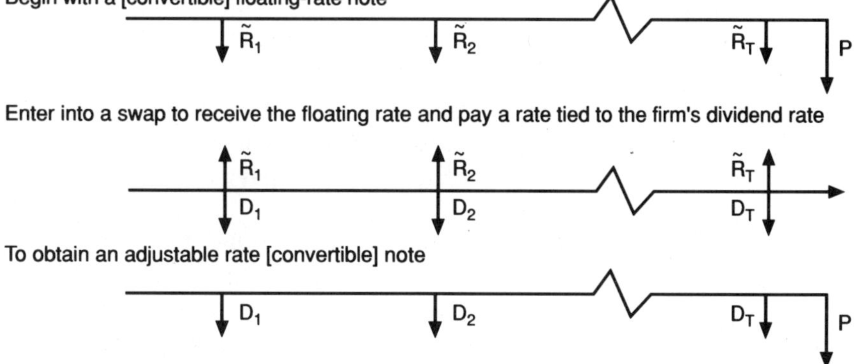

been divided into four types: (1) bonds with warrants, (2) bonds that are convertible or have their principal indexed to a financial price, (3) bonds with their coupons indexed to a financial price, and (4) bonds with options on the issuer's creditworthiness or on shareholder behavior.

Bonds with Warrants. As noted earlier, bonds with equity warrants are common in the U.S. capital market. The equity option that makes up the warrant can be American or European. Moreover, the equity option can be "detachable," permitting it to be traded independently, or "nondetachable."

Warrants now have been used wherein the options are on commodities or foreign exchange. In 1986, Pegasus Gold Corporation, a Canadian gold-mining firm, issued a Eurobond with detachable gold warrants. In 1987, General Electric Credit Corporation made a public offering made up of debt and yen–USD currency-exchange warrants.[7]

Convertible Bonds and Bonds with Indexed Principal. Like the bonds with warrants described above, convertible bonds are made up of bonds and equity options, but with one important difference. The bondholder can exercise the option embodied in a warrant and still keep the underlying bond; to exercise the option in a convertible bond, the bond must be surrendered.

Similar constructions—hybrid bonds that enable the bondholder to receive either the value of the bond or the value of the option, but not both—have appeared where the underlying asset is a commodity, some amount of a foreign currency, another bond, or an equity index, rather than equity.

1. **Principal Indexed to Commodity Prices.** The Silver-Indexed Bond issued by Sunshine Mining in 1980 is generally perceived as the first of the modern commodity-indexed bonds. Figure 16–5 demonstrates this hybrid is the combination of a fixed-rate, bullet-repayment bond and a European option on silver.[8]

It was, however, Standard Oil's Oil Indexed Note that caused the regulators to become seriously interested in these hybrid securities.[9] Figure 16–6 illustrates that the Standard Oil hybrid was the combination of a zero-coupon bond and a European-style option on oil with the same maturity.[10]

2. **Principal Indexed to Exchange Rates.** When this structure appeared with an embedded foreign-currency option, the hybrid was called an *Indexed Currency Option Note* (or *ICON*). This security, which was first underwritten by First Boston in 1985, combines a fixed-rate, bullet-repayment bond and a European option on foreign exchange.[11]

3. **Principal Indexed to Interest Rates.** In the same way that the bondholder can have an option to exchange the underlying bond for a commodity or a specified amount of a foreign currency, hybrid securities have been marketed in which the bondholder has an option to exchange the bond for another bond. Floating-rate notes that give the holder the right to convert to (exchange for) a specified fixed-rate bond appeared in 1979. Extendable bonds, bonds that give the holder the right to exchange the underlying bond for a bond of longer maturity, appeared in 1982.

4. **Principal Indexed to an Equity Index.** The year 1986 witnessed the introduction of bonds with the principal indexed to an equity index, either the Nikkei or the S&P 500. In this case, the principal repayment is linked to value of an equity index rather than to the value of an individual equity. The equity-index-linked hybrid introduced by Salomon Brothers—S&P 500 Index Subordinated Notes, or "SPINs"—can be viewed as the combination of a fixed-rate, bullet-repay bond and a call option on the S&P 500 index.[12] A similar construction intro-

FIGURE 16–5 A Fixed-Rate Bond

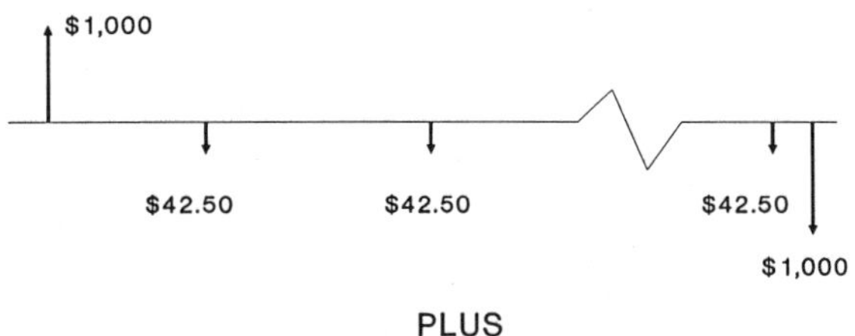

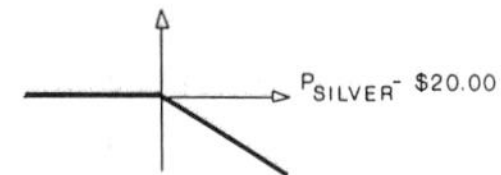

PROSPECTUS

$25,000,000

Sunshine Mining Company

8 1/2% Silver Indexed Bonds Due April 15, 1995

Interest payable April 15 and October 15

Each $1,000 Face Amount bond shall be payable at maturity or redemption at the greater of $1,000 or the Market Price of 50 Ounces of Silver ("Indexed Principal Amount"). If the Indexed Principal Amount is greater that $1,000, the Company may at its option deliver Silver to holders electing to accept such delivery in satisfaction of the Indexed Principal amount. As of the close of trading on April 9, 1980, the Spot Settlement Price of Silver on the Commodity Exchange, Inc. in New York was $16.00 per Ounce and, accordingly, at such price 50 Ounces of Silver would be valued at $800.

duced by Goldman Sachs—Stock Index Growth Notes ("SIGNs")—can be viewed as the combination of a zero-coupon bond and a call option on the S&P 500 index.[13] Subsequently, bonds have appeared with the principal repayment indexed to other equity indices (such as the NYSE index) and subsets of indices (such as the zero-coupon bond indexed to the S&P Pharmaceutical Index that United Technologies issued in 1991).

Indexed Coupons. The debt-plus-option hybrids considered so far are all combinations of debt with a single option. Hybrids have also appeared that are made up

FIGURE 16–6 Standard Oil Hybrid

AT MATURITY, the holder of the 1990 Oil Indexed Note receives $1,000 plus the excess of the crude oil price over $25 multiplied by 170 barrels

$$\$1,000 + 170 \times (P_{\text{crude oil}} - \$25)$$

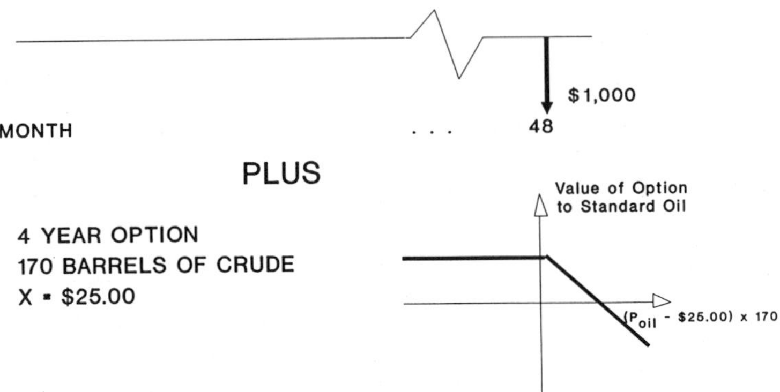

This announcement is neither an offer to sell nor a solicitation of offers to buy any of these securities. The offering is made only by the Prospectus and the related Prospectus Supplement.

NEW ISSUE June 23, 1986

The Standard Oil Company

37,500 Oil Indexed Units

Consisting of

$300,000,000 6.30% Debentures Due 2001

$37,500,000 Oil Indexed Notes Due 1990

$37,500,000 Oil Indexed Notes Due 1992

The Debentures and Notes are being offered in Units, each of which consists of eight Debentures of $1,000 principal amount each, one Oil Indexed Note Due 1990 and one Oil Indexed Note Due 1992 of $1,000 principal amount each. The Debentures and Notes will be issued only in registered form and will not be separately transferable until after July 31, 1986, or such earlier date as may be determined by the Underwriters with the concurrence of the Company.

Price $7,976 Per Unit

plus accrued interest on the Debentures from July 1, 1986

of debt and a package of options with various maturities—typically with the maturities of the options matching the coupon dates of the underlying bond.

1. **Commodity Interest-Indexed Bonds.** Magma Copper Company's 1988 Copper interest-indexed senior subordinated notes were the first of the bonds to have interest payments indexed to a commodity price.

This announcement appears as a matter of record only.

$503,000,000

Recapitalization

$200,000,000 Bank Term Loan and Revolving Credit

$210,000,000 Copper Interest-Indexed Senior Subordinated Notes

December 1988

As illustrated in Figure 16–7, this 10-year debenture has embedded in it 40 option positions on the price of copper—one with maturity three months, one with maturity six months, and so on, up to one with maturity 10 years.[14]

The result of these option positions is that the quarterly interest payment is determined by the prevailing price of copper:

Average Copper Price	*Indexed Interest Rate*
$2 or above	21 percent
1.80	20
1.60	19
1.40	18
1.30	17
1.20	16
1.10	15
1.00	14
0.90	13
0.80 or below	12

FIGURE 16–7 Magma Copper's Senior Subordinated Notes

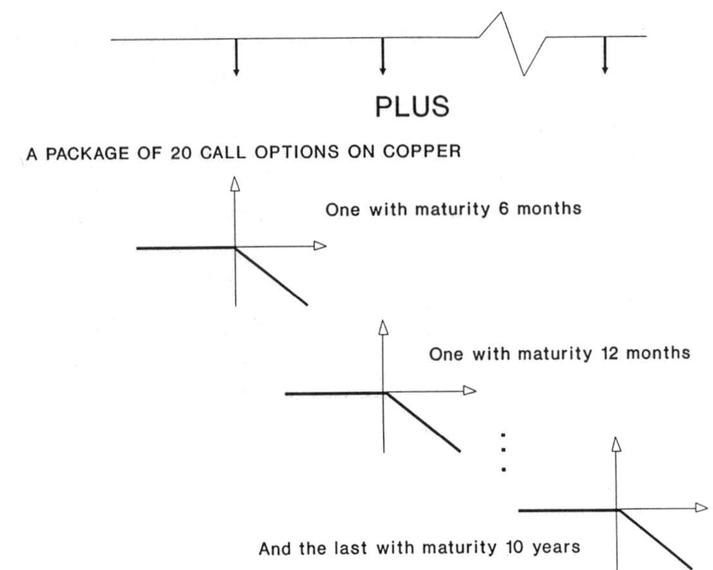
PLUS
A PACKAGE OF 20 CALL OPTIONS ON COPPER
One with maturity 6 months
One with maturity 12 months
And the last with maturity 10 years

A structure that was similar but had the coupons linked to the price of natural gas was issued by Presidio Oil Company in 1989.[15] And in 1991, VAW Australia used a similar structure—but this time to the price of aluminum—to finance expansion of its aluminum smelter north of Sydney.[16]

While the examples cited have all been firms that have a direct exposure to the price of the commodity, the same kind of structure can also be used by firms that have an inverse exposure to the price of the commodity. In 1991 Shin Etsu, a Japanese chemical manufacturer—a commodity user rather than a commodity producer—issued a private placement in which the coupon floated *inversely* with the price of oil.

2. **Floored Floating-Rate Bonds.** The combination of a standard floating-rate bond and a package of European put options on the index interest rate (with the maturities of the put options set to match the coupon reset dates) results in a floating-rate bond that has a minimum interest rate.[17] However, the cost of this minimum rate protection is the premium that must be paid for the put options. And there could clearly be times when the premiums would be too expensive. This cost can be reduced by replacing the European options with Asian interest rate options; instead of paying off if the interest falls below a specified rate, the average rate options would pay off if the interest rate falls below the average rate over a specified period prior to the reset date. The resulting security has a floor, but the level

of the floor depends on the path interest rates have followed. Such a structure is referred to as a "path-dependent floater."

3. **Inflation-Rate Interest-Indexed Bonds.** In 1988 the Franklin Savings Association issued notes called Real Yield Securities (REALS), in which the investors received interest payments calculated as the sum of 3 percent and the rate of inflation as measured by the change in the Consumer Price Index. Hence, this hybrid could be viewed as the combination of a fixed-rate, bullet-repayment bond plus a package of options on the CPI inflation rate, with the maturities of the options coinciding with the quarterly coupon payment dates.

Debt plus Options on the Issuer's Creditworthiness or on Shareholder and Manager Behavior

Puttable, Callable, Extendable Debt. Extendable debt, as we have explained, is the combination of debt and an interest rate option (a put option on interest rates held by the bondholder). Callable and puttable bonds can also be described as debt plus interest rate options in which puttable bonds (introduced to the market in 1976) contain call options on interest rates held by the bondholder, and callable bonds contain put options on interest rates held by the issuing firm.

However, these debt structures also contain embedded options on the credit spread of the issuer. With puttable and extendable debt, the bondholder holds the option. If the credit spread of the issuer increases, the right to put the bond to the issuer has value. If the credit spread of the issuer decreases, the right to extend the maturity of the bond (at the old credit spread) has value. With callable debt, the issuer holds the option. If the issuing firm's credit spread declines, the right to call the bonds (and reissue at a lower credit spread) has value.

Convertible Debt. As we have noted, convertible bonds contain embedded equity options—a standard bond plus a call option on the value of the issuing firm's equity. But this right to convert to equity also can be viewed as an option held by the bondholder on the behavior of the firm's shareholders. If the shareholders behave opportunistically so as to transfer value from bondholders to shareholders, the right to become a shareholder becomes valuable.

Earlier, we used the term "exchangeable" to refer to a bond that can be exchanged for a different bond from the same company. "Exchangeable debt" also refers to a form of convertible debt in which the debt is exchanged for equity of a company different from the one that issued the debt. Brad Barber (1993) notes that exchangeable debt has been offered since the early 1970s and, by the 1980s, accounted for 6 percent of all equity-linked debt.[18]

LYONs. While a number of bonds are puttable or convertible, the Liquid Yield Option Note℠ (LYON©) introduced by Merrill Lynch in 1985 is perhaps the best example of a hybrid security designed to deal with this potential for opportunistic behavior on the part of the shareholders. As described by McConnell and Schwartz (1986):

PROSPECTUS

$750,000,000

Waste Management, Inc.

Liquid Yield Option Notes* due 2001
(Zero Coupon—Subordinated)

The issue price of each Liquid Yield Option Note* ("LYON") will be $250 (25% of principal amount) and there will not be any periodic payments of interest. The LYONs are subordinated to all existing and future Senior Debt and will mature on January 21, 2001. The LYONs are convertible at the option of the holder at any time, unless previously redeemed, into Common Stock, $1.00 par value, of the Company at the conversion rate of 4.36 shares per LYON. The conversion rate is not adjusted for accrued original issue discount but is subject to adjustment under certain conditions. On April 11, 1985, the last reported sale price of the Common Stock on the New York Stock Exchange—Composite Tape was $52⅛ per share.

Each LYON will be purchased by the Company at the option of the holder on June 30, 1988 and on each June 30 thereafter at various purchase prices as set forth in this Prospectus. See "Description of LYONs—Purchase of the LYONs at the Option of the Holder".

Prior to June 30, 1987, the LYONs are redeemable at the option of the Company only under certain circumstances. The LYONs are redeemable at any time on or after June 30, 1987 prior to maturity. Redemption prices vary and are set forth elsewhere in this Prospectus. See "Description of LYONs—Redemption of LYONs at the Option of the Company".

*Trademark of Merrill Lynch Capital Markets

The LYONs are offered by the Underwriter subject to prior sale, when, as and if delivered to and accepted by the Underwriter and subject to its right to withdraw, cancel or modify such offer and to reject orders in whole or in part. It is expected that the LYONs will be ready for delivery in New York, New York on or about April 22, 1985.

Merrill Lynch Capital Markets

The date of this Prospectus is April 12, 1985.

and illustrated in Figure 16–8, the LYON is a puttable, callable, convertible, zero-coupon bond.

Explicit Options on the Issuer's Creditworthiness. In 1988 Manufacturers Hanover issued floating-rate, rating-sensitive notes in which Manufacturers Hanover agreed to pay a spread above LIBOR that varied, as did the corporation's senior debt rating. For every step that Mannie Hannie's credit rating[19] decreased, the investors would receive an additional 1/16 in yield. Therefore, if Manufacturers Hanover became less creditworthy, the bondholders would automatically receive a higher yield.

While this idea is attractive, there is an obvious flaw. If the option becomes valuable, the option holder must look for payment to the entity whose creditworthiness has declined. A hybrid that avoided this problem was the syndication devel-

FIGURE 16–8 A LYON©: A Puttable, Callable, Convertible, Zero-Coupon Bond*

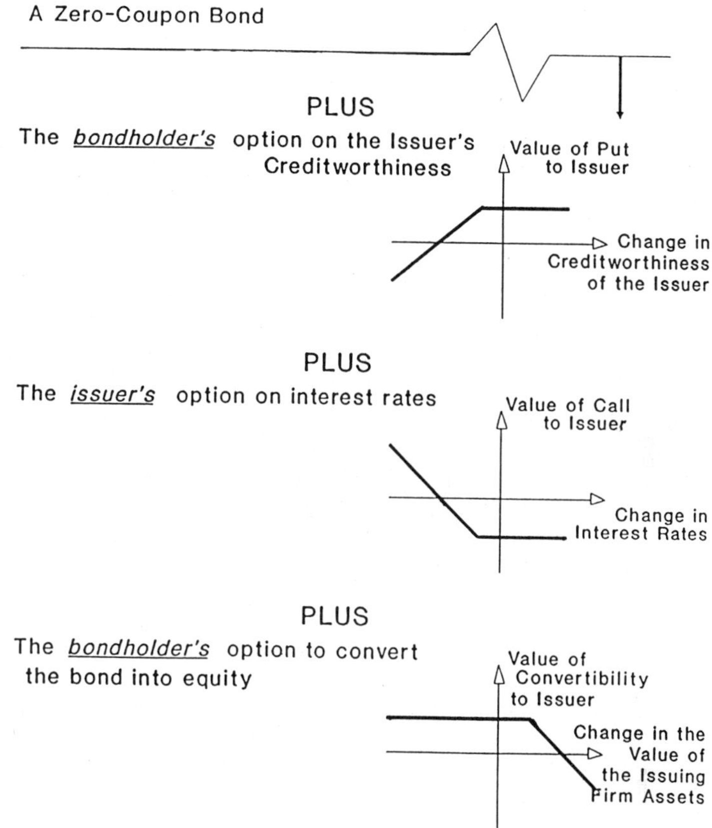

*LYON is a trademark of Merrill Lynch & Co.

oped in 1990 by the Chase Manhattan Bank for Sonatrach, the state hydrocarbons company of Algeria. If oil prices decline, the creditworthiness of Sonatrach declines, so the syndicate banks would like to have a higher return. However, if oil prices decline, Sonatrach will have less money to pay out, so a structure like the Mannie Hannie Rating Sensitive Note would not work. Instead, as Figure 16–9 illustrates, the transaction was structured so that Chase accepted two-year call options on oil from Sonatrach and then transformed the two-year calls into seven-year calls and puts that are passed on to the syndicate members. The calls Chase received from Sonatrach have desirable credit characteristics; Chase will look to Sonatrach for payment only if the oil price is high, and if the price of oil is high, Sonatrach has money. If the price of oil declines, the members of the syndicate receive a higher yield; this increase comes from Chase, not from Sonatrach.

FIGURE 16–9 Sonatrach Option

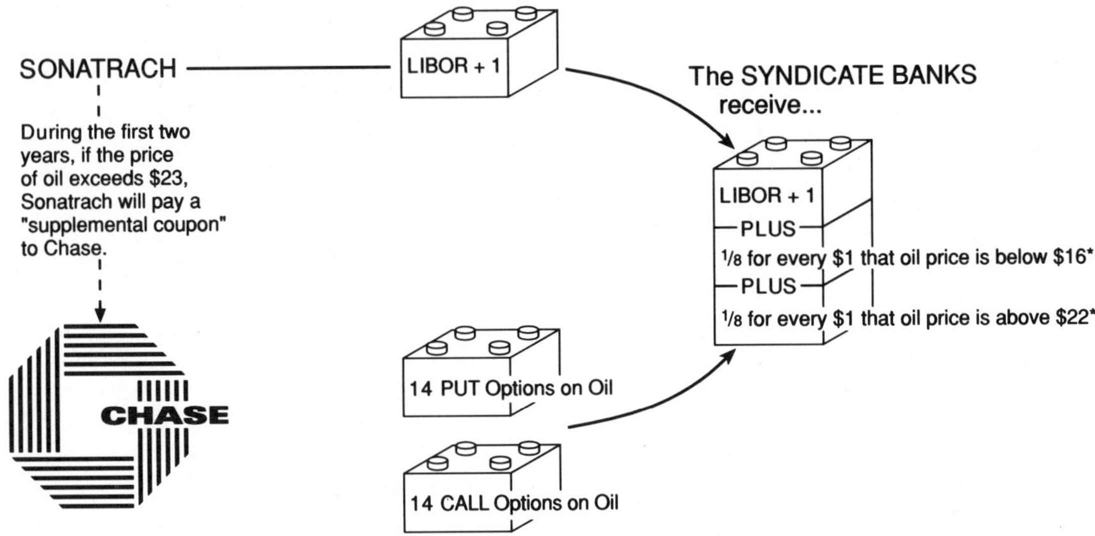
SONATRACH
During the first two years, if the price of oil exceeds $23, Sonatrach will pay a "supplemental coupon" to Chase.
CHASE
LIBOR + 1
The SYNDICATE BANKS receive...
LIBOR + 1
PLUS
1/8 for every $1 that oil price is below $16*
PLUS
1/8 for every $1 that oil price is above $22*
14 PUT Options on Oil
14 CALL Options on Oil
*In the first year, the syndicate receives additional interest of the price of oil falls outside the rage $16–$22. In year 2, the range widens to $15–$23, then to $14–$24 on year 3, and to $13–$25 in years 4 through 7.

*In the first year, the syndicate receives additional interest of the price if oil falls outside the range of $16–$22. In year 2, the range widens to $15–$23, then to $14–$24 in year 3, and to $13–$25 in years 4 through 7.

Hybrids Composed of Equity and Derivatives

While we identified five forms of standard debt, standard equity comes in only two forms, common and preferred.

Equity plus Swap. Adjustable-rate preferred stock, introduced to the market in 1982, paid a dividend that was adjusted quarterly to reflect changes in short-term interest rates. Looking at the "building block," adjustable-rate preferred stock can be viewed as the reverse of the adjustable-rate note described earlier. In the same way that we viewed an adjustable-rate note as the combination of a floating-rate note and a swap in which the bondholder pays a floating rate and receives a rate tied to the firm's dividend rate, adjustable-rate preferred stock can be viewed as the combination of preferred stock and a swap in which the preferred equity holder pays a rate tied to the dividend rate on the firm's preferred stock and receives a floating rate.[20]

Equity plus Option

Options on Equity or an Equity Index. In 1983, Americus Trusts were created to enable investors to separately trade the dividend and capital gains components of equity. From trusts of shares of certain blue-chip firms, two hybrid securities were issued: The holders of the PRIMEs (Prescribed Right to Income and Maximum Equity) would receive all the dividend income and the value of the underlying share up to a predetermined price—the termination claim. The holders of the SCOREs (Special Claim on Residual Equity) would receive the value of the underlying share above the termination claim.

The Americus Trust idea died almost stillborn because of an IRS ruling. However, the idea of decomposing the claims on equity has resurfaced in two other hybrids.

Morgan Stanley introduced Preference Equity Redemption Cumulative Stocks (PERCS) in 1991 with the first issue by General Motors. Shares of the underlying stock are held in trust (known as depository shares), and the PERCS are sold from the trust. In return for an above-market dividend, the investor grants to the issuer the right to call the equity at a predetermined price. Hence the investor has a position that is equivalent a long position in the equity and a short position in a call on the equity.

The firm of Leland–O'Brien–Rubinstein has proposed a similar idea it calls SuperShares.[21] In this case the trust would hold a portfolio made up of the S&P 500 portfolio and a portfolio of Treasury bills instead of an individual equity. Against this portfolio the trust would sell four hybrids: (1) Priority SuperShares—holders receive all dividends plus the value of the S&P 500 portfolio to a specified level; (2) Appreciation SuperShares—holders receive the value of the S&P 500 portfolio above a specified level (a call option on the S&P 500 index); (3) Protection SuperShares—holders receive the value of any decline in the value of the S&P portfolio below a specified level (a put option on the S&P 500 index); and (4) Money Market Income SuperShares—holders receive the interest from the Treasury bills plus the value of the Treasury bills after the Protection SuperShares have been paid. These SuperShares would trade on the American Stock Exchange.

Option on Managerial Behavior. In November 1984 Arley Merchandise Corporation issued puttable stock. As described by Andrew Chen and John Kensinger (1988), the investor buys a hybrid made up of a share of common stock and a right that entitles the investor to claim more stock if the market price of the stock is below a stated level at a predetermined date. At the predetermined date, if the market price of the share is above the guaranteed floor price, nothing happens; if the market price of the share is below the guaranteed floor price, the issuing firm must make up the difference in value by giving the investor additional common shares. This hybrid can be viewed as an equity security plus an equity-settled put option on the value of the equity; as Chen and Kensinger point out, this hybrid is comparable to a convertible bond.

The Economic Rationale for Issuing a Hybrid Security

Once we observe that hybrid securities can be decomposed into simpler building blocks, we must ask why firms issue these hybrid securities instead of the simpler individual components. The answer lies in these four rationales.

To Provide Investors with a "Play"

The most straightforward reason for issuing a hybrid is to provide investors with a means of taking a position on a financial price. If the issuer provides a "play" not available otherwise, the investor will be willing to pay a premium, thereby reducing the issuer's cost of funding.

The "play" can be in the form of a forward contract. Perhaps the best example of such is dual currency bonds. Dual currency bonds provide investors with foreign exchange forward contracts that have much longer maturities than those available in the standard market—that is, the forward contract embedded in dual currency bonds normally has a maturity of 10 years, while the liquidity in the standard foreign exchange forward market declines for maturities in excess of 1 year and falls dramatically for maturities beyond 5 years.

However, the "play" has more commonly been in the form of an option embedded in the bond, generally an option of longer maturity than those available in the standard option market. Examples include PEMEX's Petrobonds, Sunshine Mining's Silver Indexed Bond, Standard Oil's Oil-Indexed Note, Salomon Brothers' Market Indexed Notes, and the gold warrants issued by Pegasus Gold Corporation.

To "Arbitrage" Tax and/or Regulatory Authorities

Hybrid securities have been used to take advantage of asymmetries in the tax treatment across national boundaries and in regulations in different markets. A classic example is the case we described in Chapter 10:

> There was a tax arbitrage opportunity: Japanese tax authorities ruled that the income earned from holding a zero-coupon bond would be treated as a capital gain, and since capital gains were untaxed, the interest income on zero-coupon bonds would not be taxed for Japanese investors. In contrast, U.S. tax authorities permitted any U.S. firm issuing a zero-coupon bond to deduct imputed interest payments from income.
>
> Moreover, there was regulatory arbitrage that would allow the issuing firms to eliminate some of the resultant exposure to yen while obtaining a still lower realized

interest rate: The Ministry of Finance (MoF) limited the amount a Japanese pension fund could invest in non-yen-dominated bonds issued by foreign corporations to at most 10 percent of their portfolio, but MoF ruled that dual currency bonds qualified as a yen issue.

Hence, U.S. firms would (1) issue a zero-coupon yen bond, (2) issue a dual currency bond, and (3) hedge the remaining yen exposure with a currency swap. The result was a set of cash flows that are like that of a deep-discount dollar bond with below-market coupons.

Perhaps the most thinly disguised attempt to issue tax-deductible equity was the *adjustable rate convertible debt* introduced in 1982. Such convertibles paid a coupon determined by the dividend rate on the firm's common stock; moreover, the debt could be converted to common stock at the current price at any time (in other words, there was no conversion premium). Not surprisingly, once the IRS ruled that this was equity for tax purposes, this structure disappeared.

On a less ambitious level, a number of issuers wish to take advantage of the treatment of zero-coupon instruments by U.S. tax authorities: The issuer can deduct the deferred interest payments from current income, thus reducing potential liquidity problems faced by firms in the near term. Merrill Lynch's LYON is one hybrid structure that provides this benefit.

To Obtain Accrual Accounting Treatment for Risk Management

If a U.S. firm uses a forward, a futures, a swap, or an option to hedge a specific transaction (such as a loan or a purchase or a receipt), it is relatively simple to obtain accrual accounting (hedge accounting) treatment for the hedge. However, if the firm wishes to use one of the risk management instruments to hedge net income or an economic exposure, the current position of the accounting profession is that the hedge position must be marked-to-market. Some firms have hesitated to use risk management because this accounting treatment will make their accounting statement income more volatile.

However, if the risk management instrument is embedded in a debt security, the firm can obtain accrual accounting treatment for the entire package. Accountants, by making an analogy to convertible debt, use the accepted accounting principles for convertible debt to account for the hybrid on an integrated basis using historical cost, thereby achieving hedge accounting treatment.[22]

To Align Interests of Shareholders and Bondholders

Michael Jensen and William Meckling (1976) bring into focus the impact of conflicts between shareholders and bondholders (as well as managers, workers, suppliers, and customers) on the behavior of the firm. Clifford Smith and Jerry

Warner (1979) highlight the sources of shareholder–bondholder conflict, suggesting that potential bondholders are concerned that shareholders will behave opportunistically:

1. *Shareholders could dilute the bondholders' claims by increasing debt or adding debt senior to that held by the bondholders in question.* In the practitioners' jargon, this is referred to as "event risk"; academics refer to this as the "claims dilution problem."
2. *Shareholders could invest in more risky projects.* This is referred to as "asset substitution."
3. *If income is sufficiently volatile, the firm may pass up positive NPV Projects.* As we noted in Chapter 4, in periods in which the firm has less income, it may be induced to pass up otherwise profitable projects.[23]

Hybrid securities provide ways of dealing with these concerns.

Making the bond puttable reduces the claim dilution problem. If the shareholders attempt to dilute the bondholders' claim, bondholders have the right to cash in the bond. In this way, we might look at the put as a "golden parachute" for bondholders.

Making the bond convertible reduces the asset substitution problem. If the shareholders attempt to expropriate value from the bondholders by investing the proceeds of the debt into more risky investment projects, the bondholders can elect to become shareholders.[24]

A puttable and convertible structure, like Merrill Lynch's LYON, would therefore be attractive in situations in which shareholder–bondholder conflict is likely, such as when the issuing firm requires substantial capital investment and has available to it a wide range of alternative investment projects (with varying degrees of risk). Interestingly, the LYON structure was used early on in this context to fund firms that faced acute asset substitution problems; Waste Management and Turner Communications are two examples.

The puttable and convertible features of a LYON make it attractive to the retail investor. However, it turned out that another feature of the LYON, the call feature, lately has made it less popular with investors.

Hybrids can be structured to reduce the volatility in the underlying net income of the firm, thereby reducing the probability of default compared with straight debt. Examples of hybrid issues that have decreased the volatility of income include Magma Copper's Copper Interest Indexed Notes, Presido's Natural Gas Interest Indexed Note, and Franklin Savings' CPI Indexed Bonds. The inverse floating-rate note could effectively reduce the volatility of net income for firms that are adversely affected by interest rate increases—for instance, firms that supply materials for new home construction.

Risk Management in Practice

Are LYONs Becoming a Dying Breed?

Constance Mitchell

A few years ago, LYONs were one of Wall Street's hottest products. Brokerage firms, led by Merrill Lynch, heavily promoted the hybrid securities to small investors.

LYONs have a popular "put" option that allows the investor to sell them back to the issuer at certain intervals, usually after 5 years and then 10 years.

It all looked great. But with interest rates tumbling, many LYONs owners are getting a rude shock as they realize that LYONs can be "called," or redeemed early, much faster than most bonds.

That's just what LYONs issuers are doing; these companies know they can replace their LYONs today by selling ordinary bonds that pay lower interest rates.

"The [bond] market has rallied so much," and interest rates have declined so sharply, said Bradley Sparks, MCI's treasurer, that "it's cheaper to issue straight debt" than complex securities such as LYONs.

Constance Mitchell is a staff reporter for *The Wall Street Journal*. This article is excerpted from a March 8, 1993, article by the same title in the *The Wall Street Journal*.

No Longer King?

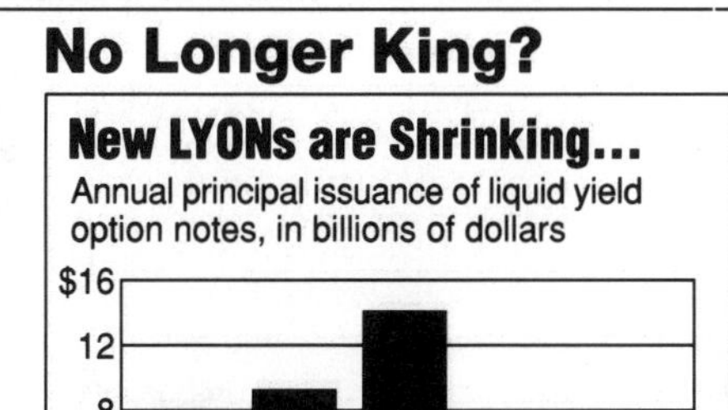

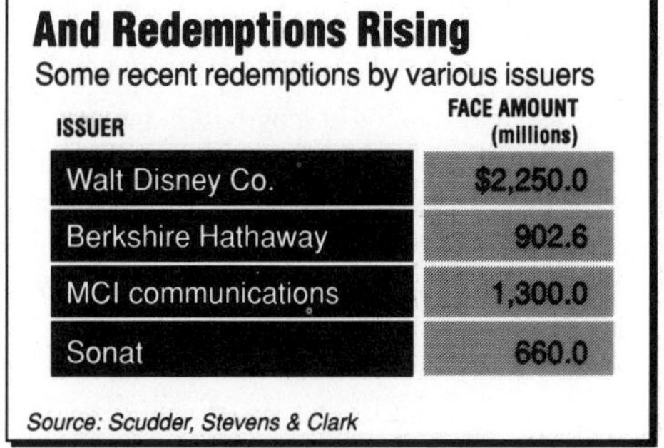

And Redemptions Rising

Some recent redemptions by various issuers

ISSUER	FACE AMOUNT (millions)
Walt Disney Co.	$2,250.0
Berkshire Hathaway	902.6
MCI communications	1,300.0
Sonat	660.0

Source: Scudder, Stevens & Clark

As an alternative to reducing the probability of default, the conflict between shareholders and bondholders could be diminished by compensating the bondholders if the issuing firm becomes more risky. Manufacturer Hanover's Rating Sensitive Notes were meant to address this problem.

Notes

1. The dates for the first issuance of convertible debt and debt with warrants are taken from Tufano (1989).
2. See McCulloch (1980).
3. *Derivatives Week* (1993).
4. LYON is a trademark of Merrill Lynch & Co.
5. The dates for the introduction of floating-rate notes and zero-coupon bonds are taken from Tufano (1989).
6. See Capatides (1988).
7. The notes and warrants were offered simultaneously, but they were sold separately, with the warrants trading on AMEX.
8. In the early 1990s—with silver trading in the $4 range— the exercise price of $20 per ounce might seem bizarre. However, between October 1979 and January 1980 the price of silver averaged $23 per ounce.
9. See Jordan, Mackay, and Moriarty (1990).
10. While this option appears to be European-style, its payoff was actually determined by the average price of oil over a specified period, making it an average-rate option (an Asian option). See Chapter 15 for more on average-rate options.
11. Finnerty (1992) notes that ICONs "were introduced and disappeared quickly."
12. For more on SPINs, see K.C. Chen and R.S. Sears (1990).
13. SIGNs are discussed at length in Finnerty (1993).
14. In effect, the owner of the note is long a call option with an exercise price of $0.80 and is short a call with an exercise price of $2.
15. It was Forest Oil Company that first considered issuing the natural gas–linked debt. However, Forest Oil subsequently felt certain that certain natural gas prices were about to rise, which would make the *ex post* price of the natural gas–linked debt too great. It turned out that Forest Oil made a large bet that went against the firm; natural gas prices fell, and Forest Oil was forced to restructure the standard debt it had issued (*The Wall Street Journal*, May 7, 1991).
16. As reported in the June 1992 issue of *Risk*, VAW Australia used a five-year US$31 million facility that had interest payments indexed to the average LME price of aluminum. As the price of aluminum rises, the interest rate VAW Australia pays rises.
17. Floored floating-rate debt was used widely in 1993 with issues by the Chase Manhattan Bank, First Union, and First Chicago (American Banker 1993).
18. For more on exchangeable debt, see Barber (1993).
19. The note specified that the lower of S&P or Moody's rating would be used.
20. Michael Alderson and Don Fraser (1993) argue that adjustable-rate preferred stock failed to flourish because the value was too volatile—the dividend rate did not change as rapidly as did the interest rate to which it was tied, and the dividend rate did not change to reflect changes in the creditworthiness of the issuing firm. They point out that adjustable-rate preferred stock has given way to a second-generation hybrid—auction rate preferred stock.
21. The idea for SuperShares was originally proposed by Nils Hakansson (1976).
22. Singleton (1991). Note, however, that the accounting treatment of derivatives tends to be a moving target. At an Emerging Issues Task Force meeting in September 1993, the SEC took the position that dual currency bonds would have to be decomposed into the underlying bonds and the long-dated forward contract and the two components would have to be accounted for separately.
23. In addition to the three sources of shareholder–bondholder conflict we consider here, Smith and Warner identify a fourth source of conflict, dividend payout. This source of conflict is normally dealt with through debt covenants.
24. See Brennan and Schwartz (1981).

CHAPTER

17

MEASURING AND MANAGING DEFAULT RISK

The magnitude of the default risk[1] inherent in an OTC derivatives transaction has been—and remains—a source of concern for both market participants and the regulatory authorities. As the 1980s neared their end, the U.S. Federal Reserve had begun to view the credit risks from intermediating OTC derivatives as "a significant element of the risk profiles of . . . the large multinational banking organizations that act as intermediaries between end users of these contracts."[2]

As we noted in Chapter 3, the spotlight focused on risk management products got a lot brighter in the early 1990s. E. Gerald Corrigan, then the president of the Federal Reserve Bank of New York, voiced the concern of many regulators when he noted that "the growth and complexity of [derivatives transactions] . . . and the nature of the credit . . . and settlement risk they entail should give us all cause for concern. . . . "[3]

The bankruptcy of Drexel Burnham Lambert and the failure of the Bank of New England[4] led the users of risk management products to attempt to do more of their derivative transactions with AAA and AA financial institutions. The bankruptcies of nonfinancial entities—notably Olympia & York—highlighted to intermediaries of the risk management products the importance of performing careful credit analyses. And, when the UK House of Lords ruled that the UK local authorities of Hammersmith & Fulham could walk away from derivative transactions they had entered into, the market realized that failure to perform can be the result of reasons other than a financial inability to pay.

Concern about credit risk led to the development of risk-based capital adequacy standards for the derivatives transactions intermediated by commercial banks. The requirements were established in July 1988 by the Basle Committee on Banking Supervision—that is, representatives of the central banks of Belgium, Canada,

France, Germany, Italy, Japan, the Netherlands, Sweden, United Kingdom, the United States (the Group of Ten countries) plus Switzerland and Luxembourg.[5] These requirements—commonly referred to as the Basle Accord—came into full force at the end of 1992.

Using the "Building Blocks" to Examine Default Risk

When the "building block" approach was introduced in Chapter 2, we began with forwards and moved toward options. To develop some insight about the default risk associated with derivatives, we can again use the building blocks. But since the determinants of default risk are most apparent for options, we begin at the other end this time.[6]

Default risk for an option is one-sided. There is no duty to perform on which the option buyer could default; once the premium payment is made, the buyer only receives payments. It is the option seller who has the obligation to perform. Two circumstances are necessary for the seller of the option to default.

First, the option must be in-the-money. Unless the option is in-the-money, the seller of the option will not be required to perform.

Second, for default to occur, the seller of the option must be released from contractual obligations by a court. In Chapter 3, we discussed circumstances in which courts have granted[7] or have been petitioned to grant[8] release from contractual obligations; the most likely circumstance—and the one that we will focus on here—is bankruptcy of the option seller.

Indeed, the default risk of this option can itself be viewed as an option. However, the value of this "default risk option" depends on two uncertain values—the underlying financial price on which the option is written and the value of the other assets of the seller of the option. Consequently, the option to default is a compound option.[9] And, if we look at the option to default as a compound option, the probability-weighted loss that could result from a distress-induced default on an option contract is determined by three things:

The value of the option, itself determined by the relation between the exercise price and the prevailing spot price, the volatility of the underlying financial price, and the time to maturity.

The credit standing of the seller of the option, determined by the critical change in the value of the other assets necessary to put the option seller into distress as well as the volatility of these other assets.

The correlation between the underlying financial price and the value of the option seller's other assets, which depends on whether the option sold is a call or a put.

As we saw in Chapter 12, selling a forward is equivalent to buying a put and selling a call. Conversely, buying a forward is equivalent to selling a put and buying a call. This equivalence has direct implications for the default risk for a forward contract.

First, evaluation of the default risk for a forward contract must involve valuation of the same default-risk "option" as with options themselves. To evaluate the default risk for a forward, it is necessary to consider the embedded "short" option positions.

Second, the default risk of a forward contract is associated with both the buyer and seller of the forward. The seller of the forward has sold a call; the buyer of the forward has likewise sold a put.

Since a swap can be viewed as a package of forward contracts, default risk for a swap is again a compound option. However, it is a more complex compound option than for options or forwards. Under "full two-way" payment, default on a swap would oblige immediate cash settlement of the contract. A swap counterparty can only default once. Therefore, there could exist an "optimal default strategy" that would depend on the joint distribution of the counterparty's asset values and the underlying asset price *at each settlement date*. Although this default option is dramatically more complex than for calls and forwards because of the multiple settlement dates, the variables that determine its value are the same.

The compound option framework is useful in developing an understanding of the default-risk problem, and we believe that this path is one that will be followed in the future. However, this approach will be quite demanding, both computationally and with respect to data collection and management.

Thus, both market participants and regulators have employed the simplifying approximation that the financial price underlying the derivative transaction and the counterparty's other assets *are uncorrelated*. With this simplifying approximation in place, any measure of risk based on the potential default-induced loss to the intermediary must be a function of two determinants:

1. *Exposure*—the amount at risk.
2. *Probability of default*—the likelihood of a loss.

Using a simple mathematical expression, we can denote potential default-induced loss as

$$\text{Potential default-induced loss} = (\text{Exposure}) \times (\text{Probability of default})$$

It is with the two components—the exposure generated by and the probability of default for risk management transactions—that most of this chapter will deal. We will, however, also consider some of the techniques used to measure credit risk, methods for reducing credit risk, and some evidence on the default history to date for risk management instruments.

Aside

The Approach of the Basle Committee on Banking Supervision

The approach we will describe in this chapter mirrors that which the Basle Committee on Banking Supervision used in developing the capital adequacy guidelines. They considered an exposure measure weighted by the probability of default, one that "applies credit conversion factors to the face value, or notional principal, amounts of off-balance sheet exposures and then assigns the resulting credit equivalent amounts to the appropriate risk category in a manner generally similar to balance sheet assets."* To make this cryptic description more clear, the following flow chart describes the manner in which the process is accomplished.†

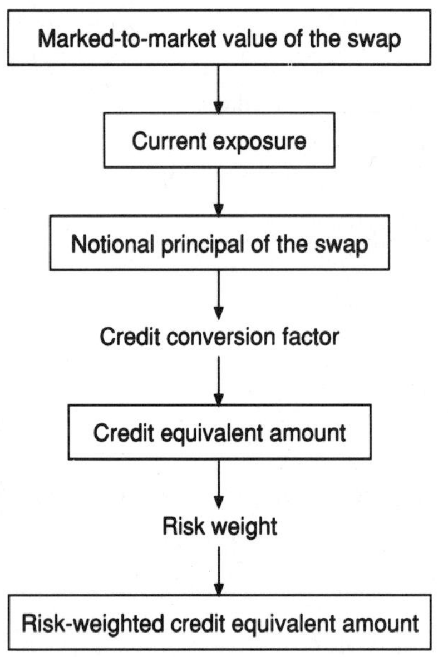

The process begins with the *marked-to-market value of the risk management product.* From this measure, the *current exposure* of the financial institution to default on the swap is defined as the positive portion of the mark-to-market value:

Max [0, marked-to-market value]
= Current exposure

Next, the current exposure is combined with the *notional principal amount* of the swap and a *credit conversion factor* to define the *credit equivalent amount* for the swap:

Current exposure
+ Notional principal of swap
× Credit conversion factor
= Credit equivalent amount

This is equivalent to the "exposure" described above.

Then, to get from this "exposure" measure to some measure of potential default-induced loss, the credit equivalent amount is multiplied by a *risk weight* to yield a *risk-weighted credit equivalent amount*:

Credit equivalent amount × Risk weight
= Risk-weighted credit equivalent amount

---

*Federal Reserve System *Capital Maintenance: Revisions to Capital Adequacy Guidelines*, 12 CFR Part 225, Appendix A (Regulation Y), January 24, 1988, pp. 61–62.

†This process is taken from the January 24, 1988, Federal Reserve System publication, pp 103–06.

Exposure

When dealing with credit risk, banks are used to dealing with loans. The exposure to the bank on a loan is straightforward: The amount of money the bank has at risk is the amount that "walked out of the bank" less any principal repayments that have occurred. However, things are not quite so simple for the risk management products:[10] At any point in time, the bank is exposed not only for the *current value of the derivative* but also for *potential changes in value*. Also, the calculation of the exposure must take into consideration the fact that the *exposure will change over the life of the transaction*. Moreover, the bank must consider two exposure measures—*maximum* and *expected*.

Current and Potential Exposures

As an example of a risk management transaction, consider an interest rate swap. In Figure 17–1, we have illustrated how the value of the swap changes as the underlying interest rate changes. Panel (a) illustrates the value profile for the fixed rate payer: If interest rates rise, the expected present value of the inflows becomes larger than that for the outflows and the value of the swap becomes positive; but, if rates fall, the

FIGURE 17–1 Marking a Swap Contract to Market (*a*) The value of a swap in which the party illustrated pays fixed, receives floating (*b*) The value of a swap in which the party illustrated pays floating, receives fixed.

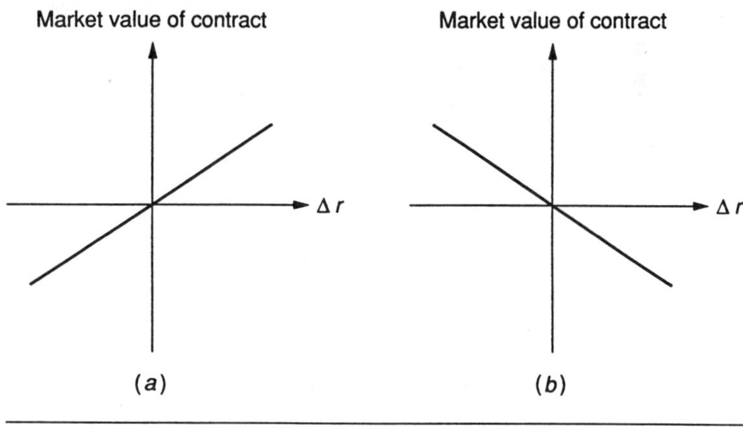

value of the swap to this fixed-rate payer becomes negative. Panel (b) illustrates the reverse, the value of a swap to the party receiving fixed and paying floating.

The current replacement cost of a swap—the current exposure of the swap—is obtained directly from the market value of the swap contract. In panel (a) of Figure 17–1, if rates have fallen since origination, there will be no loss if the counterparty defaults; if rates have fallen, the fixed-rate payer is making payments to the counterparty. For the fixed-rate payer, a default-induced loss will occur only if rates rise.

Hence, for this individual transaction, the current cost of replacing the counterparty in a swap contract is given by the positive segment of the market value profile for the swap contract. This is illustrated in Figure 17–2.

Albeit an essential element, market value—current replacement costs—alone does not accurately portray the credit risk faced. As noted by the Board of Governors of the Federal Reserve System and the Bank of England (1987), "The cost to a banking organization of a counterparty default . . . is the cost of replacing the cash flows specified by the contract"—the *total* exposure characterized by the Fed as the sum of the current replacement cost and "a measure of the potential future credit exposure that may arise from further movements over the remaining life of the instrument."

Put another way, the current replacement cost indicates the cost of replacing the swap counterparty if the counterparty defaults *today*. However, the counter-

FIGURE 17–2 Current Replacement Cost (*a*) The current cost of replacing a floating cash flow (*b*) The current cost of replacing a fixed cash flow.

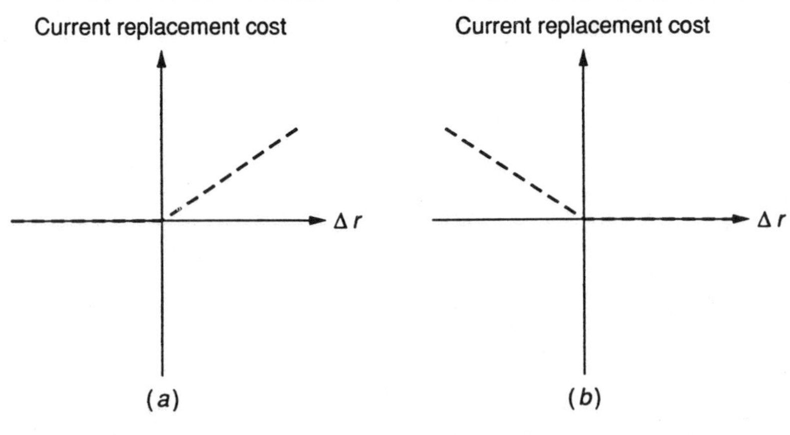

party may default not today but rather at some date in the future, at which time the interest rate may be different from that today. For example, consider default by a floating-rate payer.

Panel (a) of Figure 17–2 is reproduced as Figure 17–3. Suppose that the current interest rates are lower than those that prevailed at contract origination, $\Delta r_t < 0$—a situation illustrated by point *A* in Figure 17–3. In this case, the *current* replacement cost is zero. However, since the issue is the magnitude of the total exposure to loss today of default that may occur in the future, we need to know the current replacement cost *plus* the potential credit exposure illustrated by point *B* in Figure 17–3.

What determines this potential credit exposure? In the context of Figure 17–3, the exposure to default-induced loss depends on potential interest rate movements. For a default-induced loss to occur, the interest rate at some future default date must exceed the rate which prevailed at contract origination (r_0). Clearly, the likelihood of this increase in rates occurring depends on the volatility of interest rates, σ_r and on the remaining life of the contract, *T*. And, since the exposure is the result of lost cash flows *in some future periods*, we also require a discount factor $D = D(r,T)$ where *r* is the relevant discount rate and *T* is the time remaining to contract maturity.

FIGURE 17–3 Potential Credit Exposure

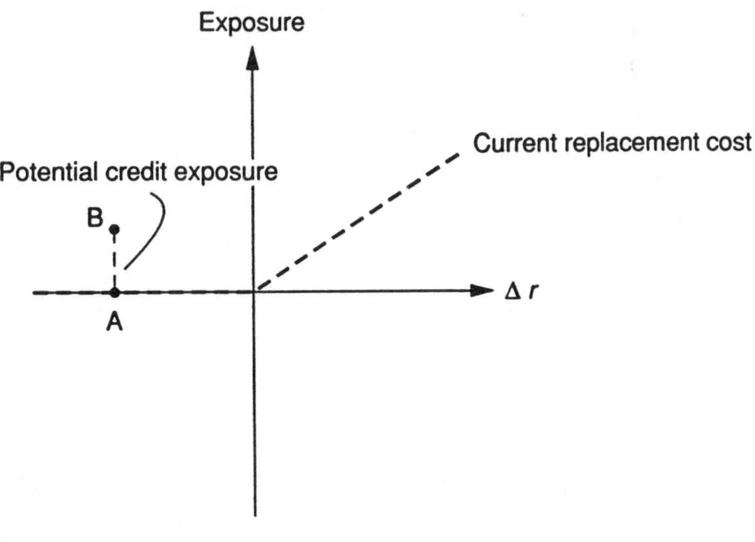

Exposure over the Life of the Transaction

For some traditional bank products, the bank's exposure to the borrower is constant throughout the life of the transaction. If the bank makes a zero-coupon loan, the principal exposure—the amount of money that left the bank at origination—is unchanged during the life of the transaction.[11] However, other products are structured so that the amortization effect reduces the bank's exposure over time. In the case of an amortizing loan, the bank's exposure to the borrower declines dramatically over time as principal is repaid. The exposure on a loan that pays regular interest payments but returns all the principal at maturity (a "bullet" repayment loan) declines over time, but not nearly as dramatically as the amortizing structure.

The credit exposure generated by intermediating risk management instruments also varies over the life of the transaction. As will be described below, there are two reasons for this changing exposure. One is the familiar amortization effect; the other is much less familiar.

The Amortization Effect. In the same way that the bank's exposure declines as principal is repaid or coupons paid, the bank's exposure to some derivative transactions also declines as the time remaining to contract maturity declines. Figure 17–4 demonstrates that the amortization effect for a 10-year interest rate swap is like that for an amortizing loan: At time 0—origination—the bank is exposed for 10 years, 20 settlements. (In the case of an amortizing loan, at month 0, the bank is

FIGURE 17–4 The Amortization Effect

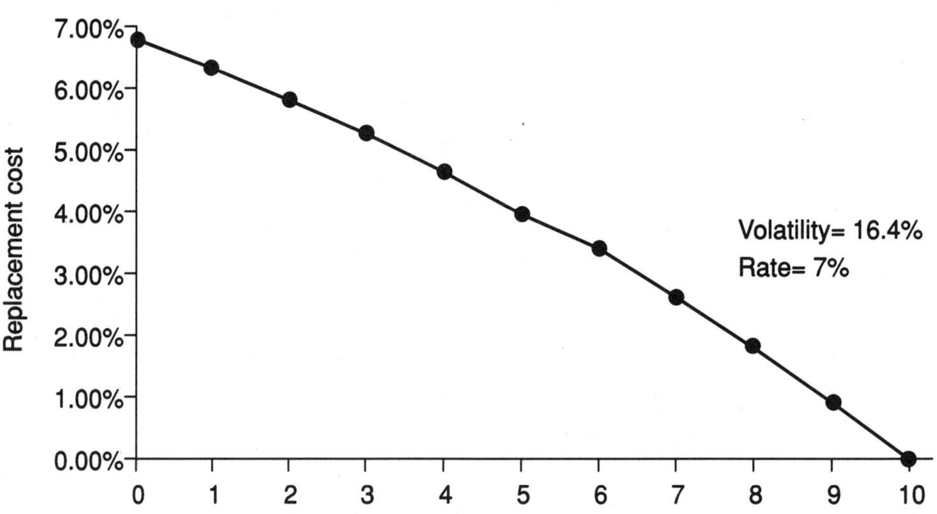

SOURCE: This figure is adapted from a presentation made to the Bank for International Settlements by Denise M. Boutross, executive vice-president, DKB Financial Products, Inc., on January 21, 1993.

exposed for the entire principal.) Over time, settlement payments are made and the bank's exposure declines. (In the case of an amortizing loan, over time, principal is repaid and the bank's exposure declines toward zero.)

The Diffusion Effect. Unlike a traditional bank product, where the bank's concern is about principal exposure, the bank's exposure to its counterparty for a risk management product is also influenced by the degree to which the underlying price can differ from the price that existed at contract origination. This effect is referred to as *the diffusion effect*.

As we described earlier, volatility deals with the amount the financial price can change in a single period. In panel (a) of Figure 17–5, we use the now-familiar lattice diagram to illustrate this concept: In a single period, the financial price could move up from P_0 to $P_0{*}u$ or down to $P_0{*}d$. The volatility for this binomial process is a function of the initial price and the size of the up-and-down movements.[12]

Diffusion deals with the amount the financial price can change over a number of periods. Panel (b) of Figure 17–5 presumes the same volatility as panel (a) but illustrates that, over three periods, the financial price could be as high as $P_0{*}u^3$ or as low as $P_0{*}d^3$.

The diffusion process illustrated in panel (b) will generate a set of distributions for the underlying financial price. Panel (c) of Figure 17–5 illustrates how, as time elapses, the diffusion process causes the dispersion of prices to increase. As more time elapses, increasingly high (low) prices will be feasible.

This probability distribution for prices provides a framework for the bank to evaluate its potential exposure. If the bank is receiving the financial price, the potential exposure becomes greater when more time to maturity remains. Figure 17–6 illustrates the effect that diffusion will have on the bank's exposure to its counterparty: With more time remaining until contract expiration, the bank's potential exposure increases—that is, the possible deviation in the financial price from its level at origination increases.[13]

Combining the Amortization and Diffusion Effects

For an interest rate swap, if we combine the amortization effect (Figure 17–4) and the diffusion effect (Figure 17–6), we obtain the familiar "humped" exposure profile illustrated in panel (a) of Figure 17–7. The rising portion of the profile indicates that the diffusion effect dominates early in the life of the swap; the falling section indicates that at some point in the swap's life, the diffusion effect is swamped by the amortization effect as the time to maturity gets short and there are fewer settlements outstanding.[14]

While standard interest rate swaps and other derivative transactions that have periodic payments and no final exchange of principal have the hump-backed exposure profile, panel (b) of Figure 17–7 illustrates that the exposure profile for a cross-

FIGURE 17–5 Volatility and Diffusion

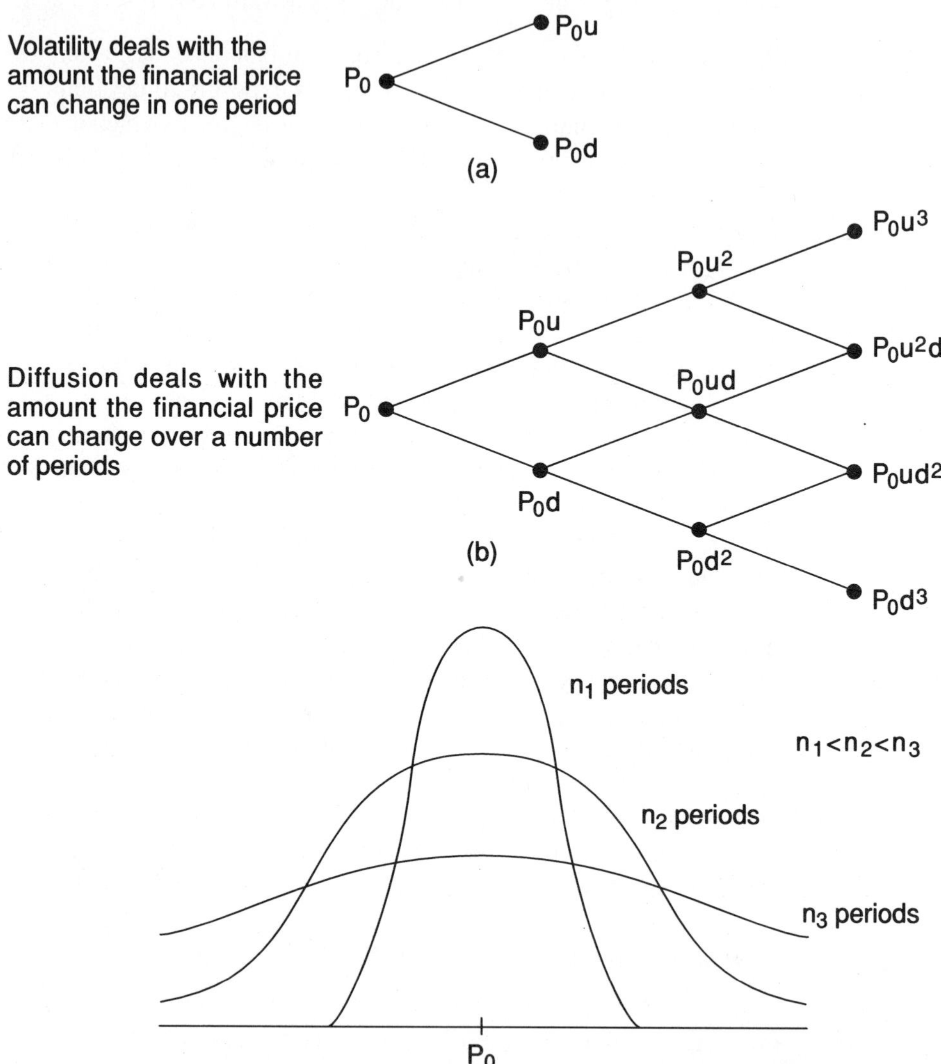
Volatility deals with the amount the financial price can change in one period
P_0
P_0u
P_0d
(a)
Diffusion deals with the amount the financial price can change over a number of periods
P_0
P_0u
P_0d
P_0u^2
P_0ud
P_0d^2
P_0u^3
P_0u^2d
P_0ud^2
P_0d^3
(b)
n_1 periods
$n_1<n_2<n_3$
n_2 periods
n_3 periods
P_0
As the number of periods increases, the dispersion of the financial price increases
(c)

currency swap rises over time. Since the bank is exposed to the principal reexchange at maturity, the amortization effect from the periodic settlements is swamped by the effect of diffusion on the principal reexchange.

FIGURE 17–6 The Diffusion Effect

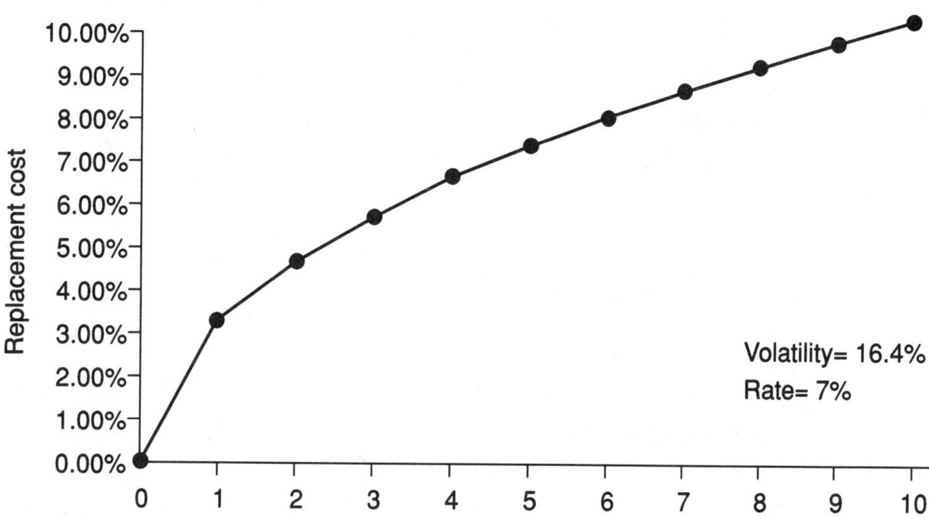

SOURCE: This figure is adapted from a presentation made to the Bank for International Settlements by Denise M. Boutross, executive vice-president, DKB Financial Products, Inc., on January 21, 1993.

Maximum versus Expected Exposures

In the process of developing the capital adequacy standards, the U.S. Federal Reserve System and the Bank of England noted that, when the swap counterparties evaluate their exposures, they should be asking about *two* exposure measures:[15]

1. What is my *maximum exposure* if my counterparty to this contract defaults?
2. What additional exposure do I accept by entering into this contract—that is, what is the *expected exposure* generated by this contract?

Note that, in the case of a loan contract, the same number—the loan principal—answers both questions. Consequently, since commercial banks have become the dominant intermediaries for swaps and since commercial banks are used to dealing with the credit risk of loans, the two-question aspect of this issue has become veiled.

Maximum Exposure. The maximum credit exposure[16] should reflect the greatest amount that the intermediary could lose were the counterparty to default. This measure is most widely used in the credit allocation function for the financial institution intermediating the transaction—to determine how much to allocate for the risk management transaction against general counterparty lines of credit.

FIGURE 17–7 Combining the Amortization and Diffusion Effects

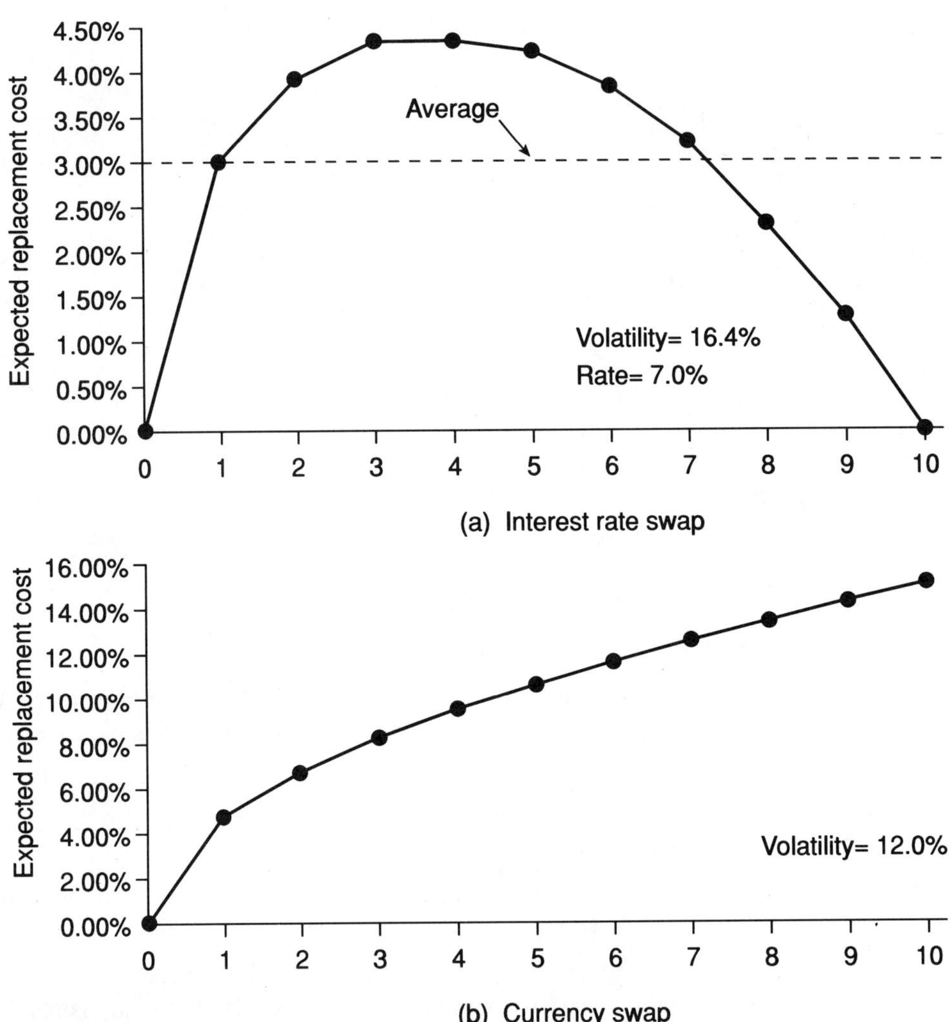

SOURCE: This set of figures is adapted from a presentation made to the Bank for International Settlements by Denise M. Boutross, executive vice-president, DKB Financial Products, Inc., on January 21, 1993.

A measure of the maximum exposure is also crucial for the credit risk control function. Maximum exposure sets some "alarm level." If the current exposure (the mark-to-market exposure) ever exceeds the exposure that was defined as the maximum when the contract was originated, "the alarm goes off." Once the alarm sounds, the duty of management is to determine whether the alarm was set off because of (1) a random draw from the interest rate distribution or (2) a change in the structure of interest rates. If the alarm rang because of (1), no response is necessary—all we know is that an unlikely event occurred. If, however, the alarm rang because of (2), the policies with respect to the next swap transaction must be reexamined.

In practice, determination of the maximum exposure for a risk management product is difficult because financial prices are stochastic. Since there is a distribution for the underlying financial price, there likewise exists a distribution for the market value of a the risk management instrument. Consequently, there can be no true *maximum* exposure for the risk management transaction. Hence, when measuring the maximum exposure for a risk management transaction, the intermediary must define some value that will be the maximum exposure with some specified probability.

To illustrate this, Figure 17–8 expands the exposure profiles presented in Figure 17–7 to provide maximum exposure profiles with confidence levels of 90 percent and 95 percent for an interest rate swap (panel (a)) and a cross-currency swap (panel (b)).

In the context of Figure 17–8, a measure of the maximum exposure could be defined as the peak exposures attained by the maximum exposure profiles. Note that these peaks are relatively small percentages of the notional principal of the transaction.

Expected Exposure. The expected exposure for a risk management instrument would reflect the likely future overall exposure of the intermediary's derivatives portfolio that would result from intermediating this additional transaction.

Expected exposure gives the intermediary an *ex ante* measure of how much, on average, it could expect to lose if the counterparty were to default. Hence, this exposure measure is the one the banking regulators have focused on in determining how much capital a bank should be required to hold against derivative transactions.

Within the firm intermediating the risk management transaction, expected exposure is used both to price and to evaluate the profitability of a transaction. Expected exposure is used to determine the appropriate credit margin to include in the pricing of a risk management transaction. Expected exposure is also the appropriate exposure to use in the denominator when evaluating the rate of return for the risk management transaction.

As its name implies, an expected exposure recognizes the probability distributions for the underlying financial prices (and the value of the risk management instrument). However, in comparison to maximum exposures that look at the exposure that will be exceeded only 1 percent or 5 percent or 10 percent of the time, the expected exposure uses the mean value. The relation between expected exposures and maximum exposures is illustrated in Figure 17–8.

FIGURE 17–8 Maximum and Expected Exposures

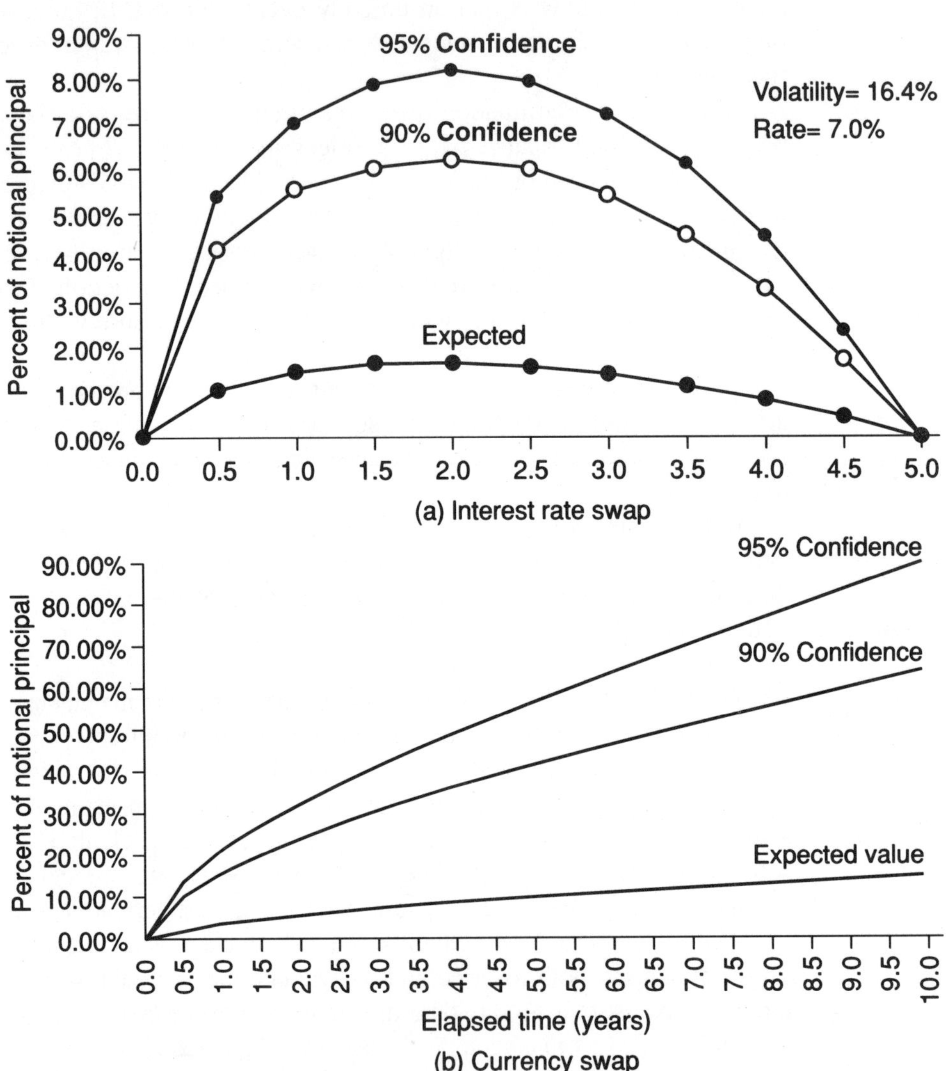

SOURCE: This set of figures is adapted from a presentation made to the Bank for International Settlements by Denise M. Boutross, executive vice-president, DKB Financial Products, Inc., on January 21, 1993.

Measuring the Exposure for an Individual Transaction

The "Worst-Case" Approach

Early measures of the credit risk for swaps and the other risk management products were based on "worst-case" assumptions about market risk and default. As Mark

Ferron and George Handjinicolaou (1987) described the process, the bank would make conservative high and low projections for the future level of replacement interest rates and then use these extreme cases to calculate the maximum cost of replacing all cash flows associated with a single swap. While the worst-case procedures are generally proprietary, the ones we have heard market participants describe provide overly conservative assessments of swap risk by assuming the worst outcome for the bank from *both* the diffusion and amortization processes. That is, they calculate the exposure by assuming that the underlying financial price moves immediately to the extreme value and that default occurs immediately after inception of the contract (so the bank will lose all future payments).

The Simulation Approach

In Chapter 5 we described how a Monte Carlo simulation could be used to assess the degree to which a firm is exposed to financial price risk. Not surprisingly, this same approach is widely used to measure a bank's exposure when it intermediates a risk management transaction. For exposition, we have broken such a simulation process into six steps:

1. *Specify the manner in which the underlying financial price behaves.* For example, the most common assumption is that interest rates follow a lognormal probability distribution.
2. *Specify the initial value for the financial price.*
3. *Specify the volatility of the financial price.*
4. Use 1, 2, and 3 to simulate a number of *paths (as few as 1000, as many as 10,000) that the financial price could take over the life of the risk management transaction.*
5. For each of the simulated financial price paths, calculate the corresponding value of the risk management product at specified intervals over its lifetime.
6. *Combine the individual estimates of the value of the transaction to obtain probability distributions for exposure at specified intervals.*

The Option Valuation Approach

When we illustrated current and potential exposure in Figure 17–3, the resulting figure is an option payoff diagram. Indeed, as we have already noted, since default occurs only if it is in the counterparty's interest, default must be viewed in an option-theoretic framework.[17]

When we discussed potential exposures, we noted that five parameters go into the determination of the exposure to default-induced losses for the interest rate swap we were considering:

1. The interest rate at the evaluation date, r_t.
2. The interest rate at origination, r_0.
3. The volatility of interest rates, σ_r.
4. The discount rate, r.
5. The time remaining to contract maturity, T.

These parameters are those needed to value an option—in this case a call option.

A standard option-pricing approach would result in a credit exposure profile like that illustrated in Figure 17–9.[18] For an in-the-money swap (one where the market value of the swap is positive because of an increase in rates), the current replacement cost rises as the swap moves further and further into the money; but at the same time, the potential credit exposure declines as time value decreases.

The Capital Adequacy Rules

To move from their simulation results for expected exposure to an implementable rule, the Basle Committee determined "credit conversion factors":

	Credit Conversion Factor	
Maturity of Transaction	*Interest Rate Transactions*	*Currency Transactions*
Less than one year	0.000	0.010
One year or greater	0.005	0.050

FIGURE 17–9 Credit Equivalent Exposure as an Option

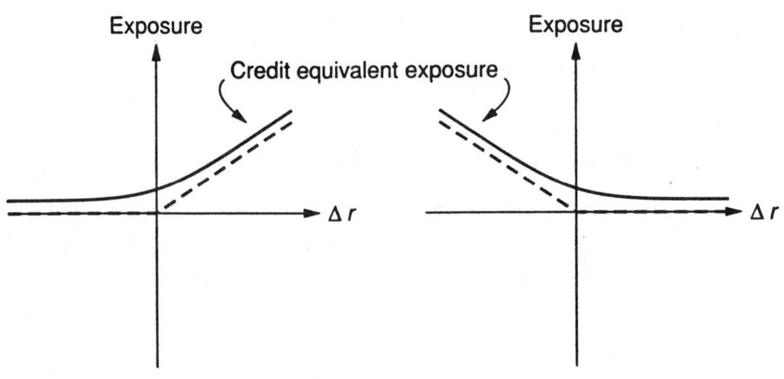

FIGURE 17–10 Capital Adequacy Rules

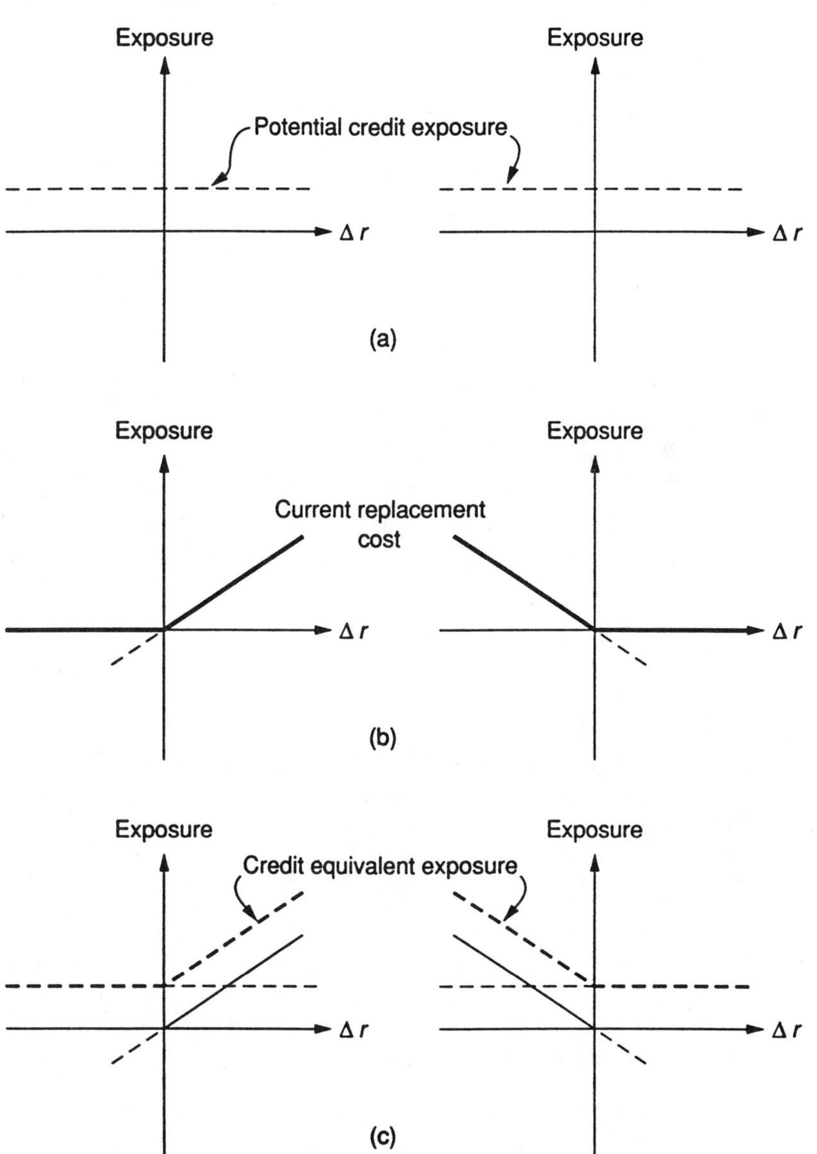

Using this credit conversion factor, the potential credit exposure is determined as:

Notional principal × Credit conversion factor = Potential exposure

As illustrated in panel (a) of Figure 17–10, the resulting potential credit exposure is invariant to the prevailing interest rate or foreign exchange rate. The poten-

FIGURE 17–11 Comparison of Capital Adequacy Rules Approach and Option-Theoretic Approach

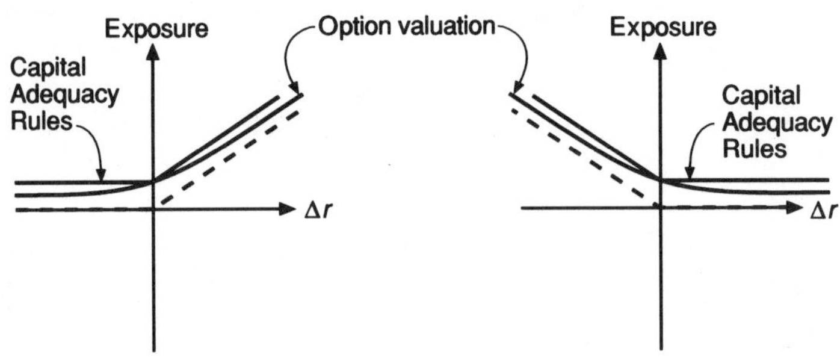

tial credit exposure varies as the size of the notional principal varies or as the time to maturity changes but it does not vary as the financial price changes.

To obtain the total credit equivalent exposure, this constant potential credit exposure is added to the current replacement cost (shown in panel (b) of Figure 17–10). But if the current replacement cost is negative, it is treated as zero. The resulting credit equivalent exposure can be summarized by the mathematical expression

$$\text{Credit equivalent exposure} = \text{Potential credit exposure} + \text{Max}[0, \text{market value of swap}]$$

and is illustrated as in panel (c) of Figure 17–10.

We noted above that simulation and option valuation approaches give similar results for expected exposure. However, the expected exposures simulated or obtained from an option-pricing approach differ substantially from those obtained from the capital adequacy rules. A comparison of the credit equivalent exposure profiles for the capital adequacy rules and for an option-pricing model is provided in Figure 17–11. This figure suggests that the capital adequacy rules overestimate the exposures for a swap that is further in- or further out-of-the-money.

Measuring the Exposure for a Portfolio of Transactions

So far, we have considered the exposure of a bank were it to intermediate a *single* derivative transaction. However, most market participants (notably financial intermediaries) hold large portfolios of risk management products.

General Portfolio Effects

As with loans, portfolio effects exist such that the exposure of the sum is less than the sum of the individual exposures. But default on derivative transactions should

Aside

Probability of Default: Swap versus Loan

Unfortunately, the similarity between loans and swaps that was so useful in examining the evolution and pricing of swaps in Chapter 10 proves counterproductive when we look at credit risk. We believe that there are three primary differences between the default implications of loans versus those of swaps.

First, the principal in a swap is not at risk; as we have described, the principal in a swap is only notional. In contrast, a significant component of the credit risk of a loan has to do with the potential failure to repay the principal.

Second, for a swap, the periodic net cash flows to be paid or received (that is, at settlement dates) are proportional to the difference in rates (for example, in an interest rate swap, I pay or receive on the basis of the difference between a fixed interest rate and a floating rate). In a loan, the periodic cash flows to be paid or received (that is, at the coupon payment dates) is determined by the level of rates (for example, with a floating rate loan, I pay or receive on the basis of the level of a floating interest rate). Hence, the periodic cash flows from a swap must be smaller than those from a comparable loan.

The third difference is that default on swaps requires that *two* conditions exist simultaneously while default on a loan requires only *one*. Default on a loan requires only that the firm be in financial distress. Default on a swap requires both that the party to the swap be in financial distress and that the remaining value of the contract to that party be negative. Hence, the probability of default on a swap is a joint probability: the probability of the value of the swap being negative and the probability of the party being in financial distress. Therefore, this joint probability (on a swap) will be less than would be the simple probability (on a loan).

be more idiosyncratic than would be default on a loan. And, because default on derivatives are more idiosyncratic, the portfolio effect should be more pronounced for derivatives than for loans.

The Effect of Netting

For an individual transaction, the current cost of replacing the counterparty in a risk management contract is given by the positive segment of the market value profile for the contract. However, for a portfolio of transactions, if the bank could net its exposures, the bank's exposure resulting from a positive-valued transaction could be offset by a transaction that has a negative mark-to-market value.

For OTC derivatives, netting is currently accomplished on a bilateral basis—positive mark-to-market values on transactions for one counterparty could be off-

Risk Management in Practice

Aggregating the Exposure for a Portfolio of Transactions

James P. Healy

Calculating measures of the potential exposure for a portfolio of transactions is much more difficult than for a single transaction. The simplest method is simply to add the measure of potential exposure of each transaction in the portfolio. Unfortunately, this procedure will, in most cases, dramatically overstate the potential exposure because it does not take into account transactions in the portfolio that have offsetting exposures or peak potential exposures that occur at different times.

To illustrate how offsetting exposures influence the exposure of the portfolio, let's look at an example that reflects the actual position of many of the firms that intermediate the risk management products.

> Suppose the intermediary has transacted two interest rate swaps with the same counterparty and that the swaps are identical in all respects except that the counterparty is receiving the fixed rate in one swap and paying the fixed rate in the other.
>
> There is no net exposure. However, if we correctly calculate the total maximum exposure as \$5 million for each transaction and if we add the exposures, the total maximum exposure for the portfolio would be \$10 million—clearly an overstatement.
>
> If the counterparty were to default in the future, only one of the swaps would result in a loss—both swaps could not have a positive mark-to-market value at the same time. The proper exposure in this portfolio is \$5 million even if netting does not apply (and zero if netting does apply).

Another shortcoming of adding the maximum exposure on a transaction-by-transaction basis in a portfolio relates to the timing of the default if one were to occur. It is not appropriate to add the peak exposures of transactions that occur on different dates. An example will help to illustrate this point:

> Suppose that the portfolio consists of a purchased interest rate cap and a long-term swap:
>
> The last rate setting on the cap has taken place and a final cap payment of \$5 million is due in two months. The credit risk on the cap is \$5 million.
>
> The swap was executed recently, and the swap currently has a zero mark-to-market value and a peak maximum exposure of \$6 million that occurs in two years (according to the hump-backed schedule discussed earlier).
>
> If we add the peak maximum exposures, the peak maximum exposure on the portfolio would be \$11 million. This is clearly an overstatement. The peak maximum exposure on the cap occurs in two months and the peak maximum exposure on the swap occurs in two years. In this situation, we should calculate the maximum exposure on the swap that could occur in two

Aggregating the Exposure for a Portfolio of Transactions continued

months. If that peak exposure were to be $2 million, we should conclude that the peak maximum exposure on the portfolio is $7 million, not $11 million.

The potential exposure of a portfolio of transactions with a given counterparty can be analyzed more thoroughly by simulation analysis. This requires sophisticated mathematical modeling and systems capability. In this approach, multiple scenarios are generated by means of a statistical model, and the stochastic properties of the derivatives portfolios are investigated. At each point in time under a given scenario, the mark-to-market value of each transaction in the portfolio is computed, and the present value of the replacement cost of the entire portfolio is calculated, taking account of netting provisions where applicable. This process is repeated for a large number of scenarios to generate a probability distribution of the present value of the replacement cost of the portfolio at each point in time. This information can be used to calculate the expected and maximum exposure profiles for the portfolio over its life span. The main advantage of this portfolio-level simulation is that it directly measures complex portfolio effects and thereby provides a much more accurate measure of expected and maximum potential exposure to a counterparty than would be obtained by aggregating exposures on individual transactions or by making an (educated) guess.

Market participants who cannot justify having such simulation and statistical systems to perform such potential exposure calculations use tables of factors developed under the same principles, making sure that the factors used differentiate appropriately by type of transactions and are adjusted periodically to reflect changes in market conditions and the passage of time.

It is extremely important to recognize that, much like current exposure, potential exposure also is constantly changing as time passes and the underlying variables move (that is, amortization and diffusion effects). Accordingly, calculations of potential maximum and expected exposures should be reviewed and updated to reflect these factors. Firms that aggregate potential exposures without quantifying portfolio effects through simulation analysis generally overstate their counterparty exposure, and therefore they do not need to perform calculations as frequently as firms that use simulation analysis to measure portfolio exposure more precisely. In any event, the frequency of calculation should be increased when credit limits are approached or exceeded. Because it is relatively simple to calculate current exposures and relatively more difficult to calculate potential exposure, several institutions update the current exposure on a daily basis but allow for potential exposure as a constant "add-on" to the current exposure. This add-on factor remains constant for the life of the transaction. This practice generally results in a material overstatement of counter

Aggregating the Exposure for a Portfolio of Transactions concluded

party risk. This inaccuracy ignores the dynamic relationship between current and potential exposure and may be avoided by periodically updating the potential exposure calculations.

In the course of The Group of Thirty Global Derivatives Study, we surveyed dealers about the way they measured credit risk. The results of this survey indicated that the methods of aggregating derivatives exposures with a counterparty vary widely. Approximately one third of the dealers surveyed aggregate exposures with a counterparty by summing the exposures as initially calculated, while two thirds of the dealers update aggregate exposures based, at a minimum, on the change in current exposure.

The survey results indicate that many dealers recognize the importance of aggregating the measurement and integrating the analyses of exposure from derivatives transactions with exposures from more traditional on-balance-sheet banking products. Almost half the dealers surveyed currently aggregate exposures from derivatives and nonderivatives activities across all products and all business lines; 73 percent of those surveyed intend to do so in the future.

James P. Healy is a managing director member of the executive board of Credit Suisse Financial Products. Prior to joining Credit Suisse Financial Products, Mr. Healy was a managing director at The First Boston Corporation and head of financial engineering and product development.

Mr. Healy received a Ph.D. in economics from Princeton University, an MSc from the London School of Economics, and a BA from Stanford University. He worked as an economist at the International Monetary Fund from 1979 to 1982 and has served as a consultant to the Board of Governors of the Federal Reserve, the National Bureau of Economic Research, and the OECD, and as a visiting professor of economics at Dartmouth College.

set by negative mark-to-market values for the same counterparty. However, multilateral netting—offsetting positive mark-to-market values on transactions with one counterparty with negative mark-to-market values for transactions with another counterparty through a clearinghouse—is being discussed.

Confining ourselves to bilateral netting, a spectrum of netting arrangements could be used:

Netting by Novation. The two counterparties agree that *matched* pairs of transactions—transactions that are based on the same underlying financial price and have the same settlement date—will be deemed terminated and replaced by a single transaction requiring a payment equal to the difference between the novated transactions. In essence, the counterparties agree to maintain a running balance. Netting by novation is common in foreign exchange spot and forward transactions in which counterparties (typically banks) are likely to have a large number of off-in which counterparties (typically banks) are likely to have a large number of offsetting payments due in the same currency on the same value date; but it is less common for derivatives.[19]

Closeout Netting. This form of netting becomes operative only in the event of default (or a triggering event such as a downgrade). For a specific product (such as interest rate swaps), the positive contract values for a particular counterparty are netted against the negative contract values. Closeout netting has become the standard (indeed, one credit officer indicated that the exception is not to have it). For example, the current ISDA master agreement specifies that if a default occurs, all transactions covered by the master will be terminated, and the values of the various transactions will be netted to a single number.

Cross-Product Netting. Bilateral netting is increasingly being extended to net across products: The bank could reduce its current exposure by offsetting positive mark-to-market values for the counterparty's interest rate swap positions with foreign exchange positions for the same counterparty that have negative mark-to-market value.

To give you some idea about the impact of netting, we use an example used in a presentation made to the Committee on Banking Supervision at the Bank for International Settlements in Basle, Switzerland on January 21, 1993:

Risk Management in Practice

The Impact of Netting on the Exposure to a Swap Portfolio

J. Matthew Singleton

To illustrate the impact of netting, consider a hypothetical portfolio of 12 interest rate swaps, each of which has a notional principal of $20 million. Of the 12 swaps, 3 were transacted with Counterparty A and 3 with Counterparty B; the remaining 6 swaps were done with various counterparties.

At any point in time, some of the swaps will have positive mark-to-market values and others will have negative values. To get this example started, assume that the current total market value of the swap portfolio is $2,070,000, with gains and losses distributed in the following table:

The Impact of Netting on the Exposure to a Swap Portfolio continued

assume that the current total market value of the swap portfolio is $2,070,000, with gains and losses distributed in the following table:

Hypothetical Swap Portfolio: Mark-to-Market Values

Positive Mark-to-Market Values		*Negative Mark-to-Market Values*	
Swap 1	$ 850,000	Swap 3	$ (60,000)
Swap 2	250,000	Swap 7	(500,000) (A)
Swap 4	330,000	Swap 9	(1,650,000) (B)
Swap 5	690,000 (A)	Swap 10	(275,000) (B)
Swap 6	760,000 (A)		
Swap 8	50,000		
Swap 11	1,500,000 (B)		
Swap 12	125,000		
	$4,555,000		($2,485,000)

(A) Swap with Counterparty A.
(B) Swap with Counterpary B.

For this portfolio, the exposure could be measured in several ways.

Gross Notional Principal

The gross notional principal for the 12 interest rate swaps is $240 million.

Sum of Gross Positives

At every point in time, every swap transaction has either positive or negative relpacement value. Only transactions with a positive replacement value expose the bank to credit risk. Thus, the greatest possible credit risk the bank could face is the sum of the gross positives. In the case of our hypothetical portfolio, this would be $4,555,000.

Sum of Net Positives

When we calculated the bank's exposure as the greater of the bank's positive and negative mark-to-market values, we assumed that with Counterparty A, the bank could lose as much as its gross exposure to Counterparty A:

$$\$690{,}000 + 760{,}000 = \$1{,}450{,}000.$$

The Impact of Netting on the Exposure to a Swap Portfolio continued

most the bank could lose is the net positive exposure the bank has with Counterparty A:

$$\$690{,}000 + 760{,}000 = \$1{,}450{,}000 - \$500{,}000 = \$950{,}000.$$

For Counterparty A, all the negative mark-to-market value can be netted against the positive value; the effect of bilateral netting is to reduce the exposure by $500,000.

However, for Counterparty B, the positive mark-to-market value, $1,500,000, is less than the negative value, ($1,650,000) + (275,000) = ($1,925,000). There is no such thing as a net negative exposure and, therefore, if negative mark-to-market values are greater than positive mark-to-market values on transactions with a single counterparty, the net exposure is zero. So, for Counterparty B, the effect of bilateral netting is to reduce the exposure by $1,500,000.

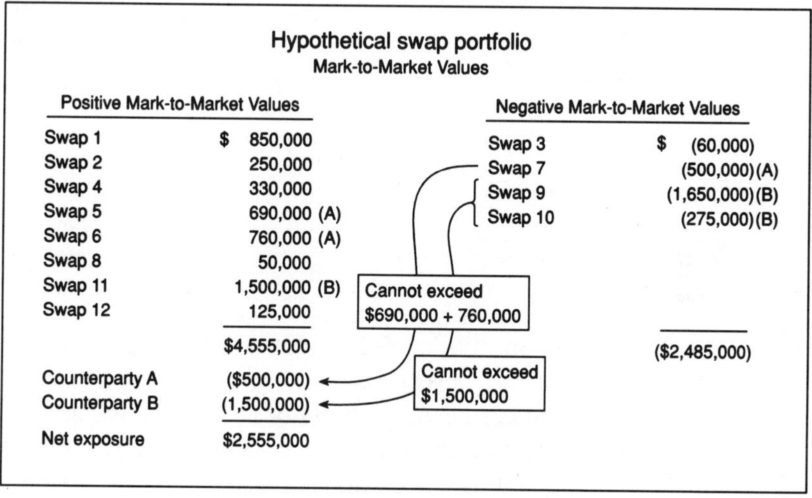

As the preceding table indicates, the effect of bilateral netting is to reduce the exposure from $4,555,000 to $2,555,000.

"Grand Slam" Netting

If all gains could be netted against losses, the bank could perform a "grand slam" net:

The Impact of Netting on the Exposure to a Swap Portfolio concluded

Gross positive M-T-M values	$4,555,000
Gross negative M-T-M values	($2,485,000)
"Grand slam" net	$2,070,000

Some banks use "grand slam" netting as the basis for preparing their balance sheets. Many accountants would regard that approach as aggressive because multilateral netting is not currently recognized by the legal system.

The following table summarizes the impact of netting on the exposure for the portfolio:

Gross notional principal	$240,000,000
Greater of "longs" or "shorts"	$ 4,555,000
Net by counterparty	$ 2,555,000
Multilateral netting	$ 2,070,000

J. Matthew Singleton is the partner in charge of Arthur Andersen's Audit and Business Advisory practice in New York and serves on his firm's Chairman's Advisory Council. Previously, he was responsibile for the New York Financial Services audit practice. He leads the Arthur Andersen team that serves as technical adviser to the International Swaps and Derivatives Association.

Between 1981 and 1983, Matt served as a practice fellow at the Financial Accounting Standards Board. Matt Singleton received a bachelor's degree in economics from Princeton and an MBA from New York University.

Given the impact of netting on the exposure, it is not surprising that the firms that intermediate the derivative products have been in favor of netting. The problem has been the legal enforceability of netting agreements. Because of the impact netting would have on exposures, the impetus is to recognize netting more widely.[20] In April 1993, the Basle Committee on Banking Supervision issued a consultative proposal[21] that recognizes the effectiveness of closeout netting and would permit banks to use bilateral netting in measuring their current exposures.

Measuring the Probability of Default

As we alluded to in the beginning of this chapter, the probability of default for an individual risk management transaction is determined by four general factors. The first two of these are familiar to those who are used to evaluating the credit risk inherent in traditional bank products:

Risk Management in Practice

The Enforceability of Netting

John P. Behof

The legal enforceability of bilateral netting agreements is paramount in order to effect any risk reduction in the case of counterparty bankruptcy. It has been substantially enhanced in the United States by recent amendments to the U.S. Bankruptcy Codes (1990), FIRREA, and FDICIA for depository institutions. The ability of conservators to "cherry pick" (that is, demand payment for trades with positive mark-to-market values and renege on trades with negative mark-to-market values) has been severely restricted in the United States by these legislative changes, but only if written bilateral netting agreements exist. Section 212 of FIRREA states that no person will be prohibited from exercising his or her right to net obligations of any qualified financial contracts with depository institutions in conservatorship or receivership. FIRREA defined *qualified financial contracts* as any securities contract, commodity contract, forward contract, repurchase agreement, swap agreement, and any similar agreement.

Despite the legal changes incorporated in FIRREA and the bankruptcy code, some uncertainty remained. For example, since the qualified categories were so broadly defined, it was never made clear whether spot foreign exchange contracts were included. In addition, it was also never made clear whether netting would be permitted across categories of individually qualified contracts. FDICIA's approach, however, is to look at the type of contracting party, not the contract. Any kind of agreement between *financial institutions* in which parties agree to net positions subject to certain contingencies would be considered a qualified netting contract. Under FDICIA, the Federal Reserve Board may determine what is a financial institution and is currently determining whether insurance companies, swap affiliates of broker-dealers, nonbank subsidiaries of banks and bank holding companies, or other entities will be included in the definition.

Outside of the United States, the legal enforceability of netting is not as straightforward. The Lamfalussy Committee on Interbank Netting Schemes concluded in its 1990 report that bilateral master agreements and other bilateral netting by novation or current account agreements are likely to be enforceable in countries where the 1988 Basle Accord is in effect. The ISDA has obtained legal opinions from counsel in Belgium, Canada, France, Germany, Italy, Japan, the Netherlands, Sweden, and the United Kingdom indicating that netting provisions contained in bilateral master agreements were likely to be

The Enforceability of Netting concluded

upheld in each of those countries. Unfortunately, constructing legally enforceable netting agreements, considering the sometimes conflicting legal structures of different countries, is often at odds with the attempts to standardize such agreements. Also, because so few derivative firms have gone bankrupt, different degrees of comfort are taken from reasoned legal opinions, especially when the more esoteric derivatives are involved and countries with less clear legal precedent are involved. In addition, regulatory authorities have expressed concern over the enforceability of netting agreements during an international financial crisis, which would have potentially widespread systemic implications.

Although they can be somewhat expensive and difficult to execute, bilateral netting agreements are gaining popularity as an immediate remedy to credit constraints, particularly since multilateral clearinghouses appear to be a year or two away from establishment. Until recent introduction of more standardized documents, standardized bilateral netting agreements were usually customized documents or somewhat customized versions of the ISDA master agreement and were negotiated by the attorneys from each counterparty. As bilateral netting agreements have gained popularity, more standardized agreements are appearing. ISDA has developed a standardized bilateral closeout netting agreement that is part of the so-called multiproduct master agreement that has recently been completed. Other agreements used in the market that have provisions for bilateral netting include the International Currency Options Market Master Agreement (ICOM), the Foreign Exchange Master Agreement, the PSA agreement for bond options and repurchase agreements, the cross-border Canadian foreign exchange agreement, and the FXNET master agreement. In addition, the ICOM group is preparing an agreement for foreign exchange spot and forward transactions that will include netting provisions. None of these netting documents has yet emerged as a clearly preferred document within the financial industry.

John P. Behof has recently joined Nations Bank in Chicago. Previously, he was a senior examiner in the Department of Supervision & Regulation at the Federal Reserve Bank of Chicago. This discussion originally appeared as part of "Reducing Credit Risk in Over-the-Counter Derivatives," which was published in the January/February issue of *Economic Perspectives* (Federal Reserve Bank of Chicago).

1. Creditworthiness of the counterparty: The more creditworthy (higher rated) the counterparty, the lower the probability of default.
2. Maturity of the transaction: The longer the maturity of the transaction, the more likely it is that the firm's credit quality will deteriorate, so the higher the probability of default is.

Risk Management in Practice

International Bank Insolvencies and the Enforceability of Multibranch Master Netting Agreements

Daniel P. Cunningham

A concern for international bank regulators is the oversight of banks that transact business through branches or agencies in other jurisdictions. A home country regulator may find significant discrepancies between its approach to bank regulation and those of regulators in other countries in which the parent bank operates branches or agencies. This conflict can be especially acute in the case of a bank insolvency involving branches and agencies in multiple jurisdictions.

While some European bank regulators have adopted a unified approach to cross-border banking insolvencies, U.S. regulators tend to view U.S. branches and agencies of foreign banks as distinct entities, subject to an insolvency proceeding independent from a proceeding in the home country. For example, New York State banking law dictates a "ring-fencing" approach to international bank insolvencies. Assets of a New York branch or agency in liquidation are first used to satisfy the creditors of the New York branch or agency; any remaining assets are then transferred to the banking authority of the country in which the bank's principal office is located.

Since different regulators would attempt to distribute the same pool of assets, this approach invites conflict. For example, when they attempted to ring-fence the assets of the New York agency of the Bank of Credit and Commerce International (BCCI) during the global liquidation of that bank, New York Banking Department regulators clashed with banking regulators from England, Luxembourg, and other jurisdictions.

Though local creditors of a foreign bank branch or agency may applaud ring-fencing (because their claims are more likely to be satisfied than if they are forced to seek satisfaction in a foreign liquidation proceeding), this policy could frustrate the intention of parties who have entered into derivatives transactions documented under master agreements that include multibranch netting arrangements. A multibranch master netting agreement permits a party to make or receive payments or deliveries under derivatives transactions that are documented ("booked") through any eligible branch or agency. A bank that enters into a multibranch master agreement expects that amounts owed to counterparties or due to it from counterparties will be netted across all branches and

International Bank Insolvencies and the Enforceability of Multibranch Master Netting Agreements continued

agencies of the bank. A liquidator applying a ring-fencing approach to a multibranch master agreement would be forced to set aside the explicit terms of the agreement and instead focus on the amounts owed under only the transactions booked through the local branch or agency.

Despite great gains that have been made toward global recognition of the enforceability of bilateral netting agreements in OTC derivatives transactions, enforceability issues regarding multibranch netting agreements have not received sufficient attention. Nevertheless, the enforceability risk may concern many participants in derivatives transactions. A recent study of global derivatives practices by the Group of Thirty indicates that multibranch master agreements have been used with some degree of frequency.

The New York Banking Department's experiences in the BCCI case led to amendment of the New York banking law in August 1993. The amendments were intended to enhance the ability of the superintendent of banks to deal with foreign regulators, while retaining the ring-fencing approach. Initial proposals attempted to explicitly apply ring-fencing to derivatives transactions, termed "qualified financial contracts." However, the final version of the amendment abandoned the ring-fencing approach for qualified financial contracts and adopted an approach that enforces multibranch netting agreements. Under the amended version of the New York banking law, qualified financial contracts are not automatically terminated upon the superintendent's taking possession of an insolvent New York branch or agency, and the superintendent shall not assume or repudiate qualified financial contracts documented under a multibranch netting agreement. Instead, the home country banking regulator of the foreign bank may assume or repudiate multibranch master agreements, and counterparties will be allowed to terminate such agreements in accordance with their terms.

Upon any repudiation or termination, netting of amounts owed under a qualified financial contract shall be calculated on both a global and New York–only basis. The global net amount is the amount owed by or to the foreign banking corporation as a whole if *all* transactions subject to the multibranch netting agreement are considered. The New York or local net amount is the amount owed by or to a foreign banking corporation after netting *only* the transactions entered into by the New York branch or agency. The superintendent shall only be liable to pay the *lesser of* the global net amount and the local net amount. Any amount due to a counterparty after payment of a local net amount can still be collected from the home office. Likewise, when a counterparty owes a net amount pursuant to a repudiated or terminated qualified financial contract, the superintendent of an insolvent New York branch or agency may demand from the counterparty a payment of the *lesser of* these two net amounts.

International Bank Insolvencies and the Enforceability of Multibranch Master Netting Agreements continued

In addition to enhancing the enforceability of multibranch master netting agreements, the amendment also enforces collateral arrangements securing net amounts due under multibranch master agreements. Upon a termination or repudiation, collateral of an insolvent branch or agency properly held by a counterparty may be applied against any outstanding claims under a multibranch master agreement, up to the global net amount owed by the bank. Such collateral therefore will not be considered an asset of the branch or agency subject to return to the branch or agency upon the taking of possession by the superintendent.

This amendment to New York banking law is an important first step toward a unified approach to international bank regulation. A multilateral regulatory treatment of qualified financial contracts during bank insolvencies would provide greater legal certainty for parties to multibranch master agreements and reduce systemic risk for all participants in derivatives transactions. Other jurisdictions (especially other major financial centers) should follow New York's lead and where necessary adopt similar laws to fully address the global concerns raised by the risk of global banking insolvencies.

Daniel P. Cunningham is managing partner of the law firm of Cravath, Swaine & Moore. His corporate finance practice includes derivative instruments, mergers and acquisitions, and receivables finance.

Mr. Cunningham is general counsel to the International Swaps and Derivatives Association (ISDA). In that capacity, he has participated in the preparation of standard master agreements for derivative transactions and has served as legal coordinator for the preparation of memoranda under UK, U.S., Canadian, French, German, Italian, Japanese, Dutch, Swedish, and Belgian law examining the status of the 1987 ISDA master agreements with counterparties that have become insolvent under the laws of those nations.

Mr. Cunningham was a member of the Group of Thirty Derivatives Project Working Group.

Mr. Cunningham received a BA degree from Princeton University in 1971. In 1975 he graduated from Harvard Law School.

However, the last two factors require us to step away from our simplifying assumption that the correlation between the underlying price and the counterparty's assets is zero. The third determinant of the probability of default for a risk management transaction deals with the use to which the transaction is put:

3. The counterparty's inherent exposure to movements in the financial price on which the swap is based.

Whether or not the firm is using the transaction as a hedge for its underlying exposure to interest rates, exchange rates, or commodity prices has a potentially significant effect on the probability of default. A derivative transaction used as a hedge has a lower probability of default. Although for more creditworthy counterparties the financial institution is less concerned with the counterparty's core business exposure, for lower-rated counterparties it is clearly in the financial institution's interest to understand their customer's exposure.

The fourth is a characteristic of most derivative transactions.

4. Volatility of the underlying financial price: The more volatile the underlying financial price, the more likely it is that there will be a price movement sufficiently large to put the counterparty into financial distress.

Firms that intermediate risk management products have all developed systems (with varying degrees of sophistication) that reflect the probability of default arising from factors 1, 2, and 4. Many firms use a set of matrices—one for each product—to assign required credit premiums, which rise as the maturity of the transaction rises or the credit rating of the counterparty declines. Such a set of matrices is illustrated in Figure 17–12.

FIGURE 17–12 Matrices for Assigning Credit Premiums

	AAA			*AA*			*A*		
Maturity of Transaction	*IRS*	*CS*	*Caps*	*IRS*	*CS*	*Caps*	*IRS*	*CS*	*Caps*
2	XXX	XXX	XXX	XXX	XXX	XXX	XXX	XXX	XXX
3	XXX	XXX	XXX	XXX	XXX	XXX	XXX	XXX	XXX
4	XXX	XXX	XXX	XXX	XXX	XXX	XXX	XXX	XXX
5	XXX	XXX	XXX	XXX	XXX	XXX	XXX	XXX	XXX
7	XXX	XXX	XXX	XXX	XXX	XXX	XXX	XXX	XXX
10	XXX	XXX	XXX	XXX	XXX	XXX	XXX	XXX	XXX

For interest rate swaps, the shape of the term structure can also have an impact on the probability of default. If the term structure is upward sloping (as it has been during most of the history of the interest rate swap market), the probability of default is reduced if the counterparty pays fixed and receives floating. To show how this can occur, in Figure 17–13 we have illustrated the relation between the fixed-rate and floating-rate payments for a three-year interest rate swap. Since the term structure is upward sloping, the expectation is that the party paying fixed and receiving floating will pay difference checks early in the term of the swap

Settlement 1:	Pay R_{36}	Receive r_6
Settlement 2:	Pay R_{36}	Receive ${}_6r_{12}$

and receive net payments in later periods

Settlement 3:	Pay R_{36}	Receive ${}_{12}r_{18}$
Settlement 4:	Pay R_{36}	Receive ${}_{18}r_{24}$
Settlement 5:	Pay R_{36}	Receive ${}_{24}r_{30}$
Settlement 6:	Pay R_{36}	Receive ${}_{30}r_{36}$

Thus, the credit risk of the fixed-rate payer is less than would be the case if the term structure were flat. An overview of the market for interest rate swaps indicates that the less creditworthy counterparties have been, by and large, paying cash flows based on a fixed interest rate. Hence, the probability of default for the portfolio of swaps is lower than if the counterparties were reversed.

The credit management systems used by many of the firms that intermediate interest rate swaps actually reflect the impact of the shape of the term structure on the probability of default. In the context of the credit premium matrices noted in Figure 17–12 above, the matrix firms use to reflect the probability of default in an interest rate swap in which the bank receives the fixed rate is different from that used in a swap in which the bank receives the floating rate.

FIGURE 17–13 Relation between Fixed-Rate and Floating-Rate Payments

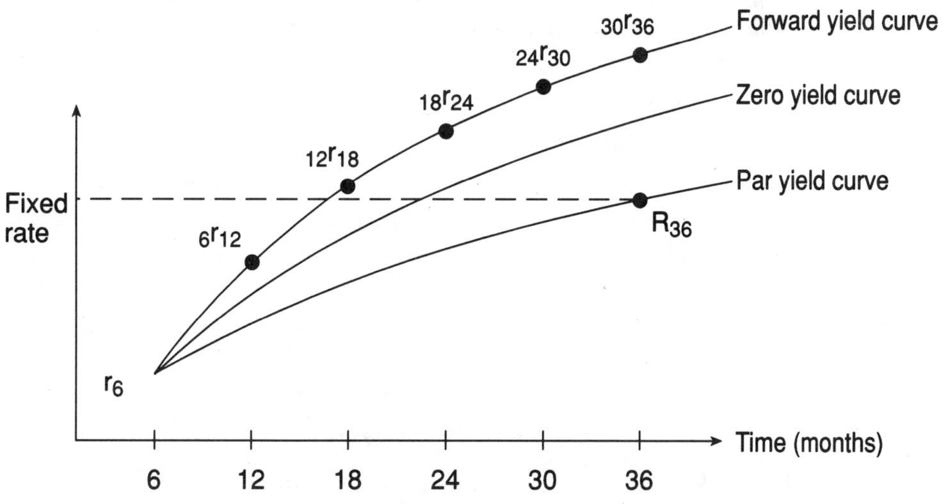

Methods for Reducing Credit Risk

The simplest and most effective means of reducing credit risk is netting. However, other methods can be employed to reduce the credit risk inherent in OTC derivatives transactions.

Collateral

For any transaction that involves an extension of credit, the credit risk can be reduced by bonding the transaction—that is, requiring that collateral be posted. In the case of OTC derivatives, the transaction is marked-to-market, and collateral, in the form of pledged assets, is posted in accordance with the mark-to-market size of the exposure.

Collateral agreements tend to be bilateral; that is, both parties are required to post collateral when the market value of their side of the contract is negative. However, collateral agreements can be unilateral—only the weaker credit is required to post collateral. To reduce the cost of a collateral arrangement, thresholds for movement of collateral are common. In such a structure, collateral is posted only if the agreement is "triggered." Two kinds of triggers have been observed in the market.

Value Trigger. Collateral is posted only if the mark-to-market value of the transaction exceeds a specified threshold. To facilitate transactions between counterparties with different levels of creditworthiness, uneven thresholds can exist; that is, the threshold for the higher-rated counterparty is set at a higher level.

Event Trigger. While value triggers are more common, agreements have been structured such that collateral is required (or the level of collateral is increased) when the counterparty is downgraded or when capital ratios fall below specified levels.

Third-Party Supports

As an alternative to posting collateral, weaker credits can be supported by letters of credit or guarantees from a third party. Guarantees, or weaker variants such as "keepwell," "support," or "comfort letters," are often required from a counterparty's parent company or affiliate. Less frequently, an unaffiliated third party will guarantee performance of one of the counterparties in a derivative transaction in return for a fee.

Settlements, Unwinds, and Assignments

Instead of posting collateral or looking to third-party support, the counterparties could agree that when the exposure reaches a specified level, the set of transactions between the counterparties will be restructured so as to reduce the exposure. This could be done in one of three ways.

The counterparties could settle all or part of the transactions. One form of such an agreement is very similar to the value-triggered collateral agreements noted above: The counterparties agree to cash-settle all exposures above a specified level. If the mark-to-market value of the transactions exceed this specified level, one party has to send cash sufficient to reduce the exposure to the specified level. Another form of this agreement is to cash-settle transactions at intermediate points in the life of the transaction. For example, the counterparties could enter into a five-year transaction that is cash-settled annually, thereby effectively reducing the credit exposure to a one-year exposure.

Second, transactions could be unwound. Instead of cash-settling the transactions, the counterparties could put in place a mirror transaction that would have the effect of putting a ceiling on the exposure. (Clearly, such a structure requires that bilateral netting be enforceable.)

Finally, transactions could be assigned to a third party. Instead of cash-settling all exposures above a specified level, the counterparties could agree that when the mark-to-market values of the transactions exceed a specified level, some transactions will be assigned to another counterparty.

Special Purpose Vehicles

In the context of the risk management markets, special purpose vehicles (SPVs) are, as Standard & Poor's describes them, "bankruptcy-remote" subsidiaries set up to transact risk management products. In all of the cases to date, the SPVs have been rated AAA; hence, these structures are also referred to as "AAA subsidiaries." As John Behof (1993) pointed out, the use of SPVs to reduce the credit risk in a derivatives transaction is analogous to more traditional asset securitization, in which a separate structure (such as a trust) is set up to isolate the assets being securitized from other risks. In the case of the SPVs, a separate organization is established to isolate the derivatives transactions from the risks in the overall firm.

As 1993 neared its end, SPVs had been established by Goldman Sachs—*GS Financial Products International, L.P. (GSFPI)*; Merrill Lynch & Co.—*Merrill Lynch Derivative Products, Inc. (MLDPI)*; Salomon Brothers—*Salomon Swapco Inc. (Swapco)*; and Banque Paribas—*Paribas Dérivés Garantis (PDG)*. Rumors in the marketplace suggested that as many as 15 other SPVs were being structured. While there are differences in the structures, there are some common features in the AAA subsidiaries:

Nonconsolidation. The SPV is structured to be legally separate from the parent. Consequently, if the parent were to experience bankruptcy, the assets of the SPV would not be consolidated with those of the parent.

Capitalization. The SPVs are overcapitalized in order that the excess capital provide a "cushion" against default. The rating agencies tend to require that the capital of the AAA subsidiary be able to withstand the most extreme stress scenario. GSFPI was capitalized by a portfolio of in-the-money Nikkei index options and warrants valued at 9.3 billion Japanese yen. MLDPI was capitalized by $300 million in common stock sold to the parent and by a $50 million preferred stock offering sold to a third party. Swapco was initially capitalized with $175 million but is required to maintain additional capital if the size or composition of the derivatives portfolio increases the risk of the SPV.

Operating Guidelines. In order to maintain the AAA rating, the behavior of the SPV is proscribed by certain parameters and guidelines within which the SPV's transactions must be conducted. These guidelines prescribe acceptable counterparties: MLDPI was initially permitted to enter into transactions with only AA or better counterparties.[22] Swapco will have to maintain more capital if it deals with lower-rated credits. The guidelines also limit an SPV's exposure to individual counterparties and its aggregate exposure to classes of counterparties (such as by credit rating or by country of origin of counterparty) to specified dollar (or percent of capital) limits.

Matching and Affiliate Transactions. Since the AAA subsidiary is set up to provide counterparties with more comfort on default, the SPV is required to take actions to limit its market risk; that is, the SPV is restricted from taking unmatched positions. In the case of MLDPI and Swapco this is accomplished by requiring that the SPV enter into a "mirror" transaction with the parent every time it enters into a transaction with a third party. By passing the interest rate or foreign exchange rate exposure on to its parent, the SPV will not be directly exposed to fluctuations in financial prices. To maintain the credit rating, the SPV's transactions with the parent are collateralized (on a net basis).

Given that a primary objective of an SPV is to avoid having the assets of the SPV made part of the parent in event of bankruptcy of the parent, it should not be surprising that two banks, Citibank and Continental Bank, withdrew bids to set up SPVs after receiving indications from the OCC that the proposals would be rejected.[23] The report in the press suggested that the OCC was concerned that the creditors of the SPVs would gain priority over the insured depositors of the bank in the event of a default.

Evidence on Defaults for the Risk Management Instruments

If we return to the conceptual discussion at the beginning of this chapter and assume that the underlying financial price for a derivative transaction is uncorrelated with the value of the counterparty's other assets, the probability of default on a derivative transaction would be one half the probability of default for a bond. If the two are independent, in half the cases in which the counterparty would default on a debt obligation, the derivative transaction is generating inflows.

Altman (1989) provides some data that are useful in estimating this likelihood. Examining data from bond issues from 1971 through 1986, he reports cumulative default rates according to the S&P rating for the bond at origination. Ten years after issuance, AAA bonds had a cumulative default rate of 0.13 percent; AA, 2.46 percent; A, 0.93 percent; BBB, 2.12 percent, and BB, 6.64 percent.

As noted above, let's assume that the financial prices underlying swaps are uncorrelated with the values of the counterparties' other assets. If we also assume that the "representative" swap counterparty is a single-A rated firm, Altman's estimates would suggest that the average probability of default on a swap would be 1/2 of 1 percent.

Moving from the conceptual, let's see what the available data indicate. At the end of 1991, the ISDA surveyed its members on their default experience. Survey respondents accounted for more than 70 percent of the total notional principal outstanding. The results of this survey, provided in Table 17–1, indicate that cumulative losses (losses over the respondents' entire history in the swap market) had been $358.36 million. The ratio of these *cumulative* losses to the respondents' notional principal *outstanding at the end of 1991* was 0.0115 percent. Perhaps a more useful ratio is that between these cumulative losses and the market value of the respondents' portfolios at the end of 1991—0.46 percent. As a rough comparison, in 1991 alone, federally insured banks charged off 1.8 percent of year-end loan balances. And, the composition of the losses is instructive. Almost half of the total losses were in transactions with UK local authorities—Hammersmith and Fulham.[24]

TABLE 17–1 Net Loss by Counterparty Type

	Amount (in millions)	*Percent*
UK local authorities	$177.7	49.6%
Corporate	94.5	26.4
Other nondealer financial institutions	60.1	16.8
Savings & loans	20.3	5.6
Other governmental entities	3.0	0.8
Non-ISDA dealers	2.0	0.6
ISDA dealers	0.6	0.2
Total	$358.2	100.0%

SOURCE: ISDA.

Settlement Risk[25]

Finally, we have to consider the risks inherent in the settlement system itself. Settlement risk exists when there is a simultaneous exchange required in the transaction.

One aspect of settlement risk results from the fact that few financial transactions are settled on a same-day basis. In the United States equity markets, for example, the difference between the trade date and settlement is at present five days. As a result, one party could suffer a loss if the price moved in his favor and the counterparty refused to exchange on the settlement date.[26]

Settlement risk in derivatives is reduced greatly by the widespread use of the payment-netting provisions of master agreements. This reduces the settlement risk of payments made in the same currency. In addition, for many derivative transactions (for example, interest rate swaps), principal amounts are not exchanged on the maturity date.

Payment netting, however, does not address cross-currency settlement risk. The largest source of settlement risk in payment systems is the settlement exposures created by foreign currency trade—spot and short-dated forwards (so-called Herstatt risk after the 1974 failure of the Bankhaus Herstatt). While derivatives activity would benefit from a reduction of Herstatt risk, it must be noted that the amounts involved in derivatives are very small relative to the amounts involved in traditional foreign exchange activities. It has been estimated by ISDA that daily global cash flows from interest rate swaps and currency swaps average $0.65 billion and $1.9 billion, respectively. In contrast, the BIS Central Bank Survey of Foreign Exchange Market Activity in April 1992 estimated daily global net turnover in foreign exchange spot and forward markets at $400 billion and $420 billion, respectively.

Risk Management in Practice

Settlement Risks for OTC Derivatives

Ronald D. Watson

For those who use derivatives, credit and market risks dominate the list of "downside" concerns—and should! However, "settlement failure" risks also deserve consideration, especially for derivatives strategies based on transac-

Settlement Risks for OTC Derivatives continued

tions that settle in over-the-counter markets. "Settlement" is the actual physical or electronic event when a financial exchange occurs and both parties satisfy their obligations under the contract terms created by the derivative transaction. Reliable, timely settlement of contracts is the "plumbing and electrical work" behind financial engineering. It isn't sexy, but the cost of not designing and maintaining it properly can be enormous.

The safest form of transaction clearance occurs in a secure, electronic exchange system where settlement is immediate and guaranteed by a central bank. The Federal Reserve's wire transfer system is ideal for settling transactions that are consummated by a single-payment transfer. Its book-entry system for U.S. Treasury and Agency securities creates a simultaneous exchange of securities and cash (called "deliver versus payment," or DVP). Any departure from this model creates risk for the transacting parties.

There are three sources of risk once settlement starts. One is the failure of either party to deliver cash, FX, a commodity, or securities at settlement. Another is the risk that a settlement agent (the bank, clearinghouse, or exchange being used to execute the money or securities transfers) will fail to perform. Finally, there is a risk that financial markets will encounter difficulties that create "systemic" settlement problems. The chances of any one of these events occurring are very low, but the risk is still real and must be anticipated.

Counterparty Failure to Perform

This is more than a simple credit risk issue. In transactions such as a foreign exchange forward contract, either party may require special steps to protect its principal from the financial weakness of its counterparty. If failure occurs *before* settlement, and the exchange of payments can't be completed, you may be at risk for the cost of replacing the hedge at current market prices but not for the value of the contract. However, once the settlement date arrives, either party may be exposed for the full value being transferred (unless they have assurance that their counterparty has already made the transfer). The counterparty's failure at this time creates a risk of losing the full transaction amount. Controlling this exposure is a matter both of counterparty credit risk management and diligence in controlling release of your funds only on confirmed completion of the other party's obligations.

Intermediary Agent Performance

To the extent that a derivative contract is structured to use agents to perform any exchanges of value or securities, the parties should monitor the agents'

Settlement Risks for OTC Derivatives continued

soundness. Securities firms, banks, clearinghouses, and exchanges all perform these "exchange agent" functions. In recent years most exchanges and organized clearinghouses have tightened their rules and operating practices to minimize the risk that they will be unable to settle all transactions entrusted to them. U.S. exchange clearinghouses use a combination of capital requirements for members, security deposits, intraday counterparty exposure limits, margin calls, lines of credit, and other risk reduction and sharing arrangements to assure their ability to make settlement for all trades on time.

When immediate, irrevocable settlement of each contract is not possible, clearinghouses often settle each business day's transactions at the end of the day. Usually transactions are "netted" to reduce settlement risks. Netting is the process of offsetting the payments obligations of each participant with cash it should receive from the same or other counterparties. Netting the transactions of each pair of participants is called "bilateral" netting, while combining and offsetting the trades of all participants into a single net settlement payment for each is called "multilateral" netting. By netting the projected payments of each participant in the exchange, a clearinghouse can reduce the aggregate number and size of settlement payments. This in turn decreases the liquidity burden of meeting the settlement and increases the probability of a successful settlement. Netting of payments is the norm for all U.S. settlement systems (except the Federal Reserve's), but the practice is not as well established in other parts of the world.

Transactions that are not settled in an exchange's clearinghouse may not enjoy the same multilayered protections. Private settlement arrangements may be efficient, but they don't operate with the same level of public scrutiny or member oversight as exchanges. The most recent innovations in over-the-counter derivatives contracts may be so specialized that they cannot be handled as "standardized" back-office settlements. The more that private agents, time-zone differences, currency conversions, different sovereign legal jurisdictions, and special covenants become involved in reaching a proper settlement, the greater the risk.

Systemic Risk

The least tangible but most troubling risk is the possibility that a single major settlement failure will "domino" throughout our highly interdependent global financial markets and create a series of failures. This can occur if an unforeseen event such as revolution or natural disaster shocks price relationships of major currencies or commodities enough to bankrupt several large players. Their rapid demise could create losses for their creditors, who in turn might

Settlement Risks for OTC Derivatives continued

then be unable to meet their obligations to others. Financial turbulence tends to produce gridlock in settlement markets as each player waits for the others to move fast. Central banks would be forced to step in to stabilize markets, but it is virtually certain that large losses would be taken by some private parties before order was restored.

Industry Efforts to Cut Risk

Appreciation of settlement exposure is growing along with the size and complexity of these markets. Central banks of the larger industrialized nations and the international finance trade associations are both taking steps to manage it. At the level of the "deal" itself, considerable private effort is being devoted to defining standardized, court tested, contract language for these new financial instruments. This is particularly challenging for contracts that require settlements in more than one sovereign jurisdiction, but progress is being made.

The central banks of the G-10 countries have been working on these problems for several years. There is general agreement among the regulators on minimum soundness standards that must be imposed on any private sector clearing system offering cross-border, multicurrency netting services to its participants. Regulators are also integrating off-balance-sheet risk exposures (including derivatives such as currency, interest rate swaps, and more complex contracts) into their common capital adequacy regulations.

Finally, the private sector is experimenting with new clearinghouse arrangements intended to deal with the settlement risks of global finance. In the foreign exchange markets, bilateral trade-matching and netting systems are being created, but so far, the participating institutions are not prepared to guarantee settlement of each other's trades. Multilateral netting systems are only in the pilot project stage.

In summary, efforts to reduce the settlement risks of nonstandard derivative products are under way, but the problems are far from solved. This is an arena in which the global financial services industry and its counterpart family of central banks have a common interest in working together to refine the laws, regulations, contract standards, and day-to-day operating procedures of the institutions conducting this business to minimize the risk of financial market disruption and potential for catastrophe.

Ronald D. Watson is the chairman of Custodial Trust Company (CTC), the securities servicing and custody bank of The Bear Stearns Companies, Inc. Before joining CTC he taught at the University of Delaware and spent 17 years at the Federal Reserve Bank of Philadelphia. He is active in the Financial Management Association and the U.S. Department of Labor's ERISA Advisory Council.

Notes

1. "Default risk" and "credit risk" are used interchangeably in the market. However, while default (counterparty) risk could refer to any failure to perform under the contract, credit risk is more specific, refering to a financial inability to pay.
2. Taylor, Spillenkothen, Parkinson, Spindler, White (1987).
3. January 1992 speech to the New York Bankers Association.
4. Chris Culp of the Federal Reserve Bank of Chicago reminded us that we should also mention the insolvencies of the British & Commonwealth Merchant Bank and the Development Finance Corp. of New Zealand.
5. The requirements are described in two publications of the Bank for International Settlements: *Proposals for International Convergence of Capital Measurement and Capital Standards*, December 1987, and *International Convergence of Capital Measurement and Capital Standards*, July 1988.
6. This discussion of the nature of default risk is adapted from Smith (1993).
7. *Hammersmith and Fulham.*
8. Cases where counterparties argued that the derivatives contract is an "illegal off-exchange futures contract"—e.g., *Dr. Tauber.*
9. Johnson and Stulz (1987) provide a mathematical discussion of these issues.
10. Nor, in truth, are things really that simple for traditional bank products. The exposure to the bank on a transaction like a standby line of credit is neither the total amount of the commitment nor only the amount of the commitment actually used to date. Instead, the amount the bank has at risk is somewhere in between these two—the question is, where in between?
11. Some readers of this chapter disagreed with referring to a zero-coupon loan as a "constant exposure" instrument. Some noted that the face value of the loan is different from the amount that "walked out of the bank"—i.e., treating the zero-coupon loan as a constant exposure instrument focuses only on principal repayment and ignores the additional loss the bank will suffer if the borrower fails to repay interest. However, as one bank credit officer noted, the traditional treatment of credit exposure is invariant to the payment of interest. Others noted that, as interest rates change, the *present value* of the zero-coupon instrument will change.
12. The variance for the price change for this binomial process is

    $$(P_0)^2[pu^2 + (1 - p)d^2] - (P_0)^2[pu + (1 - p)]d^2$$
13. Indeed, if the underlying distribution is lognormal, the dispersion increases with the square root of time.
14. The "humped" exposure profile is a characteristic of at-market interest rate swaps. If the swap is deep in-the-money, the initial exposure is positive and the hump becomes less pronounced.
15. The staffs of the Federal Reserve System and the Bank of England expressed these two questions as (1) What is the *average* replacement cost over the life of a *matched pair* of swaps? (2) What is the *maximum* replacement cost over the life of a *single* swap? See Board of Governors of the Federal Reserve System and the Bank of England (1987) and Muffett (1986).
16. As this chapter was being assembled, Cliff Smith bridled at using the word "maximum," correctly arguing that no maximum value exists for the derivative instruments. While he would have preferred using the word "extreme," we elected to remain with the market convention and use "maximum."

    Note further that this "maximum" is different from the "worst-case" exposure measures described in the next section of this chapter.
17. And this prescription is not limited to the derivatives transactions. An excellent example of an instance in which banks were damaged by not using an option-theoretic approach to default is found by looking at nonrecourse real estate development loans.
18. In implementing this approach to estimating the exposure to default-induced losses, most practitioners would view the default-risk "option" as a simple option. In fact, as we described at the beginning of this chapter, the valuation of this option-like construction would be more correctly written as a compound option that depends on (1) the value of the swap contract and (2) the value of the other assets of the counterparty. Hence, the exposure to default-induced losses would be

    $$\text{Exposure} = f(r_t, r_0, r, T, \sigma_r, \sigma_{\text{FIRM}}, \sigma_{r,\text{FIRM}})$$

    where

σ_{FIRM} = Volatility of value of counterparty's other assets and

$\sigma_{r,FIRM}$ = covariance between the interest rate and the value of counterparty's other assets.

19. "Payment netting" is similar to netting novation. The counterparties agree to net payments (settlements) that are due on the same day and in the same currency—e.g., the settlements in an interest rate swap. According to John Behof (1993), payment netting is accomplished via an unwritten agreement; if the agreement is written, payment netting becomes netting by novation.
20. The impetus toward netting is reinforced by accounting rules. SFAS 105, which went into effect in 1993, requires that gains and losses be reported separately, unless they are netted with an acceptable contract.
21. "The Supervisory Recognition of Netting for Capital Adequacy Purposes."
22. However, in May 1993, Moody's relaxed the rule to permit MLDP to deal with single-A counterparties.
23. *The American Banker,* December 17, 1992.
24. The losses attributable to the Hammersmith and Fulham transactions are understated in Table 17–1, since one of the major victims, TSB Bank, was not a member of ISDA at the time of the survey.
25. This discussion is adapted from the Report of the Group of Thirty Derivatives Project.
26. This two-sided settlement risk is similar to the two-sided credit risk for forwards and swaps.

CHAPTER

18 MANAGING PRICE RISK IN A PORTFOLIO OF DERIVATIVES

To manage the price risk—the market risk—of a portfolio of derivatives, the portfolio must be structured so that its value will not be affected by changes in the underlying price. While this underlying price might be foreign exchange rates or commodity prices, we will, for the purposes of the example used in this chapter, consider interest rates as the underlying price.

Measuring Price Risk: "Fraternity Row"

The first step in managing price risk for a portfolio of derivatives is to *quantify* the risks. As we noted in Chapter 5, several measures of price risk could be used. However, most risk managers for derivatives now use a series of Greek letters to identify the different risks that will be hedged. We like to refer to these Greek-letter measures of risk as *fraternity row*.

Delta

The first of the Greek letters to be considered—the first house on fraternity row, if you will—is *delta*. In the context of interest rates, delta measures the change in the value of a financial asset as the underlying price (in this example, interest rates) changes.

Graphically, delta is the slope of a value profile. Figure 18–1 illustrates the relation between a long bond position and interest rates: The value of the bond declines as the interest rate rises. Delta is simply the slope of this value profile.

Delta is not a new concept. In the case of interest rates, delta is simply a new name for a concept that has heretofore been referred to by bond traders as *basis-*

FIGURE 18–1 Delta

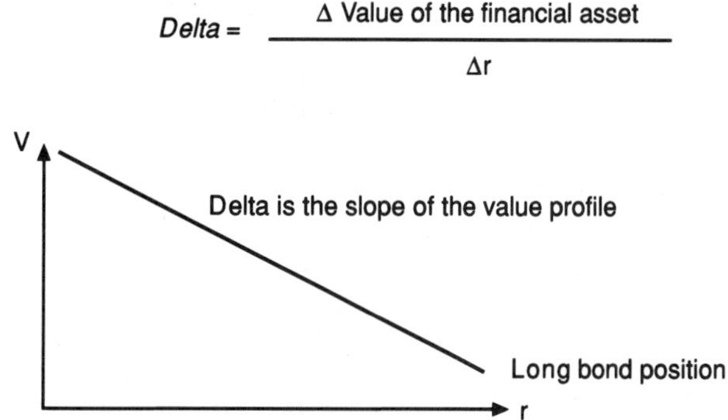

point value or *the value of an 01*. Moreover, delta and *duration* are two measures of the same risk. Indeed, as indicated in the following equation, the calculation of duration embodies delta:

$$\text{Duration} = -\frac{\text{Percentage change in the value of the asset}}{\text{Percentage change in the discount rate}}$$

$$= (\Delta V/V) \;/\; [\Delta(1 + r)/(1 + r)]$$

$$= (\Delta V/\Delta r) \times (1 + r)/V$$

$$= \text{Delta} \times (1 + r)/V.$$

In Figure 18–1, we illustrate delta as constant—that is, we drew the value profile as a straight line. However, this need not be the case. The value profile for a short-term, noncallable government bond is well approximated by a straight line. However, as the maturity of the bond gets longer or as the bond incorporates other features (for example, the right to prepay), the value profile becomes increasingly nonlinear. And for options, there is no question that delta is *not* constant. Panel A of Figure 18–2 illustrates the value profile for a long position in a call option on an interest rate—an interest rate cap. As panel A illustrates, delta (the slope of the value profile for the option) ranges from zero when interest rates are very low to one when interest rates are very high. Conversely, for the put option on interest rates—an interest rate floor (illustrated in panel B of Figure 18–2)—delta would range from negative one when interest rates are very low to zero when interest raies are high.

Gamma

The dramatic change in delta evident for options leads us to the next of the Greek-letter measures of risk (the next house on fraternity row), gamma. Gamma measures the change in delta as the underlying price—in this case, the interest rate—changes. This concept is illustrated in Figure 18–3. As the interest rate moves up and down, the delta for the option position changes; gamma measures this change.

Gamma is not a new concept. In the same way that delta is another name for basis-point value, gamma is another name for *convexity*.

Panel A of Figure 18–3 illustrates a financial instrument that has a *convex* value profile. Note that when the value profile is convex, gamma is positive. Panel B illustrates the value profile for a financial instrument that exhibits what the market refers to as *negative convexity*. In this case, gamma is negative.

If the payoff profile were linear, gamma would be zero. Indeed, interest rate futures contracts are constructed so as to have linear payoffs; hence for interest rate futures, gamma equals zero.[1]

FIGURE 18–2 Delta for Option Positions

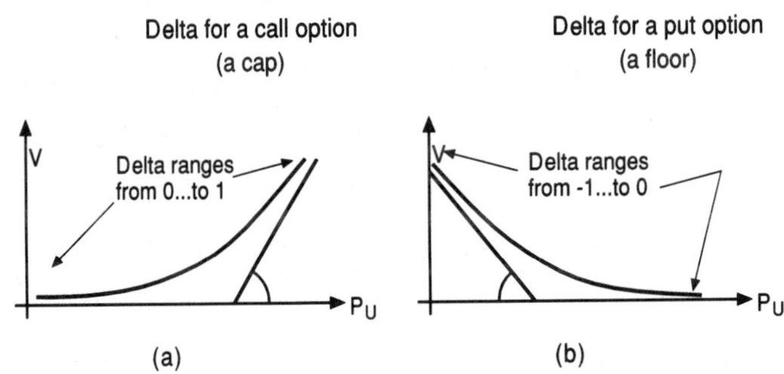

FIGURE 18–3 Gamma

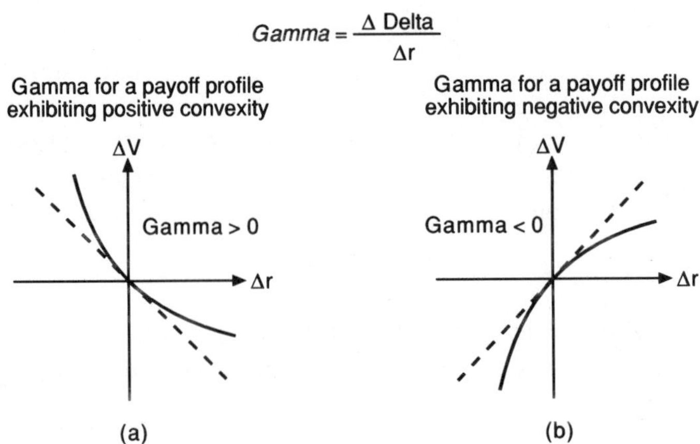

While both interest rate forwards (FRAs) and interest rate swaps exhibit gamma, this risk is primarily a characteristic of options.[2] And as Figure 18–4 illustrates, gamma is largest when the option is *at-the-money*. When the option is way out-of-the-money, the slope of the call function is very near zero, and the slope doesn't change very much for small changes in the price of the underlying. Likewise, when the option is way in-the-money, the slope of the call function is very near to one, and small changes in the price of the underlying don't have much of an impact on the slope. Only when the option is at-the-money do small changes in the underlying price have much impact on the slope of the value profile.

FIGURE 18–4 Gamma for Options

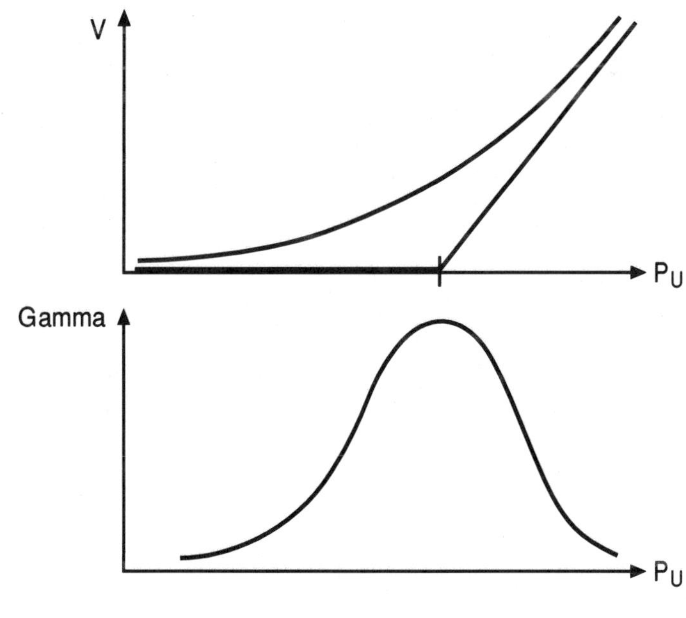

Risk Management in Practice

The Curse of Negative Convexity

Kosrow Dehnad

"Buy high and sell low." That sounds like a sure way to the poorhouse. Unfortunately, this is the dilemma managers face when they try to hedge positions

The Curse of Negative Convexity continued

after they have sold options. Their ordeal, theoretically, will not be over till they spend the last penny of the option premiums they receive to delta-hedge their positions and to break even at expiration!

The villain is negative convexity—or being "short gamma." With negative convexity, when the option increases in value, losses on the hedge can well offset the gains in the value of the option, and when the option decreases in value the hedge does not generate enough gains to compensate for the loss.

Adding insult to injury, the hedge often also exhibits slippage because of approximation error resulting from trying to use straight lines (that is, the payoff profile for the hedge instruments) to "synthetically" construct a curve (that is, the payoff profile for the option).

Since a picture is worth a thousand words, let us illustrate the above points graphically.

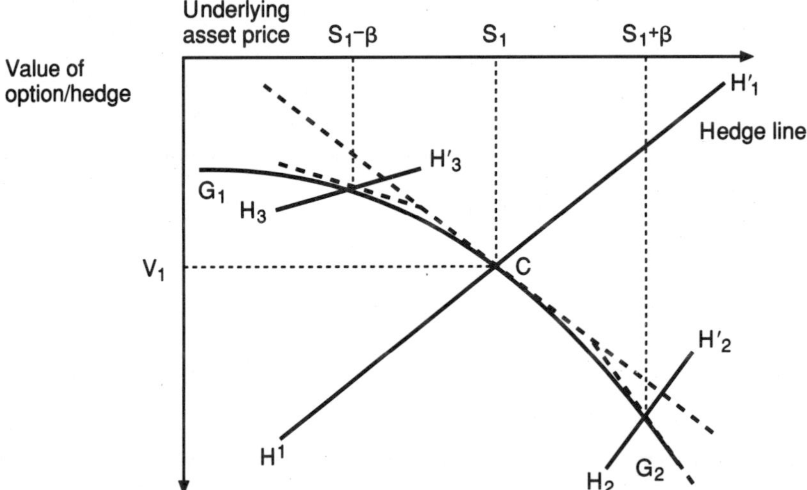

The figure shows the value of a short position in a European call (G_1 G_2) for different values of the underlying asset; for example, when the asset price is S_1, the option value is V_1. To immunize (hedge) our position against small movements in the asset price we should buy some of the underlying asset.

The size of the hedge, to first approximation, is based on the slope of the tangent to the curve at point C. In fact, the hedge position is given by the line H_1 H_1', which is the reflection of the tangent line about the line parallel to the X-axis and passing through point C. The construction reflects the fact that

The Curse of Negative Convexity continued

hedge position is opposite the option position. So, if we are short the call we should be long the underlying. In other words we approximate our option position for small changes in the price of the underlying by a straight line. The hedge using the stock should be opposite to that, so the hedge position is given by the reflected line.

Should the stock price rise to $S_2 = S_1 + \beta$, the new hedge ratio would be the slope of the line $H_2 H_2'$, which indicates that we have to add to our holding of the stock when its price is advancing—that is "buy high."

On the other hand, if the stock goes down to $S_3 = S_1 - \beta$, the new hedge ratio is the slope of $H_3 H_3'$ which indicates that we should reduce our hedge and sell when the price of the stock declines—that is "sell low."

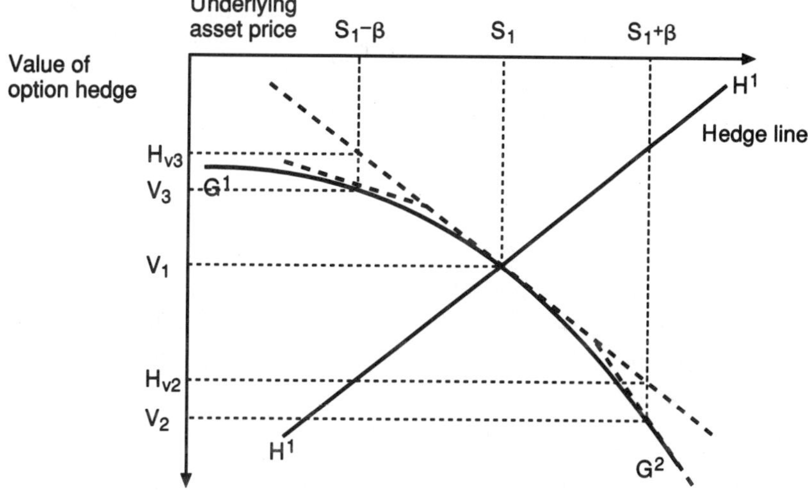

The hedge slippage that can occur because of approximating a curve with a straight line is illustrated above. Suppose the price advances to $S_1 + \beta$ and our short option position loses $V_2 - V_1$. The hedge position gains only $V_1 - H_{V2}$, that is, less than the loss on the option position; this translates into a slippage of $H_{V2} - V_2$. Similarly, if the stock price falls to $S_1 - \beta$, our short option positions will have a value of V_3 and gains $V_3 - V_1$. On the other hand, the hedge loses $V_1 - H_{V3}$. Once more, the loss on the hedge outweighs the gains on the position and we will experience a slippage of $H_{V3} - V_3$. The reason for slippage is that we are trying to hedge our position that changes nonlinearly as a function of the underlying stock (curve) with an instrument whose value

The Curse of Negative Convexity continued

changes linearly as a function of the underlying security—the asset itself or a futures contract on the asset.

All the above phenomena are reversed for the holder of the long option position: By delta-hedging the position, the holder will be selling high and buying low and theoretically should recuperate costs. Moreover, the hedge slippage will also work in the holder's favor. All this because, up front, the holder of the option paid the option premium to buy the call.

Kosrow Dehnad is a vice president and head of Hybrid Product Development and Structuring at Citicorp Securities Inc. Prior to Citicorp, he was a vice president repsonsible for new product development at the Chase Manhattan Bank. Before joining Chase in 1990, Dr. Dehnad worked AT&T Bell Laboratories. He is the author of numerous technical articles and of *Quality Control, Robust Design, and the Taguchi Method.* He has served as an adjunct professor at San Jose State University, Rutgers University, and Columbia University. Dr. Dehnad has received two doctorates, one in applied statistics from Stanford University and the other in Mathematics from the University of California at Berkeley.

Vega (a.k.a. Kappa)

The final house on fraternity row to be considered here is confusing, since some market practitioners refer to it as *vega* while others refer to it as *kappa.*[3] In this example and for the remainder of the book we will refer to this risk measure as vega (even though vega is the name of an automobile and not a Greek letter). Vega measures the change in the value of the financial instrument that occurs when the *volatility* of interest rates (the underlying price) changes.

$$\text{Vega} = \frac{\Delta \text{ Value of financial instrument}}{\Delta\sigma}$$

Of the derivative instruments—forwards, futures, swaps, and options—only the value of options is influenced by volatility. Hence while gamma is a characteristic *primarily* of options, vega is a characteristic *solely* of options.[4]

Figure 18–5 illustrates two option value profiles, one when the volatility of interest rates is σ_1 and the other when volatility is σ_2, where $\sigma_1 < \sigma_2$. The value for this interest rate option is higher with σ_2 than σ_1 for all interest rates, but the difference in value is greatest when the option is at-the-money—in other words, the magnitude of vega is largest when the option is at-the-money, the same relation we observed for gamma.

FIGURE 18–5 Vega for Options

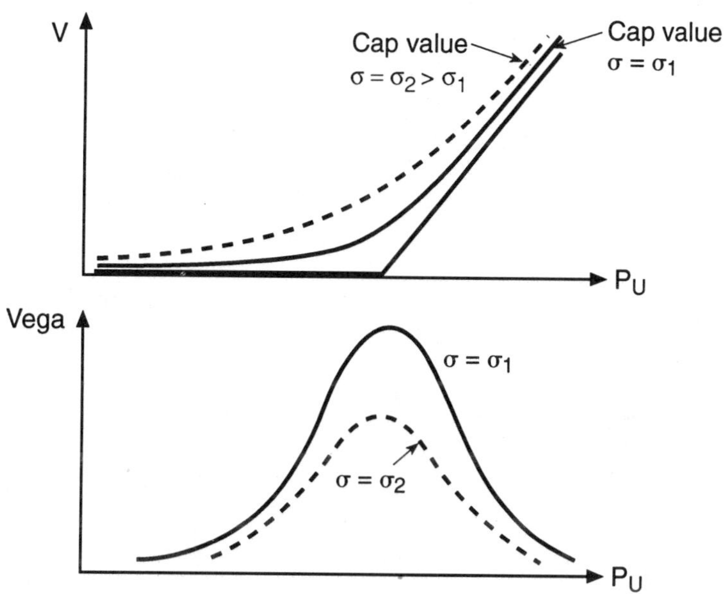

Measuring Price Risk: "Value at Risk"

While the warehouse manager uses delta, gamma, and vega (as well as some additional measures of risk we will introduce later in this chapter), senior management often wants a *summary measure* of the price risk. Many summary measures are available, but the market appears to be moving toward a measure that is variously referred to as "value at risk" (alternatively referred to "dollars at risk" or "risk management units"). The basic concept behind value at risk can be summarized as follows.

The risk manager first values the portfolio of derivatives using current prices—using today's "price list."[5] The risk manager then revalues the portfolio using some alternative price list and calculates the change in the portfolio value that would result—the difference in the value of the portfolio between today's price list and the alternative price list. As illustrated in Figure 18–6, if this is done for a number of price lists, the risk manager will obtain a distribution of changes in the portfolio value.

Once the distribution of changes in portfolio value is known, value at risk is specified in terms of confidence levels. While there is no *maximum* loss, the risk manager can tell senior management the maximum that the institution can lose *at*

FIGURE 18–6 Value at Risk

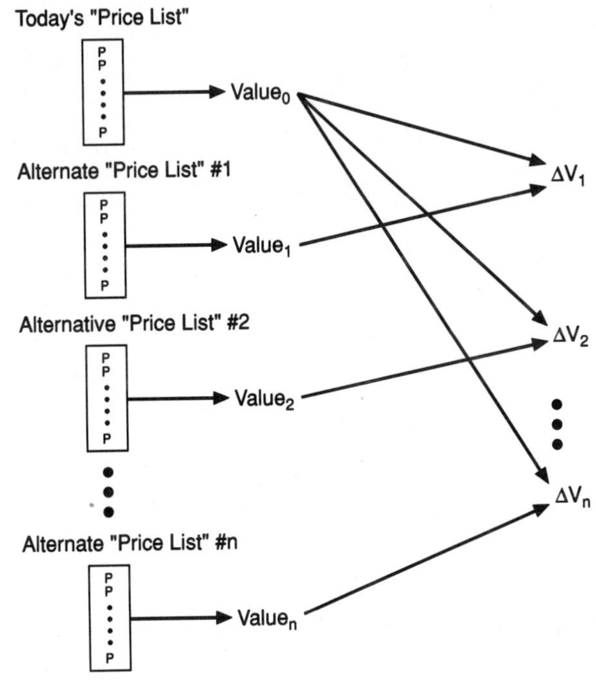

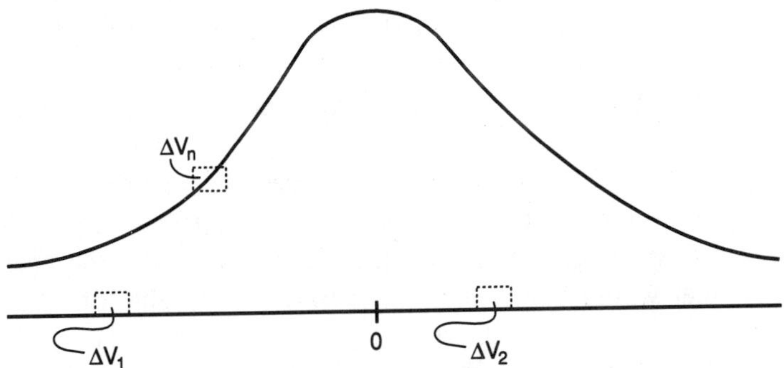

a specified probability level. For instance, the distribution will permit the risk manager to define the loss that will be the maximum loss at a 95 percent probability—that is, the loss that will be exceeded only 5 times out of 100.

Different institutions calculate value at risk over different periods. Some firms might want to know value at risk for a single trading day while others might want to consider potential value changes over a longer period.

Different institutions use difference confidence levels for determining value at risk. Senior management at one institution might want value at risk to be set so that it is exceeded in only 1 trading day in 100. Other management teams might prefer to set a lower value at risk threshold, knowing that the lower number is more likely, but knowing also that it will be exceeded more than once in 100 trading days.

Finally, different institutions use different methods of obtaining those alternative price lists. Some firms use historical price series while others prefer simulations.

Risk Management in Practice

Using Value at Risk at Chase

Victor I. Makarov

At the Chase Manhattan Bank we use *value at risk* to evaluate one-day market risk for all trading positions. Chase uses value at risk to monitor the price risk faced by the bank as it intermediates forwards, futures, swaps, and options in New York, London, Tokyo, and Hong Kong. Global management of the risk is performed using position guidelines and limits based on value at risk. Value-at-risk measures are also used for capital allocation and for the analysis of performance on a risk-adjusted basis.

We obtain a distribution of daily changes in the market value of a trading position using historical data. Then, our value-at-risk measure is a one-standard-deviation change—that is, on average, the loss is not expected to exceed this value-at-risk measure in more than 15 percent of the cases.

Since our value-at-risk measure is based on a statistical analysis of actual historical variability of returns, two features of the distributions of historical price changes are particularly important:

- Since the distributions are relatively stable over time, we can use historical distributions to assess future variability of the returns.
- Since the distributions are very close to zero-mean normal, we can describe the distributions with only one parameter—standard deviation.

Using Value at Risk at Chase continued

Value at Risk for an Individual Instrument

For individual positions, value at risk includes the following factors:

- Size and sign (long or short) of the position.
- Sensitivity (or elasticity) of its market value to changes in market factors.*
- Volatility of the markets (or corresponding market factors).

Value at Risk for a Portfolio of Instruments

For a portfolio, value at risk is calculated as the standard deviation of a time series of daily changes in the market value of the portfolio. The market risk of the portfolio is determined both by the exposures of its components and by the correlations between movements in the underlying financial prices. As a result, the risk for a portfolio of long positions is generally smaller than the sum of the risks for the individual positions. Similarly, the risk added to an existing portfolio by adding a new transaction is generally less than the risk for the new transaction on a "stand-alone" basis.

Adjustments for Illiquidity and Concentration

The market risk of an illiquid position is larger than the risk of otherwise identical liquid position because it will take longer to unwind the illiquid position. As a result, the illiquid position is exposed to the volatility existing in the market for a longer period. A liquidity measure for a position can be obtained by comparing the position size to the *liquidity threshold*—the maximum position size that can be unwound in normal market conditions during one trading day without disrupting market prices. The size of the position relative to the *threshold* determines the number of days required to close the position, which can be translated into a liquidity increment to value-at-risk measures.

When several illiquid positions are from the same narrow market, unwinding one position can significantly depress the prices of all other positions and effectively prevent immediate liquidation of the portfolio. Concentration, therefore, can lead to an increase in the liquidity risk. This can be incorporated by applying the same liquidity factor to all illiquid positions from the same market (the ratio of the combined position in all financial instruments from the same market to the liquidity threshold of the market).

---

*For a fixed-rate bond, the appropriate market factor is its yield to maturity, and the elasticity is measured in terms of duration, "the value of an 01," or "1-year equivalents." For option

Using Value at Risk at Chase continued

contracts, the appropriate market factors are the price of the underlying instrument, volatility, and short-term interest rates. For FX forwards contracts, the factors are the interest rates (domestic and foreign) and the spot exchange rate.

Victor I. Makarov is a vice president in the corporate treasury of the Chase Manhattan Bank. His responsibilities include evaluation and analysis of market risk exposure and the development of risk management strategies. Prior to joining Chase, Dr. Makarov had been a manager in the Risk Monitoring Group at Security Pacific Bank and a member of the Hedging and Arbitrage Group at Merrill Lynch. Dr. Makarov is a member of the editorial board of *Bank Asset/Liability Management*.

He holds a Ph.D. in theoretical physics and mathematics from the USSR Academy of Sciences, Moscow, and a master's degree with honors in theoretical physics from Kiev University, Ukraine.

Managing the Price Risk in a Simplified Warehouse

Given the measures of risk, we can now consider how to measure and manage the price risk inherent in a warehouse.

Delta-Hedging a Warehouse

Within a bank, a warehouse manager normally begins by hedging the delta risk, the exposure of the warehouse to movements in the underlying price. The manager wants to structure the warehouse so that changes in the underlying price—shifts in the yield curve—will have no impact on the value of the warehouse.

To see how this is accomplished, let's consider the simple warehouse of derivatives provided in Table 18–1.

TABLE 18–1 The Warehouse

Swap 1:	2-year maturity $25MM notional principal bank receives six-month LIBOR, pays fixed semiannual settlement
Swap 2:	1.5 year maturity $10MM notional principal bank receives fixed, pays six-month LIBOR semiannual settlement
Cap:	Bank has sold a one-year cap on three-month LIBOR. Notional principal $50MM, cap rate 8.5%, quarterly settlement

Continuing to keep this example as simple as possible, let's suppose that it's mid-December, and let's suppose further that a zero-coupon yield curve is the smooth, upward-sloping yield curve illustrated in Figure 18–7. To see how changes in interest rates affect this portfolio of derivatives, let's begin by looking at the transactions, one at a time.

Delta-Hedging a Swap. Figure 18–8 illustrates the cash flows for swap 1 using the same kind of illustration used in Chapter 10. In Figure 18–8, the convention we use is that arrows pointing up indicate cash flows coming into the bank; arrows pointing down indicate cash flows leaving the bank.

For swap 1, the bank is paying the fixed rate, so the amount that the bank pays at each of the settlement dates—June and December of the upcoming year and June and December of the following year—are the same.

However, the amounts the bank will receive are not going to be the same over time. The amount that the bank will receive in June—six months from now—is already known; this cash flow will be determined by the six-month LIBOR rate in effect today and the $25 million notional principal of the swap:

$$[r_6/2 \times \$25MM]$$

But the payments the bank will receive in December of next year, and in June and December of the following year, are not known; they will depend on future six-month LIBOR rates. The payment the bank will receive in December of next year depends on six-month LIBOR—not the six-month LIBOR rate in effect today, but rather the rate that will be in effect six months from now:

$$[{}_6r_{12}/2 \times \$25MM]$$

FIGURE 18–7 A Stylized LIBOR Yield Curve

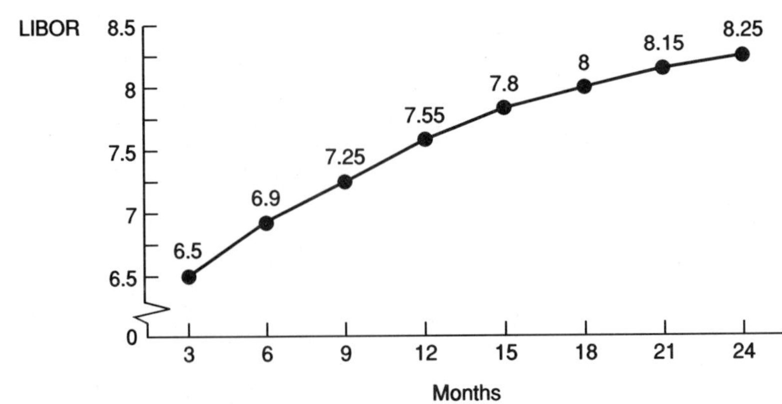

FIGURE 18–8 Swap 1: Cash Flows

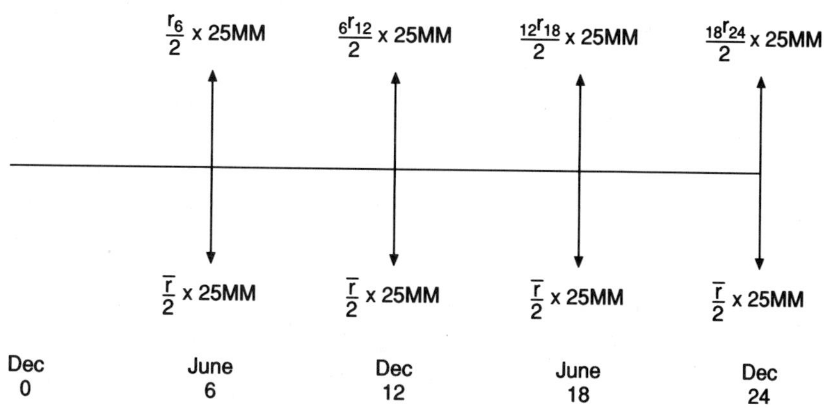

Likewise, the payments the bank will receive in June and December of the next year depends on the 6-month LIBOR rates in effect 12 months and 18 months from now:

$$[{}_{12}r_{18}/2 \times \$25MM]; \text{ and}$$
$$[{}_{18}r_{24}/2 \times \$25MM].$$

The cash flows illustrated in Figure 18–8 give us a way to think about the delta for swap 1. As we noted, only the cash flows on the floating side of the swap, the inflows to the bank, will change if interest rates change. And of these floating-side cash flows, only the payments in December of next year and the payments in June and December of the following year will change.

Table 18–2 illustrates how these cash flows will change. If interest rates rise by one basis point, the payments the bank will receive at months 12, 18, and 24 will rise by $1,250.

$$[0.0001/2 \times \$25MM = \$1{,}250]$$

But for purposes of valuation, it is not the changes in the cash flows that matter but rather the present values of these changes. Consequently, these $1,250 cash flows

TABLE 18–2 Swap 1: Calculation of Delta

Swap Period	*0–6*	*6–12*	*12–18*	*18–24*
Change in cash flow	-0-	+1,250	+1,250	+1,250
Present value	-0-	+1,162	+1,116	+1,073

$$\text{Delta} = \frac{\Delta \text{ Value of the asset}}{\Delta \text{ Interest rate}} = \frac{(1{,}162 + 1{,}116 + 1{,}073)}{1} = +3{,}351$$

have been discounted by the corresponding zero-coupon interest rates to get their present value. If interest rates rise by one basis point, the value of the payment to be received at month 12 will rise by $1,162, the value of the payment to be received at month 18 will rise by $1,116, and the value to be received at month 24 will rise by $1,073. Summing these values, the delta for swap 1—that is, the change in the value of this swap for a one-basis-point increase in interest rates—is $3,351; if interest rates rise by one basis point, the value of the swap will rise by $3,351. Conversely, if interest rates fall by one basis point, the value of this swap falls by $3,351.

We will illustrate how the deltas for swap 2 and the cap can be calculated. However, as long as we have the delta for swap 1, let's consider how this swap could be hedged.

Managers of derivatives warehouses use a range of financial instruments to hedge their positions. Swap 1 could be hedged by positions in the cash market (bonds), with forward rate agreements (FRAs), with other swaps, or with futures contracts. But to keep our example as simple as possible, let's consider hedging the swap using only futures contracts. In this example we will presume that the hedge is managed using Eurodollar futures contracts.

Table 18–3 summarizes the delta-hedge position for swap 1. The first row in Table 18–3 summarizes the delta for swap 1. (This row is taken directly from Table 18–2.) The delta of $1,161 for month 6 to month 12 is plotted against the time line at month 6, to reflect the time when the exposure is encountered. Similarly, the delta of $1,116 is plotted at month 12, and the final element of the delta for swap 1, $1,073, is plotted at month 18.

This first row indicates that we must use Eurodollar futures that expire in June and December of the next year and in June of the following year. The questions that remain are whether we must buy these futures contracts or sell them, and how many futures contracts we must buy or sell.

The second row in Table 18–3 provides the delta for a Eurodollar futures contract. As we noted in Chapter 8, a Eurodollar futures contract is a cash-settled

TABLE 18–3 Swap 1: "Delta-Hedged" Position

	0 D	3 M	6 J	9 S	12 D	15 M	18 J	21 S	24 D	
Delta for swap 1			+1,162		+1,116		+1,073			+3,351
Delta for one ED futures contract			−25		−25		−25			
Futures hedge			+46 contracts		+45 contracts		+43 contracts			
Delta for futures Contracts			−1,150		−1,125		−1,075			−3,350
			+12		−9		−2			+1

instrument whose value is determined by the value of a three-month, $1 million Eurodollar deposit. If interest rates rise, the value of this deposit—the value of a very short bond—will fall. More specifically, if interest rates rise by one basis point, the value of a $1 million three-month bond will fall by $25:

$$0.0001/4 \times \$1\text{MM} = \$25$$

Hence, the delta for a long position in a Eurodollar futures contract is −$25.

The third row of Table 18–3 describes the hedge. Consider month 6—June of next year. The delta for swap 1 is positive, so the warehouse manager requires an asset with a negative delta in June to establish the hedge. Since the delta for a long position in a Eurodollar futures contract is negative, it follows that the manager must buy futures contracts. How many futures contracts are required? If we divide the June delta for swap 1 ($1,161) by the delta for a single Eurodollar futures contract ($25) and round to the nearest whole number, it follows that the warehouse manager must buy 46 contracts.

$$1{,}161/25 = 46.44 \rightarrow 46$$

Similarly, to hedge the exposure in December, the manager must buy 45 contracts. And to hedge the exposure next June, the manager must buy 43 contracts that expire in June of the following year.

The fourth row in Table 18–3 summarizes the delta for the futures contracts that the warehouse manager bought, the number of contracts multiplied by −$25. Summing across that row, the delta for the futures contracts purchased is negative $3,350.

It follows then that since the delta for swap 1 is positive $3,351 and the delta for the futures contracts purchased is negative $3,350, the delta for the hedged position is $1.

Table 18–4 describes the delta hedge for swap 2. Note that since the bank pays the floating rate in swap 2, the delta for swap 2 is negative rather than positive. To hedge this swap, the warehouse manager must sell rather than buy Eurodollar futures contracts.

Delta-Hedging a Cap. The cap that the bank has sold is actually a package of interest rate options—what the practitioner may refer to as "caplets." Three months from now, if the three-month LIBOR rate is above 8.5 percent, the bank will pay to the holder of this option the difference between the three-month LIBOR rate and 8.5 percent. Likewise, the holder of this option will receive payments from the bank if the three-month LIBOR rate is above 8.5 percent at month 6 and at month 9.

Table 18–5 describes this cap. As noted above, the cap is a strip of three active options: one with a maturity of three months, one with a maturity of six months, and one with a maturity of nine months. The cap rate, the exercise (strike) price for

TABLE 18–4 Swap 2

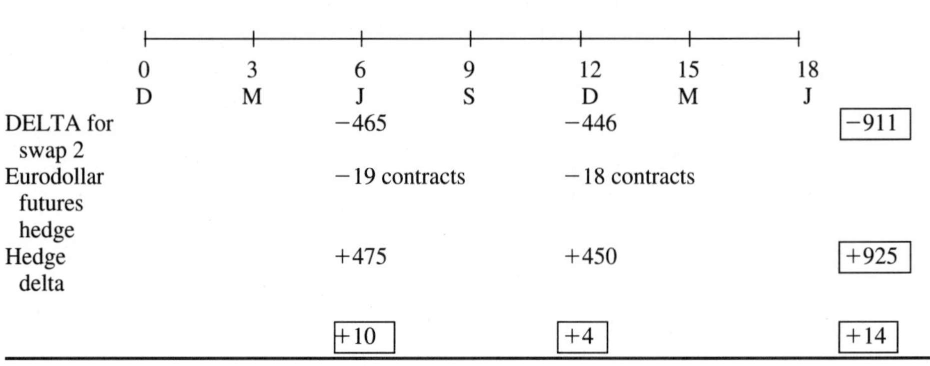

	0 D	3 M	6 J	9 S	12 D	15 M	18 J	
DELTA for swap 2			−465		−446			−911
Eurodollar futures hedge			−19 contracts		−18 contracts			
Hedge delta			+475		+450			+925
			+10		+4			+14

TABLE 18–5 The Cap = A Package of Interest Rate Options

	0	3	6	9	12
Option maturity		3 month	6 month	9 month	
Cap rate		8.5%	8.5%	8.5%	
Forward rate		${}_3r_6 = 7.18\%$	${}_6r_9 = 7.68\%$	${}_9r_{12} = 8.01\%$	
Option value basis points		0.38bp	8.95bp	23.89bp	Total
Dollars		$475	$11,188	$29,863	$41,525

the options, is specified as 8.5 percent. Since these options can be exercised only in the future, the relevant rate to compare with the exercise rate is not the current three-month LIBOR rate but rather the forward rate for three-month LIBOR. These forward three-month LIBOR rates at months 3, 6, and 9 are calculated from the LIBOR yield curve illustrated in Figure 18–7. Using a standard option-pricing model, we have valued the three interest rate options. Table 18–5 provides the value of these options, expressed both in basis points and in dollars.

However, the warehouse manager is interested not only in the value of the options but also in the Greek-letter risk measures described earlier. Table 18–6 provides these risk measures for the cap.[6] The first row of Table 18–6 provides the delta for the strip of individual interest rate options that make up the cap and the total for the cap. Note that as the maturity of the interest rate options gets longer, the forward rates are higher, increasing the delta for the options. Likewise, looking at gamma and vega, both of those numbers rise—and rise dramatically—as the options move nearer to the money.

TABLE 18–6 Greek-Letter Risk Measures for the Cap

	3-month Option	*6-month Option*	*9-month Option*	*Total*
Delta	−24	−243	−426	−693
Gamma	−100	−390	−399	−889
Vega	−200	−1,838	−3,075	−5,113

Table 18–7 illustrates how this cap could be delta-hedged using Eurodollar futures contracts. The first row of Table 18–7 is the delta for the cap (taken from Table 18–6). If interest rates rise by one basis point, the value of this cap to the bank that sold it declines by $693. Since the delta is negative, the bank must sell Eurodollar futures contracts to hedge this position. The second row of Table 18–7 summarizes the required number of futures contracts to be sold. The third row of Table 18–7 provides the delta for the Eurodollar futures contracts. The final row summarizes the hedged position, the sum of the delta for the cap itself and the delta for the Eurodollar futures contracts. A one-basis-point increase in interest rates causes the value of the cap to decline by $693. However, once the cap is delta-hedged, a one-basis-point increase in interest rates results in only a $7 increase in the value of the hedged position.

Delta-Hedging a Warehouse. So far, we've acted as if a portfolio of derivatives would be hedged transaction by transaction. However, it's probably evident that there are portfolio effects to be realized by instead hedging the entire portfolio.

Table 18–8 illustrates the delta for the entire warehouse. The deltas for the warehouse are obtained simply by summing the deltas for the individual transactions. Notice, however, that the magnitude of the total warehouse delta ($1,747) is

TABLE 18–7 Cap: "Delta-Hedged" Position

	0 D	3 M	6 J	9 S	12 D	
Cap delta		−24	−243	−426		−693
Eurodollar futures hedge		−1	−10	−17		
Hedge delta		+25	+250	+425		+700
		+1	+7	−1		+7

TABLE 18–8 Delta for the Warehouse

	0 D	3 M	6 J	9 S	12 D	15 M	18 J	
Swap 1 delta			+1,162		+1,116		+1,073	
Swap 2 delta			−465		−446			
Cap delta		−24	−243	−426				
Warehouse delta		−24	+454	−426	+670	0	+1,073	+1,747

smaller than the delta for swap 1 ($3,351). That is, by combining these transactions into a portfolio, the overall risk is reduced.

Albeit smaller, the warehouse contains residual risk that remains to be hedged. The method by which this risk is hedged is precisely that used earlier to hedge the individual transactions. At a point in time, if the delta for the warehouse is negative, the manager must sell Eurodollar futures contracts to hedge that position. If, on the other hand, the delta is positive, the manager must buy Eurodollar futures contracts.

Table 18–9 illustrates the delta-hedged warehouse. Consider month 3, March. The delta for the warehouse is a negative $24. To hedge this exposure, the manager sells one Eurodollar futures contract. The delta for short one Eurodollar futures contract is $25, so after the hedge is established, the delta for the warehouse in March of next year is $1. At month 6, June, the delta for the warehouse is $454. To hedge this positive delta of $454, the manager buys Eurodollar futures contracts as follows:

$$\$454/25 = 18.16 \rightarrow 18 \text{ Eurodollar futures contracts}$$

The delta for a long position in 18 Eurodollar futures contracts is −$450. Summing the $454 positive delta for the warehouse and the $450 negative delta for the futures contracts, the delta-hedged warehouse has a delta of only $4. This procedure is repeated for each maturity bucket.

Hedging the Warehouse against Risk Other Than Delta

Before the delta-hedge was implemented, the warehouse was quite sensitive to changes in interest rates. A one-basis-point change in interest rate would change the value of the warehouse by $1,747. After the hedge is implemented, the sensitivity of the hedged warehouse declined dramatically. As indicated in Table 18–9, once the warehouse is hedged, a one-basis-point movement in interest rates changes the value of the warehouse by only $3.

TABLE 18–9 The Delta-Hedged Warehouse

	0 D	3 M	6 J	9 S	12 D	15 M	18 J	
Swap 1 delta			+1,162		+1,116		+1,073	
Swap 2 delta			−465		−446			
Cap delta		−24	−243	−426				
Warehouse delta		−24	+454	−426	+670	0	+1,073	+1,747
Eurodollars futures contracts		−1	+18	−17	+27	0	+43	
Delta for futures		+25	−450	+425	−675	0	−1,075	1,750
Hedged Warehouse delta		+1	+4	−1	−5	0	−2	−3

But the delta-hedge is only the beginning. The delta-hedge protects the warehouse against small, parallel shifts in the yield curve. However, the warehouse manager must also protect the warehouse against rotations in the yield curve (yield curve twists), jumps in interest rates, changes in the volatility of interest rates, and other risks.

Hedging the Warehouse against Term-Structure Twists. To consider how the warehouse could be managed to hedge against rotations in the term structure, consider the delta ladders for warehouse 1 and warehouse 2 illustrated in Figure 18–10.

For both warehouse 1 and warehouse 2, the aggregate delta for the warehouse is zero—that is, the positive delta for some maturity buckets is exactly offset by the negative delta for other maturity buckets. However, the manner in which this aggregate delta of zero is obtained is quite different for the two delta ladders. In panel A-1, warehouse 1 has a very large positive delta for the three-month maturity bucket and a very large negative delta at the five-year maturity bucket. On the other hand, warehouse 2 (panel A-2) has a delta ladder that has positive and negative delta scattered through the maturity buckets.

If the manager's objective is to hedge the warehouse against rotations in the term structure, warehouse 2 is preferred to warehouse 1. To see why this is the case, consider the yield curve twist illustrated in panel B and the resultant impact on the two warehouses, illustrated in panels C-1 and C-2.

FIGURE 18–9 Hedging against Rotations of the Term Structure

Consider the delta "ladders" for two warehouses. Both of the warehouses are delta-hedged. Aggregate delta = 0

Panel A–1: Warehouse #1 has positive Delta in the 3–month maturity bucket offset by negative delta in the 5–year bucket.

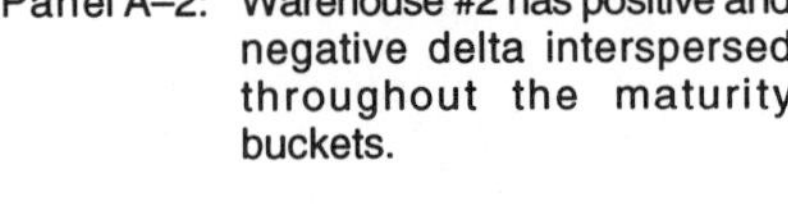
Panel A–2: Warehouse #2 has positive and negative delta interspersed throughout the maturity buckets.

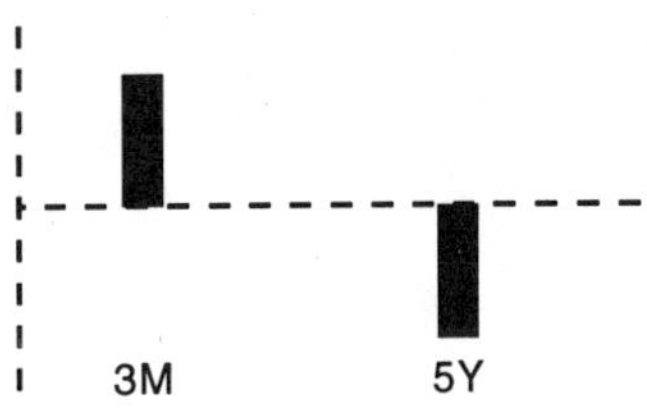

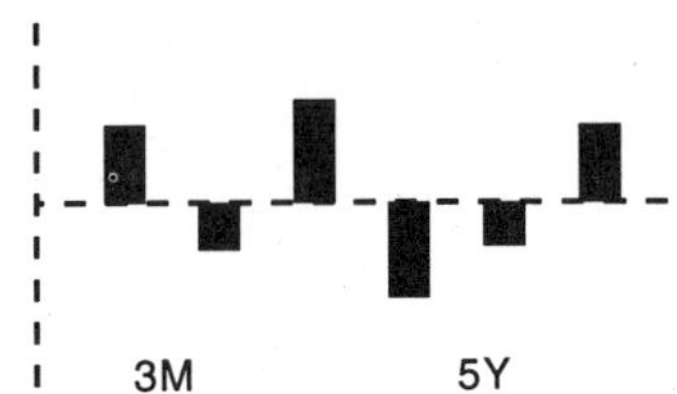

Panel B: Suppose the yield curve steepens—short-term rates fall and long-term rates rise.

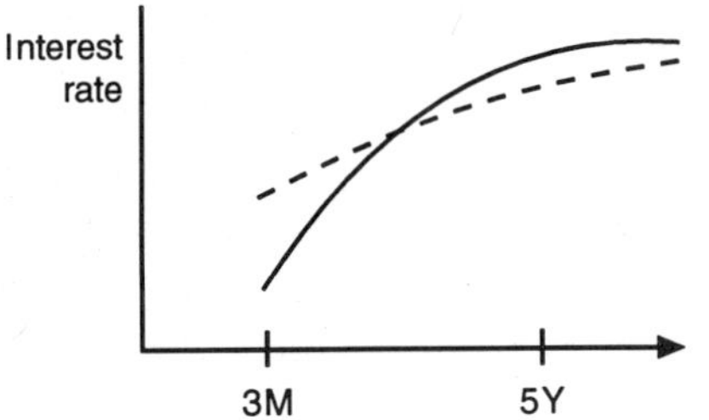

Panel C–1: Warehouse #1 loses value *both* due to the fall of short-term rates and the rise of long-term rates.

	3M	5Y
Delta	+	—
Chg in int rate	↓	↑
Chg in value	↓	↓

Panel C–2: Warehouse #2 is structured so that the rotation in the yield curve has little impact—gains and losses balance out.

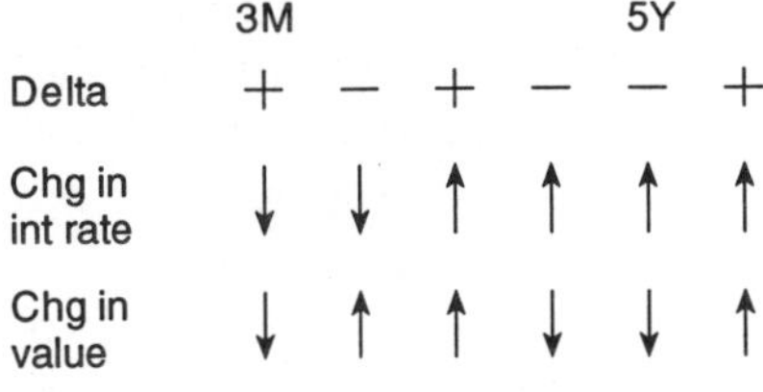

	3M				5Y	
Delta	+	—	+	—	—	+
Chg in int rate	↓	↓	↑	↑	↑	↑
Chg in value	↓	↑	↑	↓	↓	↑

As panel C-1 shows, warehouse 1 would lose value in both the three-month and five-year maturity buckets. Since warehouse 1 has a positive delta at the three-month maturity, the reduction in interest rates at the short end of the yield curve causes a loss in value. And since the warehouse has a negative delta at the five-year maturity bucket, the increase in rates at the long end of the curve also causes a loss in value. So with this twist in the yield curve, the value of warehouse 1 will decline even though the delta is zero.

However, for warehouse 2, the positive and negative deltas in the maturity buckets tend to cancel each other. Consequently, the change in value of the portfolio caused by this twist in the yield curve will be much smaller.

Hedging Gamma and Vega. When we toured fraternity row, we described the Greek-letter measures of risk: delta, gamma, and vega. However, when we've hedge this warehouse, we've hedged only the delta risk. Any gamma and vega risk in the warehouse remains. Indeed, because this bank has sold an interest rate cap, the warehouse is short both gamma and vega.

Since swaps and FRAs have gamma, the manager could use them to hedge the gamma introduced by selling the cap. (We will return to the implementation of a gamma hedge using swaps and FRAs later.) However, to hedge the vega risk in the warehouse, the warehouse manager has no choice but to buy options. The questions facing the warehouse manager are then: *Which options do I buy? How many options do I buy?*

In many cases, a warehouse manager will elect to hedge residual gamma and vega by purchasing out-of-the-money options. Figure 18–10 illustrates the vega in the warehouse for the out-of-the-money cap; since the bank sold the option, the vega is negative. And since vega is largest when the option is at-the-money,

FIGURE 18–10 Hedging against Jumps

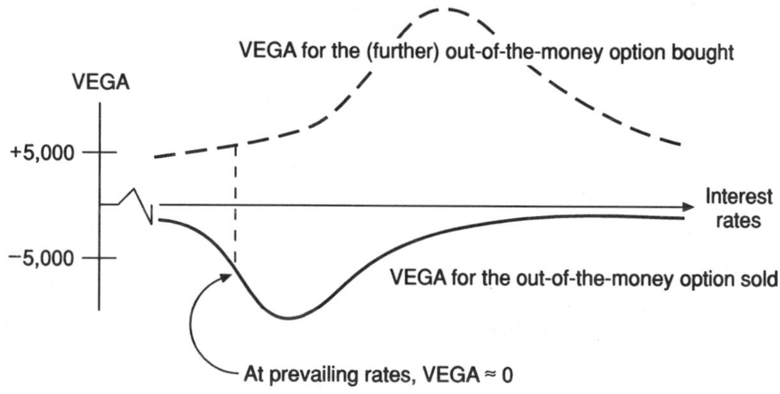

the vega in the warehouse is most negative at interest rates higher than the prevailing rate.

To hedge this vega, the warehouse manager must purchase other options. Suppose that the warehouse manager had implemented the hedge by purchasing options that were even further out-of-the-money than the ones the bank sold. As Figure 18–10 illustrates vega is now hedged—as long as interest rates remain at the current level.

Hedging the Warehouse against Jumps. So far, we have talked about hedging the warehouse assuming that the market moves continuously. However, there have been times when the market has "jumped" (or "gapped"). A recent instance was in the foreign exchange markets in September 1992.[7]

> Liquid, orderly foreign exchange markets temporarily disappeared in September 1992. This was most evident by looking at volatility. Under the ERM, volatility had been low compared with free-floating currencies. For example, before the crisis erupted, one-month UK sterling–deutsche mark volatility was as low as 3.8 percent while one-month U.S. dollar–deutsche mark volatility was in the 12–15 percent range.[8] From the end of August to September 11, one-month implied UK sterling–deutsche mark volatility was around 7 percent. Three days before sterling devalued, implied volatilities had risen to 14–15 percent. On the morning that sterling devalued, implied UK sterling–deutsche mark volatility was as high as 35 percent.
>
> And, the turmoil in the currency markets caused huge volatility in the interest rate markets as central banks manipulated short-term rates to defend their ERM parities. Short-term interest rate contracts had unprecedented trading ranges. And, highs and lows were often reached within 48 hours of each other. A case in point is the jump in the overnight Swedish krona rate from 24 percent to 500 percent.

To put this into context, consider again the vega hedge described in Figure 18–10. This hedge is valid only if interest rates stay at their prevailing level. If interest rates were to jump up or down, vega is no longer hedged.

To show how this can happen, Figure 18–11 illustrates the net vega for the warehouse. This net vega is obtained by summing the negative vega from the cap that the bank sold and the positive vega obtained when the warehouse manager bought the further out-of-the-money option.

Notice that if rates jump up a little, vega becomes negative. But if rates jump a lot, vega can actually become positive. So the warehouse manager has to consider not only the vega risk of today but also what the vega risk could be tomorrow if interest rates move a little or a lot.

Implementing the Hedge

So far, we have talked about hedging a warehouse (portfolio) of derivatives as if we first hedge delta, then hedge gamma and finally hedge vega. While this is a

FIGURE 18–11 Hedging against Jumps: Continued

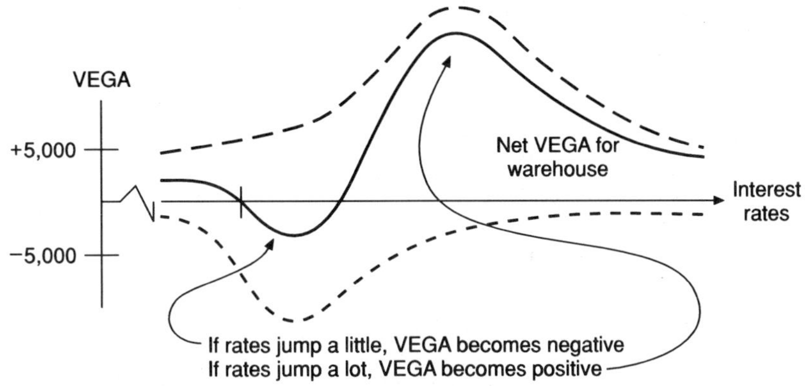

logical way to *think* about the necessary hedge, it is not a logical way to *implement* the hedge.

Table 18–10 illustrates the difficulty. Suppose the initial risk parameters of the warehouse are as provided on the first row of the table: delta = +1,750, gamma = −1,000, and vega = −5,000. Suppose that the warehouse manager first uses futures to hedge the delta risk. The results are provided in row 3: Delta is zero, gamma and vega are unchanged. So far so good. Now, suppose the manager uses swaps and FRAs to hedge the gamma. As row 5 illustrates, the manager can enter into swaps and FRAs with enough positive gamma to make the gamma of the warehouse zero, but since swaps and FRAs have delta as well as gamma, the warehouse would no longer be hedged with respect to delta. Consequently, the warehouse manager would then have to rehedge delta (see rows 6 and 7). Look what happens if the manager then purchases options to hedge the negative vega. Rows 8 and 9 illustrate that by purchasing the appropriate number of options, the manager could eliminate the vega risk, but since options have both gamma and delta, the warehouse will no longer have zero delta and gamma. Rows 10–15 illustrate the steps that would have to be accomplished to hedge the delta for the options (rows 10 and 11), to hedge the gamma for the options (rows 12 and 13), and then rehedge the delta that will be disturbed by hedging the gamma (rows 14 and 15).

As illustrated in Table 18–10, if the warehouse manager attempts to hedge delta then gamma and then vega, rehedging is constant. If I have delta hedged and I then hedge gamma, I displace the delta hedge; if I hedge vega, I displace both the delta and gamma hedges.

Hence, instead of hedging delta-gamma-vega, the warehouse manager will hedge vega-gamma-delta. This is illustrated in Table 18–11. The manager first uses options to hedge the vega (rows 2 and 3). The warehouse manager next hedges the remaining gamma with swaps and FRAs (rows 4 and 5). Since these instruments

TABLE 18–10 The Difficulties Encountered Implementing a Delta-Gamma-Vega Hedge

		Delta	*Gamma*	*Vega*
(1)	Initial warehouse	+1,750	−1,000	−5,000
(2)	Hedge delta with futures	−1,750	0	0
(3)	Warehouse after hedge	0	−1,000	−5,000
(4)	Hedge gamma with swaps and FRAs	−5,000	+1,000	0
(5)	Warehouse after hedge	−5,000	0	−5,000
(6)	Hedge delta with futures	+5,000	0	0
(7)	Warehouse after hedge	0	0	−5,000
(8)	Hedge vega with options	+500	+500	+5,000
(9)	Warehouse after hedge	+500	+500	0
(10)	Hedge delta with futures	−500	0	0
(11)	Warehouse after hedge	0	+500	0
(12)	Hedge gamma with swaps and FRAs	+2,000	−500	0
(13)	Warehouse after hedge	+2,000	0	0
(14)	Hedge delta with futures	−2,000	0	0
(15)	Warehouse after hedge	0	0	0

have no vega, hedging the gamma will not displace the vega hedge. Finally, the manager will hedge the remaining delta with futures (rows 6 and 7). Since futures have only delta, this hedge will not displace the existing hedges of gamma and vega.

Hedging beyond Delta-Gamma-Vega

While delta, gamma, and vega are risk measures used by virtually all managers of derivatives warehouses, they are by no means all of the "houses" on fraternity row. In this section we note some of the other risk measures that are commonly employed.

Theta measures the change in value of the financial asset associated with a change in the time to contract maturity. Since only options have time value, theta, like vega, is a characteristic only of options. Most trading rooms also refer to theta as "time decay" and track this change in value as part of the daily profit/loss report.

For options other than interest rate options, rho measures the change in the value of the option associated with changes in interest rate. For foreign exchange options, rho would be associated with the domestic interest rate rather than the foreign interest rate.

Lambda measures the change in the value of the options associated with changes in the dividend rate for equity options or the foreign interest rate for foreign exchange options.

TABLE 18–11 Implementing a Vega-Gamma-Delta Hedge

		Delta	*Gamma*	*Vega*
(1)	Initial warehouse	+1,750	−1,000	−5,000
(2)	Hedge vega with options	+500	+500	+5,000
(3)	Warehouse after hedge	+2,250	−500	0
(4)	Hedge gamma with swaps and FRAs	−2,500	+500	0
(5)	Warehouse after hedge	−250	0	0
(6)	Hedge delta with futures	+250	0	0
(7)	Warehouse after hedge	0	0	0

Risk Management in Practice

Managing Market Risk in a Money-Center Bank

Peter D. Hancock

J.P. Morgan is active in all segments of the markets for OTC derivatives. Our purpose is solving the risk management problems of our clients by providing customized solutions and making wholesale markets to other dealers. To effectively manage market risks involved, J.P. Morgan has established well-defined financial and operating controls. Those are developed and implemented by Corporate Risk Management Group, which reports directly to corporate office and is independent of all business groups. One of our goals is to integrate all our risk management techniques and export them firmwide.

Managing the market risk of our derivatives portfolio starts with marking-to-market. The positions are marked-to-marked daily, based on mid-market levels less following adjustments:

- Unearned credit spread adjustment. Unearned credit spread represents amounts set aside to cover expected credit losses and provide a return on credit exposure.
- Closeout costs adjustment, which represents the cost that would be incurred if all unmatched positions were closed out or hedged.
- Investing and funding costs adjustment. Since all but perfectly matched derivatives portfolios have future cash surpluses or deficits embedded in

them, the value of the book is adjusted to reflect J.P. Morgan's access to and costs of funds in various markets and currencies.
- Administrative costs adjustment. This includes, for example, systems costs, operational costs, and allocated costs of other functions affecting the derivatives activity.

These adjustments are directly related to the following sources of profit:

- Compensation for bearing credit risk.
- Origination (innovation) revenue, generated by valuing new transactions at mid-market after deducting appropriate adjustments.
- Bid/offer spread.
- Portfolio management (risk-taking ability).

Being able to distinguish in this way between the sources of revenue, and in particular being able to isolate the profit-and-loss effect of taking market risk, is essential to understanding and controlling market risk. Our business philosophy is to put capital to work to obtain the first three kinds of profit while minimizing the amount of capital at (market) risk.

Make Markets in Risk, Not Instruments

Our risk management is based on decomposing risk into its underlying factors. In that way we can focus on making markets in risks and not in instruments. Consequently, we manage our derivatives business on a total portfolio basis, not product by product. The derivatives books are organized by underlying instrument. That allows us to consider the following elements of market risk with respect to each underlying: absolute price or rate change (delta), convexity (gamma), volatility (vega), time decay (theta), basis or correlation, and discount rate (rho).

Understand Assumptions behind Risk Measurement

After identifying the elements of risk, one can proceed to measure market risk. At J.P. Morgan market risk is measured as "value at risk" (VaR), the 95 percent confidence limit on the loss from adverse market moves over a period of time. In order to be able to compare and aggregate VaR values over the entire portfolio, we use a common time horizon of one day for all the instruments, irrespective of their liquidity. We feel that the liquidity should properly be accounted for through closeout costs adjustments in marking-to-market. Those can be measured based on value at risk, and illiquidity can be accounted for by

Managing Market Risk in a Money-Center Bank continued

lengthening the time horizon in that measurement. Those assumptions about closeout costs and market access depend upon our market presence. Therefore, it is important to keep track of the size of our position relative to the market.

Balance Your Reliance on the Theoretical Models

The responses of derivatives portfolios to the simultaneous moves in many factors are best determined through simulations. This avoids reliance on any one option valuation model. In addition, care is taken that the assumptions (the type of distribution governing factor moves, the time interval over which the volatilities and correlations are sampled) going into the calculation of VaR values are continuously reviewed. A natural outgrowth of such reviews is our effort to quantify and prepare for the consequences of abnormal market conditions, such as market crashes or prolonged periods of inactivity, when those assumptions no longer apply. We perform stress simulations to determine how the portfolio would respond to stress conditions in improbable market environments.

Understand Differences Across Markets

Another important aspect of market risk management is understanding the many markets in which we are active. This includes the history of prices and volatilities, availability and transaction costs of hedge instruments, and the regulatory environment. It is on that foundation of understanding the market context that one can prepare for changes, gradual or sudden, in the characteristics of a market and in its relationship to other markets.

Peter Hancock is a managing director and the global head of derivatives at J.P. Morgan & Co. in New York. He has held a variety of positions since joining J.P. Morgan in 1980. Since returning to New York in mid-1986, Mr. Hancock has been stationed in the firm's New York office, where he served as manager of Euro-Asset and Liability Book, manager of New York Cap Desk, manager of New York Swap Trading, manager of New York Swaps, and most recently, head of Global Swaps. Before returning to New York, Mr. Hancock spent five years at J.P. Morgan's London operation.

Mr. Hancock, a British citizen, received an MA in politics, philosophy, and economics from Oxford University.

The multifactor options we introduced in Chapter 15 require that the manager also measure the risk to the warehouse from a change in the correlation between variables.

Recently, Mark Garman has suggested some additions to the list of risk measures.[9] Interestingly, this new list of risk parameters potentially reflects a shift in

FIGURE 18–12 Changes in Delta and Gamma as Time to Expiration Changes

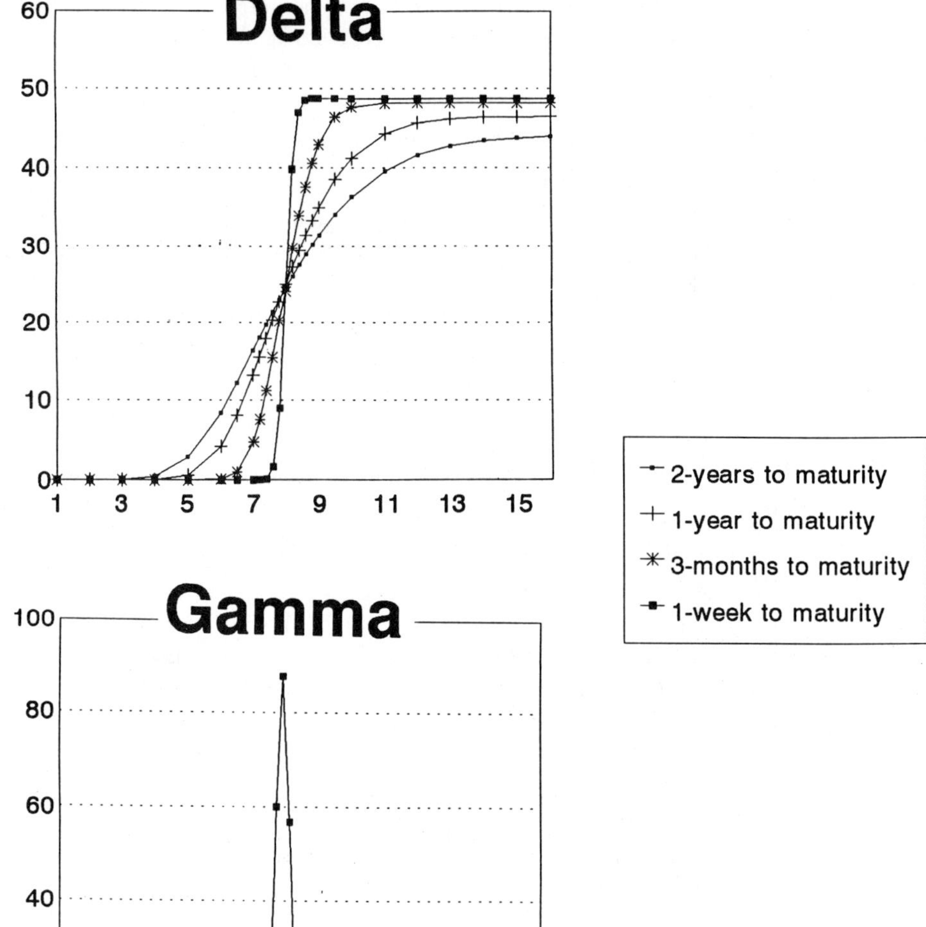

direction for the derivatives business: The language seems to be shifting from fraternity row to the jargon of physics.

As noted gamma measures the change in delta that will occur as the price of the underlying asset changes.[10] A manager of a large warehouse keeps a close eye on gamma, since this risk measure provides advance warning of the change that will be required in the hedge. Moving a step further, to obtain some advance warning of changes in gamma, some warehouse managers are now tracking the change in gamma as the price of the underlying asset changes. According to Garman, this risk measure is being referred to as *speed*.[11]

On a practical basis, one of the most stressful times for the manager of a warehouse that contains options is just prior to expiration of an option contract. As the time remaining on the option becomes short, the positions tend to become more sensitive to price changes around the exercise price. This increase in sensitivity as the time to expiration declines is illustrated in Figure 18–12. With a lot of time remaining to the expiration of the option, changes in the underlying price from below to above the exercise cause delta to change, but the change in delta is relatively smooth; that is, gamma is relatively small. However, when expiration is imminent, changes in the underlying price from below to above the exercise cause delta to change abruptly from very small to very large; that is, gamma is large. Consequently, some warehouse managers are beginning to track not only theta but also two other time effects.

Charm is the name Garman suggested for the change in delta as time to maturity changes. If the manager is attempting to keep the warehouse delta-hedged, the hedge will have to be adjusted day to day even if the underlying price does not change and Charm tells the warehouse manager how much the hedge will change.

Color measures the change in gamma as time to maturity changes. Particularly when expiration is close, the manager will want to know how small changes in the underlying price will impact the hedge.

Notes

1. Interest rate futures were designed to have zero gamma so that the change in the futures price for a given change in interest rates would be invariant to the level of rates. With this convention, a one-basis-point move in three-month LIBOR changes the value of a Eurodollar futures contract on the CME by $25, regardless of whether the move in three-month LIBOR is from 3 percent to 3.01 percent or from 6 percent to 6.01 percent. Similarly, with this convention, there is a strict linear relation between interest rate changes and the value of the futures contract—a 3-basis-point move will change the value of a Eurodollar futures contract by $75, a 30-basis-point move will change the value of a Eurodollar futures contract by $750, and a 300-basis-point move will change the value of a Eurodollar futures contract by $7,500.
2. Foreign exchange and commodity forward contracts have no gamma; delta is constant. Hence the gamma for FX and commodity swaps would also be zero.
3. To make it even more confusing, some academic textbooks have referred to this risk measure as lambda.
4. As we saw in earlier chapters of this book, changes in volatility change the value of an option but not the values of forwards, futures, or swaps.

   However, there are special cases in which one could argue that financial instruments other than options have vega. For example, suppose that the structure of interest rates follows the Cox-Ingersoll-Ross process we mentioned in footnote 8 of Chapter 13: Short-term interest rates determine the structure of bond prices. In such an environment, if the volatility of short-term rates rises while the level of the short-term rate is constant, financial instruments that have a nonzero gamma will have a nonzero vega as well.

5. This price list includes not only prices but also I volatilities.
6. The risk measures and the option valuation measures were obtained using a Black model to value the individual options—the caplets.
7. This discussion is adapted from "Things Fall Apart," an article by Richard Cookson and Lillian Chew that appeared in the October 1992 issue of *Risk*.
8. All volatilites were implied from the value of at-the-money options.
9. Garman (1992).
10. For those of you who like to think about these as mathematical derivatives, gamma is the second derivative of the value of the asset with respect to the price of the underlying asset.
11. If gamma is the second derivative of the value of the asset with respect to the price of the underlying asset, speed is the third derivative.

CHAPTER

19 THE IMPACT OF RISK MANAGEMENT

Most of this text has been devoted to showing you *how* to manage financial price risks. Before we conclude, we need to spend some time talking about *why* firms manage financial price risk. As we will describe, our perception is that risk management has a beneficial impact on the individual firm, on the markets for the underlying assets, and even on the macroeconomy.

The Impact of Risk Management on Individual Firms

The impact of risk management on the individual firm can be reflected either in the firm's net cash flows or in the firm's beta.

The Impact on Net Cash Flows

In Chapter 4, we provided the theoretical reasons risk management can increase the firm's net cash flows.

Risk management can add value by decreasing taxes. If the firm's average effective tax rate rises as pretax income rises, a reduction in the volatility of pretax income will lead directly to a reduction in the firm's future tax liabilities.

Risk management can add value by decreasing the expected costs associated with financial distress. A reduction in the volatility of the firm's cash flows reduces the probability that the firm's net income (or value) will fall low enough to trigger financial distress, and, consequently, it reduces the expected costs of financial distress. The magnitude of the cost reduction depends on two obvious factors: (1) the probability of encountering distress if the firm does not hedge and (2) the costs the firm will face if distress occurs. The benefit from risk management increases as the probability of distress and/or the distress-induced costs increase.

Risk management can add value by avoiding the errors in the investment decision that are induced by conflicts between bondholders and shareholders. The conflict between bondholders and shareholders results from differences in the kind of claims each holds: Bondholders hold fixed claims while shareholders hold claims that are equivalent to a call option on the value of firm. The conflict can result in a constraint on the debt capacity of the firm—the firm's paying a higher coupon on its debt—or in the firm's investing less than it would otherwise.

However, the question is whether or not the behavior of firms is actually consistent with these theoretical arguments. Our work with Deana Nance provides some empirical evidence.[1] The theoretical arguments we lay out indicate that the firm should be more likely to use the derivative instruments:

- To reduce its tax liability
  . . . if the firm's effective tax rate rises as pretax income rises (the effective tax function is "convex").
- To reduce the costs associated with financial distress
  . . . if the probability of default is higher.
- To avoid errors in the investment decision
  . . . if the firm's structure encourages conflicts between shareholders and bondholders.

To determine if firms actually behave in this manner, we assembled a sample of 169 Fortune 500 firms and estimated the relation between their use of risk management products—forwards, futures, swaps, and options—and the characteristics noted above. Our estimates indicate that firms that use risk management products:

- Face a more convex effective function.
  The firms that hedge have more tax credits or greater likelihood of income in the progressive region of the tax function.
- Have a higher probability of default.
  The firms that hedge have less coverage of fixed claims.
- Have a structure that increases conflicts between shareholders and debtholders.
  The firms that hedge have more growth options in their investment opportunity set and have higher debt-equity ratios.

And our study is not the only one to examine some of these issues. Indeed, our work complements other examinations of corporate hedging policy. Booth, Smith, and Stolz (1984) surveyed 238 banks and S&Ls in the western United States regarding their use of interest rate futures. Block and Gallagher (1986) surveyed 193 Fortune 500 firms regarding their use of interest rate futures and options. Houston and Mueller (1988) surveyed 48 firms regarding their hedging of foreign exchange exposures (accounting exposures). Wall and Pringle (1989) examined a group of 250 swap users obtained via a search of footnotes to annual reports. Mayers and Smith (1989) examined another form of hedging—the purchase of reinsurance by 1,276 property-casualty insurance companies. Since the samples differ, more powerful inferences can be drawn from aggregating the evidence across the studies. We summarize the results of the six studies in Table 19–1.

Our results are consistent with the proposition that firms with more convex tax schedules hedge more. Firms that use the hedging instruments have significantly more tax credits and more of their income in the progressive region of the tax schedule.

Several papers examine issues concerning the probability of default and the costs of financial distress. Booth, Smith, and Stolz find that S&Ls use interest rate futures more than do banks; Houston and Mueller find that firms with more foreign operations (firms with greater foreign exchange exposures) hedge more; Wall and Pringle find that firms with lower credit ratings are more likely to use swaps; Mayers and Smith find that firms with lower Best's ratings reinsure more.

Each study examines firm size, but the collective evidence does not suggest that a single dominant motive explains the relation between firm size and hedging. Studies examining hedging via forwards, futures, options, and swaps generally conclude that large firms hedge more. This result is consistent with significant information and transaction cost scale economies. Moreover, since futures trading does not exhibit the substantial transaction cost scale economies that are evident in forwards, options, and swaps, the Booth, Smith, and Stolz and Block and Gallagher results specifically suggest important informational scale economies. Yet Mayers and Smith's examination of insurance companies, where these scale economies should be less pronounced, indicates that small insurers hedge (reinsure) more.

TABLE 19–1 The Impact of Risk Management on the Firm's Net Cash Flows: Empirical Evidence

The Theory	The Evidence				
	Booth/ Smith Holz (1984)	*Block Gallagher (1986)*	*Wall Pringle (1989)*	*Mayers Smith (1990)*	*Nance/Smith Smithson (1993)*
A firm is more likely to use risk management if:					
. . . the firm's effective tax function is 'convex.'					✔
. . . the probability of default is higher.	✔		✔	✔	✔
. . . the firm's structure would increase conflicts between shareholders and bondholders.		✔			✔

This result is consistent with size-related tax and financial distress incentives being relatively more important hedging decisions in this industry. However, in an insurance company, management should be familiar with reinsurance, since it is a normal component of the business. Such managerial familiarity is less likely for the financial hedging instruments.

Block and Gallagher find a positive but statistically insignificant relation between the debt-equity ratio and hedging. Our results (1) that firms that use the hedging instruments have significantly higher R&D expenditures and (2) that firms with more investment options have both lower leverage and more hedging suggest that firms that use hedging instruments have more growth options in their investment opportunity set.

The Impact on Beta

If financial price risks are diversifiable, the capital asset pricing model (CAPM) would predict that financial price risk management would have no effect on beta. However, some evidence is beginning to suggest that risk management may actually have an impact on the firm's beta.

In their survey of empirical work on the effects of the introduction of derivative securities on the underlying assets, Aswath Damodaran and Marti G. Subrahmanyam (1992) note evidence that when derivatives on individual equities are introduced, *the beta for the involved firm declines*.

Using data on 32 stocks for the period 1970–76, Gary Trennepohl and William Dukes (1979) find that after options were listed on the stocks, the betas for the individual stocks declined. Robert Klemkosky and Terry Maness (1980) had similar results for a sample of 40 stocks over the period 1972–79. However, as noted in Table 19–2, the more recent studies do not find any statistically significant changes in beta.[2]

Following a much different path, Eli Bartov, Gordon M. Bodnar, and Aditya Kaul (1993) document a "beta shift" that provides evidence of an empirical relation between foreign exchange rate risk and beta. They examine a sample of 109

TABLE 19–2 The Impact of the Introduction of Options on Individual Shares on the Beta for the Shares

Study	*Number of Shares/ Period Examined*	*Impact on Beta of Individual Share*
Trennepohl/Dukes (1979)	32 / 1970–76	Declined
Klemkosky/Maness (1980)	40 / 1972–79	Declined
Skinner (1988)		No change
Damodaran/Lim (1991)	200 / 1973–85	No change

U.S. multinational firms and find that during the period surrounding the breakdown of the Bretton Woods agreement, the betas for these multinational firms increased.

Finally, the results of ongoing research at the Chase Manhattan Bank might be viewed as the other side of the coin from the Bartov, Bodnar, and Kaul results. We find evidence that for firms issuing risk-reducing hybrid securities—that is, debt that contains an embedded derivative that would decrease the firm's exposure to a financial price risk—beta declines.[3]

The Impact of Risk Management on the Markets for the Underlying Assets[4]

In marked contrast to the paucity of evidence on the impact of risk management on the performance of individual firms, we have a wealth of empirical evidence on the impact of derivatives on the markets for the underlying assets. For exposition, we will survey the evidence about the impact of the introduction of financial derivatives on the markets for the underlying assets as it relates to:

- The volatility of the underlying financial price.
- The speed of adjustment in the underlying markets.
- The bid-ask spreads in the underlying markets.
- Trading volume for the underlying asset.

The Impact on Price Volatility

> Futures and options are the tail wagging the dog. They have also escalated the leverage and volatility of the markets to precipitous, unacceptable levels.
>
> John Shad, former chairman,
> Securities and Exchange Commission

John Shad aptly summarizes the view that the introduction of derivatives has led to an increase in the volatility of underlying assets.[5] This view was widely voiced in the wake of the October 1987 stock market crash.

A more moderate position holds that there is no reason for the introduction of derivatives to have any effect on the volatility of underlying assets. Futures and options are created assets (for every long there is a corresponding short). Thus, the introduction of these contracts would have no predictable effect on trading in the underlying security.

A more radical counterargument suggests that with the introduction of derivatives, the volatility of an underlying asset should fall, not rise. After all, the newly created trading opportunity in this derivative security should increase market liquidity for an underlying asset.

The debate about the impact of the introduction of derivatives on the volatility of the price of the underlying asset has been going on for more than 20 years with no clear winner. The increased-volatility side gained credibility when this argument became a primary justification for a 1977 moratorium on expansion in options trading. (This argument also provided an interesting juxtaposition when, in 1983, the Golden Nugget—an enterprise apparently in favor of risk—argued in court that the introduction of options contracts on its shares should be prohibited because the options made buying its shares a more risky proposition.[6])

However, as summarized in Table 19–3, the empirical evidence fails to support the increased-volatility story. Indeed, the evidence supports the contention that the introduction of derivatives actually reduces the volatility in the underlying markets.

The futures market has been studied intensively. With the possible exception of the S&P 500 Equity Index, data on the behavior of the market before and after the introduction of futures contracts overwhelmingly supports the contention that the introduction of derivatives decreases rather than increases the volatility in the underlying markets.

And the recent evidence from examination of the impact of the listing of option contracts on individual shares is perhaps even more compelling. Douglas Skinner (1989) examines the volatility of share returns before and after the listing of options by observing a sample of 304 new listings of options (Chicago Board Options Exchange and the American Stock Exchange) between April 1973 and December 1986. He documents a decline in return volatility of between 10 and 20 percent following the listing of exchange-traded options on common stock. Jennifer Conrad (1989) reports similar results for option listings on the CBOE and AMEX from 1973 to 1980. Eighty-six of the 96 in her sample exhibited a decrease in share-price volatility with the introduction of an options contract. These results are reinforced by even more recent research by Aswath Damodaran and J. Lim (1991).

If the statistical evidence is so overwhelming, why do knowledgeable individuals like John Shad argue that the introduction of futures and options increased volatility? One answer may be that this is yet another instance in which cause and effect have been confused. There is no question that volatility and derivatives appear together; in Figure 19–1, we repeat a figure we showed you in Chapter 1. Some observers look at this pattern and conclude that the introduction of the derivative was responsible for the increased volatility:

$$\textit{Derivatives} \rightarrow \textit{Volatility}$$

However, as we have noted throughout this book, risk management using derivative securities is a valuable activity only if prices in the cash market are volatile. Responding to demand, the exchanges are more likely to list futures and options contracts on an asset when the underlying price becomes more volatile:

$$\textit{Volatility} \rightarrow \textit{Derivatives}$$

TABLE 19–3 The Impact of the Introduction of Derivatives on the Volatility of the Price of the Underlying Asset

Study: Asset Examined	*Change in Volatility*
Futures on Agricultural Commodities	
Working (1960): Onions	Decreased
Gray (1963): Onions	Decreased
Powers (1970): Pork bellies and cattle	Decreased
Taylor/Leuthold (1974): Cattle	Decreased
Cox (1976)	Decreased
Futures on U.S. Treasury Securities	
Dale/Workman (1981): Treasury bills	No change
Bortz (1984): Treasury bonds	Decreased
Simpson/Ireland (1985): Treasury bills	No change
Edwards (1988): Treasury bills	Decreased
Futures on GNMAs	
Froewiss (1978)	Decreased
Figlewski (1981)	Increased
Simpson/Ireland (1982)	No change
Corgel/Gay (1984)	Decreased
Moriarty/Tosini (1985)	No change
Futures on S&P 500 Index	
Santoni (1987)	No change
Stoll/Whaley (1987)	
Harris (1989)	Increased
Edwards (1988)	Decreased
Damodaran (1990)	Increased
Options on Shares	
Hayes/Tennenbaoum (1979)	Decreased
Klemkosky/Mannes (1980)	Decreased
Witeside/Duke/Dunnes (1983)	Decreased
Ma/Rao (1986, 1988)	Decreased
Bansai/Pruitt/Wei (1989)	Decreased
Conrad (1989)	Decreased
Skinner (1989)	Decreased
Damodaran/Lim (1991)	Decreased

Risk Management in Practice

Less Is Brewing in Witching Hours

Allen R. Myerson
The New York Times

The triple-witching hour, which in days past often sent stocks spinning 40 points or more in the final hour of trading, no longer casts such a possessing spell.

Only once in the last 12 triple-witching days—when three sets of options and futures contracts simultaneously expire each quarter—has the Dow Jones Industrial Average moved as much as 1 percent. [One] Friday, for example, it gained less than six points.

"It's just not the same as it used to be, where you'd see all hell break loose," said Stephen A. Mindnich, a trader at Jefferies and Company.

Once Each Quarter

The witching days result from the regular expirations of futures and options contracts, particularly a handful of contracts based on leading stock indices. These contracts, based on indices like the Standard & Poor's 500, helped bring about huge trading volume and big swings in the stocks that the indices cover. The problems were compounded when the index options and futures and options on individual stocks expired on the triple-witching days, once each quarter.

The result was jagged markets and trauma, even for savvy Wall Street professionals.

One of the sharpest swings came on a double-witching day in November 1991, when two sets of contracts expired. The Dow plunged 120 points, 80 of them in the last 90 minutes of trading.

Troubled Individual Investors

Such swings raised fears among investors that stock prices were determined not by the underlying values of companies but by the arcane strategies of big traders. The New York Stock Exchange, wary of losing investors, sought to calm these fears with rules intended to reduce volatility on witching days.

The exchange's approach, dating back to September 1986, has been to force greater disclosure and improve coordination with the options and futures markets.

Less Is Brewing in Witching Hours continued

On witching days, the exchange now publishes lists of as many as 50 stocks with large imbalances of buy or sell orders. The lists appear before the opening of trading and again several times shortly before the closing. The announcements often attract offsetting orders that can stabilize prices.

Restrictions on computerized trading on any day the market moves 50 points or more have helped bring new stability to the Big Board.

The New York Stock Exchange has also put pressure on the options and futures exchanges to have their index contract expire at the stock market's opening prices, not at the close.

The steps by the Big Board and the options exchanges have largely succeeded in limiting wild price swings.

Like commuters jamming bridges and tunnels at dawn to beat the rush hours, some traders simply execute their quarterly endgames ahead of time. Many triple-witching Fridays are now less volatile than the Thursdays before.

While new trading rules have clearly eased the last-minute crush, traders' behavior has also helped. Traders are more likely to carry out their strategies a day or more before options and futures expire. "Most of the positions were all squared away going into today, so the triple witching didn't mean that much," [says] David G. Shulman, chief equity strategist at Salomon Brothers. . . .

Many expiration strategies that paid off a few years ago are now so common that some traders have abandoned them. Price discrepancies have narrowed, making index arbitrage—the simultaneous buying and selling of futures, options, and stocks—much less profitable.

"The arbitrage opportunities were unbelievable for a few years," said Robert N. Gordon of Twenty-First Securities. "The market's gotten much more efficient since then."

Consequently, the introduction of derivatives tends to coincide with increased volatility. But the empirical evidence we have summarized clearly indicates that volatility is the impetus for the introduction of derivatives, not the result.

Another answer is that observers may be confusing volatility with speed of adjustment. So let's look at the evidence on the impact of derivatives on speed of adjustment in the underlying markets.

FIGURE 19–1 Evolution of Exchange Rate Risk Management Tools

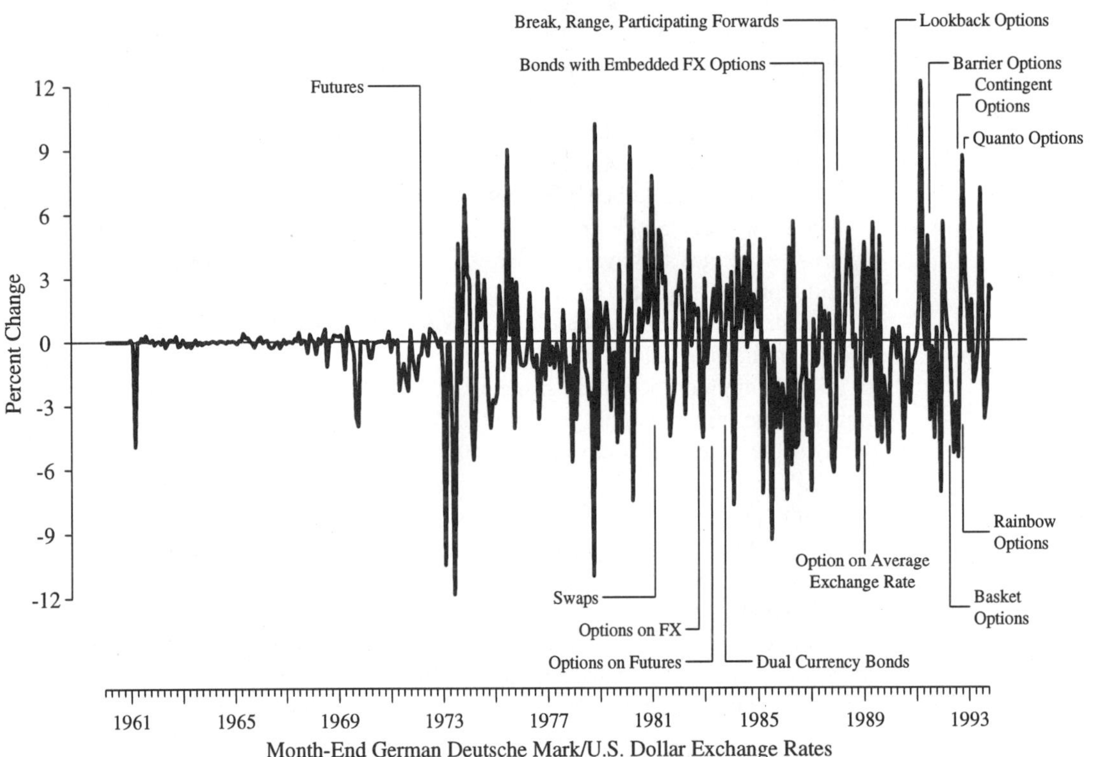

The Impact on Adjustment Speed

The impact of the introduction of derivatives on the speed of price adjustment has been examined primarily in the context of options. The available evidence, summarized in Table 19–4, suggests that the derivatives may well increase the speed with which the market incorporates information and adjusts prices.

Robert Jennings and Laura Stark (1981) examine the behavior of 180 stocks during the period 1981–82 and find that the prices of stocks that have traded options adjust *more quickly* to new information (specifically, earnings reports) than nonoptioned stocks of comparable size. Douglas Skinner (1990) considers 214 stocks for the period 1973–86 and finds that after options were listed, the reaction to earnings reports was smaller than it was without options. This evidence implies that some of the information content of the announcement already has been reflected in the share price and is consistent with the view that the option increases the incentive to invest in information about the firm. The Damodaran and Lim research we noted

TABLE 19–4 The Impact of the Introduction of Derivatives on the Speed of Price Adjustment

Study (Sample size—Period)	*Finding*
Jennings/Stark (1986) 180 stocks—1981–82	Prices of optioned stocks adjust *more quickly* to earnings reports
Skinner (1990) 214 stocks—1973–86	Reaction to earnings reports is smaller after listing of options
Damodaran/Lim (1991) 200 stocks—1973–85	Prices adjust *more quickly* to information after options are listed

earlier also finds that share prices adjust *more quickly* to information after options are listed on a stock.

The Impact on the Bid-Ask Spread

Theory suggests that the introduction of derivative contracts should cause the bid-ask spread for the underlying asset to decline. There are two components of the bid-ask spread. One is the inventory component discussed by Demsetz (1968). The higher the cost of the inventory required to supply liquidity to the market, the higher the bid-ask spread. The introduction of derivatives, especially options, reduces this inventory cost by reducing the volatility of the underlying asset price and by increasing the volume of trading. The second component of the spread comes from the information disparity among traders described by Bagehot (1971). The larger the disparity within a market, the greater the spread. When it is available, the more informed traders tend to exploit their information in the options market. This translates informed traders' private information into prices that are publicly observable, thereby reducing the information disparity in the underlying market.

As was the case with speed of adjustment, the studies that have examined the impact on the bid-ask spread have focused on the listing of new option contracts on individual shares. The results of these studies are summarized in Table 19–5.

Robert Neal (1987) examines the behavior of 16 shares during the period 1985–86 and finds that the bid-ask spreads are *lower* for those shares that have listed options. Mark Fedenia and Theoharry Grammatikos (1992) use a much larger sample of 419 firms over the period 1970–88 and find that the average bid-ask spreads *decrease* after the listing of options for the 341 New York Stock Exchange-traded stocks. However, the bid-ask spreads increase for the 78 stocks in the sample that are traded over-the-counter. For their sample of 200 stocks, Damodaran and Lim conclude that the bid-ask spreads *decline* after the listing of options.

TABLE 19–5 The Impact of the Introduction of Derivatives on the Bid-Ask Spread in the Underlying Market

Study	*Sample Size*	*Period*	*Effect on Bid-Ask Spread*
Neal (1987)	16	1985–86	Decreases
Fedenia/Grammatikos (1989)	419	1970–88	
			NYSE: Decreases
			OTC: Increases
Damodaran/Lim (1991)	200	1973–86	Decreases

The Impact on Trading Volume of the Underlying Assets

Theory suggests that trading volume on the underlying asset should increase when derivatives are introduced. As noted above, the introduction of derivatives can reduce the bid-ask spread in the underlying asset market. This reduction in transaction costs increases volume. Moreover, the derivatives market and the underlying asset market develop an important symbiotic relation. Shocks to either market are transmitted to the other by arbitragers exploiting any discrepancy in pricing between the markets.

The studies that have looked at the effects on trading volume when options are listed on the shares are summarized in Table 19–6. Unlike Tables 19–3, 19–4, and 19–5, this table reflects mixed conclusions.

In his examination of 304 shares, Skinner finds that there is an *increase* in the raw trading volume after the listing of options. For their sample of 200 shares, Damodaran and Lim report a similar increase in raw trading volume but find no significant change in market-adjusted trading volume. Vipul Bansal, Stephen Pruitt, and John Wei (1989) cast further light on this issue by categorizing option listings by time period. They find in their sample of 175 stocks over the period 1973–86 that the trading volume adjusted for the changes in the overall market *increases* after options listing prior to 1979 but not thereafter.

TABLE 19–6 The Impact of the Introduction of Derivatives on Trading Volume in the Underlying Market

			Effect on Trading Volume	
Study	*Sample Size*	*Period*	*Raw*	*Market Adjusted*
Skinner (1989)	304	1973–86	Increase	
Damodaran/Lim (1991)	200	1973–86	Increase	No change
Bansal/Pruitt/Wei (1989)	175	1973–78		Increase
		1979–86		No change

Summary

The empirical evidence discussed above on the impact of the introduction of derivatives on the markets for the underlying assets is summarized in Table 19–7. This evidence supports the following conclusions:

- With the possible exception of stock-index futures, the introduction of derivatives has reduced price volatility in the underlying market.
- The introduction of derivatives enriches the information set and increases the speed with which prices adjust to information.
- The introduction of derivatives has decreased bid-ask spreads in the underlying market.
- The introduction of derivatives has had little effect on market-adjusted trading volume in the underlying market.

TABLE 19–7 The Impact of the Introduction of Derivatives on the Markets for the Underlying Assets: Summary

		Futures on		
	Options on Individual Shares	*Commodities*	*Fixed Income Assets*	*S&P 500 Index*
Volatility of the price of the underlying asset	−	−	− or no change	?
Speed of price adjustment for the underlying asset	+			
Bid-ask spread for the underlying asset	−			
Trading volume for the underlying asset	?			

The Impact of Risk Management on the Economy

In examining the remarkable growth of the derivative securities market, most financial economists conclude that the social benefits of financial innovation far outweigh the costs. Perhaps the principal benefit from the many securities innovations over the last two decades has been an improvement in the allocation of risk within the financial system. Derivatives have dramatically reduced the cost of transferring risks to those market participants who have a comparative advantage in bearing them. As Merton Miller (1992) says, "Efficient risk sharing is what much of the futures and options revolution has been all about."

Aside

The Impact of Growth of Over-the-Counter Derivatives on Exchange-Traded Markets*

Concern has been expressed that activity in privately negotiated derivatives may divert order flow from the centralized exchange markets for futures, reducing information flow and impairing price discovery. In the extreme, the final result could be market fragmentation, a loss of liquidity, and more volatile futures prices.

In fact, the growth of these derivatives may well have had the opposite effect—acting as a complement to the development of the exchange markets. Most of the growth in global derivatives is in response to new demands by end users for customized transactions that are not met by the exchanges. Derivatives growth adds indirectly but significantly to exchange-traded volumes, as derivatives dealers rely in part on exchange-traded futures and options to hedge their net market risks.

Evidence of this is that on U.S. exchanges at year-end 1991, banks held over 50 percent of the open positions in short-term interest rate futures, over 45 percent of the open positions in calls on short-term interest rate futures, and over 42 percent of the open positions in puts. Much of this activity in interest rate futures and options is driven by the need to hedge global derivatives portfolios. For example, the Chicago Mercantile Exchange's Eurodollar futures and options contracts—two of the exchange-traded contracts most closely associated with global derivatives activity—have also been the most successful contracts. The volume of Eurodollar futures grew by over 300 percent between 1987 and 1991, a period of rapid growth for global derivatives. The Eurodollar contract also has the largest far-dated volume of any futures contract because of its use in the hedging of longer-dated swaps. Derivatives dealers are estimated to hold over 50 percent of the total open interest in Eurodollar contracts.†

The effect of this activity is to augment rather than impair price discovery by bringing more participants into the price formation process. With participants actively competing with one another, arbitrage effectively unified dispersed price information. In this regard, global derivatives activity and the exchange markets are complementary.

---

*This discussion is adapted from work by Robert J. Mackay, director, Center for Study of Futures and Options Markets, Virginia Tech University.

†Swap activity also drives a significant portion of the activity in energy futures and options. For example, in March 1992, commodity swap dealers reportedly held as hedges positions accounting for 17.5 percent of crude oil and 5.5 percent of clear products open interest on the New York Mercantiltile Exchange, up over 60 percent from the figures for September 1991. The increase in activity by commodity swap dealers as a percentage of open interest coincided with a 23 percent increase in open interest during this period. See "The Growth of NYMEX and Over-the-Counter Markets: Interrelationships, Implications, and Strategic Recommendations," New York Mercantile Exchange, March 1992.

Derivatives markets provide corporations the ability to hedge against currency, interest rate, and commodity-price risks far more quickly and cheaply than was possible before. For example, consider the developments in the mortgage market. Historically, a local institution originated, owned, and serviced the loan. Now investment bankers pool and repackage individual mortgages into securities and sell them in a national market. Local financial institutions more narrowly focus on origination and servicing, activities in which they are more likely to have a comparative advantage. The extraordinary growth of this as well as other forms of asset securitization have been made possible in part by the financial futures markets used to hedge the investment banker's exposures.

These financial innovations—futures, swaps, and securitization—have permitted massive transfers of interest rate risk from local financial institutions to well-diversified institutional investors. This transfer has not only lowered mortgage rates for home buyers, it also should help protect the financial system from another disaster like the one experienced by the savings and loan industry.

We believe that it is critical to understand that even though one party's gain is another's loss in a derivatives market, the use of derivatives can create value. The more efficient risk sharing afforded by derivatives can reduce total risk for all market participants. For example, consider an oil company. Obviously, its profitability will be affected by market oil prices. Historically, to help manage this risk, the firm might diversify its activities by also operating a chemical subsidiary. But the skills required to run an oil company efficiently are not necessarily the same skills required in a chemical firm. And this diversified firm may well face difficult compromises in establishing its financing, dividend, or human relations policies. With access to a well-functioning oil derivatives market, the firms can split. Each can choose policies more customized for its needs, and both companies can hedge by exchanging their oil price exposures in the derivatives market.

Over the past two decades, derivatives have expanded the technology available to firms and individuals to manage risk. They have reduced the costs of managing exposures, thereby increasing liquidity and efficiency. While providing precise estimates of these benefits may be difficult, the continued growth of these markets suggest they are substantial.

Notes

1. Nance, Smith, and Smithson (1993).
2. As Damodaran and Subrahmanyam point out, the difference may be that the more recent studies correct for nontrading problems in estimating beta.
3. Smithson and Turner (1993).
4. This section is based on Smith and Smithson (1989) and Damodaran and Subrahmanyam (1992).
5. *The Wall Street Journal*, January 15, 1988.
6. *The Wall Street Journal*, November 1, 1983.

REFERENCES

Altman, El (1989). "Measuring Corporate Bond Mortality and Performance." *Journal of Finance* 44.

Arak, Marcelle; Arturo Estrella; Laurie Goodman; and Andrew Silver (1988). "Interest Rate Swaps: An Alternative Explanation." *Financial Management* 17 (Summer): 12–28.

Arak, Marcelle; Laurie S. Goodman; and Arthur Rones. "Credit Lines for New Instruments: Swaps, Over-the-Counter Options, Forwards and Floor-Ceiling Agreements." *Bank Structure and Competition,* pp. 437–56.

Bachelier, Louis (1900). "Theorie de la Speculation." *Annales de l'Ecole Normale Superieure* 17: 21–86. English translation by A. J. Boness in *The Random Character of Stock Market Prices,* ed. Paul H. Cootner. Cambridge, Mass.: M.I.T. Press, 1964, pp. 17–78.

Bank for International Settlements (1987). *Proposals for International Convergence of Capital Measurement and Capital Standards,* December.

———. (1987). *International Convergence of Capital Measurement and Capital Standards,* July.

Bansal, V. K.; S. W. Pruitt; and K. C. John Wei (1989). "An Empirical Reexamination of the Impact of CBOE Option Initiation on the Volatility and Trading Volume of the Underlying Equities: 1973–1986." *The Financial Review* 24: 19–29.

Barone-Adesi, Giovanni, and Robert E. Whaley (1987). "Efficient Analytic Approximation of American Option Values." *Journal of Finance* 42 (June): 301–20.

Bartov, Eli; Gordon M. Bodnar; and Aditya Kaul (1992). "Exchange Rate Volatility and the Riskiness of U.S. Multinational Firms: Evidence from the Breakdown of the Bretton Woods System." Working Paper, 1993.

Behof, John P. (1993). "Reducing Credit Risk in the Over-the-Counter Derivatives." Federal Reserve Bank of Chicago *Economic Perspectives,* January/ February.

Bierman, H., Jr. (1967). "The Valuation of Stock Options, *Journal of Financial and Quantitative Analysis* 2: 327–34.

Bierwag, G. O., George G. Kaufman, and Alden Toevs (1983). "Immunization Strategies for Funding Multiple Liabilities." *Journal of Financial and Quantitative Analysis* 18, no. 1, pp. 113–23.

Black, Fischer (1976). "The Pricing of Commodity Contracts." *Journal of Financial Economics* 3.

Black, Fischer; Emanuel Derman; and William Toy (1990). "A One-Factor Model of Interest Rates and Its Application to Treasury Bond Options." *Financial Analysts Journal* (January–February): 33–39.

Black, Fischer, and Myron Scholes (1973). "The Pricing of Options and Corporate Liabilities," *Journal of Political Economy* 81 pp. 637–59.

Block, S. B., and T. J. Gallagher (1986). "The Use of Interest Rate Futures and Options by Corporate Financial Managers." *Financial Management* 15: 73–78.

Board of Governors of the Federal Reserve System and the Bank of England (1987). "Potential Credit Exposure on Interest Rate and Foreign Exchange Rate Related Instruments." Joint Working Paper.

Boness, A. James (1964). "Elements of a Theory of Stock-Option Value." *Journal of Political Economy* 72 (April): 163–75.

Booth, J. R.; R. L. Smith; and R. W. Stolz (1984). "The Use of Interest Rate Futures by Financial Institutions." *Journal of Bank Research* 15: 15–20.

Boyle, Phelim P. (1977). "Options: A Monte Carlo Approach." *Journal of Financial Economics* 4 (May): 323–38.

Branch, B., and J. E. Finnerty (1981). "The Impact of Option Listing on the Price and Volume of the Underlying Stock." *Financial Review* 16: 1–15.

Brealey, Richard, and Stewart Meyers (1988/3rd edition) *Principles of Corporate Finance.* New York: McGraw Hill.

Brennan, Michael J. (1986). "A Theory of Price Limits in Futures Markets." *Journal of Financial Economics* 16 (June).

Brennan, Michael, and Eduardo Schwartz (1978). "Finite Difference Method and Jump Processes Arising in the Pricing of Contingent Claims." *Journal of Financial and Quantitative Analysis* 13 (September): 461–74.

Brennan, Michael, and Eduardo Schwartz (1979). "A Continuous-Time Approach to the Pricing of Bonds." *Journal of Banking and Finance* 3 (July).

Brennan, Michael, and Eduardo Schwartz (1981). "The Case for Convertibles." *Chase Financial Quarterly,* Fall. (Reprinted in *Journal of Applied Corporate Finance*, Summer 1988).

British Bankers' Association (1985). *Forward Rate Agreements.* London, August.

Bulkeley, William H. (1989). "Tough Pitch: Marketing on the Defense." *The Wall Street Journal,* October 18.

Capatides, Michael G. (1988). *A Guide to the Capital Markets Activities of Banks and Bank Holding Companies.* W. C. Brown and Co.

Chen, Andrew H., and John W. Kensinger (1988). "Puttable Stock: A New Innovation in Equity Financing." *Financial Management* 17 (Spring).

Chesler-Marsh, Caren (1992). "Nightmare on Wall Street." *Euromoney,* February.

Chew, Lillian (1992). "A Bit of a Jam." *Risk* 5 (September).

Chicago Board of Trade (1988). "Futures: The Realistic Hedge for the Reality of Risk."

Conrad, J. (1989). "The Price Effect of Option Introduction." *Journal of Finance* 44: 487–98.

Cookson, Richard, and Lilian Chew (1992). "Things Fall Apart." *Risk,* October 1992.

Cooper, Ian A., and Antonio S. Mello (1991). "The Default Risk of Swaps." *The Journal of Finance* 46 (June).

Courtadon, Georges (1982). "A More Accurate Finite Difference Approximation for the Valuation of Options." *Journal of Financial and Quantitative Analysis* 17 (December): 697–703.

Cox, C. C. (1976). "Futures Trading and Market Information." *Journal of Political Economy* 84: 1215–37.

Cox, John A.; Jonathan E. Ingersoll; and Stephen A. Ross (1981). "The Relations between Forwards Prices and Futures Prices." *Journal of Financial Economics* 9.

Cox, John; Jonathan Ingersoll; and Stephen A. Ross (1985). "A Theory of the Term Structure of Interest Rates." *Econometrica* 53 (March).

Cox, John C. and Stephen A. Ross (1976). "The Valuation of Options for Alternative Stochastic Processes." *Journal of Financial Economics* 3 (January–March): 145–66.

Cox, John C.; Stephen A. Ross; and Mark Rubinstein (1979). "Options Pricing: A Simplified Approach." *Journal of Financial Economics,* September.

Cox, John C., Ross, and Mark Rubinstein (1985). *Options Markets.* Englewood Cliffs, N.J.: Prentice Hall.

Damodaran, A. (1990). "Index Futures and Stock Market Volatility." *Review of Futures Markets* 9.

Damodaran, A., and J. Lim (1991). "The Effects of Option Listing on the Underlying Stocks' Return Processes." *Journal of Banking and Finance* 15: 647–64.

Damodaran, Aswath, and Marti G. Subrahmanyam (1992). "The Effects of Derivative Securities on the Markets for the Underlying Assets in the United States: A Survey." *Financial Markets, Institutions, and Instruments,* December.

DeTemple, J., and D. Jorion (1990). "Option Listing and Stock Returns." *Journal of Banking and Finance* 14: 781–802.

Dickins, Paul (1988). "Fast Forward with FRAs." *Corporate Finance*, April.

Drabenstott, Mark, and Anne O'Mara McDonley (1984). "Futures Markets: A Primer for Financial Institutions." *Economic Review,* Federal Reserve Bank of Kansas City, November.

Edwards, F. R. (1988). "Futures Trading and Cash Market Volatility: Stock Index and Interest Rate Futures." *Journal of Futures Markets* 8: 421–39.

Fedenia, Mark, and Theocharry Grammatikos (1992). "Options Trading and the Bid-Ask Spread of the Underlying Stocks." *Journal of Business* 65 (July): 335–51.

Federal Reserve Bank of Chicago (1986). "Credit Lines for New Instruments: Swaps, Over-the-Counter Options, Forwards, and Floor-Ceiling Agreements." *Proceedings of a Conference on Bank Structure and Competition,* Federal Reserve Bank of Chicago.

Ferron, Mark, and George Handjinicolaou (1987). "Understanding Swap Credit Risk: The Simulation Approach." *Journal of International Security Markets* (Winter): 135–48.

Figlewski, S. (1981). "The Informational Effects of Restrictions of Short Sales: Some Empirical Evidence." *Journal of Financial and Quantitative Analysis* 16: 463–76.

Figlewski, Stephen (1986). *Hedging with Financial Futures for Institutional Investors: From Theory to Practice.* Cambridge, Mass.: Ballinger.

Finnerty, John D. (1988). "Financial Engineering in Corporate Finance: An Overview." *Financial Management* 17 (Winter).

Flannery, Mark J., and Christopher M. James (1984). "The Effect of Interest Rate Changes on the Common Stock Returns of Financial Institutions." *Journal of Finance,* September.

French, Kenneth R. (1983). "A Comparison of Futures and Forward Prices." *Journal of Financial Economics* 12 (November).

Friedman, Avner (1975). *Stochastic Differential Equations and Applications.* New York: Academic Press.

Frye, Jon (1992). "Underexposed and Overanxious." *Risk* 5 (March).

Furbush, Dean, and Michael Sackheim (1991). "U.S. Hybrid Instruments: Evolving Legal and Economic Issues." *Butterworth's Journal of International Banking and Financial Law,* September.

Garber, Peter M. (1986). "The Tulipmania Legend." Center for the Study of Futures Markets Working Paper #CSFM-139, August.

Garman, Mark B., and Steven W. Kohlhagen (1983). "Foreign Currency Option Values." *Journal of International Money and Finance* 2 (December).

Garman, Mark B. (1988). "Charm School." *Risk* (October): 16–19.

Geske, Robert (1979). "The Valuation of Compound Options." *Journal of Financial Economics* 7 (March): 63–81.

Geske, Robert (1979). "A Note on an Analytic Valuation Formula for Unprotected American Call Options on Stocks with Known Dividends." *Journal of Financial Economics* 7 (December): 375–80.

Goldman, M. Barry; Howard B. Sosin; and Mary Ann Gatto (1979). "Path Dependent Options: Buy at the Low, Sell at the High." *Journal of Finance* 34, no. 5 (December): 1111–27.

Grabbe, J. Orlin (1983). "The Pricing of Call and Put Options on Foreign Exchange." *Journal of International Money and Finance* 2 (December): 239–53.

Grindal, Izabel (1988). "Flexible Risk Control and Arbitrage." *Futures and Options World,* June.

Hakansson, Nils H. (1976). "The Purchasing Power Fund: A New Kind of Financial Intermediary." *Financial Analysts Journal,* November/December.

Harris, L. (1989). "S&P 500 Cash Stock Price Volatilities." *Journal of Finance* 44: 1155–76.

Hayes, S. I., and M. E. Tennenbaum (1979). "The Impact of Listed Options on the Underlying Shares." *Financial Management* 8 (Winter) no. 4: 72–76.

Healy, James P. (1993). "Working Paper of the Credit Risk Measurement and Management Subcommittee." The Group of Thirty Global Derivatives Study, July.

Heath, David; Robert Jarrow; and Andrew Morton (1990). "Bond Pricing and the Term Structure of Interest Rates." *Journal of Financial and Quantitative Analysis* 25 (December).

Hicks, J. R. (1939). *Value and Capital.* Cambridge: Oxford University Press.

Ho, Thomas S. Y., and Sang-Bin Lee (1986). "Term Structure Movements and Pricing Interest Rate Contingent Claims." *Journal of Finance* 41: 1011–29.

Hopewell, Michael, and George Kaufman (1973). "Bond Price Volatility and Term to Maturity: A Generalized Respecification." *American Economic Review* 62 (September).

Hopewell, Michael H., and George G. Kaufman (1974). "The Cost of Inefficient Coupons on Municipal Bonds." *Journal of Financial and Quantitative Analysis* 9, no. 2, pp. 155–64.

Houston, Carol Olson, and Gerhard G. Mueller (1988). "Foreign Exchange Rate Hedging and SFAS no. 52: Relatives or Strangers?" *Accounting Horizons* 2, no. 4 (December), 50–57.

Hull, John (1989). *Options, Futures, and Other Derivative Securities.* Englewood Cliffs, N.J.: Prentice Hall.

Hull, John, and Alan White (1987). "The Pricing of Options on Assets with Stochastic Volatilities." *Journal of Finance* 42: 281–300.

———. (1990). "Pricing Interest Rate Derivative Securities" *Review of Financial Studies* 3.

———. (1990). "Valuing Derivative Securities Using the Explicit Finite Difference Method." *Journal of Financial and Quantitative Analyses* 25, no. 1 (March): 87–100.

———. (1992a). "The Impact of Default Risk on the Prices of Options and Other Derivative Securities." Unpublished manuscript, May.

———. (1992b). "The Price of Default." *Risk* 5 (September).

Hutchins, Dexter (1986). "Caterpillar's Triple Whammy." *Fortune,* October 27.

Iben, Benjamin, and Rupert Brotheron-Ratcliffe (1991). "Principals at Stake." *Risk* 5 (December/January).

Ingersoll, Jonathan (1976). "A Theoretical and Empirical Investigation of the Dual Purpose Funds: An Application of Contingent Claims Analysis." *Journal of Financial Economics* 3 (January–March).

International Chamber of Commerce (1986). *Futures and Options Trading in Commodity Markets,* Paris.

Jarrow, Robert A., and George S. Oldfield (1981). "Forward Contracts and Futures Contracts." *Journal of Financial Economics* 9.

Jarrow, Robert, and Andrew Rudd (1982). "Approximate Option Valuation for Arbitrary Stochastic Processes." *Journal of Financial Economics* 10 (November): 347–69.

Jarrow, Robert, and Stuart Turnbull (1992). "Drawing the Analogy," *Risk* 5 (October).

Jarrow, Robert, and Stuart Turnbull (1990). "The Pricing and Hedging of Options on Financial Securities Subject to Credit Risk: The Discrete Time Case." Unpublished manuscript.

Jennings, R. H., and L. T. Stark (1981). "Earnings Announcements, Stock Price Adjustment and the Existence of Options Markets," *Journal of Finance* 41: 43–61.

Jensen, Michael C., and William H. Meckling (1976). "Theory of the Firm: Managerial Behavior, Agency Costs, and Capital Structure," *Journal of Financial Economics* 3.

Jordan, James; Robert Mackay; and Eugene Moriarty (1990). "The New Regulation of Hybrid Debt Instruments," *Journal of Applied Corporate Finance,* Winter.

Jorion, Philippe (1990). "The Exchange-Rate Exposures of U.S. Multinationals." *Journal of Business* 63.

Kemna, A. G. Z., and A. C. F. Vorst (1990). "A Pricing Method for Options Based on Average Asset Values," *Journal of Banking and Finance* 14 (March).

Keynes, John Maynard (1930). *Treatise on Money.* London: Macmillan.

Kleinbard, Edward D. (1991). "Equity Derivative Products: Financial Innovation's Newest Challenge to the Tax System." *Texas Law Review* 69 (May): 1319–68.

Klemkosky, Robert C., and T. S. Maness (1980). "The Impact of Options on the Underlying Securities." *Journal of Portfolio Management* 7: 12–18.

Krzyzak, Krystyna (1988). "Don't Take Swaps at Face Value." *Risk* 11 (November).

Lewent, Judy C., and A. John Kearney (1990). "Identifying, Measuring, and Hedging Currency Risk at Merck." *Journal of Applied Corporate Finance,* Winter.

Loeys, Jan (1985). "Interest Rate Swaps: A New Tool for Managing Risk," *Business Review,* Federal Reserve Bank of Philadelphia, May/June, 17–25.

Ma, C. K. and R. P. Rao (1986). "Market Characteristics, Option Trading and Volatility of the Underlying Stock." *Advances in Futures and Options Research* 1: 193–200.

———. (1988). "Information Asymmetry and Options Trading," *The Financial Review* 23: 39–51.

Macaulay, F. R. (1938). *Some Theoretical Problems Suggested by the Movement of Interest Rates, Bond Yields, and Stock Prices Since 1856.* New York: National Bureau of Research.

Macmillan, Lionel W. (1986). "Analytic Approximation for the American Put Option." *Advances in Futures and Options Research* 1: 119–39.

Mayers D., and C. W. Smith (1990). "On the Corporate Demand for Insurance: Evidence from the Reinsurance Market." *Journal of Business* 63: 19–40.

McCulloch, J. Huston (1980). "The Ban on Indexed Bonds." *American Economic Review* 70 (December).

McConnell, John J., and Eduardo S. Schwartz (1986). "LYON Taming." *Journal of Finance* 41.

Merton, Robert C. (1973). "Theory of Rational Option Pricing." *Bell Journal of Economics and Management Science* 4 (Spring): 141–83.

Merton, Robert C. (1976). "Option Pricing When Underlying Stock Returns Are Discontinuous", *Journal of Financial Economics,* 3 (January–March): 125–44.

Merton, Robert (1992). "Financial Innovation and Economic Performance." *Journal of Applied Corporate Finance,* Winter.

Miller, Gregory (1986). "When Swaps Unwind." *Institutional Investor*, November.

Miller, Merton (1992). "Financial Innovation: Achievements and Prospects." *Journal of Applied Corporate Finance,* Winter.

Millman, Gregory J. (1988). "How Smart Competitors Are Locking in the Cheap Dollar." *Corporate Finance,* December.

Millman, Gregory J. (1991). "Kaiser and Union Carbide Hedge Their Bets with Their Banks." *Corporate Finance*, June.

Modigliani, Franco, and Merton Miller (1958). "The Cost of Capital, Corporation Finance, and the Theory of Investment." *American Economic Review* 48 (June).

Modigliani, Franco, and Merton Miller (1961). "Dividend Policy, Growth and the Valuation of Shares." *Journal of Business* 34 (October).

Moriarity, E. J., and P. A. Tosini (1985). "Futures Trading and Price Volatility of GNMA Certificates—Further Evidence," *Journal of Futures Markets* 5: 633–41.

Muffett, Mark (1986). "Modelling Credit Exposure on Swaps." *Proceedings of a Conference on Bank Structure and Competition.* Federal Reserve Bank of Chicago, pp. 473–96.

Myers, S. C. (1977). "The Determinants of Corporate Borrowing." *Journal of Financial Economics* 5 (November).

Nance, Deana R.; Clifford W. Smith, Jr.; and Charles W. Smithson (1993). "On the Determinants of Corporate Hedging." *The Journal of Finance* 48: 267–84.

Neal, Kathleen, and Katerina Simons (1988). "Interest Rate Swaps, Currency Swaps and Credit Risk." *Issues in Bank Regulation,* Spring, pp. 26–29.

Neal. R. (1987). "Potential and Actual Competition in Equity Options." *Journal of Finance* 42: 511–32.

Powers, M. J. (1970). "Does Futures Trading Reduce Price Fluctuations in the Cash Markets?" *American Economic Review* 60: 460–64.

Putman, Bluford, and D. Sykes Wilford, eds. (1986). *The Monetary Approach of International Adjustment* New York: Praeger.

Pye, Gordon (1966). "A Markov Model of the Term Structure." *Quarterly Journal of Economics* 25 (February).

Quint, Michael (1989). "Reducing Shareholder-Debtholder Conflict on the RJR Nabisco Deal," in "Talking Deals." *The New York Times,* February 16.

Ramaswamy, Krishna, and Suresh M. Sundaresan (1986). "The Valuation of Floating Rate Instruments: Theory and Evidence." *Journal of Financial Economics* 17, pp. 251–272.

Rawls, S. Waite III, and Charles W. Smithson (1989). "The Evolution of Risk Management Products." *Journal of Applied Corporate Finance,* Winter, pp. 18–26.

———. (1990). "Strategic Risk Management." *Journal of Applied Corporate Finance* 2, no. 4 (Winter).

Rendleman, Richard J., Jr. and Brit J. Barter (1979). "Two-State Option Pricing." *Journal of Finance* 34 (December): 1093–10.

Roll, Richard (1977). "An Analytical Formula for Unprotected American Call Options on Stocks with Known Dividends." *Journal of Financial Economics* 5 (November): 251–58.

Samuelson, Paul A. (1965). "Rational Theory of Warrant Pricing." *Industrial Management Review* 6: 13–31.

Samuelson, P. A., and R. C. Merton (1969). "A Complete Model of Warrant Pricing that Maximizes Utility." *Industrial Management Review* 10: 17–46.

Schacter, B. (1988). "Open Interest in Stock Options around Quarterly Earnings Announcements." *Journal of Accounting Research* 26: 353–372.

Schuyler, K. Henderson (1985). "The Constraints on Trading Swaps," *Euromoney,* May.

Schwartz, Eduardo (1977). "The Valuation of Warrants: Implementing a New Approach." *Journal of Financial Economics* 4 (January): 79–93.

Scott, Louis (1987). "Option Pricing When the Variance Changes Randomly: Theory, Estimation, and an Application." *Journal of Financial and Quantitative Analysis* 22: 419–38.

Sharpe, William F. (1985). *Investments,* 3rd ed. Englewood Cliffs, N.J.: Prentice Hall.

———. (1987). "Integrated Asset Allocation." *Financial Analysts Journal,* September/October.

Siegfried, J. J. (1974). "Effective Average U.S. Corporation Income Tax Rates," *National Tax Journal,* June.

Singleton, J. Matthew (1991). "Hedge Accounting: A State-of-the-Art Review." *Bank Accounting and Finance.* Fall, 5, no. 1, pp. 26–32.

Skinner, D. (1989). "Option Markets and Stock Return Volatility." *Journal of Financial Economics* 24: 61–78.

Skinner, D. (1990). "Options Markets and the Information Content of Accounting Earnings Releases." *Journal of Accounting and Economics,* pp. 191–211.

Smith, Clifford W., Jr. (1976). "Option Pricing: A Review," *Journal of Financial Economics* 3 (January–March).

Smith, Clifford W., Jr., and Charles W. Smithson (1989). "Derivatives and Volatility." *Intermarkets,* July.

Smith, Clifford W., Jr., Charles W. Smithson, and Lee M. Wakeman (1986). "The Evolving Market for Swaps." *Midland Corporate Finance Journal,* Winter.

———. (1988). "Analyzing the Credit Risk of Swaps." *Simon Management Review,* Winter.

Smith, Clifford W., Jr., and David Watts (1987). "Corporate Insurance and the Underinvestment Problem." *Journal of Risk and Insurance.* Vol. LIV, no. 1, pp. 45–54 (March 1987).

Smith, Clifford W., Jr., and Jerold B. Warner (1979). "On Financial Contracting: An Analysis of Bond Covenants." *Journal of Financial Economics* 7.

Smith, Clifford W., Jr. (1993). "A Building-Block Approach to the Credit Risk for OTC Derivatives." Working paper, William E. Simon Graduate School of Business, University of Rochester.

Smith, Clifford W., Jr. (1976). "Option Pricing: A Review." *Journal of Financial Economics* 3, no. 1, 3–51.

Smithson, Charles W. (1987). "A LEGO Approach to Financial Engineering: An Introduction to Forwards, Futures, Swaps, and Options." *Midland Corporate Finance Journal* 4 (Winter).

———. (1991). "Wonderful Life." *Risk* 4; no. 9, October 1991, pp. 37–44.

Smithson, Charles W., and Donald H. Chew, Jr. (19???). "The Uses of Hybrid Debt in Managing Corporate Risk." *Journal of Applied Corporate Finance* 4, no. 4, (Winter 1992), 79–89.

Smithson, Charles W., and Christopher M. Turner (1994). "Financial Price Risk Evidenced in Share Price Behavior." Risk Management Research Working Paper, The Chase Manhattan Bank.

Sprenkle, Case M. (1964). "Warrant Prices as Indicators of Expectations and Preferences." *The Random Character of Stock Market Prices,* ed. Paul H. Cootner. Cambridge, Mass.: M.I.T. Press, pp. 412–74.

Sterngold, James (1993). "Rising Yen Rings Alarms in Tokyo." *The New York Times* (April 6).

Stevenson, Merril (1987). "The Risk Game: A Survey of International Banking." *The Economist,* March 21.

Sullivan J. (1988). "The Application of Mathematical Programming Methods to Oil and Gas Field Development Planning." *Mathematical Programming* 42, pp. 199–200.

Sweeney, Richard J., and Arthur D. Warga (1986). "The Possibility of Estimating Risk Premia in Asset Pricing Models." *The Financial Review* 21, no. 2, pp. 299–308.

Taylor, Spillenkothen; Parkinson, Spindler; and White (1987). "Uses of Interest Rate and Exchange Rate Contracts by U.S. Banking Organizations." Appendix C to "Treatment of Interest Rate and Exchange Rate Contracts in the Risk Asset Ratio." Staff Report, Federal Reserve System, March 2.

Teweles, Richard J., and Frank J. Jones (1987). *The Futures Game,* 2nd ed. New York: McGraw-Hill.

Thorpe, E. O., and S. T. Kassouf (1967). *Beat the Market.* New York: Random House.

Toevs, Alden (1984–85). "Interest Rate Risk and Uncertain Lives." *Journal of Portfolio Management* 11, no. 3, pp. 45–46.

Trennepohl, Gary L., and W. P. Dukes (1979). "CBOE Options and Stock Volatility." *Review of Business and Economic Research* 18: 36–48.

Tufano, Peter (1989a). "Three Essays on Financial Innovation." Ph.D. Dissertation, Harvard University.

———. (1989b). "Financial Innovation and First-Mover Advantages." *Journal of Financial Economics* 25.

Journal of Financial and Quantitative Analysis 26 (September): 377–89.

Vasicek, Oldrich (1977). "An Equilibrium Characterization of the Term Structure." *Journal of Financial Economics* 5 (November).

Wall, Larry (1989). "Interest Rate Swaps in an Agency Theoretic Model with Uncertain Interest Rates." *Journal of Banking and Finance* 13.

Wall, Larry D., and John J. Pringle (1988). "Interest Rate Swaps: A Review of the Issues." *Economic Review,* Federal Reserve Bank of Atlanta, November/December.

———. (1989). "Alternative Explanations of Interest Rate Swaps: An Empirical Analysis." *Financial Management* 18:59–73.

Warner, Jerry (1977a). "Bankruptcy, Absolute Priority, and the Pricing of Risky Debt Claims." *Journal of Financial Economics* 13 (May).

———. (1977b). "Bankruptcy Costs: Some Evidence." *Journal of Finance* 32 (May).

Whaley, Robert E. (1986). "Valuation of American Futures Options: Theory and Empirical Evidence." *Journal of Finance* 41 (March): 127–50.

Whiteside, M. M.; W. P. Dukes; and P. M. Dunne (1983). "Short-Term Impact of Option Trading on Underlying Securities." *Journal of Financial Research* 6: 313–21.

Whittaker, J. Gregg (1987). "Interest Rate Swaps: Risk and Regulation." Federal Reserve Bank of Kansas City *Economic Review,* March.

Wiggins, James (1987). "Option Values under Stochastic Volatility: Theory and Empirical Evidence." *Journal of Financial Economics* 19 (December): 351–72.

Wilkie P. J. (1988). "Corporate Average Effective Tax Rates and Inferences about Relative Tax Preferences." *Journal of American Taxation Association,* Fall.

Working, Holbrook (1960). "Price Effects of Futures Trading." *Food Research Institute Studies* 1: 3–31.

Zimmerman, J. L. (1983). "Taxes and Firm Size." *Journal of Accounting and Economics* (August): 119–49.

INDEX

LIST OF OTHER BOOKS

Thank you for choosing **Irwin Professional Publishing** for your business information needs. If you are part of a corporation, professional association, or government agency, consider our newest option: Custom Publishing. This service helps you create your own customized books, manuals, or other materials from your organization's resources, select chapters of our books, or both!

Irwin Professional Publishing books are also excellent resources for training/educational programs, premiums, and incentives. For information on volume discounts or Custom Publishing Services, call **Irwin Professional Publishing** at 1-800-634-3966.

Other books of interest to you from Irwin Professional Publishing . . .

The Handbook of Interest Rate Risk Management
Edited by Jack Clark Francis and Avner Wolf
This complete handbook reveals how more than three dozen experts control and preserve the value of their own fixed-income portfolios—from choosing the right risk management product to monitoring and evaluating the effectiveness of hedge management strategies. (832 pages)
ISBN:1-55623-382-5

Global Risk-Based Capital Regulation:Volume I
Capital Adequacy
Edited by Charles A. Stone and Anne Zissu
Offers rigorous insights on the effectiveness of risk-based capital regulations from Princeton's international finance Professor Ethan Kapstein, the Bank of

England's Andrew Bailey, European Investment Bank's Pier Luigi Gilibert, and many others. (630 pages)
ISBN: 1-55623-791-X

Global Risk-Based Capital Regulations: Volume II
Management and Funding Strategies
Edited by Charles A. Stone and Anne Zissu
In this second volume, the authors analyze the effect of risk-based capital regulations on the allocation of capital within the banking industry and consider the value of structured finance transactions and asset securitization as effective ways to raise capital. (446 pages)
ISBN: 1-55623-789-8

The Bond Market
Trading and Risk Management
Christina I. Ray
This one-of-a-kind reference explains the art and science of trading bonds for maximum profit with controlled risk and illustrates how the best traders apply sound theoretical techniques under battlefield conditions. Readers will learn how to use mathematics to construct positions in bonds or other derivatives suitable for different market conditions and their own market risks, how to determine the value of different securities, and more. (720 pages)
ISBN: 1055623-289-6

The Money Market, Third Edition
Marcia Stigum
More than 100,000 copies sold in previous editions! The most comprehensive, authoritative, and respected source on the money market. Completely revised with totally new chapters on medium-term notes, futures, and options, and loan participations. (1,250 pages)
ISBN: 1-55623-122-9

Available at fine bookstores and libraries everywhere.